Sports Law in Portugal

Sports Law in Portugal

Second Edition

Rui Botica Santos
Alexandre Miguel Mestre
&
Francisco Raposo de Magalhães

This book was originally published as a monograph in the International Encyclopaedia of Laws/Sports Law.

General Editors: Roger Blanpain, Frank Hendrickx
Volume Editor: Michele Colucci

Wolters Kluwer

Published by:
Kluwer Law International B.V.
PO Box 316
2400 AH Alphen aan den Rijn
The Netherlands
Website: www.wklawbusiness.com

Sold and distributed in North, Central and South America by:
Wolters Kluwer Legal & Regulatory U.S.
7201 McKinney Circle
Frederick, MD 21704
United States of America
Email: customer.service@wolterskluwer.com

Sold and distributed in all other countries by:
Turpin Distribution Services Ltd.
Stratton Business Park
Pegasus Drive, Biggleswade
Bedfordshire SG18 8TQ
United Kingdom
Email: kluwerlaw@turpin-distribution.com

ISBN 978-90-411-6677-7

This title is available on www.kluwerlawonline.com

This book is dedicated to the memory of:
José Manuel Coelho Ribeiro
Because of the passionate and sporting way in which he practiced law and promoted the value of the legal profession.

The Authors

Rui Botica Santos was born in Lisbon in 1968. He graduated from the Lisbon University Law Faculty in 1992 with a degree in law. He was admitted to the Portuguese Bar in 1995, to the Brazilian Bar in 2006 and to the Macau Bar in 2013. He has since 2012 been admitted as a practising lawyer at the Lawyer's Association of the Republic of Timor-Leste. He has been an arbitrator at the Lausanne Court of Arbitration of Sport since 2004. He has been a judge at the Fédération Internationale de l'Automobile (FIA) International Court of Appeal since 2010. He is an equity partner in the Coelho Ribeiro e Associados Law Firm (CRA) and is a founder partner of the CRA Timor Law Office. He has been the General Secretary of the Portuguese Committee of the European League for Economic Cooperation since 2010. He has taught Dispute Resolution Mechanisms in the International Sports Law Masters Programme at the Instituto Superior de Derecho y Economia (ISDE) in Madrid, since 2007, and has a vast experience in the areas of Sport and Arbitration and is frequently appointed as an arbitrator in proceedings before the CAS. Rui is also a Master *Honoris Causa* at the ISDE and a member of the Advisory Board of the European Sports Law and Policy Bulletin, established in 2010, in addition to having published various articles on the legal aspects of Sport. He was appointed by the Portuguese Government as a member of the *Commission for the Revision of Sports Justice* in September 2010.

Alexandre Miguel Mestre was born in Lisbon, in 1974. He graduated from the Law Faculty of Universidade de Lisboa, in 1998. He was admitted to the Portuguese Bar in 2003. He has a Postgraduate Course on Olympic Studies (Loughborough University/International Olympic Academy), a Master on European Legal Studies and a Master of Law and Sports Management (ISDE – Distance Learning). He holds a Ph.D. degree in EU Sports Law at Edge Hill University, Liverpool. He was a member of the Group for the foundation of the Portuguese Court of Arbitration for Sport (PCAS) in the ambit of the Portuguese Olympic Committee (POC). He has been a member of the Board of the Portuguese Olympic Academy since 2002 and is Counsel at Abreu

The Authors

Advogados, law Firm based in Lisbon He is President of the General Assembly of the Portuguese Sports Law Association. He was Secretary of State for Youth and Sport from 2011 to 2012. His preferred practice areas are Sports Law, EU Law and Competition Law. He lectures sports law related disciplines at three Portuguese Universities. He has published various books and scientific articles on the legal aspects of Sport, particularly in the context of the European Union and the Olympic movement.

Francisco Raposo de Magalhães was born in Lisbon in 1982. He graduated with a licentiate degree in law from the Law Faculty of the Universidade Nova de Lisboa in 2007. He was admitted to the Portuguese Bar Association in 2011 and was a member of the Sports Law Department of the CRA Law Firm. He has attended various training courses and conferences in the area of Sports Law and the III Postgraduate Course in the Law of Professional Sport at the Law Faculty of Coimbra University, in 2009–2010. He has published various articles on the legal aspects of Sport.

Table of Contents

List of Abbreviations

AdC	*Autoridade da Concorrência* (Portuguese Competition Authority)
ADoP	*Autoridade Antidopagem de Portugal* (Portuguese Anti-Doping Authority)
AMEF	*Associação Nacional dos Médicos de Futebol* (National Association of Football Doctors)
ANDIF	*Associação Nacional dos Dirigentes de Futebol* (National Association of Football Directors and Managers)
ANEDAF	*Associação Nacional dos Enfermeiros Desportivos e Massagistas de Futebol* (National Association of Sports Nurses and Football Masseurs)
ANPC	*Autoridade Nacional de Protecção Civil* (National Civil Protection Authority)
ANTF	*Associação Nacional de Treinadores de Futebol* (National Association of Football Coaches)
APAF	*Associação Portuguesa de Árbitros de Futebol* (Portuguese Association of Football Referees)
ASAE	*Autoridade para a Segurança Alimentar e Económica* (Food and Economic Safety Authority)
CAP	*Comissão Arbitral Paritária* (Paritary Arbitration Commission)
CAS	Court of Arbitration for Sport (Lausanne, Switzerland)
CCT	*Convenção Colectiva de Trabalho* (Collective Bargaining Agreement)
CESD	*Conselho para a Ética e Segurança no Desporto* (Council for Ethics and Security in Sport)
CFI	European Court of First Instance
CHF	*Swiss Franc*
CIRC	*Código do Imposto sobre o Rendimento Colectivo* (Corporation Tax Code)

List of Abbreviations

CIRS	*Código do Imposto sobre o Rendimento Singular* (Private Income Tax Code)
CIVA	*Código do Imposto sobre o Valor Acrescentado* (Value Added Tax Code)
CJEC	Court of Justice of the European Communities
CNAD	*Conselho Nacional Antidopagem* (National Anti-Doping Council)
NSC	*Conselho Nacional do Desporto* (The National Sports Council)
POC	*Comité Olímpico de Portugal* (Olympic Committee of Portugal)
CPI	*Código de Propriedade Industrial* (Industrial Property Code)
CPTA	*Código de Processo nos Tribunais Administrativos* (Administrative Courts Procedure Code)
CRP	*Constituição da República Portuguesa* (Constitution of the Portuguese Republic)
CSD	*Conselho para o Sistema Desportivo* (Council for the Sports System)
CTD	*Contrato de Trabalho Desportivo* (Sport Employment Contract)
DRC	Dispute Resolution Chamber
DRE	*Diário da República* (Official Journal)
DTT	Double Taxation Treaty
EBF	*Estatuto dos Benefícios Fiscais* (Tax Incentives Statute)
ECA	European Association of Clubs
ECJ	European Court of Justice
EC Treaty	European Community Treaty
EEA	European Economic Area
ESPAD	*Estrutura de Suporte ao Programa Antidopagem* (Anti-Doping Programme Support Structure)
EU	European Union
EUPD	*Estatuto de Utilidade Pública Desportiva* (Sport Public Utility Status)
EURO	European Football Championship
FEI	*Fédération Equestre Internationale* (International Equestrian Association)
FIA	*Fédération Internationale de l'Automobile* (International Automobile Association)

FIBA	*Fédération Internationale de Basketball* (International Basketball Association)
FIFA	*Fédération Internationale de Football Association* (International Federation of Association Football)
FIFPro	*Fédération Internationale des Associations des Footballeurs Professionels* (International Federation of Professional Footballers)
FINA	*Fédération Internationale de Natation* (International Swimming Federation)
FPF	*Federação Portuguesa de Futebol* (Portuguese Football Federation)
IAS	*Indexante de Apoios Sociais* (Indexing of Social Support)
ICAS	International Council of Arbitration for Sports
ICJ	International Court of Justice
ICN	*Instituto da Conservação da Natureza*
IDP	Nature Conservation Institute (*Instituto do Desporto de Portugal)*
IOC	International Olympic Committee
IP	*Instituto Público* (Public Institute)
IRC	*Imposto sobre o Rendimento Colectivo* (Corporation Tax)
IRS	*Imposto sobre o Rendimento Singular* (Private Income Tax)
LAD	*Laboratório de Análises e Dopagem* (Doping Analysis Laboratory)
LAV	*Lei da Arbitragem Voluntária* (Voluntary Arbitration Law)
LBAFD	*Lei de Bases da Actividade Física e do Desporto* (Basic Law of Physical Activity and Sport)
LBD	*Lei de Bases do Desporto* (Basic Law of Sport)
LBSD	*Lei de Bases do Sistema Desportivo* (Basic Law of the Sports System)
LdC	*Lei da Concorrência* (Competition Law)
LGT	*Lei Geral Tributária* (General Tax Law)
LOE	*Lei do Orçamento de Estado* (Budget Law)
LOFTJ	*Lei de Organização e Funcionamento dos Tribunais Judiciais* (Law on the Organisation and Working of the Courts)
LPFP	*Liga Portuguesa de Futebol Profissional* (Portuguese Professional Football League)
OC	Olympic Charter

List of Abbreviations

OECD	Organisation for Economic Co-operation and Development
PRACE	*Programa de Reestruturação da Administração Central do Estado* (Programme for the Reorganisation of the Central State Administration)
QREN	*Quadro de Referência Estratégico Nacional* (National Strategic Reference Framework)
REG	*Regime Especial de Gestão* (Special Management Framework)
RETJ	*Regulamento do Estatuto e Transferência de Jogadores* (Regulation on the Status and Transfer of Players)
RJCTPD	*Regime Jurídico do Contrato de Trabalho do Praticante Desportivo Profissional* (Legal Framework governing Employment Contracts of Sportsmen and Sportswomen)
RJFD	*Regime Jurídico das Federações Desportivas* (Legal Framework Governing Sports Federations)
RJUE	*Regime Jurídico da Urbanização e da Edificação* (Legal Framework governing Urbanization and Construction)
ROC	*Revisor Oficial de Contas* (Official Auditor)
RSTP	Regulation on the Status and Transfer of Players
RTP	*Rádio e Televisão de Portugal* (Radio and Television of Portugal)
SAD	*Sociedade Anónima Desportiva* (Public Limited Sports Company)
SEJD	*Secretário de Estado da Juventude e do Desporto* (Secretary of State for Youth and Sport)
SJPF	*Sindicato dos Jogadores Profissionais de Futebol* (Professional Football Players Union)
STJ	*Supremo Tribunal de Justiça* (Supreme Court of Justice)
TAB	*Tribunal Arbitral do Basquetebol* (Basketball Arbitration Tribunal)
PCAS	*Tribunal Arbitral do Desporto (Portugal)* (Sport Arbitration Tribunal)
TC	*Tribunal Constitucional* (Constitutional Court)
TFEU	Treaty on the Functioning of the European Union
TFS	*Tribunal Fédéral Suisse* (Swiss Federal Court)
UCI	*Union Cycliste Internationale* (International Cycling Union)
UEFA	*Union des Associations Européennes de Football* (Union of European Football Associations)

UMTS	Universal Mobile Telecommunications System
UN	United Nations
UNESCO	United Nations Educational Scientific and Cultural Organisation
VAT	Value Added Tax
WADA	World Anti-Doping Agency

List of Abbreviations

Foreword

A few months ago, José Mourinho and I were on the same flight from Lisbon to Madrid. We had a short and agreeable conversation about life in Madrid, our children's schools and the countries in which we had lived. I did not dare to talk about football with the greatest football coach in the world. However, I did not lose the opportunity to say that he was doing more for the visibility of Portugal in Spain than Portugal's entire diplomatic effort.

Sport has various aspects of which the sports competitions certainly attract the most media attention. However sport's educational, health and moral and ethical value creation aspects are also important as are its financial, legal and diplomatic facets.

What one of the authors terms international sports diplomacy has various historical antecedents. The Olympic Games were a time of sacred truce in the ancient world. The founding of the new Olympic Games founded by Pierre de Coubertin in the nineteenth century brought with it another facet of sport. For example, the so-called ping pong diplomacy, which blazed the trail for the normalization of relations between the United States and China in 1971. Another example is Mandela's use of the 1995 rugby World Cup in South Africa. There are many other similar examples.

Regrettably, sport is not always used to promote peace and concord. Sometimes, it is even used as a weapon in ideological confrontations, or in demonstrations of power and authority that far exceed its normal bounds. Sport is open to such (ab)use because the values expressed in and by it are easily comprehended by public opinion all over the world.

Just as international law is defined as the rules applicable to the international community, sports law and sports justice, which are the subject-matter of this book, concern the national and international sports community.

States are no longer the sole agents of foreign policy and international affairs. Indeed the effects of globalization have meant that the role of states in these areas is actually decreasing. This trend has given rise to a justified and increased recourse to international non-state procedures and to non-national arbitration procedures: for example in areas such as investment contracts with States, human rights and sport.

As with any branch of law, sports law also tends to create legal mechanisms, which reaffirm principles, structure procedures, codify penalties and generate the trust of all sports stakeholders, including the general public, which is always the final beneficiary of such measures and initiatives.

Foreword

By compiling the legal provisions that govern sport in Portugal and their international reflexes, Rui Botica Santos has provided a work of reference both for specialists in the field and for those interested in sports law and sports justice. This work is indispensable for those, who wish to analyse the various aspects of sport and may, in some cases, be called on to decide, by applying the law to the facts. This book also creates various interfaces with the international sports community, with participants and with public opinion, which demands that sport be characterized by transparency, safety and trustworthiness.

The merits of this work are many. Rui Botica Santos and his fellow authors have shared with their readers the knowledge that they have acquired over the years in sports law arbitration both in Portugal and internationally. This book will certainly become a work of reference, which will open up perspectives and consolidate knowledge. I therefore predict that it will be a great success. However, as the English novelist George Eliot wrote: 'Of all forms of mistake, prophecy is the most gratuitous.'

António Martins da Cruz
Ambassador – Former Portuguese Foreign Minister
Lisbon, January 2011

Acknowledgements

Everyone, whether they are professional or amateur sportspersons or spectators, can contribute to the improvement of Sport. There are innumerable ways in which to demonstrate a love of Sport, and this book is our modest contribution to it.

One of the great challenges of the twenty-first century is the struggle for a Sport that responds in a better way to the needs and concerns of those involved in it. We therefore dedicate this book to all those whose objective it is to constantly improve Sport.

We are profoundly grateful to Ana Brilha, Felix Majani and Bruno Ribeiro Comicholi for the care, effort and speed with which they have reviewed this book and also for the exceptional contribution they have made as well as the quality they have added to the final result.

We are profoundly grateful to Mark Robertson for the care, effort and speed with which he has translated and reviewed this book from Portuguese to its final version in English.

This second and revised edition had the collaboration of Matilde Costa Dias, to whom we express our sincere thanks.

Rui Botica Santos, Alexandre Miguel Mestre
& Francisco Raposo de Magalhães
Lisbon, 1 January 2016

Introductory Note

1. This Monograph on Portuguese Sports Law, which I have the honour of writing the introductory note, is the fruit of the combined efforts and knowledge of three eminent specialists in Sports Law: Rui Botica Santos, Alexandre Miguel Mestre and Francisco Raposo de Magalhães.

2. It is, without exaggeration, a book of fundamental importance. This work is an indispensable tool for all those, whether lawyers or not, who actively operate in the *teatro juris*, or who are merely interested in the immense and multifaceted cluster that Sport has become in Portugal, Europe and the World and in its special relationship with the Law.

3. As this Monograph clearly portrays, the relationship between Sport and Law is by no means an ancient phenomenon, at least so far as football is concerned. By the same token, it is not something that has only arisen in recent years.

4. While archaeological findings and ancient depictions have shown that ball games were already played in the ancient Mayan civilization at *Chichén Itza* and William Wyler, in his 1959 masterpiece *Ben-Hur*, immortalized the chariot races in the Circus Maximus, and while the passions aroused by the gladiators among the howling mobs to whom Caesar distributed bread and circus at the Roman Coliseum are legendary, there can be no doubt that it was with the creation of *The Football Association* and *The Football League* in 1863 and 1888, respectively, that the association between Sport and the Law commenced, in response to the need to organize football matches with proper rules, on a regular basis, between the teams that, following the pioneering lead of Sheffield Football Club, had been transformed into clubs, all over England.

5. In Portugal, this relationship emerged much later, constrained by the political dictates of an authoritarian and markedly interventionist regime, which remained in power for almost half a century, and by the mentality of the epoch, which originally regarded so-called professional sport with mistrust and deemed it to be a 'frivolous matter' and 'socially and morally harmful practice'.

6. However, as the professionalization of sport grew and its commercial aspects became more predominant, the codification of sport became increasingly evident. After the 1974 revolution, the new democratic State lost no time in recognizing that sport was a matter of public interest and in consecrating Sport in the Portuguese Constitution as a fundamental right.

7. It was however with the Law no. 1 of 13 January 1990 (Law of Basis of the Sports System) that the State's role in the regulation of sport was accentuated. Since then, Sport has been the subject matter of a growing volume of public legislation, which *expressis et apertatis verbis* recognizes its specific characteristics and the autonomy of sports organizations and makes a healthy separation of waters between non-professional and professional sport, whose governance, regulation and administration are then entrusted *ope legis* to the Professional Leagues.

8. Since 1990, the volume of new legislation and regulations in the field of sport has been unprecedentedly intense. This has involved not only public legislation, but also private regulations introduced by the sports movement. This framework has affirmed the duality, *rectius*, the plurality of the sources of Sports Law in Portugal. We have therefore witnessed a progressive affirmation, development and consolidation of Sports Law, as an autonomous branch of Law, based on a complex and multiform framework, in which the public and private spheres are interlinked, with State legislation co-existing with private regulations enacted by sports organizations and with national provisions mixed with the regulations issued by international sports federations. Moreover, the courts and sports dispute resolution and disciplinary bodies have been increasingly called upon to resolve disputes and to consider the disciplinary impacts of the conduct of sports actors.

9. All this profusion of national and international, public and private sources of law, including the growing role of the European Union institutions, such as the European Commission or the European Court of Justice, is masterfully described and analysed in this book.

10. We are not unaware that such complexity can make the application of the law an arduous task, particularly for the less experienced. However, it is in this apparent abundance of sources of law that the richness and attractiveness of the Portuguese sports law, as a field of study and work, is to be found.

11. As the readers of this will be able to find, the book that Rui Botica Santos, Alexandre Miguel Mestre and Francisco Raposo de Magalhães bring to us is comprehensive, deep and rigorous.

12. This is indisputably a book that I can unreservedly recommend as an indispensable exposition of Portuguese sports law, which includes the most relevant aspects of the international sports regulation, with a mandatory incursion through Competition Law and the problematic related to the principle of the specificity of sport, not to mention the main decisions regarding the players' transfer system, as well as the rules and leading cases regarding the commercial operation of sports competitions, among many other related matters of significant import.

13. There is no subject in the area of their chosen subject matter that the authors of this work have failed to consider in detail. They deal fully with the public and private regulation of sport, dispute resolution structures and procedures (particularly the Court of Arbitration for Sport, in Lausanne), the powers and duties of the various organs of the Sports Public Administration and the sports movement, the legal frameworks applicable to the prevention of violence associated with sport, doping, tax matters, collective bargaining agreements and player transfer, without neglecting the most significant aspects of International Sports Law.

14. In addition to the high quality of their texts and the analysis on which they are based, the authors have also left an indelible imprint of two other fundamental aspects throughout this work.

15. First, the commendable purpose to inform, as they have clearly stated their opinions with regard to each of the topics comprised in the subject matter of this work. In this, I detect a perhaps undeclared but nevertheless natural and inescapable desire to use this book as a window to the world through which they share the essence of the Portuguese legal thought and regulatory production in the field of sport. This is objective has been successfully and praiseworthily attained.

16. Second, an open invitation to all readers to consider and join the debate on the increasingly productive, fruitful and intense relationship between two phenomena, which formerly viewed each other askance and at a distance, and are now completely inseparable, i.e., Sport and Law. Who could indeed resist such an invitation?

Emanuel Macedo de Medeiros
Lawyer
CEO of the ICSS – International Centre for Sport Security

Introductory Note

General Introduction

Chapter 1. Introduction

17. The legislation and regulations governing sport have become increasingly extensive and complex because of the growing economic and social importance of sport. It is very evident that sport at the highest level involves other acts and contracts of great economic and legal significance, e.g., sponsorship, merchandising agreements, insurance among other matters.

18. The law firms to which the authors of this book belong already have multidisciplinary teams made up of specialists in legal practice areas such as civil, commercial, tax, criminal, administrative, EU and competition law. Sports law, as a specific area of legal practice, is a very recent phenomenon, to be found in a small number of Portuguese universities. The current sports legislation is also quite recent, as will be seen below.

19. This new version takes into consideration all of the legislative changes that have occurred as at the publication date of this second and revised edition.

Chapter 2. About Portugal

20. Portugal is located in the southwest of Europe and is bordered by Atlantic Ocean to the east and Spain to the west. The Azores and Madeira are also part of Portugal and are located in the Atlantic Ocean. These islands have their own Regional Government and Parliament, but are also subject to the National Assembly and the Portuguese Constitution.

21. Portugal is a republic, with a parliamentary democracy. Portugal had a monarchic regime between its foundation, in 1143, and 5 October 1910, with brief interruptions. The current Portuguese Constitution dates from 2 April 1976 and has subsequently been amended on several occasions. The Portuguese legal system is a civil law system. The Council of Ministers is appointed by the President, who is the head of state, on the recommendation of the prime minister, who is the head of the government.

22. The Portuguese population, in December 2015, was 10,825,309.[1] The total area of the country is 92.389 square kilometres, including the Azores and Madeira. Lisbon is the capital city.

1. According to the *CIA – World Fact Book* which can be consulted at: https://www.cia.gov/library/publications/the-world-factbook/geos/po.html.

Chapter 3. Statistics

23. According to the most recent sports' statistics published in Portugal,[2] which date from 2009, there were then 492,000 sportspersons in Portugal, who were members of sports federations, compared to approximately 266,000 in 1996. Football is by far the sport with the largest number of sportspersons, who are federation members, with almost 142,000 such members. In 2008, 77% of these were male, while only 23% were female. This means that approximately 4.63% of the Portuguese population was formally and actively involved in sport in 2008. There are estimated to be almost 16,000 coaches, approximately 12,400 referees and 12,000 sports clubs, each with an average of 40 members in Portugal.

24. In as far as public funding of sports federations and the Portuguese Olympic Committee (POC) is concerned, the evolution has also been positive. In 1996, the sports federations received approximately EUR 27 million from the State, while, in 2008, this figure was EUR 42 million, EUR 37 million of which was for the sports federations and 5 million was for the POC.

25. There was an exponential growth of infrastructures between 1996 and 2008. The increase in the area of sports infrastructures between 2005 and 2008 was 545,000 m2.

26. Despite all these increases during the period in question, there was a decline in the numbers of sportspersons in the age groups corresponding to the training levels. This indicates not only a lack of sports culture among the population in general, but also deficient national sports planning, by the State, at school and university levels. Measures are, however, gradually being taken to encourage sport in schools, above all at primary and junior levels, in order to have positive results in the medium term. Despite the clear efforts of various governments to promote a *culture of sport and physical activity* among the population, the fact is that there is not even legal provision for the production of a National Sports Development Plan,[3] which we consider to be a useful tool in the promotion not only of a true culture of sport and physical activity, but also for the implementation of a constitutional principle into everyday life, which is the responsibility of the State in conjunction with the educational institutions.

---

2. The statistics were disclosed by the Instituto do Desporto de Portugal, at a ceremony in the Auditorium of the Swimming Pools Complex at the Jamor National Sports Centre. They will be published in a forthcoming book to be entitled 'Estatísticas do Desporto 1996-2009'.
3. Compare José Manuel Meirim. *Lei de Bases da Actividade Física e do Desporto – Estudo, Notas e Comentários. Coimbra, Coimbra Editora, 2007, p. 186-188.* Coimbra, Coimbra Editora, 2007, p. 149.

Chapter 4. Institutions

27. Historically, there is no Ministry of Sport in Portugal and the State's responsibilities in the area of sport fall under the remit of one Minister, who is assisted by the Secretary of State for Youth and Sport. The State is responsible for the promotion and encouragement of sport at national level in conjunction with local authorities, educational institutions and sports associations. In as far as the private regulation of sport is concerned, the State's role is secondary and is exercised via its supervision of those associations to which it grants public powers.

28. The State seeks to pursue a policy of expansion and improvement of sports infrastructures, of increased support for high performance sport, of promotion of sports-associated tourism and of the general funding of the sports system.

Chapter 5. An Introduction to the Portuguese Legal System

§1. The Political Organization of Society

29. In Portugal, political power is sovereign as it is supreme and independent and is not limited by any other power within the internal politico-legal system. However, in the international legal system, sovereign power exists at the level of the supreme powers of other States, which exist in a state of parity and are not subject to an obligation to accept any norms other than voluntarily.

30. The acts of the State's organs of power consist of the creation and implementation of laws and in the guaranteeing of the implementation of these laws via the use of the necessary means of repression and coercion.

31. In order to achieve these objectives, the State divides its powers between sovereign organs, which decide independently, i.e., without being subject to a duty to comply with the orders or instructions of other sovereign bodies.

32. The sovereign organs of the Portuguese State, as enshrined in Article 110 of the Constitution of the Portuguese Republic (CRP), are:

(a) the President of the Republic;
(b) the Assembly of the Republic;
(c) the Government;
(d) the Courts.

33. The Portuguese sovereign organs comply with the constitutional principles of separation and interdependence of powers, and none of them, whether regional autonomous powers or local authorities, may delegate their powers to other bodies, except when the CRP and the law expressly provide accordingly.

34. The CRP contains the fundamental rules regarding the organization of political power, which is based on the concept of representative democracy and defines the formation, composition, powers and working of the sovereign organs and expressly lays down fundamental rights.

35. The government model adopted is semi-presidential and the CRP has a strong social law aspect via the detailed description of a broad series of social, economic and cultural rights.

36. The organ, which has the primary legislative powers, is the Assembly of the Republic. In Portugal, legislative powers are, however, shared between the Assembly of the Republic and the Government. The Government has the exclusive power to legislate with regard to certain matters, namely its own organization and workings.

§2. Sources of Law

I. Introduction

37. In a technical-legal sense, sources of Law are the ways in which legal provisions are formed and revealed. According to this meaning, the following are generally considered to be sources of law:

(a) the law;
(b) case-law;
(c) custom;
(d) legal theory.

II. The Law

A. Introduction

38. The Law is the most important source of order, not only because of its importance but because of its hierarchical prevalence. In the Portuguese legal system, the law is the only immediate source of law, as is stated in no. 1 of Article 1 of the Civil Code. All other sources are mediated sources of Law, i.e., they are not per se binding and serve only to assist the revelation of the law. Despite this, mediated sources of law plays an important role in the Portuguese legal system, because of the way in which they influence the formation and revelation of legal provisions.

39. According to no. 2 of Article 1 of the Civil Code, *all provisions of a general nature with their origin in the proper organs of the State*, i.e., the Government and the Assembly of the Republic, are considered to be laws. However, the process of the elaboration of law is not uniform, to the extent that each body with legislative competence acts in its own way.

40. In addition to laws, of which more is written below, Portuguese internal law also includes EU Law provisions, such as Regulations (which come into force in the international legal system, automatically) and EU Directives (which come into force once transposed into domestic law).

41. The norms and principles of general or common International Law are an integral part of Portuguese law in accordance with the principle of automatic reception. The said norms are directly applicable and do not require transposition into the Portuguese legal system.

42. The provisions of international conventions are effective in Portugal provided that they are properly ratified or approved, once they have been published in the Official Journal (DRE) and provided they are internationally binding on the Portuguese State. In as far as the acts of international organizations of which Portugal is a member are concerned, they have direct effect in the internal legal system if this is provided in the treaties, which establish the said organizations.

B. Types of Laws

1. Laws of the Assembly of the Republic

43. In as far as laws *strictu sensu* are concerned, i.e., those passed by the Assembly of the Republic, their formulation commences with the submission of a text by bodies with legislative initiative, on which the Assembly takes a position. In accordance with Article 167 of the CRP, the following bodies have legislative initiative:

(a) deputies, when the text submitted is termed a draft law;
(b) parliamentary groups, when the text submitted is termed a draft law;
(c) the Government, when the text submitted is termed a proposed law;
(d) groups of electors;
(e) regional legislative assemblies.

44. The current CRP dates from 1976.[4] There are other laws, which fall within the ambit of the powers of the Assembly of the Republic, which can be special laws, or not, as the case may be. Special laws are laws which: (i) must be passed by a two-thirds majority of the deputies in office (a qualified majority), or (ii) are the precondition of other laws, or (iii) must be complied with by other laws. The following are special laws:

(a) statutory laws;
(b) authorizing laws;
(c) basic laws;
(d) framework laws.

In addition to these special laws, there are also laws which convert or transpose EU directives into Portuguese domestic law.

a. Basic Laws in Particular

45. According to the systematic organization of the Portuguese legal system, Basic Laws have the following characteristics:

(a) they are the general basis of a legal framework and enshrine the principles to be developed by the executive branch;
(b) they are enshrined in the CRP in no. 2 of Article 112, which refers to laws, which establish the general basis of legal frameworks.

4. The CRP was revised seven times until the presente date, in 1982, 1989, 1992, 1997, 2001, 2004 and 2005.

46. According to Gomes Canotilho,[5] the establishment of general bases *means the establishment of fundamental political and legislative options, with the specific definition of the general legal frameworks being left, or not, as the case may be, to the Government and the regional legislative assemblies.*

47. The Assembly of the Republic is generally responsible for the elaboration of basic laws, and is thus guaranteed a primary involvement, with the Government being able to legislate subsequently without the need for authorization, provided that the general basis of the legislation has been established.

48. The Assembly of the Republic can also authorize the Government to legislate via the passing of a legislative authorization law. According to no. 2 of Article 165 of the CRP, the said laws must define the subject matter, meaning, extent and duration of the authorization, which may be extended.

49. In the Portuguese legal system, the legislation related to sport is based on a Basic Law, which contains its general principles, which are then developed by laws and, above all, by Decree-Laws. The Basic Law to which we refer is the 2007 Basic Law of Physical Activity and Sport (LBAFD), which was introduced by Law no. 5/2007 of 16th January, and later amended by Law no. 74/2013 which was preceded by two other Basic Laws, the Basic Law of Sport (LBD) introduced by Decree-Law no. 30/2004 of 21st July and the 1990 Basic Law of the Sports System (LBSD), introduced by Law no. 1/90 of 13 January.

2. Decree-Laws and Government Regulations

50. The Government can also submit Draft Laws to the Assembly of the Republic, which are subsequently approved by the Council of Ministers. This was the case with regard to the LBAFD, which had its origin in Government Draft Law no. 80/X.

This was also the case with regard to the Law no. 74/2013 which created, in 6 September 2013, the Court of Arbitration for Sport in Portugal (PCAS).

51. The Government legislates via Decree-Laws with regard to matters, which are not reserved exclusively reserved for the Assembly of the Republic, and which have been identified in Article 164 of the CRP, or via the authorization of the Assembly of the Republic, in relation to matters in respect of which the Assembly only has relative competence. There are however matters in respect of which the Government has exclusive competence, which include legislation with regard to its own organization and workings. There are also Decree-Laws, which transpose EU directives into Portuguese law.

52. The Government accordingly has legislative and regulatory functions, which it exercises by issuing of regulations, which either expound on the already existing

5. José Gomes Canotilho. *Direito Constitucional e Teoria da Constituição*. 3rd Edition. Coimbra. Almedina, 1999, p. 700.

law or formulate complementary or instrumental rules, with a view to the proper implementation thereof, while decree-laws merely state fundamental principles or general bases.

53. Government regulations may take the following forms:

(a) Statutory instruments
(b) Circulars
(c) Instructions
(d) Resolutions of the Council of Ministers
(e) Normative orders
(f) Ministerial orders
(g) Regulatory decrees.

3. The Methods of Interpretation and Resolution of Lacunae in the Law and the Control of the Constitutionality Thereof

54. The method used to construe the law is based on the theoretical development thereof based on the various elements in the law. No. 1 of Article 9 of the Civil Code provides the general principle that:

> the interpretation of the law must not be limited to the letter of the law, but must reconstitute the legislative intention on the basis of the texts, taking the following into consideration, above all, i.e. the unity of the legal system, the circumstances in which the law was drafted and the specific circumstances of the time when it is applied. Number 2 of the article adds that legislative intentions, which do not have the slightest, albeit imperfectly expressed, verbal correspondence with the letter of the law, cannot be taken into consideration by the interpreter.

55. Another premise of the interpretation of the law, which is provided by number 3 of Article 9 of the Civil Code, is the presumption by the interpreter that the legislator enshrined the most appropriate solutions and knew how to express its intentions in adequate terms, when it stipulated the meaning and scope of the law. It follows therefore that the historic circumstances in which the law arises, the letter of the law and the specific circumstances in which the law is to be applied have an influence in the interpretation of the law.

56. The question of the resolution of lacunae in the law is dealt with by Article 10 of the Civil Code. The rules regarding the resolution of lacunae in the law are applicable to cases not directly catered for in the law. According to no. 2 of Article 10 of the Civil Code, the law can be construed via the application of analogies. An analogy exists *whenever the factors that justify the application of provisions in the cases stated in the law apply to a case, which is not so stated.* In the absence of an analogous case, the resolution of lacunae is effected in accordance with the legal provision to be created by the interpreter within the spirit of the system.

57. In Portugal, the courts control the constitutionality of laws and have the power to consider the unconstitutionality of laws when this is pleaded in the in the specific cases before them. In Portugal, there is a single Constitutional Court to which an appeal lies from the decisions of the ordinary courts with regard to questions involving the unconstitutionality of laws. In restricted circumstances and upon request from certain entities the Constitutional Court can also control the constitutionality of laws on a first instance basis.

III. Custom

58. Custom is a legal provision that arises spontaneously in society, in which it is the community itself that plays the creative role, rather than the legislator or the proper bodies. According to the Boa Razão Law of 1769, customary law in Portugal was subject to the following preconditions:

(a) custom cannot be contrary to the express law;
(b) the custom must have existed for at least 100 years;
(c) the custom must be in accordance with common sense.

59. Currently, custom is of residual importance in the Portuguese legal system and is not considered to be an immediate source of law and cannot legitimately arise when contrary to the law. However, in as far as amateur sport is concerned and with particular regard to bullfighting in which the bull is killed in the arena, there is a case of an illegal custom, which the State recognized as an authentic source of Law, as the legal norm arose as a consequence of the will of the people. Bullfights in which the bull is killed in the arena are typical in some parts of Portugal, such as the town of Barrancos.

60. Accordingly and despite the fact that bullfights in which the bull is killed in the arena were illegal until 2002, the said prohibition was frequently violated without any significant repressive reaction on the part of the State, despite all its efforts in that regard, because the popular will was imposed in the conviction that the said practice was lawful and obligatory.

61. Law 19/2002 of 31 July put an end to the said prohibition. No. 4 of Article 3 thereof provides that:

> [the] holding of any bullfight in which the bulls are killed in the arena shall be authorised on an exceptional basis in order to comply with local traditions, which have been in force uninterruptedly for at least 50 years prior to the coming into force of this law, as an expression of the local culture and on those days on which the historic event takes place.

62. However, the Civil Code does not refer to custom in Article 1 thereof, which concerns the sources of Law. Despite this, Article 348 thereof provides that the courts may also apply norms based on custom, provided that the parties that invoke them establish the existence thereof. In such circumstances, the court has the obligation to seek to ascertain the nature of the custom on its own motion. If it is not possible to determine the content of the applicable law, the court will apply the provisions of ordinary Portuguese law.

IV. Case-law

63. Case-law is not generally considered to be an immediate source of Law, because it only applies to the specific case in question and has no binding effect beyond the specific case in which it is handed down. In as far as sport is concerned, court decisions tend only to be effective in relation to the specific case in point. To the extent that knowledge of legal technique and the perfection of legal technique evolve under the influence of other legal systems, there have been conflicting decisions from the courts with regard to the matters at issue in the cases before them, above all in relation to the employment rights of sportspersons, which have received considerable protection from the courts. This gives rise to doubt as to the interpretation and application of the law. However, although there is no doctrine of *stare decisis* in Portugal, fixed case-law amounts to persuasive precedent and can be considered to be a true, although mediated source of Law, as it interprets, develops or completes legal norms.

64. Prior to 1995, *assentos,* which were decisions of the plenary Supreme Court of Justice (STJ), were considered to be an immediate source of law and were of mandatory effect. However, the repeal of Article 2 of the Civil Code, insofar as it grants jurisdiction to the courts to make legal findings of general binding effect, by Constitutional Court Judgment no. 734/96, of 28 May, also abolished *assentos*. The said judgment stated with binding effect that *assentos* are unconstitutional because they are contrary to Article 115 no. 5 of the CRP (currently Article 112 no. 5 of the CRP).[6] *Assentos* were replaced by special judgments of the STJ, the purpose of which is to standardize and fix case-law. These judgments are of general mandatory effect.

65. Despite the fact that most authors do not consider case-law to be an immediate source of law, almost all authors acknowledge that it is impossible to become well familiarized with Portuguese law without studying the decisions of the courts and particularly those of the higher courts. Even so, it must be stressed that the judgments of the ordinary courts do not constitute binding precedent, although decisions in previous similar cases are usually taken into consideration.

66. The judgments of Portuguese courts, and particularly those of the higher courts, contain all relevant matters of fact and a detailed description of the substantive and procedural rules applicable in the abstract and in the specific case. They

6. Article 112, no. 5, of the CRP, provides that *General Laws of the Republic Are the Laws and Decree-Laws, Which Are Applicable to all of Portugal and State Accordingly.*

usually contain extensive references to legal theory and case-law in their consideration of the matters of law.[7]

67. Article 8 of the Civil Code requires Portuguese courts to decide solely *in accordance with the law and their conscience.* It is therefore irrelevant that the decision of a judge in a specific case conflicts with a judgment of a higher court, or with an analogous case previously decided by the same court.

V. Legal Theory

68. In the Portuguese legal system, legal theory is not considered to be an immediate source of law, despite the key role that it plays in the construction and comprehension of the legal system and in legislative reforms. In fact, the value of a legal opinion, however distinguished its author is, does not make it binding or give it an extrinsic value that behoves its acceptance.

69. Portuguese Legal Theory has a distinguishing characteristic, i.e., it focuses on and makes comparisons with foreign legal systems. Works of Portuguese legal theory normally contain various references to foreign legal systems, above all those systems that, like the Portuguese legal system, belong to the Romano-German group of legal systems; and also a bibliography of references to Portuguese and foreign works.[8]

70. The most relevant contributions in the area of legal theory come from academia. In recent years a large number of works based on masters and doctoral theses have been published. The approach of these works is fundamentally theoretical and based on solutions enshrined in the law and also on the hypothetical discussion of viable conclusions that can be drawn from case-law.[9]

VI. Equity

71. In the Portuguese system, equity has no autonomy as a source of law, as recourse to it is only permitted when this is permitted by legal provision, or when the parties have validly so agreed accordingly.

72. The courts can only decide in accordance with equity when there is legal provision that permits this. For example, in a case of necessity, the court can award equitable damages against a person, who has destroyed or damaged the property of another, in order to eliminate a present danger of manifestly greater damage.

7. Compare Carlos Ferreira de Almeida, *Sistemas Jurídicos Comparados* (Coimbra: Almedina, Segunda Edição, 1998), 56–57.
8. Compare Carlos Ferreira de Almeida, *Sistemas Jurídicos Comparados* (Coimbra: Almedina, Segunda Edição, 1998), 58.
9. Compare Carlos Ferreira de Almeida, *Sistemas Jurídicos Comparados* (Coimbra: Almedina, Segunda Edição, 1998), 58.

Likewise, equitable considerations are also relevant in circumstances of an abnormal change of circumstances, when the injured party is entitled to rescind the contract or to the alteration thereof, in accordance with the dictates of equity. Equity is also applicable when the acts of a person, who is under a disability, cause loss and damage. Exceptionally, the tortfeasor may be ordered to make reparation on equitable grounds. These circumstances are dealt with in Articles 339, no. 2, 437, no. 1 and 489, no. 1 all of the Civil Code.

73. Another situation in which there can be recourse to equity is when this is agreed between the parties and the legal relationship in question does not involve inalienable rights, or when recourse to equity is the subject matter of a prior agreement, in accordance with the provisions of an arbitration agreement. In fact, Article 22 of Law 31/86, of 29 August provides that arbitrators shall decide in accordance with the applicable law, unless the parties have agreed in the arbitration agreement, or in a document signed prior to the acceptance by the first arbitrator of his/her appointment that the arbitrators are authorized to decide according to equity.

74. According to no. 2 of Article 26 of Law no. 78/2001, of 13 July, which introduced Civil Law Magistrates, they are authorized to decide according to equity, provided that the parties so agree and the value of the action does not exceed the jurisdiction limit of courts of first instance.[10]

75. The content of equity is indeterminate and varies in accordance with the prevailing concepts of justice in each society and at each moment in history. Independently of whether or not Equity is a source of Law, it can be considered to be a criterion of correction in the application of the Law.

§3. The Organization of Judicial Power

I. Ordinary Courts

A. Introduction

76. Courts are sovereign bodies with the power and duty to administer justice on the people's behalf. According to no. 2 of Article 202 of the CRP, they are subject to an obligation to:

(a) defend the legally protected rights and interests of all citizens;
(b) punish violations of democratic legality;
(c) decide conflicts between private interests and public interests.

10. Article 24 of the Court Organisation and Workings Law (LOFT), approved by Law no. 3/99, of 13 January and Art. 12 of the new LOFTJ, approved by Law no. 52/2008, of 28 August fix the upper jurisdiction threshold of the Courts of First Instance as EUR 5,000 and that of the Courts of Appeal as EUR 30,000.

77. According to Article 203 of the CRP, the courts are independent and are only subject to the law. This independence is reflected in the fact that judges do not receive any orders or instructions as to how they are to decide disputes. The Laws on the Organisation and Working of the Courts (LOFTJ), which were approved by Law no. 3/99, of 13th January, and by Law no. 52/2008, of 28th August, also refers to the independence of the courts and of judges.

78. Judges decide solely in accordance with the CRP and the law and cannot be held liable for their decisions, except in exceptional circumstances laid down in the law. The independence of judges is guaranteed by the existence of a private body, which is responsible for the management and discipline of the judiciary, i.e., the Supreme Council of the Judiciary, by the fact that a judge cannot be removed during proceedings, except in exceptional circumstances, failing which the entire proceedings must be repeated, and by non-subjection of the judge to any orders or instructions, other than the duty to comply with the decisions of higher courts in appeals. The fact that judges cannot be removed or held liable is also enshrined in Article 216 of the CRP and in Articles 4, 5 and 6 of the Judiciary Statute, which was approved by Law no. 21/85, of 30th July. This law has been successively amended, most recently by Law no 63/2008, of 18th November.

79. According to Article 206 of the CRP, court hearings are generally public, which reinforces the principle of confidence in justice, except when the court itself decides otherwise through an order which states due grounds, in most cases for purposes of protecting the dignity of persons or public morals, and also to ensure the normal working of the court. Court decisions bind all public and private entities and prevail over the decisions of any other authorities.

B. Judicial Organization

80. The LOFTJ divides Portugal into judicial districts, judicial circuits and judicial areas. The courts are divided between ordinary courts and special courts. The Constitutional Court and the Public Accounts Court exist in addition to the other courts.

81. The ordinary court deal with cases that are not allocated to special court, such as the administrative and tax courts. Arbitration tribunals and civil lay magistrates can also be created.

C. Hierarchical Organization

82. The ordinary courts have civil and criminal jurisdiction. These courts are organized in three levels, with most courts being on the lowest level, i.e., 1st instance courts, with general jurisdiction, i.e., they can decide all cases whatever the subject matter thereof. There are also courts of special jurisdiction, i.e.: Criminal Investigation Courts, Family Courts, Minors Courts, Employment Courts, Maritime

Courts and Sentence Implementation courts. The major innovation in the area of sport was the creation of the PCAS, which is considered in detail in the following chapters.

83. The ordinary, or 1st instance courts, are normally district courts and are known by the name of the judicial district in which they are located. The 2nd instance is comprised of the courts of appeal, whose principal jurisdiction is to decide appeals from the judgments of 1st instance courts, in most cases whatever the subject matter thereof. The 3rd instance is the STJ, which sits in Lisbon and is divided in to specialized sections, i.e.:

(a) civil;
(b) criminal;
(c) social.

84. The STJ decides appeals from the decisions of the courts of appeal, limited to matters of law. In certain special cases laid down in the law, the STJ can decide regarding criminal matters and also directly with regard to 1st instance appeals, which, according to the law, lie directly to the STJ. There is no jurisdiction value limit in criminal courts. However, criminal law states the circumstances in which there is a right of appeal.

II. Arbitration Courts

85. No. 2 of Article 209 of the CRP provides for the possible existence of arbitration tribunals. According to no. 3 of the said article the circumstances and ways in which arbitration tribunals can be established is a subject matter of legislation. Arbitration tribunals are not part of the structure of the State and are not organs of sovereignty, but are private courts in which arbitrators can decide disputes in a binding manner. These powers of arbitration tribunals have their source in the law, but are specifically vested in them pursuant to arbitration agreements.

86. The law governing arbitration proceedings is the Voluntary Arbitration Law (LAV), approved by Law no. 63/2011, of 14th December. According to the LAV, a dispute may be referred to arbitration by the parties, who must be natural persons, pursuant to an arbitration agreement in writing, provided that the dispute does not concern inalienable rights and is not subject to the exclusive jurisdiction of a court of law, or compulsory arbitration, pursuant to a special law.

87. The LAV came into force on the 15th of March 2012 and applies to proceedings commenced after it came into force and may be applied to proceedings commenced prior to that date, by agreement between the parties, or if no opposition is raised within fifteen days of an application to that effect, by one of the parties.

88. One of the objectives of the latest version of LAV[11] is to:

> bring the Voluntary Arbitration Law closer to the provisions of the UNCITRAL Model Law on International Commercial Arbitration, in order to create an awareness among companies and professionals in various areas that frequently have recourse to arbitration in other countries, above all those with which our country has stronger economic relations, with regard to the advantages and potential of the selection of Portugal as the seat of international arbitration, i.e. those disputes which involve companies and other economic agents from Portuguese speaking countries, or when the applicable law is the law of such a country.

89. Another objective of the current LAV is the facilitation of the recognition and enforcement of foreign arbitration awards. The LAV therefore contains provisions similar to those of the 1958 New York Convention, regarding the Recognition and Enforcement of Foreign Arbitral Awards (the New York Convention).

90. Additionally the following important changes introduced by the current law should be noted:

(a) the arbitrability criterion is extended to *'any dispute regarding financial interests';*
(b) the negative effect of arbitration agreements/clauses: a negative effect of arbitration agreements/clauses is introduced, as the courts of law are required to dismiss proceedings against respondents, who successfully plead violation of an arbitration agreement/clause;
(c) the independence and impartiality of arbitrators: the LAV includes a major amendment, as independence and impartiality are now emphasized prerequisites for arbitrators in Article 9, no. 3 14 – *'Arbitrators must be independent and impartial'* – and also in Article 13, no. 1 15 – *'Those persons who are invited to be arbitrators must disclose all circumstances that could give rise to doubts regarding their impartiality and independence'*. Moreover, the law expressly provides that the said requirements are applicable throughout the entire proceedings and that further notice must be given if any of the said circumstances arise during the proceedings, or if they are only known of after the arbitrator's acceptance of his/her appointment. The major difference in relation to the previous version of LAV is that although Article 9 of the new law essentially contains the same rules; tacit acceptance of the appointment is now deemed to exist unless the arbitrator appointed states within ten days of his/her appointment, which he/she does not wish to accept the same;
(d) arbitrators' liability: it provides new circumstances in which arbitrators are liable for breach of their duties. According to the said provisions, arbitrators are liable for the loss and damage they cause by unjustifiably resigning from their position and when they unjustifiably fail to hand down their award within the time limit fixed;

11. The previous LAV was approved by Law no. 31/86, of 29 August.

(e) the rules regarding the formation of the tribunal, where there are more than one applicant, or more than one respondent: Article 11 of the new LAV provides, without prejudice to other agreement between the parties, that when the arbitration tribunal is to comprise three arbitrators, the applicants jointly appoint one arbitrator and the respondents jointly appoint another arbitrator. In the absence of agreement between the various applicants or respondents, either party may apply to a court of law for the appointment of the absent arbitrator;
(f) arbitrators' fees: according to Article 17 of the new LAV, in the absence of provision in the arbitration agreement/ clause, the arbitrators fees, the form of the reimbursement of their expenses and the form of the payment by the parties of amounts on account of the said fees and disbursements, are the subject matter of an agreement in writing between the parties and the arbitrators, which is concluded prior the acceptance by the last arbitrator of his/her appointment;
(g) interlocutory injunctive relief: this is one of the areas in which the current LAV introduces various provisions in Articles 20–29 thereof that are innovations in the Portuguese legal system and in which the solutions in the UNCITRAL Model Law are adopted. The LAV therefore permits the granting of interlocutory injunctive relief both by courts of law and by the arbitration tribunal;
(h) appeals: the rule in the previous LAV was that an appeal always lay from arbitral awards made in domestic arbitrations, unless the parties had excluded this possibility. The LAV provides that an appeal only lies from awards in domestic arbitration proceedings if the parties have so stipulated and whenever the cause has not been decided by reference to equitable criteria, or by amicable agreement;
(i) setting aside of arbitral awards: the Portuguese courts have the power to set aside arbitral awards with regard to both domestic and international arbitration proceedings that take place in Portugal. The LAV sets a sixty-day time limit for the commencement of proceedings to set aside an arbitral award (Article 46, no. 6 59), however the inalienability rule in no. 5 of Article 46 is unchanged. Furthermore, the new LAV suggests that proceedings to set aside an arbitral award are in fact an appeal, i.e., they take place in a court of second instance as if it was an appeal.

91. Article 46 no. 3 of the LAV alters the previous regime with regard to the grounds for an order setting aside an arbitral award. Accordingly and instead of referring to the possibility that the dispute is not arbitrable, or that the award was made by a tribunal that lacked jurisdiction, or was not properly formed, the updated version of the LAV provides that an award may be set aside if the applicant party that so applies proves that: (a) one of the parties to the arbitration agreement/clause was affected by a disability; or the said agreement/clause was not valid according to the law to which the parties subjected it; or, in the absence of any indication by the parties in that regard, in accordance with Portuguese arbitration law; (b) that the award decides a dispute not included in the arbitration agreement/clause, or con tains decisions that exceed the ambit thereof; In general terms, the ground based on the violation of the fundamental principles provided in Article 30, no. 1 of the LAV is retained. The violation of the requirements of Article 42 nos 1 and 3 (the agreement/clause must be in writing and signed, and the duty to state grounds for the award) is also retained as grounds for setting aside.

92. The LAV also governs the way in which arbitration tribunals are established, the appointment of arbitrators, bars and impediments, the workings of arbitration proceedings and the arbitration award. According to no. 2 of Article 26 of the LAV, an arbitration award has the same enforceability as the judgment of a court of law. Arbitration awards are enforced in 1st instance courts of law in accordance with the provisions of the Civil Procedure Code.

Part I. Organization of Sports

Chapter 1. Public Regulation

§1. Sports Law

I. The Fundamental Principles of Sport in the Portuguese Constitution

93. No. 1 of Article 79 of the CRP enshrines a general right to physical culture and sport. No. 2 of the said article, which was introduced in the 1989 constitutional reform, provides that the State is required *to promote, stimulate, guide and support the practice of sport and the diffusion of physical culture and sport,* in collaboration with schools and sports groups and associations. The final part of no. 2 of the said article provides that the State must also ensure the *prevention of violence in sport.*

94. The CRP recognizes the right to sport as a fundamental and universal right, as it considers that all citizens are entitled to sport as recreation, a source of income, profession, or leisure activity, *inter alia.* The principle of the necessity of public intervention in sport and the principle of the necessary collaboration by the State with sports associations' movements can be inferred from the said constitutional provision, as no. 2 of the article requires the State to collaborate with certain intermediate organizations. This indicates a collaborationist model of the relationship of the State with autonomous sports structures, such as clubs, associations, or sports federations, with an inherently decentralizing concept of the State's role as complementary and subsidiary.

95. However the constitutional provisions with regard to sport are not limited to Article 79 of the CRP. For:

(a) it follows from Articles 71 and 79 of the CRP that handicapped citizens have a fundamental right to sport;
(b) a general right to rest and leisure is included in the list of workers' rights in Article 59 of the CRP;
(c) Article 65 of the CRP enshrines the right to housing. In the context of social facilities, sports facilities have a specific role and amount to a requirement for the obtaining of a real and true right to housing;
(d) Article 66, no. 1 of the CRP enshrines the right of all to a healthy and ecologically balanced human living environment;

(e) Article 69 enshrines the right of children to the protection of society and the State, with a view to their complete development, i.e., it implicitly includes the right to take part in recreational and sporting activities suitable for their age;
(f) according to no. 1 and no. 2 of Article 73 of the CRP, all people are entitled to education and it is for the State to create the conditions so that education can contribute to the development of their personalities;
(g) No. 1 of Article 64 of the CRP stipulates that all people are entitled to the protection of their health and that young people are entitled to special protection in order to ensure the full enjoyment of their economic, social and cultural rights, particularly in physical education and sport, as per Article 70, paragraph d) of the CRP.

II. Sport and Fundamental Rights

A. *Introduction*

96. Sport is essentially governed by private bodies. However, there is an involvement of the political authorities and the State in the organization of sport, as one of the roles of the political authorities is the protection, promotion and dissemination of fundamental rights.

97. The first legislation relevant to sport,[12] which structured the sports system, was Decree no. 21.110, of 4 September 1932, which approved the regulations governing physical education in grammar schools. The law's preamble refers to the evil spirit of competitive sport, as a cause of *physical and moral malformation.* Competitive sport was accordingly not promoted in schools and only the various amateur sports, healthy leisure and social intercourse were legally accepted.

98. With Decree no. 32.946, of 3 August in 1943, which introduced the regulations governing the General Directorate of Physical Education, Sport and School Health,[13] the law became less harsh and began to see sport as a leisure activity to be afforded to its citizenry.

99. The first time that professional sport was referred to in a law was in 1960, but even so with clear disdain for what is referred to in Law no. 2104, of 30 May as *sport of the masses.* Only in those sports in which practice was starting to demonstrate the inevitability of the professionalization of sportspersons Even so it was

12. For a more complete description of the chronology of the laws that have governed sport in Portugal since the beginning of the twentieth century see João Leal Amado, 'Vinculação Versus Liberdade. O Processo de Constituição e Extinção da Relação Laboral do Praticante Desportivo'. Coimbra: Editora, 2002, pp. 20–26.
13. This General Directorate was created in 1942, by Decree-Law no, 32.241, of 5 September. For a detail account of the various institutions created by the Estado Novo that were in some way connected to sport see Alberto Trovão do Rosário, *O Desporto em Portugal.* Lisbon: Instituto Piaget, 1996, pp. 48–136.

with great reservation that the existence of professional sportsmen, and not of professional sport, was expressly admitted.

100. Only after the revolution of 25 April 1974 did there start to be serious and detailed talk of real professional sport, but always in connection with topics such as the ethics of sport, violence and doping, topics which acquired interest of the Portuguese legislature in the 1980s.

B. Fundamental Rights and State Intervention

101. In order to consider the problem of fundamental rights and sport it is necessary to distinguish between professional sport and amateur sport and also to provide a brief account of the development of fundamental rights in the Portuguese legal system.

102. Nowadays, the CRP sees the right to sport as a fundamental right, in the context of *social rights.* However, in most European constitutions, fundamental rights started out as merely *freedoms,* i.e., they were viewed as a *right to participate,* and arose as the basis for the construction of a free society in the context of a totalitarian and oppressive state, so that sport had nothing to do with fundamental rights.

103. The evolution of political thought resulted in the fact that fundamental rights started to be seen as having a social aspect – i.e., the welfare state, a State, which is required to promote the welfare of the general public, i.e., physical and mental well-being, which had to include *the right to sport.* In as far as the State is concerned, this means the duty to promote sports activities, which implies State promotion of *sport of the masses* and sport in schools, in order to promote and defend the fundamental rights of the general public. In the CRP, sport appears as a factor, which improves the quality of human life and culture, so that public intervention is necessary in order to ensure the right to sport and to defend it from violence, racism and intolerance, *inter alia.*

104. Accordingly, during most of the twentieth century, professional sport was prohibited in Portugal, a state of affairs, which is now inconceivable, to the extent that the State could, and subsequently was required to, intervene in sport in order to improve and promote it.

105. Today, Portugal is one of the countries where there is major public intervention in the area of professional sport because the State considers that it must play a significant role in sport, which includes professional sport. Despite the fact that professional sport is an essentially private activity, it has a social and solidarity aspect, which justifies public intervention, regulation and supervision, although it is acknowledged that sport is a free and autonomous activity.

106. The internal autonomy of the sports system is recognized as is its inter-state and trans-state autonomy, together with its external projection, as the sports system is organized internationally. The basic idea is that it is for the State, so far as necessary, to ensure that the general public have a series of fundamental rights. The right to sport cannot prejudice certain rights, freedoms and guarantees enshrined in the constitution, i.e., there are imperatives that permit the State to intervene in the sports system, despite its private nature. The purpose of this State intervention is the defence of fundamental rights, to the extent that they bind both private and public bodies.

107. The protection of fundamental rights involves individual rights such as the right to life and the right to privacy, but also the rights of people, who are members of organizations, such as freedom of association and freedom to set up an economic activity, *inter alia.*

108. Furthermore, the fundamental rights of sportspersons are frequently limited as a consequence of the fact that they are involved in professional sport, e.g., image rights and the right to privacy. In these cases, a reduction of the fundamental rights of sportspersons is acceptable, to the extent that it is appropriate and proportionate in order to meet the needs of the sport system.

109. There are some examples in which a special status is necessary for sportspersons, i.e., the fact that the general individual principles regarding assault cannot be applied to a team sport, which could pose problems in terms of the *dignity of the human person.*

C. Legal Restriction of Rights and the Specific Resolution of Conflicts of Rights

110. The CRP permits a normative limitation of rights, to the extent that the limitation is proportional and the objective is to protect another value, such as the workings of sports activities. The fundamental rights of sportspersons may only be limited, if the limitation complies with the principles of proportionality, appropriateness and necessity, not overlooking the abstract principle and absolute limit established by the principle of human dignity and the fundamental individual rights involved and the aim, which is to preserve the proper working of the sports system.

111. It is also necessary to consider the growing mediatization and general curiosity regarding some of the more popular sports, e.g., football, which is likely to give rise to greater limitation, or violations, of the privacy of some sportspersons and leaders.

112. Sportspersons involved actively in high performance sport also benefit from a higher level of health care, than the general public, because of the rapid wear and negative health outcomes involved.

113. In as far as disputes are concerned, there can also be rules and bylaws, which involve a reduction of the fundamental rights of sportspersons, in the abstract. For example, there may be a conflict between two fundamental rights, the most common of which is the conflict between freedom of information and the right to privacy and a private life.

114. Although it is understood that there is no hierarchy between two specific fundamental rights, or between a value of society and a fundamental right, attempts must be made to harmonize the two rights and, if this is impossible, to evaluate the specific case in order to ascertain the possibility of one of the conflicting rights prevailing over the other in accordance with their comparative preponderance.

115. In the case of relations in the context of sport, it is also possible to renounce fundamental rights to the extent that sports relations are frequently governed by contract, which can include the agreed limitation and reduction of certain rights. It can be queried whether this reduction of rights is lawful and whether the State should permit it, as its duty is to guarantee fundamental rights. It is however clear that the prior renunciation of rights, or consent to the limitation of fundamental rights is only valid to the extent that the consent or agreement is free and informed and insofar as the absolute limit represented by the principle of the *human dignity* is complied with. If this limit is exceeded, free and informed consent is irrelevant.

116. One of the examples of the prevalence of the protection of fundamental rights is so-called sports justice, which is generally restrictive in terms of rights to appeal to courts of law. Whenever fundamental rights are at issue, however, the matter cannot be considered to be strictly sporting because the courts will always have the power to intervene to protect those constitutional rights.

117. However great the autonomy of sport may be, or become, the State cannot negate from its duty to ensure an effective legal protection of the fundamental rights of those involved in sports relations. However, the State also must not exceed the minimum limits of intervention in the regulation of sport, when the guarantee of fundamental rights is not at issue.

III. The Organization of the Government in Relation to Sport

A. Introduction

118. The 2005 Programme of the 17th Constitutional Government identified the modernization of the Public Administration as one of the essential aspects of the country's development strategy. The Government accordingly approved the Programme for the Reorganisation of the Central State Administration (PRACE) by Council of Ministers Resolution no. 124/2005, of 4th August, in order to promote citizenship, economic development and the quality of public services, with efficiency gains as a consequence of simplification, rationalization and automation, which permitted a reduction of the number of departments and of the resources allocated to them.

119. Following the approval of PRACE, Council of Ministers Resolution no. 39/2006, of 30th March defined the general and specific orientations for the reorganization of the existing ministries, in which sport fell under the auspices of the Presidency of the Council of Ministers, which was, in turn, supported by a Secretary of State for Youth and Sport (SEJD).

120. Decree-Law no. 202/2006, of 27th October, which approved the Organic Law of the Presidency of the Council of Ministers, as outlined in PRACE, gave rise, in the area of sport, to organizational reforms i.e., the abolition of the National Council Against Violence in Sport, the Higher Council for Sport and the National Anti-Doping Council, the powers and duties of which were vested in the future National Sports Council (NSC), working together with the Portuguese Sports Institute, Public Institute (IDP, IP).

B. The Portuguese Sports Institute

121. The IDP was created by Law no. 96/2003, of 7 May, which was repealed by Decree-Law no. 169/2007, of 3 May,[14] which created a new organizational framework that came into force on 1 June 2007. The IDP exercises the powers of the Presidency of the Council of Ministers and is an organ of the *Indirect Administration* of the State and has administrative and financial autonomy and its own assets. The IDP is governed by its bylaws, which were approved by Statutory Instrument no. 662-L/2007, of 31 May, as amended by Statutory Instrument no. 573/2008, of 4 July[15] and republished by the Statutory Instrument no. 1326/2010, of 30 December.

122. The role of the IDP is to support the definition, implementation and evaluation of sports public policy, to promote the generalization of physical exercise and to support the practice of ordinary and high performance sport, via the provision of technical, financial and human resources.

123. The IDP is the body responsible for:

(a) proposing measures with a view to the prevention and combating of racism and xenophobia in sport;
(b) proposing and implementing an integrated programme for the construction and recuperation of sports facilities and infrastructures, in collaboration with local authorities, and to give an opinion regarding sports security and safety rules to be complied with in the construction and licensing thereof;

14. With exception of the provisions of Art. 12.
15. The amendments introduced by this Statutory Instrument came into force on 5 Jun. 2008.

(c) promoting the generalization of medical checks on access to sport and during sports activities;
(d) carrying out such supervisory and inspection activities and for issuing such authorizations and licences, certifications and credentials as it is charged with by law;
(e) proposing the Adoption of programmes with a view to the inclusion of physical activity in the daily habits of the general public and for providing the development of sport with technical, material and financial assistance;
(f) ensuring the valorization and qualification of sports actors;
(g) the promotion and support of the conduct of studies and research regarding the sports activity indicators and the various factors involved in the development of physical activity and sport.

124. The IDP has various departments, which are first level organizational units, which are hierarchically and functionally subject to the chairman of the IDP. It also has regional offices. Such departments are:

(a) the Human Resources and Management Development;
(b) the Human, Financial and Material Resources Department;
(c) the Sports Medicine Department;
(d) the Sports Development Department;
(e) the Sports Facilities Department.

C. The National Sports Council

125. PRACE and the Organic Law of the Presidency of the Council of Ministers, approved by Decree-Law no. 202/2006, of 27 October, abolished the Higher Council for Sport and provided for the creation of the National Sports Council (NSC).

126. Decree-Law no. 266-A/2012, of 31 December, develops and implements the legal framework established by Law no. 5/2007, of 16 January (Basic Law regarding Physical Activity and Sport), and defines the powers, duties, composition and workings of the National Sports Council, and therefore replaces Decree-Law no. 315/2007, of 18 September, which previously governed these matters.

127. This new decree-law altered the NSC, so that it now comprises a Plenary Session, as applied previously although now with an additional ordinary meeting, and a Permanent Committee, with a new structure, which is responsible for doing all things necessary in order to facilitate the Council's activities, while the Plenary Session is responsible for advising the Government with regard to matters related to national sports policy. The sections of the NSC which existed prior to the passing of this decree-law have accordingly been abolished.

128. The Council for Ethics and Safety in Sport (CESS) and the Sports System Council (SSC), i.e., the two sections of the National Sports Council, were accordingly abolished on the coming into force of the NSC's new legal framework.

129. The LBAFD gave the NSC increased powers, i.e., to make provisional decisions in disputes arising between sports federations and the corresponding professional league, with regard to the number of clubs that take part in the professional sports competition, the access conditions governing professional and non-professional competitions and the organization of the activities of national teams.

130. The NSC is made up of representatives of the Public Administration and of the voluntary sports associations' movement,[16] and operates under the immediate auspices of the Government member responsible for sport Its powers and responsibilities include the following:

(a) to monitor the development of policies to promote physical activity and sport;
(b) to give an opinion regarding draft legislation with regard to sport, when requested so to do by the Government member responsible for sport;
(c) to state its opinion regarding factors for the development of high performance sport;
(d) to state its opinion regarding measures to be taken within the ambit of the non-academic training of sports staffs;
(e) to state its opinion regarding the links between the various sports subsystems; and
(f) to recognize the professional nature of the competitions in each sport.

With the coming into force of the new decree-law the NSC, the CESS and the SSC cease to exist.

§2. SPORTS JUSTICE

I. Introduction

131. In as far as sport justice is concerned, the Portuguese Legal System is structured in such a way that certain matters are intentionally excluded from the jurisdiction of the ordinary courts of law, while not neglecting the constitutional principle of guaranteed effective legal protection of rights.

132. Even if it makes sense to exclude certain sports disputes from the jurisdiction of ordinary courts of law, or at least to require the internal dispute resolution

16. Decree-Law no. 1/2009, of 5 January increased the number of members of the NSC from 33 to 38, by adding a representative of the Ministry of Employment and Social Solidarity, a representative of the Olympic Athletes Committee of the Olympic Committee of Portugal ad by adjusting the representation of persons of recognised merit, accordingly. (Este Decreto-Lei foi alterado pelo novo decreto-lei n.° 266-A/2012, de 31 de Dezembro).

mechanisms within the federations and leagues to have been exhausted before the matter is brought before a court of law, it is nevertheless true that the constitution guarantees access to the courts and the effective legal protection of rights in accordance with Article 20, no. 1 and Article 268, no. 4 of the CRP.

II. Sports Justice in the LBAFD

133. The LBAFD used to contain a single chapter on the subject of sports justice in section II of Chapter III, which was dedicated to the subject of the sports federations. Article 18 of the LBAFD, which was entitled '*Sports justice*', had five sections, which were as follows:

(a) disputes arising from the acts or omissions of the management and supervisory bodies of sports federations and professional leagues, within the ambit of the exercise of public powers, are subject to the rules governing administrative disputes. Sports consequences that are a valid consequence of the most recent decision of the competent instance in the sports system shall, however, not be subject to alteration;
(b) there shall be no right of appeal outside of the sports dispute resolution systems against decisions and resolutions with regard to strictly sporting matters;
(c) strictly sports matters are those that are based on technical or disciplinary rules, which arise from the application of the rules of the game, or the organisational rules and regulations regarding the organisation of the corresponding competitions;
(d) for the purposes of the provisions of the preceding number, disciplinary decisions and resolutions with regard to contraventions of sports ethics, in the context of violence, doping, corruption, racism and xenophobia, shall not be deemed to be strictly sporting matters;
(e) disputes with regard to strictly sporting matters can be resolved by recourse to arbitration, or mediation, if there is a prior arbitration agreement in writing, or in accordance with the provisions of the bylaws or regulations of the relevant sports associations.

134. Article 18, no. 1 of the LBAFD confirmed the constitutional guarantee of effective legal protection with regard to disputes arising from acts or omissions of organs of sports federations and professional leagues, within the ambit of the exercise of public powers, which are made subject to the provisions governing contentious administrative matters. It should be noted that this principle has been limited, in relation to the previous Basic Laws of Sport, as it only applies with regard to disputes arising from the exercise of public powers. Legal theory[17] considers however that this was not the legislator's intention, so that the constitutional right of access to the courts and to effective legal protection prevails.

17. Namely, José Manuel Meirim, *Lei de Bases da Actividade Física e do Desporto – Estudo, Notas e Comentários*. Coimbra, Coimbra Editora, 2007, pp. 183 and 184.

135. The second part of no. 1 of Article 18 of the LBAFD sought to safeguard the valid sports effects of the last decision of the proper sports judicial body, which has been taken in the meantime. This indicates the need to exhaust the jurisdiction of the proper sports dispute resolution bodies, in order to obtain a final decision, before it is possible to appeal to the courts of law.

136. Sports res judicata[18] was accordingly safeguarded by the second part of no. 1 of Article 18 of the LBAFD. Res judicata means, for example, that legal proceedings regarding a decision, which disqualified a team or player may result in an award of damages to the injured party, but will not order the repetition of the game in question.[19] This means that when a club is relegated and the corresponding disciplinary measure is revoked by a court of law, a right to civil damages then arises with regard to the unlawful act, but the sports sanction of relegation of the club cannot be revoked. Some authors consider that the said provision should not be construed so as to be limited to an entitlement to damages and that the club should be placed in the position in which it was prior to the punishment that was set aside.

137. According to Article 2 of Article 18 of the LBAFD, there was no right of appeal with regard to strictly sports matters outside of the competent bodies in the sports system. No. 3 of the said article clarifies that strictly sports matters are those that are based on strictly technical or disciplinary rules, which arise from the application of the rules of the game, or the organizational rules and regulations of the corresponding competitions. The legal definition enshrined in the LBAFD has given rise to problems as to the ambit of matters and disputes that the same is intended to include.

138. The definition of *strictly sports matters* in the second part of no. 3 of Article 18 of the LBAFD included a wide range of circumstances, which some legal theorists consider to be unconstitutional because the definition is too broad.

139. With the publication of w no. 74/2013 of 6 September, Article 18 of the LBAFD was entirely removed since it was created the *Portuguese Court of Arbitration for Sport (PCAS).*

140. The *Portuguese Court of Arbitration for Sport (PCAS)* was created with the publication of Law no. 74/2013, of 6 September (which was later amended by Decree Law no. 33/2014 of 16 July). It has its head office at the Portuguese Olympic Committee (POC) and began its operations in October 2015.

141. The law defines the PCAS as a judicial body that is independent of the sports public administration and of the bodies that comprise the sports system,

18. An expression used by José Ribeiro e Castro. *Lei de Bases do Sistema Desportivo, Anotada e Comentada.* Lisbon, Ministry of Education, 1990, p. 80.
19. Example given by José Manuel Meirim. *Lei de Bases da Actividade Física e do Desporto – Estudo, Notas e Comentários.* Coimbra, Coimbra Editora, 2007, p. 184.

which has administrative and financial autonomy. The Court has specific jurisdiction to administer justice with regard to disputes arising within the sports legal system, or in relation to the sports activity.

142. The PCAS's jurisdiction extends to the whole of Portugal and it is required, within the ambit of its mandatory arbitration jurisdiction to decide disputes arising from the acts and omissions of the federations and other sports entities and professional leagues, within the ambit of the exercise of their rule-making, organizational, management and disciplinary powers.

143. Access to the PCAS is however only available in appeals against the decisions of the judicial bodies of the sports federations, or against the final decisions of other sports entities and professional leagues. This means that there is still a need to have recourse to internal challenge, appeal or penalization mechanisms with regard to acts or omissions practiced, in the exercise or ambit of rule-making, organizational, management and disciplinary powers and powers provided in the law, or in bylaws or regulations. However, a time limit is established for the decision of the federation judicial body and for the final decision of the federations and other sports bodies and professional leagues: i.e., thirty working days. An originating application may be filed with PCAS ten days after the expiry of the said period, in the event that the decision is not made within the same.

144. The resolution of issues arising from the application of technical and disciplinary rules regarding the conduct of competitive sport is excluded from the SDAT's jurisdiction. PCAS also has jurisdiction to decide appeals against decisions of the disciplinary bodies of the sports federations, or the Anti-Doping Authority of Portugal, with regard to violations of the anti-doping rules, in accordance with the provisions of Law no. 38/2012 of 28 August.

145. So far as PCAS' voluntary arbitration jurisdiction is concerned, it may decide all disputes that are directly or indirectly related to the practice of sport, which are not subject to mandatary arbitration, that are arbitrable in accordance with the voluntary arbitration law (Law 63/2011 of 14 December) provided that the same are the subject matter of an arbitration agreement, or a clause in the bylaws of a federation or other sports body. Disputes arising from sports employment contracts between sportspersons or trainers and agents or sports bodies may be referred to voluntary arbitration and can include the issue of the lawful or unlawful nature of dismissals. PCAS therefore has the arbitration jurisdiction of the former Paritary Arbitration Commissions.

146. The PCAS has a maximum of forty independent and impartial arbitrators appointed by the following bodies: five by those Olympic sports federations, which do not organize professional competitions, five by the non-Olympic sports federations, five by the Portuguese Sports Confederation, two by the federations that organize professional sport competitions, two by the leagues that organize professional competitions, one by each of the professional associations of sportspersons, managers, referees and umpires of those sports in which professional competitions are organized, two by the Olympic Athletes Committee, two by the Portuguese Confederation of Coaches Associations, two by the associations that represent other sports actors, which are recognized by the sports federations, one by the Portuguese Sports Law Association and five by the Executive Committee of the Portuguese Olympic Committee and the remainder by the Sport Arbitration Council.

147. The arbitrators are appointed for a renewable four year period, but may be removed at any time by the Sport Arbitration Council in certain circumstances. Inclusion in the list of PCAS arbitrators is however incompatible with practice as a lawyer in the said court.

The law also establishes specific rules regarding the workings of the PCAS, together with some general provisions that are applicable to mandatary arbitration proceedings and voluntary arbitration proceedings. The law also contains some rules regarding Court fees in mandatary arbitration proceedings, which will only be relevant once the PCAS has been established.

148. Since its creation, the PCAS has been met with various criticisms with regard to its compliance with the Portuguese Constitution. PCAS was conceived to decide disputes referred to mandatary arbitration, e.g., disputes arising from the acts and omissions of the federations and other sports bodies and professional leagues, within the ambit of the exercise of rule-making, organizational, management and disciplinary powers; and to decide appeals against the decisions of the disciplinary bodies of the sports federations, or by the Portuguese Anti-Doping Authority with regard to violations of the anti-doping rules, and disputes referred to voluntary arbitration by the parties, i.e., disputes that are arbitrable in accordance with the voluntary arbitration law, are not subject to mandatary arbitration and are directly, or indirectly, related to the practice of sport, including disputes arising from sports employment contracts.

149. The critical point of the draft law was whether it is permissible to create an arbitration tribunal with a mandatary jurisdiction without provision being made for a right of appeal to the courts against its decisions and what the scope of the said appeal provisions should be. For, by granting a complete jurisdiction to PCAS, the law removed control of the legality of the rules and acts of sports justice from the Administrative Courts.

150. Even before the law that approves PCAS came into force, the Constitutional Court declared in its Judgment no. 230/2013 that some of the provisions of Assembly of the Republic Decree no. 128/XII were unconstitutional because they were contrary to the principle of equality, the right of access to the courts and the principle of effective court protection of rights, as the Decree made no provision for any type of appeal to a court of law from the decision made. Subsequently, Law no. 74/2013, provided for an exceptional appeal from the decisions of the PCAS to the Supreme Administrative Court (SAC), by way of an intermediate solution.

151. This solution did not convince the Constitutional Court, which, in its Judgment no. 781/2013, again held that the provisions that enshrined the said intermediate solution were unconstitutional. Although it was no longer possible, in the light of the alteration of the law, to consider that the jurisdiction of CAS was complete, it is also true that the said alterations were not sufficient to create a relative jurisdiction.

152. The legislature decided to make a final attempt to overcome the unconstitutionality issues raised, via Draft Law no. 523/XII; which now provides for an urgent appeal to the Central Administrative Court against decisions of arbitration panels.

153. Law no. 33/2004, of 16 June, amends Article 3 of the Law that created the PCAS and Articles 4, 8, 52, 53, 54 and 59 of the PCAS Law. The said alterations were made following an application by the President of the Republic for the successive abstract evaluation of the constitutionality of nos 1 and 2 of Article 8, with regard to appeals against arbitral awards, when read together with Articles 4 and 5, which establish the scope of mandatary arbitration.

154. The Constitutional Court held, in its Judgment no. 781/2013, that the limitations on the right of access to the courts were unconstitutional and contrary to the principle of effective court protection of rights, as not all decisions of PCAS, in mandatary arbitration proceedings, involve a right of appeal to the Supreme Administrative Court (SAC), as the said right is limited to those decisions, which having been admitted to the chamber of appeals and are of manifest social and legal importance.

155. With the amendment of no. 1 of Article 8 all decisions of the arbitration panels are subject to appeal and it is for the parties to opt between appeal to the courts, i.e., to the Central Administrative Court (CAC) – thus resolving the issue of the exceptional nature of the appeal to the SAC, or to the PCAS appeals chamber. If the parties opt for the latter course they simultaneously renounce an appeal to the courts against the decision to be made.

156. The provisions of nos 3 and 4 are unaltered in relation to the previous draft and there is still no appeal against awards made in voluntary arbitration proceedings in PCAS, although there is a possibility of appeal to the Constitutional Court in all cases.

157. Access to the PCAS by way of appeal is only available in appeals against the decisions of disciplinary bodies and the decisions of the judicial bodies of the sports federations and, in the latter case, only when the decision is made in an appeal against decisions of another federation body, other than a disciplinary body.

158. Moreover, access to PCAS is also possible in appeals against the final decisions of the bodies of professional leagues and other sports bodies.

159. Number 3 of Article 3 of the law that created PCAS, which establishes the applicable transitional provisions, extends the duration of the exclusive or prior jurisdiction given to the arbitration commissions created by Collective Bargaining Agreements (e.g., the Paritary Arbitration Commissions of the LPFP and the SPJF), for a further year, after which the said arbitration jurisdiction will vest in PCAS, as from 31st of July 2016.

III. Case-law Comments on Sports Justice

160. Portuguese case-law has, in an effort to define the concept, indicated some matters that it considered to be included in the concept of strictly sports matter.

161. The Lisbon Court of Appeal has held that the rules governing the appointment of referees fall within the definition of *strictly sports matters.*[20]

162. According to the Supreme Court of Justice, *sports matters* are related to *conduct and circumstances that have been kept beyond all state intervention(…) for example, the so-called 'rules of the game' and competitions regulations and organisation.*[21]

163. The Constitutional Court has, in two separate judgments regarding disciplinary matters, i.e., matters of fact arising in the course of the game and matters of law arising from the application of the rules of the game, or other rules, the purpose of which is to protect the authority of referees, rejected the idea that the same are of a strictly sports nature, as what was in fact at issue were questions of mere disciplinary procedure,[22] i.e., a Rule in the FPF Regulations which made the hearing of witnesses called by the accused in disciplinary proceedings, at a place other than the headquarters of the FPF, subject to the prior payment by the accused of the travelling expenses of the person in charge of the conduct of the proceedings.

164. It follows from the above that there is evident agreement between legal theory and case-law with regard to the inclusion of *the rules of the game* and *technical rules* within the concept of *strictly sports matters.*

IV. Conclusions

165. Accordingly, both legal theory and case-law consider the *rules of the game* to be those rules that govern what occurs on the field of play, i.e., matters that arise during a competition on the field of play. There is also agreement between legal theory and case-law with regard to the definition of *technical rules*, in the light of the concept of strictly sports matters, as the rules that define matters such as premises, equipment, sports material, the size of the field of play, *inter alia*.

20. Judgment of 27 Oct. 1994.
21. Judgment of 18 Apr. 1991.
22. Judgment no. 473/98, dated 1 Jul. 1998, published in DRE, 2nd Series, no. 273, of 23 Dec. 1998 and Judgment no. 488/98, of 2 Jul. 1998, published in DRE, 2nd Series, no. 284, of 10 Dec. 1998.

166. Legal theory and case-law have also concluded in various circumstances which are not limited to violence, doping and corruption, that the matters at issue are not *strictly sports matters* but rules of law, i.e., which are challengeable on appeal beyond the sports dispute resolution and disciplinary system, in the administrative courts.

167. The possibility of recourse to arbitration, with regard to matters other than *strictly sports matter*, should exist in relation to matters concerning the conduct of sports organizations and sports-linked persons that are governed by private law.

168. The PCAS faces several challenges before it can become an effective way to resolve disputes in the world of sport. Three of these are particularly noteworthy: (i) PCAS will have to overcome the doubts regarding the constitutionality of the provisions governing appeals from PCAS to the courts, in mandatary arbitration proceedings; (ii) PCAS will have to ensure its complete independence in relation to the POC and its associated federations, which are potentially parties in the disputes to be decided by PCAS, on the one hand, and on the other hand also appoint a significant proportion of the forty PCAS arbitrators, (i.e., a closed list); (iii) PCAS must adopt a tribunal fees policy that permits effective access to justice.

§3. Sports Courts and Tribunals

I. Introduction

169. The sports system has its own dispute resolution mechanisms, which operate within the sports federations and professional leagues, as is detailed below. Nevertheless the sports federations exercise public powers delegated to them by the State. Disputes arising from acts performed or omissions committed in the exercise of the said public powers are subject to the sports dispute resolution jurisdiction, but there may be a right of appeal to the administrative courts in accordance with the rules governing administrative disputes.

170. Decisions regarding strictly sporting questions, which do not include matters related to violence, doping, corruption, racism, or xenophobia, cannot be decided other than by the dispute resolution mechanisms of the sports system, but can, in certain cases, be resolved by recourse to arbitration, or mediation, as detailed below.

II. The Disciplinary and Appeals Committees of the Federations and Leagues

171. In relation to the sports bodies with jurisdiction to decide disputes within the federations are concerned, the Legal Framework Governing Sports Federations (RJFD), approved by Decree-Law no. 248-B/2008, of 31 December, requires federations to include at least a Disciplinary Committee and an Appeals Committee in their organizational structures.

172. The role of the Disciplinary Committees is to consider and punish sports disciplinary offences in accordance with the law and the existing regulations. Sports federations are required to have regulations regarding the punishment of violations of the rules of the game or of the competition, and the other sports rules, such as those regarding sports ethics. The disciplinary framework must include the following provisions:

(a) subjection of sports actors to general and specific duties of conduct, with a view to compliance with sports ethics, fairness and truth in sports competitions and the institution penalties, that vary according to the seriousness of the violations thereof;
(b) compliance with the principles of equality, non-retroactivity and proportionality in the imposition of penalties;
(c) exclusion of the penalties of permanent disqualification or of disqualification of indefinite duration;
(d) enumeration of the grounds or circumstances, which eliminate, attenuate or aggravate the offender's liability, and the requirements for the extinction thereof;
(e) provision that disciplinary proceedings are a prerequisite of the imposition of penalties in the case of more serious offences and, in any case, when the penalty to be imposed involves a suspension for more than one month;
(f) inclusion of guarantees of the accused's rights of defence, i.e., that the charge be sufficiently clear with regard to the facts that gave rise to the exercise of disciplinary powers and the requirement that the accused be heard, in those cases that the commencement of disciplinary proceedings is necessary;
(g) that there be a right of appeal, whether or not the commencement of disciplinary proceedings in mandatory.

173. Article 43 of the RJFD makes a distinction between federations under the auspices of which professional competitions are organized, and federations which do not organize professional competitions, by requiring in the former case, that the members of the Disciplinary Committee are all law graduates and also that the Disciplinary Committee, must have sections, which are specialized according the nature of the competition. The said requirements do not apply to federations, which organize non-professional competitions, when the only requirement is that the Chairman of the Disciplinary Committee be a law graduate.

174. The Appeals Committee is also an organ of a sports federation. Its role is to decide appeals against disciplinary decisions in sports matters, but this role can be extended by the statutes of the sports federations. The requirements stated above with regard to Disciplinary Committees also apply.

III. Arbitration Tribunals

A. *The Paritary Arbitration Commission: Abolition of the Paritary Arbitration Commission via the Approval of the Law That Created the PCAS (Article 7, No. 2 of Law No. 74/2013 of 6 September)*

175. Law no. 74/2013 of 6 September is very clear as to the intention to abolish the Paritary Arbitration Commissions formed within the ambit of Collective Bargaining Agreements, in accordance with Article 30 of Law 28/98, of 28 June (the Sportsperson's Employment Contract Law), which provides that: 'the associations that represent employers and sportspersons may make provision in collective bargaining agreements for recourse to arbitration in order to resolve any employment disputes arising from the making of sports employment contracts, in accordance with the provisions of Law no. 31/86 of 29 August, via the granting of exclusive or prior jurisdiction to the paritary arbitration commissions established pursuant to Decree-Law no. 425/86, of 27 December.

176. According to the provisions of Article 7 no. 2 of Law 74/2013, of 6 September, the arbitration jurisdiction of the Paritary Arbitration Commissions, as provided in Law no. 28/98 of 26 June, is vested in the Court of Arbitration for Sport.

177. According to this new legal framework, the contracting parties must opt between referring the disputes between them either to the employment courts, to the PCAS, or to ad hoc arbitration.

178. The Constitutional Court declared, in its Judgment no. 230/13, that some of the provisions of Assembly of the Republic Decree no. 128/XII are unconstitutional because they are contrary to the principle of equality, the right of access to the courts and the principle of effective court protection of rights, as the Decree made no provision for any type of appeal to a court of law from the decisions of PCAS.

179. The second time that the appeal provisions were declared unconstitutional, this time in Law 74/2013 of 6 September, the Constitutional Court held in its Judgment 781/2013 that despite the fact that the Law provided for an exceptional appeal against PCAS's decisions, so that PCAS no longer had a complete jurisdiction, the alterations made did not involve the creation of a relative jurisdiction, with the consequence that the provisions were still unconstitutional.

180. Number 3 of Article 3 of the law that created PCAS and which establishes the applicable transitional provisions, extends the duration of the exclusive or prior jurisdiction given to the arbitration commissions created by Collective Bargaining Agreements (e.g., the Paritary Arbitration Commissions of the LPFP and the SPJF), for a further year, after which the said arbitration jurisdiction will vest in PCAS, as from 31st of July 2016.

181. The PCAS is required, within the ambit of its mandatory arbitration jurisdiction to decide disputes arising from the acts and omissions of the federations, professional leagues and other sports entities, within the ambit of the exercise of their rule-making, organizational, management and disciplinary powers.

B. The Arbitration Committee of the LPFP

182. The LPFP Arbitration Committee is one of the organs of the LPFP and its existence is included in its bylaws. The Arbitration Committee arose from a dispute between the LPFP and the football associations, which led the Government to approve the creation of the Arbitration Committee as an organ of the LPFP in 1991. The Committee started work that year.

183. The LPFP Arbitration Committee is elected by the General Meeting of the LPFP and comprises a Chairman, nine serving members and three deputy members. The members of the Arbitration Committee must be law graduates and are preferably judges or former judges. According to Article 54 of the LPFP bylaws, the Arbitration Committee has the following powers:

(a) to decide appeals against disciplinary decisions of the Disciplinary Committee, with regard to matters strictly related to the disciplinary offences provided in Chapter V of the LPFP Bylaws, i.e., any breach of the Law, the Bylaws or the General Regulations of the LPFP, whether by act or omission, committed by members of the LPFP;
(b) to decide disputes between the LPFP and its member clubs, or between those clubs. The Arbitration Committee may only decide such disputes when the parties have requested that it intervene. It should be noted that the member clubs of the LPFP are required to refer all disputes arising from understandings, contracts and agreements to the Disciplinary Committee.

184. It is for the members of the Arbitration Committee to prepare and conduct the proceedings without the involvement of the general office or any other LPFP organ. Once served with the proceedings, the respondent has eight days in which to file a defence, after which the parties are convened with a view to conciliation. If this is unsuccessful, all of the evidential measures requested must be completed before the hearing. After the hearing, the arbitrator hands down an award, from which there is an appeal to the plenary Arbitration Committee of the LPFP. Such an appeal can be based on a breach of the substantive or procedural law applicable.

C. The Arbitration Committee of the FPF

185. The FPF Arbitration Committee is created in the FPF Regulation on the Status and Transfer of Players (RETJ) as the appropriate means for the resolution of disputes that involve the determination of the sums due by way of compensation for the training of players.

186. As with the *Fédération Internationale de Football Association* (FIFA) Regulation on the Status and Transfer of Players (RSTP), on which they are based the RETJ grants clubs or SADs an entitlement to compensation in the following circumstances:

(a) signing of a player's first sports employment contract by the end of the season during which the player becomes 23 years of age, provided that the club has participated in the training of the player, i.e., provided that the player has represented the club when he was between 12 and 23 years of age, inclusive;
(b) transfer of a professional player before the end of his contract, provided that the club has contributed to the training of the player.

187. Despite the fact that the formulae for both types of compensation exist in the RETJ, there is a disagreement between the clubs involved as to the amounts payable. These are the circumstances in which the FPF Arbitration Committee can intervene to decide the dispute.

188. The FPF Arbitration Committee does not have the power to resolve disputes between clubs that compete in professional competitions, as this task falls to the LPFP Arbitration Committee.

189. The FPF Arbitration Committee does not have jurisdiction in:

(a) disputes regarding compensation for training and the solidarity mechanism that exists between clubs that belong to different federations;
(b) disputes related to the solidarity mechanism between clubs that belong to the same federation, when the transfer that gave rise to the dispute was between clubs that belong to different federations. In this case, the matter is decided by the FIFA Dispute Resolution Chamber.

190. The FPF Arbitration Committee comprises three arbitrators, one appointed by each party and a third, who is the Chairman, appointed by the Chairman of the FPF. According to the FPF Bylaws, the Arbitration Committee is not an organ of the FPF, despite the fact that it is based at the FPF headquarters.

191. Any club or SAD which has not reached agreement regarding the amount of compensation payable for the transfer of a player may submit an application to the Chairman of the FPF, which states grounds and appoints an arbitrator, requesting the calling of the Arbitration Committee to decide the dispute. Such applications must be submitted within ninety days of the date of notice of the registration of the player's first contract, on pain of being time-barred. When the Chairman of the FPF receives the application he appoints the Chairman of the Arbitration Committee from the list of experts previously indicated by the ordinary members of the FPF, to whom the application is sent. The Chairman of the Arbitration Committee will notify the other party to appoint an arbitrator from the FPF list of experts within eight days and, if it wishes, to submit a statement of the reasons justifying the non-payment of the financial compensation sought. There are two scenarios that can arise from this notification of the other party:

(a) the respondent defends and the Committee then makes its decision. Any amount awarded must be paid within thirty days;
(b) the respondent does not defend, which means that it admits that the amount claimed by the applicant is payable, when the Chairman of the Committee orders the payment thereof, also within thirty days.

192. In the event of failure to comply with the Arbitration Committee's decision or with the approval of the compensation agreement, the clubs involved are subject to the following penalties:

(a) the debtor club may be punished with a fine imposed by the FPF Disciplinary Committee of 5% of the amount due;
(b) should the clubs still fail to fulfil their obligations within thirty days following the imposition of the fine mentioned in paragraph (a) above, they may be automatically prevented from registering new contracts with players.

193. According to Article 14 of the FPF RETJ, there is no right of appeal from the decisions of the Arbitration Committee. However in accordance with a Judgment of the Supreme Administrative Court of 15 December 2004,[23] the prevailing opinion is that as the FPF Arbitration Committee is an arbitration tribunal. Consequently, the judgment of the Supreme Administrative Court of 15 December 2004 took the opinion that in accordance with no. 1 of Article 29 of the LAV, the courts have jurisdiction to hear appeals against decisions passed by the Arbitration Committee. It was the Supreme Administrative Court's understanding that since Article 8 of the now repealed RJFD stated that only the organs of the federations have the exclusive power to regulate and discipline their respective sports, it followed that the FPF Arbitration Committee, created by the FPF RETJ was not an organ of the FPF in accordance with the said RJFD provision.

D. The Basketball Arbitration Tribunal

194. Another Court of Arbitration in the area of sport was created some years ago but it no longer exists: the Basketball Arbitration Tribunal (TAB), which had a wider jurisdiction than those described above, namely to:

(a) decide disputes arising from contracts between clubs and/or SADs, coaches and sportspersons;
(b) to consider any question that arises within the ambit of the agreements between them, at the request of any of the signatory institutions of the arbitration agreement, and to exercise all of the powers specifically provided therein;

---

23. Available at: http://www.dgsi.pt/jsta.nsf/35fbbbf22e1bb1e680256f8e003ea931/f25a67bc6106d75080256f88003d79f6?OpenDocument&Highlight=0,15-12-2004.

(c) interpret the provisions of agreements made between signatories of the arbitration agreement;
(d) decide all of the matters envisaged in the said agreements.

195. No right of appeal lies from the awards of the TAB, which are enforceable by the Ordinary Courts.

IV. The Portuguese Court of Arbitration for Sport

196. The Portuguese Court of Arbitration for Sport (PCAS) has the specific jurisdiction to administer justice regarding disputes with regard to the sports legal system, or which are related to the practice of sport and is an independent judicial body, i.e., it is independent of the sports public administration bodies and the organizations comprised in the sports system, and has administrative and financial autonomy.[24]

197. The POC is charged with the establishment and operation of the PCAS.[25]

198. PCAS exercises its jurisdiction throughout Portugal and is based at the POC.[26]

199. PCAS' jurisdiction in mandatory arbitration proceedings is as follows:

(i) Disputes arising from the acts and omissions of sports federations, professional leagues and other sports entities, within the ambit of the exercise of their rule-making, organizational, management and disciplinary powers.[27]
(ii) [With the exception of disciplinary proceedings commenced by ADoP in accordance with the provisions of the Anti-Doping Law] The disputes referred to (i), whenever the decision of the disciplinary or judicial of the sports federations, or the final decision of another body is not issued within forty-five days, or when the matter is demonstrated to be complex, within seventy-five days from the day on which the proceedings are commenced [the time limit for the filing of a CAS arbitration application is ten days from the end of the forty-five or seventy-five day time limit. The said application must be in the form of an originating application[28]].

24. Cf. Art. 1, no. 1 of Law no. 74/2013, of 6 September and Art. 1 of the CAS Law.
25. Cf. Art. 1, no. 4 of the CAS Law.
26. Cf. Art. 2, of the CAS Law.
27. Cf. Art. 4, no. 1 of the CAS Law, as amended by Art. 3 of Law no. 33/2014, of 16 June – First amendment of Law no. 74/2013, of 6 September, which creates the Court of Arbitration for Sport and approves the corresponding law.
28. Cf. Art. 4, no. 4 of the PCAS Law, as amended by Art. 3 of Law no. 33/2014, of 16 June – First amendment of Law no. 74/2013, of 6 September, which creates the Portuguese Court of Arbitration for Sport and approves the corresponding law.

(iii) Appeals against the decisions of sports federation disciplinary bodies, or ADoP, with regard to violations of anti-doping rules.[29]

200. Access to PCAS's appeals jurisdiction only exists with regard to:

(a) Decisions of disciplinary bodies, or of the judicial bodies of the sports federations and, in the latter case, only when the decision is made in an appeal against decisions of a federation body, other than a disciplinary body.
(b) Final decisions of professional league bodies and other sports bodies.[30]

201. PCAS' voluntary arbitration jurisdiction includes all disputes, not covered by mandatory arbitration, which are directly or indirectly related to the practice of sport, which, according to the voluntary arbitration law are arbitrable; such disputes can be referred to PCAS pursuant to an arbitration agreement, or clause, or pursuant to a clause in the bylaws of a sports federation or other sports organization.[31]

202. All disputes arising from sports employment contracts between sportspersons or trainers and sports actors or sports organizations may be referred to PCAS, which has the power to consider the legality of dismissals. As from 1 August 2016, PCAS will have the exclusive or prior arbitration jurisdiction that the law[32,33] grants to the paritary arbitration commissions.

203. The decisions of arbitration panels may be appealed to the Central Administrative Court (CAC), unless the parties agree that an appeal shall lie to the appeals chamber, when they must expressly waive their right to appeal to CAC. The provisions of the Administrative Courts Procedure Code regarding urgent proceedings apply to appeals to the CAC so that such appeals do not suspend the enforcement of the decision appealed against and must be decided within forty-five days:[34]

– PCAS has a maximum of forty arbitrators comprised in a list that may include jurists of good standing and competence and persons of established scientific,

29. Cf. Art. 5, of the PCAS Law.
30. Cf. Art. 4, no. 3 of the PCAS Law, as amended by Art. 3 of Law no. 33/2014, of 16 June – First amendment of Law no. 74/2013, of 6 September, which creates the Portuguese Court of Arbitration for Sport and approves the corresponding law.
31. Cf. Art. 6, nos 1 and 2 of the PCAS Law, as amended by Art. 3 of Law no. 33/2014, of 16 June – First amendment of Law no. 74/2013, of 6 September, which creates the Court of Arbitration for Sport and approves the corresponding law.
32. Cf. Art. 7 of the PCAS Law and Art. 30 of Law no. 38/98, of 26 June, which introduced the new legal framework governing employment contracts with sportspersons and sports training contracts and repeals Decree-Law no. 305/95, of 18 November.
33. Cf. Art. 3, no. 3 of Law no. 74/2013, of 6 September, as amended by Art. no. 33/2014, of 16 June – First amendment of Law no. 74/2013, of 6 September, which creates the Court of Arbitration for Sport and approves the corresponding law.
34. Cf. Art. 8, nos 1 and 2 of the PCAS Law, as amended by Art. 3 of Law no. 33/2014, of 16 June – First amendment of Law no. 74/2013, of 6 September, which creates the Portuguese Court of Arbitration for Sport and approves the corresponding law.

professional or technical competence in the area of sport. The list is approved by the Sport Arbitration Council.[35]

- PCAS has a mediation service, which is a voluntary and informal procedure for the resolution of sport-related disputes, which is based on a mediation agreement and takes place under the control of a PCAS mediator (a mediation agreement is an agreement between the parties, in which they agree to refer any present or future sport-related dispute between them to mediation, either in an express clause in a contract, or in a separate document. Mediation is not applicable to the resolution of disputes subject to the jurisdiction of sports disciplinary bodies, or to disputes regarding disciplinary matters, doping or sport-related violence). [36]
- PCAS provides a consultancy service, which issues non-binding opinions with regard to sport-related legal issues, at the request of public sports administration bodies, the COP, the CCP, the sports federations with sports public utility status, the professional leagues and ADoP, for which a consultancy fee is payable in accordance with the fees regulation.[37]

V. The Court of Arbitration for Sports (Lausanne)

A. *Introduction*

204. CAS was created on 30 June 1984, and has its headquarters in Lausanne, Switzerland. From the time he took up office as the president of the IOC, in 1981, Juan António Samaranch expressed both the desire that a Supreme Court be created for sport-related questions and the willingness to make resources available for that purpose.

205. The need for an independent body, which is capable of resolving disputes that arise within international sports federations, in a rapid and flexible way, at a low cost, with guaranteed enforcement of its decisions, became evident at the beginning of the 1980s. At that time the number of sport-related disputes grew considerably and the national courts and the international sports dispute resolution bodies were unable to deal with the cases with the rapidity and specific knowledge that were then necessary and fundamental.

206. It was then that Samaranch gave Judge Keba Mbaye, who was then a Judge of the International Court of Justice (ICJ), the supreme judicial instance of the United Nations (UN) and subsequently the first President of CAS, the task of drafting the CAS bylaws.

207. Proceedings before CAS have the same advantages as normal arbitration proceedings, but are limited to sport. They are proceedings, in which:

35. Cf. Art. 20, nos 1 and 2 of the CAS Law.
36. Cf. Arts 32, 63 and 65 of the CAS Law.
37. Cf. Art. 33, no. 1 of the CAS Law.

(a) the arbitrators are prestigious professionals with a profound theoretical and practical understanding of sport-related matters;
(b) both the language to be used in and the law applicable to the proceedings can be chosen;
(c) the awards of CAS can be enforced more easily via the international sports federations;
(d) the proceedings are quicker and more simplified;
(e) the costs of CAS arbitrations are usually lower that proceedings before national courts.

B. The Gundel Case and the Creation of the ICAS

208. Despite the fact that CAS was created in 1984, its independence was only challenged in 1993 in legal proceedings commenced by the horseman Elmar Gundel before the Swiss Federal Court (TFS), the highest court in Switzerland.

209. The penalty imposed on Gundel was reduced on appeal to CAS against a decision of the International Equestrian Federation (FEI) with regard to the doping of his horse. However, still dissatisfied with the decision, he challenged the validity of the decision in the highest court in Switzerland on the grounds that it did not comply with the requirements of impartiality and independence demanded of a true arbitration tribunal.

210. In its decision,[38] the TFS held that the independence of CAS was assured with regard to that specific case, but drew attention to the relations between CAS and the IOC and particularly to the fact that:

(a) CAS was financed almost entirely by the IOC.
(b) One of the prerogatives of the IOC was the power to alter the CAS bylaws unilaterally.
(c) There were too many powers in the hands of the IOC and its President to appoint the members of CAS.

211. Despite the fact that the TFS held that CAS complied with the requirements with regard to its independence, it did not consider whether the requirements of independence and impartiality would be complied with if the IOC was a party in the proceedings before the court. The message of the TFS was clear. It was necessary to alter the CAS bylaws. With the creation of ICAS in 1994, its structure changed radically in terms of both administration and finance, as only four of the twenty members of CAS were appointed by the IOC. Amongst other duties, ICAS is responsible for the appointment of the arbitrators on the CAS arbitrators list. The creation of ICAS was one of the factors, which assisted in the reestablishment of

38. Decision of the Swiss Federal Court 4P.217/1992, of 15 Mar. 1993 *(Gundel v. FEI).*

the court's concepts of independence and impartiality, in order to safeguard parties' rights and facilitate the resolution of sport-related disputes.

C. The Organization of CAS

1. Organization

212. According to Article S20 of the CAS Code, the Court of Arbitration for Sport has two divisions, an Ordinary Division and an Appellate Division, plus a mediation structure and procedures. Each Division is seized with the corresponding proceedings and exercises the powers conferred by the CAS rules and bylaws, in order to ensure the proper processing of proceedings.

213. During major sport events such as the Olympic Games or the FIFA Football World Championships, CAS also has ad hoc Divisions, in order to rapidly resolve any disputes that arise within the ambit of these competitions.

214. Awards made by CAS arbitrators are enforceable in other jurisdictions, in accordance with the New York Convention on the Recognition and Enforcement of Foreign Arbitral Awards, of 10 June 1958.

215. Proceedings commenced in the CAS are distributed to the appropriate Division by the Court Office and this distribution cannot be challenged by the parties. In addition to the Court Office, CAS also has a Secretary-General and one or more legal advisors, who replace the Secretary-General whenever necessary.

2. Arbitrators

216. ICAS is the body responsible for the creation of the list of CAS arbitrators. According to S14 of the CAS Code:

> The ICAS shall call upon personalities with full legal training, recognized competence with regard to sports law and/or international arbitration, a good knowledge of sport in general and a good command of at least one CAS working language.

217. The CAS bylaws lay down the rules governing the selection and distribution of its arbitrators, who are selected from among the candidates proposed by the IOC, the International Federations and the National Olympic Committees and in accordance with the interests of sportspersons and via the exercise of ICAS' discretionary power to appoint arbitrators from among sports personalities. Whenever possible, ICAS is required to ensure a just and proportional representation of all continents and of the various legal cultures. The arbitrators are, in any event, subject to the general principles of confidentiality, impartiality and independence.

3. The CAS Code and Relevant Amendments Made in 2013

218. In 1994, the CAS published the CAS Code, which contains the CAS Statutes and the procedural rules applicable to the various proceedings in the CAS. This Code has been amended several times, and lately in 2013, in order to adapt to the procedural rules and to Swiss and European Law. With effect from 2010, some of the following procedures are now applied in CAS proceedings:

(a) a person whose name appears on the CAS list of arbitrators cannot appear before the CAS as a legal representative of a party in a separate suit or proceedings before the CAS;[39]
(b) the arbitral panels now have greater latitude to determine the status of third parties, their rights in the procedure and also grants them powers to admit and/or call for the filing of amicus curiae briefs;
(c) the panel also has the power to attempt to settle any appeal disputes before it by way of conciliation prior to proceeding with full arbitration, with the ICAS members, the CAS staff as well as the CAS members being exempted from any liability incurred in relation to the arbitration proceedings;
(d) parties can easily and quickly file their submissions or send notices to CAS by way of fax, or courier. Additionally, the CAS shall, with effect from 1 January 2010, also allow parties to send their communications by way of electronic mail;
(e) parties (the Respondent) are also prohibited from filing counterclaims when answering to appeal briefs filed by Appellants. Any Respondent wishing to challenge of a decision issued by a lower judicial body in proceedings before the CAS must do so within twenty-one days from the date of notification of the decision issued by the lower judicial body;
(f) upon receiving the parties' submissions, the President of the CAS Division concerned is now empowered, on being requested to rule on provisional measures, to terminate arbitration proceedings if he considers that the CAS manifestly has no jurisdiction to consider the matter;
(g) finally, it is worth noting that awards for appeal cases are now delivered within three months of transfer of the file by the CAS Court Office to the Panel.

4. Court Fees

219. The fees payable in CAS proceedings vary considerably depending on whether the proceedings are ordinary or appellate. Since January 2004, disputes regarding international disciplinary matters are effectively free of costs, despite the fact that it is necessary to pay a minimum fee – the Court Office Fee – of CHF 1000 (CHF 1,000) in all cases, without which the CAS Office will not initiate the proceedings. The administrative costs, which are predefined by the CAS Office, are directly related to the value of the dispute.

39. Once an arbitrator appears before the CAS as a legal representative of any party in proceedings before the CAS, he automatically loses his status and recognition as a CAS arbitrator.

D. Jurisdiction

220. The jurisdiction of CAS is stated in Article S12 of the CAS Code and comprises:

(a) disputes referred to CAS by the ordinary arbitration;
(b) appeals on the merits against the decisions of federations, associations or other sports bodies, whenever this is permitted by their bylaws or regulations, or a specific agreement;
(c) Resolve the disputes that are referred to them through mediation.

221. Even though Article R27 of the CAS Code provides that the court's jurisdiction is limited to sport-related disputes, CAS has never declared that it lacks jurisdiction in relation to a dispute, which is not sport-related.

E. Procedure

1. Introduction

222. The main types of proceedings that can be commenced in CAS are Ordinary Proceedings, Appeal Proceedings and Mediation Proceedings, which are briefly explained below.

223. Proceedings in the Ad Hoc Division have very specific procedural rules adapted to the need to resolve disputes with greater rapidity, frequently within twenty-four hours, while also affording the parties the maximum protection and the opportunity to exercise of their rights.

2. Ordinary Proceedings

224. The ordinary proceedings described in Articles 38 et seq. of the CAS Code are commenced pursuant to an agreement, which refers the dispute arising from the legal relations between the parties to arbitration by CAS.

225. In ordinary proceedings, the Arbitration Panel is usually comprised of three arbitrators. The definition of the number of arbitrators is normally dealt with in the agreement pursuant to which the parties submit their dispute to arbitration. In the event that the number of arbitrators, or the way in which the President of the court of arbitration is appointed is not stipulated in the arbitration agreement, these matters are decided by the President of the Ordinary Division. In order to do this, the president applies the following criteria:

(a) the amount in dispute; and
(b) the complexity of the dispute.

226. If the arbitration panel is made up of three arbitrators, each party appoints one arbitrator and the two arbitrators selected by the parties select a third arbitrator, who is the Chairman of the Panel of Arbitrators. If the arbitrators appointed fail to agree on a president, the President of the CAS Ordinary Division appoints the President of the panel.

227. On average, awards are handed down within six to twelve months. The fees are estimated in advance and divided between the parties. On the conclusion of the proceedings, the Panel of Arbitrators fixes the final court fees and the proportion in which the parties are to bear them.

3. Appeal Proceedings

228. As appellate proceedings are the most usual and important type of proceedings in the CAS, the provisions of Articles 47 et seq. of the CAS Code merit particular attention. The parties can appeal against the decisions of federation and association tribunals and other sport bodies, when their bylaws designate CAS as having jurisdiction to decide the dispute, or pursuant to a specific agreement between the parties to that effect, whenever the parties have exhausted all of the legal opportunities afforded by the corresponding internal bodies. An appeal also lies from decisions of CAS, when it acts as a first instance tribunal and whenever the said appeal is not excluded.

229. In the absence of an agreement to the contrary, appeals must be lodged within twenty-one days of notice of the decision challenged. The statement of appeal must, among other necessary documents, contain the name of the arbitrator appointed, a copy of the decision challenged and a copy of the document proving the payment of the corresponding court fees to the General Office.

230. If the President of the CAS Appeal Division considers that the case is simple or the amount involved is too small to justify the cost of three arbitrators, he may decide that the case should be decided by a single arbitrator.

231. Ten days after the filing of the statement of appeal, the appellant must submit its Appeal Brief, which pleads the facts and legal arguments, together with all of the documents that support the claim. The Appeal Brief must also identify the witnesses and experts to be called at the hearing.

232. After the giving of notice of the appointment of the arbitrator by the appellant, the respondent has ten days, following receipt of the statement of appeal within which to appoint its arbitrator to the Panel of Arbitrators, except if the parties have agreed that the case will be decided by a sole arbitrator.

233. The President of the Appellate Division is required, after consulting the two arbitrators already appointed by the parties, to appoint the third arbitrator, who will be the Chairman of the Arbitration Panel.

234. The respondent must file its answer within twenty days of receipt of the appeal brief. According to the new rules in the CAS Code, counterclaims are not permitted in appeal proceedings. Even if the respondent does not file an answer, the Arbitration Panel will proceed with the case and hand down its decision.

235. The Arbitration Panel must consider whether a hearing is necessary in order to decide the issues. Most hearings take place *in camera* in accordance with the principle of confidentiality, unless the parties agree otherwise. Cases are decided in accordance with the new rules within three months of the submission of the file to the arbitrators, on average. The Panel has powers to review the facts and the law and may decide the case *ex novo*.

236. In 2015 the e-filing service came into force to facilitate the filing of the submissions before the CAS. It can only be activated after the opening of arbitration proceedings by the CAS Court Office. This implies the prior filing of a Request for Arbitration (according to Article R38 of the CAS Code) or a Statement of Appeal (pursuant to Article R48) by facsimile or courier, within the deadline set out in Article R49 of the CAS Code, as well as the allocation of a case number for the arbitration proceedings in question.

4. Mediation

237. Mediation is a procedure in which the parties, with the assistance of a mediator, seek to find an amicable solution to disputes between them. Mediation essentially differs from arbitration because of the absence of rigid formalities and because of the non-binding nature of the procedure.[40]

238. CAS inaugurated its mediation service in 1999. Only disputes that fall within the scope of ordinary proceedings can be mediated. This means, for example, that cases of doping, disputes arising from the decision of a sport body and questions arising from the application of disciplinary rules and measures are excluded from mediation within the CAS structure.

5. The Ad Hoc Divisions

239. The Ad Hoc Division was created in 1996, at the time of the Atlanta Olympic Games. The aim of ICAS, in conjunction with the sport community, was to find a rapid and definitive way to resolve disputes derived from or connected with the Olympic Games, in order to be able to approve competition results without prejudice to the parties involved and without risking the prestige of the competition or its organizers. It was also fundamentally important to respect the right of the parties to due process and to all of the guarantees afforded in the national regulations and

40. The TAS/CAS Regulations can be consulted at www.tas-cas.org.

legislation. Since then, Ad Hoc Divisions have been created and present at the main international sports competitions, i.e.:

(a) at the Summer and Winter Olympic Games since 1996;
(b) at the Commonwealth Games since 1998;
(c) at the *Union des Associations Européenes de Football* (UEFA) European Football Championship since 2000;
(d) at the FIFA World Cup since 2006.

240. Despite the fact that the proceedings can sometimes last for only a few hours, the decisions of the Ad Hoc Divisions are enforceable in accordance with the general rules of Private International Law and in accordance with the New York Convention on the Recognition and Enforcement of Foreign Arbitral Awards, of 10 June 1958.

F. The Enforcement of Arbitration Decisions

241. One of the main advantages of the submission of disputes to CAS, so far as the parties are concerned, is the ability to enforce the arbitration awards via the international sports federations, most of which have their headquarters in Switzerland.[41] The statutes of these sports federations voluntarily and automatically recognize the mandatory enforcement of and compliance with CAS awards. Failure by the national federations to comply with CAS awards ultimately leads to sanctions by their respective international federations. This then requires the national federations to automatically enforce CAS awards against their member clubs and sportspersons. CAS awards are final and binding on the parties and have the same effect as the judgment of a national court.

242. In the unlikely event that the award cannot be enforced by the national federation by the means referred to in the preceding paragraph, CAS awards comply with the rules and requirements of the New York Convention on the Recognition and Enforcement of Foreign Arbitral Awards, of 10 June 1958, which most countries have signed. Therefore, if the unsuccessful parties fail to comply with their obligations, the successful party may enforce the award in the national courts of the country in question, provided that it is a signatory of the New York Convention.

243. In Europe, CAS is recognized by the European Convention on the Recognition of the Legal Personality of International Non-Governmental Organisations, signed at Strasbourg, on 24 April 1986. CAS awards can also be enforced by national federations, associations and national sport bodies, although not via CAS.

41. With effect from August 2011 awards rendered by the CAS in ordinary proceedings can no longer be enforced by the FIFA Disciplinary Committee (see FIFA Circular No. 1270 of 21 Jul. 2011). This therefore means that parties in possession of awards rendered by the CAS in an ordinary proceeding cannot seek FIFA's intervention in the enforcement thereof, and must instead revert to the NY Convention on the Recognition and Enforcement of Foreign Arbitral Awards, of 10 Jun. 1958.

G. Challenging of Awards

244. As a general rule, an award is final once it has been communicated to the parties (CAS Code, Article 190). There are however five grounds on which the parties can challenge the award:

(a) error in the appointment of the sole arbitrator, or in the establishment of the arbitration court;
(b) error of the Court in a decision regarding its jurisdiction, or lack of jurisdiction to hear the specific case;
(c) in its award, the Court took into consideration matters that should not have been considered, or failed to consider matters that should have been considered;
(d) failure by the Court to comply with the principle of equality of the parties or their right to present their cases and to question the other parties case;
(e) the award is contrary to Swiss public policy.

§4. Sport and Security

I. Security at Sports Facilities to Which the Public Have Access

A. Introduction

245. Until 1997, there were few legal provisions in Portugal governing sports infrastructures. Regulatory-Decree no. 34/95, of 16 December, governed the technical and safety conditions of enclosed locations for public entertainment and shows. Decree-Law no. 317/97, of 25 November, introduced the *legal framework governing the establishment and operation of public access sports facilities, independently of whether the same are publically or privately owned and whether they are operated on a non-profit basis or not.*[42] The intention recorded in the preamble to the law was to require *the creation of legal rules and a legal framework governing the conduct of sports activities in order to promote the quality of the services offered and to improve the supervisory mechanisms of the Public Administration, namely in relation to operating and safety conditions.*

246. With the passing of Decree-Law no. 317/97, of 25 November, new Regulations should have been introduced to replace Decree-Law no. 315/95, of 28 November, which governs the establishment and operation of enclosed locations for public entertainment and shows and established an extensive legal framework governing artistic shows, but which focuses above all on the prevention of risks and accidents at shows, with a series rules to facilitate the evacuation those at the location and the intervention of the emergency services.

247. Decree-Law no. 385/99, of 28 September, which defined the *legal framework of technical responsibility for sports facilities open to the public and the*

42. Article 1, no. 1.

activities carried on there,[43] was published to complement Decree-Law no. 317/97 of 25 November. The purpose of this legislation was to ensure that sports facilities have qualified technical staff, in order to ensure the proper control and operation thereof and also introduces a *compulsory insurance* requirement, covering the risks of personal injury of users, inherent in the physical activities carried on therein.

248. Access to and presence in the facilities was subject to the compulsory production of a *medical report.* Decree-Law no. 385/99, of 28 September was repealed by Decree-Law no. 271/2009, of 1 October (this Decree-Law was repealed by Decree-Law no. 39/2012, of 28 August), which defines the technical responsibility for the management of physical and sports activities carried on at sports facilities, which provide sports services in the area of fitness, i.e., gymnasiums, academies or health clubs, whatever the designation, used and the way in which the same are operated.

249. Decree-Law no. 141/2009, of 16 June (as amended by Decree-Law no. 110/2012, of 21 May) which introduced the legal framework governing public access sports facilities, repealed Decree-Law no. 317/97, of 25 November, fundamentally because of the need to render the legislation in this area compatible with the Legal Framework governing Urbanization and Construction (RJUE), introduced by Decree-Law no. 555/99, of 16 December, as amended by Law no. 60/2007, of 4 September, in order to promote the simplification of set-up procedures and to improve the legal framework of the duties of proprietors and bodies responsible for the operation and working of sports facilities.

B. *The Legal Framework Governing Public Access Sports Facilities*

250. With the coming into force of the legal framework governing public access sports facilities, the aim was also to harmonize procedures with regard to the establishment and workings of sports facilities with the provisions of various items of legislation that had been passed in the meantime, i.e.:

(a) Law no. 159/99, of 14 September, which introduced the legal provisions governing the transfer of powers and duties with regard to culture, leisure time and sport to local authorities.
(b) Decree-Law no. 309/2002, of 16 December, which regulates the establishment and operation of enclosed locations for public shows and entertainment.
(c) Decree-Law no. 310/2002, of 18 December, which governs the legal framework regarding the licensing of the conduct and supervision of various activities, such as the holding of sports events, grants licensing powers previously held by the civil governments to local authorities.

251. In accordance with the legislation listed above and in order to improve the quality and safety of the services provided to users of sports facilities, the new legal

43. Article 1, no. 1.

framework governing sports facilities and the safety of the services provided to users of sports facilities, makes some changes with regard to facility licensing, e.g., the abolition of operating licences, which are replaced, in accordance with the terms of the RJUE, with a sports activity use authorization, in the form of a licence authorizing the use of a building, or autonomous fraction of a building, where the creation of sports facilities is intended. The grant of the licence is subject to the giving of prior notice by the operator to the local authority.

252. Also introduced was a requirement that prior notice be given identifying the body responsible for the operation of the facility and the manager or person in charge thereof as a precondition of the grant of the authorization of use for sports activities.

253. Also introduced was a requirement that the IDP, IP, be given notice of the authorizations for use for sports activities granted by local authorities, which information is recorded in the Sports Facilities Map, which is part of the National Sports Map, introduced by Article 9 of the LBAFD.

254. The National Sports Map, the regulations for which have yet to be introduced, will contain the register of data and indicators, which portray the various aspects of the development of sport, in order to reveal the status of sport in Portugal, i.e., in terms of sports facilities and natural leisure and recreation spaces, *inter alia.*

255. The IDP, IP also acquires the power to issue opinions, in accordance with the RJUE, regarding:

(a) projects for specialist and special sports facilities for sports events;
(b) compliance with the applicable legal rules and regulations of projects for shooting facilities for sports competitions and events;
(c) in the said opinion, to stipulate the maximum capacity and use and maximum spectator capacity, taking the requirements of the type of facility in question into consideration.

256. The opinion of the IDP, IP concerns compliance with the functional solutions and construction characteristics proposed, in terms of the type of facilities in question and the specificities of the activities proposed, together with compliance with the rules regarding the applicable technical and safety conditions. The opinion is binding when unfavourable or, when favourable, if subject to certain conditions.

C. Types of Sports Facilities

257. Decree-Law no. 141/2009 of 16 June, updated by the Decree-Law 110/2012 of 21 May, classifies sports facilities in accordance with the following typology:

(a) basic sports facilities, which can be either recreational or training facilities;
(b) specialist or single sport facilities;
(c) special sports facilities for sports events.

258. Recreation facilities are tools, which are used for sports activities, within the ambit of recreational, fitness and active leisure activities, which are informal, or are not subject to compulsory and permanent rules.

259. Sports facilities for training purposes are facilities, which are designed and intended for basic sports education and training activities with a view to access to specialist sports disciplines, for sports improvement and training; the functional, construction and multiuse characteristics of which comply with the requirements of sports rules, which govern the sports for which the facilities are intended.

260. Specialist sports facilities are defined by the law as permanent tools, which are designed and organized for single sport activities, as a consequence of the specific adaptation thereof to the sport in question, or the natural conditions in existence at the location of the facility for education and training for that sport. The following are specialist sports facilities:

(a) sports pavilions and halls, which are intended and equipped for a specific sport;
(b) halls, which are exclusively equipped for combat sports;
(c) Olympic swimming pools, diving pools and specials tanks for sub-aquatic activities;
(d) regulation closed cycling circuits;
(e) facilities for shooting with firearms;
(f) archery facilities;
(g) circuits and infrastructures for land-based motor sport;
(h) facilities for equestrian sports;
(i) rowing and canoeing tracks and land-based infrastructures that support water sports;
(j) golf courses;
(k) sports facilities in infrastructures for the training of sportspersons, namely in high performance sports centres and sports training centres.

261. Special sports facilities for sports events are permanent facilities, which are designed and intended for the conduct of sports competitions, which combine the following factors:

(a) a significant capacity to accommodate the public and the ability to accommodate the media;
(b) principally used for high performance sports competitions and events;
(c) the incorporation of significant and specific natural and technological resources to support the holding and broadcasting of sports events.

262. The following are special sports facilities for sports events:

(a) stadiums, but the provisions of the Stadium Technical and Safety Conditions Regulations, approved by Regulatory Decree no. 10/2001, of 7 June, apply to stadiums;
(b) multiuse sports pavilions;
(c) aquatic stadiums and Olympic swimming pool complexes;
(d) horse racing tracks;
(e) cycle racing stadiums;
(f) car racing tracks, motor cycle racing tracks and motocross racing tracks;
(g) nautical stadiums.

263. The specific requirements that determine the classification of facilities intended to be special sports facilities, with the exception of stadiums, are defined by a statutory instrument issued by the member of the Government responsible for sport.

264. This legal framework covers not only all public access sports facilities, whether they are publically or privately owned, and whether or not they are part of for profit operations, but also sports facilities within establishments, which provide fitness services, whatever the description of that use, e.g., gymnasiums, health academies or clubs. This measure will permit the standardization of the quality and safety criteria applicable to sports facilities in these establishments, which are now subject to the same requirements as all other sports facilities.

265. This Decree-Law also applies to sports facilities that are included in complexes, which are intended to provide high performance preparation and training, i.e., training centres and high performance sport centres, whatever they are called and however they are operated.

D. Facilities Not Covered by the Sports Facilities Legal Framework

266. Decree-Law 110/2012, of 21 May contains extensive provisions, which exclude its application. Accordingly, sports facilities, which are intended to be used in a specific manner and are comprised in the following locations are not covered by the legal framework governing sports facilities:

(a) barracks and enclosed military facilities;
(b) enclosed locations for the private use of the security forces;
(c) prisons;
(d) spas and health and convalescent units, which are subject to medical supervision.

267. This legal framework also does not apply to facilities for the firing of firearms when the operation thereof is governed by Law no. 5/2006, of 23 February and Law 42/2006, of 25 August and the corresponding regulations.

268. The legal framework introduced by the said decree-law also does not apply to sports facilities that are accessory or complementary to establishments in which sport activities are not the main service, in the following cases, without prejudice to the need to comply with the general technical and safety conditions required for the type of facility in question:

(a) sports facilities that are part of public or private educational establishments, whatever the level thereof;
(b) sports facilities that are part of holiday undertakings, i.e., hotels, holiday villages, holiday apartments, holiday resorts, bed and breakfast accommodation, rural holiday undertakings, camping and caravan parks and nature tourism undertakings.

269. In as far as the sports facilities that are included in most holiday undertakings are concerned, which are subject to the provisions of the legal framework governing sports facilities applies; there is an exception with regard to golf courses, horse tracks and equestrian centres, car racing and karting tracks. The provisions of the legal framework governing sports facilities also do not apply to the following cases:

(a) natural recreation or sports locations, i.e., places, which have the natural conditions for certain recreational activities without the need for adaptation works or significant alterations, which are subject to the provisions of Regulatory Decree no. 18/99, of 22 September as amended by Regulatory Decree no. 17/2003, of 10 October;
(b) children's play and recreation areas that are subject to the provisions of Decree-Law no. 397/97 of 27 December and the legislation complementary therewith;
(c) locations and enclosed areas not designed for sports use, which are used for short periods to host sports events or activities, without prejudice to the need to comply with the applicable technical and safety requirements;
(d) sports facilities that are part of permanent residential housing buildings, which are intended for the use of residents.

E. Technical Responsibility in Gymnasiums, Academies or Health Clubs

270. Decree-Law no. 385/99, of 28 August, which established the technical responsibility provisions with regard to sports facilities open to the public and the activities that take place therein, which was repealed by Decree-Law no. 271/2009, of 1 October, proved to be lacking and even incoherent in terms of both its subject matter and scope. The fact that the regulations implementing this legislation were never introduced also prevented it from being fully implemented. Decree-Law no. 110/2012, of 21 May, introduced a new legal framework governing public access sports facilities, which repealed Decree-Law no. 317/97, of 25 November and which, among the new developments detailed above, introduced the requirement that sports facilities must have a manager or person in charge.

271. Article 35 of the LBAFD provides that the qualifications necessary for the exercise of the various technical functions in the area of physical activity and sport must be defined and also establishes that it is not permitted, in those cases specially envisaged in the law, to work in an occupation in the areas of physical activity and sport, namely within the ambit of sports management, exercise and health, physical education and sports training, as a principal or secondary occupation, in a regular, seasonal or occasional manner, without proper academic or vocational training.

272. Furthermore, Article 43 of the LBAFD provides that bodies, which offer physical or sports activities, which organize sports events and shows, or which operate sports facilities open to the public, are subject to the provisions of the law, i.e., in terms of the minimum training levels of the staff in charge of these activities or who manage sports facilities.

273. Sports activities in gymnasiums, health clubs, adventure sports companies and elsewhere are now commonplace in Portugal. Businesses, which are based on the supply of these types of sports-related services, have flourished in Portugal and some of them have client numbers, which far exceed the numbers of members of some sports federations.[44]

274. The aim is accordingly to seek to achieve a situation in which physical and sports activities take place safely with a view to the health and well-being of the general public.

275. Physical and sports activities, which are promoted, regulated and managed by a sports federation with EUPD are excluded from the application of this law. Also excluded are activities of certain groups of the general public, and activities that take place in sports facilities in certain establishments. The Decree-Law also does not apply to physical and sports activities in sports facilities within hotel complexes or tourist developments, provided that access thereto is exclusively reserved for users of the said complexes or resorts.

276. The responsible exercise of citizenship includes the right to undertake physical and sports activities, which take place without any technical support, when the citizen in question consciously assumes the liability involved therein.

277. This Decree-Law introduced the position of Technical Director, who is a natural person, who is responsible for the physical and sports activity or activities that take place within the sports facility. The Technical Director must have a licentiate degree in Sport or Physical Education and must attend in-service vocational training during such time as his/her registration is valid. Technical Directors must be registered with the IDP, IP, for the sports activities covered by this Decree-Law. This registration has a five-year validity.

44. José Manuel Meirim. *Lei de Bases da Actividade Física e do Desporto – Estudo, Notas e Comentários*. Coimbra, Coimbra Editora, 2007, p. 268.

278. There are two different situations so far as the qualifications required of those in charge of the orientation and conduct of physical and sports activities are concerned:

(a) those responsible for the orientation and conduct of physical and sports activities, which are not within the objects of sports federations with EUPD, must also have a licentiate degree in Sport or Physical Education;
(b) those responsible for the orientation and conduct of physical and sports activities which fall within the ambit of the objects of sports federations with EUPD, are subject to the provisions of Decree-Law no. 248-A/2008, of 31 December, which introduced the legal framework governing access to and exercise of the profession of sports coach.

279. The transitional provisions, make it possible, first, for all professionals, who do not comply with the requirements of the Decree-Law, to apply to the IDP, IP for the recognition of their current skills and, second, for those professionals, who become holders of qualifications in the area of sports within the ambit of the national qualifications system also to be able, within two years as from the publication of the Decree-Law to apply to the IDP, IP for the recognition of the qualifications so acquired.

F. Safety of Play and Recreation Areas

280. Decree-Law no. 379/97, of 27 December, subsequently amended by Decree-Law no. 119/2009, of 19 May, approved the Regulations, which establish the safety conditions to be complied with in the location, construction, design and functional organization of play and recreation areas, their facilities and impact surfaces. In addition to the changes made in line with other legislation, the powers to supervise compliance with the decree-law, which was hitherto granted to the IDP, IP, is transferred to the Food and Economic Safety Authority (ASAE).

281. Other alterations of the provisions of the original regulations were also introduced, i.e., the strengthening of the requirement that there be a barrier, which adequately protects play and recreation areas, the requirement that these spaces must be isolated from traffic, and the creation of technical solutions, which restrict movement near children's swings and other similar equipment in order to reduce the risk of accidents. There is a requirement that an efficient technical solution be found, which makes it possible to completely isolate this type of equipment and their surrounding areas so that free access to the equipment is restricted.

282. New obligations of the entity responsible for play and recreation area are also created, so that local authorities and ASAE must now conduct an inspection of all play and recreation areas in their areas, which must be at least annual. As there have been various accidents in recent years with other equipment such as inflatables, trampolines and skateboards, these are now subject to certain safety rules, which increase the level of user protection. The aim is that such equipment be used safely and with adequate supervision in order to prevent the accident risks recently reported. The amount of the compulsory insurance has been updated and the level of the fines that can be imposed was also reviewed. These Regulations apply to all enclosed play and recreation areas for public use and the corresponding equipment and impact surfaces, which are intended for children, whatever the location thereof, with the exception of locations with water amusements.

283. Article 4 of the Regulations contains a general safety obligation, which provides that play and recreation areas cannot be a hazard to the health and safety of users or third parties. Furthermore, the Regulations require play and recreation areas to be distant from environmentally degraded or dangerous areas, or areas, which are affected by noise, and impose special access and signalling conditions with a view to access by those with limited mobility and the facilitation of access by the emergency services. It also contains provisions regarding protection against vehicle traffic, weather conditions and the protection of the areas in order to prevent vandalism, or the entry of animals and conditions regarding proximity and visibility, particularly with regard to a general duty that facilities have adequate artificial lighting.

284. Chapter III of the Regulations attached to Decree-Law no. 379/97, of 27 December, as re-enacted by Decree-Law no. 119/2009, of 19 May, concerns *impact equipment and surfaces.* The chapter commences with another general safety obligation to the effect that impact equipment and surfaces for play and recreation areas, must not, when used for the purpose for which they are intended, or other foreseeable purposes, and given the habitual behaviour of children, put the health and safety of users and third parties at risk. Furthermore, they must, when placed on the market and during the entire period of the normal and foreseeable use thereof, comply with the safety requirements contained in the decree-law, which contains provisions applicable to the safety, maintenance and safety of equipment and areas.

G. The Specific Case of Goals and Baskets

285. Article 7 of Decree-Law no. 317/97, of 25 November, which introduced the legal framework governing the establishment and operation of public access sports facilities and was repealed by Decree Law no. 141/2009, of 1 October, provided for regulations governing the technical conditions of sports facilities given the special characteristics thereof. It should be noted that various accidents involving children occurred in Portugal in a short period of time, which obliged the State to intervene urgently in this area,[45] as is evident from the preamble to Decree-Law no. 100/2003, of 23 May, as amended by Decree-Law no. 82/2004, of 14 April, which states that in this area the ADoPtion of legislation governing the installation, maintenance and conservation of goals is a matter of urgency given the seriousness of the accidents that had repeatedly occurred and injured children and young people in our country. *The legal framework introduced establishes a general safety obligation,*

45. Compare José Manuel Meirim. *Segurança e Seguranças Desportivas.* Lisboa, Livros Horizonte, 2007, p. 39.

which must be complied with both when the sports equipment is placed on the market and while it is in use.

286. The Regulations apply to football, handball, hockey and water polo goals and to basketball equipment in public access sports facilities. An obligation to check safety conditions, i.e., the checking of the stability and solidity of the equipment, within ninety days, was introduced in order to rapidly check the national situation as to the installation and confirmation of goals in recreation parks and stadiums in Portugal. The Regulations also include a general safety obligation to the effect that sports equipment cannot be a risk to the health and safety of users and third parties and must, when placed on the market and during the entire period of normal and foreseeable use, comply with the safety requirements of these Regulations.

287. The definition of responsible body for the purposes of the Regulations, is important as the following are deemed to be the body responsible for equipment, for the purposes of the Regulations:

(a) any natural person in a management position and private law juristic persons;
(b) heads of departments or organizations of the local, regional or central public administration, which are responsible for the normal working of the place where these items of equipment are installed and for the installation and maintenance thereof;
(c) those persons to whom the use of the said places has been ceded for a limited duration, whether for valuable consideration or otherwise, are also deemed to be the responsible body in the same terms, namely for the purposes of the obligation to take out civil liability insurance in respect of the incorrect use of the sports equipment.

II. Safety in Stadiums

288. Regulatory Decree no. 10/2001, of 7 June was introduced, which approved the Stadium Technical and Safety Conditions Regulations, with regard to safety within stadiums and in the surrounding areas and particularly in football stadiums, given the responsibility for the organization of the 2004 UEFA European Football Championship (EURO) and the consequent need to construct a series of stadiums that complied with the most modern safety requirements at that time.

289. This legislation, which was not repealed by Decree-Law no. 141/2009, of 16 June, was the response to the need for a regulatory structure, which was more in line with modern technical and functional requirements for enclosed locations, which involve great technical complexity and an unavoidable impact in town-planning terms. Accordingly, the legal framework governing public access sports facilities applies to stadiums with the exception of technical and safety conditions to which the provisions of Regulatory Decree no. 10/2001, of 7 June apply. The conditions governed by Regulatory Decree, accordingly range from the implantation of stadiums (classifying them according to their seating capacity), access roads, user safety, and areas for spectators, sportspersons, referees, coaches, and social security.

290. The body which is responsible for the supervision of sports infrastructures is ASAE, in accordance with the provisions of Decree-Law no. 274/2007, of 30 July and in accordance with the provisions of Decree-Law 141/2009, of 16 June, without prejudice to the powers and duties of local authorities in the RJUE, and the powers and duties granted by law to other administrative and police authorities.

291. It should also be noted with regard to sports infrastructures that according to the provisions of no. 2 of Article 1 of Law no. 48/98, of 11 August, (which establishes the basis of town and country planning policy), *town and country planning policy defines and co-ordinates the measures taken by the Public Administration, with a view to ensuring the adequate use and organisation of the national territory with a view to the valorisation thereof within the European space, with the objective of the harmonious integrated and sustainable economic, social and cultural development of the Country, its various regions and urban agglomerations.*

292. Sport is increasingly assuming a significant role in the context of economic, social and cultural development, which is intended to be integrated. For this reason, Decree-Law no. 46/2009, of 20 February, i.e., the legislation regarding territorial management tools, contains the following provisions in Article 17 under the title of Public infrastructure and collective facilities networks:

(a) '[t]he fundamental networks of infrastructures and facilities, which promote the qualityof life, support economic activity and ensure the optimisation of access to culture, education, training, justice, health, social security, sport and leisure shall be identified in the territorial management tools.'.
(b) '[f]or the purposes of the provisions of the preceding number, the national Town and Country Planning Policy programme, the regional plans and the inter-municipal town and country planning plans, the relevant sectorial plans, and municipal town and country planning plans will define a coherent strategy for the establishment, conservation and development of those infrastructures or facilities, taking into consideration the social and cultural needs of the population and the prospects of economic and social evolution.'

293. As is stated above, Article 7 of Decree-Law no. 317/97, of 25 November, which created the legal framework governing the establishment and operation of public access sports facilities, which was repealed and replaced by Decree-Law no. 141/2009, of 16 June, provided that *the rules in the sports premises technical conditions regulations to be approved by regulatory decree shall apply to sports facilities.* The Decree-Law also provided, in its transitional provisions in Article 27 thereof, that Regulatory Decree no. 34/95, of 16 December, which governs the technical and safety conditions of enclosed sports and public entertainment locations, would remain in force until the publication of the said regulatory decree.

294. However, the provisions of Regulatory Decree no. 34/95, of 16 December fundamentally concern questions of the safety of spectators, via measures, which deal extensively and generally with the common types of enclosed locations for public events. This can be explained by the fact that the safety requirements of enclosed locations for events and shows have a common basis, despite the fact that there is a need to consider the specificities of each case.

295. It is accordingly necessary to complete the safety and quality requirements in those regulations, with regard to other technical and functional aspects, while, at the same time, also acknowledging the specificities associated with the various enclosed sports locations, particularly those, such as stadiums, which are paradigmatic spaces of public assembly and for mass events. Stadiums require increasingly well planned and sophisticated resources in the configuration of the types of comfort and safety afforded to sportspersons and spectators. The most recent are stipulated by Law no. 39/2009, of 30 July, which establishes the legal framework governing the combating of violence, racism, xenophobia and intolerance in sports events, which will be further detailed below.

296. The scope and complexity of the technical provisions to be included in legislation targeted at the wide range of differing types of sports facilities necessarily involves great consideration in the definition of appropriate and technically viable measures, which meant that it was, in fact, only partially possible to attain the said objective.

297. In the meantime, a series of new factors, i.e., an increasing local authority involvement in the creation and modernization of sports infrastructures and the award to Portugal of the organization of the final phase of UEFA EURO 2004, led to the construction and modernization of stadiums all over the country, but without of a set of rules that was adapted to the modern technical and functional requirements, which are applicable to enclosed locations, which involve unavoidable town planning impacts in addition to technical complexity.

298. In this specific scenario, in which unique opportunities and conditions for the development and modernization of a wide range of stadiums combine, it was necessary and a priority to promote the development of special rules with regard to the works affecting stadiums. The aim of this new legal framework is to ensure improved comfort, functionality and safety in such a way as to contribute to the promotion of town planning, functional and technical quality in the said enclosed locations and also to improve the level of the services provided to those involved in sports and to the general public within the ambit of sports events in stadiums.

III. Policing of Sports Events

299. The State is responsible for the policing of areas outside enclosed sports locations. The legal framework governing policing within enclosed sports locations is to be found in Decree-Law no. 238/92, of 29 October, which applies a limited concept of enclosed sports location for the purpose of the application of its provisions. According to Article 1 no. 2, paragraph a), an enclosed sports location is a space created exclusively for sports activities, which is permanent and has structures, which are appropriate in terms of the said use and function and which has permanent seating reserved for spectators subject to entry control. (Decree-Law 216/2012, of 9 October, repealed Decree-Law no 238/92, of 29 October, as amended by Laws nos 38/98, of 4 August and 39/2009, of 30 July, with the exception no. 1 of Article 7, Article 8 and the corresponding annexes)

300. According to this legislation, it is for the organizer of the sports event, which is defined by paragraph b) of the said article as the entity, which promotes, co-ordinates or holds events of the sport in question, in accordance with the law, to ensure safety and maintain order within enclosed sports locations. In order to do so, they are required to request police assistance in order to ensure the safety of all involved, whenever they consider the same to be necessary. When the organizer considers that the policing of a sports event is not necessary, the responsibility for the maintenance of order within the enclosed sports location lies with the *organizer of the sports competition*. This principle that the requesting of the presence of security forces is not obligatory applies except when an order has been made prohibiting the use of an enclosed sports location, when a request for policing is obligatory.

301. The legislation also establishes the criteria for the classification of events as high risk events, when the clubs involved are required to take security and control measures, to control the access of and groups of supporters and to monitor them, and normal risk events when a request for police assistance is optional. This legal provision, which establishes the criteria for the risk classification of sports events, was recently repealed by Law no. 39/2009, of 30 July, which introduced the legal framework governing the combating of violence, racism, xenophobia and intolerance at sports events, while the rest of the legislation remained in force.

302. The new law substantially amended the event classification criteria. Accordingly, the following national sports events are deemed to be high risk events:

(a) finals of a European or World Championships of sports to be defined annually by the CESD, after having consulted the security forces;
(b) events, which are declared by International, European or World organizations of the sports in question, to be high risk, on the basis of incidents caused by supporters of at least one of the teams, or for exceptional reasons;
(c) events in which the supporters of the visiting team will presumably account for more than 10% of the capacity of the enclosed sports location, or are 2,000 or more people;
(d) when the enclosed sports location is expected to be full to capacity, or when the probable number of spectators exceeds 30,000 people.

303. The following national sports events are deemed to be high risk:

(a) events that are defined as such by the CESD, after having consulted the security force responsible for the area and the corresponding sports federation, or the professional league, in the case of professional competitions;
(b) events, which are the quarter or the semi-finals of a competition;
(c) when the expected number of spectators is equal to 80% of the capacity of the enclosed sports location;
(d) when the probable number of supporters of a visiting team equals 20% of the expected number of spectators;
(e) when the supporters of the clubs involved have caused serious incidents at previous games;
(f) when sports events are decisive for both teams in terms of the winning of a trophy, access to international competitions or divisional promotion or relegation;
(g) sports events not included in the situations described above are deemed to be normal risk events.

304. The costs of the policing of sports events are borne by the organizer of the sports competition. There is provision for a State contribution to the costs of the policing of sports events, which involve national teams, or which take place as part of national championships of age groups lower than the senior age group, and district championships.

305. The law makes no distinction between professional and non-professional competitions in enclosed sports locations, for the purposes of the application of measures to prevent violence in stadiums. The criterion is whether or not the sports competition is considered to be high risk or not.

306. It is for the *organizer of the sports competition*, i.e., the corresponding league or federation, to decide whether the sports spectacle should be considered high risk or not, in accordance with the criteria established by Law no. 39/2009, of 30 July.

307. Article 3, no. 2 of the LBAFD, following the principle contained in Article 79 of the CRP, strengthens this principle, i.e., it is for the State to take measures with a view to the prevention and punishment of anti-sporting conduct, i.e., violence, doping, corruption, racism, xenophobia and all types of discrimination.

IV. The Security Co-ordinator

308. The security co-ordinator is the person in charge of security within the enclosed sports location, without prejudice to the powers and duties of the criminal police. The said co-ordinator shall co-ordinate the work of the stewards, with a view, in co-operation with the sports competition organizer, the security forces, the ANPC and health services, to ensuring that the sports event takes place without adverse occurrences, by meeting with the said entities before and after each sports event and by preparing a final report, which is submitted to the organizer of the sports event, with a copy thereof being submitted to the CESD. It can thus be seen that the security co-ordinator is in charge of the management of and is responsible for all aspects of it that can give rise to a lack of security, or violence,[46] and are not purely sporting in nature.

309. The position of security co-ordinator, which appears in Article 10 of Law no. 39/2009, of 30 July, is not new and appeared in the previous laws that combated violence in sport, i.e., Law no. 38/98, of 4 August, as continued in Law no. 16/2004, of 11 May.

310. Law no. 39/2009 (as amended by Decree-Law no. 52/2013, of 25 June, which introduced the legal framework governing the combating of violence, racism, xenophobia and intolerance at sports events, so that the same may take place securely), of 30 July only established the functional content of the position of security co-ordinator, which matters related to the necessary vocational training of those human resources that wish to occupy the said position were to be the subject matter of a subsequent statutory instrument. Accordingly, the legal framework governing the training of security co-ordinators was introduced by Statutory Instrument no. 181/2010, of 26 March, which provides that security co-ordinators are subject to the legal framework governing private security in Decree-Law no. 35/2004, of 21 February. Security co-ordinators must comply at all times with all of the following requirements, some of which are also necessary requirements for those seeking work in private security, i.e.:

(a) be a Portuguese citizen, a national of a Member State of the European Union (EU), a State that is a party to the European Economic Area (EEA) Agreement, or of a State where Portuguese is an official language, subject to reciprocity;
(b) be of full civil capacity;
(c) not have a criminal record for intentional crimes against human life, of assault, or against privacy, against property, of forgery, against telecommunications security, against public order, of resistance to or disobedience of public authority, of illegal possession of arms, or any other intentional crimes punishable by a term of imprisonment exceeding three years, without prejudice to the rehabilitation of offenders;
(d) not to have occupied any supervisory position, or had any supervisory duties, in the private security business in the three preceding years;
(e) not to have been definitively excluded from the Armed Forces, the services comprising the Information System of the Republic, or the security forces.

46. On this see, Alexandre Miguel Mestre, 'Comentários à Lei n.º 39/2009, de 30 de Julho, que Estabelece o Regime Jurídico do Combate à Violência, ao Racismo, à Xenofobia e à Intolerância nos Espectáculos Desportivos, de Forma a Possibilitar a Realização dos Mesmos em Segurança', *A Nova Legislação do Desporto Comentada*, Walters Kluwer/Coimbra Editora, Colecção PLMJ, Lisbon (2010), 303.

311. Candidates for the position of security co-ordinator must comply with the following specific requirements:

(a) have concluded secondary education;
(b) be physically fit and have the psychological make-up necessary for the position, as substantiated by an aptitude sheet and an obligatory psychological assessment by an employment medical practitioner in accordance with the legislation in force, or as substantiated by an aptitude sheet or equivalent test carried out in another Member State of the European Union;
(c) successful completion of a training course in accordance with the provisions of the statutory instrument, or identical courses given and recognized in another Member State of the EU;
(d) proof of at least three years' work in the area of private security.

312. Statutory Instrument no. 181/2010, of 26 March, however requires security co-ordinators to prove that they comply with all of the requirements listed above and to prove that they have worked in that area for more than three years. They are also required to attend a security co-ordinators training course, the details of which are attached to the Statutory Instrument, within 180 of the same coming into force. This obligation means, in practice, that those, who prove that they have successfully completed a course, which is identical to that provided in the Statutory Instrument, but which is recognized in another Member State of the European Union, are required to take the Portuguese course.

V. Stewards

313. The need arose to create a form of private security in the world of Portuguese sport, as a consequence of the organizational and security requirements of UEFA EURO 2004. Decree-Law no. 94/2002, of 12 April, not only introduced the concept in the context of private security activity, but requires that the private security system be adopted at the time of the holding of some events in enclosed sports locations, in accordance with statutory instrument 1522-C/2002, of 20 December. According to Article 2 of the statutory instrument, the use of stewards is obligatory *in professional football competitions in enclosed sports locations with a capacity of 25,000 or more, which comply with the Stadium Technical and Safety Conditions, approved by Regulatory Decree no. 10/2001, of 7 June*. The use of *stewards* is optional in all other competitions.

314. Statutory Instrument no. 1522-B/2002, of 20 December, defines the specific role of stewards and establishes the circumstances in which they must be used. The Statutory Instrument also establishes the duration and content of the training course and the evaluation system for candidates for the position of steward, and the specific training units the purpose of which is to instil sufficient knowledge of the specificities and demands of the duties to be performed. According to the statutory instrument, stewards have the following duties:

(a) to oversee the enclosed sports location and security perimeters and ensure compliance with the regulations regarding the use of the enclosed location by spectators;
(b) to control access points, including the detection and prevention of the introduction of objects and substances, which are prohibited, or which could facilitate acts of violence;
(c) to check entry tickets and control the proper working of the equipment installed for that purpose;
(d) to oversee and monitor spectators in the various parts of the enclosed location and to provide information regarding organization, infrastructures and emergency exits;
(e) to prevent, monitor and control the occurrence of incidents and to communicate the same immediately;
(f) to orient spectators in all emergency situations, particularly those that involve the evacuation of the enclosed location;
(g) to monitor groups of supporters, who travel to other enclosed sports locations, in order to contribute to the security of the game;
(h) to inspect the premises before and after each sports event, in accordance with the security rules and regulations;
(i) to prevent spectators from moving from one sector to another, within the enclosed location;
(j) during games, to prevent spectators from abandoning their seats in such a way that they obstruct or hinder the accesses and emergency accesses and exits.

315. According to the current *legal framework governing private security services*, in Decree-Law no. 35/2004, of 21 February, as amended by Decree-Law no. 38/2008, of 8 of August, which includes the position of *steward, stewards* are permitted to conduct security and preventive searches in their control of access to the enclosed sports location, but strictly in order to assist in the prevention of the introduction of prohibited or potentially dangerous articles. To do this, they are authorized to use metal and explosives detection paddles. The purpose of these powers is not and cannot accordingly be confused with the objective of obtaining evidence of the commission of a crime, as provided in the criminal law. Stewards do not have powers to seize any objects, or to make arrests.

VI. Sport Medicine

316. Paragraph b) of no. 2 of Article 64 of the CRP includes the promotion of physical and sports culture in the implementation of the right to health protection. The Basic Law of Health approved by Law no. 48/90, of 24 August, provides that sport must be involved in the promotion of health. This concern is no novelty. Even during the Salazar regime there were evident concerns with regard to the relationship between health and sport, which were enshrined in the constitution of the Corporative Chamber, by Decree-Law no. 29 111, of 12 November 1938, which included a representative of hunters associations and a medical practitioner who was a physical education specialist.

317. In 1999, two items of legislation were passed in this area: Law no. 119/99, of 11 August, which governed 'Sport Medicine assistance' and Decree-Law no. 345/99, of 27 August, which introduced the legal framework governing sports medicine.

318. Article 17 of the LBSD as amended by Law no. 19/96, of 25 June, gave the State the task of promoting the institutionalization and regulation of sport medicine services and access to sport within the ambit of the federations, via a medical examination, which attests to the absence of any counter-indication.

319. It is necessary, with a view to the prosecution of an effective policy for the support and protection of sportspersons, and in the light of the increasing technical evolution of sports activity, to establish specific measures, which will permit an increased link between sportspersons and the specific diagnoses and the scientific procedures involved in sport medicine.

320. Medical examinations are an indispensable tool in the evaluation of the fitness or unfitness of athletes for sport and amount to a key way in which to identify certain pathologies, or clinical conditions, particularly among young people. Sports medicine examinations are accordingly obligatory in all circumstances and for all sportspersons, referees, judges and timekeepers, who are members, or who wish to become members, of federations with sports public utility status. Also defined, is a system, which links the various sport medicine services and departments and the specific qualifications that are required of those, who head these services and who work in the said departments.

321. Nos 1 and 2 of Article 40 of the LBAFD introduces a specific obligation to which persons actively involved in physical and sports activities, that do not take place under auspices of the federations, are subject, i.e., to confirm that they have no relevant counter-indications prior to involvement in the said activities. This rule appears to conflict with the annual requirement to submit a medical examination as a precondition of access to and frequency of sports facilities, which was to be found in Article 14 of Decree-Law no. 385/99, of 28 September, which established the legal framework governing the technical responsibility for sports facilities open to the public and the activities carried on there. The said Decree Law was repealed by Decree-Law 271/2009, of 1 October, and the submission of a medical certificate as a condition for the attendance of sports facilities for physical and sports activities, which do not take place under the auspices of a federation, is no longer obligatory. The risk is accordingly assumed by the user. According to no. 1 of Article 40 of the LBAFD, access to sports activity under the auspices of a sports federation is subject to proof that the sportsperson has sufficient physical aptitude, which must be certified via a medical examination certificate, which states that there are no counter-indications.

322. Another legal provision with regard to medical examinations, which also makes no provision regarding the cost thereof is Article 33.º nos 1 and 2 of Decree-Law no. 272/2009, of 1 October, under the heading of 'Medical support', the text of which is as follows:

(a) [s]pecialist medical care of sportspersons in high performance sport shall be provided by the sports medicine services;
(b) [h]igh performance status presupposes proof of physical aptitude, via medical examinations to be conducted by the sports medicine services.

323. According to Article 6 of Law no. 119/99, of 11 August, *the Government shall, after having consulted the Medical Association, approve the regulations necessary for the proper implementation of this law, i.e. regarding the rules governing medical examinations and the grant of credentials.*

324. Ministerial Order no. 11318/2009 issued by the Secretary of State of Youth and Sport on 4 May 2008, provides further that:

(a) sports-medicine examinations shall be valid for one year;
(b) sports medicine examinations shall be carried out when the sportspersons in question register with the sports federations for the first time;
(c) without prejudice to the provisions of the following number, sports medicine examinations shall be repeated only in the month in which the person in question has his/her birthday;
(d) sportspersons, who are federation members and who, as at the date of the publication of this Order, have a sports medicine examination, which expires prior to their birthday must, if necessary, have an interim examination to cover the period until the renewal in accordance with this Order;
(e) sports federations shall adapt their regulations in order to ensure that the same are compatible with the rules introduced by this Order;
(f) within the ambit of each sport, this Order shall take effect as from the commencement of the sports season immediately after its publication date.

325. Finally, nos 1 to 4 of Article 10 of Decree-Law no. 345/99, of 27 August (which was later amended by Decree Law no. 225/2012 of 29 November), provide as follows with regard to the cost of sports medicine examinations:

(a) [t]he cost of sports medicine evaluation examinations carried out by IND [now IDP, IP] Sports Medicine Centres shall be fixed annually by order of the Government member responsible for sport;
(b) [t]he costs referred to in the preceding number shall be included in the IND Sports Medicine Services Department (now IDP, IP) price list;
(c) [t]he price list referred to in the preceding number shall be approved by order of the Government member responsible for sport and shall be published in the 2nd series of the Official Journal;
(d) [s]ports medicine evaluation examinations and all support provided at IND Sports Medicine Centres (now IDP, IP) to high performance sportspersons shall be free of charge.

326. Health and safety are fundamental values that are present in sport and sometimes combine, e.g., in Article 32 of the LBAFD, regarding certain sports events that occur in public locations, when the corresponding sports federation is required to approve the sport event regulations in order to ensure compliance with the health and safety protection rules that protect participants. Such sport events must also be preceded by an opinion issued by the corresponding sports federation.

327. However, the said article only includes sports events or contests, which comply with all the following requirements:

(a) they take place on the public highway or in other public spaces;
(b) they are open to participation by sportspersons, who are members of the sports federations; and
(c) prizes in cash or kind are awarded in them, which exceed the amount fixed in the law.

328. Opinion no. 74/2001, of the Consultative Council of the Attorney-General's Department, which was published in no. 265 of the 2nd Series of the Official Journal on 15 November 2001, concerns the effect and reconciliation of these legislative provisions.[47]

329. The aim was to increase the quality of medical training and consequently to increase the prestige of the qualifications provided thereby via the reformulation of the legal framework governing medical internships introduced by Decree-Law no. 203/2004, of 18 August, via the amendments introduced by Decree-Law no. 11/2005, of 6 January, Decree-Law no. 60/2007, of 13 March and Decree-Law no. 45/2009, of 13 February and by Statutory Instrument no. 183/2006, of 22 February. The fundamental measure involved in this was the establishment of a duly updated training programme for each occupational area, or speciality, which defines the curricular structure of the training process, with durations and general activity plans, and establishes overall and specific objectives for each area and stage and the assessment event times and methods.

330. In addition to the range of specialities already envisaged in Statutory Instrument no. 183/2006, of 22 February, another has been identified, which is a

47. The conclusions of which are transcribed below: '*1. Law no. 119/99, of 11 August, and Decree-Law no. 345/99, of 27 August, are legislative acts of equal value (article 112, no. 2, of the Constitution), which legislate in respect of matters included within the joint exclusive legislative competences of the Assembly of the Republic and the Government; 2. Articles 4 to 7 of Decree-Law no. 345/99, of 27 August, tacitly repealed articles 1 and 2 of Law no. 119/99, of 11 August; 3. Sport medicine assessments are obligatory for sportspersons, referees, judges and timekeepers, who are members of, or wish to be members of federations with sports public utility status; 4. No medical specialization or specific medical qualification is required in order to conduct the general sports medicine examination referred to by articles 5, no. 1, and 7, no. 1, of Decree-Law no. 345/99, of 27 August; 5. In those cases in which sport medicine advice is justified in the light of counter indications with regard to the proposed sport, the sportspersons in question should, alternatively, be directed to: a) The sport medicine centre for the geographic area in question; b) To a medical practitioner with specific training recognised by the sport medicine section of the Portuguese Medical Association; or c) A medical practitioner with a post-graduate qualification in sport medicine approved by the said body (no. 2 of article 5 of Decree-Law no. 345/99); 6. The sport medicine assessments of sportspersons included in the high level competition provisions shall be conducted solely at the Sport Medicine Centres of the National Sport Institute (no. 4 of the said article 5)*'.

specific response to the needs of the health sector, i.e., the sports medicine speciality, which should be included in the range of medical speciality internships.

331. The occupational area of the sports medicine speciality was created by Statutory Instrument no. 302/2009, of 24 March. The Statutory Instrument also approved the corresponding training programme, which came into force on 1 January 2010. The programme will be applied and implemented by the bodies and persons responsible for training in the internships, which are required to ensure maximum national uniformity. The sports medicine speciality was added to the list in annexe I of the Medical Internship Regulations, approved by Statutory Instrument no. 183/2006, of 22 February.

332. The ambit and objective of the specific training were stated to be the fact that sports medicine is a medical speciality, which is concerned with the prevention, treatment, diagnosis and treatment of the various pathologies associated with physical exercise and sports activities in all age groups and is an area of knowledge which, because of its specific characteristics, is closely linked to other medical specialities and plays a fundamental role in the development of exercise and sports programmes for the general public. Sports medicine also plays a fundamental role in the prevention of cardiovascular, metabolic, neoplastic, psychiatric and other illnesses via, the prescribing of regular physical exercise.

333. Sports medicine is multidisciplinary, covers all age groups and all levels of involvement in exercise and sport, it uses various diagnostic, therapeutic and investigation techniques, which need to be learned in depth. Sports medicine is accordingly considered to be a speciality that should be encouraged both quantitatively and qualitatively. It demands that interns have a good knowledge of the various areas of medical knowledge related to physical exercise, if they are to be able to practice medicine effectively.

VII. Sports Insurance

334. Portuguese law provides, with regard to certain sports and leisure activities, that they are subject to an obligation to obtain insurance covering the risk of personal injury to the sportsman or woman, i.e., insurance of a person or persons – and damage to property or third parties as a consequence of the risk inherent in the said activities, so as to safeguard the liability of the insured in respect of personal injury or material loss or damage that may be caused involuntarily to property, animals or third parties, i.e., civil liability insurance.

335. Personal insurance is intended to cover risks affecting the physical or bodily integrity of persons and fundamentally pays a fixed sum, i.e., the compensation is not calculated according to the specific injury incurred.

336. In certain situations both types of insurance cover are obligatory, as those who take part in dangerous sports are required to obtain their own personal insurance cover and also to obtain cover with regard to any loss or damage sustained as a consequence of the said activity, which can per se give rise to loss and damage to people and property.

337. In any event, such compensation is only payable if the loss or damage was caused involuntarily, because intentional conduct, or conduct of a person for whom the insured is civilly liable will not render the insurance company liable to pay compensation, as per no. 3 of Article 437 of the Commercial Code, approved by Carta de Lei of 28 June 1888.

338. In the light of the risks inherent in sports activity, the obtaining of such insurance cover has been obligatory in Portugal since the publication of Decree-Law no. 146/93, of 26 April, which governed sports insurance and a provision of the LBSD, which was regulated by Statutory Instrument no. 757/93, of 26 August (in the case of insurance of sports actors, professional and non-professional sportspersons and competitions open to the public), and by Statutory Instrument no. 392/98, of 11 July (in the case of insurance of high performance non-professional sportspersons). Prior to Decree-Law no. 146/93, of 26 April, there were two other decree-laws, which concerned sports insurance, i.e., Decree-Law no. 205/83, of 21 May and Decree-Law no. 162/87, of 8 April. The following were among the main aspects of Decree-Law no. 205/83, of 21 May:

(a) the organization of group sports insurance to be taken out by the federations for non-professional sportspersons and sports actors;
(b) the obligatory nature of sports insurance for all professional sportspersons, to be taken out by the sportspersons in question, or by their club, or company with sports objects or by the company group of which it is a member;
(c) the introduction of a broader-based support scheme for non-professional high performance sportspersons, which combines insurance and social support aspects;
(d) the introduction of obligatory insurance of sports events, to be taken out by any entities that promote or organize competitions open to the public;
(e) the simplification of sports insurance subscription procedures and of the definition of the corresponding premium contribution criteria;
(f) the option granted to sports actors with regard to alternative insurance arrangements, which are capable of providing the same, or a better, cover.

339. In both of these types of insurance contracts, i.e., personal cover and civil liability cover, the policyholder is generally not the beneficiary of the insurance cover. This is the case of sports, which are under the auspices of a sports organization, when the organization is the policyholder (and therefore responsible for the payment of the premium) and the beneficiaries are sportspersons and other sports actors in the case of the personal insurance or, third parties, in the case of civil liability cover. Sports organizations, particularly sports federations, make insurance contracts termed group insurance contracts, which insure a minimum of ten people, who are connected with each other and with the insurer by a common bond, or interest.

340. Sports insurance of professional sportspersons is obligatory for all professional sportspersons, whether or not they are members of federations with sports public utility status, in accordance with no. 1 of Article 7 of Decree-Law no. 146/93, of 26 April. If a sportsperson is covered by insurance, which covers occupational accident risks, he or she is not required to obtain sports insurance cover, as per no. 5 of Article 70 of the LBD.

341. Article 4 of Law no. 8/2003, of 12 May, which introduced a specific legal framework for the reparation of loss and damage arising from occupational accidents involving professional sportspersons, provided that sports insurance was complementary in relation to occupational accident insurance. This law fixed a compensation level for complete or partial disability caused accidentally, which is higher that the levels provided in Law 98/2009, of 4 September, which governs the compensation and integration of ordinary workers injured in occupational accidents. The law also introduces special provision for medical care and rehabilitation of injured persons, who are professional sportspersons. The law further introduces the possibility that the periodic payments for life payable in the event of occupational accident that result in death or permanent disability in which the victim is a professional sports person, who is a foreign national, may be capitalized, if he or she decides to leave Portugal. Otherwise the provisions of the general legal framework governing occupational accidents approved by Law no. 98/2009, of 4 September, are applicable.

342. Decree-Law no. 10/2009, of 12 January, which introduced a specific legal framework with regard to obligatory sports insurance, repealed the legal framework then in force pursuant to Decree-Law no. 146/93, together with Statutory Instrument no. 757/93, of 26 August and Statutory Instrument no. 392/98, of 11 July. The aim of the new legislation is to implement the provisions of Article 42 of the LBAFD, which guarantees the creation of an obligatory insurance system for sports actors that are members of sports federations. This insurance provides special cover for high performance sports persons with regard to the special risks to which they are exposed. Article 43 of the said legislation requires bodies that provide sports services to have obligatory insurance cover with regard to accidents or illness arising from sports activity.

343. Legal theory had previously indicated a number of risks that should be covered by the new sports insurance regime, i.e., risks to the physical wellbeing of players, spectators or third parties, to which the human resources involved in the game are exposed, and also the risks inherent in travel to and from the place where the game takes place. However, the risks covered by sports insurance had to be defined precisely, i.e., it only covered health risks caused by active involvement in a sport. Risks arising from active involvement in various sports were however excluded.

344. Also, the experience in the meantime and the reforms that commenced with the coming into force of the LBAFD, indicated that the system should be reformed in order to deal, on the one hand, with the criticisms regarding the quantitative limits on cash compensation and, on the other hand, with the life insurance provided for high performance athletes. A working group was accordingly established, which comprises representatives of the State, sportspersons, sports federations and insurers, with a view to the implementation of new sports insurance rules in order to standardize the different situations of the various sports actors. The said Decree-Law accordingly provides that sports actors, sportspersons in sports facilities open to the public and participants in sports events must have sports insurance.

345. Sport is, by definition a predominantly physical and competitive activity so that the covering of risks via the introduction of compulsory insurance is an absolute necessity for the safety of those taking part. Compulsory insurance meets a fundamental social need, i.e., to ensure that the beneficiary has the effective benefit of the cover provided. A system of insurance obviously does not prevent the risk but is does deal with the risk that victims will not be compensated.

346. However, as the vast majority of people actively involved in sport in Portugal are not high performance sportspersons, the previous Basic Law of Sport provided for the introduction of a system of compulsory insurance for facilities open to the public and for sports events and left it to the law to define the corresponding sports and risks. Decree-Law no. 10/2009, of 12 January accordingly provides a compulsory sports insurance requirement for:

(a) sports actors;
(b) those taking active part in sports activities in public access sports facilities;
(c) participants in sports events.

347. To summarize, in the case of sports actors, the responsibility for obtaining sports insurance will now lay with the sports federations. In the case of those actively involved in sports activities in public access sports facilities, those, who operate the said facilities, are required to obtain sports insurance cover. In the case of participants in sports events, the responsibility lies with the event organizer. The risks arising from sports activities within the ambit of sport in schools are excluded from the application of the Decree-Law. So, the following persons are deemed to be sports actors:

(a) sportspersons, who are members of a sports federation;
(b) referees, judges and timekeepers;
(c) sports coaches;
(d) sports managers and directors.

348. The compulsory insurance legal framework also applies to all handicapped or disabled sports actors, with a view to their complete social integration and participation with other sports actors on an equal opportunity basis.

349. The prohibition of exclusion clauses in sports insurance policies, which, when construed individually or together, are contrary to the nature of the sports activity, or defeat the object of the insurance contract, is also noteworthy.

350. So far as high performance sportspersons are concerned, the system of two parallel insurance policies remains in force, as is also the case with regard to professional sportspersons. The mechanisms for the establishment of invalidity in terms of a specific sport or sports speciality were also clarified. High performance sportspersons are covered by health insurance and so have obligatory cover that provides a capital sum on permanent disability, without prejudice to the cover provided by group sports insurance. Invalidity in respect of a sport or sports speciality of high performance sportspersons is established by a tripartite committee. The IDP, IP is responsible for taking out and paying the premiums of these insurance contracts. The minimum cover levels for sports insurance and the insurance cover for high performance sportspersons was also updated and corresponding provisions for automatic review in January each year in accordance with the consumer price index in the previous year were introduced.

351. In the event of accidents arising from sports activities, entities that fail to take out sports insurance contracts and keep in force are liable on the same terms as the insurer would have been liable had the insurance been obtained. It should be noted that sports facilities in which physical and sports activities take place and which provide fitness sports services, i.e., gymnasiums, academies or health clubs, are required to have sports insurance and to display information regarding the existence of the said cover in a place visible to users in all facilities.

352. Promoters or organizers of sports events open to the public are also legally required to obtain temporary insurance cover for those participants, who are not included in the sports actors' insurance cover, schools insurance or who are insured because they are users or clients of sports services providers. The persons in question are on cover as from the moment they register for the event.

353. These are some of the new amendments introduced by the Decree-Law no. 95/2013, of 19 of July:

Owners of Leisure Craft

- Owners of type 1, 2, 3 and 4 Leisure Craft (LC) and type 5 LCs that have at least a motor as a means of propulsion are required to have a third party civil liability insurance policy with regard to the LC; this obligation also applies to owners of yachts with a length in excess of 7 metres.[48]

48. Cf. Art. 42 of Decree-Law no. 124/2004, of 25 May – which approves the Leisure Boating Law.

Touristic entertainment agents

- Without prejudice to the general and specific exemptions with regard to the provision of services,[49] touristic entertainment companies and maritime touristic operators that operate in Portugal are required to have the following valid insurance cover regarding the health and safety risks of the services or third parties that arise from their activities:
  (i) Personal accident insurance for clients of the services.;
  (ii) Assistance insurance cover for clients of the services that travel abroad from Portugal within the ambit of the service provided or as a consequence thereof.;
  (iii) Civil liability insurance covers material damage, pain and suffering caused by accidents in the course of the provision of the service.[50]

Providers of diving services

- Providers of diving services as legally defined,[51] which are established or provided services in Portugal are required to have insurance cover for personal accident risks during the provision of their services.[52]

354. Finally, a new enforcement framework is introduced in which the IDP, IP may, when expressly authorized by the interested party, defend the interests of sportspersons and other non-professional sports actors in legal proceedings.

VIII. Sport in the Natural Environment

355. Sport in the natural environment is an increasingly frequent phenomenon in contemporary society and this has led to an increasing intervention by the Law in terms of sport and the environment.[53]

49. Cf. Art. 28 and 28-A of Decree-Law no. 108/2009, of 15 May, as amended by Decree-Law no. 95/2013, of 19 July.
50. Cf. Art. 27 no. 1 of Decree-Law no. 108/2009, of 15th May, as amended by Decree-Law no. 95/2013, of 19 July.
51. Cf. Art. 20 of Decree-Law no. 108/2009, of 15th May, as amended by Decree-Law no. 95/2013, of 19 July.
52. Cf. Statutory Instrument no. 1049/2004, of 19 August.
53. Legislative measures in the area of the environment commenced with international legal instruments, the first of which was the UNESCO International Charter on Physical Education and Sport, the title of which states that *facilities and material appropriate for physical education and sports are indispensible*. The article provides, *inter alia*, as follows: (i) Governments, public authorities, schools and the proper private organizations, at all levels, shall combine forces and concentrate on the planning of the location and optimal use of facilities, equipment and materials necessary for physical education and sport; (ii) urban development plans and rural land zoning plans shall include long term needs in terms of facilities, equipment and materials for physical education and sport, taking the possibilities afforded by the natural environment into consideration. Also to be noted is Art. 10 of the Council of Europe's European Sports Charter, which is entitled, *Sport and the principle of sustainable development*, which provides as follows: *To ensure and to improve the physical, social*

356. Article 31 of the LBAFD establishes the following basis for a series of measures with regard to *sport in nature. (…) physical activity and sport in natural areas must be governed by the principles of respect for nature and the preservation of its resources, together with compliance with the provisions of the town and country planning instruments in force, i.e. those with regard to classified areas, in order to ensure the conservation of biological diversity, the protection of ecosystems and the management of resources and waste and the preservation of natural and cultural heritage.* These measures are also intended to contribute to the dissemination and interpretation of natural and cultural heritage, environmental awareness and education and the promotion of nature tourism.

357. Assembly of the Republic Resolution no. 19/2006 – *Environmental management of golf courses* – was approved for preventive purposes. In it the Portuguese Parliament resolved *(…) to recommend to the Government that it legislate in order to introduce a code of conduct applicable to golf courses, and with a view to the development of impact monitoring programmes, in relation to town and country planning matters, water resources, the soil, biodiversity and habitats.*

358. Also noteworthy as steps of a non-binding nature taken with preventive intent are the successive resolutions passed by the Council of Ministers, calling variously for *the preparation of a code of conduct for nature tourism,*[54] and drawing attention to the importance of *stimulation of business internationalisation processes, which associate cultural and sports co-operation projects in the areas of the social responsibility and sustainable development of undertakings, particularly within the context of sponsorship.*[55]

359. Council of Ministers resolutions show the extent to which access to community funds is aided or hindered by matters related to the relationship between sport and the environment. The National Strategic Reference Framework (QREN) is a paradigmatic example of this. Council of Ministers Resolution no. 86/2007, of 3 July, which includes QREN 2007–2013 as an annexe, calls *for the creation of new tourism products, namely event-based tourism in order to promote a proper*

---

and mental well-being of the general public, from generation to generation, requires that physical activities, including those that take place in an urban, rural or aquatic environment, are adapted to the planet's limited resources and take place in harmony with the principles of sustainable development and a balanced management of the environment. This means, inter alia, that it is necessary to: I. Take nature and the environment into consideration in the planning and construction of sports facilities; II. Support and stimulate sports organisations in their efforts to conserve nature and the environment; III. Seek to ensure that the general public becomes more aware of the relationship between sport and sustainable development, and learns to know and understand nature better. International sports organizations are also a significant example of the defence of environmental principles and values, particularly the International Olympic Committee, which, in 1996, altered the Olympic Charter so as to include the environment in the powers and duties of that Swiss juristic person and which subsequently included the environment in the Code of Ethics of the International Olympic Committee.

54. Compare para. d) of no. 9 of Council of Ministers Resolution no. 112/98, of 25 August.
55. Compare Council of Ministers Resolution no. 109/2007, of 20 August, which approved the *National Sustainable Development Strategy*, point 29.

international insertion of some cultural, sports and scientific and technological facilities within the ambit of the *deepening of the process of economic integration within the European Union.*

360. Those who are involved in water sport either as amateurs or professionals are confronted by a wide range of legislation, which includes the provision that it is an offence punishable by a fine, to conduct tourist sports competitions and marine navigation outside of the areas in which the same are permitted.[56] It is also stressed that prior authorization must be obtained for the private use of public water resources for *sports competitions and navigation, and for the corresponding support infrastructures and facilities.*[57] It is also noted that the opinion of the IDP, IP is required prior to the necessary consideration of architecture and technical projects for enclosed facilities including aquatic leisure facilities by the local authority.[58] Finally the existence of *restrictions affecting recreational fishing*, whether *sport fishing* or *leisure fishing*, which includes *the prohibition or restriction of the recreational fishing of certain species, in certain areas, at certain times*[59] should also be noted.

361. Those who prefer motor sport must bear in mind the need for an opinion of the Nature Conservation Institute (ICN) for the purposes of the authorization or licensing of *motor sport activities*[60] and that *when certain grounds related to municipal land use plans are lacking*, the intervention of the ICN and the regional co-ordination and development committee in the area of *motorized activities and sports competitions outside of urban areas*[61] is required.

362. A key aspect in this area are the specific regulations governing *environmental recreation activities in the forms of recreation, environmental interpretation and nature sport in protected areas,* of which those involved are not always aware. This type of recreation is part of *nature sport,* which is defined as *sport, which brings Man into contact with nature in a healthy way, and which is in accordance with the management of protected areas and a sustainable development policy.*[62]

363. This question is even more important if it is realized that *nature sport*[63] is part of a wider concept of *nature tourism,*[64] which is increasingly common. *Nature*

56. Compare para. n) of Art. 81 of Decree-Law no. 226-A/2007, of 31 May. Statutory Instrument no. 1450/2007, of 12 November, was enacted in order *to introduce the outstanding rules on which the application of the said legislation depends.* Point 12 of the Statutory Instrument lists the use and the details of maritime tourism sports competitions and sailing.
57. According to para. i) of no. 1 of Art. 60 of Law no. 58/2008, of 29 September.
58. According to Art. 7, no. 1, of Decree-Law 65/97, of 31 March.
59. Article 10 of Decree-Law no. 246/2000, of 29 September; cf. also Statutory Instrument no. 868/2006, of 29 August.
60. Paragraph h) of Art. 8 of Decree-Law no. 140/99, of 24 April, as amended by Decree-Law no. 49/2005, of 24 February.
61. Paragraph i) of Art. 9 of Decree-Law no. 140/99, of 24 April, as amended by Decree-Law no. 49/2005, of 24 February.
62. Paragraph l) of Art. 2 of Regulatory Decree no. 18/99, of 27 August.
63. According to no. 3 of Art. 3 of the said legislation under the title of *Typology*, of initiatives or projects, which include: (i) walking; (ii) mountain climbing; (iii) a orienteering; (iv) rock climbing;

sports activities and services comply with general and specific requirements and each protected area is required to *possess a nature sports charter and the corresponding regulations, which must be approved by a joint statutory instrument of the government members responsible for sport and the environment.*[65]

364. Tourist resorts that provide accommodation services to tourists in classified and other areas with natural attractions, which have appropriate premises, structures and facilities and complementary services related to environmental pursuits, visits to natural areas, nature sport, and environmental interpretation may be granted recognition as nature tourism, or be associated with a national brand of classified areas by the Instituto de Conservação da Natureza e das Florestas, I. P. (Nature Conservation and Forests Institute) in accordance with criteria defined by statutory instrument of the members of the Government responsible for the areas of nature conservation and tourism.[66]

365. There are some sport activities practised in the natural environment which demand for proper equipment, facilities and infrastructures. It is therefore appropriate to conduct an environmental impact study of public and private projects that are likely to have significant environmental impacts, e.g., sports infrastructures, premises and facilities,[67] in order to preserve the National Ecological Network.[68] Furthermore, equipment for the artificial lighting of sports fields and stadiums *is required to be designed in accordance with the applicable national and international quality standards applicable to enclosed sports locations of this type,* taking

---

(v) rapel; (vi) speleology; (vii) ballooning; (viii) parapent; (viii) hang-gliding; (ix) mountain biking; (xi) horse riding; (xii) canooing; (xiii) rowing; (xiv) sailing; (xiv) surfing; (xv) windsurfing; (xvi) diving; (xvii) rafting; (xviii) diving; (xix) powerboat racing; and (xx) other sports and leisure activities, which do not have a negative effect in terms of nature conservation.

64. According to para. c) of no. 2 of Art. 2 of Decree-Law no. 47/99, of 16 February, which was re-enacted by Decree-Law no. 56/2002, of 11 March. *Nature tourism* is defined by no. 1 of Art. 1 of the said decree-law as *the artistic product comprised by establishments, activities, accommodation services and tourism and environment related activities and entertainment that takes place and is provided in areas that are within the national network of protected areas, hereinafter referred to as protected areas.*
65. Article 6 of Decree-Law no. 56/2002, of 11 March.
66. Cf. Art. 20 of Decree-Law no. 39/2008, of 7 March – which approves the legal framework governing the establishment, operation and working of tourist resorts, as amended by Art. 2 of Decree-Law no. 15/2014, of 23 January.
67. Some are to be found in annexe to Decree-Law no. 69/2000, of 3 May, i.e., aerodromes; fishing ports; permanent motor sport racing and training tracks; ski slopes, ski elevators and telphers and support infrastructures.
68. Within the ambit of *leisure and recreation, green areas for public use, which facilities for the use of the general public and which comply with all of the following requirements* are considered not to prejudice the continued existence of ecological resources, values and processes that the National Ecological Reserve is intended to preserve and can therefore be authorised: (i) *Support structures that use perishable or removable materials, not involving significant earth movement;* (ii) *That are adapted to the topography of the site and do not involve significant earth movement;* (iii) *The ground is not rendered impermeable;* (iv) *Ensures the preservation of the existing vegetation, particularly riparian vegetation;* (v) *Ensures waste collection.*

the following factors into consideration, *inter alia, the contribution of the lighting to the creation of an attractive and agreeable environment.*[69]

366. Another chapter stresses the fact that the protection of the environment and natural resources is a criterion for the recognition of the public interest of a given sports infrastructure[70] and for restricting the use of certain land for sports competitions.[71] Furthermore: it is necessary to *identify the basic level infrastructures and facilities that promote quality of life, support economic activity and ensure the optimisation of access (...) to sport,*[72] *in land use management instruments.* It should likewise not be overlooked that the scope of the application of the General Noise Regulations[73] includes *sports events,* which are *likely to cause inconvenience,* and affects both *permanent noise producing activities* and *temporary noise producing activities.*[74]

367. These are just some examples, which although they may, at the outset, appear to be somewhat unrelated, are frequently interconnected because their lowest common denominator is the legal connection between sport and sustainable development.

IX. Persons Involved in Sports Events and Liability Provisions

A. *Organizers and Promoters of Sports Competitions*

1. The Duties of Organizers of Sports Competitions

368. The law provides that organizers of sports competitions are subject to a duty to ensure the security of spectators within the enclosed sports location with

---

69. Paragraph c) of Art. 24 of Regulatory Decree no. 10/2001, of 7 June.
70. This was what occurred in connection with the recognised public interest of the Portimão Motor Sports Park – Algarve International Autodrome, in Order no. 665/2005, of 28 July, or in the area of the implementation of the project called the Northeastern Highway – Phase 4 by Oliveira de Azeméis Municipal Council. Order no. 2378/2007, of 24 January, stressed the contribution to *a lesser environmental impact.*
71. According to the provisions of para. d) of no. 1 of Art. 6 of Law no. 48/98, of 11 August (the Basic Law of town and country planning policy), town and country planning are required to promote *the preservation and defence of land with a natural aptitude, or which is used for agriculture, animal breeding or forestry, and to restrict the use of such land for other purposes to those cases in which the name is proved to be necessary.* (Our underlining).
72. Article 17 of Decree-Law no. 380/99, of 22 September, most recently amended by Decree-Law no. 316/2007, of 19 September. A consultative committee exists for this purpose, which, in accordance with the provisions of no. 1 of Art. 56 of the said decree-law, includes *representatives of sport, among other representatives or organisations and departments of the direct and indirect State administration, who ensure the prosecution of matters relevant to the public interest.*
73. This is a regulation which is an annexe to Decree-Law no. 9/2007, of 17 January, which, according to Art. 1 thereof, *established the legal framework for the prevention and control of sound polution, with a view to the safeguarding of humasn health and the well-being of the general public.*
74. In the light of para. b) of Art. 3 of the General Noise Regulations, this expression means activities, which although not isolated acts have a non-permanent character and produce a noise, which is noxious or a nuisance to those who live or are present in the places where the effects of the said sound source are felt, e.g., (...) sports competitions (...).

recourse to both preventive and repressive measures. They are also subject to a duty to provide and maintain adequate resources to ensure the security of all those involved in the sports event.

369. Law no. 39/2009, of 30 July provides that it is for *the federation of the sport in question, in relation to non-professional or international competitions that take place under the auspices of the international federations, and the professional leagues of clubs and local associations with regard to the corresponding competitions,* to appoint the organizer of the sports competition.

370. Organizers of sports competitions are also responsible for the ADoPtion of sports regulations for the prevention and control of violence.

371. The abovementioned regulations must contain a list of the *preventive procedures to be complied with in the organisation of sports competitions, in the event of violent incidents and the corresponding penalties to be imposed on sports actors, the legal procedures for the imposition of the said penalties and a list of the types of objects and substances prohibited.*

372. In as far as the violence prevention regulations are concerned, the same must comply not only with the rules introduced by Law 39/2009, of 30 July, but also with the provisions of the said law, which have yet to be implemented by regulations and the provisions of the international conventions regarding violence associated with sport, which bind the Portuguese Republic, i.e., the *European Convention on Spectator Violence and Misbehaviour at Sports Events and in particular at Football Matches,*[75]signed at Strasbourg on 4 September 1985.

373. The regulations must *inter alia* contain the following matters:

(a) preventive measures to be adopted in the organization of sports competitions;
(b) a list of the forms of violence, racism, xenophobia and intolerance in sports events and the corresponding penalties to be imposed on sports actors;
(c) the procedures leading up to the imposition of the penalties referred to in the preceding paragraph;
(d) a list of the types of objects and substances, which are prohibited or are likely to give rise to the possibility of violent acts;
(e) organizers of sports competitions are also subject to a duty to publicize the said regulations.

374. The proper authority for the purposes of the approval of the abovementioned regulations is the CESD, which is a section of the NSC that was created by the Decree-Law no. 315/2007, of 18 December, and replaced the former National Council against Violence in Sport. The non-approval of the abovementioned regulations, or the failure of a sports competition organizer to adopt the same, or the

75. The Convention came into force in Portugal on 1 Aug. 1987 after having been approved for ratification by Resolution of the Assembly of the Republic no. 11/87, of 10 March.

ADoPtion of regulations that the CESD has declined to register, means that the organizer of the sports competition cannot, while the said situation continues, receive any kind of public support, and, that its sports public utility status, if any, is suspended.

375. Sports federations and professional leagues are also required to include measures and programmes to promote good practices, which safeguard sports ethics and the sporting spirit, in their annual activity plans, particularly in the area of violence associated with sport.

376. In as far as the penalties are concerned, these may be pecuniary, *or, when they are imposed on sports event promoters, may involve the interdiction of enclosed sports locations, or the obligation to hold sports events without spectators.*

2. The Duties of Promoters of the Sports Competitions

377. Promoters of sports events, whether they are *local associations, sports clubs or companies, and the federations and leagues, when they are also the organisers of sports competitions,* are required to approve internal regulations regarding safety and the use of public access areas. The regulations must contain measures, the implementation of which must be preceded by co-ordination with the security forces, the National Civil Defence Authority (ANPC), the medical emergency services and the organizer of the sports competition. The said regulations must be registered with CESD and are only valid if so registered.

378. If a promoter of a sports event fails to adopt regulations, or they are rejected by the CESD, the consequence is that sports events cannot be held in the corresponding enclosed sports location, and that it is either not possible to obtain an operating licence, or operations are suspended immediately, as the case may be, for such time as the said situation continues. The law requires the inclusion of the following measures in the regulations:

(a) physical separation of supporters in separate areas set aside for them, in both professional and non-professional competitions considered to be high risk;
(b) in professional competitions and non-professional competitions deemed to be high risk, control of ticket sales by using mechanical, electronic or electromechanical means in order to control the spectator entry flow, preventing the reuse of tickets and permitting the detection of forged tickets;
(c) surveillance and control in order to prevent the over-occupation of any part of the enclosed location and to ensure that accesses are unobstructed;
(d) installation or assembly of security perimeters and the obligatory ADoPtion of access control systems in order to prevent the introduction of objects or substances that are prohibited, or are likely to enable or give rise to acts of violence, in accordance with the provisions of this law;

(e) prohibition of the sale, consumption and distribution of alcoholic drinks, drugs and psychotropic substances within the inner security perimeter and the ADoPtion of a system to control intoxication with alcohol, drugs and psychotropic substances;
(f) creation of areas, within the enclosed sports location, in which the consumption of alcoholic beverages is permitted, subject to compliance with the legal limits;
(g) surveillance of groups of supporters, namely during travel to professional sports competitions, or non-professional sports competitions deemed to be high risk, which take place other than at the enclosed sports location of the sports event promoter;
(h) definition of the conditions governing media activity and the movement of media personnel and resources within the enclosed sports location;
(i) elaboration of an internal emergency plan, which provides for and defines the role of stewards, if any, in emergency situations.

379. The enclosed sports location in which professional sports competitions, or non-professional competitions deemed to be high risk, take place, must comply with a series of rules, which ensure spectator safety, failing which the organizers and promoters of the said sports competitions are liable. The aim of this is the protection of supporters and the prevention of violence between them, i.e., via the obligation that spectator accommodation must be seated, the provisions of seating suitable for the handicapped, the installation, when appropriate, of sectors duly identified as *buffer zones* and physical separation between the spectators of rival clubs. The rapid evacuation of the enclosed sports location in emergency situations must also be ensured.

380. The law requires sports event promoters to have a video-surveillance system, which permits the visual control of the entire enclosed sports location and the corresponding security perimeter, and which has fixed or movable cameras, with audio and image recording, which must be retained for at least ninety days. Notices must be displayed in visible locations in places subject to video-surveillance. The video-surveillance system may be used by members of the security forces and the organizer of the sports competition may access the images recorded but solely for disciplinary purposes, although compliance with Law no. 67/98, of 26 October, which introduced the legal framework governing the protection of natural persons in relation to personal data and the free circulation thereof, must be complied with.

381. Enclosed sports locations in which national and international professional competitions, or non-professional competitions that are deemed to be high risk, take place, must have sufficient car parking facilities in terms of their spectator capacity and have parking for the disabled and handicapped, in accordance with the legislation in force, plus parking for the referees, judges and timekeepers and the representatives of the corresponding federation and league.

382. Enclosed sports locations must also have special accesses for the disabled and handicapped in accordance with Decree-Law no. 163/2006, of 8 August, which establishes the legal framework governing access to buildings and establishments to which there is public access, public highways and residential buildings. Promoters of sports events must strive to ensure that handicapped and/or disabled persons have access to enclosed sports locations, although there is no penalty provided for failure to comply with this legal requirement. Disabled and handicapped people may enter enclosed sports locations with their guide-dogs, in accordance with the provisions of Decree-Law no. 74/2007, of 27 March, which establishes that persons with a sensory, mental, physical or motor disability may access places, means of transport and public establishments together with their guide-dogs.

383. The IDP, IP may, on the basis of a proposal made by the CESD, or on the basis of a proposal made by the security forces to the CESD, order that improvement works be carried out at enclosed sports locations in which national or international professional or high risk non-professional sports competitions take place, in order to improve the safety, security, sanitary and hygiene conditions thereof.

384. Promoters of sports events have the following duties, in addition to such other duties as are imposed on them:

(a) To be responsible for security within the enclosed sports location and the security perimeters, without prejudice to the powers and duties of the security forces present at the location, i.e., the commander thereof, who is solely responsible for a decision to evacuate the enclosed sports location either partially or completely and who also has the power, at any time during the sports event, to assume responsibility for security within the enclosed sports location, whenever a lack of security places people and the premises at risk.
(b) To encourage an ethical and sporting attitude among its supporters, particularly in relation to organized groups of supporters.
(c) To impose penalties on their members, who are involved in disturbances of public order by banning them from enclosed sports locations in accordance with the terms and conditions of the corresponding regulations, or by expelling them.
(d) To protect persons, who are threatened, and their assets and property, i.e., by facilitating their safe exit from the sports complex, or their transfer to a safe sector, in collaboration with members of the security services.
(e) To adopt safety regulations and regulations regarding the use of areas within the enclosed sports location to which the public have access.
(f) To appoint a security co-ordinator.

385. With the exception of the duty to appoint a security co-ordinator, the said powers and duties also apply *mutatis mutandis* to organizers of sports competitions and to promoters of sports events, who must, in co-ordination with the State, implement socio-preventive educational measures, with regard to ethics in sport, violence, racism, xenophobia and intolerance at sports events, namely via:

(a) approval and implementation of plans and measures, particularly those targeted at those of school age;
(b) implementation of publicity campaigns that promote sportsmanship, fair play and integration, particularly among those of school age;

(c) implementation of measures to ensure that families may attend sports events, i.e., via the ADoPtion of more favourable entrance terms;
(d) implementation of measures that cater for supporters and promote conviviality between then;
(e) to support the creation of *supporters' embassies*.

386. So far as the position of security co-ordinator is concerned and as is stated above, promoters of sports events that are part of national or international professional sports competitions or competitions that are high risk non-professional sports competitions are responsible for the appointment of a security co-ordinator. Promoters of sports events are required, prior to the beginning of each sports season, to submit a list of the security co-ordinators and their corresponding enclosed sports locations to the CESD. The list must be organized in accordance with the provisions of the personal data protection law.

3. The Liability of Organizers and Promoters of the Sports Competitions for the Safety of the Sports Events in their Charge

387. The State is responsible for the security and policing of areas outside enclosed sports locations. The State is required to adopt measures with a view to the prevention and punishment of anti-sporting phenomena, i.e., violence, and it has the special obligation and the duty to support initiatives and projects that promote good sportsmanship and tolerance. However, in the case of sports competitions organized by public or private entities, the State transfers the risks of the consequences of the organization of the sports events in question to another entity, i.e., the sports organizer, who is subject to a duty to ensure the security of all those involved in the event.

388. According to the provisions of Article 500 of the Civil Code, the principal is liable even if it has no fault, but is only so liable if the agent has acted negligently or wilfully in the act or omission in question and is liable in damages. Furthermore, *omissions*[76] can be a source of civil liability, provided that there is a breach of the legal duty to perform the act omitted. The said breach of legal duty is the specific feature of the required *unlawfulness*.

389. The best known case of a judgment holding a sports event organizer civilly liable for an omission is the STJ Judgment of 12 February[77] Kindly provide a valid URL 2004, in which the FPF, the organizer of the sports event in question, was held liable for the death of someone, who was struck by a very light flare in the stadium, which had been fired from the seats opposite during the Portuguese Cup Final, in 1996. The FPF was found liable because it had failed to take all of the security

76. Article 486 of the Civil Code: *Mere omissions give rise to the duty to repair loss and damage when there is a legal duty to perform the act omitted by force of law or contract, independently of other legal requirements.*
77. Available at http://www.dgsi.pt/jstj.nsf/0/de8b2558b414874c80256f070054208a?OpenDocument.

measures at its disposal appropriate to the specific case, as it was a high risk game, and had therefore acted *unlawfully* by failing to comply with the legal provisions in force.[78] It had particularly failed to implement appropriate surveillance and control measures and had failed to carry out the required control of supporters at the stadium access points in order to prevent the introduction of objects likely to facilitate acts of violence. As the FPF failed to act in accordance with the standard of diligence to be expected of a body responsible for security at events, in accordance with what could be expected of a reasonable man, i.e., the *bonus pater familiae* standard, the said breach was also considered to be *blameworthy*. This was a case of liability for poor organization and for breach of a legal duty to take measures to prevent the firing of the *Very light* flare.[79]

390. As a consequence of this case, conduct likely to place life and physical integrity at risk as a consequence of the use and carrying of weapons and explosive or pyrotechnical substances or devices, governed by Law no. 8/97, of 12 April, since repealed by Law no. 5/2006, of 23 February, which introduced the legal framework governing the manufacture, assembly, repair, import, export, transfer, storage, movement, sale, acquisition, loan, possession, listing, custody, safety and security, use and carrying of weapons, weapon components and munitions, and the legal framework for special crime prevention operations, and completed the penalty provisions in the previous law; in the context of civic, religious, artistic, cultural or sports events, became a crime.

B. *Spectators*

1. Spectators' Rights

391. At the beginning of each season, sports event organizers are required, in advance, to establish the characteristics of the tickets and the maximum and minimum price limits. The aim of this provision is to protect the rights of spectators as consumers, *to prior information as to the sum payable at sports events throughout the season,* in accordance with Article 49 of the LBAFD. This article in the LBAFD, provides that *[the] law defines the consumer protection measures with regard to the protection of economic interests and the right to advance information as to the amount payable at sports events* throughout the season, is a new feature so far as sports legislation is concerned and is a direct application of the constitutional principle with regard to *consumer rights,*[80] as per Article 60 of the CRP, to sport, which resulted in a decision to protect sports events under the heading of consumers' rights.

---

78. Which, at that time, was Decree-Law no. 270/89, of 18 August.
79. The facts established amounted to a crime of negligent homicide. There was no question of intentional conduct as the accused neither foresaw nor was aware that his specific conduct could affect some spectators and that, if that happened, it could cause their death.
80. No. 1 of Art. 60 of the CPR states that *consumers are entitled to the goods and services they consume being of good quality, to training and information, to the protection of their health, safety and economic interests and the reparation of loss and damage.*

392. According to no. 2 of Law no. 24/96, of 31 July, which introduced the legal framework applicable to consumer defence, a consumer is defined as *a person to whom goods or services, or any other rights, intended for non-occupational use, are supplied by a person, who carries on an economic activity by way of an occupation with a view to profit,* and is entitled to be informed and to the protection of his/her rights.

393. The aim of the decision to impose this obligation with regard to consumers rights on sports event organizers was to prevent the not infrequent imposition of an exaggeratedly high price for attending a sports event, such as the case that occurred during the 1999/2000 season as recounted in Legal Theory,[81] which occurred during the final of the National Football Championship, when Sport Comércio e Salgueiros and Gil Vicente Futebol Clube hosted the teams that were competing for the national title, in their stadiums, i.e., Sporting Clube Portugal and Futebol Clube do Porto, and decided to increase their ticket prices exponentially thus obliging spectators to pay an abnormally high price in order to watch those two games. Furthermore, a major requirement with regard to ticket characteristics increases the security of sports event by preventing ticket forgery and consequently reducing the number of entries to enclosed sports areas and improving the control thereof, thus preventive overcrowding of enclosed sports locations.

394. The new legal framework governing the combating of violence, racism, xenophobia and intolerance at sports events, approved by Law no. 39/2009, of 30 July, introduced new provisions with regard to the unauthorized distribution and sale of tickets for sports events and makes the said acts a crime. Two general approaches were adopted, both of which involve the imposition of a term of up to three years imprisonment, or a fine:

(a) one which seeks to safeguard security and safety at sports events and which punishes those who sell, attempt to sell, or distribute for sale, forged or anomalous tickets, or without having received the express authorization of the sports event organizer;
(b) and other, which renders the activities of those who seek to profit from the sale of tickets at sport events, when the demand for tickets far exceeds the supply thereof.

395. Accordingly, whosoever attempts to obtain financial benefit by selling tickets without being authorized to do so, is guilty of a crime. A computerized ticket issue and sale system was established in order to make it possible for sports events to take place in security. Tickets must comply with control requirements, such as the ticket sequence number and the number of the seat in the stadium to which it relates.

81. João Lima Cluny. 'A Lei de Bases da Actividade Física e do Desporto e os Direitos dos Consumidores'. *Desporto & Direito. Revista Jurídica do Desporto,* Year IV, No. 11 (2007): 302.

396. The club that organizes the sports event is required to assign specific zones for organized groups of supporters, better known in Portuguese as *claques*, of the clubs that are competing in the sports event and to strive to protect the security of all. Accordingly, whoever sells or attempts to sell tickets without being authorized so to do, or who does so in violation of the ticket issue system, the purpose of which is the safety, security and identification of those inside the stadium and to avoid the overcrowding thereof, is guilty of an offence.

397. So far as the prohibition of the sale of tickets for a price in excess of the established price, with intent to obtain a financial advantage for the seller, or others, is concerned, we consider that this prohibition applies not only to tickets touts but also, by association, to websites. These websites facilitate ticket sales and the unauthorized enrichment of the seller and the website may or may not receive a commission for the business opportunity so created. Even if this situation does not amount to a crime under the current law, it is nevertheless always a crime of speculation.

398. The crime of speculation was created by Article 35 of Decree-Law no. 28/84, of 20 January, which creates anti-economic offences and offences against public health. The decree-law provides that a person is guilty of the crime of speculation if he or she:

(a) sells goods or supplies services for prices in excess of the prices permitted by the legal provisions to which they are subject;
(b) alter the normal prices of goods or services, such as result from the normal conduct of the said activity, on any pretext or by any means with the intention to obtain and unlawful profit, or independently of the said intention, alter such prices as are provides by legal regulations in force;
(c) sells goods or supplies services for a price that exceeds the price stated on price tags, labels, signs or in price lists prepared by the seller or service provider.

399. So far as the market freedom argument is concerned, the application of the law is not so clear. This is particularly true in the case of major sports competitions, such as the World Cup, European Championships, the Olympic Games or UEFA matches, when the demand for tickets by far outstrips the available supply and tickets have to be allotted on the basis of a draw. There are frequently websites that subsequently organize ticket exchanges because it is natural that the tickets allotted are not always those that the allottees want most.

400. Another example is the sale of *follow my team* tickets, which can be sold at less than face value, when the team supported is eliminated early in the competition. Exchange services are therefore of use to the market and, despite the fact that they may be unauthorized, their existence is nevertheless justified as they provide consumers with a quality service, provided that they comply with the rule that the exchange must not give rise to a financial advantage.

401. Finally a note regarding the frequent offer of tickets in television and radio game shows and even on the internet, when tickets are allocated to each number of calls or SMS. Despite the fact that the law does not make specific provision with regard to this type of supply of tickets, it must be authorized by the organizer of the competition in question.

2. Spectators' Duties

402. The legislation includes the conditions governing access to and presence in enclosed sports locations, to which spectators are subject. More specifically, spectators have a duty to comply with the following rules, as a condition of being granted access to enclosed sports locations:

(a) possession of a valid ticket;
(b) compliance with the rules regarding security and the use of public access areas;
(c) not to be under the influence of alcohol, drugs, psychotropic substances, or products with a similar effect and to agree to submit to control and screening tests, to be administered under the direction of the security forces. Those persons, who have a blood/alcohol level of 1.2 g/l will be deemed to be under the influence of alcohol, to whom the duly adapted procedures, tests, devices and measurement methods provided in the Highway Code, approved by Decree-Law no. 114/94, of 3 May, with regard to drivers under the influence of alcohol, drugs and psychotropic substances, shall apply;
(d) not to transport or bring with them objects, which are prohibited or are likely to give rise to or facilitate acts of violence;
(e) Not to display placards, flags, symbols or other signs with offensive racist or xenophobic content;
(f) not to sing racist or xenophobic songs or songs, which incite violence;
(g) to consent to personal searches for preventive and security purposes in order to detect and prevent the introduction of objects and substances that are prohibited, or are likely to give rise to or facilitate acts of violence;
(h) to consent to video and audio recording in accordance with Law no. 67/68, of 26 October.

403. The police on duty at a sports event may require persons, who appear to be under the influence of alcohol or other toxic substances, or who conduct themselves in a violent manner, or who threaten the security of the sports event, to submit to a test for alcohol or other toxic substances. In the event that the said test results are positive, the persons in question are refused access to the enclosed sports location. Persons who refuse to submit to the said texts may also be excluded from the enclosed sports location.

404. The presence of spectators in enclosed sports locations is subject to compliance with the following rules:

(a) not to display placards, flags, symbols or other signs with offensive, violent or intolerant racist or xenophobic content at sports events, which incite violence or any other form of discrimination, or which involve manifestations of political ideology;
(b) not to obstruct access and evacuation routes, particularly emergency routes, without prejudice to the use thereof by handicapped and disabled persons;
(c) not to commit violent acts, or acts that incite violence, racism or xenophobia, or intolerance at sports events, any other form of discrimination, or which amount to manifestations of political ideology;
(d) not to insult or disrespect the Portuguese national symbols in any form of communication with the general public;
(e) not to sing racist or xenophobic songs that incite violence, racism or xenophobia, or intolerance at sports events, any other form of discrimination, or which amount to manifestations of political ideology;
(f) not to enter areas, which are restricted, or which are not intended for the public;
(g) not to move between sectors;
(h) not to throw any objects within the enclosed sports location;
(i) not to use any fireworks, other pyrotechnic devices or devices with similar effects;
(j) to comply with the regulations of the enclosed sports location;
(k) to comply with the security conditions laid down in the regulations of the enclosed sports location.

405. Breach of the conditions to which presence in the enclosed sports location is subject will result in immediate expulsion from the enclosed sports location by stewards or the police on duty there, as the case may be, without prejudice to such other penalties as may be imposed.

406. Particularly noteworthy is the legal framework, which governs *organised supporters groups*, which are defined as *groups of supporters, that are usually termed 'claques' in Portuguese, which take the form of an association in accordance with the law, the purpose of which is to support clubs, associations or sports companies in the sports competitions in which they take part* and which must be registered with the CESD. Law no. 39/2009 introduced the obligatory registration of organized supporters groups, which include the so-called *claques,* with the CESD. Organized supporters groups are now required to possess a list which identifies all of the members present during journeys to sports events, which must be included in the register.[82] Each member will also have a special card that affords access to the areas reserved for organized supporters groups,[83] within enclosed sports locations.

82. The register is obligatory and governed by Art. 13. It is required to contain the up-to-date identification of the members of the *claque* and must be submitted to the promoter of the sports event and to the CESD. Organised groups of supporters which do not comply with the conditions described above are not permitted to enter enclosed sports locations.
83. Promoters of sports events are required to reserve specific areas for persons, who are members of organised supporters groups, and to issue a special entrance card for the said areas, possession of which is the *sine qua non* of access thereto.

407. According to the new legislation, the grant of facilities for use by these supporters groups must be the subject matter of an agreement, to be signed at the beginning of each season, which deals with the provision of premises, technical or material support,. Supervision in order to ensure that the above grant of the said facilities does not result in the storage of objects, which are prohibited, or are likely to facilitate or give rise to acts of violence, is the responsibility of the promoter of the sports event. In order to receive support from the clubs they support, *claques* must have an up-to-date record of each member including the member's personal details and a photograph of the member. The penalty for breach of this provision, if illegal aid to *claques* is proved, is that the club is require to play its matches behind closed doors. The law expressly prohibits the provision of support to *claques*, which display *symbols or words, which incite violence, racism, xenophobia or any other form of discrimination.*[84]

408. It is a well-known fact that there are major clubs that are supported by one or more organized supporters groups, which are not only sometimes mutually antagonistic but also fail to comply with the requirements as to the registration of their members. The law does not, in fact provide that such *claques* cannot continue to exist, but merely that they cannot receive any type of support from the clubs they support because they are not registered as such. The said aid involves the provision of cheaper tickets to *claques* for one part of the stadium, the provision of club premises for the head office of the *claque,* or to store its materials, provided that the same do not amount to objects that are prohibited or likely to give rise to acts of violence, racism, xenophobia or intolerance. However some of the *claques* that are still illegal are well-organized and have been in existence for many years. It is accordingly difficult to imagine that they wish to become legal, as their members are normally members of the club and have had reserved seats in the same part of the stadium for many years.

409. In as far as premises are concerned *claques* certainly have their own headquarters and storage facilities for materials and objects, which are independent from the club's premises. In principle, clubs are unlikely to encourage the legalization of their *claques*, provided that they do not give them any type of assistance. However, it is with regard to the team's away games that the legalization regarding *claques* is advantageous to both *claques* and clubs. This is because legalized *claques* have a different type of protection during travel to and from and at away games, as they have specially allocated areas in the stadiums, plus increased police protection while at the game in order to ensure the security of all. Although there is no express provision in the law to this effect, it is possible, on the basis of the intention of the law, for the host club to refuse to make tickets available for visiting clubs that are supported by illegal supporters groups. The grounds for the refusal would be the need to ensure the security of the sports event, as the promoter club, by making tickets available to the visiting club, is unable to control who they are given to. Clubs would also benefit from the legalization of their *claques,* as they would then be

84. Article 12, no. 3. Non-compliance with the said provisions has the consequence that the promoter is required to hold sports events behind closed doors.

much less likely to be held liable for any damage caused by their supporters. Another argument is that if the visiting club is allocated too many tickets there is a risk that they will be obtained by illegal *claques,* as such tickets are normally distributed by 'supporters clubs' that are not controlled by the clubs. This would amount to the provision of illegal assistance by the club to the *claque*, which is punishable by having to play games behind closed doors, for so long as the illegality continues, which would be catastrophic for clubs in terms of revenue and negative publicity. There are not only direct benefits for *claques* and clubs in the legalization of *claques* but also for sportspersons and supporters generally.

410. The legal conditions and mechanisms have been created to safeguard the security of all those involved in sports events, thus contributing to a more healthy coexistence, which, if implemented, should bring more supporters to the stadiums. More specifically, organized supporters groups are required to have an organized and updated register of their members, which is updated whenever there is any alteration in relation to their members, and which complies with the provisions of Law no. 67/98, of 26 October, containing the following information:

(a) name
(b) identification card number
(c) date of birth
(d) photograph
(e) parents names, in the case of minors
(f) address.

411. As stated above, organized supporters groups must also possess an up-to-date list that identifies all of their members, who are present during a specific journey to a sports event, which must be produced to the police and the CESD whenever requested. The persons responsible for organized supporters groups that do not comply with the abovementioned requirements can be barred from access to the interior of any enclosed sports location by decision of the IDP, IP on the basis of a proposal by the CESD.

412. So far as the conditions to which access by organized supporters groups is subject, promoters of the sports event are required to allocate one or more specific areas in their enclosed sports locations for members of organized supporters groups. In national and international professional competitions and in national and international non-professional competitions that are deemed to be high risk, promoters of sports events cannot provide or sell more tickets to organized supporters groups than they have members, who are duly identified in the register provided. The member's name must appear on each ticket provided or sold. Access and entry to the reserved areas is only permitted to holders of personalized tickets.

413. Exceptionally, organized supporters groups may use the following materials or articles within the enclosed sports location:

(a) noise producing items, usually megaphones and drums, must be authorized in advance by the promoter of the sports event, who is required to inform the police;
(b) smoke producing fireworks, which must be authorized and monitored by the police, in collaboration with the ANPC and the promoter of the sports event.

C. *Sportspersons*

1. Civil Liability for Acts Committed between Sportspersons

414. We refer to the liability of sportspersons in relation to other sportspersons within the ambit of sports played side-by-side, player against player, or in which they play against each other and there is a risk of injury. Breaches of the rules of the game that result in the serious injury of a sportsperson can give rise to civil liability and the obligation to pay damages; provided that the corresponding requirements are complied with.

415. Civil liability and the corresponding obligation to pay damages is a way to eliminate the loss or damage (incurred by the player), which can be financial, if it involves property and interests, which can be valued in monetary terms, or non-financial, if they cannot be valued in monetary terms, such as life, body, honour, health and even looks. However liability varies according to the sport in question. There are sports, such as *combat sports,* above all boxing, which are violent by definition, in which assaults by the competitors on each other are a matter of voluntary consent. There are however team sports, such as football and basketball, which involve physical contact between players, which is not necessarily accepted or consented to.

416. The preconditions of extra-contractual civil liability as stated in Article 482, no. 1 of the Civil Code, are as follows:

(a) the act or omission;
(b) unlawfulness;
(c) the act or omission is caused by the tortfeasor;
(d) the loss or damage;
(e) the causal nexus between the act or omission and the loss or damage.

417. This Civil Code article does not describe the legal assets protected but there is a clear distinction between *unlawfulness* and *negligent or intentional conduct.* The latter is most characteristic of the Portuguese civil liability system. There are two types of unlawfulness:

(a) *violation of others rights,* which is understood to include *absolute rights,* such as rights of personality, real rights and intellectual property rights;

(b) *breach of a law that protects third party interests.*[85]

418. According to this criterion, the violation of the *physical integrity* of a sportsperson on the field of play is an indicator of unlawfulness. The law provides that liability can be excluded, *inter alia,* by the consent of the injured party (prior to the loss or damage), as provided by no. 1 of Article 340 of the Civil Code and Articles 38 and 149 of the Penal Code. The act is however unlawful if it is contrary to *generally accepted rules of moral and social conduct,* or a legal provision, however loss or damage incurred by the injured party is deemed to be consented to if in accordance with his/her presumed intentions (in accordance with Article 340, nos 2 and 3). Most authors consider *the consent of the injured party* to be the best justification of injuries incurred during sport as a consequence of negligence, subject to certain limits. Accordingly, the concept of *the consent of the injured party* is applicable to sports, which, because of the very nature thereof, involve direct injury of the players involved, e.g., *combat sports,* in which it is considered that there is tacit consent of the injured party, excluding criminal conduct, provided that the rules of the game are respected and the injurer does not act intentionally.

419. So far as team sports, like football, are concerned, the question that arises is whether there is tacit consent by the injured party, when the injuries are serious. Case-law has considered[86] that the said situation is contrary to *generally accepted rules of moral and social conduct*, as respect for the rules of the game does not involve a risk of serious injury to the players.

2. The Theory of Consent to the Risk

420. The acceptance of the risk *essentially means that the injured party willingly exposes him or herself to a known typical or specific risk, without being obliged so to do, but in the hope that the risk will not result in injury.*[87] However, in the case of damage that occurs in the ambit of sports that are not considered to be dangerous, legal theory[88] has contrived a concept to deal with the problem of future loss and damage consequent upon serious injuries, as the loss and damage in such cases is neither desired nor foreseeable.

---

85. Both provided in no. 1 of Art. 483 of the Civil Code. There are authors, who include *abusive exercise of a right*, as *provided* in Art. 334 of the Civil Code, as a type of *unlawful conduct.*
86. Judgment of the Supreme Court of Justice of 17 Jun. 2004, published in *Colectânea de Jurisprudência – Acórdãos do Supremo Tribunal de Justiça*, Year XII, Tome II, 2004, 90–92.
87. José Carlos Brandão Proença, *A Conduta do Lesado como Pressuposto e Critério de Imputação do Dano Extracontratual,* Coimbra, Almedina, 1997, 615.
88. For a more detailed overview on the subject, see André Gonçalo Dias Pereira, *Responsabilidade Civil em Eventos Desportivos*, Desporto & Direito. Revista Jurídica do Desporto, Year V, No. 14, Coimbra, Almedina (2008): 227 et seq and André Gonçalo Dias Pereira, *Assunção do Risco em Actividades Desportivas no Direito Português*, Desporto & Direito. Revista Jurídica do Desporto, Year III, No. 9, Coimbra, Almedina (2006): 421 et seq.

421. The difference between the concepts of *acceptance of the risk* and the *consent of the injured party* is that the former is intended to include *probable, indeterminate injuries,* while the former occurs normally as a consequence of a *precise, foreseen and specific assault by an identifiable aggressor.*[89] So far as sport is concerned, the concept of the injured party's consent to future loss and damage is the most appropriate as such damage is neither foreseeable nor desirable.

422. The theory of acceptance of the risk within the ambit of sport can cover not only sportspersons, but also:

(a) spectators;
(b) those transported to a sports event free of charge;
(c) those, who enter third party premises without authorization;
(d) those, who consciously use defective products and those, who willingly expose themselves to the risk represented by certain animals.

423. In the absence of express legal provision, the concept of *acceptance of the risk* should be included, by analogy, in the general rule in Article 81 of the Civil Code, regarding the *voluntary limitation of personality rights,*[90] and in Article 340 thereof.[91]

424. It was held in a judgment of the Supreme Court of Justice of 17 June 2004[92] that the player had failed to conduct himself in accordance with the duty of care to which he was subject pursuant to Article 487 of the Civil Code and had failed to comply with the rules of the game and was therefore held to be liable in damages in accordance with the law. As the conduct was held to be unlawful, neither Article 570 of the Civil Code[93] regarding *contributory negligence,* nor Article 494[94] regarding the *limitation of damages in the case of negligence*, are applicable.

89. Compare André Gonçalo Dias Pereira, *Assunção do Risco em Actividades Desportivas no Direito Português*, Desporto & Direito. Revista Jurídica do Desporto, Year III, No. 9, Coimbra, Almedina (2006): 426.
90. Article 80 of the Civil Code (voluntary limitation of personality rights): *All voluntary limitation of the exercise of personality rights is null and void if contrary to public policy. 2. Voluntary limitation, when legal, is always revocable, although subject to the duty to pay damages to the other party for loss and damage caused to its legitimate expectations.*
91. Compare André Gonçalo Dias Pereira, *Assunção do Risco em Actividades Desportivas no Direito Português*, Desporto & Direito. Revista Jurídica do Desporto, Year III, No. 9, Coimbra, Almedina (2006): 434.
92. Published in *Colectânea de Jurisprudência – Acórdãos do Supremo Tribunal de Justiça*, Year XII, Tome II, 2004, pp. 90–92.
93. In this case, an act of the injured party must have contributed to the occurrence of the loss and damage, in accordance with the criteria in Arts 563 et seq. of the Civil Code.
94. The power granted by this article is limited to cases of negligence and the courts cannot apply it in cases of intentional conduct, in accordance with the provisions of Art. 483, when the quantum of damages is calculated on the basis of the criteria in Arts 562 et seq. of the Civil Code.

X. Violence in Sport and Violence Associated with Sport

A. Introduction

425. Violence in sport means violence by and between sportspersons, in the context of a competition, whatever the nature thereof (amateur or professional). Violence associated with sport refers to acts of violence that occur before, during and after sports competitions, including acts outside of the enclosed sports location where the competition takes place. Normally, violence associated with sport is triggered by spectators of the sports event and the supporters of the teams or clubs that compete with each other in a specific sport.

426. The final part of no. 2 of Article 79 of the CRP imposes a duty on the State *is to ensure the prevention of violence in sport.* This provision was added to the CPR in the 1989 constitutional revision. This principle is based on the *general right to physical culture and sport,* enshrined in Article 79, which is to be implemented in collaboration with schools, associations and sports organizations.

427. The fight against violence in sport and violence associated with sport seeks to protect various legal assets, i.e., public and private safety, public order and the individual life and health of those involved, i.e., passive spectators of the event, and finally, property.

428. As *violence associated with sport is not a recent phenomena,*[95] the corresponding legislation is also not recent and dates back to Decree-Law no. 339/80, of 30 August, the purpose of which was to *establish a minimum number of measures with a view to the control, in the short term, of violence in enclosed sports locations* and which only covered violence off the field of play, i.e., solely violence among spectators. This legislation was amended by Law no. 16/81, of 31 July and repealed by Decree-Law no. 61/85, of 12 March. The objective of the latter decree-law was to *permit sports events to take place in accordance with the ethical spirit inherent in sport.*

429. However, the decisive step, which resulted in the passing of Portuguese laws, which expressly included measures to combat violence in sport was the ratification[96] of the *European Convention on Spectator Violence and Misbehaviour at Sport Events and in particular at Football Matches,* which was approved in Strasbourg on 19 August 1985. The primary aim[97] of this Council of Europe Convention was to require its signatories to implement measures to prevent and eradicate violence in sport and particularly to:

95. Judgment of the Supreme Court of Justice dated 6 Jul. 2004, Case no. 1050/02, published at http://www.dgsi.pt/jstj.nsf/0/de8b2558b414874c80256f070054208a?OpenDocument.
96. Approved by Assembly of the Republic Resolution no. 11/87, published in DRE, *1st Series*, of 10 Mar. 1987.
97. See Art. 3, no. 1, paras a), b) and c), and no. 2.

(a) ensure the provision of sufficient police to deal with violence and excesses in stadiums and in the vicinity thereof and also throughout the access routes used by spectators;
(b) set up close co-operation and information exchange between the police forces of the various localities involved, or that are likely to be involved;
(c) apply, or, if necessary, introduce, legislation, which imposes appropriate penalties on those, who are proved to be guilty of offences related to violence or spectator misbehaviour, or appropriate administrative measures, when necessary;
(d) encourage responsible organization, the good conduct of supporters and the appointment of stewards, who are responsible for facilitating the control of and the provision of information to supporters during games and to monitor the groups of supporters that travel to away games.

430. Subsequently, three fundamental items of legislation were passed with regard to violence associated with sport, i.e.:

(a) Decree-Law no. 270/89, of 18 August, the purpose of which, according to Article 1 thereof, is to prevent and control violence associated with sport (the legislator was accordingly no longer concerned only with discipline, social order and ethical conduct, but also with the control and combating of violence, and thus opened up a range of measures to deal with the negative aspects of the problem).
(b) Law no. 38/98, of 4 August, which established *the preventive measures to be adopted and penalties to be imposed in relation to violence associated with sport.*
(c) Law no. 16/2004, of 11 August, which established *the preventive measures to be adopted and penalties to be imposed in relation to violence associated with sport.*

431. Law no. 8/97, of 12 April, which criminalized certain conduct likely to be a threat to life and limb arising from the use and possession of weapons and explosives, or pyrotechnic substances, or devices in the context of civic, political, religious, artistic, cultural or sports events, is also noteworthy. Despite the fact that it appears last in the list of the *events* covered, it was the sport that triggered this legislation, after the death of a supporter in a stadium, who was killed by a *Very light* flare during a football match. Article 1 no. 4 of the said law provides that sports event organizers were required to display warning notices next to ticket booths and entrances to enclosed sports locations, to inform the general public that the introduction of weapons or explosive substances or devices is prohibited in their interest.

432. After successive items of legislation, which implemented the European Directives on the prevention of violence in enclosed sports locations and which were repealed before they had been fully implemented and could give rise to consistent case-law,[98] the law currently in force is Law no. 39/2009, of 30 July, which introduced the legal framework of the fight against violence, racism, xenophobia and intolerance in sports events, in order to ensure that the said events could take place in security.

433. Also in force since 31 October, is Law 93/2009, of 1 September, which introduced the legal framework governing the issue and transmission of decisions by the Portuguese judicial authorities that impose monetary penalties, with a view to the recognition and enforcement thereof in other Member States of the European Union, and the recognition and enforcement in Portugal, of decisions imposing monetary penalties taken by the proper authorities of other Member States of the European Union. This law transposed Council Framework Decision no. 2005/214/JAI of 24 February, as amended by Council Framework Decision no. 2009/299/JAI, of 26 February, into Portuguese law.

B. *Criminalization of Violence Related to Sport*

434. Former Law no. 16/2004, of 11 May, was the first law to criminalize violent conduct associated with sport, which had previously been subsumed within the crimes defined in the Penal Code. Until 2004, the law did not criminalize certain types of conduct, so that violence associated with sport was dealt with in criminal law terms by being subsumed in the types of crimes provided in the special part of the Penal Code, or in specific criminal law legislation. The following were the crimes then created:

(a) illegal distribution of tickets;[99]
(b) criminal damage aggravated by the fact that it is committed during travel to or from a sports event;
(c) affray during travel to or from a sports event;
(d) throwing of objects;
(e) invasion of the field of play;
(f) riot.

435. The crime of illegal distribution of tickets is intended to prevent the overcrowding of stadiums, via a proper control of the ticket distribution circuit, which makes it possible to comply with the principle of the physical separation of spectators. Article 15 of Law no. 16/2004, of 11 May, contained the general minimum conditions with which ticket issue systems are required to comply. The crime was committed when the intention is to *cause public disturbances,* in contrast to the concept of *public peace*, when the *mens rea* of the crime is the *intention to obtain*

98. We refer particularly to Decree-Law no. 270/89, of 18 August, to Law no. 38/98, of 4 August and Law no. 16/2004, of 11 May.
99. Regarding this, see Recommendation Rec (2002) 1, of the permanent Committee established by the European Convention, which, in annexe, indicates the fundamental principles with regard to the issue and sale of tickets recommended for ADoPtion by the Parties.

a pecuniary advantage for the offender, or another, or when *there is no express prior authorization by the event organizer* to that effect. The problem of the requirement that offenders must act as part of a group is the adduction of evidence that they have taken part in public disorder, as findings of individual guilt are an essential basis of the sentence imposed.

436. The crime of *throwing objects* was a crime of *specific risk*, i.e., the risk must be real The objects in question must be capable of placing the general public and the sportspersons at risk, i.e., petards, walking sticks, fireworks, smoke or gas producing devices, materials which besmirch or contaminate; heavy objects, *inter alia.*

437. Article 25 of the said law created the *crime of invasion of the field of play,* which is a crime of abstract risk, which is committed by the mere unauthorized or hostile invasion of the area allocated for a sports event, during the occurrence thereof, provided that the offender acts *intentionally.*

438. So far as the crime of criminal damage aggravated by the fact that it is committed during travel to or from a sports event, affray during travel to or from a sports event and riot are concerned, Law no. 39/2009, of 20 July, continued with the criminalization of this conduct, but abolished the first two crimes and simplified the definition of the latter crime.[100] All that is required is that the offenders act *as a group against the physical integrity of others,* during a sports event, while the other aspects of the definition, i.e., that the said conduct must give rise to *reactions on the part of other spectators* was abolished.

439. The current law made changes with regard to the conduct considered to be criminal with the result that the following courses of conduct are crimes:

(a) *[d]istribution and sale of forged or unauthorised tickets,* which amounts to the sale or distribution for sale, of tickets contrary to the ticket issue and sale system enshrined in the Law, or without having received the express prior authorization of the organizer of the sports event. Attempt to commit this offence is also an offence;
(b) *[u]nlawful distribution and sale of tickets, i.e. the sale of* tickets or distribution of tickets for sale, without being authorized so to do, with intent to cause the over-occupation of the enclosed sports location, or with intent to obtain a pecuniary advantage for the offender or another;
(c) *[a]ggravated damage within the ambit of a sports event,* this crime is committed by anyone, who, being a member of a group of supporters, whether or not the said group is organized, destroys, disfigures or renders unusable any public

100. The description of the crime of *riot* in Art. 26 of Law no.16/2004 was: *Whosoever at the time of the occurrence of a sports event, at any time from the start until the end thereof, acts, within an enclosed location, in a group, against the physical integrity of others, thereby provoking a reaction by other spectators and placing safety within the enclosed sports location at risk, shall be punished by a term of imprisonment of from 6 months to 3 years, or by a fine of not less than 500 days.*

transport vehicle, premises or facilities used by the public or with public utility status;

(d) *[p]articipation in an affray during travel to or from a sports event,* this offence is committed by whoever intervenes or takes part in an affray involving two or more people, which results in the death or injury of persons, or involves risk or danger to or assault of third parties, or causes alarm of disquiet to members of the general public;

(e) *[t]hrowing of objects or liquid products,* this crime is committed when someone throws objects or liquid products, and thus gives rise to risk to the life or limb of third parties, provided that the offence is committed within an enclosed sports location during a sports event;

(f) *[i]nvasion of an enclosed sports location,* this crime is committed if someone invades the field of play or enters areas to which public entry is prohibited, provided that the offender is within an enclosed sports location where a sports event is taking place;

(g) *[g]roup assault*, this crime is committed when a person, who acts as a member of a group, assaults a third party, provided that the group that commits the crime is within an enclosed sports location where a sports event is taking place.

440. This is the first of various provisions of the current law regarding crime in the context of sport, which in line with the process that was initiated by Law no. 16/2004, of 11 May, and brings the State's *ius punidendi* to bear in the area of violence, racism, xenophobia and intolerance at sports events. The fact that the State criminalizes conduct of this type is particularly relevant when considered in the light of the principle of the minimum intervention of the criminal law, i.e., that the criminal law should only intervene in the last resort, or as the legal system's final option. No. 2 of Article 18 of the CRP provides that the involvement of criminal law is only justified if one or more legal assets can be identified, which confer penal dignity on the interest that underlies each incrimination, and if there is a need for legal protection, in relation to each of the conducts selected, if any. As the legislator wished to make the said conduct subject to the penal law, it evidently considered that the legal assets to be protected and the seriousness of the offences justify increased intervention.

441. We agree with the approach that underlies this legislation to the extent that disturbance of the normal conduct of a sports competition is a violation of the freedom of the sportspersons and spectators alike and amounts therefore to private violence. Furthermore, violent conduct obliges players and competitors to suspend their activity, or prevents spectators from viewing the competition; not to mention the associated risks to life and limb. The said conduct therefore merits a considered legal response by the State. Moreover the concept of public order, in contradistinction to public disorder, is the legal asset on which this provision is based. The legal asset that can emerge from a specific sports event cannot, in any event, be superimposed on the socially accepted risk that is incorporated in sports legislation.

C. *The Legal Framework Governing the Fight against Racism, Xenophobia and Intolerance at Sports Events*

1. Introduction

442. Law no. 39/2009, of 30 July, repealed Law no. 16/2004 as explained above, and clarifies the objectives of the legislature. The new law amounts to the performance by the State, *qua* legislature, of its duties with regard to violence linked to sport. It develops Article 3 of the LBAFD, no. 1 of which provides that *sports activity shall be undertaken in accordance with ethical principles, the defence of the principles of sportsmanship, sporting truth and the overall training of all participants,* while no. 2 provides that *the State shall adopt measures to prevent and punish anti-sporting conduct, namely violence, doping, corruption, racism, xenophobia and all types of discrimination.*

443. According to the Statement of Reasons for Draft Law no. 249/X, which led to the passing of the Law, the first measure to be noted is the widening of the law's scope, via the creation of preventive and penalty measures with a view to the eradication of violence, racism, xenophobia and intolerance at sports events, in order to make possible the holding of sports events in safety and security and in accordance with the ethical principles that are inherent in it.

2. The Scope of Application of the Law

444. Law no. 39/2009, of 30 July extends the ambit of the previous legislation, which was limited to the *prevention and control of violence associated with sport.* The new law accordingly deals not only with violence in a unitary and global manner, but compiles various different and autonomous types of violations of good sportsmanship, such as racism, xenophobia and intolerance at sports events, in a single piece of legislation. However, even though racism and xenophobia fell outside of the ambit of the repealed Law no. 16/2004, of 11 May, it did not overlook them. Paragraphs a), c) and d) of Article 11 established the following conditions to which the presence of spectators in an enclosed sports location is subject:

(a) [n]ot to display placards, flags, symbols or other signs with offensive racist or xenophobic content;
(b) [n]ot to practice acts of violence, which incite violence, racism or xenophobia;
(c) [n]ot to sing racist or xenophobic songs.

445. In material terms, violence at sports events involves two types of violence: both endogenous violence between players during the competition, and exogenous violence, which, although it originates within the enclosed sports location where the sports competition takes place, involves persons not involved in the sports event, i.e., persons other than the sportspersons.

446. Prior to the coming into force of Decree-Law no. 270/89, of 18 August, the legislation regarding violence associated with sport did not cover all sports, but only handball, basketball, football and roller-hockey (cf. the final paragraph of the preamble of Decree-Law no. 339/80, of 30 August) and no. 1 of Article 15 of Decree-Law no. 61/85, 12 March.

447. The fight against racism and xenophobia in sport is part of an approach, which seeks to promote multi-ethnic coexistence and cultural integration in sport. The legal subject matter protected is the inviolable right of all people to be treated equally with others, whatever their race or ethnic origin, on the basis of the principle of equality stated in Article 13 of the CRP.

3. Analysis of the Legal Framework of the Fight against Violence in Sport

448. Draft Law no. 249/X, commenced by focusing on a series of preventive measures to be implemented by both sports competition organizers and promoters. Particularly noteworthy were the provisions regarding the ADoPtion of violence prevention and control regulations, the obligatory activity plans requirement, which require sports federations and professional leagues to include measures and programmes to promote good practices, which safeguard ethics and good sportsmanship, in their annual activity plans, particularly in the area of violence associated with sport. There are also a series of measures that support the promotion of ethics in sport, which include the encouragement of an equal presence of men and women on the terraces in order to ensure the family aspect of sports events, and support for the creation of *supporters' embassies*.

449. The penalties were reworked so as to fall in line with the current criminal law provisions and the penalties for misdemeanours were increased. Furthermore and in addition to the necessary CESD regulations and other aspects flowing from the contents of the draft law, it also seeks to simplify the legislation by repealed miscellaneous legislation and by incorporation of some of the provisions thereof, e.g., the provisions regarding the classification of events, or policing levels. The draft law also proposes that penalties be increased according to the nature of the victim. Accordingly, the minimum and maximum terms of prison sentences will be increased by one third when the victims are sports actors or media bodies.

450. Law no. 39/2009, of 30 July, not only criminalizes certain conducts, as described above, but goes further and considerably broadens the scope of the penalties that can be imposed. It does this by creating a series of misdemeanours and disciplinary offences. So far as misdemeanours are concerned, the following administrative offences are created to which the legal framework regarding misdemeanours, approved by Decree-Law no. 433/82, of 27 October,[101] applies subsidiarily:

(a) the introduction, sale and consumption of alcoholic beverages within the security ring or perimeter;
(b) the introduction, transport and sale in enclosed sports locations of drinks or other products contained in containers that are not made of light and non-bruising material;
(c) the introduction, sale and rental or distribution in enclosed sports areas of cushions, which are not made of a light and non-bruising material;
(d) acts or incitement of violence, racism, xenophobia and intolerance at sports events, without prejudice to other applicable penalties. Depending on the seriousness of the offence and the fault of the offender, a conviction for this administrative offence may result in the imposition of an ancillary penalty of a ban from enclosed sports locations for up to one year;
(e) the use in enclosed sports locations of electrical, battery powered or other horns and any fixed noise producing instruments, with the exception of the sports event promoter's sound system;
(f) the use of lasers or similar devices, which, because of their intensity, are capable of causing physical damage to or perturb the concentration and performance of the athletes or players;
(g) the introduction or use of explosive or pyrotechnic substances or devices, or of objects, which have similar effects, without prejudice to other penalties applicable, with the exception of permissions given to organized supporters groups, subject to certain requirements, to carry and use certain objects, which spectators, who are not members of the said groups, are forbidden to use;
(h) the throwing of objects, excluding the throwing of objects or liquid products, which involve a threat to life or limb, which is involved in the commission of crimes punishable by a term of imprisonment of no more than three years, or a fine.

451. The determination of the quantum of the administrative fine, within the limits laid down by Law no. 39/2009, of 30 July, is in accordance with the seriousness of the administrative offence, the fault of the offender, the offender's financial circumstances and the financial benefit obtained by the offender as a consequence of the commission of the administrative offence. Attempted administrative offences and those committed as a consequence of negligence are also punishable, but the minimum and maximum limits of the administrative fines that can be imposed are halved. The IDP, IP is responsible for the prosecution of administrative offence proceedings. The general principles of the legal framework governing misdemeanours apply, with the consequence that:

101. Successively amended by the Declaration of 6 Jan. 1983, Decree-Law no. 356/89, of 17 October, Declaration of 31 Oct. 1989, Decree-Law no. 244/95, of 14 September, Decree-Law no. 323/2001, of 17 September and by Law no. 109/2001, of 24 September.

(a) only acts or omissions that are stated to be administrative offences punishable by the imposition of a fine, by the law in force at the time they occur, may be punished as misdemeanours;
(b) the punishment of administrative offences is determined by the law in force at the time of the commission of the act or omission, or when the prerequisites for the commission thereof were complied with;
(c) if the law in force at the time of the commission of the act or omission is amended subsequently, the law most favourable to the accused is applied, unless the accused has already been convicted and that decision is final and has passed into judgment or has already been implemented;
(d) when the law is in force for a specific period of time, administrative offences committed during that period continue to be punishable thereafter;
(e) the act or omission is deemed to have taken place when the offender acted, or, in the case of an omission, should have acted, irrespectively of the time when the typical results thereof occur;
(f) acts or omissions are deemed to take place at the place where the offender acted, or in the case of an omission, should have acted and at the place where the typical results thereof occur.

452. Disciplinary offences are punishable by the imposition of the following penalties in accordance with the seriousness the offence:

(a) The banning of the enclosed sports location and the loss of the sports effects of the results of sports competitions, i.e., titles and qualifications, which are related to the acts practiced plus a total, or partial, loss of points in the sports classifications.
(b) The requirement that sports events take place behind closed doors.
(c) A fine.

453. When an enclosed sports location is banned, the sports competitions that fall to be organized by the host promoter of sports events that would otherwise have taken place at the banned sports location, take place at another enclosed sports location indicated by the federation, or the professional league, depending on whether the competition in question is professional or non-professional, in accordance with the regulations adopted. The penalty of the banning of enclosed sports locations and the loss of the sports effects of competitions applies to the clubs, associations and sports companies involved in the sports event in question, whose members, supporters or sympathizers commit one of the following offences:

(a) assault of sports actors, members of the police forces on duty, security co-ordinators, stewards, and all persons authorized by law or regulation to remain within the area of the sports event, which justifiably cause the referee not to commence or recommence the event, or even to abandon it before the regulation full time;
(b) invasion of the area of the sports event, which justifiable prevents the start or conclusion of the sports event;

(c) the occurrence of assaults of sports actors, members of the police forces on duty, security co-ordinators, stewards and all persons authorized by law or regulation to be in the area of the sports event, before, during or after the sports event that cause injuries that are particularly serious, either because of the nature thereof, or because of duration thereof and degree of incapacity caused.

454. The penalty of the holding of sports event behind closed doors is also applicable to the clubs, associations and sports companies involved in the sports event in question whose members, supporters or sympathizers commit any of the following offences:

(a) assault of sports actors, members of the police forces on duty, security co-ordinators, stewards, and all persons authorized by law or regulation to remain within the area of the sports event;
(b) the occurrence of disturbances, or the invasion of the area of the sports event, which unjustifiably gives rise to a delay in the commencement or recommencement of the sports event, or result in the temporary interruption thereof;
(c) assaults of spectators or of media personnel, within the enclosed sports location, before, during or after the sports event, which cause injuries that are particularly serious either because of the nature thereof or because of the duration of the incapacity.

D. *Violence in Sport and Fundamental Rights*

1. The Prohibition of Conduct Which Amounts to Expressions of Political Ideology

455. Paragraph e) of Article 23 of Law no. 39/2009, of 30 July provides that one of the precondition for a spectator, who is not a member of an *organized supporters group* being permitted to be present in an enclosed sports location is that he or she *does not sing racist or xenophobic songs that incite violence, intolerance at sports events, any other form of discrimination, or amount to expressions of political ideology.* Breach of these conditions *will result in immediate expulsion from the enclosed sports location by stewards, without prejudice to such other penalties as may be imposed.* While we understand and applaud the first part of the article in order to safeguard the principle of public order, we have serious reservations with regard to the final part of the article, which refers to expressions of political ideology. Some authors consider that the final part of the provision may be unconstitutional because it restricts a right that may only be restricted so far as is strictly necessary.

456. The FIFA and UEFA regulations also contain prohibitions of political demonstrations. The said prohibition can be justified in extreme cases, i.e., when national or club teams are supported by adherents of opposing political ideologies.

We therefore consider that these organizations included this prohibition in their regulations in order to ensure the occurrence of the sports event and public order.

457. There is in fact an excessive trend in contemporary society for prevention and precaution and there is consequently a risk that these excessive general prohibitions lead to limitations of fundamental rights that have no obvious or practical application. However, the *specificity of sport* could justify a prohibition that appears to restrict some fundamental rights excessively.

2. The Obligatory Nature of the Registration of Organized Supporters Groups

458. According to the legal framework governing the combating of violence, racism, xenophobia and intolerance at sports events, *organized supporters groups* are obliged to register with the CESD, and to supply it with personal data, in accordance with Law no. 67/98, of 26 October. The purpose of this record is *inter alia* linked to the identification of *claques* in the event of disturbances of public order.

459. Some organized supporters groups have refused to register with the CESD because they do not want to have any connection with violence. Here again, it is a question of proportion, because the State has the duty to ensure security in stadiums and may create mechanisms that provide for improved access to and identification of miscreants.

460. The law should perhaps have included a provision to the effect that only organized supporters groups that can be easily identified because of their use of banners, scarves and other artefacts are required to register, instead of the current blanket requirement.

3. Child Trafficking

461. Law no. 93/2009, of 1 September, was recently passed and introduced the legal framework governing the issue and transmission of decisions by the Portuguese judicial authorities imposing monetary penalties, with a view to the recognition and enforcement thereof in other Member States of the European Union, and the recognition and enforcement in Portugal, of decisions imposing monetary penalties taken by the proper authorities of other Member States of the European Union.

462. According to no. 1 of Article 3, decisions to impose monetary penalties in respect of a series of offences can be recognized and enforced without the need for the acts or omissions in question to be crimes in both the state of origin and the receiving state, provided that they are punishable in accordance with the law of the state of origin, including those committed in the context of sports events, i.e., the following offences *inter alia*:

(a) criminal association;
(b) trafficking in human beings;
(c) trafficking in drugs, psychotropic substances, hormonal substances and other growth stimulants;
(d) corruption;
(e) fraud in the obtaining of subsidies or aid or misappropriation thereof, include fraud contrary to the financial interests of the European Communities, in accordance with the provisions of the Convention on the Protection of the Financial Interests of the European Communities of 26 July 1995;
(f) money laundering;
(g) aiding and abetting of illegal immigration;
(h) racism, xenophobia, vandalism and theft;
(i) fraud;
(j) forgery, imitation and illegal use of trademarks or products, violation of intellectual property rights and smuggling;
(k) forgery of administrative documents and trafficking therein, and forgery of means of payment.

463. So far as trafficking of human beings and particularly of young people, which is sport-related and specifically football-related, is concerned, FIFA has introduced some rules, which seek to increase the rights and protection of sportspersons, who are minors. The Executive Committee of FIFA recently[102] altered the FIFA Regulation on the Status and Transfer of Players (RSTP) by amending three articles and by adding a fourth, which concerns the registration and notification of the information held by club academies, which host minors. Another relevant alteration is the creation of a Committee for the Protection of Minors, which has the duty to enquire into international transfers of minors, in order to ensure that the transferee clubs comply with the minimum obligations laid down in the RSTP. FIFA has also altered the compensation for training provisions in order to protect minors and requires transferee clubs to pay more in the case of the hiring of an athlete between the age of 12 and 15, when the transfer takes place before the end of the sports season in which the athlete has his 18th birthday.

464. The Declaration of the Rights of the Child, which was proclaimed by the General Assembly of the UN, resolution no. 1386, of 20 November 1959, was the first document to refer to the global protection of the rights of minors. The Convention on the Rights of the Child, which was adopted and ratified by the General Assembly of the United Nations, resolution 44/25, of 20 November 1989, defines the concept of child as a human being, who is less than 18 years old, with the exception of those children from a country where the age of majority is less than 18.

465. FIFA also plays a role in relation to the protection of the rights of players, who are minors, although it recognizes the common practice of football clubs in attracting potential talent at a very young age. These young talents are viewed by

102. The alterations were the result of the meetings of the FIFA Executive Committee on 18 Dec. 2008 and 19 Mar. 2009.

clubs as investments, which may bring considerable sports and financial returns in the future. Article 19.1 of the FIFA RSTP contains the fundamental rule regarding the transfer of players, when it provides that international transfers of players are only permitted if the player is older than 18. However, the commentaries on the RSTP prepared by FIFA in order to facilitate the interpretation of the principles enshrined therein, state that the rules governing transfers of footballers, who are minors, are strictly supervised in order to ensure that the minors in question will have a stable environment in terms of their education and training in the transferee club and in order to ensure, so far as possible, that they are not subject to the abuses and abandonment that minors have suffered in the past, by requiring all national federations to ensure compliance with these rules.

466. Article 19.2 of the FIFA RSTP accordingly establishes three exceptions to the general rule with regard to transfers as stated in Article 19.1. These exceptions apply when:

(a) the player is accompanied by his parents or legal representatives to the destination country, for reasons unrelated to football;
(b) the destination country is located in the EU or EEA and the player is aged between 16 and 18 and the transferee club have given certain minimum guarantees, related to the education and training of the player;
(c) the player lives within 50 kilometres of the national border and the transferee club in the neighbouring federation with which the player wishes to register is also located within 50 miles of the border and the maximum distance between the player's home and the club is 100 kilometres. In this case, the player must continue to reside at home and the two federations must expressly consent.

§5. Taxation

I. Introduction

467. In Portuguese law and specifically in Portuguese tax law there are few sport-specific features and it cannot accordingly be said that there is a sport-specific area of tax law. Portuguese tax law does however have various points of contact with sport and particularly professional sport.

468. The general codes and rules, i.e., the Personal Income Tax Code (CIRS), approved by Decree-Law no. 442-A/88, of 30 November, the Corporation Tax Code (CIRC), approved by Decree-Law no. 442-B/88, of 30 November, the Value Added Tax Code (CIVA), approved by Decree-Law no. 394-B/84, of 26 December, the General Tax Law (LGT), approved by Decree Law no. 398/98, of 17 December, the Tax Incentives Statute (EBF), approved by Decree-Law no. 215/89, of 1 July and subsequently reformulated and republished annexed to Decree-Law no. 108/2008, of 26 June, *inter alia,* which include some sport-specific provisions.

469. There are also some special provisions in miscellaneous legislation that take the specificity of sport into consideration, and adapt the general tax rules to the realities of sport, or create exceptions to the said rules.

II. Taxation of Sportspersons

470. Sportspersons have uncertain and short careers (when compared to the length of time during which other occupations normally continue). This involves an inherent and major concentration of income in a period of time, which is normally short. The profession of sportsperson is normally associated with highly demanding physical effort and a high level of occupational risk. There are random factors arising from the risk or from other imponderables, which can affect sports activities and which may have a decisive effect on the duration of a sportsperson's working life, as a consequence of premature physical deterioration and an above average risk of *occupational illnesses.*

471. Until 2003, only 50% of the income of professional sportsmen was taxable because they were included in the category of *rapid depletion occupations,* listed in Article 27 of the CIRS, as approved by Decree-Law no. 442-A/88, of 30 November. Sportspersons were accordingly taxed not only in respect of their class A income, directly arising from their employment contract, but also in respect of their class B income, arising from sport activities on a self-employed basis. These provisions were introduced in 1988, at the time of the revision of the Personal Income Tax Code via the amendment of Article 3-A, as transitional provisions to be in force during 1989, 1990 and 1991, but which remained in force thereafter. According to no. 6 of the said article only sportspersons and referees are deemed to be sports actors, so that sports managers and directors and coaches are excluded, from the said provisions.

472. In 2003 however, the government decided, in Law no. 32-B/2002, of 30 December, to increase the 50% tax base by 10% per annum, which meant, in practice, that by 2007 both sportspersons and referees were taxed on 100% of their income. The consequence of this was that there was no longer any interest in taxation pursuant to Article 3-A of the CIRS.

473. Sportspersons can carry on their sports careers in accordance with two different tax arrangements. In both cases, they are taxed in accordance with the general tax provision rules applicable to those two tax classes, although there are some special provisions. The said tax arrangements are:

(a) employee, corresponding to Class A;
(b) self-employed person, corresponding to Class B.

474. In as far as Personal Income Tax (IRS) is concerned, there are exceptions to the general rules in Article 12 of the CIRS, which provides that the following are not subject to a charge to IRS:

(a) grants awarded by the POC / Portuguese Paralympic Committee and the corresponding federation, to sportsmen and women involved in high performance sport;
(b) sports training grants awarded by the corresponding federation to non-professional sports actors – subject to a certain maximum annual amount;
(c) bonuses awarded to sportspersons involved in high performance sport and their coaches, in respect of classifications achieved in very prestigious and competitive sports competitions, which are recognized as such in an order of the Minister of Finance and the member of the government responsible for sport.

474.1. There is also an IRS tax incentive for rapid depletion occupations, which includes sportspersons. Accordingly, sums spent on health insurance, personal accident insurance and life insurance, which only cover the risks of death, invalidity and old age retirement, and, in the latter case, provided that the cover benefits are available to the beneficiary after the age of 55, are fully deductible from income, provided that the payment is not guaranteed and is not made, i.e., by way of redemption or advance of any capital sum during the lifetime of the insured, during the first five years until the limit of five times IAS.[103]

475. In relation to international taxatioin rules for artists and sportsmen, is bound by the Organisation for Economic Co-operation and Development (OECD) Model Convention.

III. Social Security

476. In 1989, i.e., prior to the publication of the LBSD, Decree-Law no. 300/89, of 4 September was published, which established the contributory obligations of employers of professional footballers covered by the general social security provisions. The stated objective was *to reconcile the demands of social solidarity with the particularities of professional sports activities (extreme competitiveness; rapid depletion; income dependent on criteria that are uncommon in the market and during time periods, which terminate much earlier than retirement age).*

477. The *specific circumstances of professional football* dictated the fixing of lower contribution rates and a special calculation of the income to be taken into consideration:

(a) the income on the basis of which contributions are calculated: 1/5 of real income;
(b) Employers pay 17.5% and the players 11%.

478. It was stipulated that professional football players are entitled to the benefits of the general social security scheme for employees, with the exception of

103. IAS: Social Support Index. The current IAS is EUR 419.22.

sickness pay. Subsequently, no. 3 of Article 16 of the LBSD provided as follows under the title of *Sports insurance and social security*: '[the] *integration of professional sportspersons in the social security system shall be defined in special regulations'*. Seven years later, Statutory Instrument no. 456/97, of 11 July extended the social security scheme created for professional footballers to professional basketball players. On the 15 of February 1999, a working group was set up by Joint Ministerial Order no. 220/99 with the objective of extending the scheme to sports other than football and basketball. The work of this working group did not however have any practical results. The contribution rates were altered, as follows by Decree-Law no. 199/99, of 8 June, which revised the contribution levels of the general social security scheme for employees:

(a) 17.5% for employers;
(b) 11% for employees.

479. So what was done was to invert the contribution rates so that the employer paid what was formerly paid by the employee and *vice versa*. However, with the publication of Law no. 110/2009, of 16 September, the employers will pay 22.3%, and the professional players pay 11%, with progressive tax increases until 2014.[104] Also, the value of the signing fee is considered to be part of the player's remuneration, and the value is divided in equal parts by the remaining months of the contract. The income on the basis of which contributions are calculated is still 1/5 of its remuneration.

480. We consider that the social security regime applicable is discriminatory, for the following reasons: so far as sportspersons are concerned, the existence of more favourable contribution rate is based on the fact that the sportspersons in question are professionals, as defined by paragraph b) of Article 2 of the RJCTPD. Nevertheless the sportsperson must also be a footballer or basketball player, i.e., the professional or non-professional nature of the sports competition is also a factor. Consequently professional footballers and basketball players, who play in non-professional competitions are discriminated against, as are all athletes of other sports (even though the rate is the same, i.e., 11%, the income base used to calculate the contributions is not 1/5 of real earnings but 100% thereof). Furthermore the employers of these athletes, who are discriminated against, are also discriminated against (because instead of having a contribution rate of 22.3%, their rate is 23.75%).

481. In as far as clubs and sports companies are concerned, we consider that an irrefutable conclusion can be arrived at: the current scheme prejudices employers (clubs and sports companies) other than football and basketball employers, and even

104. The progressive tax increase spans for a period of four years. So, for 2011, the total contribution rate for professional players is 30.5%. In 2012, the total contribution rate will increase to 31.5%, and then to 32.5% in 2013, until it reaches the fixed total of 33.3% in 2014. The professional players always pay 11%, and the remaining, the one which is actually subject to the progressive tax increase, is paid by the player's employer.

football and basketball employers with regard to lower divisions in which the competition is not professional. Accordingly, it is precisely the employers with the greatest financial difficulties that have to pay the highest social security contributions, which, with all due respect, makes no sense.

IV. Taxation of Consumption

482. In as far as the taxation of consumption is concerned the general rules of the CIVA apply.[105] Non-profit sport and physical education associations are exempt from Value Added Tax (VAT), in accordance with Article 9 of the CIVA, in the following cases:

(a) supplies of services and of goods connected therewith in the interests of the association or its members, when the only consideration is a membership fee fixed in accordance with the association's bylaws;
(b) organization of courses, conferences and seminars;
(c) the operation of sports or physical education facilities;
(d) library services;
(e) occasional fund-raising events.

483. In as far as the allocation of reserved seats in football stadiums to members for payment is concerned, the Tax Authorities[106] consider that this situation also falls within the exemption.

484. Before January 2011, List I attached to the CIVA, at item 2.15., transposed Annexe H of the 6th VAT Directive,[107] which provided that entry to sports events and the use of sports premises can benefit from reduced rates. Certain public amusements did not benefit from a reduced VAT rate, but games, which are recognized as sports, are not included in this. According to the Tax Authorities[108] tennis, billiards, snooker and bowling are in the nature of sports and are therefore also taxed at the reduced rate. Consequently, before January 2011, all entry tickets for sports events and the use of sports facilities, i.e., the use of swimming pools, tennis courts and golf courses also benefited from the reduced rate, provided that the space and facilities were used directly for sports activities.[109] After January 2011, the entry into force of Law 55-A/2010, of 31 December, altered item 2.15 of List I attached to the CIVA, in order to exclude the use of sports facilities to benefit from the reduced tax rate. Those activities ceased to benefit from the exemption and the general regime is now applicable to them.

105. The current normal VAT rate is 23%.
106. IVA Department Official Circular no. 56623, of 18 May 1998.
107. VAT Directive 77/388/CEE.
108. VAT Department Official Circular no. 30047, of 18 Apr. 2002.
109. VAT Department Official Circular no. 30088, of 19 Jan. 2006.

V. Taxation of Corporate Income

485. In as far as sports activity is concerned, there are two types of entity that promote sports activity, which are dealt with in the tax legislation:

(a) SADs;
(b) private non-profit associations, which are, in the present case, sports clubs which opt not to set up a SAD.

486. The regulations, which implement the LBSD, as amended by Law no. 19/96, of 25 June, establish that professional sports clubs can opt to become sports companies or can continue to be non-profit juristic persons, so that they are subject, in the latter case, to a Special Management Framework (REG).

487. Despite the fact that they can compete in the same competitions, they are legal persons with different structures and objects. The Legal Framework governing SADs and clubs which opt for the REG is to be found in Decree-Law no. 67/97, of 3 April, which grants them the necessary tools to enable them to be an important element in the promotion of professional sport in Portugal, which includes the Adoption of a new and specific tax scheme, which takes into consideration the specificities that distinguish this type of company from other companies.

488. Law no. 103/97, of 13 September approved the specific SAD tax scheme, which differs from the general tax scheme applicable to Corporation Tax (IRC) and the other taxes, although the general tax scheme still applies subsidiarily. The derogations from the general provisions include the possible:

(a) establishment of a legal framework governing the amortization of the contract rights of professional players, provided that they are registered in competitions by their employers;
(b) the obtaining of capital gains via reinvestment in the hiring of players;
(c) that amortizations may be made during the contractual term;
(d) the Adoption of a financial year that does not coincide with the calendar year;
(e) transferability of the club's losses to the corresponding SAD, or between one SAD and another;
(f) exemption from stamp duty and the corresponding fees.

489. In as far as IRC is concerned the basis of the tax incidence in the case of SADs is their profits, while, in the case of non-profit associations, whether or not they are subject to the REG, the basis is their total income. Existing associations have the benefit of an IRC exemption regime, which covers some activities, i.e.:

(a) income from subsidies and membership fees are not subject to IRC, in accordance with Article 49, no. 3 of the CIRC;
(b) income directly derived from the supply of cultural, recreational or sports services, according to Article 11 of the CIRC;

(c) donations made to sports associations, which have EUPD status, which are considered to be costs or losses of the financial year of the donors, in accordance with Articles 56-C et seq. of the EBF;
(d) so far as all ancillary activities are concerned, such as sponsorships, bars, advertising and sports material, *inter alia*, there is no express exemption but there is however a reference to Article 52 of the EBF, although the said activities should not be deemed to be IRC exempt.

490. A sports club may benefit from IRC exemption in respect of income directly derived from its sports activities, if it complies with all of the requirements in no. 2 of Article 11 of the CIRS, i.e.:

(a) they may, in no circumstances, distribute results and the members of their governing bodies must not have any direct interest in the results of the activities pursued, either individually or via a nominee;
(b) they must have accounts or books of account with regard to their entire operations and make them available to the tax authorities.

491. It should be noted moreover that according to no. 3 of Article 49, the following are, *inter alia*, not considered to be subject to IRC: membership fees paid by members in accordance with the bylaws and subsidies received to finance the pursuit of their objects.

492. It should also be noted that the LBAFD requires the updating of some IRS and IRC provisions, i.e., Article 12, no. 5 and Article 27, both of the IRS Code, under the headings of *Negative delimitation of incidence* and *Rapid depletion occupations: deductions*. The LBAFD widened the scope of the subjective negative delimitation, stipulated by no. 5 of Article 12 of the CIRS, which now covers bonuses given to sportspersons in *high level competition (high performance)* and includes technical staff and referees, in addition to coaches.

VI. Taxation of Clubs and Public Limited Sport Companies

493. Decree-Law no. 67/97, of 3 April, which establishes the legal framework governing clubs and SADs sets the tone by providing that all sums granted by the sports company to the original club, which has sports public utility status, are deemed to be costs or losses provided that they are invested in premises or sports training.

494. Without prejudice to this principle, Law no. 103/97, of 13 September – amended by Decree law 56/2013 of 14 August introduces the specific tax regime of sports companies and provides, first that sports companies may, on application to the Ministry of Finance stating the reasons therefore, adopt an annual tax accounting period other than the calendar year. Sports companies have opted for an accounting year that commences on 1 July and ends on 30 June. Nevertheless the period chosen must be adopted for at least five years, if other than the normal accounting year.

495. In as far as amortizations are concerned, the right to hire professional players is deemed to be part of the company's intangible fixed assets, provided that the players are registered in professional sports competitions on behalf of the sports company. The said rule does not permit amateur players, or players that have become members of the main team directly from the club's trainee levels to be treated as assets. This sometimes prejudices clubs whose teams are based on players, who were previously the club's trainees.

496. In as far as investment of sale proceeds is concerned, it is considered that if the positive difference between capital gains and capital losses made with regard to the sale of players, in terms of the total sale price, is reinvested in the hiring of players, or in the acquisition of tangible fixed assets used for sports purposes, the capital gain is not taxable, provided that the reinvestment occurs by the end of the third financial year after the sale.

497. Sports companies that reorganize in accordance with the law have increased tax incentives. The following are examples of reorganization:

(a) the formation of sports companies via the integration of all or part of the assets of the sports clubs, which are used in connection with an activity, which is, from a technical point of view, an autonomous operation, provided that the said activity is no longer undertaken by the sports club and is undertaken by the sports company;
(b) incorporation by sports companies of all or part of the assets of sports clubs, which are used in connection with an activity, which is, from a technical point of view, an autonomous operation, provided that the said activity is no longer undertaken by the sports club and is undertaken by the sports company;
(c) the formation of sports companies via the integration of all or part of the assets of sports clubs, which are used in connection with an activity, which is, from a technical point of view, an autonomous operation, provided that the said activity is no longer undertaken by the sports club and is undertaken by the sports company, the majority of the share capital of which is owned by a sports company, or the founding club;
(d) the incorporation, by an existing company, of all or part of the assets of the sports clubs, which are used in connection with an activity, which is, from a technical point of view, an autonomous operation, provided that the said activity is no longer undertaken by the sports club and is undertaken by the sports company, the majority of the share capital of which is owned by a sports company, or the founding club.

498. The reorganization of sports companies is exempt from Municipal Property Tax with regard to the transfer of the land and buildings necessary for the reorganization, provided that the municipal interest of the reorganization is recognized by the corresponding local authority, and also from Stamp Duty, with regard to the fees and other legal costs due in respect of the transactions involved in the reorganization process.

499. Decree-Law no. 74/98, of 27 March, approved the Official Accounts Plan for sports federations, associations and groups of clubs. The said Accounts Plan is an economic and financial management tool, which permits a more rigorous and transparent evaluation and improved judgment as to the criteria used and the rational use of State aid to the sports associations' movement. The Decree-Law was passed given the need for an accounting standard for the sports associations' movement, i.e., the sports federations, associations and groups of clubs, which takes account of their specificity, which means that they require special rules for the application of a suitable accounts plan.

500. Law no. 56/2013, has been published and alters the specific tax provisions with regard to sports companies (the previous Law was Law no. 103/97), following the changes made to the legal framework governing such companies. The new provisions have been in force since 15 August 2013 and are applicable to tax periods that commence after they came into force. The new law introduces a range of specific expenditure items not referred to in the previous law.

501. The following are accordingly now considered to be operating costs:

(a) All sums paid to the founder club, provided that it has public utility status and the same are invested in premises or sports training – this is an innovation in the new provisions.
(b) 20% of the sums paid with regard to the exploitation of image rights of sports actors (i.e., players and coaches engaged by the sports company) – this provision is an innovation.
(c) Amortizations of intangible assets with regard to the contract rights of professional players, provided that they are registered in professional sports competitions (whether for the sports company, as was already provided in the previous legal framework, or for other sports companies when on loan – as the new provisions provide) – in this case the value of the contract right that is tax deductible is equal to the acquisition costs, or, if none, to the player's training costs, provided that they are certified by an independent public auditor. The amortization method is unchanged from the previous provisions: i.e., the straight-line method, with the annual amortization amount being the result of the application of the amortization rates as determined in accordance with the duration of the contract. The straight-line method is one of the methods most used to calculate amortizations and assumes that the assets depreciate at a fixed rate during their useful life. Using this method, amortizations are calculated by dividing the value of the acquisition by the number of periods comprised in the assets useful life.
(d) The amounts paid by the sports company to holders of players' economic sports rights in consideration of the transfer of the player, as was already provided in the previous provisions.

(e) The amounts paid to the company's players for the signing or renewal of their contracts, as was already provided.
(f) The amounts paid by sports companies to agents and representatives with regard to the transfer of players, which is an innovation introduced by the new provisions.

None of the amounts referred to above are deductible if paid to non-resident entities, which are subject to a clearly more advantageous tax regime.

Reinvestment of Sale Proceeds

502. There have been no changes in relation to the previous provisions: only 50% of the proceeds of the sale of a player are deemed to be a capital gain (i.e., the positive difference the gains and losses made with regard to the sale of the player). The sale proceeds, i.e., the total intangible assets corresponding to the contract rights of professional players, must be reinvested in the hiring of players, or in the acquisition of tangible assets for sports purposes.

503. The reinvestment must take place by the end of the third financial year following the sale.

Exemptions

504. Sports companies that are reorganized in accordance with their new legal framework may be entitled to a total or partial exemption from:

(a) IMT, with regard to transfers of land or buildings necessary for the said reorganization, which must be approved by the relevant local authority and be recognized as of municipal interest, which was already provided in the previous provisions, with regard to the previous municipal sisa tax.
(b) Stamp Duty (SD) due with regard to all acts comprised in the reorganization process – which was also provided in the previous provisions.

505. In order to obtain this exemption, sports companies must make a written application to that effect, which proves the necessary requirements, e.g., municipal interest. The exemptions are granted by order of the Minister of Finance, on the basis of an opinion of the AT, to be issued within thirty days of the date on which the application is submitted, failing which the application is deemed to be tacitly approved. The AT must also request an opinion from the ministry responsible for sport (in order to establish the municipal interest of the exemption) and from the Directorate-General of Registers and Notarial Affairs (in order to establish that the reorganization requirements are complied with). There are therefore no changes in relation to the previous provisions.

506. The reorganization referred to in the Law in respect of which exemptions may be granted are the same as in the previous provisions.

Liability

507. The liability provisions are unaltered: The sports company is jointly liable with the founding club, regarding all tax and social security debts, with regard to the period prior to the effective date of the reorganization. The said liability is limited by the value of the assets transferred by the founding club to the company.

Reorganization in Relation to IRC (Corporation Tax)

508. There are also no changes with regard to this aspect: the special provisions of the CIRC (Corporation Tax Code) with regard to mergers, divisions and asset capital contributions apply to the transfer of the assets of the sports club to the sports company, or to another company, the share capital of which is majority owned by the sports company, or by the founding club, during the first five years from the commencement of trading.

VII. The Former Legal Provisions regarding the Joint and Several Liability of Sport's Directors and Managers

509. Until 2007 there were special provisions in force with regard to the liability of members of the management of clubs, which did not opt to form a SAD, and took part in professional competitions.

510. The legal position with regard to the liability of managers of clubs that opted for the REG was that their liability was deemed to be personal, joint and unlimited with regard to debts to the tax and social security authorities in respect of sums not paid during their period of office. Furthermore, the chairman of the club's management, the chairman of the supervisory board, or the single auditor, the manager responsible for the financial area and the managers in charge of the management of the said professional sections were also deemed to be liable for their management of the professional sections of clubs that have opted for the REG.

511. Accordingly, no. 2 of Article 39 of Decree-Law no. 67/97, of 3 April provided that the said members were jointly and severally liable for debts to the Tax and Social Security Authorities. However, according to José Manuel Meirim,[110] this liability is additional and not general, as it is necessary, in order for no. 2 to be effective, for there to be criminal liability for the crimes of tax fraud and/or social security fraud. Accordingly personal, unlimited, joint and several liability for the payment of tax and social security only exists if one of these two crimes has been committed.

512. However, these provisions were held to be unconstitutional by Constitutional Court Judgment no. 311/2007, of 16 May, because they violated the combined provisions of Articles 103, no. 2 and 165, no. 1, paragraph i), of the CRP,

110. Meirim, José Manuel. *Regime Jurídico das Sociedades Desportivas Anotado*. Coimbra. Coimbra Editora, 1999, 147.

insofar as they provide for personal, unlimited and joint and several liability of chairman of the club's management, the chairman of the supervisory board, or the single auditor, the manager responsible for the financial area and the managers in charge of the management of the said professional sections, with regard to tax debts. Such matters do in fact fall within the exclusive jurisdiction of the Assembly of the Republic, unless it authorizes the Government to legislate in these areas, as taxes must be created by Assembly legislation that stipulates the incidence, rate, tax incentives and guarantees of taxpayers.

VIII. The Taxation of Persons and Transactions in Professional Football

513. Sports management decisions, particularly in the case of football, do not comply with the same standards of rationality as decisions taken with regard to ordinary businesses, while the corresponding market definitions are not even comparable. It is therefore necessary for the purposes of tax law, to take into consideration the existence of specific sport-linked factors and aspects, e.g.:

(a) the success of clubs in terms of the winning of competitions and championships;
(b) the management and motivation of supporters, which is linked to the first factor;
(c) the very frequent problematic relations between clubs, the players and their representatives;
(d) the transnational nature of the markets and those active in it;
(e) the injuries, including players' state of mind that can have a decisive effect on the success or lack of success of a club;
(f) games of chance and fortune.

514. In order to adapt the general tax scheme to the most frequent relevant general transactions in the case of professional football, the Tax Authorities prepared an internal document entitled *Tax Treatment of Operations effected by Entities Linked to the Professional Football Sector,* which identifies and provides guidelines with regard to three types of operations, i.e.:

(a) international transfers of football players;
(b) image rights transactions;
(c) loan of football players.

A. The Role of Players' Agents in the Transfers of Football Players

515. According to the Corporation Tax Code, the taxation of the transfer of football players disregards certain amounts, i.e., intermediation services expenses. According to Article 23 of the CIRC, *costs and losses, which are proved to be indispensable for the making of the profits or gains subject to tax, or for the maintenance of the productive source, shall be treated as such*, but this does not include intermediation expenses.

516. From the point of view of the clubs and SADs, intermediation services are in fact indispensable. For example, in some well-known clubs it is only possible to sell a certain player via the exclusive agent, who works with the club. It follows therefore that it is impossible, for certain clubs, not to incur expenses in respect of intermediation services.[111]

517. The applicable provisions are that the costs incurred in these operations are not deductible and are accordingly taxable, when the entity in receipt of the said income is resident in a territory with a more favourable tax regime, as defined in accordance with the provisions of Article 59 and no. 8 of Article 81 of the CIRC.

518. These tax provisions give rise to a capital gain for the clubs, as a consequence of the increased sale price arising from the disallowal of costs, or by the reduction of the purchase price, also as a consequence of the disallowal of costs.

519. In as far as the Tax Authorities are concerned, the question of the disallowal of the cost of intermediation services is related to the lack of a written contract between the club or SAD and the agent or entity. The mere submission of the invoice or the declarations of the club or SAD, do not suffice, even when the case

---

111. The LBSD contained no reference to players' agents. The first legal reference to players' agents was in the LCTD, Ch. IV – Arts 22–25 of which make provision with regard to players' agents, i.e., the conduct of their profession, registration, remuneration and limitations on the exercise of the profession. With the LBD the position of players' agent acquired the dignity of a fundamental law. This legislative option was also adopted by the LBAFD. The work of a players' agent is multidisciplinary and is associated with a vaste range of specific acts, i.e.: (i) prospecting and negotiation of contracts (employment, transfer, sponsorship and other contracts) for a sportsperson, club or federation; (ii) registration of players, a club or federation in official/friendly or commercial events; (iii) elaboration and management of career plans for sportspersons; (iv) providing sportspersons with technical advice (training/coaching); (iv) development of marketing strategies for sportspersons; (v) organization/preparation of sportspersons' travel arrangements; (vi) management of the daily problems of sportspersons such as housing, and diet, *inter alia*; (vii) advising sportspersons on matters of tax, law, social security, insurance and other matters; (viii) monitoring of the school education of sportspersons; (ix) financial planning for sportspersons, etc. In any event, the fundamental role of a player's agent is to know how to assist the player in the making of sports contracts, or, in the words of para. d) of Art. 2 of the LFECS '*(…) occasional or permanent representation or intermediation in the making of sports contracts, for remuneration (…)*'. It is a contract that the LCT, in no. 4 of Art. 22, classifies as an agency contract. Most legal theorists and case-law agree with this opinion. We consider however that it is possible to classify the specific activity of a players' agent, i.e., the assisting of sportpersons in negotiations for the making of a sports employment contract, as an activity that is typical of a commercial agency agreement, or something very similar, as is the case in the United Kingdom. The preparation, celebration and performance of a contract between a player and a players' agent involves the essential aspects of a commercial agency agreement, i.e.: (i) the obligation of the agent to seek out potential contracts; (ii) on behalf of the other party; (iii) with autonomy; (iv) stability; and (v) for remuneration. We are not unaware of the fundamental distinction that is normally made between commercial agency contracts (Art. 1, no. 1 of Decree-Law no. 178/86, as amended by Decree-Law no. 118/93, of 23 April) and agency contracts (Art. 1157 of the Civil Code): even if the commercial agent is authorised to make contracts, this is merely an ancillary activity, which is complementary to the fundamental activity of seeking out potential contracts. In both cases, someone (the player's agent or the mandatary) act on behalf of another (the principal or the mandant, respectively), but the circumstances differ: While a player's agent fundamentally performs material acts, a mandatary performs juristic acts.

is a matter of public knowledge. Even so and so far as the Tax Authorities are concerned, it is only possible to deduct one amount for intermediation services, while the reality is very different.

520. The reality is that most player transfer transactions require double intermediation, not only in relation to the transferor or transferee club, but also in relation to the players involved, in order to protect their interests in the transaction.

521. This is however rejected by the Tax Authorities, which frown upon the high commissions demanded by the intermediary agents, which are between 5% and 10% of the global value of the transfer transaction.

522. Players' agents can also have financial rights related to the player's transfer rights, which is why they receive additional income from transfer transactions. These payments are unrelated to the provision of intermediation services and fit with difficulty into the general tax scheme.

523. The fact is that intermediaries and particularly FIFA Agents play a fundamental role in the success, or otherwise, of clubs in relation to their hirings, because:

(a) they are responsible for the management of the careers of top ranking footballers and coaches, who are the principle human resources of the clubs;
(b) they have an unequalled knowledge of the world market and have representatives in all of the main markets, i.e., Europe and Latin America;
(c) *the nominee effect,* which is advantageous for the transferee club and the transferor club in terms of the speed of agreement, which is a fundamental characteristic of this type of transaction;
(d) the relationship between supply and demand is marked by the rapid identification and satisfaction of purchase, sale and loan requirements.

In Portugal, the costs incurred by clubs in relation to intermediation services are disregarded for tax purposes, but are nevertheless taken into consideration as taxable income of resident intermediaries, so that the Tax Authorities benefit both ways.

B. Image Rights

524. The operation of image rights has become an increasingly important aspect of the hiring of players. From the point of view of the clubs or SADs, the sports potential of a player must be associated with a commercial potential, because this enables both of them to earn a considerable income. This means that clubs are willing to pay increasingly high amounts in addition to the amount paid with regard to the players transfer value, financial rights and player registration rights.

525. The business of the operation of these rights has grown exponentially as image rights are, in most cases, owned by companies, which operate them for the player's benefit. These companies are sometimes based in tax havens.

526. The Tax Authorities challenge the economic substance of image rights in most transactions and accordingly the said costs are disallowed for deduction as costs by clubs or SADs, on the basis of:

(a) Article 59 of the CIRC, when the payments in question are to entities based in tax havens, unless it can be proved that they relate to transactions that have in fact taken place and that the same are not abnormal and that the amount thereof is not excessive. If this cannot be established such payments are taxed separately in accordance with no. 8 of Article 81.
(b) Article 23 of the CIRC, which defines costs and losses as *costs or losses, which are proved to be indispensable for the earning of the income or the making of the gains subject to tax, or for the maintenance of the productive source,* on the grounds of alleged lack of documentation, or the lack of a connection between the costs and the income or gain generated.

527. When players earn income based on image rights, the Tax Authorities reclassifies the income as:

(a) employment income, which is subject to the general provisions applicable to Class A income for IRS purposes;
(b) income with regard to the use of intellectual property rights, or arising from an ordinary supply of services, which are treated as class B income for Personal Income Tax purposes, to which the general tax provisions apply.

528. In the case of companies:

(a) if there are resident, the income is subject to Corporate Tax in accordance with the CIT Code;
(b) if they are non-residents, the income is treated as royalties and is subject to the deduction of tax at source. Double Taxation Treaties (DTTs) between Portugal and other countries may be applicable.

C. Loans of Football Players

529. In the vast majority of loans of football players between clubs or SADs in Portugal no payment is agreed. The Tax Authorities consider that these contracts involve the use of a service for purposes that are foreign to the club, which service, being free of charge, is subject to VAT. The price taken into consideration is the *normal market price.*

530. Lender clubs or SADs have a financial interest in such loans, i.e., in the maintenance of their players' competitive form and the affirmation of the player in the market, with a view to re-joining the lender club, or a profitable sale.

IX. Payment to Non-resident Entities

531. The following payments are subject to different withholding tax rates:

(a) payments to non-resident entities: 25%;
(b) payments to non-resident entities located in tax havens: 35%;
(c) Waiver or reduction of the withholding tax rates in accordance with a Double Taxation Treaty between the Portuguese State and the State of residence of the beneficiaries of the income, on production of certificates of tax residence.

§6. Financing of Sports

I. Sports Development Aid Programme Contracts

A. Introduction

532. Financial aid and subsidies for sport granted by the State, the Autonomous Regions and local authorities are required to be granted pursuant to sports development aid programme contracts. The form of the programme contract and the obligations and requirements directly related thereto are defined by law and can currently be found in Decree-Law no. 273/2009, of 1 October, which introduced the corresponding legal framework. The principle that the aid and subsidies granted by the State to the various entities within the sports system, i.e., the sports federations, was introduced into Portuguese law by the first Basic Law of Sport, the LBSD, although it should be noted that financial aid to sports associations was already provided for in the constitution and is implicit in no. 2 of Article 79 of the CRP.

533. However, prior to the LBSD, the making of sports development aid programme contracts was already part of the practice of the Ministry of Education, via the Sports Development Fund, as a vehicle for technical and financial co-operation between the central administration and the municipalities, as provided and governed by Decree-Law no. 384/87, of 24 December. This legislation introduced the legal framework governing the making of sectorial or multisectorial programme contracts within the ambit of technical and financial co-operation between the central administration and one or more municipalities, associations of municipalities, or their concessionary undertakings, and sectorial collaboration agreements. It was therefore necessary to define the legal framework applicable to the making of programme contracts with sports organizations by the central, regional and local administration, which would be compulsory for all subsidies, with the exception of those, which because of their low amount, do not justify such demanding formalisms.

534. After the introduction of the principle of the grant of State subsidies to sport via the signing of sports development aid programme contracts, it was necessary to implement this principle in the law. This gave rise to Decree-Law no. 432/91, of 6 November, which established the legal framework applicable to programme contracts signed with a view to the payment of subsidies within the ambit of the system of aid to the sports movement. The said subsidies included all subsidies, whatever the proportion of the costs they cover, which were granted by the State, the autonomous regions, or the local authorities and whether granted directly, or via agencies working under their auspices.

535. Regional and local development aid granted in the context of technical and financial co-operation between the Government and the municipalities has been implemented via the signing of programme contracts. The purpose of these financial instruments was the investment in sporting areas and facilities which are central to local and regional development.

536. The experience of the application of Decree-Law no. 432/91, of 6 November, was considered to be positive, however the current Basic Law of sport, the LBAFD, introduced new requirements and demands with regard to the public funding of the various private structures that are comprised in, or direct the sports system, which had to be included in the decree-law, which governs sports development aid programme contracts. The legislation was accordingly repealed and replaced by Decree-Law no. 273/2009, of 1 October. The said requirements include:

(a) the need for a prior binding opinion issued by the member of the Government responsible for sport for the grant of State funding for the construction of public and private sports facilities;
(b) the subordination of the granting of public financial subsidies for the construction or improvement of privately owned sports facilities, when the nature of the investment so justifies, and the granting of permission to the said private bodies to use or manage public sector sports facilities, free of charge, to the assumption by them of commitments in the public interest;
(c) the prior recognition of the public interest status of sports events, by order of the Government members responsible for sport, as a precondition of the public funding thereof;
(d) the introduction of the principle according to which sports clubs that take part in professional competitions cannot benefit, in that context, from aid or subsidies from the State, Autonomous Regions and local authorities, with the exception of the funding of the construction or improvement of sports premises or facilities with a view to the holding of sports competitions of public interest, which are recognized as such by the member of the Government responsible for sport;
(e) the requirement that the accounts of entities that receive public funding must be certified, when the amounts of the funding expected to be granted during the financial year exceeds EUR 50,000;

(f) the prohibition of the grant of further public funding to entities that are in breach of their tax or social security obligations. The financial benefits of any programme contracts in force must be suspended until such time as the said default is remedied;
(g) the fact that funds provided out of public funds in the context of programme contracts cannot be subject to judicial seizure or charging orders, as the said funds are deemed to be usable solely for the purposes for which they were granted.

B. Beneficiaries

537. According to the LBAFD, in line with the approach adopted by the previous Basic Laws of the Sports System, sports associations and sports events with public interest status that are recognized as such by the member of the Government responsible for sport, can receive aid or subsidies from the State, the Autonomous Regions or the local authorities. The legislation, which establishes the legal framework governing sports development programme contracts, widens the definition of public interest of sports events or competitions, from not only those that are recognized in an order of the member of the Government responsible for sport, but also includes those sports events that are comprised in the regular competitions of the corresponding national and international sports federations. This broadens the criterion to include almost all competitions taking place within the federations, provided that they are regular.

538. The following can be granted aid and subsidies:

(a) the Olympic Committee of Portugal and the Portuguese Paralympic Committee;
(b) the Portuguese Sports Confederation;
(c) the sports federations;
(d) the association or confederations of sportspersons, coaches and referees and the sports clubs;
(e) sports companies, subject to limitations;
(f) other natural and juristic persons provided that the aid or subsidies are to be employed, directly or indirectly, to support sports activities, pursuant to an order of the member of the Government responsible for sport.

539. Publicly funded subsidies, within the ambit of aid to the sports associations' movement, may only be granted in the context of sports development programme contracts that have been published officially, so that the same are only in force once they have been published in the Official Journal. The contracts must also be in writing. Furthermore, the financial subsidization of the construction of private or public sports facilities by the State is subject to the prior binding opinion of the member of the Government responsible for sport.

540. Sports clubs and public limited sports companies, which take part in professional competitions, cannot receive any aid or subsidies from the State, the

Autonomous Regions or the local authorities, with regard to the said competitions. An exception to the preceding prohibition is when a club or public limited sports company is competing in professional competitions and wishes to construct or improve sports infrastructures or facilities with a view to the holding of sports competitions with public interest status, which are recognized as such in an order of the member of the Government responsible for sport.

541. A broad concept of *sports development programme* has been adopted in order to prevent certain activities from being unjustifiably excluded from receiving financial aid, i.e., the construction of infrastructures and sports facilities. It is indeed such works that are the main beneficiaries of public subsidies and which are most appropriate in terms of the demanding formalism imposed by the law with regard to the signing of programme contracts.

542. The legislation, which governs programme contracts, also includes a provision regarding the granting of sports sponsorship to sports actors, whose activity, in that capacity, promotes Portugal internationally, and natural or juristic persons, who promote or organize sports events. The rules governing programme contracts are applicable to sponsorship, with the exception of the provisions governing sports development programmes.

C. *Sports Development Programmes*

543. Another aspect is that financial aid and subsidies may only be granted when a sports development programme has been submitted by the interested parties. The law defines these programmes as:

(a) regular action plans of entities that promote and control the practice of the various sports at national, regional or local level;
(b) specific action plans with a view to the promotion and dissemination of physical activity and sport, the organization of competitions of social interest, or in order to support the participation of Portuguese sportspersons in international events;
(c) projects for the construction or improvement of sports facilities and infrastructures;
(d) measures taken with a view to the development and improvement of the practice of physical activity and sport, i.e., in the areas of training, documentation, research, or relations with international organizations.

544. The recipients of the funding may be both the sports federations and the associations that are members thereof and the clubs themselves, in addition to the Olympic Committee of Portugal. The restriction of financial aid and subsidies to federations with sports public utility status does not affect the provision of aid to clubs, but they must obtain the said funding from special programmes that do not conflict with the powers of the associations or federations. Public limited sports companies are completely excluded because of their commercial nature.

545. Indeed, the legislation only authorizes financial aid to professional sport when what is funded is the organization of competitions of manifest public interest in order to channel the available resources to the dissemination and promotion of sport among the general public.

546. The grant of financial aid is subject to the signing of programme contracts with a view to the achieving of the following objectives, as defined by law:

(a) the inclusion of the financial aid in the execution of specific sport promotion plans;
(b) to give greater flexibility to the financial aid grant procedure, so that the aid granted in each case is most suited to the sports development programme of which it is part;
(c) to combine the grant of financial aid with a complete evaluation of the costs of each plan or project, and of the levels of financial, technical, material and human autonomy involved in the implementation thereof;
(d) to permit the intervention and mutual commitment of various entities in the implementation of a single sports development programme;
(e) to strengthen the sense of responsibility of the parties with regard to compliance with the obligations freely assumed by them;
(f) to ensure the full publicity and transparency of the conditions subject to which the financial aid was granted.

547. Other entities, or agencies, that are jointly interested in the implementation of a certain sports development programme, may take part in programme contracts, in addition to the grantors and recipients of the financial aid. The rights and obligations of the said third parties are defined by the contracting parties. Accordingly, the contracting parties have complete autonomy to regulate third party positions within the ambit of the multilateral relationship created.

D. The Programme Contract Procedure

548. The programme contract formation procedure is based on certain standard acts of the grantor and recipient of the financial aid, although there is an inevitable area of lawful informal negotiations between the parties. It is for the entities that wish to receive the corresponding financial aid, which always have the contractual initiative, to submit proposals for the making of programme contracts. These proposals must contain the following information:

(a) a general description and characterization of the sports development programme;
(b) a social justification of the programme stating the benefits of the programme to third parties, or the general public;
(c) a sports justification of the programme, namely in terms of the development of the sports in question and the events or competitions to be held;
(d) quantification of the expected results of the implementation of the programme;

(e) an estimate of costs and public funding requirements, including the corresponding time charts or stage payments;
(f) a demonstration of the level of financial, technical, material and human autonomy offered by the proposer for the implementation of the programme, including the indication of any other subsidies, funding or sponsorships and the terms thereof, if any;
(g) identification of any entities that are involved in the management and implementation of the programme, defining the nature of the said involvement and their powers and responsibilities;
(h) any complementarity with other programmes that have already been implemented or that are being implemented in the same area or in associated areas;
(i) the time schedule and overall duration of the implementation of the sports development programme;
(j) the intended use of the assets to be acquired, or constructed, pursuant to the programme, if they will not belong to the proposer, together with a definition of the entity in charge of the management and maintenance thereof.

549. When the programme involves the construction of sports infrastructures or facilities, the proposal must, in addition to the information referred to in the preceding paragraph, also contain a location plan and the preliminary studies or technical specifications necessary to evaluate the same.

550. If the participation of third party entities in the programme contract is envisaged, they must also be identified in the proposal together with their rights and obligations. The LBAFD also requires that other proposed or actual funding sources must be identified. This new condition is important because it permits a better management of the public funds granted to sport and prevents overlapping of different public investment funding of the same sports project.

551. Provision is made with regard to those proposals, which merit approval but, which cannot, for budgetary reasons, proceed immediately to the signing of a programme contract. Such proposals are valid until the end of the financial year, which permits the renewal thereof during the following financial year, on favourable terms. Accordingly, such proposals have priority in relation to proposals submitted subsequently, which have not yet been approved, as the proposer may renew the proposal for the following financial year by making a simple declaration.

552. Special care is also taken in the regulation of rejections of contractual proposals, in order to ensure the complete fairness and integrity of relations between the Administration and proposers. Grounds must be stated for the rejection of contractual proposals. If the reasons for the rejection do not amount to a definitive obstacle to the acceptance of the development programme proposed, the entity that made the rejection decision must indicate the terms and conditions on which the proposal must be reformulated in order to be accepted. Decisions that expressly or tacitly reject proposals for the signing of programme contracts may be challenged in legal proceedings in accordance with the law.

E. Public Interest and Non-performance

553. One of the most important matters that must be included in programme contracts is a rigorous definition of the public interest benefits that are the reasons for the funding, namely when the programme contract involves the acquisition or construction of sports infrastructures. Compliance with the obligations assumed by the recipient is secured via a real public use right, which the legislation terms a sports easement. The content and duration of this easement is defined by the parties on a case-by-case basis. The enforcement of the easement is controlled by the public entity that grants the funding (or by such other entity as is identified as the proprietor of the easement in the contract) via the exercise of powers which, together with the general power to supervise the performance of the contract, are the only enforcement powers granted by the Decree Law 273/2009, of 1 October.

554. Provision is made with regard to the non-performance of the contracts in order to prevent excessively rigid or disproportionate solutions, while preserving the necessary liability. The non-performance of the contract may involve various circumstances, the causes and consequences of which vary from case to case. In certain circumstances, the grantor of the funding is granted the power to establish new time limits or performance schedules, or to reduce the funding, or to assume responsibility for the conclusion of incomplete works, in exchange for further public interest rights. The repayment in full of the sums paid and the personal liability of the members of the bodies charged with the implementation of the programme are accordingly reserved for the most serious cases of non-performance. The recipient of the funding is, in turn, entitled to be compensated when it is compelled to have recourse to other funding sources, in the event of failure to pay, or delay in the payment of the funding granted.

555. One of the innovations in the new legal framework governing programme contracts is the reduction of the aid arising from sports development programme contracts in the event of the suspension of the EUPD, which reduction is proportional to the duration of the suspension. The corresponding amount is included in the working budget of the IDP, IP.

556. Another innovation is that non-compliance with the legislation with regard to the combating of doping in sport and racism, xenophobia and intolerance at sports events, and non-compliance with the decisions of the proper authorities in these areas, involves the suspension of State funding for as long as the non-compliance continues.

557. Finally, we stress the importance of the arbitration system created in order to resolve disputes arising from programme contracts, at first instance. This involves no reduction of legal guarantees, as an appeal lies from the arbitration award to the administrative courts, which includes the reconsideration of the matters of fact. It is hoped that this system will contribute to providing interested parties with a rapid and credible conflict resolution mechanism.

II. Financial Aid for Professional Competitions and the Special Case of the Autonomous Regions

558. No. 2 of Article 46 of the LBAFD prohibits any form of State, autonomous region or local authority aid to sports clubs that compete in professional competitions, unless the subject matter of the aid is related to the improvement of sports infrastructures or facilities, with a view to the holding of sport competitions of public interest. The State defines which competitions are of public interest, by order of the member of the government responsible for sport.

559. There is some disparity with regard to such matters between Continental Portugal and the autonomous regions, particularly Madeira, as Regional Legislative Decree no. 4/2007/M, of 11 January, which introduced the fundamentals of the sports system in the Autonomous Region of Madeira permits aid to SADs in relation to taking part in professional sports competitions. Paragraph q) of Article 12 of this Regional Legislative Decree includes financial and material aid to sport, including high performance and professional sport, as a general principle of the sports policy of the Autonomous Region of Madeira.

560. Articles 22, 55 and 56 of the said Regional Legislative Decree include various provisions that conflict with the provisions of the LBAFD, with which the said regional legislative decree should comply. The said provisions concern aid to teams that compete at a high level, which are defined as *teams, which have sports merit in national and international terms,* which *benefit from specific aid measures detailed in specific regulations.* The decree states later that the aim of the public financing of sport is to ensure the means, *inter alia, to fight inequalities, difficulties and limitations arising from insularity* and *the fundamental role of high level competitive sport is the promotion of the Autonomous Region of Madeira as a tourist destination.* No. 1 of Article 56 states that the public funding of sport includes, *inter alia*, the subsidization of the costs associated with the following aspects:

(a) travel of people and property to regional, national and international competitions;
(b) organization and participation in federation sports competitions;
(c) high performance sport activities.

561. Paragraph m) of Article 228 of the CRP recognizes that sport is a matter of specific interest to the autonomous regions and gives them legislative and administrative autonomy in this area. However, no. 4 of Article 112 of the CRP provides that regional legislative decrees cannot include provisions that are contrary to the fundamental principles of the general laws of the Republic, while paragraph a) of no. 1 of Article 227 reaffirms that the autonomous regions have powers to legislate, but always subject to the fundamental principles of the general laws of the Republic.

562. The final part of no. 2 of Article 46 of the LBAFD excessively widened the powers of the member of the government responsible for sport to define sport competitions of public interest. We consider that the said power does not apply to the definition of competitions of this type in the autonomous regions.

563. It can be stated in conclusion that the LBAFD is the greatest intrusion of political power into sport since the 25th of April 1974, when the first all-embracing sports legislation began to appear, and above all, in the area of professional sport and in combination with the RJFD, which contains various provisions that are materially unconstitutional.

III. The Aid System for High Performance Sportspersons, Coaches and Referees

A. Introduction

564. The introduction of an integrated aid system for the development of high performance sport is a relatively recent factor in Portugal. It was only following the publication of the LBSD that Decree-Law no. 257/90, of 7 August was passed. This decree-law established a series of aid measures targeted at what was then called the high performance sub-system. This series of aid measures was subsequently perfected by Decree-Law no. 125/95, of 31 May, as subsequently amended by Decree-Law no. 123/96, of 10 August.

565. Subsequently, the LBAFD introduced a new approach to high performance sport. New provisions were also included in the CIVA by Decree-Law no. 442-A/88, of 30 November, with a view to exempting the prizes received by high performance sportspersons as a consequence of the good sports results they achieve and the grants they receive in a more appropriate manner, by exempting them from VAT. Decree-Law no. 10/2009, of 12 January, also established a new insurance system that covers the special risks to which high performance sportspersons are subject, within the context of a general revision of the sports insurance system.

566. The experience gained during the one and a half decades during which an aid system for high performance sport has been in force and the new approach introduced by the LBAFD gave rise to the need to carry out a general reform with regard to these matters.

B. Innovations in the Legal Framework Governing Aid to High Performance Sport

567. The reforms that commenced with the publication of Decree-Law no. 272/2009, of 1 October, involve profound changes in the way in which high performance sportspersons are supported.

568. The aim was to remedy the principle weakness of the previous system, which was based on an excessively permissive definition of high performance sport, which had inherent consequences in terms of the state aid granted to sportspersons whose results hardly justify the aid received.

569. A new register of sportspersons, coaches and referees is created in which applicants for assistance under the high performance provisions must be registered. Registration is subject to proposal by the corresponding sports federation to the IDP, IP.

570. The legal framework introduced by Decree-Law no. 272/2009, of 1 October distinguishes between Olympic sports and non-Olympic sports, in order to better channel the available public aid to the former.

571. The provisions applicable to high performance sportspersons in the sports reserved for those with disabilities and handicaps, so that they too can benefit from the public support envisaged in the Decree-Law.

572. High performance sportspersons are also classified in three levels, A, B and C, in order to be able to reserve the most significant public aid for those with the high levels of sports performance.

573. The general criteria governing the classification of certain sports competitions as high level competitions for the purposes of inclusion of the participants in such competitions as level C high performance players and athletes are defined in Statutory Instrument no. 325/2010, of 16 June. These criteria are based on the participation of a minimum number of countries, teams or athletes or players, with a certain position in the ranking of each event. In the case of those sports that do not have a European or World championship, the relevant sports results or positions in the corresponding rankings of the athletes or players, must be defined, with a view to their inclusion in levels A to C as referred to in Decree-Law no. 272/2009, of 1 October. The same provisions apply to the conditions governing the classification of international referees as high performance referees.

574. This approach enables the state to give significant support to sportspersons, who have achieved real results in highly competitive competitions. In some cases this support is comparable with the support provided in other countries in similar circumstances.

C. The Increased Obligations of High Performance Sportspersons

575. High performance sport is of special public interest to the extent that it is an important factor in the development of sport and represents a country in international sports competitions.

576. High performance sportspersons must seek to conduct themselves in all circumstances in an exemplary manner, in order to benefit the image of the sport, the national team to which they belong and Portugal. They must be available to take part in public measures to promote their sport and sport in general. These sportspersons are regularly subjected to random tests during competitions and otherwise, by the proper sports authorities in order to check whether they are under the effect of doping and are also required to comply with the plans submitted by the IDP, IP and to take their part in national teams if selected for them.

577. Sportspersons, who are included in the register of high performance sports actors, are required to make a contract with the corresponding sports federation and the IDP, IP, which stipulates their rights, obligations and the penalties for breach of the contract. In the case of Olympic and Paralympic sportspersons, the said contract is made with the Olympic Committee of Portugal or the Paralympic Committee of Portugal. Breach of the additional duties referred to above and any other duties imposed by law or sports regulations, can result in the suspension or cancellation of the high performance sport aid measures, according to the seriousness of the case. These sanctions are imposed by order of the member of the government responsible for sport.

578. So far as doping is concerned and in addition to the special duty to which high performance sports persons are subject, sports actors with high performance sport responsibilities are required to strive to ensure that the corresponding sportspersons do not breach any anti-doping rule.

D. Educational Aid and Aid to Access to Higher Education

579. The Decree-Law introduced some measures, which facilitate the reconciliation of high performance sport in schools and promote it. The IDP, IP is responsible for informing the Ministry of Education of the sportspersons involved in the high performance scheme and is also required to convey the information provided by educational establishments, i.e., regarding the educational achievements of sportspersons, to the sports federations.

580. High performance sportspersons can register at educational establishments located outside of their areas of residence and may apply to be transferred when this is justified by their sports activity. They can also have timetables and examination dates that are more compatible with their sports training. Absences during periods of training for, and participation in, sports competitions, are not penalized and there may be special lessons to make up for lessons missed.

581. The entitlement to school support measures is directly related to the educational achievements of high performance sportspersons, taking the various variables involved in the sportsperson's school and sports activity into consideration.

582. Academic scholarships may also be provided to sportspersons, who wish to attend educational establishments in Portugal or abroad, which have educational programmes which combine studies with training so that they can train abroad if they comply with certain requirements. The rules governing the grant of scholarships will be published in a joint statutory instrument of the members of the Government responsible for education and sport.

583. High performance sportspersons, who have completed secondary education or a legal equivalent thereof can take advantage of special provisions governing access to higher education in accordance with Decree-Law no. 393-A/99, of 2 October, and obtain a transfer to another educational establishment, via a confirmatory declaration issued by the IDP, IP. These sportspersons, who comply with the higher education or specialized training entry criteria have priority with regard to the attendance of trainer training courses for their sport, whatever the sport and the promoter of the training courses.

E. Measures to Aid Employees, Coaches and Referees

584. The Decree-Law provides that high performance sportspersons, who are civil servants or public employees, may be granted special leave of absence for the time necessary for their preparation for and participation in sports events included in the plan produced by the corresponding federation. The said grant of leave of absence means that the sportsperson is temporarily release from the obligation to work, without prejudice to seniority, length of service, retirement, pension and benefit entitlements. During the leave of absence, the sportspersons remuneration is paid by the IDP, IP, via recourse to funds set aside by the sports federations to support high performance sports persons, which is also subject to the deductions provided in the law.

585. So far as private sector workers are concerned, high performance sportspersons may be excused from work by their employers for such time as is necessary for preparation for and participation in sports events, at the request of the IDP, IP, and the said absences are classed as unpaid justified absences.

586. If they are not excused from work and if other attempts at a negotiated solution fail, sportspersons may be requisitioned on the grounds of the public interest of the events in which they are to take part. In all cases, the remuneration paid by the IDP, IP via recourse to the funds allocated by the sports federation to support high performance sport, is subject to deductions in accordance with the law.

587. The professional career, receipt of perquisites or benefits, i.e., with regard to good time keeping and work attendance of workers, who benefit from these aid measures, cannot be prejudiced.

588. Provision is made for the signing of an agreement between the IDP, IP and employers, in connection with regard to the grant of assistance by employers, who risk being deprived of their high performance sportsperson employees for long periods of time, with a view to compensating them and taking advantage of a commercial opportunity, via the promotion of the images of their businesses.

589. The Decree-Law also introduces measures to support high performance sports coaches and referees, who also benefit from the employee support measures detailed above together with the school aid measures, but only those with regard to school hours and attendance, the justification of absences and the possible alteration of test and exam dates. High performance coaches are entitled to specialist training.

F. Post Career Aid Measures

590. Another innovation was the introduction of a series of measures to assist high performance sportspersons after the end of their sports careers, in accordance with an orientation to that effect in the LBAFD. The Decree-Law accordingly introduces measures such as the temporary reintegration subsidy, of an amount equal to the level of the last grant received by sportspersons within the ambit of the Olympic project of which they were part.

591. At the end of their careers, high performance sportspersons are entitled to a voluntary social insurance, which is paid for by the IDP, IP, subject to certain legal limits. There is a tax benefit for those who hire high performance sports persons, such contracts are treated, for Social Security contribution purposes, as contracts made with a young person seeking first employment, provided that the requirements are complied with and the contract is of indefinite duration. High performance sportspersons are also granted special conditions in access to public recruitment procedures and in access to higher education.

Chapter 2. Private Regulation

§1. Sports Federations

592. Sports federations are defined in the LBAFD as juristic persons formed as non-profit associations, whose members are clubs or sports companies, regional associations, professional leagues, if any, sportspersons, judges and referees, and other entities that promote, compete in, or contribute to the development of the sport in question and comply with all of the prerequisites for the grant of sports public utility status, and have the following general objects enshrined in their bylaws:

(a) to promote, regulate and govern the practice of a sport, or a group of similar or associated sports, at national level;
(b) to represent the interests of their members in dealings with the Public Administration;
(c) to represent their sport, or group of similar or associated sports, in international sports organizations and to ensure the participation of national teams in competitions.

593. It is noteworthy that the law makes the existence of a federation subject to the prior grant of EUPD, which is granted by order of the member of the Government responsible for sport. Therefore, according to the legal definition of a sports federation it is prima facie not possible to create a sports federation, which is a private organization, without the involvement of the public authorities, exactly because with the grant of EUPD, a federation becomes a hybrid public/private organization *ab initio*.

594. There is a principle of independence in the law in order to ensure that sports federations are independent of the State, political parties and religious institutions. Sports federations are civilly liable to third parties for the acts and omissions of their officers, employees, and the legal or auxiliary representatives, on the same terms as a principal is liable for the acts or omissions of its agents. The principle of the publication of decisions also applies so that federations are obliged to publish their decisions via the publication of all information regarding their activities on their internet pages, in accordance with the personal data protection provisions, i.e., with regard to the decisions of its disciplinary and dispute resolution organs.

595. Sports federations can be of two types, i.e., single or multisport federations. Single sport federations are federations whose members are involved in a single sport, which may include various events or a group of similar or associated sports. Multisport federations are federations, which are involved in various different sports, in specific social areas, e.g., within the ambit of sport for the handicapped and sport within the educational system. Federations also have a duty to organize national teams and to award national or regional sports titles. This duty cannot be delegated.

I. National Sport Federations

596. Sports federations are juristic persons formed as non-profit associations, whose members are clubs or sports companies, regional associations, professional leagues, if any, sportspersons, umpires and referees, and other entities that promote, compete in, or contribute to the development of the sport in question and comply with all of the following requirements:

(1) They have, *inter alia*, the following general objects in their bylaws:

- (i) Promote, regulate and govern the practice of a sport, or a group of similar or associated sports, at national level.
- (ii) Representation the interests of their members in dealings with the Public Administration.
- (iii) Representation of its sport, or group of similar or associated sports, in international sports organisations and responsibility for the participation of national teams in competitions.

(2) They obtain sports public utility status,[112] for which they must first have obtained ordinary public utility status.[113]

597. Federations can be single sport federations or multi-sport federations; single sport federations are federations whose members are persons or bodies are involved in the practice of the same sport, including the various disciplines comprised therein, or a number of similar or related sports; multi-sport federations are those dedicated to the practice of different sports, in specific areas of social organisation, i.e. sport for the handicapped and sport in the education system.[114]

598. Sports federations have the following rights in addition to their other legal rights:

- (i) The right to participate in the definition of national sports policy.
- (ii) The right to representation on the National Sports Council.
- (iii) The right to the revenue allocated to them by law.
- (iv) The right to the recognition of the teams and national representations organised by them.
- (v) The right to participate in the international organisations that govern the sport.
- (vi) The right to use Portuguese national symbols.
- (vii) The right to make regulations governing competitors in the sport.
- (viii) The right to award national titles.
- (ix) The right to take disciplinary measures with regard to the sports agents under its auspices.

112. Cf. Art. 15 of the BLPSA and Art. 2 of the LFSF.
113. Cf. Art. 20, no. 1 of the BLPSA.
114. Cf. Art. 15 of the BLPSA and Art. 3 of the LFSF.

(x) The right to use the designation 'sports public utility' or 'UPD' following the federation's name.[115]

(xi) The right to all of the rights that derive from the prosecution of the federation's objects and the rights attributed to them by their members in their bylaws.[116]

599. Sports federations are also required, without prejudice to their other obligations, to comply with the objectives to develop and spread sports activities, to ensure their internal representativity and democracy, particularly via the limitation of terms of office, and to ensure that they are managed fairly and properly.[117]

600. Sports public utility status grants a sports federation the exclusive authority to exercise the rule-making, disciplinary and other public powers, with regard to a sport or series of sports and entitles it to the rights and subject to the obligations provided in the law.[118]

601. Sports public utility status is granted for a four-year period, which coincides with the Olympic cycle, to a single juristic person for each sport or group of similar sports, which has public utility status and also complied with the requirements stipulated in the LFSF and demonstrates that it has relevant national sporting interest and intends to adopt the following objectives:

(i) To promote, regulate and direct the practice of a sport or group of similar or associated sports, at national level.

(ii) Representation of the interests of their members in dealings with the Public Administration.

(iii) Representation of its sport, or group of similar or associated sports, in international sports organisations and to ensure the participation of national teams in competitions.[119]

602. If an application for sports public utility status is made after the beginning of the first year in the Olympic cycle, grant of the status is deemed to be made until the end of that Olympic cycle.[120]

603. For the purposes of the grant of sports public utility status, organisations that belong to an international federation for a sport that is included in the programme of the Olympic or Paralympic Games and which comply with the following criteria are deemed to be of relevant national sporting interest:

115. Cf. Art. 13, no. 1 of the LFSF.
116. Cf. Art. 19, no. 1 of the BLPSA and Art. 13, no. 3 of the LFSF. Paragraph e) has been amended by Art. 2 of Decree-Law no. 93/2014, of 23 June – Effects the first amendment of Decree-Law no. 248-B/2008, of 31 December, which introduced the legal framework governing sports federations and the conditions governing the grant of sports public utility status.
117. Cf. Art. 13, no. 3 of the LFSF.
118. Cf. Art. 10 of the LFSF.
119. Cf. Art. 15, no. 1 and Art. 2 (iii) of the LFSF.
120. Cf. Art. 15, no. 2 of the LFSF, as amended by Art. 2 of Decree-Law no. 93/2014, of 23 June.

(a) They have a sufficient national presence and prove that they have a national membership of 500, or more, sportspersons, who are sufficiently scattered throughout Portugal.
(b) Their sports activity contributes to the sports development of Portugal, or of one of its regions, via the organisation of competitions, sport events or demonstrations that are likely to promote the image of Portugal internationally.[121]

604. Sports public utility status may be suspended[122] or cancelled,[123] and must be renewed on a four-yearly basis.[124]

605. Sports public utility status can be suspended by a detailed order of the member of the Government responsible for Sport in the following circumstances:

(a) Acts or omissions in the exercise of the public powers conferred by sports public utility status that amount to serious illegalities or irregularities, or reiterated violation of the rules in the decree-law.
(b) Failure to comply with the anti-doping obligations in sport legislation and the legislation regarding the fight against violence, corruption, racism and xenophobia.
(c) Failure to comply with tax obligations or to make social security payments.
(d) Violation of contractual obligations to the State pursuant to programme contracts.
(e) Other circumstances expressly provided in the law.[125]

606. The suspension of sport public utility status may have one or more of the following consequences as is fixed in the said detailed order of the member of the Government responsible for sport:

(a) Suspension of aid pursuant to one or more programme contracts.
(b) Suspension of other aid in the form of technical, material or human resources.
(c) Banning from new programme contracts with the State while the suspension is in force.
(d) Banning from benefitting from declarations of public utility for the expropriation of property, or rights inherent therein, which are necessary for their purposes.
(e) Suspension of applications for any tax benefits pursuant to the Tax Benefits Statute.
(f) Banning of the governing bodies of sports federations from the exercise of public powers for a fixed period.

---

121. Cf. Art. 19, paras a) and b) of the LFSF, as amended by Art. 2 of Decree-Law no. 93/2014, of 23 June.
122. Cf. Art. 21 of the LFSF.
123. Cf. Art. 23 of the LFSF.
124. Cf. Art. 24 of the LFSF.
125. Cf. Art. 21 of the LFSF.

(g) The results of the events and competitions organised by sport federations and professional leagues are disregarded for the purposes of sport and the regulations, while the suspension is in force.

607. Sports public utility status ceases:

(a) On the extinction of the sports federation.
(b) When cancelled.
(c) At the end of the term for which it is granted, if not renewed.

608. Sports public utility status is cancelled by a detailed order of the member of the Government responsible for Sport in the following circumstances:

(a) When the legal prerequisites for the grant of the status no longer exist.
(b) At the end of the status suspension period, if the sports federation has failed to remedy the reasons that gave rise to the said suspension [the federation in question is subject to the consequences of the suspension of its sports public utility status until the final decision in the cancellation procedure.]

609. Sports federations that wish to apply for the renewal of their sports public utility status must do so during the year in which the summer Olympic Games take place; Applicants' sports public utility status is deemed to be renewed for a further four years, if no decision is made in response to the application within 90 days of the submission thereof.

610. Sports federations must have at least the following statutory bodies in their organisational structure:

(i) General meeting.
(ii) President.
(iii) Board of management.
(iv) Supervisory board.
(v) Disciplinary council.
(vi) Judicial committee.
(vii) Refereeing council.[126]

611. Persons, who are of full age and are not subject to any disqualifying factor, who are not indebted to the federation in question, who have not been punished for any criminal, administrative or disciplinary offence involving violence, doping, corruption, racism and xenophobia, for up to five years after completion of the sentence/penalty, who have not been punished for crimes committed in the exercise of management duties in sports federations, or for crimes against the property of the

126. Cf. Art. 32 of the LFSF.

said sports federations, for up to five after completion of the sentence/penalty, unless some other penalty has been imposed by a judicial decision.[127]

612. The following are incompatible with membership of a federation governing body:

(i) Holding of another office in the same federation.
(ii) Direct or indirect involvement in contracts with the federation in question.
(iii) In the case of governing bodies of federations or professional leagues, occupation in the said organisation of the position of club or association director, referee, umpire or coach in an active role.[128]

613. The terms of office of members of the governing bodies of sports federations and the professional leagues or territorial associations of clubs that belong to them, is four years, which generally coincides with the Olympic cycle.[129]

614. National or regional sports titles are awarded by the existing federations and only they may organise national teams,[130] membership of national teams organised by a sports federation is restricted to Portuguese nationals.[131]

615. The form that must be submitted for the purpose of applications for sports public utility status can be found in a Statutory Instrument,[132] which also stipulates the documents that must be submitted with such applications.[133]

616. Sports federations must submit a plan containing the following information to the PISY annually in order to benefit from public funding of support for high performance sport:

(i) A statement of the sports results that justify the inclusion of its sportspersons in the register of high performance sportspersons.
(ii) The sports curriculum of each sportsperson, containing the main results and classifications obtained in national and international competitions and also their position in the ranking of the sport in question, in the case of individual sports, and the data that identifies and describes high performance sportspersons, in terms of sport and their educational and occupational status.
(iii) Proof of the physical aptitude of the sportpersons and statements of the dates of the medical examinations to be conducted by the federation's medical services during the year.

127. Cf. Art. 48 of the LFSF.
128. Cf. Art. 49 of the LFSF.
129. Cf. Art. 50, no. 1 of the LFSF.
130. Cf. Art. 16, no. 1 of the BLPSA.
131. Cf. Art. 63, no. 1 of the LFSF.
132. Cf. Art. 16, no. 2 of the LFSF and Art. 2 of Statutory Instrument no. 345/2012, of 29 October, and the Annexe thereof – Approves the application form for use in applications for sports public utility status.
133. Cf. Art. 3 of Statutory Instrument no. 345/2012, of 29 October.

(iv) International technical rules and regulations of the sport in question on which the sportspersons' classification as high performance sportpersons is based.
(v) A statement of the support measures available for sports clubs that include high performance sportspersons.
(vi) The measures to be taken by the federation with regard to high performance sport.
(vii) Specification of the sport objectives to be achieved both overall and with regard to each of the measures included in the plan.
(viii) The financial, technical or human resources that are considered to be necessary for the high performance development programmes for the sport in question.
(ix) Funding sources and distribution thereof detailed according to source.[134]

617. POCFAAC (the accounting plan for Sports Federations Associations and Groups of Clubs) applies to federations,[135] their accounts must be organised in accordance with the accounting plan provided therein, which must be appropriate in terms of the economic and financial management requirements of sports federations, associations and groups of clubs and permit permanent budgetary control, and easy checking that accounting entries accurately reflect assets values.[136]

A. *Professional Leagues*

618. Single sport federations in which professional competitions, as defined by the law, take place, belong to a professional league, in the form of a non-profit organisation, with a legal personality and administrative, technical and financial autonomy.[137]

619. Clubs and sport companies that compete in professional competitions[138] must belong to professional leagues, which may also include representatives of other sports actors, in accordance with the law and their bylaws.[139]

620. Professional leagues are required to exercise the powers and duties with regard to organisation, management, discipline and refereeing in accordance with the law.

621. If, after having been given express notice to desist, a professional league continues not to comply with an obligation that involves, or could involve, the suspension of the sports public utility status of the corresponding federation, it must give notice of the said fact to the member of the Government responsible for sport,

134. Cf. Art. 11 of Decree-Law no. 345/2012, of 1 October.
135. Cf. Art. 2, no. 1 of Decree-Law 74/98, of 27 March.
136. Cf. Art. 2, no. 2 of Decree-Law 74/98, of 27 March.
137. Cf. Art. 20, no. 1 of the BLPSA.
138. Cf. Art. 27, no. 4 of the LFSF, as amended by Art. 2 of Decree-Law no. 93/2014, of 23 June.
139. Cf. Art. 22, nos 2, 3 and 4 of the BLPSA.

who may, having consulted the NSC, order the termination of the delegation of the federation's powers and duties to the league and the temporary exercise thereof by the sports federation. This termination of the delegation of powers may be lifted on the basis of the disappearance of the circumstances that were the grounds therefore.[140]

622. The relationship between the sports federation and the corresponding professional league is governed by a contract between them in accordance with the law,[141] which is valid for four sports seasons,[142] in which the number of clubs that will participate in the professional sports competition, the rules governing access between professional and non-professional competitions, the organisation of the activity of national teams and support for non-professional sport[143] are agreed, inter alia.

623. The competitions managed by the professional league are the highest level of the sports competitions that take place within the ambit of the corresponding federation.[144]

624. The professional league is responsible for the drafting and approval of the regulations governing its competitions, refereeing, and discipline, which must be submitted to the general meeting of the federation to which it belongs, in accordance with the law.[145]

625. Members of the governing bodies of professional leagues serve a four-year term of office, which generally coincides with the Olympic cycle.[146]

II. Olympic Committee of Portugal

A. *Introduction*

626. The strength and dynamism of the modern Olympic movement lays in the combined action of the various international sports federations. The role and vigour of the international sports federations has been of fundamental importance to the construction of the modern Olympic movement.

627. The POC is part of the Olympic Movement and is governed by its Statutes and regulations, and also by the principles and rules of the Olympic Charter (among other principles of the IOC), and by the WADA anti-doping code. The POC is an institution in the nature of an association, which has sports public utility status, and

140. Cf. Art. 27, no. 2 of the LFSF, as amended by Art. 2 of Decree-Law no. 93/2014, of 23 June.
141. Cf. Art. 23, no. 1 of the BLPSA.
142. Cf. Art. 28, no. 1 of the LFSF.
143. Cf. Art. 23, no. 2 of the BLPSA and Art. 28, no. 2 of the LFSF.
144. Cf. Art. 28, no. 3 of the LFSF.
145. Cf. Art. 24 of the BLPSA and Art. 29 of the LFSF.
146. Cf. Art. 50, no. 1 of the LFSF.

was created in accordance with the rules laid down by the IOC and is independent of the Government. Among its duties and other powers, the POC represents the national sports federations in dealings with the Portuguese government and, together with them, co-ordinates all Olympic preparation and representation programmes.

628. Created in 1909, the Portuguese Olympic Committee, subsequently renamed the Olympic Committee of Portugal, has increasingly become subject to a legislative framework. Gradually, the POC became consolidated as the body at the apex of the Portuguese sports association movement, so that even fundamental laws were unable to remain immune to this reality. In this way, the three Basic Laws, which still today define the bases of Portuguese sport, focussed on the POC, with noteworthy systematic and even substantive options.

629. Accordingly, in 1990, the OCP was included in the LBSD, in Chapter III thereof, which concerns *Sports Organisations*. The chapter is divided into two sections: section I, with regard to the *Sports Associations Movement* – which primarily includes provisions regarding *sports clubs, sports federations, sports dispute resolution* and *national teams*, and section II, which solely concerns what was then still called the Portuguese Olympic Committee, which is also the title of the Section. The only provision in the section is contained in Article 28, under the title of *legal framework*, and had the following text:

1. The Portuguese Olympic Committee is granted the powers that arise from the International Olympic Charter, i.e. the power to organise the Portuguese team in the Olympic Games and the power to authorise the holding of sports events for Olympic purposes.
2. Only the Portuguese Olympic Committee shall be entitled to use the Olympic symbols in Portugal.
3. Special regulations shall ensure the rights referred to in the preceding numbers and shall define the specific State aid to be granted in this context and the way in which the various private and public sector organisations active in the area of sport shall interact, within the ambit of the preparation for and participation in the Olympic Games.

630. According to José Ribeiro e Castro,[147] the mentor of the provision:

> [the] article contains the principles in the International Olympic Charter with regard to the Portuguese Olympic Committee and recognised the rights considered to be suitable for inclusion in a Basic Law (…) without prejudice to other rights to be introduced by regulation. The enshrinement of the OCP at such a high legislative level and the devotion to it of an entire chapter – Section II of Chapter III, are significant and certainly no accident. This fact means that without having to alter the structure of the law, the said article or Section

147. José Ribeiro e Castro. Lei de Bases do Sistema Desportivo, anotada e comentada, Lisbon, Ministry of Education, 1990.

II can be modified or developed in the future, as the powers and duties of the Portuguese Olympic Committee grow, evolve and widen.

631. In general terms, we have only praise for the inclusion of the POC in the Basic Law of Sport. For, from this inclusion results the recognition and inclusion of the highest level of the Portuguese associations movement in a fundamental law. It should particularly be noted that the law refers the question of the legal nature, powers and duties of the POC to the OC,[148] although it 'imported' some of them by way of example, perhaps because it deemed them to be the most relevant; i.e., *to organise the Portuguese team at the Olympic games and to authorise the holding of sports events for Olympic purposes.*

632. No. 2 of the law refers to the exclusive right of the POC to use the Olympic symbols in Portugal, which right, eight years earlier, in 1982, had been the sole subject matter of a decree-law, which is referred to further below, as also stated below that decree-law was repealed in 2012. No. 3 of the law provides that the State is required to grant specific aid to the POC and in line with no. 1 stipulates that the said funds are to be used for, or primarily for: *the preparation for and participation in the Olympic Games.* Six years later, the title of section II and numbers 1 and 2 were amended by no. 2 of Article 2 of Law no. 19/96, of 25 June, which revised the Basic Law of the Sports System, as follows: All references to the *Portuguese Olympic Committee* shall be amended to read the *Olympic Committee of Portugal.*

633. The LBD made some amendments to the provision regarding the POC, which coincidentally retained the same numbering. The text of Article 28, entitled the Olympic Committee of Portugal was as follows:

1. The Olympic Committee of Portugal is a non-profit association, with a legal personality, which is governed by its bylaws and regulations, in accordance with the law and the principles and rules in the International Olympic Charter.
2. The Olympic Committee of Portugal has the exclusive right to form, organise and manage the Portuguese team at the Olympic Games and in the multisport competitions sponsored by the International Olympic Committee, by collaborating in the preparation and promotion thereof and in the practice of the sports comprised in the said competitions.
3. The Olympic Committee of Portugal shall keep an up-to-date record of Portuguese Olympic Athletes.
4. The Olympic Committee of Portugal is entitled to the exclusive use, in Portugal, of the Olympic emblems, logo, anthems and symbols.
5. Special regulations ensure the rights referred to in the preceding numbers and define the specific State aid to be granted in this context and the way in which the various private and public sector organisations active in the

148. The Portuguese Communist Party proposed an alternative solution: in Art. 34 of Draft Bill no. 336/V of the Basic Law of Physical Culture and Sport Law, under the title Portuguese Olympic Committee, the POC was stated expressly to be a not-for-profit organization.

area of sport interact, within the ambit of the preparation for and participation in the Olympic Games.

634. We shall now consider this summarily, starting with the systematic inclusion of the provision in the structure of the law: the POC was included in section II entitled *Private Organisation of Sport*, with two subsections: the first of which is dedicated to the *Sports Associations Movement* while the second concerns the *Non-federated Organisation of Sport*. This is a change in relation to the 1990 model: for while the POC had previously been dealt with separately from the Associations Movement, it was now a part of the legal and programmatic framework applicable to it. So far as the provision itself is concerned, no. 1 introduces an innovation by defining the legal nature of the POC.

635. José Manuel Meirim[149] disagreed with this legislative technique, and stated as follows: *Indeed we also do not agree with the LBD when it allows itself to define the Olympic Committee of Portugal and to indicate is power, duties and missions. We are still of the view that such matters can only be determined by the Olympic Committee of Portugal.* (Our underling).

636. With all due respect, we disagree with the said author for the reasons briefly stated below:

(a) while it is true that the OC makes no provision as to the legal nature of the National Olympic Committees – a matter to which we give some attention in this study – the truth is that the POC, which has existed for almost 100 years, has always been a non-profit entity and we think it very unlikely that this will ever change. If the non-profit nature of the OCP were to change, the alteration of the said provision would certainly meet with the unanimous approval of the Assembly of the Republic;
(b) the definition of the legal nature of a National Olympic Committee in a state law dealing with sport is not exclusive to Portugal. It also occurs in countries, whose legislation is frequently praised and/or adapted and included in the Portuguese legal system, such as Spain and Brazil;[150]
(c) it is untrue that it is solely for the POC to define its own powers, duties and mission. It suffices to read Rule 28 of the OC, which is entitled *The Mission and*

149. José Manuel Meirim. *Lei de Bases do Desporto Anotada*, 1st edition, Coimbra, Coimbra Editora, 2005, p. 66.

150. In Spain, Art. 48 of the Sport Law – Law 10/1990, of 15 October – provides as follows: The Spanish Olympic Committee is a not-for-profit association, with legal personality, the object of which is the development of the Olympic movement and the dissemination of Olympic ideals. The Spanish Olympic Committee is granted public utility status in order to pursue the said objects. In Brazil, Art. 15 of Law no. 9.615, of 24 Mar. 1998, which introduced general legal provisions regarding sport and introduces other measures, provides as follows: The Brazilian Olympic Committee – COB, a private law organization, shall represent the country at Olympic, Pan-American and other events of similar status and in the international Olympic movements, and promote the Olympic movement in Brazil in accordance with the provisions of the Federal Constitution and the provisions of the bylaws and regulations of the International Olympic Committee and the Olympic Charter. (Emphasis added).

role of the National Olympic Committees, with which the POC is required to comply by virtue of no. 2.2 thereof, in order to understand that the essence of the mission, powers and duties of the POC is dictated by the IOC, via the OC approved by the corresponding Session. There is however nothing to prevent a state law from referring to the objects of a National Olympic Committee. We again refer to the Spanish and Brazilian legislation and also to the French and Italian legislation[151] by way of example.

637. In no. 1 the law is also innovative when it does not limit the activity of the POC to strict compliance with the OC, while also providing that it must necessarily comply with the law, which must naturally be construed in the broadest sense, as the legislative framework, which must shape and guide the provisions to be included in the bylaws and regulations of the POC, which is referred to for the first time in a Basic Law.

638. To complete the reference to no. 1, it is noted that, for the first time, the legislation refers to the *principles to be found* in the OC. We consider that this reference is vital, although we would have preferred the text in Article 28 of Draft Law no. 80/IX, which was deleted, which made specific reference to the POC's mission to develop and protect the Olympic movement in Portugal and to disseminate the *fundamental principles of Olympism in the area of sport.* This would, in our view, be the best way to link the mission and role of the POC with the OC. As is still the case of the OC currently in force, in 2004, when the LBD was published, no. 1 of Rule 28 of the OC provided that the mission of the National Olympic Committees is to promote and protect the Olympic Movement in their respective countries and, in no. 2, it prioritized the promotion of the fundamental Olympic principles and values, among the other roles of the National Olympic Committees. Furthermore: in Article 6 of its bylaws regarding Objects, the POC enshrines the following object in the first of fifteen paragraphs: *to disseminate and defend the Olympic Movement and sport in general, in accordance with the Olympic Charter.*

639. Otherwise, the new no. 2 is in similar terms to the former no. 1 at the end of Article 28 of the LBSD, while the new no. 5 is practically a copy of the former no. 3 of the said law.

151. See some parts of the current version of Art. 19 of Law no. 84-610 of 16 Jul. 1984, regarding the organization and promotion of physical and sports activities: '(…) II. The French Olympic and Sport Committee initiates and participates in activities of common interest on behalf of the federations or together with them (…) and is associated with the promotion of the various sports in programmes of audiovisual communications companies (…) It can delegate part of its mission to decentralised bodies, which it establishes (…) it is charged with the resolution of disputes between members, sports groups and sports federations (…)'. In Italy, para. 1 of Art. 1 of Decree Law 'Riordino del Comitato Olimpico Nazionale Italiano – CONI' of 23 Jul. 1999, N. 242, the *Italian National Olympic Committee hereinafter referred to as CONI is a public law juristic person (…).* Article 2, as amended by Legislative Decree of 8 Jan. 2004, no. 15, assigns missions to the IOC within the ambit of the promotion of national sport, particularly with regard to the Olympic Games and the fight against doping, violence and discrimination in sport.

640. In as far as no. 3 is concerned, which concerns the updating of a record of Portuguese Olympic athletes, we consider that the law should have used the expression sportspersons and that the new no. 4, which unlike the previous law, does not limit the exclusive right of the POC to the use the Olympic symbols but also includes other Olympic assets, which the OC enshrines as emblems, symbol and anthem.

641. Another novelty in the LBD could be found in Article 26, under the heading of the *Paralympic Committee of Portugal*, which did not then existed but was in the process of being formed. The text of the said provision was as follows:

> The provisions of the preceding article with regard to handicapped sportspersons and the Paralympic Games shall apply to the Portuguese Paralympic Committee, with the necessary adaptations.

642. This law also necessarily dealt specifically with Olympic and Paralympic phenomena in Chapter III which was entitled 'Sports Associations Movement', which comprised three sections: Section I concerns *Olympic Organisation*; section II concerns the *Sports Federations* and section III concerns *sports clubs and companies*.

643. The text of Article 12, which entitled the *Olympic Committee of Portugal*, is as follows:

1. The Olympic Committee of Portugal is a non-profit association, with a legal personality, which is governed by its bylaws and regulations, in accordance with the law and the International Olympic Charter.
2. The Olympic Committee of Portugal has the exclusive right to form, organise and manage the Portuguese team at the Olympic Games and in the other sports competitions organised under the auspices of the International Olympic Committee, by collaborating in the preparation thereof and in the practice of the sports comprised in the said competitions.
3. The Olympic Committee of Portugal shall keep an up-to-date record of Portuguese Olympic athletes.
4. According to the law, only the Olympic Committee of Portugal is entitled to use the Olympic symbols in Portugal.

644. There are three noteworthy matters in this text, i.e.:

(a) first, the absence of any innovation in relation to the previous law. The only differences with the previous law are minor drafting changes;
(b) the second matter is the return to the provisions of the 1990 law, the LBSD, by referring only to Olympic symbols. We have already stated our disagreement with this, which may be a consequence of a wish not to eliminate the terminology used in Decree-Law no. 1/82, of 4 January, to which we refer to below;

(c) the third aspect is the non-inclusion of a legal framework that was enshrined in the previous laws. As José Manuel Meirim[152] states, *in the LBSD and the LBD, there was a provision, which envisaged regulations that defined the state aid to be granted with regard to participation in the Olympic Games, and with regard to the ways in which the said aid would be provided, within the ambit of the preparations for the Olympic Games and the collaboration between the various public and private organisations involved in the area of sport.*

645. It is still too early to be able to understand the real reasons for this option. We are reluctant to believe that the Government wished to cease the transfer of funds to the POC, i.e., by putting an end to the current system, which is based on programme contracts.

646. Article 13 concerned the *Paralympic Committee of Portugal* and provided as follows: *The provisions of the preceding article shall apply, with the necessary adaptations, to the Paralympic Committee of Portugal, with regard to handicapped sportspersons and the corresponding international sports competitions.*

647. The following differences in relation to the corresponding provisions in the LBD should be noted: the references to Paralympic now read Paralympic; and the reference to *necessary adaptations* now reads *required adaptations*, and the *corresponding international sports competitions* now reads as merely the *Paralympic Games*. Nothing of any great significance therefore.

648. There are several items of ordinary legislation that affect the activity of the POC, e.g.:

(a) Decree-Law no. 155/2012, of 18 July, which includes provisions intended to protect Olympic symbols and enshrines *(…) measures that prohibit the generalised use of the Olympic symbols in order to prevent their degradation via the indiscriminate use thereof and which reserves the use thereof to the authorities.*
(b) Within the ambit of the legal framework governing sports federations, i.e., the RJFD.
(c) In the area of financial and fiscal aid, paragraph 1 of Statutory Instrument no. 738/91, of 1 August and paragraph a) of no. 1 of Article 3 of Decree-Law no. 273/2009, of 1 October – the legal framework applicable to sports development programme contracts.
(d) Statutory Instrument no. 393/97, of 17 June grants prizes to handicapped citizens, who come in the first three places in events at the Paralympic Games or in the European or World Championships or the Boccia World Cup. Statutory Instrument no. 211/98, of 3 April, fixes the prizes to be awarded to sportspersons in sports included in the Olympic programme, who come in the first three

152. José Manuel Meirim, *Lei de Bases da Actividade Física e do Desporto: Estudos, Notas e Comentários*, 1st edition. Coimbra, Coimbra Editora, 2007, p. 158–159.

places in the Olympic Games, the European and World Championships, in absolute terms.[153]

(e) The CIRS.
(f) In the area of the exercise of the duties of a sports manager, Article 4 of Decree-Law no. 267/95, of 18 October.
(g) So far as POC's membership of the various organisms within the ambit of the sports public administration is concerned, the POC is a member of the National Sports Council, an eminently consultative body, which is governed by Decree-Law no. 315/2007, of 18 September.

649. In addition to the said legislation, the POC is governed by its bylaws (which are drafted in accordance with the principles in the Olympic Charter), by its General Regulations and by the Civil Code,[154] i.e., the provisions applicable to associations.

650. Its objects are to participate at national level, in actions in favour of peace, the promotion of women in sport, to support and encourage the promotion of sports ethics, the fight against doping in sport and to act responsibly in relation to and create an awareness of environmental problems. Its primary object and task is obligatory participation in the Olympic Games and for this it has the exclusive duty to organize and manage the national team that represents Portugal at the Games. As

153. The purpose of these two statutory instruments is primarily to register a further recognition by the legislature of the value of the contribution that the OCP can make. We refer to Statutory Instrument no. 211/98, of 3 April, that fixes the value of the prizes to be awarded to sportspersons, in sports included in the Olympic programme, who come in the first three places in the Olympic Games, the European and World Championships, in absolute terms, which provides as follows: '*the member of the Government responsible for sport may authorise that the World or European Championships of sports and events that are not included in the Olympic programme, be supported on the basis of a detailed proposal by the corresponding federation and a favourable opinion of the Olympic Committee of Portugal and the Portuguese Sports Confederation*'. Given the importance of the topic it is important to note the differences between the amounts awarded pursuant to the first statutory instrument, which are less than those awarded by the second, even though the Constitutional Court has held that Statutory Instrument no. 393/97, of 17 June, is constitutional, i.e., that it does not violate the principle of equality. In an attempt to systematize and summarize the arguments employed by the Constitutional Court in its decision, i.e., Judgment no. 486/03, of 21 Oct. 2003, in case no. 182/2000 – we note first that the Constitutional Court justified the difference between the amount of the prizes on the basis of the differing social and cultural relevance of obtaining the highest rankings in the games and championships in question, which the State cannot ignore, given Portugal's differing international projection. Going into greater detail, the Constitutional Court held as follows: (i) It is difficult to compare the differing universes and realities of the Olympic Games, World and European Championships, on the one hand, and Paralympic Games, World and European Championships for the Disabled and the Boccia World Cup, on the other hand, objectively; (ii) The two classes of event differ and have differing universes of competitors and the events in question are also organised differently (in one case, the sports events are open to all, while, in the other, they are limited to disabled players and athletes); (iii) There is an obvious difference between the public profile of these two types of events, which involve inherent differences in terms of the prestige and international projection of the country. Classification in one of the first places at the Olympic Games is certainly not the same thing as a similar ranking in the Paralympic Games.

154. We refer to Arts 157 et seq.

such, it is accordingly *jointly*[155] liable for the conduct of its members. It is responsible for the definition of the criteria for the selection of the athletes to be included in the Portuguese team at the Olympic Games and in all other competitions sponsored by the IOC.

651. According to the rules in the Olympic Charter, only one federation for each sport may become an ordinary member of the POC. Federations initially become a provisional member and become a full member once they are recognized by the corresponding international federation, as the representative of the sport in Portugal. The POC accordingly has the power to consider the possibility and the necessary requirements for the inclusion of new sports that want to members of the POC and the feasibility of their recognition by the IOC.

B. *Funding*

652. As a public institution independent of the Government, the POC must ensure the necessary funding resources via revenue not prohibited by the Olympic Charter. The funding is provided via the collection of membership fees from its members, receipt of subsidies from the State, or other private or public entities, revenue from the making of advertising or sponsorship agreements, sales of marketing products and subsidies from the IOC, *inter alia.* The POC is authorized to issue commemorative coins and stamps and to accept inheritances and legacies.

653. According to the amount of the revenue generated by its activities, the POC gives annual subsidies to the sports federations and, according to their specific requirements, supports the creation of new sports facilities, contributes to funds for sports activities at school and university level, in addition to the funding of the Mission that takes part in the Olympic Games.

C. *Governing Bodies*

1. Plenary Meeting

654. The Plenary Meeting is the supreme organ of the POC and is made up of ordinary and extraordinary members and is chaired, as of right, by the Chairman of the POC. The ordinary members of the POC are the national sports federations, or equivalent bodies, which are recognized by the IOC, or which have sports public utility status. All athletes or former athletes, who represent, or have represented, Portugal at the Olympic Games are also ordinary members. The associations that

155. According to the general part of the Civil Code with regard to juristic persons, in Art. 165, associations are civilly liable for the acts or omissions of their representatives, agents or mandataries in the same terms as a principal is liable for the acts or omissions of his agent. Articles 500 et seq. governs the civil liability of principals. Cf. also the sub-chapter on the *civil liability* provisions in the chapter on *safety in sport.*

represent sport at school and university level are extraordinary members of the POC.

655. The Plenary Meeting is responsible for the drafting and defining of the major policies of the POC. It considers and votes on the annual budget, reports and accounts as well as the report and accounts of the Mission to the Olympic Games. It elects the members of the Executive Committee, approves the proposals of the Executive Committee and the Supervisory Board and is responsible for the admission of new members to the POC. It decides disciplinary matters directly or on appeal from the Executive Committee.

656. In questions related to the Olympic Games, only those federations, or equivalent entities, whose sports are included in the Olympic Programme, are entitled to vote. In other decisions and in the constitution of the Plenary Meeting, the sports federations are entitled to a number of votes that cannot be less than 2/3 of all votes.

2. Executive Committee

657. The Executive Committee comprises a chairperson, five vice-chairpersons, a secretary-general, treasurer, seven ordinary members, plus the Portuguese representative on the IOC, the Presidents of the Olympic Academy of Portugal and the Olympic Athletes Committee, all as of right. The Executive Committee is the organ that administers and manages the POC in accordance with the guidelines established by the Plenary Meeting.

658. The Executive Committee is responsible for the preparation of the annual budget, accounts and report to be submitted to the Plenary Meeting for approval. The Executive Committee can create such committees as it deems necessary in order to ensure the prosecution of the POC's objects. The Executive Committee has disciplinary powers in respect of POC members. An appeal lies from its decisions to the Plenary Meeting. The Executive Committee is also responsible for the drafting of the General Regulations of the POC and for the resolution of doubts and lacunae in the Bylaws and Regulations. Its decisions are subject to ratification by the Plenary Meeting.

3. Supervisory Board

659. The Supervisory Board is comprised by a chairman, a secretary and a reporter. It is the supervisory body *par excellance*. It is responsible for the supervision of the accounts and all the accounting documentation of the POC and of the Mission to the Olympic Games and issues an opinion with regard thereto prior to their submission to the Plenary Meeting for approval.

D. Dispute Resolution

660. The national sports federations, their representatives and any organizations that are members of the POC, and their representatives, together with natural persons, who are members of the POC, are subject to the internal disciplinary rules of the POC.

661. The Executive Committee has the power to impose the disciplinary sanctions of warning, rebuke and suspension, from which an appeal lies to the Plenary Meeting. The disciplinary sanction of expulsion is imposed by the Plenary Meeting on the basis of a proposal by the Executive Committee. Any of the said measures may be imposed by direct decision of the Plenary Meeting.

662. When the POC is an interested party in a dispute, it recognizes the CAS as an appeals jurisdiction with regard to sports and financial disputes.

E. The Exclusive Rights of POC

1. General Aspects

663. COP has the exclusive right to use the Olympic symbols (Olympic assets) in Portugal, in accordance with specific legislation:[156] POC therefore has the exclusive right to use Olympic or equivalent assets, independently of any registration, deposit or other formality, and also has the exclusive authority to authorise the holding of sport events in Portugal for Olympic purposes.[157]

664. The said exclusive right entitles POC to prevent third parties from using any identical or similar symbol in products or services in the context of any economic activity, which, as a consequence of the similarity of the symbols in question, could give rise to a risk of confusion or association with the Olympic or equivalent assets in the mind of the consumer, without its consent.[158]

665. The use of Olympic or equivalent assets for commercial, associative or sports purposes is prohibited in the absence of the express authorization in writing of POC, granted on the basis of a valid decision of POC. This prohibition includes the organization of sports and association events, commercial activities, the manufacture, supply, storage, transport, import or export, advertising or use of a product

156. Cf. Art. 12, no. 4 of the BLPSA and Decree-Law no. 155/2012, of 18 July – Establishes the legal framework for the legal protection of Olympic symbols and the mechanisms to combat any form of unlawful use of the benefits arising from the use thereof, and repeals Decree-Law no. 1/82, of 4 January.
157. Cf. Art. 3, no. 1 of Decree-Law no. 155/2012, of 18 July.
158. Cf. Art. 3, no. 2 of Decree-Law no. 155/2012, of 18 July.

that imitates or copies all or part of one or more Olympic, equivalent or similar assets.[159]

666. POC is represented in the Plenary Session of the NSC by its President,[160] by the president of the Olympic Athletes Committee[161] and by the president of the Portuguese Olympic Academy[162] – and on the NSC Permanent Committee, by its president.[163]

667. So far as doping is concerned, POC is one of the organisations to which ADoP is required to:

(i) Distribute the list of forbidden substances and methods.[164]
(ii) Nominate a medically qualified expert as a member of the National Anti-doping Council (NADC), with is an ADoP consultative body.[165]
(iii) Request the conduct of anti-doping measures.[166]

III. Portuguese Paralympic Committee

668. The legal provisions applicable to POC shall apply, with the necessary adaptations, to the Portuguese Paralympic Committee (PPC), with regard to handicapped sportspersons and the corresponding international sports competitions.[167]

669. The PPC plays the following role in anti-doping:

(i) It is one of the bodies to which ADoP must distribute the list of prohibited substances and methods.[168]
(iii) It nominates a medically qualified expert to be a member of the NADC.[169]
(iii) It may request the conduct of anti-doping measures.[170]

670. Preparation for and participation in international competitions by Portuguese national teams under the auspices of PPC have the benefit of specific support

159. Cf. Art. 3, no. 1 of Decree-Law no. 155/2012, of 18 July.
160. Cf. Art. 5 no. 1, para. e) of Decree-Law no. 266-A/2012, of 31 December, as amended by Decree-Law no. 153/2013, of 5 November.
161. Cf. Art. 5, para. k) of Decree-Law no. 266-A/2012, of 31 December, as amended by Decree-Law no. 153/2013, of 5th November.
162. Cf. Art. 5, para. m) of Decree-Law no. 266-A/2012, of 31 December, as amended by Decree-Law no. 153/2013, of 5th November.
163. Cf. Art. 6, no. 1, para. f) of Decree-Law no. 266-A/2012, as amended by Decree-Law no. 153/2013, of 5 November.
164. Cf. Art. 8, no. 2 of Law no. 38/2012, of 28 August.
165. Cf. Art. 27, no. 2, para. e) of Law no. 38/2012, of 28 August.
166. Cf. Art. 33, no. 2, para. b) of Law no. 38/2012, of 28 August.
167. Cf. Art. 13 of the BLPSA.
168. Cf. Art. 8, no. 2 of Law no. 38/2012, of 28 August.
169. Cf. Art. 27, no. 2, para. f) of Law no. 38/2012, of 28 August.
170. Cf. Art. 33, no. 2, para. b) of Law no. 38/2012, of 28 August.

measures,[171] on the basis of the public interest involved,[172] for sportspersons, their coaches, support staff and managers,[173] and can cover matters such as education rules;[174] temporary leave of absence from work;[175] use of infrastructures;[176] and medical support.[177] The PPC must give notice of all national teams or other representations under its auspices to the Instituto Nacional para a Reabilitação, I.P. (INR, I.P.).[178]

671. The PPC is represented in the Plenary Session of the NSC by its President and by the President of its Paralympic Athletes Committee,[179] and on the Permanent Committee by its President.[180]

672. CAS has a consultancy service, which is required to issue non-binding opinions regarding sport-related legal issues at the request of COP.[181]

673. *P*reparation for and participation in international competitions by Portuguese national teams under the auspices of COP have the benefit of specific support measures,[182] on the basis of the public interest involved,[183] for sportspersons, their coaches, support staff and managers,[184] and can cover matters such as education rules;[185] temporary leave of absence from work;[186] use of infrastructures;[187] and medical support.[188]

674. COP must be consulted with regard to applications to the member of the Government responsible for sport, by sports federations, for sports public utility status. COP.[189] COP must issue its opinion within thirty days of receipt of the corresponding request.[190]

---

171. According to the provisions of Decree-Law no. 45/2013, of 5 April. Cf. Art. 2, paras d) and f) particularly.
172. Cf. Art. 3 of Decree-Law no. 45/2013, of 5.
173. Cf. Art. 2, para. e), Arts 13 and 15 of Decree-Law no. 45/2013, of 5 April.
174. Cf. Arts 5 to 10 of Decree-Law no. 45/2013, of 5 April.
175. Cf. Arts 11 and 12 of Decree-Law no. 45/2013, of 5 April.
176. Cf. Art. 14 of Decree-Law no. 45/2013, of 5 April.
177. Cf. Art. 15 of Decree-Law no. 45/2013, of 5 April.
178. Cf. Art. 4, no. 3 of Decree-Law no. 45/2012, of 5 April.
179. Cf. Art. 5, no. 1, para. l) of Decree-Law no. 266-A/2012, as amended by Decree-Law no. 153/2013, of 5 November.
180. Cf. Art. 6, no. 1, para. g) of Decree-Law no. 266-A/2012, as amended by Decree-Law no. 153/2013, of 5 November.
181. Cf. Art. 33, no. 1 of the CAS Law, which is an annexe to Law no. 74/2013, of 6 September.
182. According to the provisions of Decree-Law no. 45/2013, of 5 de Abril – Establishes the specific aid measures with regard to the preparation and international participation of national teams and other national sports representation – Cf. particularly, Art. 3 and Art. 2, paras d) and e).
183. Cf. Art. 3 of Decree-Law no. 45/2013, of 5 April.
184. Cf. Art. 2, para. e), Arts 13 and 15 of Decree-Law no. 45/2013, of 5 April.
185. Cf. Arts 5 to 10 of Decree-Law no. 45/2013, of 5th April.
186. Cf. Arts 11 and 12 of Decree-Law no. 45/2013, of 5 April.
187. Cf. Art. 14 of Decree-Law no. 45/2013, of 5 April.
188. Cf. Art. 15 of Decree-Law no. 45/2013, of 5 April.
189. Cf. Art. 17, no. 1 of the LFSF.
190. Cf. Art. 17, no. 2 of the LFSF.

675. So far as CAS is concerned:

(i) COP is responsible for the establishment and operation of CAS,[191] and the law provides that the court is based at COP.[192]
(ii) Two of the eleven members of the Sports Arbitration Council are nominated by COP and must be jurists of recognized merit and good standing, with experience in the area of sport.[193]
(iii) The plan for the creation of the list of CAS arbitrators provides that the Executive Committee of COP submits the names of five arbitrators to the Arbitration Council[194] and that the Olympic Athletes Committee submits two names for the same purpose.[195]
(iv) CAS has a consultancy service, which is required to issue non-binding opinions regarding sport-related legal issues at the request of COP.[196]

IV. The Portuguese Sports Confederation

676. Unlike the previous legal framework for sport, the PSC – which is a private law juristic person in the nature of an association, the function of which is to combine the sports federations into a single organisation and to act as a tool for co-operation, consultation and representation is not expressly referred to in the basic law of sport.

677. The non-remunerated serving members of the governing bodies of the PSC are classed as volunteer sport leaders and have the benefit of the corresponding legal provision.[197]

678. The PSC must be consulted with regard to applications to the member of the Government responsible for sport, by sports federations, for sports public utility status.[198] PSC must issue its opinion within thirty days of receipt of the corresponding request.[199]

679. There is a representative of the PSC on the Technical Committee, which operates under the auspices of the member of the Government responsible for internal administration, within the ambit of issues linked to the policing of sports events.[200]

191. Cf. Art. 1, no. 4 of the CAS Law, which is an annexe to Law no. 74/2013, of 6 September.
192. Cf. Art. 2, of the CAS Law, which is an annexe to Law no. 74/2013, of 6 September.
193. Cf. Art. 10, no. 1, para. a) of the CAS Law, which is an annexe to Law no. 74/2013, of 6 September.
194. Cf. Art. 21, no. 1, para. k) of the CAS Law, which is an annexe to Law no. 74/2013, of 6 September.
195. Cf. Art. 21, no. 1, para. g) of the CAS Law, which is an annexe to Law no. 74/2013, of 6 September.
196. Cf. Art. 33, no. 1 of the CAS Law, which is an annexe to Law no. 74/2013, of 6 September.
197. Cf. Art. 2, no. 1 of Decree-Law no. 267/95, of 18 October.
198. Cf. Art. 17, no. 1 of the LFSF.
199. Cf. Art. 17, no. 2 of the LFSF.
200. Cf. Art. 6, no. 1, para. e) of Decree-Law no. 216/2012, of 9.

680. The President of the PSC is a member of the Plenary Session of the NSC[201] who is also a member of the NSC Permanent Committee.[202]

681. CAS Sport Arbitration Council has eleven members two of whom are nominated by the Portuguese Sport Confederation. Those nominated must be jurists of recognised merit and good standing, with experience in the area of sport.[203]

682. Five of the arbitrators on the CAS list of arbitrators are nominated by the PSC.[204]

V. Portuguese Football Federation

A. *Introduction*

683. The FPF was founded in 1914 and is a not-for-profit private law juristic person, which is governed by its Bylaws and by the FIFA and UEFA Bylaws and Regulations, by the Regulations and decisions of its General Meeting and by the other applicable legal provisions. Its objects are to promote, organize, regulate and control the teaching and practice of football in all events and competitions, by co-ordinating its activities and initiatives with its members, clubs and sports actors that belong to them and to defend the prestige, ethics, sporting spirit and all of the material interests of football. According to no. 1 of Article 16 of the LBAFD, the FPF is also the sole representative of Portuguese football at both national and international levels and is responsible for the award of national or regional sports titles in the competitions it organizes.

B. *Types of Members*

684. The FPF has the following classes of members:

(a) ordinary members;
(b) honorary members, who are natural or juristic persons, who are considered to merit this distinction;
(c) meritorious members, who are sports actors, who because of their worth and actions are worthy of this distinction.

685. The following are included in the category of ordinary members:

201. Cf. Art. 5, para. g) and Art. 5, no. 1, para. g) of Decree-Law no. 266-A/2012, of 31 December, as amended by Decree-Law no. 153/2013, of 5 November.
202. Cf. Art. 6, no. 1, para. h) of Decree-Law no. 266-A/2012, of 31 December, as amended by Decree-Law no. 153/2013, of 5 November.
203. Cf. Art. 10, no. 1, para. a) of the CAS Law, which is an annexe to Law no. 74/2013, of 6 September.
204. Cf. Art. 21, no. 1, para. c) of the CAS Law, which is an annexe to Law no. 74/2013, of 6 September.

(a) district and regional associations of football clubs, that are registered in accordance with geographic criteria, which are also members of the LPFP, if they compete in professional competitions;
(b) LPFP;
(c) SJPF;
(d) National Association of Football Coaches (ANTF);
(e) Portuguese Association of Football Referees (APAF);
(f) National Association of Football Directors and Managers (ANDIF);
(g) National Association of Football Doctors (AMEF);
(h) National Association of Sports Nurses and Football Masseurs (ANEDAF).

686. Ordinary members cannot be members of another Football Federation, or take part in competitions in the territory of another Federation, without the authorization of the FPF or FIFA, except in exceptional circumstances. The FPF and its ordinary members recognize the jurisdiction of CAS to resolve cross-border disputes involving FIFA, FPF, and UEFA, leagues, clubs, players and other sports actors. Such disputes are subject to the CAS Code.

C. Governing Bodies

687. The governing bodies of the FPF are as follows and the members of which are elected for a four-year term of office, which coincides with the cycle of the FIFA Senior World Cup:

(a) General Meeting
(b) Chairman of the FPF
(c) Management
(d) Supervisory Board
(e) Appeals Board
(f) Disciplinary Council
(g) Refereeing Council.

1. General Meeting

688. The general meeting of the FPF is made up of ordinary members with the right to vote. The allocation of votes between ordinary members is established in the RJFD. Honorary and meritorious members and members of FPF governing bodies are entitled to participate but not to vote.

689. According to Article 17 of the LBAFD, proxy voting is not permitted at general meetings of federations and leagues. Elections of officers or decisions involving the consideration of the conduct or qualities of any person must be taken by secret ballot. This is a novelty that has no parallel in previous Sports Basic Laws and has been confirmed by the most recent RJFD.

690. The general meeting has the power to decide all matters submitted to it for its consideration, which are not the exclusive remit of other governing bodies of the FPF and particularly has the power to:

(a) elect the members of the governing bodies of the FPF and remove them from office;
(b) authorize the FPF to take legal proceedings against members of its governing bodies with regard to acts and omissions practiced during their term of office;
(c) approve the budget, report, balance sheet, financial statements, supplemental budgets and all decisions, which involve costs not included in the budget;
(d) approve and amend the Bylaws, Regulations and Rules;
(e) admit and expel ordinary members and elect honorary and meritorious members;
(f) approve proposal to dissolve the FPF;
(g) award medals and accolades to natural or juristic persons that have made a relevant contribution to the FPF, or to football in Portugal;
(h) fix the remuneration of the Chairman of the FPF and take decisions regarding the professional or semi-professional status of members of the FPF's governing bodies;
(i) authorize the acquisition, encumbering or disposal of land and buildings or of rights in respect thereof;
(j) decide or ratify FPF's membership of national or international organizations;
(k) ratify the Protocol (with the LPFP);
(l) approve Match, Disciplinary, Arbitration and Economic and Financial Regulations of all competitions, without prejudice to the powers of the LPFP;
(m) have all other powers granted by the Bylaws or Regulations.

2. Chairman

691. The Chairman of the FPF is the representative organ of the FPF *par excellance* in dealings with public and private bodies, similar national and international organizations and in legal proceedings.

692. The Chairman is a full-time officer of the FPF and has the powers to propose the hiring and dismissal of the Manager of the Portuguese national football team and the rest of the technical team.

3. Management

693. The management is responsible for managing the FPF and has specific duties to:

(a) ensure compliance with its bylaws and the decisions of the FPF's governing bodies;

(b) prepare the annual activities plan;
(c) annually, submit the Budget, the balance sheet and the Report and the financial statements to the supervisory board for its opinion;
(d) organize national non-professional teams and sports competitions;
(e) register the employment contracts and sports commitments of sportspersons;
(f) undertake and ensure compliance with obligations arising from commitments or agreements made within the ambit of the international organizations of which the FPF is a member (which include FIFA, UEFA and the IOC, *inter alia*);
(g) without prejudice to the powers of the disciplinary committee and the league disciplinary committee, to decide the imposition of protective measures on sports actors, i.e., suspension, whenever the prestige of the FPF, healthy coexistence and sports ethics are at issue, or when the competitions organized by them are vitiated in some way;
(h) approve and implement, on a compulsory basis, the manuals, regulations and directives of FIFA and UEFA, which have obligatory force in their member countries, in accordance with the provisions of Article 1, no. 4 of the FPF Bylaws.

4. Supervisory Board

694. The supervisory board is the body responsible for the issue of opinions regarding the Budget, Balance Sheet, Report and financial statements and Supplemental Budgets. The FPF's accounts are always certified by an external Official Auditor (ROC), unless one of the members of the supervisory board is an official auditor.

D. *Regulatory and Disciplinary Powers*

695. The FPF has disciplinary powers in respect of its ordinary members and in respect of sports actors, who work within the ambit of the objects of the FPF. The said powers arise directly from the EUPD, which grants the FPF the competence to exercise regulatory and disciplinary powers and other public powers defined by law, on an exclusive basis, with regard to football.

696. The Public Administration supervises the use of these public powers via the conduct of enquiries, inspections and audits. According to this grant of powers, one of the permanent organs of the FPF is the Enquiries and Audits Committee, which has technical autonomy and the power to:

(a) conduct disciplinary enquiries, bring charges, conduct proceedings and take any evidence-taking measures;
(b) promote the implementation of the decisions of the Disciplinary Council, the Appeals Council and the Arbitration Tribunal, always without prejudice the disciplinary powers of the LPFP;
(c) comply with the orders and conduct the audits ordered by the Management.

697. The Appeals Council has the following disciplinary powers:

(a) to hear and decide appeals from the decisions of the Chairman of the FPF and the Management;
(b) to hear and decide appeals against decisions of the FPF Disciplinary Council and the League Disciplinary Council;
(c) to hear and decide appeals against decisions of the Refereeing Council of the Portuguese Football Federation, the plenary meeting of the Refereeing Council and the decision of the members thereof;
(d) to hear and decide appeals against acts and decisions of the Executive Committee and the League Refereeing Committee;
(e) to exercise disciplinary powers in respect of the members of the organs of the FPF, its ordinary members and leaders.

698. The Disciplinary Council has the power, in accordance with the applicable regulations, to consider and punish all offences alleged to have been committed by persons subject to the disciplinary powers of the FPF, without prejudice to the specific powers of the LPFP.

699. The FPF Refereeing Council also operates within the FPF. The FPF Refereeing Council, together with the League Refereeing Committee, form the Plenary Session of the Refereeing Council, which has the following powers in accordance with the Refereeing Regulations:

(a) to approve the overall guidelines of refereeing in Portugal;
(b) to establish the technical parameters of training within the national refereeing system;
(c) the make the technical and final classification of referees and observers in all competitions;
(d) to appoint international referees.

§2. The Organization of Sports Competitions

I. The Organization of Professional Sports Competitions

A. Introduction

700. The organizational model of sports competitions was altered significantly throughout the twentieth century. The first texts did not include the possibility of professional competitions.

701. The first legislation to deal with the topic was Decree-Law no. 32.946, of 3 August 1943, which provided that sports competitions were to be organized separately for each sport, in which each sport has its own federation, whose only members were district or regional associations. All clubs were required to be members of an association according to the location of their headquarters, which meant that the model did not distinguish between clubs, their size or objectives.

702. At that time, there was no legal provision that envisaged professionalism in any sport. This situation changed in 1960, with Law no. 2.104, of 30 May, which provided for the existence of three professional sports, while all other sports were considered by the law to be amateur sports. The three professional sports were:

(1) football
(2) cycling
(3) boxing.

703. Only in 1990, when the LBSD came into force, as implemented by Decree-Law no. 144/93, of 26 April, was the concept of *leagues of clubs* introduced for certain sports. According to these two items of legislation, leagues of clubs started by being professional sport organizations autonomous of the federations, without a legal personality, which had to be formed by the federations and within the ambit of which professional competitions were organized, which were obligatorily subject to recognition by the Higher Council of Sport.

704. The LBSD was considerably amended by Decree-Law no. 19/96, of 25 June, which altered the structure and working of the leagues in relation to the federations. The leagues were consequently required to be created with legal personality, administrative, financial and technical autonomy, within the federations and to include all clubs that play in professional competitions. According to no. 2 of Article 24 their main powers and duties were to:

(a) [o]rganize and regulate professional competitions, which take place within the ambit of the federation in question, in accordance with the technical rules established by the proper organs of national and international federations;
(b) [p]erform the roles of supreme authority, control and supervision in accordance with the law, the bylaws and sports regulation, in relation to the clubs that belong to it;
(c) [e]xercise disciplinary powers and manage the specific area of refereeing in accordance with the legislation, which implements this law;
(d) [e]xercise such other powers as are granted to them by law or the federation bylaws.

705. The solution for professional sportspersons of a sport in which the federation does not organize professional competitions was the creation of a body to represent them.

B. The Criteria for the Recognition of Competitions as Professional

706. Article 8 of the European Sports Charter, which was approved in Rhodes in 1992, distinguishes between professional sport and sport in general. For, given the economic and social nature of professional sport, it should be considered as a sub-system within the sports system, which needed to be regulated so that its specificity and its objectives could be attained and so that the problems to which it gives rise can be dealt with in the best way possible.

707. Decree-Law no. 303/99, of 6 August, established the general criteria for the characterization of a sports competition as professional. According to the said decree-law, the power to initiate the procedure leading to the recognition of a competition as professional lay with the chairman of the corresponding federation, who was required to obtain the parameters from the body under whose auspices the sport operated, which, at that time, was the Higher Council of Sport, which was replaced by the IDP. Application for the recognition of a competition as professional must contain information with regard to the following parameters, previously approved by a two-thirds majority at a meeting of the clubs and companies that intend to participate therein:

(a) the minimum and maximum number of sports clubs and companies taking part, plus the corresponding organization in levels and divisions;
(b) the lower limit of the salaries of sportspersons and coaches, to be included in the total of the corresponding budget;
(c) lower limit of the independent budgets of each club for the corresponding competition;
(d) average number of spectators at each game played within the ambit of the competition;
(e) minimum requirements regarding facilities, i.e., as to the number of individual seats and the security rules in force, as required by Decree-Law no. 38/98, of 4 August.

708. After stating the figures identified above, the application for recognition must be justified in terms of the economic importance of the competition, the number of sports contracts it will generate, the resulting possibilities of participation in international competitions and the social aspect of the competition, *inter alia*.

709. A number of general rules were also approved in order to oblige clubs to be up to date with their payments in order to ensure the financial equilibrium of professional competitions. Clubs were accordingly subject to a requirement:

(a) to submit an independent budget solely with regard to the competition in which they wish to participate;
(b) that ordinary revenue in the budget must cover ordinary expenditure, thus permitting the financial equilibrium of the clubs;
(c) submit a certificate prior to the beginning of each sports season that proves that the club's tax and social security obligations have been complied with; and

(d) after the above, the opinion was sent to the IDP, IP and then approved by the member of the Government responsible for Sport.

710. Until such time as the parameters for the various professional sports competitions were fixed, the 1st and 2nd Division of Honour Football Championships and the Professional Basketball League Championship were, at that time, deemed to be professional, on a provisional basis.

711. Decree-Law no. 303/99, of 6 August, was repealed by Decree-Law no. 248-B/2008, of 31 December. After the repeal, the existence of professional sports ceased to be subject to the federations and leagues, or participants. The final word in the recognition of a sports competition as professional always lies with the State, in accordance with rules established in a statutory instrument issued by the member of the Government responsible for sport, which has yet to be published.

C. Professional Competitions in Portugal

712. The member of the Government responsible for sport approved the favourable opinions of the Higher Council of Sport, establishing parameters for professional competitions.

713. Currently, only football has professional competitions, which have two levels, i.e., the Zon Sagres League and the Orangina League. The Basketball Clubs League was announced for the 2008/2009 season, but has been discontinued in the meantime. At the end of that season, the abolition of the Portuguese Handball League was announced, so that the competition at the highest level of that sport was once again organized by the Portuguese Handball Federation.

D. The Organization of Professional Sports Competitions in the LBAFD and the Professional Leagues

714. Articles 22 et seq. of the LBAFD regulates the organization of sports competitions and it provides, in the case of federations with EUPD, that they have exclusive competence with regard to the regulation of the sport and disciplinary matters related thereto. The said powers are defined as being public in nature, but it is also recognized that the leagues have a preponderant role with regard to professional competitions. For this reason powers originally granted to the federations were delegated to the leagues, e.g.:

(a) the organization and regulation of professional competitions, which take place within the ambit of the federation in question, in accordance with the technical rules established by the proper organs of the national and international federations;
(b) exercise of such control and supervisory functions in respect of its members as are established in the law and in the corresponding bylaws and regulations;

(c) definition of the sporting, financial and organizational prerequisites of access to professional competitions, and the supervision of the conduct thereof by the participant entities. Nevertheless, despite the fact that the league has the power to draft and approve competition regulations, it is for the federation of which the league is part, to ratify the refereeing and discipline regulations of professional competitions at a general meeting.

715. As these powers are delegated by the federations, the acts of the leagues are public acts and are, as such, subject to the rules governing administrative disputes.

716. An innovation in the LBAFD with regard to the refereeing of professional competitions can be found in Article 24, which requires that referees be appointed by bodies other than the bodies that evaluate their performance. The situation that existed was that the body that appointed referees also evaluated them, which gave rise to debate and suspicions. The aim was to create a more transparent legal framework. This article will have to be implemented by the new RJFD.

717. The LBAFD established that single sport federations, in which professional competitions are organized, in accordance with the recognition criteria for competitions of that sort, which are to be defined in a statutory instrument, must be organized by a professional league and not by a league of clubs, which is formed as a non-profit association and is subject to the legal framework governing non-profit associations and has administrative, technical and financial autonomy.

718. It should be noted that the competitions delegated to and managed by the professional leagues, in conjunction with the federations, are required to be at the highest level of the sports competitions within the corresponding federation.

719. Professional leagues are required by law to be made up of the clubs and sports companies that compete in professional competitions. Their bylaws may also provide that representatives of other sports actors, i.e., sportspersons and coaches, may also be league members. As they are part of the concept of a federation, the federation rules apply to their decisions, i.e., proxy voting is not permitted and decisions appointing members of governing bodies, or which involve the consideration of the conduct or qualities of persons, must be taken by secret ballot. Furthermore, professional leagues are required to have organized accounts, in accordance with the current provisions of the Accounting Standardisation System,[205] in order to ensure the transparent management.

---

205. According to the Civil Code, a sports club is an association and its accounts must accordingly be organised in accordance with the Official Accounting Plan for Federations, Associations and Groups of Clubs (PROFAC), as approved by Decree-Law no. 74/98, of 27 March. The ADoPtion of PROFAC is obligatory for the bodies in question and is intended to *'(...) permit permanent budgetary control and checking of the matching of assets values and accounting figures'*. (Art. 2, no. 1). If a sports club has revenue from commercial, industrial or agricultural activities, even if the same are undertaken on an ancillary basis, it is required to have organised accounts with regard to

720. The Law appears, with regard to relations between the sports federation and the professional league, to define a series of powers that are shared by the professional league and the corresponding federation. In the LBSD and the LBD, the expression used was *protocol*, which term was subsequently abandoned in favour of *contract*. Accordingly, the contract between the league and the sports federation must state the number of clubs that take part in the professional sports competition, the rules governing access by clubs to professional competitions, the organization of the activities of national teams and support for non-professional sport. The contract is valid for four sports seasons, which are not required to coincide with the Olympic cycle.

721. If the federation and league fail to reach agreement in the contract regarding the way in which the league will exercise the powers delegated to it by the federation, the NSC is required to make temporary provision regarding the matters stipulated in the contract, except for those with regard to disagreement as to the amounts to be allocated to non-professional sport, which differences are subject to compulsory arbitration in accordance with Law no. 31/86, of 29 August.

722. Competitions organized by the federations and leagues via the exercise of delegated powers, which involve the award of national, regional, local or other official titles, and competitions intended to select the sportspersons, or clubs, to represent Portugal in international competitions, must comply with the following general conditions:

(a) free access by all sportspersons and clubs based in Portugal, who are full members of the corresponding federation and comply with the participation requirements stipulated by it;
(b) equality of all competitors in the conduct of the competition, without prejudice to levels created solely on the basis of exclusively sports criteria;
(c) publication of the regulations of each competition and of the decisions applying them and, when the decisions are written, publication of the grounds therefore;
(d) impartiality and lack of bias in the deciding technical and disciplinary matters.

723. There is a high level of involvement of the State in the powers of the federations and leagues to designate and organize competition schedules. These schedules are stipulated by the Secretary of State of Youth and Sport, who has the power to approve the obligatory opinion of the NSC, which establishes a system for the designation of competition schedules for all sports and which distinguishes and names them in terms of importance, level and ambit. The federations can only use approved designations and if the breach this requirement their EUPD may be suspended. Improper use of the name, image and activities carried on by sports federations is an administrative offence.

---

those activities, in accordance with no. 2 of Art. 116 of the IRC Code, and must therefore have an Accountant subject to Decree-Law no. 452/1999, of 5 November, which approved the Accountants Professional Regulations.

724. According to the law, sports federations have the exclusive power to grant national and regional titles. All competitions leading to the award of a Portuguese title must take place in Portugal.

725. The LBAFD provides that sportspersons, who are Portuguese nationals and who are selected to be members of Portuguese national teams, have a duty to take part in them. Sportspersons, who have received any type of financial support pursuant to the high performance sport programme, are subject to the same obligation.

II. Sports Companies

A. Introduction

726. The LBSD introduced the concept of a company with sports objects. The original version of no. 2 of Article 20 of the LBSD stated that:

> Special legislation will define the conditions subject to which sports clubs may, without prejudicing their legal nature and status, form companies with sports objects, in order to promote the specific organisational and operational needs of sectors of their sports activity.

727. Decree-Law no. 146/95, of 21 June, created the legal framework of clubs and sports companies (the creation of which is optional), which was amended as a consequence of Law no. 19/96, of 25 June, in order to put an end to the (unsustainable) prohibition of the distribution of profits. However this legal framework had no practical effect as not a single sports company was formed while this law was in force.

728. Without prejudice to the respect and encouragement that are always due to amateur sport and to the social benefits it has produced over the years, professional sport and the associated competitions needed innovative solutions, based on a new legal framework for the entities that are the legal support for sports activity, which, in a non-discriminatory manner, distinguished between professional and amateur sport, which should co-exist in properly regulated manner.

729. The LBSD granted sports clubs the power to form sports companies and this was not altered by the following Basic Laws. Clubs were accordingly able to have recourse to a structure with increased economic and financial dynamism for their professional activities, which is able to meet the management and economic demands for which more traditional models are unsuited.

730. As the aim was neither an absolute separation nor a discrete structure for professional sport, the model and spirit of the club was recognized and preserved as the entity, which generates the fan support and enthusiasm, which is profoundly entrenched in local and regional communities and in the tradition of the Portuguese associations movement. This phenomenon is of fundamental importance in the promotion and dissemination of sport.

731. The principle of the prevalence of the club, which is affirmed in relation to any other idea or model, was ensured by the fact that the power to create sports companies is granted exclusively to clubs. The aim was for professional sport to have more solid and responsible management processes and the financial rigour necessary to ensure their stability and development, although always via the clubs, but assisted by the innovative solution of the sports companies.

732. No. 3 of Article 20 of the LBSD, as amended by Article 1 of Law no. 19/96, of 25 June read as follows:

> the terms according to which sports clubs, or their professional teams, which compete in professional sports competitions, may adopt the form of a for profit sports company, or the management framework to which those which do not opt to form such a company, shall be subject, shall be established by suitable legislation.

733. It was necessary for the legislation to provide a new framework for sports companies. Accordingly, two separate decree-laws were passed in order to create the said framework: Decree-Law no. 146/95, of 21 June, and Decree-Law no. 67/97, of 3 April, which will be considered in greater detail below.

734. The provision made by Decree-Law no. 146/95, of 21 June with regard to sports companies was generally considered to be inadequate, to the extent that it prohibited the distribution of profits by sports companies and accordingly defeated one of the main reasons for forming them. It was accordingly important to alter the said legal framework by giving the companies the instruments they required so that they could, at least in theory, be an important factor in the promotion of professional sport in Portugal. This alteration was also used as an opportunity to create a tax regime for these companies, which takes their specificities, in relation to other companies, into consideration.

B. Sports Companies in General

735. Sports companies are a new type of company, that are governed secondarily by the general rules applicable to public limited companies, but with some specificities arising from the special demands of sports activity, which are their main object. Decree-Law no. 67/97, of 3 April introduced the legal framework governing sports companies and the special management framework, which will apply to those sports clubs that opt not to form such a company and repealed Decree-Law no. 146/95, of 21 June. According to Decree-Law 67/97, of 3 April, sports companies differ from ordinary companies as follows:

(a) the minimum share capital and the way in which it is paid up;

(b) the special system whereby the company is tied to the founding sports club via the grant of special rights to the shares held by the founding club;
(c) the possibility that the Autonomous Regions, municipalities and associations of municipalities can subscribe up to 50% of the share capital of sports companies with their registered office in the area of their jurisdiction; and
(d) the establishment of special rules for the transfer of assets of the founding club to the sports company.

736. Sports clubs, which compete in professional competitions and which do not opt for this new legal form are subject to a special legal framework, which essentially introduces minimum rules that ensure the indispensable transparency and rigour in the management thereof. The following aspects of the said legal framework are noteworthy:

(a) the principle of personal liability of club executives for certain acts of management;
(b) the accounting transparency requirement, via the certification of the accounts by an official auditor;
(c) the obligatory ADoPtion of the accounting standardization system; and
(d) the provision of bank guarantees, or the posting of an insurance bond, to secure the reparation of the consequences of acts that prejudice the said clubs.

737. A sports company is a private law person, formed as a public limited company, the object of which is participation in a sport, in professional sports competitions, the promotion and organization of sports events and the promotion or development of activities related to the practice of that professional sport. There is a principle of subsidiarity that is justified by the specificities of the sport and which culminates in the creation of a special legal framework, to which the provisions applicable to public limited companies apply on a secondary basis. The Securities Code approved by Decree-Law no. 486/99, of 13 November, applies to the public subscription of shares in this type of company.

738. Sports companies can be formed in the following ways:

(a) via the transformation of a sports club that competes, or intends to compete, in professional sports competitions, when a sports company takes the place of the club. The sports club thus ceases to exist as such and is transformed into a juristic person that is part of a miscellaneous legal category. The sports company has the benefit and burden of all the legal relations to which the sports club was party. The club's economic and financial liabilities are transferred *in toto* to the new sports company;
(b) the transformation of teams that compete in, or intend to compete in professional sports competitions, into an entity with a legal personality, so that the sports club continues to exist alongside the new sports company, which is centred on the management of the participation in professional competitions. In this case, unlike the transformation of a sports club, there are two juristic persons, both of which can be bearers of a nucleus of rights and duties;

(c) formation *de novo*, which is not a consequence of the transformation of a sports club, or the transformation of a team into an entity with a legal personality, so that, in this case a new company is formed.

739. So far as the formation of sports companies is concerned, there is a principle of irreversibility, i.e., sports clubs that opt to form a sports company, or to transform their professional team into an entity with a legal personality, cannot, subsequently, compete in professional competitions other than as the new sports company. Once the company has been formed, it cannot change its legal status while it continues to compete in professional competitions. The company can only change its form, if it competes in non-professional competitions either originally or because it has been relegated, although when it once again competes in professional competitions, it has to do so as a sports company. The formation of sports companies other than in the context of professional competitions is also possible, in which case the minimum share capital is EUR 250,000. The minimum share capital in professional competitions is as follows:

(a) EUR 997,595.80 for sports companies, which compete in the football first division organized by the LPFP.
(b) EUR 498,797.90 for sports companies, which compete in the football second division organized by the LPFP and, in the event of promotion of the sports company to the football first division organized by the LPFP, the promotion is subject to an increase of share capital to a figure of no less than the amount in the preceding paragraph.
(c) EUR 249,398.95 for companies that are formed in order to compete in professional basketball competitions, which is the same amount as applies for those companies formed to compete in non-professional sports competitions.

740. These amounts differ from the general rule in the Commercial Companies Code, which is that the nominal minimal share capital is EUR 50,000. There is another specific rule regarding increases of share capital, which applies only to sports companies, which compete in professional competitions, i.e., that the minimum share capital must be successively increased, during the five-year period following the formation of the company, to an amount equal to 30% of the average budget of the company in the first four years of its existence, failing which the company will be excluded from professional competitions. If, during or at the end of that period, the sports company no longer competes in professional competitions, it is released from the obligation to increase its share capital, but cannot compete again in such competitions until such time as the share capital has been duly increased.

741. The share capital must be fully paid up in cash, although the payment up of 50% of the nominal value of the shares may be deferred for up to two years. The payment up of the shares subscribed by the founding club is not covered by this provision and may be paid up in kind. Existing shareholders of the company and members of the founding club, if any, have a right of first refusal in increases of share capital. The bylaws of sports companies stipulate the rules governing increases of share capital in the latter case.

742. In order to prevent a company, which has major losses, which significantly affect its share capital, from continuing to trade, Article 35 of the Commercial Companies Code includes a mechanism to the effect that a company, which according to the accounts prepared by its management organ, has lost half of its share capital, or if there is good reason to consider that there has been such a loss, must inform its shareholders of the said situation, by calling a general meeting, so that they may decide what measures to take, which must include the following:

(a) dissolution of the company;
(b) reduction of share capital;
(c) payments in by the shareholders to make up the share capital coverage.

743. The previous version of Article 35 of the Commercial Companies Code provided that the creditors could apply for the dissolution of the company, if half of the share capital was lost in two consecutive financial years. The original version of the article also provided that any shareholder or creditor could apply for the company to be dissolved in the event of a loss of half the share capital.

744. The permitted share classes, which are always of registered shares, are as follows:

(a) class A, which are shares for subscription by the founding club, when the company has been formed via the transformation of the team into a sports company. Ownership of these shares confers a special right on the founding club, as these share can only be judicially seized or charged to public sector juristic persons, which clearly prejudices private sector creditors;
(b) class B shares, i.e., the remaining shares.

745. The founding club is granted other special rights, when the sports company arises from the transformation of the team into an entity with a legal personality. Accordingly, the direct participation of the founding club in the share capital can never be less than 15% or more than 40%. The founding club's class A shares always grant the club:

(a) the right to veto general meeting decisions for the merger, demerger, transformation or dissolution of the company and for the alteration of its bylaws, the increase and reduction of its share capital and moving of the registered office;
(b) the power to appoint at least one of the members of the governing organs, who has a right to veto the decisions of the organ. The company bylaws may also stipulate that certain general meeting decisions are also be subject to the authorization of the founding club.

746. The founding club may hold its shares in the share capital of the sports company via a holding company provided that it holds the majority of the holding company's share capital. However the rule that stipulates a maximum holding of 40% of the share capital is unaffected by this provision.

747. The bylaws of sports companies must stipulate that their management organs must have an uneven number of members and a minimum of three members, who must be professional managers. The following persons cannot be directors of sports companies:

(a) persons, who were, during the previous year, officers of another sports company formed for the same sport;
(b) officers of sports federations or associations of the same sport;
(c) professional sportspersons, coaches and referees, who are active in the said sport in the said capacities.

748. A sports company cannot have shares in the share capital of another sports company. There is also a limitation on the exercise of shareholders' rights by shareholders, who have shares in more than one sports company, to the effect that the exercise of shareholders rights in one sports company precludes the exercise of the said rights in other sports companies involved in the same sport. The following rights are excluded: the right to divide and receive dividends and the right to transfer shares. The company's bylaws cannot restrict the transfer of shares, which means that shares are freely transferable. This can give rise to conflicts of interest. The said prohibition, together with the conflict of interests rules and the rules restricting the exercise of shareholder's rights, seek to prevent murky situations that can arise from the holding of such offices, or similar positions, in sports companies that compete in the same sport, in addition to being a reflection of the prohibition of multi-ownership of clubs or sports companies.

749. It should be borne in mind that the Autonomous Regions, municipalities or associations of municipalities can be shareholders in sports companies, which have their registered office within their areas. Such shareholdings cannot, however, exceed 50% of the share capital, which means that not only are public holdings in the share capital of sports companies permitted, but they are also regulated.

750. The transfer of the assets of sports companies is subject to special rules. Accordingly, the disposal or encumbering, on any basis, of assets comprised in a sports company's immovable assets must be authorized by a general meeting at which shareholders representing at least two thirds of the total votes, are present or represented, when the meeting is called for the first or second time. Acts, which exceed the budget provisions, must also be authorized by a general meeting, which can decide such matters, if shareholders with at least two thirds of the total votes are present or represented, when the meeting is first called, or whatever the number of members present, when the meeting is called for the second time.

751. In companies that are created as a consequence of the transformation of teams into entities with a legal personality, the founder club is entitled, but not required, to transfer all or part of its rights and obligations linked to participation in professional competitions of the sport, which is part of the company's objects, to the sports company, when it is formed. The transfer of the founding club's rights and obligations is not subject to the other party's consent, as the sports company is liable to the club's creditors for such reduction of their guarantee, as represented by the club's assets, as is occasioned by the transfer of the club's position in any contracts to the company. However the rights to participate in the competitions in which the founding club competed, and the sports employment contracts and professional sport training contracts with sportspersons of the sport that is comprised in the company's objects, are obligatorily transferred to the sports company.

C. *The Special Provisions Governing the Management of Clubs That Compete in Professional Competitions*

752. Sports clubs, which compete in professional competitions that do not wish to form a sports company, can opt for a REG, which is structured in such a way that the club's professional sections are autonomous from its other sections. This means that they must have separate accounts for each such section, which clearly identify the revenue and expenditure of each of them.

753. Before the beginning of each sports season, the management of each club that has adopted the special management arrangement must submit a bank guarantee, an insurance bond, or some other equivalent guarantee that covers their liability to their club, to the corresponding professional league of clubs, which is in the same terms as is required of directors of public limited companies. The amount of the guarantee is fixed by the professional league of clubs and cannot be less than 10% of the budget of the club's professional department.

754. The balance sheet and other accounts of sports clubs that have adopted the special management arrangements cannot be approved by their general meetings without a prior opinion of an official auditor, or of a firm of official auditors.

Part II. Sport and Employment

Chapter 1. Sports Regulation

§1. Employment Contracts of Sportspersons

I. Introduction

755. The Portuguese employment law system is complex to the extent that its historical evolution is marked by a proliferation of miscellaneous legislation. For this reason, there are many provisions scattered in various items of legislation that apply to sportspersons and their employers.

756. There are, in any event, various specificities or particularities in relation to sports employment law, which require a specific legal framework: we therefore consider that a sport employment contract (CTD) is a special employment contract to which the standard legal provisions governing individual employment contracts cannot be applied immediately and automatically. There is therefore a need for a structured relationship between the traditional and classic protection of sports employees and the protection of the specificities and particularities of sports competitions.

757. The general employment rules are not suited to the sports employment relationship. For example, the general employment rules regarding the following aspects are entirely inadequate:

(a) the trial period
(b) non-compete clause
(c) reinstatement
(d) the *right to withdraw*
(e) temporary loan
(f) individual redundancy dismissal
(g) the ordinary rules governing working hours, and the calculation of the time spent in training and journeys, weekly rest days, the definition and alteration of working hours and the booking of holidays, *inter alia.*

758. This being so, sports employment law was specifically governed, for the first time, by Law 85/95, of 31 August, which led to the passing of Decree-Law no. 305/95, of 18 November. This Decree-Law was subsequently repealed, in order to meet the demands of the new reality created by the *Bosman* case, by Law no. 28/98, of 26 June which was later amended by Law no. 114/99 of 3 August and by Law no. 74/2013.

759. The RJCTPD subjects' employment contracts not so much to the general employment law provisions, because they are inappropriate, but adapts the Employment Law rules to the particularities of sport, so that, in some cases, the provisions are quite different from the general employment provisions. Given the nature of their work and their working environment, sportspersons have a series of specific contractual rights and duties, which are counterbalanced by a series of perquisites and benefits, with regard to their contractual and legal relationship and legal with the club or company for which they play.

760. The RJCTPD continues in force practically unamended despite the very large number of amendments made to the general legal framework. The RJCTPD was drafted at a time when employment legislation was still dispersed.[206] It was subsequently aggregated into a more coherent and systematic Employment Code, introduced by Law no. 99/2003, of 27 August, which was repealed by the new Employment Code introduced by Law no. 7/2009, of 12 February whose latest amendment took place through Law no. 120/2015.

761. In addition to the said legislation, the Collective Bargaining Agreement[207] between the Portuguese Professional Football League and the Professional Footballers Union, which governs the specificities of professional football, is also applicable to sports employment relations. So far as coaches are concerned, there is a Collective Employment Contract for Coaches, which was made between the LPFP and the National Association of Football Coaches, on 9 November 1996. This collective contract was extended to all coaches and clubs or SADs with their registered offices in Portugal, by statutory extension instruments, but is no longer in force.

762. Article 3 of the RJCTPD provides that the provisions of the Employment Code are applicable secondarily and are accordingly only applicable in the absence of sports law provision. However, subsequent laws such as Law no. 8/2003, of 12 May, which introduced a special legal framework with regard to the reparation of loss and damage arising from work accidents involving professional sportspersons, the Employment Code[208] introduced by Law no. 7/2009, of 12 February and the Law, which introduces the Regulations for the Implementation of the Employment Code,[209] apply to professional sportspersons pursuant to the said article.

206. The key Law, *inter alia*, are the Employment Contract Law, the Termination of Employment Contracts and Fixed Term Employment Contracts Law (LCCT), the Working Hours Law (LDT), the Collective Regulation Instruments Law (LIRC), the Temporary Employment Law (LTT), which were repealed with the coming into force of the first Employment Code in 2003.

207. The Convention in question was signed on 15 Jul. 1999 and was published in the 1st Series of the Work and Employment Bulletin, no. 33 on 8 Sep. 1999.

208. That is Law no. 7/2009, of 12 February.

209. That is Law no. 35/2004, of 29 July, as amended by Decree-Law no. 38/2008, of 8 August, which introduced the regulations to implement the previous version of the Employment Code, approved

763. In Portugal, it is generally accepted that the relationship between players and the club or SAD for which the former works for a salary and bonuses, is an employment relationship.[210] It is also fixed case-law[211] that the said relationship is a special employment relationship. The minimum age at which a Sports Employment Contract can be signed is 16. It must also be signed by the player's legal representatives, if the player is less than 18, failing which contract is voidable. This provision is based on the concern to protect players, who are minors, from signing a contract, which deals with rights, which the minor does not yet legally possess. Article 31 of the RJCTPD provides that Training Contracts, which are also governed by the RJCTPD, may be signed by minors aged between 14 and 18.

II. The Form and Registration of Sports Employment Contracts

764. The CTD must be in writing, failing which it is invalid. The requirement not only proves the existence of the sports employment contract, but operates to immediately provide the player with a minimum level of legal protection of his rights. The Collective Employment Agreement between the Professional Players and the SJPF provides that a CTD that is not in writing is null and void.

765. If the player plays for a club, which is a member of a Federation with EUPD, the CTD must be registered with the corresponding federation. In the absence of the said registration the player cannot compete in any competition organized by the federation. The employer accordingly has the obligation to register its players and players prejudiced may seek a finding of liability against their employers on the basis of this provision.

766. The obligation to register CTDs with the corresponding Federation referred to in Article 6 of the RJCTPD gives Federations important powers. According to the stipulations regarding the form of the contract, it is for the Federations to decide how the standard CED, which is the annexe of the Collective Bargaining Agreement between the Portuguese Professional Football League and the Professional Footballers Union, is negotiated. While some Federations are content with a simple

---

by Law no. 99/2003, 27 August. This Law is still in force although it is expected to be repealed soon, in accordance with the new legislation in force.

210. Compare Bernardo Xavier, *Curso de Direito do Trabalho*, 2nd Edition, Lisbon, Verbo, 1993, p. 15, Pedro Romano Martinez, *Direito do Trabalho*, 3rd Edition, Lisbon, Almedina, 2006, p. 40, João Leal Amado, *Rescisão do Contrato de Jogadores de Futebol*, Questões Laborais, no. 4, Coimbra, Coimbra Editora, 1995, pp. 50 et seq., André Dinis de Carvalho, Da Liberdade de Circulação dos Desportistas na União Europeia, Coimbra, Coimbra Editora, 2003, p. 60, Lúcio Correia, *Limitações à Liberdade Contratual do Praticante Desportivo*, Lisbon, Livraria Petrony Editores, 2008, p. 47.

211. See the decision of the Supreme Court of Justice of 9/10/1996, which states: *A contract between a sports club and a volleyball player, in which the player is required to work on a continuous basis together with other players and under the orders and instructions of the club, is an employment contract and not a contract for the supply of services.* (Available on the Internet at: http://www.dgsi.pt/jstj.nsf/954f0ce6ad9dd8b980256b5f003fa814/2b6029ad462d8c69802568fc003b1ec6?OpenDocument&Highlight=0,VOLEIBOL)).

contract, which refers to the provisions of the RJCTPD or to the Collective Bargaining Agreement, others require the CTD to contain all of the clauses in the Collective Bargaining Agreement before they can be registered.

767. In the case of professional football, notice of and the obligation to register CTDs involves a larger number of entities. Once a CTD has been signed, copies of it must be sent by the employer to the LPFP, the Professional Footballers Union and the FPF within five days.

III. The Obligatory Nature of the Contractual Term

768. The standard employment relationship is based on the rule of employment for an indefinite period, as is clear from Article 129 of the Employment Code. This provision is not suited to the realities of sports employment given the nature thereof and its temporary character, i.e., the fact that it is an ephemeral activity and a rapid depletion occupation. The rule which applies and to which there are no exceptions, is the fixed term contract. The said terms are stipulated in the contract and have a stabilizing effect,[212] i.e., the sportsperson cannot, in the absence of due cause, terminate the contract prior to the expiry of the contractual term.[213]

769. The term of a CTD must be at least one season[214] and no more than eight seasons. This requirement differs greatly from the general provisions in the Employment Code, in which the general rule is a contract for an indefinite period. It should also be noted that the principle of automatic renewal is inapplicable to CTDs. This being so, the general principle of the giving of notice to the other party to terminate the contract on the previously agreed date does not apply, unlike the provisions of the Employment Code.[215]

770. The justification of the obligatory nature of the term is the nature of the occupation in question, which is a rapid depletion occupation. This means that in most sports the average duration of high performance activity is no more than ten

212. Article 8 SECL.
213. Article 26 SECL.
214. The minimum duration of a sports season is subject to the two exceptions in no. 2 of the LFECS. The first is when the CTD is signed after the commencement of the sports season to take effect until the end thereof. The case is typical of player transfers that take place when the market is open in January each year. The second exception is a CTD in which the sportsperson is engaged to play in a competition, or is a certain number of events, which amount to an identifiable unit within the ambit of the corresponding sport. Although it is not very common in Portugal, this exception refers to the very common contracts in which a certain sportsperson is engaged to play only in a specific sports competition, which is defined in terms of season, or only in a specific number of games in a competition, normally the final. Such contracts are commonly used to attract top players, or formerly top players, to play in championships and competitions, in which it is, in principle, unthinkable that players of such a high profile would play.
215. Article 149, no. 2 and Art. 344, no. 1 of the Employment Code introduced by Law no. 7/2009, of 12 February.

to fifteen years.[216] Other justifications of the term requirement are the protection of sport, sports competition and the employers.[217]

771. In sports employment contracts there is no automatic renewal of the contract and consequently no need for the employer to give the prior notice of termination required by general employment law. According to this approach, which is supported by most Portuguese legal theory, there is also accordingly no place for the type of compensation provided in the general employment legal framework, which is payable when the contract terminates as a consequence of notice by the employer to that effect. The general understanding is that the employer should not be ordered to pay compensation to a player because of the precarious nature of the contract, because the law does not permit the making of a contract for an indefinite period.

772. Contracts for a fixed term are not automatically renewable given their strictly temporary nature. As we shall see, the termination of a CTD, which is a fixed term contract *par excellance*, also differs from the general employment law provisions.

IV. Definition of Professional Sportsperson

773. Article 2, paragraph b) of the RJCTPD defines a professional sportsperson as *a person, whose exclusive or main occupation, pursuant to a sports employment contract and after the necessary occupational and technical training, is a sport, for which he or she is paid.* In the said Article 2, the law individualizes and distinguishes professional sportspersons from others involved in sport, who receive payment for work done in the general world of sport, e.g., players' agents and trainee sportspersons.

774. This definition of sportsperson involves some interpretation problems, above all in relation to the part of the definition, which requires the sports occupation as the sole or main occupation.[218] We adopt the majority approach in Portuguese legal theory[219] to the effect that a sportsperson, who has another occupation, may be considered to be a professional sportsman, if the aspects of *legal direction and control of the employee, and payment* are present, and that the question as to whether or not the sportsperson's said sports occupation is his or her principal or secondary occupation, is a matter of secondary concern.

216. Lúcio Correia, *Limitações … supra*. pp. 58 et seq.
217. João Leal Amado, *Vinculação … supra.*, p. 109.
218. On this question see Lúcio Correia, *Limitações à Liberdade Contratual do Praticante Desportivo* (Coimbra: Coimbra Editora, 2007, pp. 54 et seq.
219. That is João Leal Amado, *Vinculação Versus Liberdade – O Processo de Constituição e Extinção da Relação laboral do Praticante Desportivo* (Coimbra: Coimbra Editora, 2002), p. 50. See also Lúcio Correia, *Limitações à Liberdade Contratual do Praticante Desportivo. Coimbra*, Coimbra Editora, 2007, p. 56.

775. It should also be noted that the said definition requires a sportsperson's sport's occupation to be their *sole* or *main* occupation, before he or she can be considered to be a professional sportsperson. This has been a source of debate among most Portuguese authors.[220] It is debated whether a sportsperson, who signs a sports employment contract with a club and then decides that this is not going to be his or her main activity automatically loses professional sportsperson status, merely because he or she has some other paid activity. The legislation makes no provision for this situation, but legal theory considers that there is no such loss of professional sportsperson status. The RJCTPD in Law no. 28/98 will apply to workers who are employed as sportspersons, whether this is their main activity or not.

776. The RJCTPD appears to exclude its application to amateur sportspersons, as amateur sport has different characteristics, *inter alia* the absence of a salary. In principle, amateur sportspersons are not paid for what they do, although they may receive some payments, which are not deemed to be a salary.

777. In the case of football, no. 4 of Article 2 of the FIFA RSTP provides that *an amateur player is a football player, whose aims are healthy leisure and the conservation of his physical condition and who receives no remuneration or any direct or indirect benefit (...) for the said sports activity.* This definition has a limited practical scope as, in Portugal, most amateur clubs and sports adopt strategies identical to those of professional clubs, i.e., with regard to the intensity and duration of training. They are sportspersons, whose sole or main income source is football, even though they do not have a formal CTD. This precarious situation involves problems in relation to proof of the existence of an employment relationship, which in the world of sport is primarily proved by the obligatory registration of CTDs with the corresponding federation.

V. The Trial Period

778. The definition of *trial period,* in no. 1 of Article 111 of the Employment Code refers to it as the period of time *corresponding to the initial period of the performance of an employment contract, during which the parties consider whether they wish the same to continue.* No. 2 adds that during this period *the parties must act in such a way as to be able to evaluate the interest in the continued existence of the employment contract.*

779. During the trial period,[221] either party is at liberty to rescind the contract without prior notice in as much as ignorance on the part of the employer of the player's skills and aptitudes and possible ignorance on the part of the player regarding

220. See João Leal Amado, *Contrato de Trabalho Desportivo ... supra.*, pp. 17 e 18.; André Dinis de Carvalho, in da *Liberdade de Circulação ... supra.*, p. 55;.Lúcio Correia, *Limitações ... supra.*, p. 54 e ss.

221. That is João Leal Amado, *Vinculação Versus Liberdade – O Processo de Constituição e Extinção da Relação laboral do Praticante Desportivo,* Coimbra: Coimbra Editora, 2002, pp. 205 et seq.

the conditions of the club or company to which he is transferred or by which he is hired; mean that they are unable to properly consider their interest in the maintenance of the contract for the entire period initially agreed. Sport in general, and football in particular, as the sports spectacle *par excellence,* is widely publicized and disseminated in the media. This means for example that fans are informed about various circumstances of the life of players or clubs. This means that sportspersons can be evaluated prior to the trial period.[222]

780. The RJCTPD provides that the trial period cannot exceed thirty days. In the case of a trainee's first employment contract made with the training body after the termination of a Training Contract, there can be no trial period as the objectives of mutual knowledge and evaluation have already been complied with while the training contract was in force. The Collective Bargaining Agreement between the SJPF and LPFP provides that *in the absence of provision to the contrary, it shall be presumed that the parties have excluded the possibility of a trial period.* This special rule does not apply to other sports, which, in the absence of a CCT, are bound by the general employment law provisions.[223]

781. The trial period terminates:

(a) when the player first takes a part in the competition that precludes him playing for any other club in that competition;
(b) when the player sustains an injury and the recovery period extends beyond the trial period.

782. In as far as the circumstances in case (b) are concerned, if the trial period was permitted to continue, it would give rise to the possibility that it could be invoked by the club as grounds for rescission, without having the need to invoke just cause, which would amount to abusive invocation of a legitimate contractual mechanism.

VI. The Employer's Duties

783. The main duties of employers are related to the conditions that must be afforded to sportspersons in order to enable them to work in their profession. So far as employment law in general is concerned, the position of Portuguese case-law is that the employer is subject to a duty to provide actual employment. In the area of sport also, Article 12 of the RJCTPD provides that sportspersons are entitled to effective occupation, which is limited to training and other activities, which are preparatory or linked to sports competition, but not actual participation in sports competitions. This duty was recently enshrined in the general law in Article 122,

222. Albino Mendes Baptista, *Estudos Sobre o Contrato de Trabalho Desportivo.* Coimbra: Coimbra Editora, 2006, p. 74.
223. Albino Mendes Baptista, *Estudos Sobre o Contrato de Trabalho Desportivo.* (Coimbra: Coimbra Editora, 2006), p. 75.

paragraph b) of the Employment Code. According to the provisions of paragraph a) of Article 12 of the RJCTPD, sports employers are subject to a duty to provide sportspersons with the conditions necessary for participation in sport, and actual participation in training and other activities, which are preparatory or linked to sports competition, but this obviously does not amount to a right to be selected to play in such competitions. A sportsperson cannot be prevented from training, or from taking part in activities that are preparatory or linked to sports competition (except on medical or technical grounds), or be excluded from the normal working group, or be improperly selected to play in so-called 'B teams'. Paragraph d) of Article 14 of the CCT between the LPFP and the SJPF expressly prohibits clubs from altering the player's working conditions in such a way as *prevents the player from working as a member of the normal working group, other than in special circumstances for medical or technical reasons.* This does not however mean that the club is obliged to use players in all games of all the competitions in which it competes. The club has the power to take the technical decision whether or not to use a certain player in competitions. This protection is above all at the level of the prohibition of exclusion from training, or the isolation of the player during non-training activities. It is common practice in Portugal to invoke *technical reasons* in order to justify the exclusion of a player from the normal working group.[224]

784. In order to comply with the duty to provide actual work, clubs have the option to include players in so-called *B teams,* which were originally created to enable younger players, who were being trained, to achieve the competitive pace and experience needed in order to play in main teams. This purpose of the existence of *B teams* justifies the existence of age limits for membership thereof. Accordingly, only four senior category players may be included in *B teams* without any age or nationality restrictions. Nationality restrictions are justified by the other purpose of the creation of *B teams,* i.e., the promotion and training of young Portuguese talent.

785. However, *B teams* are frequently used to manage large squads by keeping them in better physical condition and playing in matches, so they do not to lose market value and competitive pace. While there are championships in which players accept this situation, other players view relegation to the *B team,* on completion of the training period, as a demotion,[225] which has consequences in terms of the player's short career in sport. Article 15 of the 2009 version of the FIFA Player Status and Transfer Regulations provides that players are entitled to rescind their contracts with just cause if they can establish that they played in only 10% of the official matches played by the club during a season. This just cause will always be established on a case-by-case basis depending on the player's specific circumstances.

224. For further detail, see Albino Mendes Baptista, *Estudos Sobre o Contrato de Trabalho Desportivo.* (Coimbra: Coimbra Editora, 2006), pp. 140. et seq.

225. In fact, according to the Portuguese Football Federation B Team Regulations, such teams can only be created by 1st Division clubs. B teams must play in the 2nd Division B National Championship and cannot take part in the Portuguese Cup.

786. The duty to provide actual employment must include not only the physical conditions necessary for the participation and inclusion of the player in training and other activities preparatory to the competition, but also adequate psychological conditions, i.e., a working environment that favours sport activities.[226]

787. One of the obligations arising from the specificities of the RJCTPD is that the employer is required by the FPF regulations to permit its players to take part in the work of the Portuguese national teams. Article 45 of the LBAFD classifies participation in the work of national teams as a *mission in the public interest,* which should be particularly supported and ensured by the State. Articles 12 and 13 of the RJCTPD also impose an obligation to take part in the training and games of the national team, which is also binding on clubs. In the Portuguese case, the Federations have the power to regulate the terms on which sportspersons are released to play for national teams. If there is a League within the Federation, the question of the release of players to play in the national team must be governed by a contract between the Federation and the corresponding League. So far as financial compensation payable to the clubs is concerned, it is debated whether it should not be granted *in order to preserve the unpredictability of competition outcomes and therefore their integrity.*[227] The clubs have got together to lobby FIFA for the creation of a solidarity-based compensation mechanism with regard to the release of players for national teams. Cases related to the liability for injuries sustained by a player while in the service of the national team can be expected.

VII. The Duties of Professional Sportspersons

788. Sportspersons are obliged to take part in the work of national teams and to keep in good physical condition, i.e., to *maintain the physical condition, which enables them to compete in the sports competition that is the subject matter of the contract,* as per paragraph c) of Article 13 of the RJCTPD. Legal theorists have debated whether the extra-mural activities of players, i.e., their *nocturnal outings* can be regarded as a breach of the said provision. According to the provisions of the RJCTPD, sportspersons are subject to a duty to refrain from placing themselves in circumstances that are likely to affect their physical condition, in order not to run the risk of not performing at the best level pursuant to their employment contract. There is therefore a possibility that players could be punished for extra-mural conduct, which is likely to damage their physical or psychological condition, even if there are in fact no such consequences. Furthermore, employers have *internal regulations* with specific rules restricting the personal freedom of players that are, in principle, admissible, provided that the principle of *proportionality* is complied with. Players are also subject to a duty not to be involved in dangerous activities or

226. See Lúcio Correia, in *Limitações … supra.*, p. 63, note 107.

227. Emílio A. Garcia Silvero, '*A Libertação de Desportistas Para as Selecções Nacionais: Aspectos Jurídicos e Económicos*', Desporto & Direito Revista Jurídica do Desporto, Year III, No. 9, 2006, 382.

in other sports activities that have not been approved by the club, in order to preserve their physical condition, despite the absence of express provision to that effect.

789. Given the specificity of sports employment obligation and in order to ensure and control the physical condition of sportspersons on an *a priori* basis, Article 13 of the RJCTPD prevails over Article 19 of the Employment Code, which provides that employers may not, *require job applicants, or employees to submit to medical tests or examinations of any type with a view to the establishing their physical or psychological condition for the purposes of engagement or the continuation of employment (...).* The practice of clubs, i.e., to carry out medical examinations before signing contracts with players is acceptable in order to safeguard the clubs' legitimate interests. It is not however acceptable for a club, after having made the contract with the player, to claim just cause on the basis of a clause in the contract, which subjects the validity of the contract to the conduct of subsequent medical examinations. This is as provided in the 2008 version of the FIFA RSTP and is implicit in FIFA Circular no. 1171, of 24 November 2008, which established the Professional Football Player Contract Minimum Requirements.

790. Compliance by players with the ethics and discipline rules prevails over the general duty of obedience to the employer in Article 128 of the Employment Code. In this case, a player can legitimately refuse to take some substances even if they are obligatory in accordance with the employer's internal regulations.

VIII. Remuneration Clauses

791. Clauses that stipulate the variation of the remuneration payable to sportspersons in the event of promotion or relegation of the club or company are valid. This question is controversial however as it may amount to a breach of the principle of *equal work for equal pay.* However the justification for the rule is the changes wrought by a change of division in terms of alterations of sponsorship agreements, television broadcasting rights and other advantages and disadvantages, may reduce the income of the employer club and consequently of its employees.

792. In the absence of agreement to the contrary, when the remuneration includes a part that is related to the obtaining of certain sports results, the said amounts are deemed to fall due during the month following the month in which the results in question occurred.

IX. The *Normal Working Period*

793. For the purposes of the limitations of the normal working period in the Employment Code, time spent engaged in training programmes, and the journeys that precede or follow participation in sports competitions are not taken into consideration.

794. The weekly rest period in the RJCTPD differs, as the general law provides that the preferred weekly rest day is Sunday, which, in sport, is a day on which competitions take place.

795. The rules to be complied with in the definition and alteration of working hours also differ from the general law to the extent that it is the coach that decides on the times of training sessions, while competition times are fixed by the federations, or leagues.

796. The freedom to book holidays is also limited so that the holiday period is the period during which there are no official sports activities, which is frequently at the end of the season at the club for which the player plays.

X. Loan of Sportspersons

797. Given the specificity of CTDs, the rules and terms that permit the loan of an employee are, given the parties' legitimate interests, much broader than in the general law. On the one hand, the employee is put to profitable use while the lender is freed from a cost for which it was not receiving the corresponding benefit, and, on the other hand, a period of player inactivity is avoided, which is always prejudicial to both player and employer. Finally, the borrower is able to use the services of a player, which, if the player had been made available on any other basis, it might not have been able to afford.

798. Loans are only possible by agreement between the parties and if there is no alteration of the subject matter of the sports activity. The best way to effect the loan of a sports worker involves the inclusion of a statement by the player that he agrees to the loan and to obligations stipulated as to form. This statement must be registered in accordance with the RJCTPD.

XI. Option Clauses

799. Option clauses were commonly accepted as legal provided that they are agreed on by the parties, given the specificity of Sports Employment Contracts, but were held to be unconstitutional by a recent judgment of the FPF Paritary Arbitration Commission. Normally, options are granted to clubs, but there have been recent cases in which options have been granted to players. That is what happened in the Marcelo case, regarding a player for Associação Académica de Coimbra, in the 2004/2005 season, which resulted in a judgment of the Coimbra Employment Court on 26 August 2005. In this decision, the Court ordered the club to pay compensation to Marcelo. One of the clauses in the Sports Employment Contract between the parties was that *the contract shall also be valid for the 2004/2005 season, if the player considers that he is in possession of all his capacities and so wishes. In this case, the Club undertakes to pay the net sum of (…) € to be paid in 10 equal monthly net instalments of (…) €.*

800. The notice in due time given by Marcelo to the Club, stating that he complied with the preconditions and stating his wish to continue, were considered by the Court to be sufficient and the renewal of the contract took place merely by virtue of that expression of intent and the club's position to the effect that it was *not interested in the continuation of the employment of the player* was of no avail, for when an employer terminates an employment contract, in accordance with no. 2 of Article 27 of Law no. 28/98, of 26 June, the employee is entitled to be reinstated. According to the provisions of the CCT between the LPFP and the SJPF, i.e., Articles 48 and 49 thereof, the player was awarded compensation *equal to the amount of the remuneration that he would have received if the contract had run its full term (...).*

801. With the exception of the circumstances referred to above, it is clubs that normally have this type of option, i.e., the club has the right to renew or not to renew the contract, which amounts to a situation in which one of the parties is contractually bound to offer to renew, while the other party is entitled to accept or reject the offer and consequently to renew the employment contract for more seasons, or not.

802. What was at issue later in the N'Doye case was whether this right to compel the renewal of the contract is legally permissible. In the opinion of João Leal Amado,[228] Law no. 28/98, of 26 June does not permit employees to surrender both their freedom and stability simultaneously. Accordingly, an option agreement that makes the employee legally subject to the *club's mere whims* is inadmissible. According to this line of reasoning, no. 1 of Article 18 of Law no. 28/98, of 26 June, seems to support this solution when it provides that *clauses in a sports employment contract that seek to limit the sportsperson's freedom to work after the expiry of the contractual term, or to make it subject to conditions, shall be null and void.*

803. According to Paulo Leite Gonçalves,[229] *the legality of an option freely and knowingly agreed by the parties, in a sports employment contract (...) cannot be queried, given the special form of this type of employment contract*, provided that it does not *excessively restrict contractual freedom and does not amount to an agreement in fraudem legis.*

804. In fact this specificity of CTDs features in no. 1 of Article 17 of the FIFA Player Status and Transfer Regulations, which established that one of the factors to be taken into consideration in the calculation of the compensation due in respect of the rescission of an employment without just cause is the specificity of sport, so that Article 18 of the RJCTPD must be applied on a case-by-case basis in order to ascertain whether the sportsperson's freedom to work is prejudiced.

805. In the *N'Doye* case, the Paritary Arbitration Commission considered that in the case of a contract signed for one season, with an option in the club's favour for

228. João Leal Amado, *Temas Laborais 2*, Coimbra, Coimbra Editora, 2007, p. 153.

229. Paulo Leite Gonçalves, *O Direito de Opção na Prestação do Desportista Profissional. Memórias, II Congresso de Direito do Desporto, Almedina, 2006, p. 270.*

a further two seasons, *violates and restricts the player's/applicant's freedom to work, which is a legal asset that the legal provision in no. 1 of article 18 of Law 28/98, of 26 June in intended to protect,* because the player was subject the whim of the club. The judgment held that the clause was contrary to Article 47, no. 1 of CRP, which provides that *all people are entitled to freely choose their occupation or type of work, with the exception of the legal restrictions imposed in the collective interest, or that are inherent in their own capacity.* In this specific case, the option clauses were accordingly considered to be invalid and ineffective, and therefore null and void.

XII. Arbitration Clauses

806. It is evident from the RJCTPD that it is possible for a collective bargaining agreement to grant jurisdiction, in relation to labour disputes, to an arbitration tribunal.[230] However, the possibilities for the use of arbitration clauses are not limited to strictly employment matters. Private legal disputes relating to the parties' alienable rights may also be decided by arbitration tribunals. It is also possible to grant jurisdiction to an arbitration tribunal with regard to appeals against decisions made by an organ of a federation, association or any sports entity, which has been granted disciplinary powers by law.

807. It is to be supposed that, with the appearance of an Arbitration Tribunal with a special jurisdiction with regard to sports disputes, the Bylaws that govern each of the sports governed by, or subject to the authority of the Olympic Committee of Portugal, will have to be adapted in order to give exclusive, or at least prior, jurisdiction to these courts, with regard to disputes, which arise within a formal or de facto contractual relationship between two parties.

808. The possible powers and jurisdiction of the Portuguese Court of Arbitration for Sport is also an option. It should be noted that until such time as there is a collective bargaining agreement between the trade unions representing sportspersons and the equivalent employers' associations, there will be freedom to submit matters directly to CAS, whenever this is permitted by Portuguese law.

XIII. Sportspersons and the Right to Form and Belong to Associations

809. Freedom of association is a constitutional right that is enshrined in Article 46 of the CRP and is the right of individuals and associations to protect their interests and working conditions and the organizational forms and means in order to implement the protection of these rights.

810. In Portugal, all workers are entitled to belong to a trade union and to take part in its activities. The purpose of this mechanism is to enable workers to protect

230. Article 30.1 LFECS.

themselves from unjust discrimination, or to enforce rights that are not being respected by the employer.

811. Trade union freedom, as so defined, also includes the individual right not to belong to any type of trade union. The SJPF, unlike ordinary trade unions, which are primarily concerned to negotiate their members' salaries, has another type of aims, such as the abolition of temporary restrictions imposed on workers by employers, the provision of legal advice, the establishment of a salary guarantee fund for players whose employers become insolvent, protection of workers from any abuses of their image rights, life insurance, *inter alia,* by clubs. The SJPF is a member of the International Federation of Professional Footballers (FIFPro), an organization that defends the interests of football players in approximately forty countries.

812. It has been established that there could only be one trade union representing the employees in each sport. So far as the employers are concerned, it is incorrect to treat the federations as the employers' representative, as they are not associations or organizations, which can be joined freely and they have a system of voting and election procedures for their governing bodies that differ from the usual method. Nevertheless this inconsistency in the defence of employers' rights has been resolved since the creation of the professional leagues, which represent the clubs' interests.

XIV. The Right to Strike

813. Strikes are viewed historically as a collective reaction of workers against their employer in order to force home a point of view or to defend their collective rights. The right to strike is enshrined in Article 57 of the CRP, although the CRP does not include a definition of a strike and refers the regulation of the exercise of this right to sub-constitutional legislation. The limits of the exercise of the right to strike can be regulated by legislation, by the courts and by the agreement of the parties involved. The right to strike is an individual right that can never amount to breach of contract. Despite the fact that it is an individual right, it is normally exercised collectively. The law does, in exceptional circumstances, also admit the possibility of a one-person strike.

814. In Portugal, sport strikes are a recent and rare phenomenon. The most recent strike stories have involved groups of players, whose employers have not paid their salaries for a long time. In sport, the right to strike is seldom exercised. This is partially a consequence of a series of sports regulations, which provide in team sports, that failure by a team to appear for a game is always penalized *by loss of the game.* There is no record of the right to strike being claimed on the basis of the CRP in order to prevent the said consequences. Even when both teams fail to turn up for a match and both invoke a strike as grounds both teams are treated as having lost that game, which is understandable in order to safeguard and protect the normal conduct of competitions and because of the immense public interest in sports competitions and particularly football matches. It is nevertheless a matter of public knowledge that the SJPF has achieved many victories and agreements between parties by merely threatening strike action, without ever having actually led a players' strike.

XV. The Termination of Sports Employment Contracts

815. The possible causes of the termination of a CTD are as follows:

(a) effluxion of time
(b) revocation
(c) dismissal with just cause
(d) rescission with just cause
(e) abandonment of employment.

816. So far as the general legal framework is concerned, the grounds of individual redundancy and dismissal on the grounds of unsuitability do not apply to CTDs. Rescission of the contract without just cause is likewise inapplicable even though there is some doubt regarding this.

817. Even though there is no express legal provision regarding the admissibility of the inclusion of resolutive conditions in a CTD, there are doubts whether this is permissible, particularly in the case of clauses to the effect that the contract expires if the club or company is relegated. There are also doubts regarding the legality of a clause pursuant to which the contract expires if a player receives an offer from a specific club, or which provides for the payment of compensation to the player if the employer does not accept an offer of a certain amount.

818. While some authors maintain that clauses of this type are illegal, there are others that consider them to be justified on the grounds of the specificity of this type of contract.

819. Whatever the form of the termination of a sports employment contract, the termination is only effective once notice thereof has been given to the entities responsible for the obligatory registration of the contract, i.e., the Federation of the sport in question.

820. When just cause is invoked by a player as the grounds for the termination of the contract, the player is not required to pay the sums normally due to the employer pursuant to valorization clauses.

821. The legal provisions governing the termination of CTDs is very specific and have been the subject matter of much litigation as the CTD provisions in Portugal were primarily conceived with regard to sports employment contracts that involve large sums of money and there are no middle range provisions. The consequence of this is that the said provisions are wholly out of line with the realities of sport in Portugal. The fact that there is a great disparity in Portugal between the salaries of sportspersons depending on the sport in question and the circumstances of the employer club. This means that the Legal Framework governing CTDs is too general and is inappropriate for most sportspersons.

822. Constitutional Court Judgment no. 199/2009, published in the Official Journal, 2nd series, on 1 June, found that Article 27, no. 1 of the RJCTPD was unconstitutional, when interpreted to mean that *the rescission of a fixed term contract by a player, on the grounds of just cause only entitles the player to compensation that cannot exceed what the player would have been entitled to had the employment contract terminated at the end of the contractual term,* on the grounds of violation of Article 13 of the CRP, which establishes the *principle of equality.* According to Constitutional Court Judgment no. 409/99, *the principle of equality […], requires that equal treatment be afforded to what is essential equal and that matters that are essentially different be treated differently. The principle of equality, when considered as a limitation of legislative discretion, does not in fact prevent the ADoPtion of measures, which create distinctions. It does however prohibit the creation of measures that create discriminatory distinctions, i.e. unequal treatment that is unjustified or without any reasonable, objective and rational basis. The principle of equality as a binding legal principle amounts to a general idea of the prohibition of arbitrariness.*

823. The Constitutional Court also held in the said judgment that the provision in the RJCTPD prejudices sportspersons in two ways, i.e.:

(a) it does not entitle sportspersons to a minimum level of compensation;
(b) by capping the maximum amount of compensation payable there is a risk that the compensation will not include compensation for loss and damage incurred by the sportsperson that can be proved, merely because they fall outside the maximum compensation level.

824. As the contract to which the ordinary employment law framework applies is not very different from the contract that governs a player's employment relations with his club, the difference created with regard to this form of compensation, i.e., the limits introduced by the RJCTPD are considered to be inappropriate and contrary to the constitutional principle of equality.

825. No. 4 of Article 396 of the Employment Code retained the wording of Article 443 of the former law, i.e., Law no. 99/2003, of 27 August, i.e., that, in the general legal framework, the compensation payable to employees, whose employment terminates in the same circumstances is calculated on the basis of at least the payment that would have been due and payable until the end of the contractual term, i.e., the amount to which the employee would have been entitled if the contract had terminated on the expiry of the contractual term.

826. The case in question concerned a dispute between a basketball player and a club, in which the 1st instance Court ordered the payment of compensation to the player by the club corresponding to the amount that the player would have been entitled to throughout the season, less the amounts that the player received during that same season, from another club.

XVI. Player Transfers

A. *The Compensation for Formation and the Solidarity Mechanisms to Protect Training Clubs*

827. Recognizing the impact of the Bosman judgment on the transfer market and the imbalances it caused between clubs, FIFA altered the Player Status and Transfer Regulations in 2001, so as to bring them into line with the recommendation of the European Commission, which recognized the *specificity* of international transfers in football, as commercial exchanges between Member States.

828. The FIFA RSTP introduced financial compensation for clubs, which have had an influence on the players' training between the ages of 12 and 21, as a way of distributing the future profits produced by that work, at the time of a transfer for a large sum. Accordingly, if a player aged 23 or less is involved in an international transfer, the clubs involved in the training of the player between the ages of 12 and 21 are entitled to receive financial compensation, as soon as the player is registered for the first time as a professional player and is transferred between clubs that belong to different federations, whether the player is transferred as a player pursuant to the sports employment contract, or as a Free Player. The amount of compensation payable is calculated on the basis of the foreseeable costs that the new club would have had to incur if it had trained the player up until the time he was transferred.

829. In addition to the financial compensation for training mechanism, a *Solidarity Mechanism* was also created, which is only triggered if there is a financial transaction between clubs that are members of different federations, while the contract is in force, by way of temporary or definitive transfer, whatever the player's age on the transfer date. 5% is deducted from the transfer fee, which is then distributed to the clubs involved in the training of the player between the ages of 12 and 23. If any club does not claim its due, the corresponding sum is paid to the federation to which the club responsible for training the player belongs.

B. *The Locally Trained Player Concept*

830. With the increasing risk that the championships organized by federations that are members of UEFA will lose their national character, because of the exponential increase in the number of foreign players in club teams, UEFA created the concept of the *Locally Trained Player*.

831. In order to be a Locally Trained Player, a player must have been trained, between the ages of 15 and 21, by the club he is currently playing for *(Player Trained by the Club),* or by a club that is a member of the federation in which the player is registered *(Player trained in the Federation)* whatever the player's nationality. The relevant period for this purpose is the length of presence and registration in the federation during the said specific period when the player was being trained. The main effect of this rule is that young players are obliged to establish themselves and remain with their club of origin.

832. Portugal has adopted the Locally Trained Player concept in its internal competitions and has interpreted it to mean that a player complies with the obligatory period if he spent it not only with the club played for on his registration date, but also if time was spent with a club that is a member of the FPF *(Player Trained in the Federation).*

833. As from the 2006/2007 season there has been a requirement in matches organized by UEFA that four of the twenty-five players selected for the either the Champions League or the UEFA Cup must be Locally Trained Players and that of those at least two must have spent their training period with the club that registered them. Clubs may accordingly only field twenty-one players, who are not deemed to be locally trained. This number of Locally Trained Players was increased by two for the 2007/2008 season (one according to each understanding of the concept, with a minimum of three players who are Players Trained by the Club), thus reducing the number of other players to nineteen. Finally in 2008/2009, the number of Locally Trained Players was increased to eight, of which four must be Players Trained by the Club, which, in practice, reduces the number of players permitted in UEFA matches, who are not Locally Trained Players from twenty-five to seventeen.

834. The aim of this new concept is to protect training and to promote the national identity of football. Clubs with more financial weight have, for a considerable time, been willing to hire players in lower and lower age groups in order to comply with the training period obligatory for the Locally Trained Player concept. This may not be in line with the FIFA rules, which prohibit the international transfer of players aged less than 18, except when the player's legal representatives change domicile along with the player, for reasons unrelated to football. In the EU, the age limit for player transfers is 16.

835. As Rita Figueira[231] well observes, the solution found by UEFA *may not meet the purpose for which it was created.* With the liberalization of the market on the basis of a criterion that does not involve the players' nationality, what major clubs are doing is to hire players earlier. This poses great problems for child players, who may be unable to live up to the expectations created. The international

231. Rita Figueira, *Reflexões sobre a liberalização do mercado no Futebol*, Desporto & Direito n.º 14, Coimbra Editora, pp. 45 et seq.

sports jurisdictional bodies have as yet not taken steps to deal with this evident conflict. In Portugal, the existing legislation regarding training contracts, i.e., Decree-Law no. 28/98, of 26 June, is out-of-date and needs to be altered, given the new problems that have arisen, and the recent LBAFD.

836. Accordingly, mechanisms have been created, which, to a certain extent, re-established the equilibrium between championships that are essentially exporters and championships that are essentially importers. However, experience demonstrates that exporter clubs frequently experience difficulties in enforcing their rights, which has led FIFA to intervene in many cases.

C. The 6+5 Rule

837. In February 2008, FIFA proposed to invoke the so called '6+5 rule'. This rule seeks to compel all clubs to field a minimum of six local players, who would be eligible to play for the national team of the country, in which their club is domiciled, in any given match. FIFA intended to have this rule fully operational by 2010. Its first step towards attaining this goal took place on 30 May 2008, when the rule received the required two-thirds majority at the FIFA congress.[232]

838. This rule was however strongly opposed by the European Association of Clubs (ECA), led by the now extinct G14 group of clubs.[233] The European Union also expressed their criticism of this proposed rule, and stated that it was unlawful and a violation of the freedom of work and movement guaranteed by EU law[234] as provided by Article 39 of the EU Treaty.

839. At its 60th Congress on 11 June 2010, UEFA pulled back from its intention to implement this rule in 2012, without prejudice to considering new forms of 'eligibility'. This ultimately led FIFA to abandon its intention to introduce this rule as the same was deemed to be contrary to the EU laws.

D. The Home-Grown Player Rule

840. In sharp contrast to the FIFA 6+5 rule, the UEFA home-grown players rules seem to have carried the day in the eyes of the EU. The key difference between the

232. Interestingly, a number of members from the African and south American confederations whose football has vastly benefited outside the 6+5 rule voted in favour of this rule, which could well have repercussions on the standards of their national teams.
233. The ECA view the 6+5 rule as unnecessary, and instead endorse the home-grown players proposals.
234. 'Compared with the 6+5 plan proposed by FIFA, which is incompatible with EU law, the Commission considers that UEFA has opted for an approach which seems to comply with the principle of free movement of workers while promoting the training of young European players' EU Press release of 28 May 2008, see http://europa.eu/rapid/pressReleasesAction.do?reference=IP/08/807&format=HTML&aged=0&language=EN&guiLanguage=en.

home-grown players rule and FIFA 6+5 rule is that unlike the FIFA rule, the home-grown players rule involves no restrictions based on players' nationalities.

841. Introduced in 2005, the UEFA home-grown players rule require clubs participating in the Champions League and the UEFA Cup to have a minimum number of home-grown players, i.e., players who, regardless of their nationality, have been trained by their club or by another club in the same national association, for at least three years between the age of 15 and 21. A minimum of eight home-grown players must be included in the twenty-five man squad fielded by clubs in all UEFA club competitions.

842. Despite having received EU backing, questions still linger as to the compatibility of this rule with EU law and possible avenues for challenging it. This leads us to the question – How different are the UEFA home-grown players rule and the FIFA 6+5 rule? What are the features of the rules that make them compliant with the EU laws of freedom of work, movement and equal treatment, in so far as non-discrimination is concerned? It appears feasible to challenge these rules under EU laws in as far as they discriminate indirectly between players rights to move and work within the EU, contrary to Article 39.

843. The main aim of the UEFA home-grown players rule is to promote and to protect the quality training of young footballers within the EU and to consolidate the balance of competitions. It aims to encourage clubs to invest in training and in the setting up of football academies for children rather than investing in the hiring of footballers from foreign countries. The idea is that the national football teams of all UEFA member countries will be provided with a flow of talent from their club academies.

844. The home-grown players rule only applies to UEFA club competitions, i.e., the Champion's League and the UEFA Cup. It does not apply to domestic competitions, although UEFA has encouraged its members to adopt the rule in their own competitions. These rules favour of all home-grown players trained by clubs in the national association they play in.

845. Home-grown players have been defined by UEFA as players who, regardless of their nationality or age, have been trained by their club, or by another club in the relevant national association, for at least three years, between the ages of 15 and 21. The UEFA rule does not contain any nationality conditions.

846. The rules adopted by UEFA have been implemented gradually in successive stages and began with the inclusion of four home-grown players out of 25 in the 2006/07 season. This was followed by six home-grown players in the 2007/08 season. The 2008/09 season saw the full implementation of the rule, with clubs being required to field eight home-grown players out of twenty-five. The rule only applies to UEFA club competitions.

E. The Andrew Webster Case

847. One of the most recent decisions with a significant effect on sports employment law is the CAS decision on the *Andrew Webster* case.[235] In this case, the professional footballer rescinded his contract with the club. The player was accordingly required, by Article 17 of the FIFA RSTP, to compensate the club for the absence of just cause for the rescission and on the basis of the *Principle of contractual stability between players and clubs,* to which the FIFA RSTP refers.

848. The key aspect of the case was the amount of the compensation payable by the player. The player considered that he was only required to pay the amount of the remuneration to which he would have been entitled had the contract run its full term, which was approximately EUR 200,000. The club claimed compensation corresponding to the player's market value, i.e., an amount to be determined equitably in expectation of the amount to which the club would have been entitled if it had sold the player, all other factors being equal, i.e., the player's physical and psychological condition and development.

849. The arguments and the way the decision was reasoned are important and merit citation *verbatim.* The arbitration panel wrote that:

> 142. From an economic perspective there is no reason to believe that a player's value on the market owes more to training by a club than to a player's own efforts, discipline and natural talent. An empirical study might even demonstrate the contrary, i.e. that a talented and hardworking player tends to fare well, stand out and succeed independently from the exact type of training he receives, whereas an untalented and/or lazy player will be less successful no matter what the environment. Also market value could stem in part from charisma and personal marketing. In any case, it is clear that a club cannot simply assume it is the only source of success of a player and thus claim his entire market value, without bringing any proof (which would be very difficult) of its paramount role in the player's success leading to his market value. In this case, Hearts have underlined the player's success and alleged his market value but have brought no evidence that the club entirely or even predominantly generated the alleged market value in question through its training and education.
>
> 143. In addition from an economic and moral point of view, it would be difficult to assume a club could be deemed the source of appreciation in market value of a player while never be deemed responsible for the depreciation in value. Consequently, if the approach relied on by Hearts

235. Judgment of 30 Jan. 2008 (CAS 2007/A/1298-1299-1300), with a panel of arbitrators comprising Quentin Byrne Sutton, (Switzerland), Jean-Jacques Bertrand (France), Michael Beloff (United Kingdom).

were followed, players should be entitled to claim for example that they are owed compensation for the alleged decrease in market value caused by such matters as being kept on the bench for too long or having an incompetent trainer etc. Obviously such a system would be unworkable and would not serve the good of football.

144. From a regulatory standpoint, to allow clubs to claim market value of players as lost profit under article 17 of the FIFA Status Regulations would not make sense and would amount to double counting, since, as mentioned earlier, article 20 and annex already provide for a system of compensation to clubs for the training and education of players, and it is not by chance that such compensation is not based on the players market value but on demonstrable investments made and cost incurred by the club.

145. Moreover, since a club's possible entitlement to the transfer or market value of players is entirely absent from the criteria of compensation listed in article 17(1) and there is no reference to any such form of compensation in favour of Hearts in the player's employment contracts, to apply such a criteria and thereby imply it into the contract would contradict both the principle of fairness and the principle of certainty.

146. Finally, because of the potentially high amounts of compensation involved, giving clubs a regulatory right to the market value of players and allowing lost profits to be claimed in such manner would in effect bring the system back to pre-Bosman days when player's freedom of movement was unduly hindered by transfer fees and their careers and wellbeing could be seriously affected by them becoming pawns in the hands of their clubs and a vector through which clubs could reap considerable benefits without sharing the profit or taking corresponding risks. In view of the text and history of article 17(1) of the FIFA Status Regulations, allowing any form of compensation that could have such an effect would clearly be anachronistic and legally unsound.

147. For the above reason, the panel finds that Hearts is not entitled to claim any part of the player's alleged market value as lost profit or on any other ground and that as a result its corresponding claim for £4.000.000, must be rejected.

850. In Portugal, a Judgment of the Supreme Court of Justice, in proceedings commonly referred to in the world of sport as the *Zé Tó* case,[236] similarly reduced the compensation payable by the player, who had rescinded his contract with the club unilaterally, to the amount of the remuneration that he would have earned if the contract had run its full course, as provided in Article 27 of the RJCTPD.

236. Judgment of the STJ, dated 7 Mar. 2007. Available at http://www.dgsi.pt/jstj.nsf/954f0ce6ad9dd8b980256b5f003fa814/6fcf637fd779f32880257297005966c1?OpenDocument.

F. The Matuzalém Case

851. The most recent case of clear relevance to employment relations between clubs and players is the famous *Matuzalém* case.[237] Matuzalém Francelino da Silva signed a contract for five years with the Ukrainian club Shakhtar Donetsk, effective as from 1 July 2004 and expiring on 1 July 2009. The Ukrainian club paid the Italian club *Brescia Calcio Spa*, the sum of EUR 8,000,000 for the player's services. After completing three years of the contract, corresponding to three sports seasons and some salary increases and an offer for the player of EUR 7,000,000, which Shakhtar Donetsk declined on 2 July 2007, the player decided to rescind his sports employment contract unilaterally, without claiming just cause. On 19 July 2007, the player signed a new sports employment contract, this time with the Spanish club Real Zaragoza SAD, for three seasons.

852. Taking advantage of a clause in the sports employment contract, which required the Ukrainian club to release the player in the event of an offer to acquire him for EUR 25,000,000, the club considered that the player could only release himself from his obligations to the club for that sum, and demanded the said sum from the player and the Spanish club. As neither the player nor the Spanish club paid the amount demanded by the Ukrainian club, the latter club commenced proceedings in the FIFA Dispute Resolution Chamber seeking the payment of the said sum of EUR 25,000,000, on the grounds of facts related to the unjustified unilateral rescission by the player.

853. On 2 November 2007, the FIFA Dispute Resolution Chamber held, in a decision that was based on few palpable arguments or criteria, partially in favour of the club, *Shakhtar Donetsk,* that it was entitled to compensation in the sum of EUR 6,800,000. Both parties appealed to CAS in terms similar to those of the complaint submitted to the FIFA Dispute Resolution Chamber.

854. This time the decision was somewhat more detailed and based on more specific criteria and was to the effect that the compensation of EUR 11,858,934 was payable by the player to *Shakhtar Donetsk,* as a consequence of the unilateral rescission of his sports employment contract without just cause, in accordance with the criteria in Article 17 of the FIFA RSTP. The factors that the arbitrators took into consideration in accordance with the said regulations were as follows:

(a) the player's remuneration, not only with the previous club, but also with the new club;
(b) loss of profits;
(c) sums expended in the hiring of the player;
(d) costs inherent in the replacement of the player;
(e) amount expended in training the player;

237. Judgment of 19 May 2009 (CAS 2008/A/1519-1520), with a panel of arbitrators comprising Michele Bernasconi, (Switzerland), Ulrich Haas (Switzerland) and Jean-Jacques Bertrand (France).

(f) the legislation in the country (the Ukraine in this case); and
(g) the specificity of sport.

855. Having considered the abovementioned criteria, CAS considered that the real value of the services of the player Matuzalém was EUR 11,258,934. To this amount was added the sum of EUR 600,000 under the heading of the *specificity of the sport,* although without providing objective quantitative criteria as to how the said amount was arrived at. CAS also held that the Spanish club Real Zaragoza was jointly liable with regard to the payment of the compensation.

856. This decision amounts to a case-law reversal in relation to the *Webster* case and demonstrates that there is, as yet, no fixed case-law in this type of case, or even criteria that can be used in advance in order to determine the compensation payable by the player in the event of unilateral rescission without just cause by the player. On the one hand, this is a source of legal uncertainty, which is much to be avoided in an organized system of law. On the other hand, it is clear that each case will be considered separately and that the decision with take the reasons and circumstances that resulted in the rescission, into consideration. The court will seek to preserve the stability of the employment relationship, a principle, which should govern contractual relations between clubs and players.

857. This uncertainty is of fundamental importance, so that players carefully consider the economic and sports effects of unilateral rescission without just cause. Clubs are aware that they can be held to be jointly liable with the player to pay any compensation and will therefore ponder the risks and financial repercussions of the hiring of a player in such circumstances.

858. On a critical note, both FIFA and CAS appear to be unable to define *the specificity of the sport* criterion, which appears to be determined at random, without any specific grounds for its inclusion as a head of damage. This legal uncertainty has no positive aspects. It is very important that these matters be considered on a case-by-case basis but it is also very important to define clear criteria on which the considerations and decisions of decision-making bodies can be based.

859. The message that CAS wished to transmit is that rescission without just cause is not a player's right but unlawful conduct within the ambit of a contractual relationship, which may have serious consequences in terms of compensation.

G. Webster versus Matuzalém

860. There are two fundamental differences between these two cases. In the Matuzalém Judgment, there is a significant alteration of the calculation of the compensation in accordance with Article 17 of the FIFA RSTP, in that the amount of remuneration to which the player would have been entitled if the player's sports employment contract had run its full term, is not the sole criterion adopted. The court sought to determine the real value of the loss and damage to the club prejudiced as a consequence of the rescission of the contract without just cause, via the application of criteria, which permit the identification of the real value of the player's services to the club.

861. Another clear difference that can be observed on comparing the two decisions is their differing interpretations of the objective of Article 17 of the FIFA RSTP. While, in the *Webster* case, the understanding was that the rescission of a sports employment contract without just cause by the player was the player's right, it was demonstrated in the *Matuzalém* case that the performance of the sports employment contract is a duty, which the player cannot evade, and that, if he does, he runs the serious risk of having to pay compensation to his former club.

862. What is now considered to be more important and which was perhaps overlooked at the time of the *Webster* case, because of the specific peculiarities of that case, in which the sportsman was treated unjustly because he did not want to renew his contract, is that the performance of the contract is obligatory. This is fundamentally a question of contractual good faith and the enforceability of the *pacta sunt servanta,* which should also govern contractual relations in professional sport. For this reason, in cases of unilateral rescission without just cause, the decision should contain a punitive element in order to create awareness of the need to comply with the important principle of contractual stability.

863. Notwithstanding the fact that the amount of the award in the *Matuzalém* case was exorbitant according to normal standards, given the care taken by CAS to consider all of the requirements of Article 17 of the FIFA RSTP, and despite the lack of coherent grounds and quantification criteria with regard to the head of the *specificity of sport* could be faulted, this case is, for the time being, the leading case with regard to damages for unilateral breach of a sports employment contract without just cause, by the sportsperson.

864. Nevertheless, until such time as there is an alteration or announcement by FIFA, which determines the way in which Article 17 of the RSTP should be construed in order to resolve the current doubts and introduce greater legal certainty, plus some supporting case-law, many other cases will give rise to the same, or greater, polemic in this area.

§2. EMPLOYMENT CONTRACTS OF COACHES

I. Introduction

865. As professional coaches do not fall within the concept of sportsperson, it is necessary to establish what legal framework is applicable to contracts between clubs or SADs and professional coaches. The case-law is almost unanimous in considering that the contract in question is an employment contract and that the RJCTPD applies to coaches, as the ordinary employment law framework is inappropriate for this type of contract. In practice and without prejudice to the application of the ordinary employment legal framework, the provisions in force with regard to sportspersons are applicable when the said framework is inappropriate in terms of, or incompatible with, the specific nature of the contractual relationship between Clubs or SADs and professional coaches.

866. In November 1996, the LPFP and the ANTF signed a CCT, which was subsequently extended administratively. Article 2 of the said CCT defines the subjective aspect of the application thereof to *professional coaches, who are engaged on an exclusive basis, in the preparation, technical orientation and training of football teams for remuneration, pursuant to an established and regular relationship with and under the direction and control of a club or sports company.* Article 8 thereof provides that *the employment contract shall always be for a fixed term and shall terminate on the expiry of the term stipulated therein. However the contract can be extended by mutual agreement of the parties for a period equal to the initial term, or for some other period.*

II. Professional Coaches

867. Coaches in Portugal therefore have a special status so far as their contractual status and employment conditions are concerned. The Collective Labour Agreement specifically applies to the employment relations between professional coaches and clubs, which are members of the Portuguese Professional Football League.

868. The CCT has special provisions relating to remuneration, termination of contracts, compensation, rights, duties and obligations of coaches towards clubs and vice versa. The provisions of this CCT prevail over the contractual agreements agreed between the club and the coach, but only if the application of the provisions of the CCT is more favourable to the coach.

869. Annexe 3 Article 1 of the CCT sets out the minimum professional requirements with which a coach and his technical staff must comply in order to be eligible for employment by a club.

870. Coaches' employment contracts are required to be in writing, signed by the club and the coach and must be for a fixed term.[238] According to Article 9 of the CCT, coaches cannot start to perform their duties until their contracts have been registered with the Portuguese Football Federation, the Portuguese Professional Football League and the National Association of Football Coaches. The CCT allows clubs to hire a coach on the basis of a temporary loan, subject to the consent of the coach. Such loans are subject to the registration required under Article 9.

871. The club owes the coach a number of duties pursuant to this contract, which include the duty to respect the coach as a member of staff, to pay his salary on time,

238. Articles 6 and 8 of the CCT.

and to provide him with good working conditions. Clubs must also ensure that coaches can exercise their right to join and participate in trade unions and must also compensated for any illnesses, loss or damage sustained as a result of an accident at work. Conversely, a coach is obliged to respect the club, as his employer, the players and his superiors. He is bound to comply with the orders and instructions of the club and its representatives in matters related to performance of his work and the sport in question. Clubs have the disciplinary power to fine, dismiss, warn or suspend coaches. Such sanctions are without prejudice to further action by other sports disciplinary bodies.

872. One of the features of the CCT, which takes the specific nature of sport into consideration, is that it makes coaches exclusively responsible for preparing and making decisions in matters related to the technical, tactical and physical organization of the team. Coaches have the right to chooses the players, who will play in any match, to stipulate the times when players will be required to report to the changing rooms, to designate training sessions, hours, locations and, where necessary, to recommend the holding of friendly matches to the club. According to Article 13(f), the coach has disciplinary powers in respect of the players and technical staff, who are responsible to him, and is required to inform the employer of the disciplinary sanctions, of which he is aware, for purposes of disciplinary proceedings. In all these actions, the club is not entitled to prejudice the coaches' working conditions or to require him to provide services, which have not been contracted for. Conversely, coaches are prohibited, in the absence of the club's express consent, from performing any other remunerated sports activity while their contracts are in force.

873. Coaches are entitled to an annual holiday of thirty days per season. Coaches with contracts of less than one year are entitled to a minimum holiday of two and a half days for every thirty days of work actually done. The CCT establishes minimum basic salaries payable to coaches by clubs, depending on the division the club plays in. Coaches, who train 1st division clubs are entitled to a minimum basic salary equivalent to eight times the normal minimum salary in Portugal. The salary scales for other coaches are as follows, their assistants being entitled to half of these amounts:

(a) in the 2nd national division club coaches – 4 x the minimum national salary;
(b) in the 2nd national division B club coaches – 3 x the national minimum salary;
(c) in the 3rd national division club coaches – 2 x the national minimum salary;
(d) other divisions and juvenile club level coaches – 1 x the national minimum salary.[239]

874. Contractual relations between coaches and clubs can be terminated by mutual agreement, effluxion of time, rescission by either party, or by dismissal by the club with or without just cause. Coaches are entitled to rescind with just cause when the club:

239. These amounts are inclusive of match bonuses as well as Christmas and holiday bonuses. See Arts 30 and 31 of the CCT.

(a) wilfully neglects to pay the coach's salaries on time, or fails to pay the coach at all;
(b) violates the coaches' rights and privileges, physical integrity, honour or dignity;
(c) improperly imposes disciplinary sanctions on the coach.[240]

875. When a coach rescinds with due cause, the coach is entitled to a compensation equal to the remuneration he would have received had the employment contract terminated on the expiry of its term, provided that at least six months prior notice is given of the intention to rescind. This sum includes bonuses. Failure to give the said notice renders the coach liable to pay compensation to the club equal to the remuneration corresponding to the period of notice not given. A club can dismiss a coach with just cause if he engages in any of the following acts:

(a) wrongful failure to comply with the orders of his employer or his employer's representatives;
(b) repeated provocation of or involvement in conflicts with members of the team and members of the club's governing bodies;
(c) repeated failure to comply with the applicable conduct and disciplinary;
(d) seriously damaging the club's financial interests;
(e) physical violence, insults or offences against the person;
(f) persistent failure to comply with sporting ethics and rules of conduct;
(g) unjustified absence from work for five consecutive days, or ten interpolated days resulting in serious loss or damage to the club.

876. The situation is different in cases of unilateral termination of the contract by the coach. In such instances, the coach is liable to compensate the club in an amount not less than half the as yet unaccrued remuneration. Where the damage incurred by the club exceeds this amount, then the club/employer is entitled to commence legal proceedings against the coach to recover the additional amounts.

877. A special Arbitration Committee has been established to decide any dispute between the parties arising from an employment contract made in accordance with the CCT. The decisions of the Arbitration Committee are final and are not appealable to the courts.

878. The conclusion reached is that the legal framework applicable to contracts between coaches and non-professional clubs is that of general employment law, although it is admitted that this solution is not the most appropriate given the specificity of the contractual relationship between coaches and clubs.

879. As was also the case of sportspersons, it would be desirable if there was legislation introducing a legal solution adapted to the needs of sports coaches, in addition to the existing Collective Bargaining Agreement, which is of limited application.

240. See Art. 39 of the CCT.

III. The Legal Framework Governing Access to the Profession of Sports Coach

880. The State has, from early on, been concerned to regulate sports activities and those involved in sport. This concern appeared for the first time in Decree-Law no. 553/77, of 31 December, which was subsequently ratified by Law no. 63/78, of 29 September, which gives the State the direct responsibility for the training of technical staff, with the exception of physical education teachers. Subsequently, Decree-Laws 98/85, of 4 April, 163/85 and 164/85, of 15 May, reformed the 1977 policy, by regulating the training of sports coaches and other sports actors.

881. In 1991, the provisions regarding the training of coaches and players agents respectively were introduced by Decree-Laws nos 350/91 and 351/91, of 19 September, within the ambit of the LBSD. Via this legislation, the State transferred the powers and responsibilities with regard to the organization of the entire training process to the federations. Consequently the profession of sports coach was given a scale structure and there was an increase in the supply of training, which was now offered by the federations. However the regulations governing admission plans and conditions were never introduced by the State.

882. In 1999, the training and certification of players' agents was included in the National Vocational Certification System, via the publication of the Legal Framework governing Sports Training included in the Vocational Training Framework, in Decree-Law no. 407/99, of 15 October. In this way the State regulated the training system, while permitting public and private bodies to contribute to it.

883. Decree-Law no. 248-A/2008, of 31 December, introduced the legal framework governing access to and the exercise of the profession of sports coach, in accordance with the provisions of the Legal Framework of Sports Training in the Vocational Training Framework, established by Decree-Law no. 407/99, of 15 October and Decree-Law no. 396/2007, of 31 December, which introduced the Legal Framework of the National Qualifications System and defined the structures involved in the workings thereof. This decree-law was long-awaited and amounts to a return to a policy which seeks to increase the professionalization of this profession, given the need to protect essential legal assets such as the health of the sportspersons and others with whom coaches work.

884. This legislative initiative in accordance with the provisions of Articles 35 and 43 of the LBAFD, is based on the recognition that the existence of duly qualified coaches is an indispensable measure not only in order to ensure the qualitative and quantitative development of the various physical and sports activities, but also in order to ensure that sports activities proceed in accordance with the rules that ensure sports ethics, the development of the sporting spirit and the protection of the health and safety of sportspersons.

885. This Decree-Law also includes some matters, which were omitted from Decree-Law no. 407/99, of 15 October, i.e., supervision, fees and penalties. The

Decree-Law also established the equivalence of diplomas issued pursuant to the now repealed Decree-Law no. 351/91, of 19 September, and the degrees in this Decree-Law.

886. The exercise of the profession of sports coach by a person, who is not a holder of a sports coach's licence, is made illegal and provision is made regarding the corresponding penalty provisions. According to the new legal framework, possession of a Qualifications Diploma is obligatory for coaches, who work as such on an exclusive or habitual basis, independently of whether or not the said activity is remunerated.

887. The scope of the application of the diploma goes beyond circumstances in which there is a full-time activity as a sports coach and also includes those circumstances in which the activity is habitual.

888. According to the new legal framework, coaches, who work as such exclusively or habitually – whether seasonally or occasionally – whether or not they are remunerated, are obliged to possess a Qualifications Diploma. The training of coaches is organized with a view to two different occupations:

(a) coaching of sportspersons for sports competitions: within the ambit of sports federations with Sports Public Utility Status;
(b) coaching of sportspersons for sports competitions: within the ambit of other physical and sports activities, whether or not the same are organized under the auspices of the said federations.

889. The provisions of the decree-law are therefore not limited to full-time coaches, but also include coaches, who only work on a regular basis. For each competitive level of sport there must be an equivalent coaching qualification level, which ranges from assistant coach, to coach, senior coach and head coach.

890. Working as a coach without a Qualification Diploma has the consequence that the underlying contract is null and void and is an administrative offence that may result in the imposition of a fine (cf. Article 280 of the Civil Code). The consequence is the same if the coach is employed (cf. Article 113 of the Employment Code) although in this case the void contract is treated as valid, while it is in force, as to the effects thereof. This aspect is relevant to the extent that the rules governing the termination of employment contracts apply pending a declaration of nullity, or the setting aside of the contract, so that there can be no dismissal without just cause.

891. Another essential aspect of this decree-law is the transitional provisions with regard to those currently working as coaches. According to the provisions of the legal framework now approved, holders of coach training course certificate are required, within one year of the coming into force of the Decree-Law, to apply to exchange their qualification certificate for the corresponding Qualification Diploma. After the said period, the former certificates will no longer be valid for the purposes of work as a coach.

§3. Players' Agents

I. Introduction

892. The position of players' agent is a specific feature of the RJCTPD, which has no parallel in any other employment relationship. An agent can represent either a player or a club in one transaction but may not represent both the player and the agent in the same transaction. However, players agents are of fundamental importance in the sports legal system, as they are a type of promoter and intermediary who play an essential role in the negotiation of the sportsperson's CTD.

893. According to João Leal Amado,[241] the *third man* is gaining increasing pre-eminence in the world of professional sport, above all in the making of employment contracts. This is made possible because of *the triumph of professional sport and the colossal expansion of the sport-entertainment industry (...), combined with the progressive dismantling of the rules that limit the contractual freedom of the sportsperson/employee.*

II. Legal Framework

894. The definition in no. 1 of Article 37 of the LBAFD describes players' agents as *duly licensed natural or juristic persons, who are in the occasional or permanent business of representation or intermediation in connection with the making of sports training contracts, sports employment contracts, or contracts with regard to image rights.*

895. The RJCTPD was the first Portuguese law to refer to the concept of a player's agent. Entry to the profession is limited to those natural or juristic persons, who are authorized by the proper national or international sports bodies, e.g., FIFA. Portugal does not as yet have specific regulations with regard to this profession.

896. The law establishes the principle that a player's agent may only act for and on behalf of one of the parties in the contractual relationship during the negotiation of the CTD and which prohibits players' agents from acting for and on behalf of sportspersons, who are minors. This limits their activity, as a significant proportion of the CTDs signed pursuant to the RJCTPD are sports training contracts that are signed by sportspersons aged between 14 and 18. The prohibition does not prohibit acting for and on behalf of sportspersons in sports training contracts, as they can be signed by a sportsperson over 18, but is only a restriction as to the age of the person represented.

897. The RJCTPD makes the following provisions regarding the incompatibilities between the profession of players' agent and other professions:

---

241. João Leal Amado. 'Vinculação *Versus* Liberdade. O Processo de Constituição e Extinção da Relação Laboral do Praticante Desportivo'. Coimbra: Coimbra Editora, 2002, pp. 487 et seq.

without prejudice to other limitations introduced by national or international federation regulations, the following are prohibited from being players agents:

(a) [s]ports companies;
(b) [c]lubs;
(c) [s]ports managers and directors;
(d) [o]fficers of sports companies;
(e) [c]oaches, sportspersons, referees, physicians and masseurs.

898. No. 3 of Article 37 of the LBAFD, for the first time, creates a duty of professional secrecy in relation to facts concerning the private or professional lives of professional sportspersons of which a player's agent becomes aware by virtue and in the performance of his/her duties. The LBAFD also widens the ambit of the role of players' agents, when it expressly provides that a player's agent can represent one of the parties with regard to image rights contracts.

899. Legal provisions apart, the real role of a player's agent involves considerably more that the negotiation of CTDs and includes various areas, such as management of the sportspersons career and income, which involves a knowledge of marketing, accounting, sponsorship and taxation. Given the wide range of services that a player's agent can provide, payment agreements are frequently made, which prevent the application of the legal provision to the effect that, *in the absence of agreement otherwise, which shall be in writing and included in the initial contract, the maximum amount receivable by the players' agent shall not be more than 5% of the global value of the contract.*

900. Generally, the player's agent requires the contract to include a clause according to which the sportsperson cannot make any contract directly with third parties so that all proposals must accordingly be addressed to the agent.

901. According to the law, *players' agents, who wish to work as intermediaries in the engagement of sportspersons, are required register as such with the sports federation of the sport in question, which must have an organised and up-to-date register for that purpose.* The said registration may be made with the corresponding league, when it exists within the federation on a form that identifies the agent. The law also provides that agency agreements made with a player's agent and contractual provisions that provide for the remuneration of the players agent, which are not duly registered, are null and void.

III. FIFA Regulations Governing the Profession of Player's Agent

902. So far as football is concerned, the example followed is the FIFA Players Agents Regulations, which, until 2001, required the candidate players' agents to post a non-repayable bond of CHF 200,000 in order to obtain a licence and registration. This requirement was not included in the Regulations that came into force on 1 September, after the European Commission, in its communication no. IP/99/

782, of 21 October 1999, entitled *Commission launches formal proceedings on FIFA rules governing players' agents,* considered that the requirement of such a bond, of such a considerable amount, was an unjustifiable limitation of access to free employment and a violation of the freedom to supply services. The said communication also concerned the restrictions regarding the exercise of the activity of players' agent by a juristic person and the restrictions imposed on recourse by sportspersons to unregistered agents. FIFA adopted the recommendations of the commission and abolished all of these limitations in the Regulations, which came into force in 2001, which were subsequently amended and expanded in the version currently in force since 1 January 2008.

903. The Players' Agents Regulations deal with relations between FIFA agents, players and professional clubs, and not only introduced penalties, but introduced the criteria for access to qualification as a FIFA agent, established a code of conduct and proposes a standard form contract between the agent and the player or club.

904. The most relevant points in the Regulations are the prohibition that prevents any player or club from seeking or engaging the services of an agent other than an agent licensed by FIFA and the stipulation of the conditions that must govern contractual relations with a FIFA-licensed agent. In fact the national federations are entitled to organize written examinations twice a year with a view to the registration of any natural person as a FIFA agent.[242] Another noteworthy point is the requirement that candidates for FIFA agent status must take out civil liability insurance cover with an insurance company in the country where they took the exam after having passed the written examination and in order to be accepted for registration.[243] The policy must include cover of any risk arising from acts comprised in the activity of Players Agents, during and after the termination of the contractual relationship. Alternatively, the candidate may post a bank guarantee for at least CHF 100,000 in favour of FIFA with any Swiss bank.[244] This requirement once again raises a question regarding another possible unjustified limitation of free access to employment. However, this question has not yet been raised before the European courts.

905. The remuneration of Players' Agents may be paid by either the club or the player represented, as is clear from Article 24 of the RJCTPD and it is established, in the absence of other agreement between the parties that the remuneration is subject to a maximum limit of 5% of the contract total. However, the Agent may only represent one of the parties in the negotiations and may likewise only be paid by one of these parties.

906. According to the FIFA Regulations,[245] when an agent is representing a club, the agent can only be paid for the work done for that club and the other club cannot

242. Article 5 of FIFA RSTP.
243. Article 6 of FIFA RSTP.
244. Article 7 of FIFA RSTP.
245. Article 29 of FIFA RSTP, 2008 version.

pay any amount or percentage with regarding the current or future transfer of any player involved in the negotiations between the clubs. The agent may accordingly only receive a commission from one of the parties involved in the transaction.

907. We note, on reflection, that there is a need for an alternative in order to improve the control and supervision of Players' Agents; as the reality is very different from what is required by national legislations and federation rules, above all in matters concerning the rules governing professional conduct and standards.

908. It is in a fact a common practice that agents, who are not holders of a FIFA licence, negotiate with clubs and players. If they neglect to comply with the established rules, they are not subject to the FIFA rules and cannot be punished by them. There are according conditions, which favour the creation of an unjust situation, which differs from the situation desired by the legislation, which can only be resolved via a joint effort by States, clubs, players and trade unions.

IV. New FIFA Intermediaries Regulations

909. In June 2014, following the 64th FIFA Congress held in São Paulo, the alterations of FIFA bylaws were approved, which abolish the activity of FIFA licenced agents, which will be replaced by intermediaries.

910. According to the new FIFA Intermediaries Regulations, intermediaries will be engaged by clubs or players to act solely in the preparation and negotiation of employment contracts and player transfer contracts, via the signing of a Representation Contract, a draft of which will be provided by FIFA and must be adopted by clubs, players and FIFA associate bodies.

911. The major change with regard to the activity of FIFA agents, which will come into force on 1 April 2015, concerns the issue of licences. Currently those interested in becoming FIFA agents must pass the examinations set by FIFA's member associations; however according to the new regulation applicants, who wish to become intermediaries must comply with a series of prerequisites and register with the associations without the need to obtain an exclusive licence in order to be able to work as a FIFA intermediary.

912. The main aspects of the new Intermediaries Regulation in comparison with the FIFA Agents Regulation are as follows.

A. Definition of Intermediary

913. According to the FIFA Intermediaries Regulation, an intermediary is a natural or juristic person that represents players or clubs, either for payment or free of charge, with a view to the negotiation of an employment contract, or a transfer contract

B. Payment of Intermediaries

914. Article 20 of the current FIFA Players Agents Regulation provides that the remuneration of an agent that has been engaged to represent a player is calculated with regard to the gross annual remuneration that the player will receive from the new club. No maximum limit is fixed for payments. All that is provided is that if the parties fail to agree, or if there is no express provision as to the amount of the agreed payment, the agent is entitled to a payment equal to 3% of the gross annual income of the player, arising from the contract negotiated or renegotiated by the agent.

915. Article 7 of the new FIFA Intermediaries Regulation establishes a maximum commission percentage of 3% of the value of the transaction that is due to the intermediary and that the service provided by the agent shall be taken into consideration, as follows:

(i) the remuneration of an intermediary engaged to represent a player cannot exceed 3% of the player's gross salary during the term of the contract;
(ii) the remuneration of an intermediary engaged to represent a club in the signing of an employment contract with a certain player, cannot exceed 3% of the player's gross salary during the term of the contract; and
(iii) the remuneration of an intermediary that acts on behalf of a club in the making of a transfer contract cannot exceed 5% of the transfer value.

So far as players who are minors, are concerned, FIFA included more rigorous provisions in the new Regulation, Article 7., no. 7 of which expressly prohibits the payment of commissions to intermediaries in transactions involving players, who are minors.

C. Information Recording and Publication System

916. Article 13 of the FIFA Agents Regulation provides that associations must keep and publish an updated register of all agents subject to the Regulation and submit the updated register to FIFA whenever new licences are issued, or when that are surrendered. Associations must also keep FIFA informed with regard to any penalties imposed on an agent. The associations must also provide FIFA annually with statistical data regarding agents' activities, i.e., the number of agents, details regarding the commencement and termination of their activities, any penalties imposed and criminal records, *inter alia.*

917. Moreover according to the provisions of Article 6 of the new FIFA Intermediaries Regulation, players and clubs must provide their association with details of all remuneration or payments of any type that have been made, or will be made to an intermediary.

918. This new Regulation will also introduce new provisions with regard to transfers. Some information, such as intermediaries' fees, and the contracts and agreements signed by them will be published in order to improve transfer transparency.

919. Article 6, no. 3 provides that associations that are members of FIFA must publish the names of all intermediaries registered with them, annually at the end of March. Moreover, associations must also provide details of the total payments by players and clubs to intermediaries.

D. Representation Contract

920. According to the provisions of Article 5 of the new Regulation, intermediaries must sign a Representation Contract with their clients, which must stipulate certain basic information, such as the parties' names, the duration of the legal relationship, the scope of the service, the amount of commission paid, rescission clauses and the parties' signatures, in addition to the nature of the legal relationship that the intermediary has with his/her/its clients.

921. Intermediaries must also sign a document termed Intermediary's Declaration (in Annexe 1 of the Regulation), for natural or legal persons, in which the intermediary declares that he/she/it will honour and comply with the provisions of the bylaws and rules of FIFA, federations and associations, with regard to the matter and the conditions governing the disclosure of the information regarding the transaction.

E. Conflicts of Interest

922. Article 8 of the new Regulation makes provision regarding conflicts of interest between parties, which operates as a general rule. This new regulation includes the possibility that the intermediary may make disclosure in writing of any potential conflict of interest with regard to a certain transaction in which he/she/it is involved.

923. Accordingly double representation is permitted, particularly with regard to clubs and players, if the agreement in writing of all parties involved is obtained prior to the commencement of the negotiations.

924. In the event of double representation, the contract between the parties must establish which party (i.e., the club or the player) will be liable with regard to the intermediary's remuneration.

F. Penalties

925. According to Article 9 of the new Intermediaries Regulations, the power to penalize parties (players, clubs and intermediaries) that violate the provisions of the new Regulation lies with the associations. Nevertheless, the associations must publish the penalties imposed and give notice of them to FIFA, which must, in turn consider whether the penalties should have worldwide effect, in accordance with the FIFA Disciplinary Code.

V. Prohibition of Third Party Ownership

926. FIFA prohibits clubs from entering into contracts which will enable 3rd parties (presumably players' agents) to acquire the ability to influence the independence, policies or performance of a club in employment and transfer related matters. (Articles 18*bis* FIFA Regulations).

927. In *Tevez* case,[246] Kia Joorabcian, a players agent, bought Tevez from Corinthians through his personal company. He sold Tevez to West Ham United but retained part of his ownership rights. The English premier league ruled that West Ham had breached the premier league rules by allowing the agent's company to retain part of Tevez's ownership rights. This meant that West Ham did not fully own Tevez and that any club which wanted to buy him from West Ham would also have to pay a transfer fee to his agent's company. The agent's company was therefore in control of matters related to his transfer.

928. Despite this, agents continue to own part of player's rights in Portugal. The English Premier League is however strict in complying with its rules and ensured that both Chelsea and Manchester city fully owned Ramires and Tevez upon signing them. Clubs outside the Premier League seem not to abide by this FIFA rule, and FIFA does not appear to be very keen on enforcing it.

---

246. In the matter of an arbitration pursuant to section S of the rules of the Football Association Premier League and in the matter of the Arbitration Act 1996 between Sheffield United Football Club and Football Association Premier league Limited, 3 Jul. 2007.

Part III. Doping in Sport

Chapter 1. Doping

§1. The Anti-doping Legal Framework

I. Introduction

929. In Portugal, from the end of the 1960s and during the 1970s, most anti-doping controls were carried out in cycling, in accordance with the regulations of the International Cycling Union (UCI). The first Portuguese legislation regarding doping was introduced in 1970: i.e., Decree-Law no. 470/70, of 3 September 1970, and nine years later in September 1979, the first legislation regarding what was then termed *anti-doping control,* Decree-Law no. 374/79, of 8 September, was published.

930. The Council of Europe Anti-Doping Convention was approved in Strasbourg on 16 November 1989 and was signed by Portugal in 1990 and ratified in 1994 by Decree-Law no. 2/94, of 20 January. As a consequence of the convention and the new definition inherent in it, the Portuguese legislation was updated by Decree-Law no. 105/90, of 23 March and implemented in detail by Statutory Instrument no. 130/91, of 13 February.

931. In 1997, Portugal adopted anti-doping legislation, which remained in force until 2009, i.e.: Decree-Law no. 183/97, of 26 July, which introduced the anti-doping legal framework, and was amended by Law no. 152/99, of 14 September and by Decree-Law no. 192/2002, of 25 September.

932. At the beginning of 1999, because of concern regarding the scale of the use of doping substances, the IOC organized the first World Conference on Doping in Sport, at which various organizations from the sports movement and countries all over the world decided to create the World Anti-Doping Agency. Portugal participated actively in this conference and in the working group established by the IOC in order to draft the first bylaws of WADA. Portugal also played an active part in the drafting of the International Anti-Doping Code and the International Standards produced by WADA. In March 2005, WADA organized the second World Conference on Doping in Sport, which took place in Copenhagen and at which the World Anti-Doping Code was approved. The 14th Government of the Republic signed the

Copenhagen Declaration. Portugal was one of the countries, which, via this declaration, recognized the fundamental role of WADA and agreed to co-finance it.

933. Portugal also took an active part in the drafting of the United Nations Educational Scientific and Cultural Organisation (UNESCO) International Convention Against Doping in Sport, which is of fundamental importance so that all countries in the world can recognize WADA, the World Anti-Doping Code and the International Standards and establish common principles within the ambit of the fight against doping. This Convention was approved at the General Conference of UNESCO in October 2005 and Portugal ratified it in 2007, by Decree no. 4-A/2007, of 20 March. On 17 November 2007, the Founding Council of WADA approved amendments of the World Anti-Doping Code and the new version came into force on 1 January 2009.[247]

934. A new version of the World Anti-Doping Code will come into force on 1 January 2015 and contains some important changes, the most noteworthy of which is the alteration of the duration maximum penalty of suspension from sport activity in cases of intentional violations of the provisions of the Code from two to four years.

II. The Legal Framework of the Fight Against Doping in Sport

935. The reform of the legal framework in force with regard to the fight against doping in sport is therefore based on the latest version of the World Anti-Doping Code. Law no. 27/2009, of 19 June, introduced the legal framework of the fight against doping in sport, and already included the alterations made to this important legal document. Portugal accordingly continues to be in the vanguard of the fight against this scourge.

936. The most important new feature in the law is the punishment of the trafficking of any prohibited substances or methods, as a breach of the anti-doping rules and therefore as a crime. The law continues the classification of the administration of prohibited methods and substances as a crime, but increases the penalties, when the victim is particularly vulnerable, by reason of age, handicap or illness, when deceit or intimidation is been used, or when the offender has taken advantage of a hierarchical, financial, employment or occupational relationship. So far as penalties are concerned, the significant increase in the severity of the penalties applicable, which can result in suspension for a maximum of twenty years, is noteworthy. The law also provides that the Portuguese Anti-Doping Authority (ADoP) may, at any time, assign to itself the enforcement of disciplinary penalties imposed by the sports federations, alter decisions not to proceed, to acquit or convict made by the disciplinary organs of a sports federation, and impose new decisions, from which an appeal lies to CAS.

247. A new version of the World Anti-Doping Code will come into force on the 1 Jan. 2015.

937. In as far as the structure of the fight against doping is concerned, the law introduces the regulations governing ADoP as the national anti-doping authority with a role in the control of and fight against doping in sport, i.e., as the authority responsible for the AdoPtion of rules with a view to the triggering, implementation, or application of any phase of the doping control process. In order to provide this new structure with the means required for the performance of its duties, ADoP has a Doping Analysis Laboratory (LAD) and an Anti-Doping Programme Support Structure (ESPAD), in addition to a President and an Executive Director. ADoP has increased powers in comparison to the National Anti-Doping Council (CNAD), which now becomes the specialist body responsible for the issue of technical and scientific opinions.

938. Finally, the law introduces the principle of mutual recognition, i.e., ADoP recognizes and respects the controls, therapeutic use authorizations and the results of hearings, or other final decisions of any anti-doping organization or organization responsible for a sports competition or event, which are in accordance with the World Anti-Doping Code and its powers and duties.

939. According to the provisions of no. 1 of Article 3, under the heading *Prohibition of doping and violation of anti-doping rule, all doping of sportspersons both in the context of sports competitions organised in Portugal and otherwise is prohibited.* According to no. 2 of the said provision, *violation of the anti-doping rules by sportspersons, or their support staff,* exists in the following circumstances:

(a) [p]resence of a prohibited substance, its metabolites or markers, in a sample taken from a sportsperson;
(b) [u]se of a prohibited method;
(c) [u]se by a sportsperson of a prohibited substance, or method, as proved by admission of the sportsperson, witness evidence, documentary evidence, longitudinal profile conclusions, or other analytic information, that do not comply with the criteria established for the verification of violations of the abovementioned anti-doping rules;
(d) [r]efusal, resistance or unjustified failure to submit to a doping test, whether in the context of a competition or otherwise, after having been given notice thereof, and any conduct amounting to obstruction of the taking of a sample;
(e) [o]bstruction, unjustified delay, concealment and other conduct that prevents or obstructs the taking of samples within the ambit of doping control, whether by act or omission;
(f) [f]ailure to submit information within the time limit stipulated, or the submission of incorrect information three times by the sportsperson within a consecutive 18-month period, without a valid reason, after having been duly given notice by ADoP with regard to each such failure;
(g) [i]n the event of three tests declared not to have been conducted, on the basis of the rules laid down by ADoP, during a consecutive 18-month period, for no valid reason, after the sportsperson has been given due notice by ADoP in relation to each such test declared not to have been conducted;

(h) [a]lteration, forgery or tampering with any part of the doping control procedure;
(i) [p]ossession of prohibited substances or methods, either by the sportsperson or by any member of the sportsperson's support staff.

940. Law no. 38/2012, of 28 August, inspired by the revisions of the WADA Code, changed the definitions which are now the following:

(a) the mere presence of a prohibited substance, its metabolites or markers, in a sample A of sportsperson, when the athlete waives analysis of sample B and sample B is not analysed, or when the analysis of sample B confirms the presence of a prohibited substance, its metabolites or markers, found in sample A;
(b) use of a prohibited method;
(c) use of a prohibited substance, or method, by a sportsperson, as proved by admission of the sportsperson, witness evidence, documentary evidence, conclusions of longitudinal profiles or other analytical information, that do not comply with the criteria established for verification of violations of the anti-doping rules in (a) and (b) above;
(d) refusal, resistance, or unjustified failure to submit to a doping test, whether in a competition context or otherwise, after having been given notice, and any conduct amounting to the obstruction of the collection of a sample;
(e) the obstruction, unjustified delaying, concealment and all other conduct that, by act or omission, prevents or disrupts the collection of samples, and the alteration, falsification, manipulation or adulteration, or attempted adulteration of any part of the doping control procedure;
(f) failure by the sportsperson to submit information within the stipulated time limit, or submission of incorrect information three times within a consecutive eighteen-month period, without a valid reason, after having been duly given notice by AdOP with regard to each such failure;
(g) in the event that three tests are declared not to have been conducted, on the basis of the rules laid down by AdOP, during a consecutive eighteen-month period, for no valid reason, after the sportsperson has been given due notice by AdOP in relation to each such test declared not to have been conducted;
(h) possession of any prohibited method or substance in a competition context, or possession of any prohibited method or substance in an out-of-competition context, which is not permitted in an out-of-competition context, unless it is demonstrated that it is based on an authorization for medical use, or some other acceptable reason;
(i) possession of any prohibited substance or method by a member of the sportsperson's support staff who is linked to the sportsperson, the competition or training location, unless it is demonstrated that it is based on an authorization for medical use by the sportsperson, or some other acceptable reason.

941. It is evident from the list of prohibited types of conduct that the law seeks to typify practically all of them. There are scattered legal provisions that suggest that the general legal principle of *in dubio pro reo* does not apply to sportspersons, so that in the event of accusation by the property authorities, or even an anonymous complaint, it is for the sportsperson to prove his or her innocence, which is, in principle, contrary to the legal rules governing the burden of proof.

942. Despite all of this, Article 9 of the law states that the burden of proof of doping in disciplinary proceedings lies with the ADoP, which is responsible for deciding whether there is a violation of an anti-doping rule. However viewing the law in general terms it should be noted that this inversion of the burden of proof is more than justified, as there are important legal assets to protect, such as life, health, physical integrity, human dignity and even the honour of the individual and third parties. Moreover, it is necessary to:

(a) safeguard the correctness and fairness of sports competitions;
(b) put an end to the increasing and uncontrolled sale of doping medicines on the internet and to the public health risk involved therein;
(c) reduce the real risk to sportspersons, particularly those, who auto-medicate themselves, as it is known that the falsification of medicines and the illegal use of resources or distribution channels is increasing exponentially.

943. All of this demands truly deterrent measures, of a criminal law type. We consider that by creating a specific crime – *trafficking of prohibited substances and methods* – the State's specific interest in this matter is being demonstrated – i.e., a public interest, which justifies the creation of a criminal offence. Accordingly, the legislature intends to punish, not only those who breach, but also those who *intend to breach,* the anti-doping rules, with a term of imprisonment of from six months to five years. It is noted that the purpose of no. 1 of Article 43 is not necessarily directed at the question of the alteration of a result, or the alterations of events or performance of sportspersons, but rather at the sportsperson's entourage. What most concerned the legislator was not the criminalization of the consumer's conduct but rather the criminalization of the conduct of those around the sportsperson, who are, in some way, involved in doping, or facilitate it.

944. The attention given to the doping of animals, within the ambit of the corresponding sports, which have a long tradition in Portugal but were absent from Portuguese legislation, which protected only the *persons, who compete in organized sports events,*[248] is a positive move.

945. Another matter that is relevant to the law is related to the rules that should merit the consideration of those who apply and interpret the law. We particularly refer to the provisions regarding access to, processing and communication of personal data and other information with regard to sportspersons. Without prejudice to the fact that these practices are already known to be common internationally and the subject matter of various normative provisions, the truth is that it is important to protect the fundamental rights of sportspersons. It is important to preserve the rights

248. Animal doping is an ancient practice related to the participation of men and animals in competitions or events of a ludic or ritual nature, which consists of the use of stimulant or tranquilizing substances to increase or reduce the performance of the animals during training or competition.

to privacy, reputation and good standing and also the presumption of innocence. Furthermore, it is necessary to ensure the confidentiality of access to, processing and communication of data and other information with regard to doping. It is also necessary to avoid negative parallel judgments engendered by the publicity given to doping cases. Linked to this question is the possibility that tests may be carried out other than in the context of a competition. The concern for the defence of fundamental rights is more than necessary, because according to international rules and practices, sportspersons are vulnerable given the time taken from their leisure (nightly rest, weekends, holidays) and are sometimes even subject to the violation of their homes. Is a less restrictive and more proportionate solution to this problem not possible?

946. The following is a list of some other aspects of the law that merit criticism:

(a) the fact that the law contains no legal definition of doping but rather opts for a *negative approach* and provides an exhaustive list of circumstances, which amount to a *violation of the anti-doping rules;*[249]
(b) the possibility that anti-doping control teams (administrative staff, without police authority) can, and without prior notice, inspect gymnasium premises with a view to the detection of doping substances, and can demand unrestricted access even to users' lockers, all of which again raises the question of the compatibility of the draft law with citizens' rights, liberties and guarantees;
(c) the imposition of temporary disciplinary suspensions at the time of the first analysis and of definitive suspensions for very long periods of time, which, together with other loss and damage, prevents or practically excludes the sportsperson from having access to his or her occupational activity (and does not reinstate him or her therein), given the calendar and specificities of the various sports, may amount to a violation of the constitutionally protected right to work.

947. Finally, a very important practical reality should not be overlooked. The sports federations and the professional leagues will be required to *adapt their anti-doping regulations* to the following:

(a) the rules laid down in the applicable law and regulations;
(b) the rules laid down by international anti-doping conventions of which Portugal is, or becomes, a party;
(c) the rules and guidelines laid down by WADA and the corresponding international sports federations.

948. The said regulations will be registered with the Portuguese Anti-Doping Authority, which operates under the auspices of the Instituto do Desporto de Portugal, IP, a national anti-doping organization, which has duties with regard to the control of and fight against doping in sport, i.e., as the body responsible for the

249. Article 3.

adoption of rules with a view to the triggering, implementation or application of any phase of the doping control procedure.

949. The following principles must be observed in the drafting of federation anti-doping regulations:

(a) doping control can be carried out both in the context of sports competitions and otherwise and, in order to be effective, should normally take place without prior warning, i.e., in controls other in a non-competition context, even if this may give rise to some doubts as to the constitutionality of such a procedure on the grounds of violation of fundamental rights;
(b) doping control can be carried out both in competitions that are part of national championships and in the other competitions within the ambit of each sport;
(c) all those, who violate the rules regarding the confidentiality of the doping control procedures, should be subject to the imposition of the penalties that should be listed in the corresponding regulations. It is this principle of confidentiality that gives rise to the greatest misgivings with regard to the law. A code of conduct should be provided for and adopted, which can be applied to all those with direct or indirect responsibilities in this area;
(d) sportspersons to be subjected to controls should be selected by lot, without prejudice to recourse to other criteria, formulated in general and abstract terms, or the subjection of sportspersons, whose conduct, in the competition context or otherwise, has been anomalous in medical or sports terms, to controls;
(e) sportspersons and others suspected of breach of the regulations must be guaranteed the right to defend themselves and to a hearing, in accordance with the most elementary rights of defence and the presumption of innocence.

950. In addition to compliance with the principles enunciated above, the imposition of penalties on sportspersons and their support staff by sports federations must take all aggravating and mitigating circumstances into consideration, in accordance with the recommendations in the World Anti-Doping Code.

951. The regulations to be produced by the federations and leagues are further required to include the following:

(a) a precise definition of the competitions in the events of which anti-doping control can be carried out and the circumstances in which controls will be carried out other than in a non-competition context;
(b) a definition of the methods to be used to select the sportspersons to be subjected to each control;
(c) definition of the disciplinary penalties applicable to those responsible for violation of the anti-doping rules, whether they are sportspersons, or their support staff;
(d) a definition of the disciplinary penalties applicable to all those involved in the doping control procedure, who breach the confidentiality obligation;
(e) procedural details of the enquiry and disciplinary phases of the proceedings, which seek to punish those responsible for violation of the anti-doping rules,

indicating the means of appeal and the bodies to which a right of appeal lies. The regulation must provide that separate entities are responsible for the enquiry and the disciplinary phases;

(f) definition of the cases in which clubs or public limited sports companies can be punished for the violation of the anti-doping rules by their staff, and the identification of applicable penalties.

952. It should be noted with regard to the confirmation of national records that the law provides that such confirmation can only take place after the conduct of an anti-doping test of the sportsperson in question. Given the real impossibility of conducting anti-doping tests at all sports events, the law establishes a twenty-four-hour window for the conduct of tests, if it was not, for good reason, possible to conduct the test at the event. A question arises regarding circumstances in which it is only possible to carry out the anti-doping control after the said twenty-four-hour period, through no fault of the sportsperson, who has broken a national record, as to whether the record in question can be challenged and not be approved, e.g., when a new national record is set abroad. The sports federations are required by law to take the necessary steps in order to ensure that new records are not approved without a prior anti-doping test.

953. Another noteworthy matter concerns the suspension of a sportsperson. Two samples are always taken when the test is carried out and the sportsperson is suspended immediately on a provisional basis, if the result of the first test indicates any possibility of a violation of an anti-doping rule. The analysis of second sample, commonly known as sample B, involves much greater formality, i.e., the care taken with the analysis is greater. The sportsperson and the federation can be represented by a lawyer, which means that the provisional suspension and the results of the first analysis can be challenged. However, the law does not impose provisional suspension, if the positive results of the first test can be attributed to physiological or pathological causes, when complementary analyses are conducted and the sportsperson is not suspended. The sportsperson should therefore always apply for the analysis of sample B, as this increases the protection of his rights and prevents provisional suspension, which occurs immediately after the test period.

954. ADoP is responsible for the imposition of disciplinary penalties, but this power is delegated to sports federations that have sports public utility status, which are also responsible for the conduct of the disciplinary proceedings. These proceedings must include an appeal body to which a sports actor, who is punished, can appeal, without suspensive effect, and which must be a body other than, and independent of the body that imposed the penalty at first instance. The ADoP may, at any time, assign to itself the imposition of disciplinary penalties imposed by the sports federations, alter decisions not to proceed, to acquit or convict made by the disciplinary organs of a sports federation, and impose new decisions, from which an appeal lies to CAS.

955. The law makes the following provision regarding the sports effects and the corresponding ancillary penalties arising from doping:

(a) voiding of individual results;
(b) the effects on teams, clubs or public limited sports companies;
(c) cancellation of the results of competitions held after the collection of samples.

956. In as far as ancillary sports penalties are concerned, violation of an anti-doping rule within the ambit of the anti-doping control of a competition leads automatically to the invalidation of the individual results obtained in the said competition and to all of the consequences flowing therefrom, including the withdrawal of medals, points and prizes. In cases of violation of an anti-doping rule during a sports event leads to the invalidation of all of the individual sports results obtained by the sportsperson during the same, including the loss of all medals, points and prizes, by decision of the body responsible for the organization thereof. The sportsperson has the burden to prove that there was no wilful or negligent conduct on his or her part at the source of the offence. However the voiding of results also applies when the results of the sportsperson in question in other competitions of the same sports event, other than that in which the violation of the anti-doping rules occurred, were influenced by the offence, even if it is demonstrated that there was no wilful or negligent conduct on the part of the sportsperson.

957. In as far as the ancillary penalties that can be imposed on teams and clubs are concerned, they can be disqualified or subject to some other disciplinary measure if it is established that more than one sportsperson violated an anti-doping rule during a sports event.

958. Accordingly, all other sports results achieved from the day on which the positive sample was taken until the commencement of the provisional suspension or suspension, whether the testing was in a competition or non-competition context, or in which other violations of the anti-doping rules have occurred, are cancelled with all the consequences thereof, unless some other treatment is demanded for reasons of equity.

959. A court or tribunal decides in accordance with the rules of equity when the judge or arbitrator decides a dispute in accordance with the justice of the case without recourse to pre-established legal provision. Deciding in accordance with equity accordingly means to decide a dispute in a way that appears to be most just having regard only to the facts of the case and without recourse to any law that may be applicable thereto. These considerations with regard to recourse to equity are made because this is perhaps the best way to decide cases arising directly or indirectly from violation of the anti-doping rules and to which the law has no response. What should be done, in the case of someone placed second in an event of international prestige, when it is discovered, months, or years later, that the person placed first took part in the event in breach of the anti-doping rules, and how should the person placed second be compensated? For, so far as damages for distress are concerned, there is clearly harm that falls outside of what the courts can award. The sportsperson is deprived of the podium ceremony, the celebrations with the family, the gold medal, the title, the national anthem, the honour to which the champion is undeniably entitled and the sportsperson's only recourse is to the courts.

960. The fact is that the anti-doping legislation, which follows the recommendations of the proper international authorities, cannot punish sportspersons severely, when they have a positive test result as a consequence of medical error, or by their support staff. In fact, the principle that the sportsperson is responsible for all substances that enter his or her body can sometimes result in breaches of the fundamental rights of sportspersons, even if the decisions are correct from a legal point of view. There are measures, which must be taken urgently in order to prevent the occurrence of many cases similar to those of the tennis player Guillermo Canas,[250] or the footballers Daniele Mannini and Daniele Possanzini.[251]

961. The abovementioned tennis player was suspended for twenty-four months, which was later reduced to fifteen months by the CAS, because he had not taken due care with a medicine supplied in error by the medical panel of a tournament in which he was playing. In the case of the footballers, they delayed reporting for an anti-doping check test on the direct orders of their superior at the club with which they had an employment contract, which sufficed for them to be suspended from competing for a long period of time.

962. We consider that one of the measures that should be taken in order to ensure that such cases do not constantly arise would be to create an autonomous institution, under the auspices of the WADA, which is independent of the national federations and leagues, comprising all of the medical and support staff responsible for the administration of substances to players, which would keep a record of all their activities together with a medical profile of each sportsperson. Sportspersons are frequently unaware of the composition of the medicines they take and are also primarily preoccupied with career-related matters, or with the game being played when he receives treatment and would no longer be responsible for the administration of substances which responsibility would lie with the medical and support staff.

963. Another important measure would be to make the entire procedure completely confidential, at least until the analysis of sample B. This is because it is well-known that sponsors have cancelled their sponsorship of teams on the slightest suspicion of doping by members of the team, because of negative publicity, without the sponsorees having an opportunity to prove otherwise and with the corresponding financial and other consequences for those involved.

III. Implementation Regulations

964. Law no. 27/2009, of 19 June introduced the legal framework governing the fight against doping in sport. The corresponding implementation regulations were introduced by Statutory Instrument no. 1123/2009, of 1 October. It was accordingly

250. CAS 2005/A/951, with a panel of arbitrators comprising Maidie Oliveau (United States of America), Christopher Campbell (United States of America) and Yves Fortier (Canada).
251. CAS 2008/A/1557, with a panel of arbitrators comprising Dirk Reiner-Martens (Germany), Quentin Byrne-Sutton (Switzerland) and Andreas Zagklis (Greece).

established that anti-doping controls are only conducted with regard to sports within the ambit of sports federations with EUPD and all sportspersons.

965. This legal framework has since been replaced by Law no. 38/2012, of 28 August, and by Statutory Instrument no. 11/2013, of 11 January, which alter the penalty provisions with regard to violations of anti-doping rules that are committed within the ambit of the Sportsperson Location System.

966. According to Article 7 of Law no. 38/2012, of 28 August which was amended by Law no. 33/2014 of 16 June and Law no. 93/2015 of 13 August, this system applies to sportspersons, who are included by ADoP in the Target Group of sportspersons to be subjected to doping controls outside of a competition context.

967. In order to implement an information system with regard to the localization of sportspersons, sportspersons, who informed by ADoP that they have been included in the Target Group of sportspersons to be subject to out-of-competition testing, must submit completed localization forms, containing precise and up-to-date information regarding their location, on a quarterly basis.

968. A target group of sportspersons that can be subject to anti-doping controls in a non-competition context has been established. The group includes sportspersons, who:

(a) are subject to the high performance sports framework, with the exception of those who are part of the target group of the corresponding international federation;
(b) are members of national teams;
(c) compete in professional competitions;
(d) whose behaviour, body morphology, state of health or sports results indicates a risk of the use of prohibited substances or methods;
(e) who are currently suspended for violations of the anti-doping rules.

969. The Statutory Instrument also introduced the regulations to implement the anti-doping rule that sportspersons, who have been identified by ADoP for inclusion in a target group for the purposes of testing in a non-competition environment are required to provide precise and up-to-date information regarding their whereabouts during the three months following being so identified, i.e., in relation to the dates when and the places where they take part in training or events, not included in competitions. Statutory Instrument no. 1325/2010, of 30 December – List of Forbidden Substances and Methods for 2011 and ADoP Order no. 349872010, of 9 December – Procedures Inherent in the System for the Authorisation of the Therapeutic Use of Prohibited Substances and Methods for 2010 are also noteworthy.

970. This legal framework has since been replaced by *Law no. 38/2012, of 28 August*, and by *Statutory Instrument no. 11/2013, of 11 January*, which alter the penalty provisions with regard to violations of anti-doping rules that are committed within the ambit of the Sportsperson Location System.

Chapter 2. Corruption in Sport

§1. The Legal Framework Governing the Fight against Corruption in Sports

I. Introduction

971. Corruption has existed since the beginning of political history. Since there has been an unprecedented increase in the financial dimension of sport, which, together with its specificity, has transformed sport into a market that is very attractive and suitable for large scale investment, this has inevitably meant that sport has also become subject to various corrupt practices.

972. In order to fight the phenomenon to occur in sport, corruption is a crime and is also a disciplinary offence, which is punishable by the regulations of the federations and leagues that organize competitions.

II. The First Specific Legislation regarding Corruption in Sport

973. Legislation regarding corruption in sport was introduced in 1991 when the decision was to adopt a model of specific criminal jurisdiction in sport, i.e., criminal law legislation that was not part of the Penal Code, and which defined the anti-sports conducts punishable as crimes.

974. It was sought to advance the fight against corruption in sport in response to the phenomena, facts and events that fraudulently distort the truth and honesty of sports competitions and results, which vitiate genuine sports activity, in two complementary ways:

(a) prevention via training and education of sports actors; and
(b) in the final analysis, via repressive measures and the definition of offences and the corresponding penalties.

975. The fundamental interests in question to be protected are the honesty and fairness of the competition and its result and respect for sports ethics. It is a matter in the public interest, as revealed and manifest in the collective interest of all those (supporters, sympathizers and spectators), who expect that public sports events and the results of sports competitions are not affected and falsified by the fraudulent conduct of the corresponding sports actors, who seek to vitiate them.

976. In the defence of the public interest, particular emphasis is given to the selection and development of preventive measures, which are essentially informative, training and educational measures, targeted at young people, in general and at all sports actors in particular. The sports federations, associations and sports clubs particularly, have the fundamental task to educate and train their sports actors.

977. Another aspect of the protection of the public interest, fairness, truth and rectitude of sports competitions and the final result thereof is the definition of fraudulent conduct, described in types, the aim of which conduct is to vitiate the truth and ethics of sports competition and the results thereof and the definition of the corresponding penalties. It was decided that such fraudulent conduct would be a crime given the seriousness thereof in terms of the dignity and social significance of the interests to be so protected.

978. The imposition of penal punishment only applies in the cases of public sport or competitions, given the value and significance of the interests protected. A competition is deemed to exist whenever the sports activity is organized, regulated and takes place under the auspices of the bodies that are, in some way, responsible therefore.

979. Decree-Law no. 390/91, of 10 October accordingly classified three fundamental types of corruption:

(a) passive corruption
(b) active corruption
(c) administration to a sportsperson of substances or products, or the use of methods likely to alter his or her sports performance.

980. The first two offences each have a parallel in the Penal Code, but the third offence does not. Moreover the law does not go as far as the Penal Code in that it does not include so-called passive corruption for a lawful act, within the overall definition of corruption, and opted to reduce the prison sentences provided, in comparison to those in the ordinary criminal law. When the sports or events in question are team events or sports, the members of a team that is disqualified because one or more of its members violated anti-doping rules are also entitled to seek restitution but only by way of damages.

981. During the sixteen years that Decree-Law no. 390/91, of 10 October was in force, there was only one conviction in the higher courts, i.e., the *Guímaro* case,[252] which held that the type of corruption defined by Decree-Law no. 390/91, of 10 October, is a formal crime, or a crime of anticipated commission, because all that is required for the commission of the crime is the mere promise of an improper benefit. If the promise is fulfilled it is correct to say that the offence was committed continuously until the delivery of the benefit, i.e., it is a crime of continuous commission.

982. This legislation did not include the offence of passive corruption to procure a lawful act, i.e., it was not forbidden to offer prizes to sportspersons on condition that they win a certain game or event, as the purpose is lawful given the fact that

252. Judgment of the Supreme Court of Justice dated 30 Oct. 1997, available at: http://www.dgsi.pt/jstj.nsf/954f0ce6ad9dd8b980256b5f003fa814/0814cd360e14b3a6802568fc003b6279?OpenDocument.

winning is the normal sports objective of teams and sportspersons. So far as penalties are concerned there was a difference between the provisions in the Decree-Law and those in the Penal Code. The penalties in the Penal Code are clearly much more severe than those in the decree-law. However, unlike the Penal Code, the specific legislation provided for the imposition of the following ancillary penalties on sports actors:

(a) suspension from participation in sports competitions for from six months to three years;
(b) disqualification from the right to receive official subsidies for from one to five years;
(c) suspension from an office or position for from two to six years, in the cases of referees or the equivalent or officers of federations, associations, leagues or similar organization and leaders of sports clubs or officers of companies with sports objects.

III. The Legal Framework Governing Criminal Liability for Anti-sporting Conduct that Is Contrary to the Values of Truth, Honesty and Rectitude and Is Likely to Fraudulently Alter Competition Results

983. Law no. 50/2007, of 31 August, amended by Law no. 30/2015 of 22 April repealed all of the articles of Decree-Law no. 390/91, of 10 October (which was repealed by Law no. 27/2009 of 16 July and by Law no. 50/2007), except for Article 5, which made provision for crimes related to doping and which was repealed by Law no. 27/2009, of 19 June.

984. The new legislation made significant alterations with regard to the fight against corruption in sport and introduced the crimes of graft and criminal association associated with sport. Another relevant provision was the introduction of criminal liability of corporations and equivalent organizations, within the ambit of sport. In the previous legislation only natural persons could be punished, so this innovation resolved an important lacuna.

985. Provision was also made to reduce the penalty if the offender provides specific assistance in the gathering of decisive evidence for the identification or arrest of other offenders. The offender is not subject to the imposition of a penalty, if the offender voluntarily repudiates the offer or promise, previously accepted, prior to the act, or in the case of fungible property, the value thereof. In the crime of criminal association the penalty can be particularly attenuated, or no penalty at all is imposed, if the offender prevents, or strives seriously to prevent the continuation of criminal groups, organizations or associations, or inform the authorities of the existence thereof so that they can prevent the commission of offences.

986. The penalties were revised and increased by the new law so as to be more in line with those in the Penal Code. The crime of passive corruption, which was previously punishable by a maximum term of imprisonment of two years, is now punishable by a maximum term of five years. The new legislation also provides for the imposition of fines, unlike the previous legislation.

§2. Famous Cases

I. The *Apito Dourado* and *Apito Final* Cases

987. In 2004, news stories appeared in the Portuguese media about the involvement of clubs and personalities in the world of sport in alleged crimes of corruption. Several legal proceedings were commenced following investigations by the Judicial Police, which were collectively referred to as *Apito Dourado* (Golden Whistle). These criminal proceedings triggered a series of linked disciplinary proceedings, which were known as *Apito Final* (Final Whistle).

988. As corruption is a crime, which appears in both the Penal Code and in miscellaneous legislation, it is also a disciplinary offence in most sports and is typified and punished in the regulations of sports federations and leagues. The subject matter of the disciplinary proceedings and the legal proceedings were, in many cases, the same.

II. The *Apito Dourado* Case and Recourse to the Court of Arbitration for Sport

989. This dispute concerned a claim by SL Benfica and Vitória SC against FC Porto, as the principal respondent and UEFA as a subsidiary, or second respondent. Briefly, SL Benfica and Vitória SC wanted CAS to declare FC Porto ineligible to participate in the 2008/09 UEFA champions league competition, because it had allegedly violated the UEFA regulations to which all clubs must submit before being admitted to UEFA competitions.

990. The UEFA rule in question, Article 1.04(d) read:

> To be eligible to participate in the competition, a club must satisfy the following criteria;
>
> d) [i]t must not be or have been involved in any activity aimed at arranging or influencing the outcome of a match at national or international level.

991. It was the case of both SL Benfica and Vitória SC before CAS that FC Porto was involved in acts of corruption and match fixing at both the national league and UEFA competition level during the 2003/2004 season. Accordingly, they asked CAS, in accordance with UEFA rule 1.04(d), to exclude Porto from the UEFA Champions League, for the 2008–2009 season, because it had failed to meet the qualification criteria.

992. In April 2004, Portuguese criminal proceedings known as *Apito Dourado*, (*Golden Whistle)* were commenced, following media allegations in Portugal that several referees and their assistants had been involved in corruption and match fixing. The allegations were that the said referees had received bribes or favours from FC Porto in order to fix the outcome of matches in favour of FC Porto, during the 2003–2004 season. *Apito Dourado* prompted the Portuguese authorities to commence investigations, and subsequently criminal charges were brought against both FC Porto and its officials (the Chairman).

993. Although the criminal charges were dropped, the Disciplinary Committee of the Portuguese League took up the matter and found FC Porto and its chairman guilty of two attempts to bribe referees in matches, one between FC Porto and Deportivo La Coruna, and another between FC Porto and Estrela da Amadora. On 30 June 2008, the Disciplinary Committee fined FC Porto's chairman EUR 10,000 and suspended him for two years, while FC Porto was fined EUR 150,000 and forfeited six points from its 2007/2008 season. As a result of this ruling, on 4 June 2008, UEFA's Control and Disciplinary Body issued a ruling confirming FC Porto's guilt of two attempts to bribe referees and excluded it from the (2008/2009) UEFA Champions League. FC Porto's Chairman appealed to the UEFA Appeal Body and to the Appeals Committee of the Portuguese Football Federation. On 13 June 2008, the UEFA Appeals Body overruled the earlier decision of the UEFA Control and Disciplinary Body and the Disciplinary Committee of the LPFP. It admitted FC Porto to the UEFA Champions League. It based its arguments on the fact that an appeal by FC Porto's chairman was pending before the Portuguese courts, and that if the appeal was successful, FC Porto would have suffered irreparable loss, as a consequence of the exclusion. It therefore admitted FC Porto to the UEFA Champions League. However, the FPF Appeals Committee rejected the appeals filed by the chairman. This rejection was preceded by a turbulent meeting and disagreement between the members of the Appeals Committee, which saw the Chairman and Vice-Chairman walk out of the meeting, after which the remaining members took the said decision rejecting the appeal by a majority vote.

994. However, it was not the decision of the FPF Appeals Committee that led to the appeal to CAS, but rather an appeal against the decision of the UEFA Appeals Body by both SL Benfica, and Vitória SC. Both clubs had a clear interest in the matter as they were on the verge of gaining admission to the Champions' League, if CAS were to find FC Porto guilty of corruption. The main submissions by SL Benfica and Vitória SC against FC Porto and UEFA were that:

(a) FC Porto ought not to have been admitted to the 2008/09 champions league competition, as it had violated Article 1.04(d) of the UEFA Champions League rules. These rules admitted only those clubs, which had not been involved in any activity aimed at influencing or arranging the outcome of a match at national or international level.
(b) The decision against FC Porto at the first instance and the imposition of a fine on it and its failure to appeal against the same was proof that FC Porto had

violated Article 1.04(d) of the UEFA Champions League regulations. The appeal filed by its chairman did not alter this fact.
(c) Article 1.04 of the UEFA Champions League rules is an administrative and not a disciplinary rule. It is not subject to the principle of non-retroactivity, and therefore Article 1.04 ought to be applied *in toto* – which would mean the exclusion of FC Porto from the competition.

995. UEFA submitted that the appellants had failed to exhaust all the internal remedies available before UEFA's disciplinary, dispute resolution and appeal bodies, thereby rendering the appeal before CAS inadmissible within the meaning of R47 of the CAS Code. They accordingly asked CAS to dismiss the appeal. In its defence, FC Porto made four key arguments:

(a) that the appeal was inadmissible by virtue of R47 of the CAS Code, because it was still subject to review before UEFA and therefore not final;
(b) that failure by FC Porto to appeal against the decision of the LPFP Disciplinary Committee could not be interpreted as an admission of guilt. That the appeal by the club's chairman had, in any event, also filed on behalf of the club in his capacity as the club's chairman;
(c) that the principle of non-retroactivity was inapplicable to the case. In essence, FC Porto were saying that no sanction could be imposed on it because the rules of Article 104 came into force in the 2008/09 season, whereas the alleged corruption offences took place in the 2003/04 season;
(d) that the exclusion (Article 104(d) from the Champion's League was a disciplinary measure;
(e) that since Article 104(d) is a disciplinary measure; it was not only subject to the legal principles of non-retroactivity but was also subject to the principles of certainty and clarity. They accordingly requested CAS to dismiss the appeal.

996. The decision issued by CAS on 15 July 2008 made a series of observations:

(a) CAS ruled that all disciplinary measures are also administrative. It observed that in order to assess whether Article 1.04(d) was a disciplinary measure, it was necessary to consider the consequences that the application of the rule would have had on FC Porto, or any club.
(b) CAS held that the rule had the effect of excluding FC Porto from the Champions League competition – 'the most prestigious competition', and that this exclusion amounted to a penalty.
(c) It held that the criminal law prohibition of non-retroactivity is inapplicable to sports disputes.
(d) That Article 1.04 is unreasonable and disproportionate, because it has the consequence of imposing a lifetime ban from the Champions League competition provided that the club was at one time involved in irregularities, regardless of the time or year when the said irregularities occurred.
(e) That Article 1.04 treats clubs unequally by, on the one hand, failing to act against clubs that are found guilty of bribery and have not met the criteria established by UEFA for qualifying for the Champions League, while, on the

other hand, acting against clubs which qualify for the Champions League in future and happen to have been previously found guilty of match fixing.

(f) That the appellants had failed to prove, on the basis of the facts adduced, that FC Porto's conduct amounted to a violation of Article 1.04(d).

(g) That FC Porto's failure to appeal against the PPFL Disciplinary Committee decision was not an admission of guilt, as it had no reason to appeal, because they had already won the national league by a 20 point margin and the deduction of points would have no effect.

(h) That the decisions of the FPF Appeal Committee and the PPFL Disciplinary Committee did not demonstrate with certainty that FC Porto, or its chairman, were involved in illegal activity. The appeal was accordingly dismissed.

997. CAS erred on a number of issues, both in fact and in law. Specific errors were made with regard to the following findings:

(a) that the principle of retroactivity is applicable to Article 1.04 of the UEFA Champions League Regulations;

(b) that Article 1.04 of the UEFA Champions League Regulations is a disciplinary and not an administrative rule;

(c) that even though Article 1.04 was applicable to the case, the evidence adduced by the appellants was insufficient proof of a violation of Article 1.04;

(d) that Article 1.04 is disproportionate and unreasonable;

(e) that the facts and evidence submitted were insufficient proof that FC Porto had been involved in illegal activities. The circumstances under which the FPF Appeals Committee decision was made and the fact that the decision had been appealed to the administrative courts sufficed to convince CAS that the appellants had failed to meet their burden of proof.

998. The CAS observed that the principle of non-retroactivity, which prevents the application of rules to offences committed prior to the coming into force of the rules, was not applicable in this case. This therefore meant that Article 1.04(d) was applicable to FC Porto even though it came into force in the 2008/09 season, and the alleged offences were committed in 2003/04. This was an error of law. CAS jurisprudence has always held that laws enacted after the commission of an offence are inapplicable to the offence. A case in point was the *Chelsea FC v. Adrian Mutu* case, CAS 2006/A/1192. This case however concerned an issue as to whether the relevant regulations were the 2001 or the 2005 FIFA Player Status and Transfer Regulations. It was held that the 2001 edition was applicable because the breach committed by Mr Mutu had occurred in 2005, but before the 2005 edition had come into force.

999. Despite ruling that Article 1.04(d) was applicable, the court nevertheless declined to apply it, on grounds that it was unreasonable and disproportionate. This also amounted to an error of law and fact, because the issue under consideration was not the reasonableness or proportionality of this provision, but rather whether or not it was applicable, and the consequences that its provisions would have on any team, which violated it.

1000. Administration involves the making of rules and criteria for entry into any competition. Once a team that wishes to participate in a competition has met the entry requirements, it will thereafter be bound to follow certain playing rules set by the body in charge of the competition while participating in that competition. Should the club fail to meet the entry criteria, it will not be allowed to compete; consequently, the rules of play governing that competition will not be applicable to it.

1001. Take for example, rules imposed by a nightclub, which forbid entry to all people with long hair. This is a purely administrative rule. Any long haired person, who is denied entry into the said night club, cannot claim that he has been disciplined because he has suffered no loss. However, if the rules of the night club state that any long haired person, who gains access to the club illegally, or otherwise, shall be fined EUR 1,000, then this is clearly a disciplinary measure, because the person affected stands to be prejudiced as a consequence of violating the said administrative rules.

1002. FC Porto had failed to meet the basic requirements for entry to the competition. The wording of Article 1.04(d) reads 'to be eligible to participate in the competition, a club must satisfy the following criteria'. The words eligibility and criteria are more administrative than punitive. Indeed the factual issues before the UEFA's dispute resolution and appeal bodies concerned whether FC Porto had fulfilled the admission criteria – an administrative rule, and not whether FC Porto were liable to be penalized and/or sanctioned. The exclusion was not a sanction – it was a managerial and operational tool, aimed at protecting the image of UEFA's competitions as provided for under Article 1.04. There is no alternative but to consider CAS's evaluation of Article 1.04(d) as a disciplinary rule as a factual error.

1003. In law, discipline is the imposition of a punishment or penalty with the objective of correcting conduct. An administrative measure can only be disciplinary, if it also has an inherent penalty or punishment. The CAS overlooked UEFA's own disciplinary rules. Although these disciplinary rules were not raised by the appellants, the CAS was nevertheless obliged to refer to them. Had it given a closer assessment of these rules, it could have brought out the differences between UEFA's administrative and disciplinary regulations. According to Article 2.2(e) of the UEFA bylaws, the UEFA disciplinary rules are intended to ensure that the objectives of UEFA are met. These administrative objectives are to 'prevent *all methods or practices, which might jeopardise the regularity of matches or competitions or give rise to the abuse of football; and (f) to ensure that sporting values always prevail over commercial interests*'. Under Article 2.2, UEFA is empowered to use any measures it deems appropriate to achieve the said objectives, one of which could include the establishment of any rules. These include the UEFA Champions League Regulations 2008/09, of which Article 1.04(d) is part and parcel. It is therefore a part of UEFA's administration.

1004. Furthermore, Article 52 of the UEFA bylaws lists all the actions which can result in disciplinary measures. The exclusion of a team from the UEFA Champions

League competition is not listed as a disciplinary sanction. It is therefore clear, contrary to CAS' reasoning that UEFA intended to separate administrative rules from disciplinary rules. Whereas the latter (the UEFA Disciplinary rules) could, by implication, be said to be the fruit of the former (the UEFA bylaws) as observed by CAS, it is however worth noting that the UEFA disciplinary rules were enacted by UEFA to assist it in the performance of its administrative duties. Nowhere do the disciplinary rules include match fixing as an act giving rise to a sanction. CAS therefore erred in law in ruling that the UEFA Champions League rules 2008/09 are disciplinary.

1005. It is a fact that both FC Porto and its chairman were found guilty of match fixing by more than one judicial body. The disciplinary committee of the Portuguese Professional Football League and the LPFP Disciplinary Committee found both FC Porto and its chairman guilty of attempted bribery of match officials. Despite this, FC Porto appealed to the UEFA Control and Disciplinary body. The outcome was similar to that of the LPFP Disciplinary Committee. It found FC Porto guilty of two attempts to bribe referees in accordance with the wording of Article 1.04(d) and therefore declined to allow FC Porto to participate in the Champions League.

1006. On 4 July 2008, the FPF Appeals Committee rejected the appeals filed by both FC Porto and its chairman and upheld the decision of the LPFP Disciplinary Committee. The CAS ruling itself acknowledged that FC Porto and its chairman were involved in activities aimed at influencing the outcome of matches. CAS also confirmed that the decisions issued by the Portuguese national associations formed part of the factual circumstances of the case. Unlike criminal matters, parties to arbitration and civil matters are not required to prove the facts adduced beyond a reasonable doubt. The standard of proof has always been the balance of probabilities. Once this standard has been met, an arbitration body is required to put the other party to its defence, i.e., it is required to ask the other party to adduce evidence negating its liability. The facts highlighted above are enough evidence of the existence of a reasonable case i.e., that on a balance of probabilities and without rebuttal evidence indicates guilt. CAS was obliged to put FC Porto to its defence once these facts had been established. In failing to do so, it erred on a point of law. It was therefore an error in both fact and law, for the CAS to hold that the findings – by three separate judicial bodies, were not substantial proof, on a balance of probabilities, that FC Porto had been guilty of illegal activities. The failure by FC Porto to appeal against the deduction of points because it *would have no effect on their status as champions because they had a 20 point lead* as observed by CAS did not change the fact that the fine was imposed as a result of a finding of guilt on their part by the said judicial bodies.

1007. It was not for CAS to rule on whether or not Article 1.04 was proportionate or unreasonable. The proportionality or otherwise of Article 1.04 was not the issue before CAS. It is a fundamental principle of law that once a law has been established, it is up to the legal enforcers to apply it, regardless of, whether or not it is unfair or unjust. The only instance when a court can overlook a regulation because it is disproportionate or unequal is when a party affected by the said regulation has raised a specific plea before the court challenging the legality of that regulation i.e., when the provisions of that law are in issue before the court. Furthermore, the sole purpose behind the permanent or temporary exclusion of teams from competitions for bribery and match fixing whenever the same occurred, by UEFA or any other sports association's is to protect and preserve the integrity and image of the sport.

1008. The interest in keeping the sport free of such conduct via strict administrative rules such as Article 1.04(d) far outweighs any inequities arising from that rule. CAS was therefore obliged to apply Article 1.04(d) in its entirety and to exclude FC Porto from the UEFA Champions League competition, albeit having erroneously ruled that Article 1.04(d) was not subject to the rules of non-retroactivity. The manner in which the CAS identified the relevant facts yet failed to apply the law to them is bizarre. It may well be that CAS was not immune to the influence and power of FC Porto. It is difficult to understand how three separate and independent judicial bodies can all arrive at a single conclusion, only to see it reversed by a fourth body. Such things can occur, but not in cases where the *accused* party has not been put to its defence, on the basis of the factual convictions issued by the three previous judicial bodies. CAS is a well-known and well-regarded sports court. However, it is possible, on the basis of this decision that parties involved in sports litigation may be compelled to look elsewhere for justice.

Part IV. Sport and Commerce

Chapter 1. Sport and EU Law

§1. Competition Law and Sport

I. General Outline of the EU Competition Rules

1009. The main articles of the Treaty on the Functioning of the European Union (TFEU) governing EU competition law are Articles 101 and 102 (former Articles 81 and 82, before the changes introduced by the Treaty of Lisbon, which provide the general outline of the corresponding legal framework.

1010. Article 101 of the TFEU prohibits:

> all agreements between undertakings, decisions by associations of undertakings and concerted practices which may affect trade between Member States and which have as their object or effect the prevention, restriction or distortion of competition within the common market, and in particular those which:
>
> (a) directly or indirectly fix purchase or selling prices or any other trading conditions;
> (b) limit or control production, markets, technical development, or investment;
> (c) share markets or sources of supply;
> (d) apply dissimilar conditions to equivalent transactions with other trading parties, thereby placing them at a competitive disadvantage;
> (e) make the conclusion of contracts subject to acceptance by the other parties of supplementary obligations which, by their nature or according to commercial usage, have no connection with the subject of such contracts.

1011. Article 101, no. 1 of the TFEU accordingly prohibits:

(a) agreements between undertakings;
(b) decisions of associations of undertakings;
(c) concerted practices between undertakings.

1012. The said article is applicable to all sectors of the economy without exception. The application of the article is subject to the existence of a restrictive effect on the relevant market, to be defined on a case-by-case basis.

1013. Article 102 of the TFEU states that:

> any abuse by one or more undertakings of a dominant position within the common market or in a substantial part of it shall be prohibited as incompatible with the common market in so far as it may affect trade between Member States.
>
> Such abuse may, in particular, consist in:
>
> (a) directly or indirectly imposing unfair purchase or selling prices or other unfair trading conditions;
> (b) limiting production, markets or technical development to the prejudice of consumers;
> (c) applying dissimilar conditions to equivalent transactions with other trading parties, thereby placing them at a competitive disadvantage;
> (d) making the conclusion of contracts subject to acceptance by the other parties of supplementary obligations which, by their nature or according to commercial usage, have no connection with the subject of such contracts.

1014. Article 102 of the TFEU generally prohibits abuse of a dominant position, i.e., a situation of economic power of one or more undertakings, which permits them to prevent the existence of effective competition in the market in question and to conduct themselves independently in relation to their competitors, clients and end consumers.

1015. The jurisdictional criterion common to the prohibitions in the articles is the affecting of trade between Member States. There is however an exception to Article 101 in no. 3 of the TFEU thereof, which involves the conduct of a cost-benefit analysis. The application of the exception in no. 3 of Article 101 of the TFEU must therefore comply with following four cumulative conditions despite the fact that they are established in the light of the specific circumstances of the case rather than mechanically, i.e., that the arrangement in question:

(a) contributes to improving the production or distribution of goods or to promoting technical or economic progress; and
(b) that the existing restrictions are indispensable in order to obtain the progress generated by the agreement;
(c) that consumers/users receive a fair share of the resulting benefit;
(d) that competition with regard to a substantial part of the products in question is likely to be eliminated.

1016. Provided that they contribute to improve production or distribution or products or to promote technical or economic progress, provided that users receive a fair share of the benefits arising therefrom, and do not impose any restrictions that are not indispensable for the achievement of the said objectives, or give these undertakings the opportunity to eliminate competition with regard to a substantial part of the products in question, the exception in no. 3 of Article 101 of the TFEU is applicable:

(a) to any agreement or category of agreements between undertakings;
(b) any decision, or category of decisions, of associations of undertakings;
(c) any concerted practice, or category of concerted practices.

1017. The subjection of sport to the competition rules does not necessarily imply a negative posture by the European Commission and the National Competition Authorities, but merely means the inclusion of a new supervisory body in the sports sector, which, in this case, is concerned with its commercial aspects. If the benefits arising from the agreement or decision of the association of undertakings exceed its competition restricting effects, the European Commission Guidelines regarding the application of no. 3 of Article 81[101] of the TFEU apply.[253]

II. Regulation (EC) No. 1/2003

1018. Regulation no. 17/62,[254] introduced a centralized control system according to which, notice of agreements likely to restrict and affect trade between Member States must be given to the Commission before they can have the benefit of an exemption. This power of the Commission to authorize agreements that restrict competition and comply with the conditions in no. 3 of Article 101 (formerly no. 3 of Article 81) of the TFEU, led undertakings to give notice of innumerable agreements, which undermined the efforts, which sought to promote a rigorous and decentralized application of the competition rules.

1019. As from 1 May 2004, when Regulation (EC) no. 1/2003, of 16 December, regarding the implementation of Articles 101 and 102 of the TFEU, came into force, which replaced Regulation no. 17/62, the provisions of the said articles were applied by the National Courts and Competition Authorities. This created an added level of responsibility for Undertakings/Associations of Undertakings, which include e.g., SADs and sports federations, as they now had the obligation to evaluate whether or not their *agreements and concerted practices and decisions of associations of undertakings* complied with EU competition rules (without any possibility of prior guarantees).

1020. Furthermore, the burden of proof of offences contrary to Articles 101 and 102 of the TFEU lies with the party or the competition authority, which alleges the existence of the offence, but lie also with the undertakings or associations of undertakings when the benefit of Article no. 101, no. 3 of the TFEU is claimed.

253. Published in the Official Journal of the European Communities of 27 Apr. 2004, under no. 2004/C 101/08, p. 117–135.
254. Published in the Official Journal of the European Communities of 21 Feb. 1962.

III. The Concepts of Undertaking, Economic Activity and the Definitions of *Market*

1021. Community case-law has for some time established a broadly based concept of an *undertaking,* which includes *any entity that carries on an economic activity, whatever its legal status and form and the manner it is financed,* which includes commercial companies and incorporated civil partnerships, business associations, public institutes and the liberal professions.

1022. The concept of *economic activity* is defined by the European Court of Justice as the *offer of goods or services on the market,* which naturally includes the activities of players, sports clubs, and national and international sports associations.[255]

1023. Since the 1970s the European Court of Justice has held that sport is subject to EU law to the extent that it is an economic activity.[256] As we shall see in greater detail later, this view was completely overturned by the Meca-Medina judgment, which applied EU Law even to 'purely sporting' activities or rules.

1024. In Commission Notice 97/C 372/03 of 9 December 1997 the Commission defined *Relevant Market,* i.e., the concepts of *product market in its ongoing enforcement of Community competition law* and *geographic market.*

1025. The Commission's definition of *Product/service market* takes the fungibility of the products or services on the supply side and the demand side into consideration. For example, in the case of rights to broadcast sports events on different supports, it is necessary to take the *attractiveness* of the content, the characteristics of the audience, advertising revenue and brand image and the technological convergence process, into consideration.

1026. The Commission's definition of *geographic market* delimits supply and demand in territorial terms. For example, broadcast rights markets are generally national, for linguistic and cultural reasons and because of the system used to sell the said rights.

IV. EU Law and Transfers of Sportspersons

A. Free Movement of Sportsmen in the EU and Portugal

1027. Portugal has not hidden itself from the realities of the specificity of sport, which carries with it certain characteristics such as the need for clubs to survive, the principle of promotion and relegation and above all the development of players.

---

255. Judgments in *Walrave,* of 12 Dec. 1974, case 36/74, and *Doná* of 14 Jul. 1976, case 13/76, *Piau,* of 26 Jan. 2005, case T-193/02.
256. *Ibid.*

This specificity has certainly been reflected in the EU treaty provisions on free movement of workers, of which Portugal is a member and signatory.

1028. Players and EU nationals engaged in team sports such as football, rugby, basketball, volleyball handball etc. have the right to procure and/or change clubs freely within the EU territory, including Portugal.

1029. This right has specifically been safeguarded under Article 45 of the TFEU (former Article 39 of the EU Treaty), which provides for the free movement of workers within the EU territory while prohibiting the EU Member States from discriminating on grounds of nationality.

1030. This prohibition is yet to extend to the prospective employers themselves, as there still exist football clubs such as Athletic Bilbao of Spain with policies which exclusively provide for the non acquisition of foreign players.

1031. However, clubs are within their own rights to adopt policies of their own choice, and it has not been proved that policies such as the one adopted by Athletic Bilbao contravene the EU laws on free movement of workers.

1032. There so far exists no Portuguese club which has any policies that directly or indirectly limit the free movement of players. It is of course worth noting the UEFA Home-grown Players Rule as well as the FIFA 6+5 Rule when addressing the free movement of sportsmen.

B. Free Movement of Sportsmen and Minors

1033. Article 45 of the TFEU accords freedom of movement to workers. Under EU laws, minors, who are normally children aged 18 years and below are not considered as workers. Therefore, in restricting the right and freedom, for example of a 17 year old minor to play in UEFA club competitions because he has not met the criteria established by the home-grown players rules, UEFA have in effect considered the said minor to be a worker, who is not entitled to 'work' by representing his club in UEFA competitions unless he fulfils the criteria fixed by UEFA.

1034. The European Court of Justice has interpreted the concept of worker as encompassing a person who:

(a) undertakes genuine and effective work;
(b) under the direction of someone else;
(c) and for which he is paid.[257]

257. *FMW – Online Journal on free movement of workers within the European Union No. 2 (page 10)*; Luxembourg: Publications Office of the European Union, August 2011 (ISBN 978-92-79-16355-5 doi:10.2767/2234).

1035. Even if one were to view the UEFA home-grown players rules as being contrary to EU law by regarding minors as workers, these rules could in one way be justified on the ground that there are legitimate and largely non-economic in nature in that they are (i) aimed at promoting the training of young players, (ii) maintaining balance in competitions and (iii) inherent to the general interests of sporting activity.

1036. Article 45 precludes the application of rules laid down by sporting associations under which football clubs may field only a limited number of professional players who are nationals of other Member States.[258] Such rules are contrary to the principle prohibiting discrimination on the basis of nationality. The only exception applies to matches which are purely of sporting rather than economic nature, such as competitions between national teams.

C. The Bosman Case

1037. These days, it is generally accepted that Sport, which was originally a leisure activity, has important social and economic aspects. Professional football players are now sold for record figures, a phenomenon unheard of until the mid-1990s.

1038. The case, which undoubtedly changed the way in which the transfer market operates forever, was the case of *Jean-Marc Bosman*[259] in the European Court of Justice (ECJ).

1039. When his sports employment contract was about to expire by effluxion of time, Bosman received an offer from his club to renew for a further season but for a lower salary, which he rejected.

1040. According to the procedures in force at that time, the player was placed on the transfer list with a manifestly excessive transfer price, with the result that no clubs were interested in the player.

1041. The player sought out another club and signed a contract with a French club, subject to the sending of the player's international certificate, which should have been sent by the Belgian Football Federation to the French Federation, which did not occur, thus rendering the contract null and void.

1042. In response to the player's claim in the Belgian Courts, the *cour d'appel de Liège* posed a preliminary question to the Court of Justice, which was whether *articles 48, 85 and 86 of the Treaty of Rome, of 25th March 1957, should be interpreted so as to prohibit a football club from demanding and receiving the payment of a sum of money for the engagement by a new club, of one of its players whose*

258. The same prohibition was expressed in the Bosman case.
259. The case resulted in the Judgment of the ECJ, of 15 Dec. 1995, URBSFA -v- Jean-Marc Bosman et al. and UEFA -v- Jean-Marc Bosman, Case no. C-415/93, p. I-4921.

contract had expired? The European Parliament had already responded in the affirmative to this question[260] and the ECJ took the same position.

1043. In a decision, which held that *transfer compensation* was incompatible with EU law, the ECJ considered that transfer compensation restricts the free movement of players, as it alters the circumstances in which employment is offered and reduced the possibility of players finding employment. Article 48 of the Treaty also establishes a general prohibition of all restrictions of the freedom of movement of workers, which excludes any possibility of transfer compensation from a non-discrimination point of view.

1044. The FIFA Player Status and Transfer Regulations accordingly had to be altered so as to comply with the Treaty of Rome so that the principle of free movement and work of players in the community space was implemented. In this incident, political will prevailed over the self-determination of the sports associations.

1045. Before the decision in the *Bosman* case, the football players transfer market operated in accordance with two rules:

(a) there was a limitation on the number of foreign players in each team, in accordance with the UEFA competition rules, which was adopted by the member federations in their countries, including the FPF in Portugal;
(b) the international professional player transfer system was based on a *transfer compensation mechanism.* This compensation was payable by the contracting clubs to the club of origin even if the player was no longer subject to a sports employment contract. The reason for this payment was to compensate the club of origin for its contribution to the development training and valorization of the player.

D. The Impact of the Bosman Judgment in Portugal

1046. After the *Bosman* case became known, the FPF abolished the rule which provided for compensation for training and valorization of players, following the lead of the international Federations. This led to the emergence of the *free player* and *free transfer* concepts in the legal panorama and in the European Football Market.

1047. The end of the player transfer system based on *transfer compensation* altered the organizational system of Portuguese football, above all because there was no transitional period between transfer regulations, which meant that the alterations were more difficult.

260. See European Parliament Resolution dated 11 Apr. 1989, on the freedom of movement of professional footballers in the European Community – JOCE, no. C120, of 16 May 1989.

1048. In this way, Portugal, which, in 1994/1995, had a football championship that was considered to be attractive, with good players, low salaries, and top teams that achieved good results in direct competition with better-known adversaries with greater financial power, rapidly began to lose its potential and force after 1996.

1049. The fact is that the arrangements in force until 1996 ensured that the club of origin was entitled to receive compensation for the supposed investment made in the training of the player and for the valorization of the player. Moreover, the existence of the compensation was a disincentive to the hiring of a player, whose contract had expired. This facilitated the renewal of the player's contract with the club of origin, which gave some stability to club squads and enabled clubs in championships with less financial force to conserve their best players for a long period.

1050. The limit on the number of foreign players permitted in each team was another factor that led to the conservation of Portuguese talent, although there was a clear feeling that there were major restrictions on the freedom of movement of these professional players. However until the *Bosman* case, the attempts to challenge the regulatory power of the associations in sport, and, above all, in football, were fruitless. The problem was that when the awareness of player's rights emerged everything happened too quickly, with the result that the European football transfer market changed completely, without the benefit of a period for a natural transition.

1051. From the player's point of view, the fact that he is free after the expiry of the employment contract, had a decisively increased the level of remuneration the player could command, as this became the main criterion for the selection of the average player. This has clearly benefited clubs in championships with greater financial power. In order to be able keep up with the salaries earned by players with free player status recently hired, the richest clubs increased the level of the basic remuneration paid to their players, which resulted in a certain distancing between European championships. Small countries, which had had competitive championships and clubs that were well ranked in European terms, such as Belgium, the Netherlands and Portugal, lost status, while the championships in Eastern Europe practically ceased to have any presence in the new Europe of post-Bosman football.

1052. Furthermore, the hiring of foreign players, including extra-community players, started to proliferate all over Europe. There was still a restriction on the number of foreign players in football teams, but this applied only to non-naturalized extra-community players. The exception, in the Portuguese championship, were Brazilian players, who were granted equal status, i.e., were treated as if they were naturalized Portuguese citizens, for sports purposes.

1053. The clubs' reaction to this insecurity in the maintenance of their contractual ties with their players was felt immediately, and it became common for clubs to want to retain their players for a greater number of seasons, by stipulating rescission clauses with record compensation levels. These rescission clauses, which became generalized in the post-Bosman period, enable purchaser clubs to reduce the risk of a player leaving the club without it receiving any compensation. These clauses permit players to rescind their contracts without having to invoke just cause.

1054. In the *Portuguese* case, there can be little doubt that the Bosman judgment resulted in decline of the competitiveness of Portuguese teams in relation to other teams. In fact, Portuguese clubs of recognized merit in the production and training of young players, above all in football, were no longer able to compete financially with the more attractive championships and to ensure their financial survival, because they ran the risk of losing their best players as Free Players, without compensation.

1055. It should be noted, in addition to the matters stated above, that the Bosman judgment was the source of an alteration of the legal framework governing professional sportspersons. Accordingly, Decree-Law no. 305/95, of 18 November, was repealed by Law no. 28/98, of 26 June, and provided as follows with regard to 'transfer compensation' in no. 2 of Article 18 (which replaced no. 2 of Article 22:

> A sports employer that enters into a contract with a sportsperson after the termination of a previous contract, may be required by a collective bargaining agreement, to pay fair compensation in respect of the promotion or valorization of the sportsperson, to the previous employer.

1056. No. 2 of the said Article 18 includes the proviso that 'the collective bargaining agreement referred to in the preceding number shall apply only in relation to transfers of sportspersons between Portuguese clubs that have their headquarters in Portugal'.

1057. The essential aspect of this provision is that notwithstanding the prohibition at Community level, the legislator wished to retain the possibility of transfer compensation at the national (inter-state) level, which can always give rise to doubts as to the legality of any 'inverse discrimination' and, above all, with regard to interstate transfers, which are not 'purely internal circumstances' according to community case-law.

E. The Kolpak Judgment and the Nihat Order

1058. Some association agreements made between third countries and the EU contain provisions that prohibit discrimination on the grounds of nationality with regard to the working conditions and remuneration of workers legally employed in a Member State. Sportspersons from these countries can benefit from the Bosman Judgment to the extent that professional sportspersons that have been hired legally cannot be victims of discrimination when they play in a Member State. Accordingly, sportspersons from a State that has made an association agreement with the EU cannot be excluded from the team on the field of play on the grounds of their nationality.

1059. This question was considered in the *Kolpak* judgment,[261] with regard to a Slovak handball player in Germany. The Court of Justice held that a rule that restricts the number of professional players authorized to play in certain games was related to working conditions and restricted the opportunity of Slovak players to play in certain games in relation to players, who are nationals of a Member State of the European Economic Area, is discrimination prohibited by the association agreement. This prevents the application of a rule introduced by the federation of a Member State to the effect that clubs are only authorized to field a limited number of players from third countries, which have not signed the agreement regarding the European Economic areas, in Cup and Championship matches, to a professional sportsperson of Slovak nationality, who was properly engaged by a club based in the said State.

1060. In the case of the footballer Nihat Kahveci,[262] the Court held, in an order stating grounds, that the prohibition of all discrimination in terms of pay and other working conditions, against Turkish workers working in the legal employment market of the Member States, must be interpreted to the effect that a rule imposed by a sports federation in the said state according to which clubs are only authorized to field a limited number of players from third states, which are not parties to the Agreement regarding the European Economic Space, cannot apply to a professional sportsperson, who is a Turkish national, who has been properly hired by a club based in a Member State.

F. The Igor Simutenkov Judgment

1061. In a judgment dated 12 April 2005, the ECJ considered the legality of a limitation on the number of extra-community players in the teams of clubs eligible for national competitions. It is a fact that the Bosman judgment had not eliminated the distinction between players from countries that are members of the European Economic Area, who are deemed to be community players, and players from countries outside the EEA, who are deemed to be extra-community players. Igor Simutenkov, a Russian footballer, who was a member of a Spanish team, claimed equal status on the basis of the partnership agreement between the EU and Russia. As the EU expanded its agreements and partnerships with countries outside the EEA, the distinguishing criterion between community and extra-community players ceased to make sense and was abolished in some EU countries.

1062. In Portugal, the last season in which this distinction was effective was 2005/2006, in which the squads of the teams that competed in the championships organized by the LPFP had a maximum of six extra-community players. This rule was also in force in the levels of the championships organized by FPF. The Secretary of State of Youth and Sport, via order no. 1/SEJD/2005, ordered all federations with EUPD to remove the said limitation from their regulations. The criterion was

261. Judgment of the Court of Justice of 8 May 2003, case C-438/00.
262. Order of the Court of Justice of 25 Jul. 2008, case 152/08.

abolished as from 2006/2007, so that club squads could be exclusively comprised by foreign players, if that was the clubs decision.

1063. The total liberalization of the market had the obvious effect that players trained locally are no longer able to have normal career advancement and to progress to a place in their club's main team. This is prevented not only by the presence of foreign players, but also because it became much easier for talented players to move to any country because of the abolition of player quotas.

V. The Specificity of Sport

A. *Introduction*

1064. The relationship between sport and business is now so close that it can be stated, particularly with regard to professional sport, that the one cannot exist without the other.

1065. There are a growing number of business activities that have sprung up around sports competitions and those involved in them, i.e., clubs and players, e.g., sale of merchandising articles, broadcasting rights, tickets to sports events, sale of players transfer rights and sponsorship agreements *inter alia.* What were formerly small scale businesses generated by professional sport, above all football, are now difficult to ignore because of the large sums involved.

1066. As there are specific markets for all these business activities, which take place within territories covered by the Treaty, they are subject to competition law, even though sport involves a series of specificities that cannot be ignored.

1066.1. The European Commission and Council have, since the end of the 1990s, acknowledged that sport has special features. Among the most emblematic of these documents is the Commission Report to the Helsinki European Council, December 1999 (COM (1999) 644), and the Declaration attached to the 2001 Treaty of Nice, which refer to the importance of the autonomy of sports organizations and their right to organize themselves via the appropriate organizational structures, and also the reference to the role played by sports federations in the necessary solidarity between leisure sport and high level sport. Finally, Article 165, nos 1 and 2 of the TFEU refer to the *specificities* of sport and to its *social and educational role.* It is these factors that justify the exceptional treatment of sport in relation to Articles 101 and 102 of the TFEU, and the EU configuration of sport, primarily its role as a promoter of cultural and social integration, above all with regard to the distribution of resources, i.e., the contribution made by professional sport to amateur sport.

1067. The European Commission has, over the years, taken the following factors into consideration *inter alia,* the interdependence between sporting adversaries, for unlike other industries and sectors, sportspersons and sports clubs do not seek to benefit from the weakness of their adversaries, or to eliminate them.

1068. There is also a need to preserve the uncertainty of competition results, the fairness of sports competitions, i.e., equality of opportunities and also the need to maintain the balance between sporting adversaries, in order to attract the interest of consumers. Particularly relevant in this regard is the relevance of the principle of solidarity with regard to the redistribution of financial resources from professional sport for the development and subsistence of amateur sport, in order to support the existence of smaller clubs, the training of players, *inter alia.* Finally, the internal autonomy of sports associations and their regulatory authority in relation to genuine 'sports rules' is particularly noteworthy, which recognizes the monopolistic pyramid structure that characterizes the organization of sport in Europe.

1069. Unlike undertakings in a normal commercial market, in which the aim is to eliminate competitors; in the sports market, the aim is not to eliminate adversaries, but, on the contrary to ensure their preservation and economic viability, in order to ensure the continuity of the events and the interest and attention of spectators, which can only be achieved via the number of adversaries in the same competition their competitive capacities and qualities, which benefits the events and investors in the competition.

B. The Meca Medina Case

1070. The initial distinction between rules regarding the economic aspects of sport, which are therefore subject to the EU competition rules, and the rules regarding strictly sports matters, which have no economic aspect and are therefore excluded from the EC Treaty, was made by the Court of First Instance of the European Communities in the *Meca-Medina* judgment of 30 September 2004.[263]

1071. The Judgment of the European Court of Justice in the *Meca-Medina* case of 18 July 2006[264] set aside the judgment of the CFI and deemphasized the special treatment of purely sporting rules and widened the scope of the sporting rules subject to Articles 101 and 102 of the TFEU. The Court considered that the mere circumstance that a rule is purely sporting does not exclude the application of the Treaty to the person, who carries on an activity regulated by that rule, or the organization that introduced it and established a mechanism for the assessment of sports rules in the light of Articles 101 and 102 of the TFEU, which involves the identification of:

(a) the overall context in which the rule was adopted, or is effective and the objectives of the rule;
(b) whether the restrictions arising from the rule are inherent in the objectives pursued;
(c) whether the rule is proportionate to that end (fair, objective and non-discriminatory application).

263. Case T-313/02.
264. Case C-519/04.

1072. The *Meca-Medina* judgment was based on the *Wouters* judgment, of 19 February 2002,[265] regarding the rules of the Dutch Bar Association, which prohibited Dutch lawyers from forming partnerships with accountants, which is a leading case with regard to the application of the EU competition rules to the liberal professions.

1073. The legitimate objectives concerned the organization and proper conduct of sports competitions, such as equality of opportunity of all players in a competition, the assurance of the uncertainty of the final results, the protection of players' health, the protection of the safety of spectators, the encouragement of the training of young players, the assurance of the financial stability of sports clubs and teams and the assurance of the uniform and consistent playing of a certain sport (rules of the game). However, restrictive rules may also be justified pursuant to no. 3 of Article 101 of the TFEU, if their positive effects outweigh their restrictive effects.

1074. The conclusion is that there can be no general exemption or exceptional treatment for sports rules with this objective. The concept of a *purely sporting rule* is not relevant to the question of the applicability of the EU competition rules to the sports sector. However the methodology defined by the Court of Justice allows the specificity of sport to be taken into consideration on a case-by-case basis according to the specific characteristics of the sport in question. The consequent need to classify a rule as *strictly sporting* arises, for example in the case of the obligation of Portuguese players to play for the Portuguese national team in international competitions, if selected, and certain rules of the game such as the *off-side* rule in football and the rules regarding the duration of matches.

1075. The application of the EU competition rules to sport was defined and fixed by the *Meca-Medina* Judgment of the European Court of Justice, which clarified that:

(a) the application of the rules regarding the workings of the Internal Market (i.e., freedom of movement and the freedom to provide services) does not exclude the analysis of the practices in question in the light of Articles 101 and 102 of the TFEU. The contrary is also true;
(b) sport does not receive an especially favourable treatment in the context of EC competition law and all the rules regarding sport must, in principle, be considered in the light of Articles 101 and 102 of the TFEU, even if they can, from the outset, be classified as *purely sporting* rules;
(c) the objectives of sports rules must be considered as part of an objective analysis that takes the details of each case into consideration in accordance with the principle of proportionality;
(d) the decision of the European Commission has to a certain extent revealed special consideration of the specificity of sport in the formal decisions taken and in

265. Case C-309/99.

the positions it has adopted, which have prioritized dialogue with sports organizations, negotiations with a view to the alteration of restrictive practices, while safeguarding access by third parties on fair, equitable and non-discriminatory terms;

(e) the Commission will now follow the guidelines laid down by the Court of Justice's judgment in *Meca-Medina* and may always investigate the possible justification of restrictive practices in accordance with no. 3 of Article 101 of the TFEU;

(f) sports organizations are increasingly receptive to the application of EU competition rules to their economic activities, and now have greater legal certainty thanks to the European Court of Justice.

C. *The Specificity of Sport and EU Competition Law, or the Antinomy between Sporting Competition and Economic Competition*

1. The 'Specificity of Sport'

1076. The 'Specificity of sport' is a very nebulous concept, which has random and uncertain legal effects. Some writers identify a need to clarify,[266] and explain this concept,[267] in order to achieve greater legal stability, predictability and uniformity,[268] in order to surpass the current case-by-case approach.[269] As Carol COUSE states:

> [a]s *sport*, and particularly football, has developed socially, culturally and economically over the last decade, EU law has tried to react accordingly. However, in the absence of a clear, stable and predictable legal framework, matters have inevitably been determined by the ECJ, resulting in EU law being developed in a piece meal 'case-by-case' basis.[270]

1077. Article 165(1), paragraph 2 of the Treaty on the Functioning of the European Union (TFEU) states that '[t]he Union shall contribute to the promotion of

---

266. '4.22 In the EESC's view, the relationship between the specificities of sport and European legislation is a question of crucial importance, and there is a major need to clarify this point for sports organizations – Opinion of the European Economic and Social Committee on the White paper on sport', *COM(2007) 391 final,* (2008/C 151/12), OJEU C 151, 17.06.2008, p. 36.
267. No strict concept of the specificity of sport has been formally recognized by the EU Courts.
268. '*The need for legal uniformity is one of the most obvious* [specificities of sport]' – CAS 2005/A/983 & 984, para. 102.
269. Opinion of the Committee of the Regions on 'The White Paper on Sport', (2008/C 105/09), C 105/40 OJEU, 25.4.2008: '56. Feels that the specific characteristics of sport are fundamental and feels that the White Paper fails to take a clear position on this point. The Committee is concerned that a case-by-case approach to dealing with the specificity of sport will be unsatisfactory from the perspective of sporting organizations and will entrench existing legal uncertainty.'
270. 'The International Transfer System and the Principle of Specificity of Sport', Sports Law Bulletin no 10, June–October 2012, Nyon, EPFL, p. 75.

European sporting issues, while taking into account of the specific nature of sport, its structures based on voluntary activity and its social and educational function.' The expression 'specific nature of sport' is not defined.

1078. The European Commission has stated that '[t]he concept of the specific nature of sport is taken into account when assessing whether sporting rules comply with the requirements of EU law (fundamental rights, free movement, prohibition of discrimination, competition, etc.)[271]'. (Emphasis added). In its White Paper on Sport,[272] the Commission attempted to define the specificity of European sport, a concept that it considers can be approached in two ways:

(i) The specificity of sporting activities and of sporting rules, such as separate competitions for men and women, limitations on the number of participants in competitions, or the need to ensure uncertainty of outcomes and to preserve a competitive balance between clubs taking part in the same competition; and

(ii) The specificity of the sport structure, including notably the autonomy and diversity of sport organizations, a pyramid structure of competitions from grassroots to elite level and organized solidarity mechanisms between the different levels and operators, the organization of sport on a national basis, and the principle of a single federation per sport.

1078.1. The following aspects of the *specificity* of sport have been suggested:

(iii) The specificity of sport contracts, which require a specific legal framework adapted to the specific nature of sports activity and sports actors – employment contracts are a paradigmatic example of a case in which general or normal rules are not appropriate;

271. Communication from the Commission to the European Parliament, the Council, the European Economic and Social Committee and the Committee of the Regions – Developing the European Dimension in Sport, {SEC(2011) 66 final}{SEC(2011) 67 final}{SEC(2011) 68 final}- point 4.2. The specific nature of sport.

272. Prior to the White Paper, the Independent European Sport Review 2006 provided a detailed and motivated description of the legal specificity of sport, with a special focus on professional team sports. The Arnaut Report believed that this legal definition should be considered as the main starting point for the Commission as regards professional football. In terms of priorities the Report highlighted the following: (i) A sports justice system (notably following the recent Meca-Medina case but also other upcoming cases) including recourse to properly-constituted arbitration panels; (ii) Measures to ensure the training capacity of clubs, encourage the local training of young talent and to improve competitive balance in competitions; (iii) Rules relating to the selection and make-up of national teams; (iv) Systems for club licenses and appraising the management of licensed clubs; (v) Central marketing (in line with the existing Commission decisions); (vi) Transfer system (in line with the existing settlement between FIFA, UEFA and the Commission dated March 2001); (vii) Measures aimed at controlling betting and its influence on matches and competitions; (viii) Regulation of players' and clubs' agents; (ix) Measures against the multiple ownership/control of clubs.

(iv) The sports world;[273]

(v) The double and triple affiliation system: i.e. the fact that a person can be simultaneously a member of two different associations with regard to the same sport and that membership of one association involves membership of one or more other associations, that superintend the first association;[274]

(vi) The case law criteria (e.g. within FIFA and CAS) that has developed with regard to the calculation of compensation in the context of contractual litigation ;[275]

---

273. Albino Mendes Baptista describes such specificities quite well: (i) Special consideration should be given to the following aspects: the time chosen for the termination of contractual relations during sporting competitions; the competition or competitions entered by the club; the importance of the sportsperson to the team and his/her position in the team; existing alternatives within the work group; consequences in terms of the team's performance; consequences of termination in terms of the work group; effects on the club's image; advertising agreements, which may be frustrated; future projection of the sportsperson; (ii) However, respect for fans should never be ignored, because the spectacle cannot exist without them or, for that matter, without the true 'sporting values', which should be safeguarded by those who have 'sport judicial' responsibilities. If this effort is made, we will surely have a better understanding of what the specificity of sport should be; (iii) Protecting smaller clubs is one of the expressions of sport specificity; (iv) As is known, the standard employment model is based on hiring for an indeterminate period, which is not adequate and does not fit the reality of employment of sportspersons, which, due to its specific nature, is temporary and thus requires that the general and exclusive rule be hiring for a fixed period; (v) Sportspersons cannot terminate their employment agreement *ante tempus,* unless there is just cause to do so. This highlights the relevance of contractual stability in the balance and proper functioning of sporting competitions; (vi) The general rules regarding trial periods are also not appropriate with regard to sporting employment relationships; (vii) The standard rules regarding working hours are also not adequate for the sporting employment relationship. For example, consider the time spent on travelling and training, weekly rest days, the fixing and alteration of working hours (matches, which are held in the evening because of television broadcasting requirements) and the scheduling of holidays; (ix) The issue of disciplinary power also has its specificities, which are noteworthy. Dismissals are very rare in the sports employment because sportspersons are 'financial assets'). Termination normally occurs at the instance of the sportsperson and this is the most common way in which sports employment relationships are terminated; (x) The freedom to work cannot be reflected in sports employment in the same way it is normally. For example, in sports employment contracts, termination of the contract by the sportsperson is, and rightfully so, not permitted; (xi) On the other hand, a non-competition clause makes no sense in a sports employment contract; (xiii) The 'equal pay for equal work' principle has no place in a sports employment contract; (xiv) Another issue specific to sport concerns which is dealt with in sports employment contracts is the temporary loan of sportspersons. While ordinary employment law discourages such arrangements, they are looked upon favourably in sports employment contracts; (xv) Reinstatement, (…) is completely inadequate to sport's legal and employment environment; (xvi) 'Cancellation rights' cannot be included in a sports employment contract.

274. According to Denis Oswald, within the 'sport specificities' one must include 'double affiliation' – the fact that a person can be simultaneously a member of two independent associations, which are active in the same sports – and 'triple affiliation' – i.e., membership of an association (at the grassroots) automatically involves being a member of one or more associations, which are, in principle, hierarchically superior 'Associations, fondations et autres formes de personnes morales'.

275. FIFA Decision of the Dispute Resolution Chamber passed in Zurich, Switzerland, on 10 Dec. 2009, *Udinese Calcio v. Morgan de Sanctis and Sevilla*, FC:

> 37. The Chamber then turned its attention to the aspect relating to the 'Specificity of sport' which is equally explicitly referred to in Article 17 par. 1 of the Regulations. At the outset, the

(vii) The vulnerabilities, risks and imponderable factors of sport that account for the specificity of sport as a product: i.e. sport is subject to multiple risks[276] – vulnerability of the coaches/managers; cancellation of sport events due to the absence of 'stars', with the inherent contractual consequences, e.g. with regard to broadcasting; problems that may reduce the value of the 'product', such as doping, corruption, match-fixing, and violence;[277] player injuries[278] – the damage that such misfortunes may cause to a club are evident; the condition and characteristics of the pitch can have a decisive impact on the results of a football match; rumours and exacerbated emotional responses can have a negative impact on sport clubs and undertakings in terms of share price.[279] In short, success always depends on such random factors including weather conditions, which cannot be controlled by the service providers, which account for the specificity of sport and the sport product;

(viii) The results of a sport event are not determined by the financial investments made in the opposing teams or sportspersons, unlike other areas of activity, in which greater investment and greater size are generally accompanied by increased possibilities of gain. Major investment in a sport, a sportsperson, or a club do not necessarily guarantee successful results; the 'core-product' is beyond the control of the 'bosses', who are unable to ensure either the result or the product. This aspect is inherent in sport, and attracts spectators and investors but also separates sport from the market and economic competition;

> Dispute Resolution Chamber recalled that this important aspect has been recognized by the European Union and has repeatedly been referred to by the CAS for the purpose of establishing the applicable amount of compensation in case of contractual breach, ensuring that the decisions rendered are not only just and fair from a strictly legal point of view, but that they also correspond to the specific needs and interests of the football world and its stakeholders. (Emphasis added)

276. See Battista, Jasmin, 'Lo sport et il dirito comunitario della concorrenza', in Lo sport e il Diritto. Profili istituzionali e regolamentazione giuridica, Edited by Michele Colucci, Hovene editore, 2004, p. 74.
277. Patrice Bouvet adds issues regarding economic crisis, administrative reforms or legislative developments, particularly in the audio-visual market. According to her, the media are the 'banks of the system' and their situation has a major influence on sport entities, p. 17. This is why clubs are very dependent on the financial calculations of other 'players'.
278. From the point of view of a sponsor, the fact that a player is injured in the team's first match could mean the end of the team. This explains why sponsors frequently prefer to focus on the values of the sport, the team and/or the player.
279. Lombard Cardia, President of the Italian stock exchange market (Consob):

> The listing of clubs on the stock market was a mistake (…) I believe the value of football undertakings was and still is a mistake. This sector is structurally plagued by the dissemination of rumours and indiscretions, which are frequently amplified by an exacerbated emotional response (…) Sometimes all it takes is an enthusiastic statement from a fan or the good or bad result of a game and there you have it – hiring of players skyrockets, or just plummets, And

(ix) The lifetime of the product is normally '*extremely short*';[280]

(x) The specificity of sports law – sports law is an autonomous[281] area of law. Some of the principles applicable in sports litigation are part of the *Lex Sportiva.*

(xi) Disciplinary framework, namely the principle of par condition and the principle of *pro competitionae* – the need for fast decisions sometimes results in limitation of defence rights, via short time limits and fewer procedural guarantees

(xii) The publicity of the sport sanctions in the media – due to the specific characteristics of sport, disciplinary sanctions are more visible than other sanctions;[282]

(xiii) The specificity of the games of chance, in the framework of the Services Directive – Article 25 of the Services Directive contains an explicit reference to the '*specificity of the game*' and sport escapes from the scope of the application of EU Law;[283]

(xiv) The autonomy of sport: – '*The autonomy of sport is, within the framework of national and international law, the possibility for*

---

although this is not a case of real manipulation (of the value) it still causes some disruption to the proper functioning of the market', Jornal O Jogo.

280. See KEA-CDES: Study on the economic and legal aspects of transfers of players, January 2013, p. 123.

281. 'Acknowledgement of its autonomy is based on the creation and development of its own set of rules, even when these rules interfere with the general legal systems due to the increasingly plural positioning of the homo sportivus. Finally, the sport legal system is international for it is created as an 'extra-State', 'inter-State' and even 'supra-State' legal system with thousands of addressees in different countries', Gomes Canotilho.

282. See Olmeda, Alberto Palomar, 'Un Nuevo régimen disciplinario para el deporte profesional?', in Las Leyes del deporte de la democracia: bases para una Ley del siglo XXI, Edited by Nicolás de la Plata Caballero, Madrid, Dykinson, 2002, p. 183.

283. *Samuli Miettinen states that:*

> Every word of this proposed amendment survived and became Recital 35 in the final instrument. However, one crucial qualification was added: the final draft recognised the conflict between this exclusion and the Court's constant reiteration of the limits of the sporting exception and as a consequence inserted 'should' into the final sentence, transforming an attempt to exclude an activity into a more tentative, inaccurate restatement of case law: '(35) Non-profit *making amateur sporting activities are of considerable social importance. They often pursue wholly social or recreational objectives. Thus they might not constitute economic activities within the meaning of Community law and should fall outside the scope of this Directive.' 'It will be recalled that between the April 2006 redraft and the final text of the directive, the ECJ decided the Meca-Medina case in which it clarified some limits of the special relationship between sport and the EC Treaty.'* 'Recital 35 outlines one fundamental tenets of the 'sporting exception' thesis – that the aims and social importance of an activity should exclude Treaty interference even in economic activity.', '*Regulating sports services in Community Law', in EU, Sport, Law and Policy: Regulation, Re-Regulation and Representation, Edited by Simon Gardiner, Richard Parrish, Robert C.R. Siekmann, The Hague, T.M.C. Asser Press, 2009,* pp. 276-277.

> *non-governmental, non-profit-making sports organisations to: 1) establish, amend and interpret rules appropriate to their sport freely, without undue political or economic influence; 2) choose their leaders democratically, without interference by states or third parties;3) obtain adequate funds from public or other sources, without disproportionate obligations; 4) use these funds to achieve objectives and carry on activities chosen without severe external constraints; 5) negotiate legitimate standards proportionate to the achievement of these objectives with the public authorities.'*[284,285,286]

1079. The specificity of other sectors, such as culture, have legal recognition.[287] The specificity of cultural goods, which are not goods like others,[288] and are distinguished by a permanent oscillation between the commercial and non-commercial spheres, with major and frequent situations of porosity between both spheres.[289]

2. *Sporting Competition versus Economic Competition*

1080. There is a substantial difference between '*economic competition*' and '*sporting competition*'.[290] This is a consequence of the 'unusual'

---

284. Jean-Loup Chappelet, 'Autonomy of sport in Europe', Strasbourg, Council of Europe Publishing, 2010, p. 49.
285. *'The special nature of sport, referred to in 'Eurospeak' terms as the 'specificity of sport', is seen as valued and protected by the ability of sport to self-govern in certain critical respects (referred to as the 'autonomy of sport',* Dikaia Chatziefstathiou and Ian P. Henry, Discourses of Olympism: From the Sorbonne 1894 to London 2012, p. 269.
286. The Committee of the Regions '(…) together with the Commission, acknowledges the autonomy of sporting organisations and representative structures, and feels that the White Paper fails to emphasise the importance of such autonomy as described and acknowledged in the Nice Declaration' (Emphasis added) – Opinion of the Committee of the Regions on 'The White Paper on Sport', (2008/C 105/09), OJEU C 105, 25.04.2008, p. 55.
287. *A paradigmatic example is the Convention on the Protection and Promotion of the Diversity of Cultural Expressions 2005,* Adopted in Paris, 20 Oct. 2005. Paragraph 18 of the Preamble of the Convention states: *'Being convinced that cultural activities, goods and services have both an economic and a cultural nature, because they convey identities, values and meanings, and must therefore not be treated as solely having commercial value.' Additionally, Art. 1 ('Objectives') (g) makes reference to the need to give recognition to the distinctive nature of cultural activities, goods and services as vehicles of identity, values and meaning* (Emphasis added).
288. 'An alternative view affirms the 'specialness' of culture as a federating force in pluralistic democracies (Baker 2000). Such a view draws attention to the fact that, over and above their commercial dimension, cultural products are importantly vehicles of social communication that promote a wider sense of belonging and cultural identity. Cultural patrimony can thus be seen as a crucial component of the identity and self-understanding of a nation. Accordingly, countries should have the right to protect and promote their own culture internally' (Emphasis added) – See Pierre Sauvé and Karsten Steinfatt, 'Towards multilateral rules on trade and culture: protective regulation or efficient protection?'
289. See Françoise Behhamou, *Les dérèglements de l'exception culturelle : Plaidoyer pour une perspective européenne*, Éditions du Seuil, Paris, 2006, pp. 161–162.
290. Canivet states that the evident specificities of the sports sector had made the application of EUCL to sport 'reticent', *Le droit de la concurrence appliqué au sport, Cour de Monsieur CANIVET, Sciences Po 2006–2007.*

characteristics,[291] or special features, of sport, which mean that it is difficult to apply the underlying reasons for the application of EUCL to other areas of activity, to sport.[292] Some of these special features, which are also an expression of the 'specificity of sport' are listed below:

- *Sport is based on values and has objectives, which are very different from the values and objectives that govern the market.* This much is evident from the statement made by the Commission with regard to the educational, social, cultural, recreational and economic functions of sport,[293] of which only the latter is linked to the market.
- *In a sporting organization, profit is not the main objective*:[294]

> whilst profit is the aim of commercial undertakings (as well as civil ones) it is not the main purpose or aim of the activity of sporting associations, *whether* groups of associations or clubs. The main activity of a sporting association is winning sporting titles or, in the case of a Federation organizing sporting competitions. In the specific case of professional sport the activity is profit oriented, but only in so far as to ensure that the clubs stay in the black financially and are able generate revenues in order to stay in the competition.[295]

- One of the key features of sport is *constant uncertainty as to results,*[296] even when the competitors have diametrically opposed sporting and economic

291. Stephen Weatherhill, 'Resisting the Pressures of "Americanization": The influence of European Community Law on the "European Sports Model"', *Law and Sport in Contemporary Society*, Ed. By Steve Greenfield e Guy Osborn, Frank Class, London, 2000, p. 159.
292. As F. Latty states, even when played at a high level and notwithstanding the economic aspects associated with it, sports competition differs from economic competition, despite the fact that the same term is used in the language of Shakespeare ('competition'), *La Lex Sportiva: recherche sur le droit transnacional*, Martinus Nijhoff Publishers, Leiden-Boston, 2007, p. 731.
293. European Commission, Directorate-General X, Working Document, 29 Sep. 1998.
294. According to Pedro Silva Pereira:

> it should however be pointed out that whilst profit is the aim of commercial undertakings (as well as civil ones) it is not the main purpose or aim of the activity of sports associations, whether groups of associations or clubs. The main activity of a sports association is the winning of sports titles or, in the case of a Federation, the organizing of sports competitions. In the specific case of professional sport, the activity is profit oriented, but only in order to ensure that clubs stay in the black financially and are able generate revenue in order to stay in the competition. The economic activity created by sport has the following specificity: it does not aim to generate profit as its ultimate objective. This ultimate, even if there were no other objectives, should be enough to admit that it is not possible to combine undertakings with differing objectives and apply the same regulations to them.

295. The economic activity created by sport has the following specificity: it does not aim to generate profit as its ultimate objective. This ultimate, even if there were no other objectives, should be enough to admit that it is not possible to combine undertakings with differing objectives and apply the same regulations to them.
296. Stefan Szymanski says that:

profiles. If sport events are to be of interest to the spectator, such uncertainty of the results is vital. It follows therefore that a certain degree of competitive equality is needed and this distinguishes sport from other sectors, where competition between undertakings serves to eliminate inefficient undertaking from the market. Indeed, it is this uncertainty of results and the drama that is a consequence thereof, a phenomenon which does not even occur at concerts or at the theatre that is central to sport. This leads to the existence of differing categories in sport, according to age, weight, gender and competitive level, as it is necessary, in order to ensure an event of quality in which the outcome is not certain from the outset, that there is an approximate equality of forces, or quality of competitive opportunities.

- Furthermore, the uncertainty of results leads to relations between undertakings, which are marked by a fundamental ambiguity because *competitors need to make partnerships and are interdependent* (in a joint production by the various undertakings – the production functions of the various undertakings are inseparable) – so that these undertakings are, at the same time, economic partners and sporting opponents.[297]

> '[t]eams *in a league compete for success. Absent intervention, competition will generate an equilibrium distribution of success (wins, points, etc.). The obvious condition for a competitive equilibrium should be that the marginal revenue of a win equals the marginal cost. In a competitive labour market it might be expected that the marginal cost of a win would be identical across teams (competition should equalise the marginal cost per unit, otherwise talent could profitably move from one team to another), and therefore the equilibrium condition reduces to the equalization of win marginal revenues across teams. It is commonly argued that the distribution of wins at this equilibrium will not generate enough outcome uncertainty in the league, thereby inhibiting demand and even threatening the viability of the league. It is therefore argued that teams should be allowed to enter collusive agreements (such as roster limits, salary caps, draft rules, revenue sharing) in order to ensure a more balanced distribution of outcomes (…) Empirical studies find remarkably weak evidence in support of the uncertainty of outcome hypothesis. For example, Borland and Macdonald (2003) surveyed 18 studies across a variety of countries and sports and found that only about three provide strong evidence of an effect on attendance … Other studies provide mixed evidence that suggest a negative effect on attendance of increasing home-win probability only when that win probability is above about two thirds' (p486). 'In other words, home team fans are not interested in a well balanced contest: they want their team to win, and are more likely to attend when the probability of that event is large. The evidence that demand may decline at very high home win probabilities also needs to be interpreted cautiously, since there are very few games that are this unbalanced, and hence the estimates are based on a very small number of observations. The result that attendance at a match is almost everywhere increasing in the success of the home team is not very surprising, since most popular clubs grow by being successful, but it does suggest that some caution is required in the use of the uncertainty of outcome hypothesis. The evidence does not suggest that the hypothesis is false, but it does suggest that its importance is not as great as is often suggested'.*

'Uncertainty of outcome, competitive balance and the theory of team sports', in *Handbook on the Economics of Sport,* Edited by Wladimir Andreff and Stefan Szymanski, pp. 597–598.

297. The battled waged between them seek to ascertain who the best is without eliminating the worst (since there can be no best without the existence of worst or no second without a first,). Ultimately, competitors play *against*, but necessarily also *with* each other.

- Competition between sporting undertakings is paradoxical, i.e. a certain equality of opportunities and economic and financial solidarity is necessary in order to ensure the continued existence of championships and competitions. This mutual interdependence of participants/competitors in sporting competitions requires major partnership commitments and solidarity between participants. This means that *sport is probably the only sector of activity in which there must be solidarity between competitors.*[298] For example, in a football championship: a team has no *raison d'etre* if it cannot compete with other teams and the championship cannot take place unless a sufficient number of clubs are incapable of winning it. Accordingly, the survival of the clubs depends on a certain level of co-operation and, accordingly, the coexistence of small and large clubs becomes an essential prerequisite. Competitive cohesion is to be found in the contribution which clubs make to the success of other clubs. Participants in a competition can neither produce nor sell their product without competitors as the product is the competition in which they take part. The said product is not only collective but is also indivisible, for, if divided, it would cease to be a product, as no club can produce an official game by itself and only a large number of clubs can ensure the existence and competitiveness of the product.
- A *competitive balance* must exist in order to ensure the uncertainty of results.[299] Uncertainty of results is a key to supporter loyalty,[300] so that in addition to the first level of solidarity between clubs, i.e. coexistence and partnership in the context of sporting competition, there is a second level, which comprises *the need*

298. This is also the position of R.H. Bork: '[S]ome activities can only be carried out jointly. Perhaps the leading example is league sports.' *The antitrust paradox. A policy at war with itself*, 2 ed., New York, 1993, p. 278.
299. Giving the example of football, Andersson affirms that:

> [i]t is accepted that there must be a competitive balance between clubs in order to preserve some sort of integrity of sporting competition, to keep fans interested and to enjoy commercial success. However, if a few teams were able to collect all the best players so that the other teams were not able to provide reasonable competition, results would become predictable, the financial gap between the rich and the poor clubs would grow and fans, advertisers and broadcasters would all lose interest. Consequently, a competitive imbalance could be devastating for football- See The Legality of Transfer Windows in European Football I: A study in the light of Article 39 and 81 EC.

Master's thesis in Sports Law and EC Law, JÖNK ÖPING INTERNATIONAL BUSINESS SCHOOL, Jönköping University, January 2009, p. 34.

300. *Stephen F. Ross* states that:

> *[c]ompetitive balance occurs where 'there is relative parity among the member teams [and] each team has the opportunity of becoming a contender over a reasonable cycle of years and a reasonable chance of beating any other team on any given night. By placing the outcome of any given game in doubt, competitive balance enhances a fan's enjoyment of a sport.*

See 'Break Up the Sports League Monopolies', in 'The Business of Professional Sports', Edited by Paul D. Staudohar and James A. Mangan, Illinois, Illini Books Edition, 1991, p. 156.

for economic solidarity[301] that is primarily in the form of mechanisms for the redistribution of the funds directly and indirectly generated by the competition (ticket sales, television broadcasts arising from the final classification, *inter alia*).All the participants contribute to a 'cake', the slices of which are redistributed in accordance with criteria of proportionality and fairness.

- For these two levels of solidarity to exist, it is necessary to create appropriate institutional and regulatory mechanisms. This is why clubs are organised in federations, which sometimes include leagues, with the power to organise, regulate and direct the competitions in which the clubs take part.[302] It should be noted, that *the 'single federation' principle*, according to which there is only one federation and/or league in each country applies within the EU. The fact that there are not two or more federation structures in the same country and therefore no duplication of organisations and regulations means that these federations or leagues can be described as authentic 'natural monopolies',[303] for the benefit of supporters, who clearly prefer that one team to be officially recognized as the champion of that country at the end of the competition, instead of a multiplicity of competitions, of which only one would be official. Such a model would clearly be inefficient and give rise to imbalances, as there would be competition between each federation/league to attract the best players to play in their competitions.[304] The single federation principle forestalls competition in the organisation, regulation and direction of the specific sport in question, in accordance with a model which, in other sectors of activity, would only be comparable to natural monopolies.
- *Sport fans are not consumers in the normal free market sense*. They do not behave as rational economic actors. They are consumers of supportership and are bound to a single club. It has been argued that support for football clubs is a culturally determined irrational choice and amounts to 'fan equity'. Fans' are emotionally committed to their club and a transfer of their support to a rival club is unthinkable. The consumer has no viable choice other than to withdraw from the market. This makes sport a peculiar market. 'When compared to other forms of

301. Only by acting this way can they maximize both individually and collectively the available resources derived from ticketing, sponsorships, television rights, by-products, etc.
302. The US Supreme Court has stressed that sports played in leagues are perhaps the main example of a commercial activity, which can only be carried on collectively – *National Collegiate Athletic Association v. Board of regents of University of Oklahoma*, 468 US 85, 101.
303. 'Football leagues are natural cartels, because otherwise they would not exist', Elisabeth Eklund, 'Following the Rules of the Game. A Competition Law Study of the Collective sale of Sports Broadcasting Rights', EUI Working Paper Law No. 99/1, European University Institute, Florence-Department of Law, Italy, 1999, p. 47; 'As producers of sport, sports federations and sports leagues are "natural monopolies"' *Professional Sport in the European Union: Regulation and Re-regulation*, Ed. Andrew Caiger and Simon Gardiner, TMC Asser Press, The Hague, 2000, p. 54.
304. See. Roger G. Noll, 'The organisation of sports leagues, Oxford Review of Economic Policy', Vol. 19, No. 4, p. 531; 547; Gary R. Roberts, 'The Case for Baseball's Special Antitrust Immunity', Journal of Sports Economics, Vol. 4, No. 4, November 2003, p. 303; Michael A. Flynn and Richard J. Gilbert, 'The analysis of professional sports leagues as joint ventures', *The Economic Journal*, 111, February, p. 44.

mass entertainment, sport reveals a fundamental difference – above all, its fans want to win. They want to win first and only then have fun'.[305,306]

1081. There is a substantial difference between *economic competition* and *sporting competition,*[307] which is the result of the fact that sport has a series of *unusual* characteristics,[308] or special features, which mean that it is difficult to transpose the underlying reasons for the application of EU Competition Law to other areas of activity, to sport.[309]

1082. First, sport is based on values and has objectives, which are very different from the values and objectives, which govern the market. This much is evident from the statement made by the Commission with regard to the educational, social, cultural, recreational and economic functions of sport,[310] of which only the latter is linked to the market.

1083. Moreover, one of the key features of sport is constant uncertainty as to results, even when the competitors have diametrically opposed sporting and economic profiles. A major financial investment in a sport, in a sportsman or in a club, does not necessarily guarantee successful results, to the extent that there are random aspects, which are specific to sport, which are immune to the influences of the market, e.g., the physical condition of the sportsperson, the methods adopted by coaches and weather conditions, unlike other areas of activity, in which greater

305. *A way of explaining how we all contribute to 'specificity' – sport behaving differently to any other business – is to analyse the behaviour of sports fans. Fans – all of us – are not 'rational consumers', and therefore normal rules don't apply. Let's say you buy a season ticket to a rubbish football team (£150); plus club shirt (£30); plus travel to matches and a half-time pie every week (£20 p/w) plus a Sky Sports subscription (£40 p/m – just in case they make the FA Cup 3rd round!). They win four matches at home all year and almost get relegated. But you will probably spend that money (almost £1000) again next season to experience even more pain, heartache, and that cruellest of all the sporting Gods: hope. Does that sound rational to you? Not a bit of it. If a company in a 'normal' business sector charged you £1000 for eight months of pain, heartache and failure, you'd never pay it.*', Keith Newman, '"Specificity" – or how sport breaks the law all the time'. http://www.sportspromedia.com/guest_blog/keith_newman_the_specific_nature_of_sport/, acceded on 12 Oct. 2011.

306. Ken Foster invokes *'(...) the dual nature of the 'consumer'. He is both buyer and fan. (...) Fans who cease to go to games do not normally start supporting another club, even if there is one readily available geographically*', p. 273.

307. Guy Canivet states that the evident specificities of the sports sector had made the application of EU Competition Law to sport 'reticent'. Cf. Guy Canivet, *Le Droit de la Concurrence Appliqué au Sport, Cour de Monsieur Canivet, Sciences Po 2006-2007.*

308. Stephen Weatherhill, 'Resisting the Pressures of "Americanization": The influence of European Community Law on the "European Sports Model"', *Law and Sport in Contemporary Society*, Ed. By Steve Grennfield and Guy Osborn, Frank Class, London, 2000, p. 159.

309. As Frank Latty states, even when played at a high level and notwithstanding the economic aspects, which are associated with it, sporting competition differs from economic competition, even if the same term is used in English ('competition'). Cf. Frank Latty. *Le Degré d'Autonomie de la 'Lex Sportiva' à l'Égard de l'Ordre Juridique Communitaire. La Lex Sportiva: Recherche sur le Droit Transnacional'*, Martinus Nijhoff Publishers, Leiden-Boston, 2007, p. 731.

310. European Commission, Directorate-General X, Working Document, 29 Sep. 1998.

investment and greater size are generally accompanied by increased possibilities of major gain.

1084. Indeed, this uncertainty of results and the drama that is a consequence thereof is a phenomenon which does not even occur at concerts or at the theatre. This leads to the existence of varying categories in sport, according to age, weight, gender and competitive level, on the correct premise that it is necessary, in order to ensure an event of quality in which victory is not certain from the outset, that there is an approximate equality of forces, or equality of competitive opportunities.

1085. Furthermore, and this is a fundamental aspect, the uncertainty of results leads to relations between undertakings, which are marked by a certain fundamental ambiguity because the competitors need to make partnerships and are interdependent. The competition in question is singular, or paradoxical, i.e., it seeks to enshrine a certain equality of opportunities and economic and financial solidarity, in order to ensure the continued existence of championships and competitions.

1086. The mutual interdependence of participants demands deep and unequalled partnership commitments and solidarity between participants. This leads us to affirm that sport is probably the only sector of activity in which there is a necessary solidarity between competitors.[311]

1087. An example of this is a football championship: a team has no *raison d'être* if it cannot compete with other teams and a championship cannot take place unless a sufficient number of clubs are capable of winning the championship. Accordingly, the survival of the clubs depends on a certain level of co-operation and, accordingly, the co-existence of small and large clubs becomes an essential prerequisite.

1088. Competitive cohesion is to be found in the contribution, which clubs make to the success of other clubs. Participants in a competition can neither produce nor sell their product other than to competitors as the product is the competition in which they take part. The said product is not only collective, but also indivisible, for, once divided, it would cease to be a product, as no club can produce an official game by itself and only a large number of clubs can ensure the existence and competitiveness of the product.

1089. In addition to this first level of solidarity between clubs, i.e., coexistence and partnership in the context of a sporting competition, there is a second level, which comprises the need for economic solidarity, which primarily takes the form of mechanisms for the redistribution of the funds directly and indirectly generated by the competition (ticket sales, television broadcasts arising from the final classification, *inter alia*). All the participants contribute to a 'cake', the slices of which

311. This is also the position of Robert Heron Bork: '[S]ome activities can only be carried out jointly. Perhaps the leading example is league sports.' Cf. Robert Heron Bork. *The Antitrust Paradox. A policy at War with Itself*, 2nd edition, New York, 1993, p. 278.

are redistributed in accordance with criteria of proportionality and fairness. For these two levels of solidarity to exist, it is necessary to create appropriate institutional and regulatory mechanisms. This is why clubs are organized in federations, which sometimes include leagues, with the power to organize, regulate and direct the competitions in which the clubs take part.[312]

1090. It should be noted, that the 'single federation' principle, according to which there is only one federation and/or league in each country, is complied with in the EU. The fact that there are not two or more structures in the same country and therefore no duplication of organizations and regulations means that these federations or leagues can be described as authentic 'natural monopolies',[313] for the benefit of the supporters, who clearly prefer that one team is officially recognized as the champion of that country at the end of the competition, instead of a scenario of multiple competitions, of which only one would be official. Such a model would clearly be inefficient and give rise to imbalances, as there would be competition between each federation/league to attract the best players to play in their competitions.[314] The single federation principle forestalls competition in the organization, regulation and direction of a certain sport, in accordance with the model, which, in other sectors of activity, would only be comparable to natural monopolies.

D. *The Olivier Bernard Judgment: Impact on Training and on the Emergence of a Specificity of Professional Football in the EU*

1091. According to the Commission:[315]

> [t]he Community Courts and the Commission have consistently taken into consideration the particular characteristics of sport that set it apart from other economic activities that are frequently referred to as *the 'specificity of sport'. Although no such legal concept has been developed or formally recognized by the Community Courts*, it has become apparent that the following distinctive

312. The US Supreme Court has stressed that sports played in leagues are perhaps the main example of a commercial activity, which can only be carried on collectively – *National Collegiate Athletic Association v. Board of regents of University of Oklahama*, 468 US 85, 101.
313. 'Football leagues are natural cartels, because otherwise they would not exist', Elisabeth Eklund. *Following the Rules of the Game. A Competition Law Study of the Collective Sale of Sports Broadcasting Rights*. EUI Working Paper Law No. 99/1, European University Institute, Florence-Department of Law, Italy, 1999, p. 47; 'As producers of sport, sports federations and sports leagues are "natural monopolies"'. Andrew Caiger et al., *Professional Sport in the European Union: Regulation and Re-regulation*, Ed. Andrew Caiger and Simon Gardiner, TMC Asser Press, The Hague, 2000, p. 54.
314. Compare Roger G. Noll, *The Organisation of Sports Leagues*. 'Oxford Review of Economic Policy', Vol. 19, No. 4, Oxford University Press, 2003, p. 531; 547; Gary R. Roberts, *The Case for Baseball's Special Antitrust Immunity*, Journal of Sports Economics, Vol. 4, No. 4, November 2003, p. 303; Michael A. Flynn & Richard J. Gilbert, *The Analysis of Professional Sports Leagues as Joint Ventures*, *The Economic Journal*, 111, February 2001, p. 44.
315. Commission Staff Working Document The EU and Sport: Background and context Accompanying document to the White Paper on Sport, 2007, p. 35. The document is available at: http://ec.europa.eu/sport/white-paper/whitepaper100_en.htm.

> features may be of relevance when assessing the compliance of organisational sporting rules with Community law. (Emphasis added)

1092. Further to the second paragraph of Article 165(1) of the Treaty on the Functioning of the European Union (TFEU):

> the Union shall contribute to the promotion of European sporting issues, while taking account of *the specific nature of sport*, its structures based on voluntary activity and its social and educational function. (Emphasis added)

1093. Bearing in mind those quotations, we move directly to paragraph 40 of the Olivier Bernard judgment:[316]

> In considering whether a system which restricts the freedom of movement of such players is suitable to ensure that the said objective is attained and does not go beyond what is necessary to attain it, account must be taken, as the Advocate General states in points 30 and 47 of her Opinion, of *the specific characteristics of sport in general, and football in particular, and of their social and educational function. The relevance of those factors is also corroborated by their being mentioned in the second subparagraph of Article 165(1) TFEU.* (Emphasis added)

1094. The relevance of the said paragraph lies in the fact that it deals with the application of the principle of proportionality, as can be inferred from the first part of the text. It is important to note, in this regard, that after the (recent, but already famous) *Meca Medina* Judgment, this matter has had important practical consequences in the sporting sector. In fact, according to that judgment, persons, who have an activity regulated by a rule with a purely sporting nature, and the body which created that rule, are not exempt from the provisions of the Treaty. Furthermore, the assessment of the compatibility of a purely sporting regulation with Competition Law lies mainly in whether the means used to attain the objectives in question are proportioned, or not.[317]

1095. Therefore, in sport, there are a growing number of situations that are subject to European Law, and are therefore likely to be subject to the 'proportionality test'. This test is subjective and is applied on a case-by-case basis and discretionary. The way in which the ECJ establishes the limits for the application of the test– as with the paragraph in question – is, therefore, very important, because this can result in a reduction of the court's discretion – whether it is a national or European court, or an administrative authority, such as the European Commission, or the Competition Authority of any Member State of the EU.

---

316. Judgment of the ECJ, *Olympic Lyonnais SASP v. Olivier Bernard and Newcastle United FC*, Case C-325/08, 16 Mar. 2010.
317. § 42.

1096. The first aspect to be noted is the fact that the ECJ intentionally did not use the expression used in Article 165 TFEU, and previously mentioned in *Piau* case[318] – i.e., the *specific nature of sport,* but rather refers to the *specific characteristics of sport.* We consider this to be more than just a question of semantics, but is rather the adoption of the terminology used in the famous *Nice Declaration,* which has the full title of *Declaration on the specific characteristics on sport and its social function in Europe of which account should be taken in implementing common policies.*[319]

1097. The reference made by the ECJ to the *Nice Declaration* is even clearer when we consider the specific reference to paragraph 47 of the conclusions of Advocate General Sharpson,[320] in which the specific or special character of sport was specifically based on the *Nice Declaration,* in the following terms:

> On the one hand, professional football is not merely an economic activity but also a matter of considerable social importance in Europe. Since it is generally perceived as linked to, and as sharing many of the virtues of, amateur sport, there is a broad public consensus that the training and recruitment of young players should be encouraged rather than discouraged. More specifically, *the European Council at Nice* in 2000 recognised that 'the Community must ... *take account of the social, educational and cultural functions inherent in sport and making it special,* in order that the code of ethics and the solidarity essential to the preservation of its social role may be respected and nurtured'. (19) In addition, the Commission's White Paper on sport (*20*) and the Parliament's resolution on it (*21*) both place considerable stress on the importance of training. (Emphasis added)

1098. Further to the importance, which in our opinion, the ECJ wanted to give to the *Nice Declaration,* it is important to emphasize the terms in which the ECJ introduced Article 165 of the TFEU: i.e., it did not consider it to be the true and innovative legal basis for the concept of the specificity of sport, but rather as an instrument, which corroborates a previously established understanding that sport has *specific characteristics.*

1099. It seems, at a first glance, that we are faced with a paradoxical subordination of a Treaty provision to a political declaration. It could even be argued, on the basis of an even hastier and inattentive reading, that the Court was 'lazy' or cautious, in avoiding the definition of a line of thought or reasoning on this issue and

---

318. Compare *Judgment* of the Court of First Instance of 26 Jan. 2005, *Laurent Piau v. Commission of the European Communities,* n Case T-193/02., ECR 2005, p. II-209, § 105.
319. Compare *Annex* IV of the Presidency Conclusions for the Nice European *Council,* December 2000. A few months earlier the European Council of Santa Maria da Feira, held on 19 and 20 June, had made the following reference to the expression in question in point 50 of the conclusions, dedicated to sport: '*The European Council requests the Commission and the Council to take account of the specific characteristics of sport in Europe and its social function in managing common policies.*' (Emphasis added).
320. Opinion delivered on 16 Jul. 2009, not yet published.

that it contented itself with a pre-existing definition, or, ultimately, it could also be argued that the Court wasted a long awaited opportunity: i.e., the opportunity to define the concept of *specificity of sport* on the basis of Primary EU Law.

1100. However, this is not our view of this matter. We are convinced that what the ECJ wanted to state very clearly was, on the one hand, that the notion of *specificity of sport* had already been sufficiently defined even before sport achieved its place in the Primary law of the EU, and on the other hand, that the TFEU was in line with and strengthened the existing concept of the specificity of sport.

1101. Accordingly, it seems that the ECJ is also indicating that the text of Article 165 of the TFEU namely the expression *specific nature of sport* should be interpreted in accordance with the *Nice Declaration.*

1102. In addition to the reference to paragraph 47, the Court also made another reference to paragraph 30 of the Sharpson Conclusions, thus indicating that it shared or accepted the opinion of the Advocate General. In view of this, it is therefore important, to take a closer look at that paragraph, which reads as follows:

> *The specific characteristics of sport in general, and football in particular*, do not seem to me to be of paramount importance when considering whether there is a prohibited restriction on freedom of movement. They must, however, be considered carefully when examining possible justifications for any such restriction – just as the specific characteristics of any other sector would need to be borne in mind when examining the justification of restrictions applicable in that sector. (Emphasis added)

1103. If this paragraph in read in conjunction with paragraph 40 of the *Olivier Bernard* judgment, a formal recognition of the existence not only of a *specificity of sport* is revealed, but also of a *specificity of football*, as a sporting activity with distinctive and specific characteristics.

1104. This is no novelty, as the Court had already pointed out, in paragraph 106 of the Bosman judgment:

> In view of the considerable *social importance of sporting activities and in particular football* in the Community, the aims of maintaining a balance between clubs by preserving a certain degree of equality and uncertainty as to results and of encouraging the recruitment and training of young players must be accepted as legitimate. (Emphasis added)

1105. At any rate, in our opinion, it is very important to point out that the Court has maintained its view on this matter more than fifteen years after the *Bosman* judgment, with all that this entails, namely if we consider how the economic and entertainment aspects of football have, since then, grown exponentially (largely due to the *Bosman* judgment). It should be noted that the view of the Court has not been hindered by those who argue that football is no longer a cultural, social and entertaining event, but just an economic activity. On the contrary, and rightfully so, the ECJ continues to recognize the significance of football in society.

1106. It is stressed that the ECJ's view is far from fragmentary. For example, the revealing nature of the reference made by the ECJ to the *White Paper on Sport,*[321] mentioned in paragraph 47 of the Conclusions of the Advocate General Sharpson. It is quite revealing that football is singled out and mentioned on eight different occasions in the twenty-one pages of this important European Commission document, in contrast to other sports, which are not referred to individually at all.

1107. This reasoning of the European Commission follows another very important document, the Arnaut Report,[322] which despite dealing with sport in general, took football as a *case study*, and in doing so resorted to arguments, which were later included in the Olivier Bernard judgment:

> 1.18 Due to the economic importance of football there is more potential (and there have been more examples) for rules and practices in football to be examined under European Community law. As confirmed in the Terms of Reference for the Review, *football is arguably the only truly global game and its influence cuts across economic, political, social and cultural spheres*. Perhaps more than any other sport, football is often seen as 'big business', even though this does not accurately reflect the wider role that it plays in the community. It is necessary to reconcile this business side of football with its specific sporting nature in order to achieve the correct overall balance. (Emphasis added)

1108. There is, in fact, no way of avoiding reality, i.e., there is something different about football, i.e., its unique social relevance, which justifies calling it 'The King of Sports'. This must be taken into consideration, when considering a rule or conduct prohibited by EU law – i.e., an infringement of the fundamental liberties or competition law and whether there are any grounds to consider that the rule or conduct at issue complies with EU Law.

1109. There are therefore reasons not to dwell on the recurrent discussion about the characteristics, which set football apart from other sports. This discussion was the basis of the argument that a specificity of sport exists – and to go even further and acknowledge the specificities of a certain sporting activity in particular, football, which sets it apart or separates it from sport in general. We are, therefore, in the presence of a new concept: i.e., the specificity of football.[323]

---

321. Brussels, 11 Jul. 2007, COM (2007) 391 final.
322. Or the *Independent European Sport Review*. The team which produced the report was lead by Portuguese José Luís Arnaut. The full report is available at http://www.euractiv.com/section/sports/news/sports-is-not-only-about-football/.
323. We believe it not to be too farfetched to argue for a specificity of each sport per se. In support of this understanding is the fact that the Commission believes *that each sport has its specificities and deserves to be treated differently according to these*. (Cf. Commission Staff Working Document The EU and Sport: Background and context Accompanying document to the White Paper on Sport,

1110. Perhaps this also helps explain why the ECJ emphasized the *Nice Declaration* rather than the TFEU: for, while the latter mentions the specificity of sport – sport as a whole, as a reality with characteristics and values shared by all sports – the former permits reference to the specificity of a particular sport, i.e., football. In fact, football is the only sport specifically mentioned in that declaration, which is an acknowledgement of its greater relevance. Let us look at the key paragraph:[324]

> The European Council is keenly supportive of dialogue on the transfer system *between the sports movement, in particular the football authorities*, organisations representing professional sportsmen and women, the Community and the

---

2007, p. 43) or the argument of Advocate General Cosmas, in Case *Deliège*: *On that premise, I shall now address an issue which, in my opinion, is crucial to a precise definition of the economic dimension of a sporting activity. I shall no longer be examining the individual conduct and subjective intentions of sportsmen, but the sporting event itself, viewed objectively, that is to say the specific characteristics of sporting competition. Indeed sportsmen can only be assessed by reference to the competitions they enter, their individual performances being largely meaningless unless combined with success in particular competitions in which they pit themselves against their rivals. The question therefore arises whether sporting activities – in the present case, international Category A judo tournaments – exhibit an economic interest. If the significance of the sports event does not relate purely to sport, in the sense that it does not merely represent confrontation and reward for being the best, but also exhibits an intrinsic economic interest, then the economic dimension of the sporting event is clearly such that the event in itself constitutes an economic activity within the meaning of Article 2 of the Treaty.* (Opinion delivered on 18 Mar. 1999, *Christelle Deliège v. Ligue francophone de judo et disciplines associées ASBL, Ligue belge de judo ASBL, Union européenne de judo and François Pacquée*, in joint cases C- 51/96 and C-191/97, ECR [2000], p. I – 2549, § 54, Emphasis added). In the same way and on the issue of illegal bets, a recent study argues that specific rules of each sport should also take into consideration specific challenges that might be of special relevance in their specific sport (Cf. Examination of threats to the integrity of sports, Oxford Research A/S, April 2010, p. 25). In our opinion, the specificity of each sport also lies in the characteristics and values associated with that sport – this issue has been studied by the International Olympic Committee at the time of the requests for the inclusion of new sports in the programme of the Olympic Games – and in the extent of the economic aspect of each sport, based on which, for example, there will not be an equal distribution of television revenues among the 28 Olympic Sports Federations which will be included in the Programme of the Summer Olympic Games in London 2012 (Cf. 'Sports federations to review §375 m TV revenue share', http://www.guardian.co.uk/football/feedarticle/9049588). Obviously, what we have just argued, as well as our conviction that there is a 'specificity of sport' is not incompatible with another, rather more generally accepted view that there is a common denominator to all sports, based on which the concept of specificity of sport has been built. It is this common denominator that justifies common positions on the TFEU, of which we would like refer to the *Common position of the Olympic and Sports Movement on the implementation of the new Treaty of the Functioning of the European Union (TFEU) on sport (Lisbon Treaty), January 2010*, or even the institutionalization of platforms for the defence of common interests, shared by several sports such as the European Team Sports (ETS), which aggregates basketball (FIBA Europe), handball (EHF), ice hockey (IIHF), volleyball (CEV) and football (UEFA). It is worth mentioning ETS's testimony based on the Bosman judgment, that the judgments of the Court, on football issues may, due to a snowball effect, have implications for other collective sports, which is why that the ETS has been calling for a full recognition of the specificity of sport by all the European Institutions (Cf. Création de l'Association des sports d'équipe européens. Les sports d'équipe unissent leurs forces, uefadirect No. 95, 3.10, pp. 10–11, Cf. also 'Safeguarding the heritage and future of team sport in Europe, July 2008', ETS, July 2008, p. 10.

324. Point 16 (Transfers).

> Member States, with due regard for the specific requirements of sport, subject to compliance with Community law. (Emphasis added)

1111. We also consider that it is possible to perform an even finer tuning of what is specific in the context of football. We believe that there is also perhaps leeway to argue that professional football has specific characteristics, which set it apart from football as a whole, i.e., there are reasons to defend the existence of something even more specific, i.e., the specificity of professional football.

1112. Indeed, this is the view of the European Parliament, which not only passed a specific resolution on professional football,[325] but also, in that same act, even if only once, specifically mentioned the specificity of professional football:

> F. whereas it is thus the responsibility of the national and European political and sports authorities to ensure that, when Community law is applied to professional football, it does not compromise its social and cultural purposes, by developing an appropriate legal framework, which fully respects the fundamental principles of *specificity of professional football*, autonomy of its bodies and subsidiarity. (Emphasis added)

1113. The European Commission also seems to share this view, as it created a specific platform for Professional football within the scope of social dialogue: the European Sectoral Social Dialogue Committee for professional football, launched on 1 July 2008.

1114. In the light of the above we consider that the specificity of professional football should be taken into consideration by the courts when applying EU law to it. We also consider that there is still a long way to go in defining concepts such as the specificity of sport, the specificity of football, or the specificity of professional football. Accordingly, if the football authorities fail to continue to stress this matter, they will inadvertently contribute to what they criticize in those who do not recognize the specificity of football: i.e., legal uncertainty and insecurity.

1115. To be more specific, in the case of the *Webster*[326] and *Matuzalém*[327] judgments of the Court of Arbitration for Sport, in Lausanne, both judgments failed to contribute to a further deepening of the concept of specificity of sport. In our view, these contradictory judgments have also shown, beyond any doubt, that there is still

---

325. European Parliament resolution of 29 Mar. 2007 on the future of professional football in Europe (2006/2130 (INI)), OJEU C 27 E of 31 Jan. 2008, pp. 232–240.
326. Arbitral award of the Court of Arbitration for Sport of 30 Jan. 2008, CAS 2007/A/1298,1299 & 1230 – *Heart of Midlothian v. Webster & Wigan Athletic FC.*
327. Arbitral award of the Court of Arbitration for Sport of 19 May 2009, CAS 2008/A/1519 – *FC Shakhtar Donetsk (Ukraine) v/ Mr. Matuzalem Francelino da Silva (Brazil) & Real Zaragoza SAD (Spain) & FIFA & CAS 2008/A/1520 – Mr. Matuzalem Francelino da Silva (Brazil) & Real Zaragoza SAD (Spain) v/ FC Shakhtar Donetsk (Ukraine) & FIFA.*

a wide discretionary margin in the interpretation of this concept,[328] which is specifically provided in Article 17(1) of the FIFA Player Status and Transfer Regulations entitled *Consequences of terminating a contract without just cause*; hence the discrepancies in legal analysis.[329]

1116. However, it will be of no avail to qualify the specificity of sport as an objective criterion if, in practice, the margin for the exercise of discretion is very wide. Not everything should fall within the remit of the courts (or administrative authorities) of the EU and its Member States). The football authorities should be the first to contribute to the clarification of the matters that fall within their powers, i.e., the production of regulations. This would certainly strengthen the legitimacy of the claims of the football authorities in the eyes of the EU institutions.

E. Difficulties and Contradictions in Applying EU Competition Law to Sport

1117. The decisions of the European Commission and the case-law of the EU regarding the application of EU Competition Law to sport, lack consistency, coherence and legal certainty. The contradictions are twofold:

(a) contradictions within EU institutions and EU courts;
(b) contradictions between EU institutions and EU courts.

1. Contradictions within the Commission and the European Court of First Instance

1118. For, while it is true, that the Commission has applied the *Wouters* judgment and has, in the *Mouscron* and *ENIC* cases and in some legal articles written by officers of the Directorate General of Competition, supported the contention that EU Competition Law applies to sport, it is also true that, the Report prepared for the Hearing in the *Meca-Medina* case, by the same Commission stressed that the *Wouters* judgment was cited only residually and only in order to 'complete' the argument. The European Court of First Instance (CFI) has, in turn, within a very short space of time, adopted differing approaches with regard to the analysis criteria

328. Compare *Webster* award, § 132: *[t]he specificity of sport is a reference to the goal of finding particular solutions for the football world which enable those applying the provision to strike a reasonable balance between the needs of contractual stability, on the one hand, and the needs of free movement of players on the other hand*; Cf. also Matuzalem award, § 155: *(…) the judging body shall therefore assess the amount of compensation payable by a party under art. 17 para. 1 of the FIFA Regulations keeping duly in mind that the dispute is taking place in the somehow special world of sport. In other words, the judging body shall aim at reaching a solution that is legally correct, and that is also appropriate upon an analysis of the specific nature of the sporting interests at stake, the sporting circumstances and the sporting issues inherent to the single case. (…) professional football is a special sector (…).*

329. *In all cases, the party in breach shall pay compensation. Subject to the provisions of Art. 20 and annex 4 in relation to Training Compensation, and unless otherwise provided for in the contract, compensation for breach shall be calculated with due consideration for the law of the country concerned, the specificity of sport, and any other objective criteria.* (Emphasis added).

to be used in the application of EU Competition Law to sport. For, while in the *Meca-Medina* judgment, the non-application of EU Competition Law to sport was based on the case-law established by the *Wouters* judgment, only a few months later, the criterion applied was the application of 81(3) EC.

1119. Even the approach adopted in the *Piau* judgment is to a certain extent contradicted in that same judgment. For, the CFI commences (§ 100), by acknowledging that the Commission's decision was based on the argument that the restriction inherent in the agents licensing system was necessary for, and proportionate to, the protection of players and clubs. However, a few paragraphs further on (§ 105), the CFI states that the said Commission decision was not based on arguments related to the specificity of sport but rather on purely economic considerations.

2. Contradictions between EU Institutions and EU Courts

1120. The *Meca-Medina* case is paradigmatic in terms of the discrepancies between the analyses made by the EU institutions and by the EU courts. The Commission's approach was contradictory and somewhat confused. It hesitated between considering that the issue involved a purely sporting rule, which had indirect economic effects, and considering that the rule in question was economic in nature, but had a sports objective and was therefore subject to EU Competition Law. By hesitating, it ended up by combining these two approaches, for it commenced by considering that the limitation of athletes' freedom of action by the IOC anti-doping rules was not necessarily a restriction of competition in accordance with Article 101, to the extent that such a restriction can be inherent in the organization and proper conduct of the sporting competition (§ 42) only to subsequently consider the said regulation in the light of EU Competition Law, in accordance with the *Wouters* judgment (albeit in a subsidiary manner).

1121. It should be noted that the CFI, unlike the Commission, did not commence by establishing whether the regulatory bodies – the International Swimming Federation (FINA) and IOC – were undertakings for the purposes of EU Competition Law, thus adopting an approach, which differs from the traditional discussion, i.e., whether the activity in question is economic or not, and immediately focused on the examination of the nature of the anti-doping rules at issue. In other words, while the Commission considers that the non-prosecution of an economic objective was a justification for the rules in question, so far as the CFI was concerned this was the initial question to be considered, which resulted in the fact that it was not necessary to consider the applicability of EU Competition Law, or the existence of any justification.

1122. However, while the CFI demonstrated that its conception of competition stresses the promotion of the efficiency and the freedom of action of the parties and showed that the concept of economic activity is not infinite and must sometimes be interpreted restrictively – which almost resulted in a veritable *sports exception* – the ECJ considered, on the contrary, and with less determination than could be expected of a court other than a sports tribunal in the consideration of a matter such as doping, that whether or not it is economic in nature, a sports rule or activity must be subject to EU Competition Law, thus distancing itself from the automatic and abstract manner in which the CFI excluded the regulation in question from the ambit of the application of EU Competition Law.

1123. If the CFI granted a considerable margin for the free consideration by the sports federations, the ECJ, on the contrary, restricted the scope of the application of the sporting specificity, despite the fact that it recognized that the anti-doping rules are justified by reason of the objectives of equality of opportunity, health and the protection of the ethical values of sport. The ECJ's position diverges not only from that of the CFI but also from the opinion of Advocate General Léger, which was completely ignored. The said opinion proposed that the appeal should be dismissed on the grounds that, notwithstanding the fact that the commercial context of sport creates an economic interest in the anti-doping rules, this interest is purely secondary and cannot expunge the purely sporting nature of the said rules (§ 28).

1124. However, the *Meca-Medina* judgment not only reveals contradictions between institutions. We consider that the most serious contradiction is to be found in the ECJ judgment itself, to the extent that it seeks to innovate, by adopting an approach contrary to the preceding case-law, but at the same time defends the case-law which it seeks to overturn. For example: in § 22, the ECJ refers to the entire previous case-law regarding sport and states that *'It is to be remembered that, having regard to the objectives of the Community, sport is subject to Community law in so far as it constitutes an economic activity within the meaning of Article 2 EC (...)'*. However, only a few paragraphs later, in § 27, there is a totally contradictory innovation, which reads as follows: *In light of all of these considerations, it is apparent that the mere fact that a rule is purely sporting in nature does not have the effect of removing the person engaging in the activity governed by that rule or the body which has laid it down, from the scope of the Treaty.* All of which leaves us exactly where?

1125. We shall now conduct a brief critical analysis of the EU White Paper on Sport. The Commission, the guardian of the Treaties, proposed the *Meca-Medina* judgment as the methodological basis for the application of EU Competition Law to sport. It curtailed the ECJ's judgment and merely commented that both the CFI and the ECJ have *reiterated that sport is subject to Community Law to the extent that it is an economic activity...* as if to give the impression that the overall approach of both decisions was one and the same.

1126. Moreover, it must be underlined that despite seeking to recognize the 'specificity of sport', the European Commission ended up by distinguishing it from '*other economic activities*' (2.1.5, our underlining), i.e., it considered sport itself always to be the expression of an economic activity ... .

1127. Furthermore, the Commission also contradicts its own position: on the one hand, in accordance with the *Meca-Medina* judgment, the Commission stated that the 'rules of the game' should be subject to European Competition Law: on the other hand, in the same item (point 2.2), the Commission, in a 'hidden' footnote, stated that some 'rules of the game' are not subject to EU Competition Law, if they do not involve an economic activity.

1128. It is accordingly legitimate to ask what the Commission's position really is. Is there subjection to EU Competition Law in all sport cases, by means of the application of the criteria in Articles 101 and/or 102 of the EC Treaty, followed by the conclusion, in some cases, that EU Competition Law is not breached; or, on the contrary, is there only subjection to EU Competition Law when the rules in question involve an economic activity?

1129. However, this is not the extent of the Commission's contradictions. In its attempt to defend the application of EU Competition Law to sport on an '*ad hoc* basis', the Commission considered, initially, that 'it is not possible' to categorize sports rules and to exempt certain types of rules from EU Competition Law (points 2.1.7 and 2.2.1) only to state subsequently (point 2.4.) that it no longer considers the said tasks to be impossible but only 'difficult' (although it made no attempt to resolve the said difficulty and insists on an ad hoc approach).

1130. For the reasons stated above, there appears to be no doubt that, as yet, no minimally coherent case-law and decision-making practice has been developed. The impression gained is that of an ad hoc or case-by-case approach, with no pragmatic and scientific criteria, which obviously results in divergent solutions contrary to the principle of the uniformity of EU law.

1131. Unless a new route is followed, we will continue to have a 'never ending story' of contradictions, which jeopardizes both the 'specificity of sport' and the process of European integration through sport.

VI. The European Commission White Paper on Sport

1132. White papers are documents issued by government organs within the European Union, which identify conduct or propose measures in relation to a wide range of topics relevant to the organization of society, with a view to the future development of new regulations with regard to the said topics.

1133. In the case of sport, a white paper was proposed in order to seek solutions for a wide range of problems, based on the *Independent European Sport Review*. The following matters were considered:

(a) the role of sport in society
(b) the economic dimension of sport
(c) the organization of sport
(d) the specificity of sport
(e) freedom of movement and nationality

(f) transfers
(g) protection of minors
(h) corruption of players' agents
(i) money laundering
(j) financial crimes associated with sport
(k) the club licence system
(l) *media* regulation in sport.

1134. On 11 July 2007, the European Commission issued various proposed solutions to the problems identified, the so-called White Paper on Sport. The White Paper is in line with the Nice Treaty, which recognizes the duty of sports organizations and federations to organize sports activities, always in accordance with both national and EU laws.

1135. The Commission document stresses the importance of sport as a tool in the promotion of public health and physical activity, and demonstrates its opposition to *doping* and the use of drugs in sport and calls for all the entities involved in the world of sport to join forces with organizations such as Interpol and WADA in order to achieve their objectives.

1136. The White Paper stresses the role of society and the need to fight against racism, discrimination and hooliganism in sport and equal access to sport by men, women and the disabled. The White Paper also stresses the importance of sharing the values of the EU with other countries via the creation of a system for the rapid issue of visas to high performance athletes.

1137. The document acknowledges the importance of sportspersons for the economic development of the EU and refers to questions of taxation, intellectual property rights, and demonstrates the importance of appropriate tax provisions, which are able to create conditions for access to sport on an egalitarian basis and to ensure the survival of the federations, given their importance for the organization of physical activity and sport.

1138. The White Paper does not give particular emphasis to the EU competition rules, despite the line adopted by the European Commission in its decisions and the case-law of the Court of Justice in this area: only the working document, which accompanies the White Paper, deals with this matter in Annexe I – 'Sport and EU Competition Rules', and, in particular details the analysis to be made in the light of the recent case-law developments and identifies the formal decisions and positions adopted by the Commission and the Judgments of the Court of First Instance and the Court of Justice.

1139. The White Paper also maintains the idea that the EU competition laws and domestic legal provisions should be applicable to sport, as it is undoubtedly an economic activity. The document not only makes proposals in this area, but analyses the possible consequences thereof, particularly with regard to the following topics:

(a) prohibition of law and federation rules that discriminate against sportspersons in terms of gender, pay or nationality, on the basis of the free movement of sportspersons within the EU;
(b) federations must be required to ensure that all clubs are managed in a transparent manner, particularly in economic terms, before taking part in any competitions and to ensure that they have obtained the relevant licences in order to be able to prove their financial liquidity. Each federation must establish its own rules with regard to the issue of the said licences, which must however comply with the national and community competition legislation;
(c) clubs and federations must have an information and checks system with regard to the transfer of players with a view to greater transparency in the market;
(d) clubs and Federations must ensure that players have access to the national courts and retain the existing training compensation mechanisms;
(e) European governments must be advised to reduce and/or apply a special tax rate to Federations in order to keep them operative and to promote the sport in question;
(f) federations must co-operate with the EU with regard to the trafficking of people, sexual harassment and the abandonment of minors in foreign countries;
(g) clubs must augment the protection of their image, brand and intellectual property rights.

1140. On 8 May 2008, the European Parliament approved a Report on Sport, which welcomed the Commission's White Paper, but also called for the adoption of clear guidelines regarding the application of EU Law to the sector rather than a case-by-case approach. Stressing the role of self-regulation in the resolution of specific questions related to the sector, the European Parliament also considered sports event television broadcast rights and suggested the collective sale of the media rights in order to ensure an equitable redistribution of the revenue arising therefrom between the clubs and leagues and between professional and amateur sport and even the funding of voluntary and non-profit activities in this area.

1141. On 18 January 2011, the European Commission adopted a Communication entitled 'Developing the European Dimension in Sport', accompanied by a Staff Working Document on the free movement of professional and amateur sportspeople in the EU Following a similar structure of the White Paper on Sport, the Communication sets out the Commission's ideas for EU-level action in the field of sport and proposes concrete actions for the Commission and/or the Member States within three broad chapters: the societal role of sport, the economic dimension of sport and the organization of sport. The main targets of the Communication are to encourage debate among stakeholders, to address challenges in sport and to help the sector develop.

VII. EU Competition Law as Applied to Sport (Articles 101, 102, 106 and 107 TFEU)

A. Rules regarding Selection Criteria

1142. Sportsing rules commonly make provisions regarding the criteria for the selection of players or clubs to take part in certain national and international sportingsports events.

1143. In the *Deliège* case, the two preliminary questions submitted by the Namur *Tribunal de première instance* to the ECJ in the two cases, concerned rules of this type, and the application of EUCL thereto.[330]

1144. Advocate-general Cosmas[331] commenced by stating that a sportingsports activity is only subject to community law, namely the free movement rules, if and when the economic aspects thereof are not merely marginal or ancillary.[332] *It can therefore be inferred that, according to Cosmas, only when the economic aspect of the sportsing activity is principal is it subject to EUCL.*

Thereafter Cosmas stated that the Walrave and *Dona* case-law reveals that the ECJ accepts the '*specificity of sport*' as grounds for the exclusion of the application of community law to sport.[333]

---

330. In the first case, the preliminary question was as follows:

> Whether or not rules requiring professional or semi-professional sportsmen or persons aspiring to such status to have been authorised or selected by their national federation in order to be able to compete in an international competition and laying down national entry quotas for similar competitions are contrary to the Treaty of Rome, in particular Articles 59 to 66 and Articles 85 and 86.

The preliminary question in the second case was only slightly different:

> Whether or not it is contrary to the Treaty of Rome, in particular Articles 59, 85 and 86 of the Treaty, to require professional or semi-professional athletes or persons aspiring to professional or semi-professional activity to be authorised by their federation in order to be able to compete in an international competition which does not involve national teams competing against each other.

331. *Conclusions of advocate-general Cosmas submitted on the 18th of March 1999, Deliège, Consolidated proceedings C-51/96 and C-191/97, E.C.R. 2000 p. I-2549.*

332. *'(...), I think it appropriate to point out that, in order for a sportingsports activity to be subject to the Community rules on freedom of movement, the economic dimension of that activity must not be merely marginal. In other words, the economic component of the sports event must be significant, that is to say quite distinctive and separate from the purely sporting aspect of the event. This is particularly so where the economic component of the sporting activity affects the sporting event as a whole, in the sense that, without it, the sporting event would be dramatically different, or could not take place at all'*, No. 50.

333. *' (...) certain rules or practices relating to sport do not fall within the scope of Article 59 of the Treaty. Secondly, in order for that exception to apply, the rules or practices in question must be justified by specific, non-economic reasons which relate purely to sport'* (Emphasis added) no. 68.

1145. The Advocate-general also stated that notwithstanding the fact that there is a substantial difference between the free provision of services rules and the competition rules, both can converge and apply simultaneously to the same matter.[334]

1146. So far as the sportingsports rules at issue are concerned, Cosmas considered that they did not have a significant effect on intra-community trade and possibly even strengthened it,[335] and that, even if they did limit competition, there is no breach of EUCL, to the extent that the restriction is indispensable to the pursuance of its legitimate objectives, which arise from the specificity of the sport in question, i.e., judo.[336]

---

334. *'(…) It is ultimately debatable whether the same question may be addressed from the point of view of Article 59 et seq. of the Treaty, but not from the point of view of Article 85 et seq. There is, however, an essential difference between the rules on freedom to provide services and those on the protection of competition. In the first case, the point of law is examined in its individual dimension: the question is whether the relationship between certain persons is that of supplier and recipient of a 'service' within the meaning of Community law. It is therefore sufficient to ascertain the extent to which a sportswoman provides services only for remuneration in order to determine whether the articles of the Treaty relating to freedom to provide services are in principle applicable to her. An activity examined from the point of view of the rules on competition, on the other hand, must be considered in its overall institutional dimension. The examination focuses not on the assessment of an individual activity but on the description and delimitation of a global market. Defining the market conditions and the overall conduct of all those trading on it is clearly a more complex affair than ascertaining whether, in a particular case, there is a provision of services within the meaning of the Treaty. Similarly, the issues of fact and law of which the Community judicature must be aware in order to give a correct and satisfactory answer to a question relating to competition law are quite clearly more numerous than those which must be taken into account in order to deal with a case concerning the Community rules on freedom of movement.'*, no. 100.
335. *'(…) It is an attempt by the EJU (which it is entitled to make) to adapt to the needs of the market. (76) More specifically, it prefers to organise tournaments featuring athletes from as many countries as possible, rather than tournaments involving only a few countries where judo is already well developed. Not only does that choice not hinder intra-Community trade, it may strengthen it, in so far as it ensures that international judo tournaments are entered by athletes from all Member States and not just from those where the sport is developed.'*, no. 108 (Emphasis added).
336. *'(…) I am still of the opinion that there has been no infringement of Article 85(1) of the Treaty in the present case, since there has been no unlawful restriction of competition. I would say first of all that I agree with the Commission's argument that measures Adopted by a sports federation in the field of access for athletes to international tournaments may constitute a restriction of competition. It must also be recognised, however, that Article 85(1) does not apply to restrictions on competition which are essential in order to attain the legitimate aims which they pursue. (… .)'; 'As Advocate General Lenz pointed out in his Opinion in Bosman, (81) the above legal construction must be transposed to the relationship between sport and Community competition law. Applying that reasoning to this case, I also take the view that, even if they were to be regarded as reducing competition, in the sense that they prevent certain judokas from taking part in certain international tournaments, the contested rules do not fall within the scope of Article 85 of the Treaty because they are indispensable for attaining the legitimate objectives deriving from the particular nature of judo. (82) As regards the description and legitimacy of those objectives, I refer to the analysis above, (83) which shows that the contested sports rules were intended, first, to establish a mechanism for selecting national teams to represent Europe in the Atlanta Olympic Games and, secondly, to ensure that certain international judo tournaments are as representative as possible. Consequently, there is, in my view, no infringement of Article 85(1) of the Treaty. (currently article 81., no. 1, EC), no. 110 and no. 112'* (Emphasis added).

1147. In its judgment, the ECJ[337] stated first of all[338] that it is for the national judge to decide whether the sportingsports activities in question – those of the judo athlete ca Deliège –, i.e., her participation in international tournaments, do, or do not, amount to an economic activity in accordance with the then article 2 EC, or more precisely, a provision of services in accordance with the then Article 59 EC.

1148. The ECJ continued by stating that, on the assumption that there is a supply of services, there will be no restriction of the freedom to provide the same to the extent that the restriction arising from the rule in question is inherent in the conduct of the sportingsports competition in question, i.e., the organisation and financing[339] of the sport.[340]

1149. So far as the possible application of EUCL is concerned, the ECJ did not devote a single line in order to explain this omission.

1. Doping Issues

a. Sanctions Applicable for Violations of Anti-doping Regulations

1150. The Commission and the EU courts were called upon to decide with regard to sanctions applied within the ambit of an anti-doping regulation in the context of the so-called *Meca-Medina* case, which was dealt with differently by the Commission, on the one hand, and the CFI, on the other hand.

1151. The issue involved a complaint made against the IOC, by two swimmers who had been excluded from competition because of doping. The swimmers considered that the rules adopted by the IOC and FINA with regard to the definition of doping, by defining the level above which the presence of a prohibited substance is classified as doping, and with regard to appeal to the Court of Arbitration for

337. ECJ Judgment of 11 Apr. 2000, *Deliège, Consolidated proceedings C-51/96 and C-191/97, E.C.R. 2000 p. I-2549.*
338. No. 59.
339. *'64. (...) although selection rules like those at issue in the main proceedings inevitably have the effect of limiting the number of participants in a tournament, such a limitation is inherent in the conduct of an international high-level sports event, which necessarily involves certain selection rules of criteria being Adopted. 65. (...) the Adoption for purposes of an international sports tournament of one system of selecting participants rather than another must be bases on a large number of considerations unconnected with the personal situation of any athlete, such as the nature of the organization and the financing of the sport concerned*'.
340. Commenting the judgment at stake, Eleanor Spaventa states that '[t]*he Deliège line of reasoning (...) is conceptual: when the alleged barrier coincides with the very purpose of the rules (...) provided the aim in itself is legitimate, any effect that the rule might have on movement is inherent in the rules at issue and therefore cannot be scrutinisedeses.*' – 'The Outer Limit of the Treaty Free Movement Provisions: Some Reflections on the Significance of Kech, Remoteness and Deliège', in *The Outer Limits of the European Union Law*, Edited by Catherine Barnard and Okeoghene Oduddu, Hart Publishing, 2009, p. 26.

Sport,[341] amount to practices which limit competition, as defined by the then Article 81 EC, and to an unjustified restriction of the freedom of the swimmers to provide services, as defined by the then Article 49 EC.

1152. The Commission[342] considered that the rules and practices at issue do not appear to amount to economic activities,[343] but even so the Commission considered the said rules in order to confirm that the same were compliant with the then Articles 81[344] and 82[345] EC.

1153. The Commission concluded that the rules in question did not have a negative effect in terms of competition law and that, notwithstanding the fact that they restricted the freedom of action of an athlete, they did not necessarily limit competition, because the limitation is '*inherent in the organisation and good conduct of the sportingsports competition*', i.e., the effects which restrict competition are inherent in the prosecution of the objectives in question, i.e., '*to ensure the identification and punishment of athletes, whose conduct is contrary to the obligations to which they are subject with regard to the use of prohibited substances and the use of prohibited methods*'.[346] However, even on the assumption that the anti-doping rules in question were the result of an arrangement, the same were not intended to limit competition between economic operators, but to combat doping.

1154. The Commission also referred to the clear, fair, objective, justified and non-discriminatory nature of the rules,[347] and to the public, precise, objective, justified, reasonable, balanced and necessary nature thereof.[348]

1155. Later in its decision, the Commission reached the conclusion, on the basis of an analysis based on the *Wouters* Judgment,[349] that the anti-doping rules in question are intimately related to the proper conduct of the sportingsports competition and necessary for an effective fight against doping and that the restriction of the athlete's freedom does not exceed what is necessary in order to achieve the said

341. '(…) it is remarkable that the ECJ did not consider that their European Union law claims has been expressly rejected by a prior CAS award, which the swimmers had agreed would be final and binding, or whether the fact that Switzerland, Spain and Slovenia are parties to the New York Convention should preclude relitigation of their merits. Although the ECJ's decision effectively upheld the CAS award, Meca-Medina establishes precedent that permits future judicial challenges to the merits of CAS awards based on European Union law' – see J. Mitten and Hayden Opie, '"Sports law": implications for the development of international, comparative, and national law and global dispute resolution', in *CAS Bulletin* 1/2012, p. 12.
342. *Judgment of 01/08/2002 – SG (2002) D/231051, Meca-Medina.*
343. No. 38.
344. No. 40.
345. No. 70. It is noted in this point that the conduct imputed to the IOC is not such as can be described, in accordance with Art. 82 EC, as the relevant markets in which the IOC allegedly has a dominant position were not even identified.
346. No. 41.
347. No. 54.
348. No. 53.
349. No. 25.

objective. Accordingly, following the Commission, the rules in question are not affected by the prohibition in the then Article 81 EC.

1156. Accordingly, in this decision, the Commission, although it does not classify the activity in question as economic, proceeds as if it was an economic activity, as it applies community law, i.e., EUCL. This approach is accordingly different from the approach adopted in the case-law cited above, to the effect that EUCL is only applicable to economic activities.

1157. On appeal against the Commission's decision, the CFI[350] commenced by adopting the position that community law is not applicable to '*purely sporting rules*', which concern the sport per se and are inherent in the organisation and proper conduct of the sportingsports competition, and which, to that extent, are foreign to economic activity.[351] Given the nature of these rules they are not subject to community law. However the application of competition law should be restricted to its specific object. So far the approach adopted by the CFI adds nothing to the existing case-law.[352]

The CFI continued by arguing that the social or public health objectives of a rule, which are intimately connected and essential so that the sport, whether amateur or professional, can exist, must be considered in such a way that the rule in question is not considered to pursue any economic objective, but rather to be based on '*purely sportingsports considerations*', and is accordingly not subject to community law.[353]

1158. For this reason, the CFI considered that it was not necessary to consider the said rules in the light of EUCL.[354]

---

350. SEEI Judgment of 30/09/2004, *David Meca-Medina and Igor Majcen –v- Commission*, T-313/02, E.C.R. 2004, p II-3291.

351. Agreeing with the SEEI's decision not to classify doping as an economic activity, See. Laurence IDOT: *'(…) l'affaire Meca-Medina, dans laquelle le Tribunal avait nié, à juste titre, cette qualification'*, *Europe* No. 3, Mar. 2005, p. 24 (pp. 23–24).

352. No. 41.

353. *'It is appropriate to point out that, while it is true that high-level sport has become, to a great extent, an economic activity, the campaign against doping does not pursue any economic objective. It is intended to preserve, first, the spirit of fair play, without which sport, be it amateur or professional, is no longer sport. That purely social objective is sufficient to justify the campaign against doping. Secondly, since doping products are not without their negative physiological effects, that campaign is intended to safeguard the health of athletes. Thus, the prohibition of doping, as a particular expression of the requirement of fair play, forms part of the cardinal rule of sport'; 'In view of the foregoing, it must be held that the prohibition of doping is based on purely sporting considerations and therefore has nothing to do with any economic consideration. That means, in the light of the case-law and the considerations set out in paragraphs 37 to 42 above, that the rules to combat doping cannot, any more than the rules considered by the Court of Justice in Walrave, Donà and Deliège, come within the scope of the Treaty provisions on the economic freedoms and, in particular, of Articles 49 EC, 81 EC and 82 EC. The anti-doping rules are intimately linked to sport as such. l'*, no. 44 and no. 47 (Emphasis addes).

354. *'On the more general question of the Commission's subjection, in the alternative or for the sake of completeness according to its own words, of the contested anti-doping rules to an analysis under competition law, the Court considers that such an examination was not necessary in fact since the rules are purely sporting, and in view of Walrave, Donà and Deliège'*, no. 64 (Emphasis added).

1159. The CFI stated further that the *Wouters* case-law is not applicable to purely sportingsports rules as the said case-law is concerned with a market conduct and is applicable to an economic activity.[355]

1160. In accordance with the logic of its approach, the CFI stated that no analogies could be made with the *Wouters* Judgment, as the regulations in that case were with regard to market conduct and were applicable to an economic activity.

1161. A clear division, or clear friction, between the Commission and the CFI can therefore be seen with regard to the methodology to be used with regard to the relationship between the anti-doping regulations in question and EUCL. For the CFI, this is a matter of '*purely sportingsports*'[356] rules, while, for the Commission, the said rules should not even have been analysed in order to see whether they are compatible with EUCL. While the Commission sees a parallel with the *Wouters* Judgment, the CFI rejects such a parallel.

1162. On appeal to the ECJ against the judgment of the CFI,[357] the advocate-general Philipe Léger submitted his conclusions on the 23 March 2006,[358] which also concerned the sport/EUCL binomial.

1163. According to Léger, an anti-doping regulation is, per se, alien to an economic activity and is therefore purely sportingsports in nature. All that is associated with it is an accessory economic interest or dimension, which is why the Treaty is not applicable,[359] provided that what the ECJ said is not interpreted restrictively.[360]

---

355. *'It must also be pointed out that this case differs from that which gave rise to the Wouters judgment. The rules at issue in Wouters concerned market conduct – the establishment of networks between lawyers and accountants – and applied to an essentially economic activity, that of lawyers. By contrast, the rules at issue in this case concern conduct – doping – which cannot, without distorting the nature of sport, be likened to market conduct, and they apply to an activity, sport, which, in its very essence and as explained in paragraph 45 above, has nothing to do with any economic consideration.'*, no. 65.
356. These are rules, which, per se, located outside of the ambit of the application of community law. See. François Alaphilippe, 'Normes Sportives et Droit Communautaire de la Concurrence (à propos d'un récent arrêt de la Cour de justice des Communautés européennes', *Revue Juridique et Economique du Sport*, No. 80, Dalloz, Paris, September 2006, p. 11.
357. OJEU 16/09/2006, C 224, p. 8.
358. ECR 2006, p. I-6991.
359. *'Given the commercial and financial stakes which surround high-level sport, I think it may be impossible for purely sporting rules, such as anti-doping rules, to possess no economic interest. However, that interest is purely secondary, in my opinion, and cannot prevent anti-doping rules from being purely sporting in character. As the Commission rightly observed, the appellants' proposition effectively favours, under the cover of the argument that sporting activity is indivisible, a secondary aspect – the economic dimension – in order to ensure that the rules of the Treaty are wholly applicable to the professional or semi-professional practice of sport.'*, no. 28 (Emphasis added).
360. *'(...)The appellants seem to be adopting an especially restrictive reading of those judgments in so far as in those cases the Court has, in my view, excluded in general terms purely sporting rules from the scope of Articles 39 EC and 49 EC'*, no. 29.

1164. The advocate-general also added that the CFI was correct when it did not apply the *Wouters* Judgment to the anti-doping regulations in question, as the said judgment was made in respect of a regulation with regard to market conduct, and this was not true in this case.[361]

1165. The ECJ set aside the judgment of the CFI and rejected the appeal to set aside the Commission's decision.[362] This judgment has evident repercussions for the world of sport.[363]

1166. The ECJ commenced by emphasising that it is important to bear in mind the *Bosman* and *Deliège* judgments, when considering the relationship between the economic and sportingsports aspects of a sporting activity, i.e., the strict way in which the ambit of the application of EUCL can be limited.[364]

1167. One of the most relevant passages of the decision in question is that in which it is stressed that the fact that a rule is purely sporting in nature does not mean that it is not subject to EUCL,[365] i.e., the rule is not removed from the ambit of the application of EUCL,[366] so that it is accordingly necessary to establish whether the rule in question is purely sporting in nature and whether it is, or is not, restrictive

---

361. *'It is enough to note that the rules at issue in Wouters and Others concerned market conduct – namely, the establishment of networks between lawyers and accountants – and applied to an essentially economic activity, that of lawyers. However, because the rules in dispute are purely sporting rules, which have nothing to do with any economic consideration, the Court of First Instance could rightly, in my view, hold that examination of the rules on the basis of criteria established in that judgment was not necessary.'*, no. 44.
362. ECJ Judgment of 18/07/2006, *David Meca-Medina* and *Igor Majcen –v- the. Commission*, C-519/04 P, ECR 2006, p. I-6991.
363. *'(...) the decision [ECJ] should be read carefully by all those involved in sport'*, Fernando Seara, 'Europa, futebol e direito', Jornal 'A Bola', 25/03/2007, p. 14. UEFA described the decision as *'obscure'*, and consider that it was *'absurd'* to apply CCL to a disciplinary measure related to doping, See. Gianni Infantino, 'Meca-Medina: a step backwards for the European Sports Model and the specificity of sport'.
http://pt.uefa.com/uefa/keytopics/kind=2048/newsid=480606.html, 13/04/2007.
364. *'With regard to the difficulty of severing the economic aspects from the sporting aspects of a sport, the Court has held (in Donà, paragraphs 14 and 15) that the provisions of Community law concerning freedom of movement for persons and freedom to provide services do not preclude rules or practices justified on non-economic grounds which relate to the particular nature and context of certain sporting events. It has stressed, however, that such a restriction on the scope of the provisions in question must remain limited to its proper objective. It cannot, therefore, be relied upon to exclude the whole of a sportingsports activity from the scope of the Treaty (Bosman, paragraph 76, and Deliège, paragraph 43)'*, no. 26.
365. *'In light of all of these considerations, it is apparent that the mere fact that a rule is purely sporting in nature does not have the effect of removing from the scope of the Treaty the person engaging in the activity governed by that rule or the body which has laid it down.'*, no. 27.
366. *'If the sporting activity in question falls within the scope of the Treaty, the conditions for engaging in it are then subject to all the obligations which result from the various provisions of the Treaty (...)'*, no. 28.

and consequently prohibited by community law, i.e., by the rules of the free movement of persons, or the free provision of services[367] and by EUCL.[368]

1168. According to the ECJ, the fact that a rule does not restrict the free movement of workers and the free provision of services does not necessarily also mean that it is not in breach of EUCL,[369] so that the ECJ's view is that the CFI was simply mistaken when it decided that the rules at issue were not subject to EUCL, simply because they are purely sporting in nature.[370]

1169. Contrary to the position adopted in the judgment of the CFI, the ECJ based its decision on the *Wouters* case-law,[371] so that, given the overall context in which the anti-doping rule was adopted, or takes effect, i.e., the purpose of the rule is fair and equal sportingsports competition, it was considered to be compatible with EUCL,[372] although any effects of the rule which limit competition must be

---

367. ''*Thus, where engagement in the sporting activity must be assessed in the light of the Treaty provisions relating to freedom of movement for workers or freedom to provide services, it will be necessary to determine whether the rules which govern that activity satisfy the requirements of Articles 39 EC and 49 EC, that is to say do not constitute restrictions prohibited by those articles (...)*', no. 29.
368. '*Likewise, where engagement in the activity must be assessed in the light of the Treaty provisions relating to competition, it will be necessary to determine, given the specific requirements of Articles 81 EC and 82 EC, whether the rules which govern that activity emanate from an undertaking, whether the latter restricts competition or abuses its dominant position, and whether that restriction or that abuse affects trade between Member States.*', no. 30.
369. '*Therefore, even if those rules do not constitute restrictions on freedom of movement because they concern questions of purely sporting interest and, as such, have nothing to do with economic activity (Walrave and Koch and Donà), that fact means neither that the sporting activity in question necessarily falls outside the scope of Articles 81 EC and 82 EC nor that the rules do not satisfy the specific requirements of those articles.*', no. 31.
370. '*However, in paragraph 42 of the contested judgment, the Court of First Instance held that the fact that purely sporting rules may have nothing to do with economic activity, with the result that they do not fall within the scope of Articles 39 EC and 49 EC, means, also, that they have nothing to do with the economic relationships of competition, with the result that they also do not fall within the scope of Articles 81 EC and 82 EC.*'; '*In holding that rules could thus be excluded straightaway from the scope of those articles solely on the ground that they were regarded as purely sporting with regard to the application of Articles 39 EC and 49 EC, without any need to determine first whether the rules fulfilled the specific requirements of Articles 81 EC and 82 EC, as set out in paragraph 30 of the present judgment, the Court of First Instance made an error of law.*', no. 32 and no. 33.
371. Stephen Weatherhill adopts a position, in relation to the dichotomy between the approaches of the SEEI and the ECJ to this case, which favours the ECJ. He describes the formula of purely sporting interest, which he considers was overruled by the ECJ, as '*unfortunate*'. He also describes the position that sport is only subject to CL if and to the extent that it is an economic activity, as '*judicially orthodox*''. According to this author, rules should not be separated into sporting rules and economic rules. He considers that there are sporting rules with economic implications, which are subject to, but not necessarily prohibited by, CCL. Stephen Weatherhill also considers that the *Wouters* formula is the most satisfactory basis for the consideration of sporting rules with economic effects, in the light of Art. 81 EC, and it is '*extremely important*' for the future application of CCL to sport as it provides room for the albeit conditional autonomy of sport, 'Is the pyramid compatible with EC Law?', *The International Sports Law Journal* 2005/3-4, p. 4.
372. '*Next, the compatibility of rules with the Community rules on competition cannot be assessed in the abstract (see, to this effect, Case C-250/92 DLG [1994] ECR I-5641, paragraph 31). Not every*

necessary for the prosecution of the rule's legitimate objectives, i.e., the limits imposed must be shown to be inherent in the organisation and proper conduct of the sportingsports competition.[373]

1170. The ECJ added that the limitations on competition created cannot be excessive and must otherwise be proportionate and limited to what is necessary in order to ensure the proper conduct of the sportingsports competition.[374]

b. The *Cañas Case*

1171. This is a case of an Argentinian tennis player, Cañas, who was sanctioned by tennis federations for accidentally taking a banned substance during a tournament in Mexico. He lodged a competition complaint with the European Commission, claiming that (i) the arbitration clause-giving jurisdiction to CAs infringed EUCL; (ii) WADA infringed EUCL by setting anti-doping rules; (iii) the sanction imposed for accidental ingestion of the substance was disproportionate.

---

agreement between undertakings or every decision of an association of undertakings which restricts the freedom of action of the parties or of one of them necessarily falls within the prohibition laid down in Article 81(1) EC. For the purposes of application of that provision to a particular case, account must first of all be taken of the overall context in which the decision of the association of undertakings was taken or produces its effects and, more specifically, of its objectives. It has then to be considered whether the consequential effects restrictive of competition are inherent in the pursuit of those objectives (Wouters and Others, paragraph 97) and are proportionate to them.'; 'As regards the overall context in which the rules at issue were Adopted, the Commission could rightly take the view that the general objective of the rules was, as none of the parties disputes, to combat doping in order for competitive sport to be conducted fairly and that it included the need to safeguard equal chances for athletes, athletes' health, the integrity and objectivity of competitive sport and ethical values in sport.', no. 42 and no. 43 (our underling).

373. *'In addition, given that penalties are necessary to ensure enforcement of the doping ban, their effect on athletes' freedom of action must be considered to be, in principle, inherent itself in the anti-doping rules.'; 'Therefore, even if the anti-doping rules at issue are to be regarded as a decision of an association of undertakings limiting the appellants' freedom of action, they do not, for all that, necessarily constitute a restriction of competition incompatible with the common market, within the meaning of Article 81 EC, since they are justified by a legitimate objective. Such a limitation is inherent in the organisation and proper conduct of competitive sport and its very purpose is to ensure healthy rivalry between athletes'*, no. 44 and no. 45 (Emphasis added).

374. *'(...) It must be acknowledged that the penal nature of the anti-doping rules at issue and the magnitude of the penalties applicable if they are breached are capable of producing adverse effects on competition because they could, if penalties were ultimately to prove unjustified, result in an athlete's unwarranted exclusion from sporting events, and thus in impairment of the conditions under which the activity at issue is engaged in. It follows that, in order not to be covered by the prohibition laid down in Article 81(1) EC, the restrictions thus imposed by those rules must be limited to what is necessary to ensure the proper conduct of competitive sport (see, to this effect, DLG, paragraph 35).'; 'Rules of that kind could indeed prove excessive (...)'*, no. 47 and no. 48 (Emphasis added).

1172. The Commission dismissed the complaint,[375] which was upheld on appeal by the ECJ,[376] stating the following: (i) it was not clear that an Argentinian player has *locus standi* for an event outside EU; (ii) WADA and CAS are not subject to EU competition law as they exercise judicial functions and not economic activities; (iii) the arbitration clause imposed by tennis federations is not contrary to EU competition law unless it facilitates an infringement of EU competition law; (iv) In any event, sanctions took into account the fact that the ingestion was accidental.

1173. For the purpose of this thesis, the most relevant here is to emphasize the European Commission's assessment on WADA and CAS:

> 19. Articles 81 and 82 of the Treaty are applicable to undertakings. Sport fall within the scope of Community law in so far as it constitutes an economic activity.
> 22. (…) In accordance with constant jurisprudence, the notion of undertaking comprises all entities engaged in economic activity (…)
> 23. Thus, the Commission in their letter of 16 July 2008 clarifies that neither WADA nor ICAs organize sportingsports competitions which give rise to economic activities and they also do not exploit any rights concerning these competitions. ICA's activity consists mainly in overseeing the management and funding of the CAS, which settles disciplinary disputes within the framework of Olympic sports. CAS's role is equivalent to that of a court. It settles disputes and delivers arbitral awards which are equivalent in strength to rulings from common law jurisdictions. These jurisdictional activities as well as the management and funding of these activities are very unlikely considered economic activities. Instead, they are comparable to those of a legislator or of a supervisory authority («a sports police»). Consequently, it seems difficult to qualify ICAS (or CAS) or WADA as undertakings or associations of undertakings within the meaning of Articles 81 and/or 82 of the Treaty EU.
>
> (…)
>
> 25. (…) ATP's marketing activities and the organisation of the ATP circuit, with the assistance of the organizers of the individual tournaments which are part of the ATP Circuit, through which it enforces the anti-doping rules can then be considered economic activities. Thus, the ATP can be qualified as an undertaking within the meaning of Community competition law. (Emphasis added)

2. Territoriality Rules

1174. The Commission was called upon to take a position with regard cases of the delocalisation of club, which challenged the territorial organisation of the sport.

375. Comp. 39.471.
376. Case C- 269/12 P – Appeal brought on 1 Jun. 2012 by Guilhermo Cañas against the order of the General Court (Third Chamber) delivered on 26 Mar. 2012 in Case T-508/09 *Cañas v. Commission*, OJ C 235, 4.08.2012, p. 8.

1175. The *Wimbledon* and *Mouscron* cases the relevant authorities in this area.

1176. In the *Wimbledon* case, the Commission was called upon to state whether the EC Treaty could entitle a club to establish itself within the territory of a national federation, but continue to play in the league of another national federation of which it is a member, and whether the competition rules prevent such a delocalisation.

1177. The English club Wimbledon and the Scottish club Clydebank were studying the possibility of moving to Dublin, in the Irish Republic, a large city, which does not have a major team in the Irish league. The intention was to play there but in the more competitive league,[377] with a view to increased attendance figures.

1178. The Irish Football Federation claimed that what was at issue was a question related to the territorial organisation of football within the ambit of its exclusive jurisdiction in respect of Ireland, so that it was therefore entitled, if necessary, not to authorise the entry of these foreign clubs.

1179. In a reply to an oral parliamentary question, the Commission explained that, although it had not been formally notified of the case, it had taken a position with regard thereto and had stated that the application of EUCL could not be excluded, but that the consideration of the case was dependent upon the consideration of the facts in their specific legal and economic contexts, and that the territorial organisation of football appears to be determined by the organisation of matches per se and not by reasons of an economic nature.

1180. In the *Mouscron* case, the Commission was called upon to state whether a sportingsports rule, which contains provisions according to which home games in the context of a competition must be played at the ground of the host team, at another ground in the same city or possibly at a ground in another city within the territory of the National Federation of the host club, but never at the ground of the National Federation of the visiting club, is or is not admissible.

1181. This case involved the Belgian club Royal Excelsior Mouscron, which is a small Belgian team which, in 1997, qualified for the UEFA cup. However, given

377. In the USA, the league bylaws make provision regarding the viability or non-viability of the relocation of teams, and generally require a qualified majority, if not unanimity, to authorise relocation. Various pro-competitive justifications of the restrictions to which relocations are subject have been suggested, i.e.: (i) it is necessary to retain control of relocations, so as to prevent the creation of gaps (few teams) and to ensure the existence of geographic diversity within the country; (ii) it is necessary to preserve a certain loyalty by the supporters of a team (the relocation of a team could terminate existing rivalries with a nearby team); (iii) it is necessary to protect local authorities and taxpayers as both generally contribute to the construction of the stadiums for a specific team; (iv) so as not to prejudice the overall competition, its competitive balance – the value of a league is a function of the overall value of the clubs, which comprise it, so that relocation may involve a loss of television markets and create difficulties in the preparation of competition calendars; (v) negative externalities arising from phenomena such as free riders should be avoided., See. Alfonso Rincón, *La regulación por las ligas americanas de las conductas de los equipos bajo la óptica del derecho antitrust*, a document supplied by the author, not yet published.

the size of its stadium and for safety reasons, UEFA restricted the sale of tickets to the maximum of 4,500 places. The club accordingly decided to move the game with Limassol Cyprus to the stadium of Lille in France, which has a 21,000 place capacity. UEFA did not oppose this move. In the second game however, (Mouscron-Metz), UEFA adopted a different position and argued that Metz would have be at an unfair disadvantage by playing 'away' from its own country,[378] and invoked the 'home and away from home' rule (in UEFA international competitions, each club must play two games, one away and the other at home).

1182. Following a complaint lodged by Excelsier Mouscron, together with the municipality of Lille, the Commission[379] stated that the '*home and away from home*' rule and the application thereof was in non-discriminatory, and was comprised in the exercise by UEFA of regulatory power, which was compatible with EUCL.[380] Accordingly what was involved was a rule, which is purely sporting, the purpose of which was to ensure sporting fairness. The rule was accordingly not subject to EUCL. The Commission also stated that it was not in possession of sufficient information to enable it to conclude that the conduct of UEFA was abusive.

1183. According to the Commission, community law not only does not challenge the power of self-management and self-regulation of sportingsports entities in non-economic matters, which are linked to the specific nature of the sport, but also recognizes that sportingsports institutions have the power to promote a sport in such a way that they proceed in a close accordance with their objectives, provided that their choices are not discriminatory and do not conceal economic interests.[381]

1184. In this case, the Commission was not in possession of sufficient information to enable it to consider whether the rule at issue concealed economic interests, so that, in principle, the provisions of the rule sought to establish a sporting principle, which is indispensable to the proper conduct of national and international competitions between clubs in order to ensure equal opportunities.[382]

1185. In addition to the position that the '*home and away from home*' is not subject to the then Article 81(1) EC and cannot be contrary to the then Article 82. EC if its exceptions are applied objectively and in a non-discriminatory manner,[383] the Commission stressed the fact that the rule in question has restrictive consequences in terms of economic activities is per se insufficient, to exclude the rule from being classified as a purely sportingsports rule and accordingly escape the application of

378. In favour of the relocation of clubs, in accordance with the rules applicable to banks, See. Arnd Krüger, 'Comments on the Working Document on the Economics and Consumer Aspects of Professional sports in the Internal Market', EP Hearing.
379. Case IV/D.3: 36.851 *C.V. Lille –v- UEFA*.
380. No. 3 and no. 27.
381. No. 17.
382. No. 20.
383. No. 20.

EUCL, provided that the restrictions in question do not go further than is strictly necessary in order to safeguard the sporting interest in question.[384]

1186. It is furthermore noted that the Commission decided as it did, not because the rule in question was a sporting rule but because it had insufficient information, and because there was no community interest sufficient to justify a more detailed investigation of the matter in order to be able to give a definite reply to the two questions linked to a possible abuse by UEFA of its dominant position.[385]

1187. References also made to the more recent position of the Commission expressed following a Parliamentary question in which MEP A. Alavanos – who proposed the permanent installation of the Olympic Games in Greece.[386] The Commission stated clearly that the said matter was a matter for the IOC, which, according to Frank LATTY,[387] demonstrates unsurprisingly that the Commission considers that the rules governing the place where competitions take place are purely sporting rules and accordingly that community law is not applicable to them.

3. Rules Which Prohibit Multi-Ownership (or Multi-Control) of Clubs

1188. The *ENIC* case concerned the so-called multi-ownership of clubs,[388] i.e., the prohibition of cross-holdings in different teams, or the prohibition of the ownership by one natural or juristic person of holdings, which enables that person to influence the management/administration/activity of more than one team, or public limited sportingsports company, which take part in the same competition.[389]

1189. The specific rule at issue was an UEFA *entitled 'Integrity of UEFA competitions between clubs: Club independence'*[390] *which is known as the rule which*

384. No. 21. Evelyn Clerc says that 'the apparent sport exception recognized in the Mouscron case remains an isolated case' – See 'L'autonomie des associations sportives face au droit de la concurrence'.
385. No. 23 and no. 24.
386. OJEC C 289, 122/10/1999, p. 145.
387. *Supra*, p. 753.
388. In this case, ENIC, plc, Sociedade de Investimento had holdings in six European clubs (Glasgow Rangers FC in Scotland – 25.1% - ; FC Basle in Switzerland – 50% -; Vicenza Cálcio in Italy – 99% - ; Slavia de Praga in the Czech Republic – 96.7% - ; AEK Atenas in Greece - 47% and Tottenham Hotspur, in England – 21.9%.
389. This case was also submitted to the Lausanne Court of Arbitration for Sport, in which the outcome, in terms of the final decision, was identical – TAS 1998/200, Matthieu Rub (éd), Recueil des Sentences du TAS II 1998–2000, Kluwer Law Edition, The Hague, 2002, pp. 38 et seq.
390. This rule was also considered by the Court of Arbitration for Sport – Award of 20 Aug. 1999, CAS 98/200, *AEK Athens and SK Slavia Prague v. UEFA*- which held that CCL was applicable, given the '*economic nature*' of the rule in question. The arbitrators, who defined the relevant market as the '*market for the interests of owners of football clubs, which are capable of taking part in UEFA competitions*', considered that the rule protects and promotes economic competition between club owners and economic and sportingsports competition between clubs and is objectively necessary in order to provide consumers with a credible sportingsports event (nos 133; 150, 162). Paragraphs 76 and 82 deserve to be quoted:

prohibits multi-ownership of clubs, which, appears to restrict competition by preventing certain operators (team owners) from having a holding in the said entities.[391]

1190. ENIC lodged a complaint against UEFA on the grounds that the rule in question was anti-competitive to the extent that it restricted opportunities to invest in European clubs.

1191. Having been informed of the said rule, the Commission[392] *commenced by seeking to establish whether the restrictions on competition 'are limited to the minimum necessary in order to preserve the integrity of the UEFA competitions between clubs and in order to ensure the uncertainty of the results',* i.e., and in other words, *'(...) to confirm, whether or not there are less restrictive ways in which to achieve the same objective'.*[393]

1192. According to the Commission, the aim of the rule at issue, which is a decision of an association of undertakings, is not to distort competition.[394] The reason for the rule is evident: if two or more clubs, which participate in the same competition, are controlled or managed by a single entity, conflicts of interest will arise and the public will not have confidence in the fairness and integrity of the game and will accept the possibility that results are fixed.[395]

> 76. The Panel shares the EC Commission's position that the application of competition rules to sports regulations is a particularly complex task because of the peculiarities of sport and because of the inescapable link between sporting and economic aspects. Therefore, all the relevant elements of competition law have to be carefully weighed in this award together with the peculiar sporting elements, in order to ascertain whether the Contested Rule violates Articles 81 (ex 85) and 82 (ex 86) of the EC Treaty or not. (...) 82. The Panel observes that it is quite difficult to deduce the extent of the 'sportingsports exception' from the mentioned case law by the Court of Justice. It is clear that a sporingsports exception of some kind does exist, in the sense that some sportingsports rules or practices are somewhat capable of, as the Court put sit, 'restricting the scope' of EC provisions. In the light of the Court's jurisprudence, it seems that a sportingsports rule should pass the following tests in order not to be caught by EC law: (a) it must concern a question of sportingsports interest having nothing to do with economic activity; (b) it must be justified on non-economic grounds, (c) it must be related to the particular nature or context of certain competitions, and (d) it must remain limited to its proper objective.

391. Massimo Coccia asserts that this rule is legal and states that: *'Like in other sectors of the economy - for instance in the television sector - it appears appropriate that in sports it is avoided a concentration of ownership in a few hands'*, 'Multi-ownership of professional sports clubs', I Congresso de Direito do Desporto – Estoril/October de 2004, Coord. Ricardo Costa and Nuno Barbosa, Coimbra, Almedina, p. 132.
392. Decision of 25 June, Case COMP/37 806: ENIC/UEFA, 'Integrity of UEFA competitions between clubs: club independence', at http://europa.eu.int/comm/competition.
393. *Council communication pursuant to no.3 of Art. 19 of Regulation no. 17 regarding a request for a negative certificate, or an exemption, pursuant to no. 3 of Art. 81 of the EC Treaty, Case no. 37.632 – UEFA Rule regarding 'Integrity of UEFA competitions between clubs: Club independence', OJ C 363, 17/12/1999, pp. 2–4.*
394. No. 32.
395. No. 35 and no. 38.

1193. The possible effect of the rule on the freedom of action of the clubs and investors is therefore inherent in the existence of credible UEFA competitions between clubs.[396] Moreover, the rule does not result in a limitation of the freedom of action of clubs and investors, which exceeds what is necessary in order to ensure its legitimate objective of protecting the uncertainty of results and in order to give the public a correct perception of the integrity of UEFA competitions.[397]

1194. The Commission also stated that because the said rule does not restrict competition and because it is applied objectively and in a non-discriminatory manner, it is not subject to the provisions of the then Article 81(1) EC.

1195. The Wouters Judgment was cited[398] in order to identify the 'particular context in which the rule is applied': 'without the rule, the proper workings of the market in which the clubs carry on their economic activities would be threatened, to the extent that the public perception that the sportingsports competition is just and honest is an essential precondition of the retention of interest therein and the mercantile nature thereof'.

1196. Furthermore, the Commission stated that the rule does not result in the application of the then Article 82 EC:[399] if UEFA has a dominant position in any market considered, the fact that it adopts the rule in question does not per se amount to an abuse of a dominant position, as it is proportionate in terms of its objectives and non-discriminatory. It is not plausible that the use of a less restrictive rule could achieve the same objectives and the Commission found no evidence of abuse.

1197. This case, which has started at the CAS – a court that apparently was not enough for solving the problem [400] - took into consideration the economic particularities of sport,[401] contrary to the common decision making practice,[402] in

396. No. 32.
397. No. 40. In support of this argument, See. Stefaan Van Den Bogaert and Ann Vermeeersch, 'Sport and the EC: a tale of uneasy bedfellows?', *European Law Review*, Issue 6, Sweet & Maxwell, 2006, p. 831. According to both of these authors the judgment avoided the consequence that the result of a football match could be decided in a board room rather thatthan on the pitch. The mere possibility that the former could occur, for any reason, would threaten the very essence of the sport.
398. No. 31.
399. No. 45 and No. 46.
400. According to Richard Parrish, *'[t]he limitations of the CAS as a venue for final settlement was demonstrated in the ENIC case. Having failed with its challenge to UEFA' s multiple club ownership rules before the CAS, ENIC lodged a complaint before the European Commission'* – 'Advocacy Coalitions in European Union Sports Policy', *59th Political Studies Association Annual Conference*, 7–9 Apr. 2009, The University of Manchester, p. 10.
401. See Stephen Weatherhill, *'The White Paper on Sport as an Exercise in 'Better Regulation', in EU, Sport, Law and Policy: Regulation, Re-Regulation and Representation, Edited by Simon Gardiner, Richard Parrish, Robert C.R. Siekmann, The Hague, T.M.C. Asser Press, 2009, p. 105.*
402. For S. Den Bogaert, *'[h]aving regard to several decisions of national courts and competition authorities in similar cases, it appears that this decision might also have gone the other way, forcing the conclusion that the UEFA cannot complain about its treatment under EC competition law.'- Sport in the European Constitution: All sound and no fury?'*, Maastricht University, pp. 20–21.

the name of the integrity of the competition.[403] However some doubts were raised.[404]

4. Nationality Clauses in the Composition of Professional Teams

1198. A significant part of the rules at issue in the *Bosman* judgment were related to so-called nationality clauses, i.e., clauses which establish a maximum number of foreign players (even EU players) per team.

1199. Although the ECJ made no comment regarding the compatibility of this type of clause with EUCL, we consider that it is arguable that such clauses prevented different clubs from competing for players, to the extent that they are prevented from completing freely for the services of professional footballers in the community market. In our opinion, this limitation of the freedom of action of clubs with regard to the recruitment of players and, particularly, foreign (non-community) players, is not only the consequence but also the objective intended by clubs and federations. This leads to an allotment of the sources of supply and therefore amounts to a restriction of competition between clubs, in accordance with the then 81(1)(c) EC.

---

403. For Daniel Geey:

> [i]n analysing the ENIC decision, it could be suggested that one person or company having an Interest in two clubs could face two significant conflicts, which UEFA was keen to nullify. One interesting situation could arise a person or company had a 100% ownership stake in a non-PL European club (Team A) competing in the Champions League and had a 49% shareholding (but not an Interest) in a Premier League club (Team B). That person or company would have a significant shareholding, as defined under the Premier League Rules ('PL Rules') (as it is greater than 30%), and would be required to pass the PL FPPT, but the 49% shareholding would not breach the UEFA Integrity Rules. Both teams would be allowed to play in the same competition. The contrast such a situation presents to the transparent and fair competition rationale espoused in the ENIC decision is a matter of degree. Such questions relating to the integrity of the competition would be heightened for example, if Teamif Team A needed to win a match against Team B to qualify for the next round, whilst Team B was not in a position to qualify for the next stage. Accusations of match fixing and footballing impropriety would almost certainly follow if Team B fielded a weakened team. Transparency and integrity of the game.

404. Riccardo Croce and Stephen Sampson raise the following doubts:

> a competition lawyer might query how legitimate this rule is, particularly given the broad definition of 'control' that is typically adopted in the context of mergers. Should an investment fund be prevented from buying more than one club, if it is a mere financial holding company with no right to influence the club's management? An interested investor might wonder whether the Commission has overstepped the mark on this matter, imposing unnecessary restrictions on purely commercial transactions.

'Section 3: Sports', in The European Antitrust Review 2010.

5. Transfer Compensation on the Termination of an Employment Contract

1200. Another of the matters at issue in the *Bosman* judgment was related to rules which provide for the obligatory payment of compensation by the transferee club to the transferor club, in the event of transfer, even if the player's contract with the transferor club has already terminated.

1201. Although the ECJ has also not stated a position regarding this matter,[405] we consider that such rules are clearly in breach of EUCL.[406] The Commission[407] and the European Parliament[408] also consider that the transfer compensation on the termination of an employment contract.

---

405. 'EU competition law constitutes another front, which was untouched in the Bosman case. However, it was clear since the outset that competition law was lurking in the background and could be a powerful tool to harness the transnational regulation of sport' – See Antoine Duval, Lex Sportiva; A Playground for Transnational Law, at http://ssrn.com/abstract=2317826, acceded at May 27 2014, p. 18.
406. Alfonso Rincòn has a different opinion:

> [c] ontrary to what has been argued in several occasions, transfer clauses are not discriminating. The concept of restrict access is therefore among the set of difficulties sportsmen face when they enter the employment market. This restriction derives from an agreement between the clubs, as participants in football competitions, on the way the business should managed. This restriction's effect would be elimination of demand, curtailing production in the player market. What the Advocate General considers a perpetuation of the structure of competence is viewed as a restriction on production. The transfer clause has also been deemed a restriction of production. In fact from the point of view of the stronger clubs, what occurs is a limitation in the ability to attract new players which would limit their financial capacity. In any case, it would still be the same concept or at least the same logic since both definitions concern control over the market which would prevent free movement of players. On the other hand, the Advocate General argued that transfer clauses could not be considered restrictive of competition in the sense that they did not create a barrier preventing access to the market. According to him, the clause was an economic barrier which could be overcome by paying large sums of money. The measure could constitute an abuse of a dominant position within the meaning of Article 82 of the Treaty. In fact, in this case the FIFA and the national leagues would be competitors. They would be competing in the sporting events market. The raw material used to produce the events would be the players themselves, who are controlled by the FIFA. The fact that players' interests are not taken into account at the moment when decision are made concerning their future could constitute a restriction, i.e., an abusive conduct contrary to Article 82 TEU.

407. See White Paper on Sport:

> In the absence of transfer rules, the integrity of sport competitions could be challenged by clubs recruiting players during a given season to prevail upon their competitors. At the same time, any rule on the transfer of players must respect EU law (competition provisions and rules on the free movement of workers) … The Commission considers such a system to constitute an example of good practice that ensures a competitive equilibrium between sport clubs while taking into account the requirements of EU law, p. 15.

408. *See European Parliament Report 'Professional Sport in the Internal Market (PE 358 378), point 4.2.4 Restrictions in the labour market, on "Transfer regulations*": (…) *As the Commission states, "Competition between the clubs is impeded since those regulations replace the normal regime of supply and demand with a uniform mechanism that leads to a preservation of the existing situation*

1202. In fact, the stipulation of high and disproportionate transfer compensation permits the transferor club to ensure the 'retention' of the player as a consequence of the competitive risk that this could give rise to, and can thus prevent the transfer of the player to a certain club. The problem of the 'substitutability' of players is well known. Although there are comparable parameters, each player has his own distinctive and individual characteristics. Transfer compensation accordingly prevents clubs interested in hiring a player from carrying on their economic activity, i.e., it interferes with the opportunities of these clubs to hire certain players.

1203. Moreover, if the transferor club intends to proceed with the transfer, the transfer will involve the payment of large sums of money by the transferee club, which will accordingly be obliged to compensate the transferor club, even when the transferor club's contractual relationship with the player has terminated.

1204. Furthermore, the player is also prejudiced by the existence of such rules, as they amount to a clear restriction of the player's ability to move to a new employer of his choice. If the transfer becomes feasible, the player will very probably receive less at the new club then he would have received had the new club not been required to pay the compensation, i.e., players' salaries are reduced as a consequence of the fact that certain financial resources have to be consumed by the payment of the compensation (a deflationary effect on players' remuneration).

1205. This type of obligatory compensation consequently has the effect of restricting the supply of players, who are undoubtedly the main production factor, or source of demand, of the clubs. This restriction on the output of the 'player acquisition market' is therefore reflected in a division of markets and sources of supply of players, in accordance with the provisions of Article 101(1)(c) TFUE.[409]

1206. Such obligatory compensation, by restricting trade at the time when transfers take place, affects the club's commercial activities in markets associated with the '*player acquisition market*', e.g., the '*television rights exploitation market*' and the '*sportingsports merchandising market' inter alia.*

1207. There are two other circumstances within the context of transfer compensation, which are noteworthy.

1208. It is noted firstly, that notwithstanding the fact that the *Bosman* Judgment considered that the rules regarding transfer compensation are contrary to the then

---

and deprives the clubs of the possibility to make use of the opportunity to employ players who under normal competition circumstances would offer their services in the Community and the European Economic Area"'.

409. For the European Commission, '*competition between clubs to hire players is no more than a hypothetical market for the acquisition of players. Accordingly, for the purposes of a competition law analysis the said market cannot be established (the market for the supply of players in which clubs are mutually involved in the supply of and demand for players) – the relationship between the club and the player is an employment relationship, which is not at all relevant in terms of CCL*' – Notice of Non-compliance, Case IV/36/583- SETCA-FGRB/FIFA, no. 41.

Article 48 EC, the fact is that almost two years later, the Commission has received a number of complaints regarding FIFA Circular no. 616, of the 4 June 1997, no. 2 of which makes provisions, which include possible refusal to issue international transfer certificates in the event of the rescission of contracts of employment by non-amateur players prior to the end of the corresponding contractual term, independently of whether or not the rescission was by mutual agreement, or involved the payment of remuneration due by the player, in the event of a unilateral rescission by the player, in accordance with the relevant employment legislation.

1209. On the 15 December 1998, the Commission sent a non-compliance notice to FIFA, which considered that the said Circular was contrary to the then Article 81 EC, and that there were no grounds for the application of no. 3 of the said provision, as the objective or effects of the agreements were to significantly restrict the freedom of action of clubs.

1210. The second circumstance involves the so-called *Balog* case, in which the following preliminary question was formulated on the 2 July 1998:

> Is the fact that a football club established in the territory of a member state of the EU wishes, on the basis of the regulations and circulars of national and international federations (URBSFA, UEFA, FIFA) to obtain the payment of transfer compensation on the occasion of the hiring of one of its former employees, a professional football player with a non-community nationality, at the end of this contract, by a new employer established in the same member state of the EU, the EEA or even a third state, compatible with article 85 of the Treaty of Rome and/or article 53 of the EEA?

1211. It should be noted first of all that the national judge curiously did not query the compatibility of the rules in question with the EC-Hungary Association Agreement, but only raised the competition question.

1212. Also noteworthy is the fact that an agreement was made between FIFA and the Commission on the eve of the publication of the advocate-general's conclusions, which, together with the monetary compensation paid to the Hungarian player led to the withdrawal of the complaint to the Belgian court, with the result that the judge at first instance informed the ECJ that the preliminary question was abandoned.

1213. In any event and so far as the substantive question is concerned, our view is as follows: the obligation to pay transfer compensation would not significantly affect competition in the common market in a scenario in which the new employer is established in the EEA and the former employer is established in a third country, as the effects will be felt outside of the EEA. On the contrary, there would only being any consequences in the opposite situation, i.e., transfers from a third-country to the EEA, to the extent that the 'seller' club would not commercialise to other clubs in the EEA in the hope of receiving compensation.

1214. One could then consider that competition refers to the moment when players are being employed under contract or to the moments concerning the exploitation of the sportingsports spectacle (publicity, television rights, etc.). In what concerns the first moment, there is a clear anomaly in sport, since the clubs do not negotiate (they do not compete with one another to negotiate) with a universe of third parties who acquire their product but rather enter into contractual relationships amongst themselves.

6. The Rescission Clauses

1215. The rescission clauses constitute an economic barrier to market accession since they replace the normal demand and offer system with a uniform mechanism which, as an immediate result, preserves the existing competition situation and prevents clubs form benefiting from the opportunity to hire players whom they would count on in regular competition.

1216. Conditions (undoubtedly, the exaggerated amounts in some of these clauses impedes the clubs from hiring certain players). On the other hand, these 'economic barriers' are clearly beneficial to the major European teams for only they possess the financial means (whether real or virtual …) to pay such amounts thus preventing the smaller clubs to from even dreaming about hiring these players. However, from a different perspective, the smaller clubs may benefit from those clauses; First, when they realize that they have an exceptional player under contract with a clause for a large sum of money and that becomes discouraging to other clubs which might want to hire that player and second because it allows them to maintain that player at their service, even if against his will, with the latter clearly becoming the most affected party in this hard relationship.

1217. A number of scholars argue that even the termination clauses can constitute an abuse of a dominant position in the market and that this situation would occur 'whenever the professional sportsmen's contract of employment included a termination clause for an amount which would vary depending on which team hired the player'. In such cases, third contracting parties would face different conditions for equivalent services, and the club paying for the onerous and more expensive clause would be faced with a competitive disadvantage in relation to other clubs, something which both Article 81 paragraph d) and Article 82 paragraph c) of the Treaty do not allow.

7. Discriminatory Transfer Time Limits

1218. This topic is related to the *Lehtonen* case, which commenced with the following preliminary question, which was posed to the ECJ by the *Tribunal de première instance de Bruxelles*:

> Are the rules of a sports federation which prohibit a club from playing a player in the competition for the first time if he has been engaged after a specified date contrary to the Treaty of Rome (in particular Articles 6, 48, 85 and 86) in the case of a professional player who is a national of a Member State of the European Union, notwithstanding the sporting reasons put forward by the federations to justify those rules, namely the need to prevent distortion of the competitions.

1219. First of all we shall summarise the main conclusions of advocate-general Alber.[410] He commenced by commenting that the preliminary question does not indicate any of the factual circumstances, which should lead to the application of CCL and that the question should accordingly be rejected as inadmissible.[411] In his analysis of the application of EUCL, which he made on a merely secondary basis, Advocate-General Alber recalled, in the light of the *Bosman* judgment, that transfer periods are contrary to the free movement rules, as the said judgment held that once such a breach was identified there was no need to consider the application of EUCL.[412]

1220. Unlike the position adopted by the Commission, which had no doubts as to the application, in principle, of the EUCL to the matter at issue, i.e., the existence of restrictions of competition within the area of the hiring of professional players during a sportingsports season, and abuse of a dominant position – Alber was of the opinion that the information provided by the national court was an insufficient basis for such a conclusion.[413] Nevertheless, he still defended the position that transfer

410. Presented on *22/06/1999, E.C.R. 2000, p. I-2681.*

411. *'(...)the order for reference contains no information as to what facts are thought to justify the application of competition law, even though the Court of Justice has consistently held that especially careful statements of reasons are necessary in that field. In particular, there is no indication of how economic activities are divided up in Belgian basketball between the clubs, the Belgian League and the federation, what economic importance Belgian basketball has, and what is the economic situation of players of Belgian clubs in the Belgian league. There are thus no facts on which to base an assessment of central questions of competition law, such as the clubs' status as undertakings, the possibility of trade between Member States being affected, the distortion, obstruction or restriction of competition, the presence of a dominant position and its abuse. The question is therefore inadmissible in so far as it relates to Articles 85 and 86 of the EC Treaty (now Articles 101 TFEU and 102 TFEU)'*, no. 28.

412. *'It must be stated to begin with that the applicability of the rules on competition is being considered only in the alternative. (...) the contested provisions on transfer periods - as has been shown - infringe the rules on freedom of movement for workers under Article 48 of the EC Treaty, in so far as citizens of the Union may rely on that fundamental freedom. The Court already held in Bosman that there is no need to rule on the interpretation of Articles 85 and 86 of the EC Treaty when there is already a breach of Article 48 of the EC Treaty'*, no. 94.

413. *In the Commission's view, the application in principle of Articles 85 and 86 of the EC Treaty to the present facts is beyond doubt. Both the players and the clubs constitute undertakings, with the consequence that the federations may very well be associations of undertakings. Trade between Member States is affected in so far as the freedom of clubs to enter into contracts with professional players even during a current league season is restricted. The same applies to restriction of competition within the common market. The question arises, however, whether the rules concerning transfer periods are necessary for organising a sporting competition between the clubs. In principle they are not unsuitable for achieving that objective; however, it follows from the phasing of*

periods can restrict the free movement of professional sportsmen and women, and that intra-community trade is also affected, to the extent that the said fundamental liberty is obstructed.[414]

1221. He further stated that notwithstanding the fact that the effect of transfer periods is to restrict competition, by preventing clubs from carrying on their economic activities and increasing their product via the hiring of new players, this could be necessary in order to ensure or permit the creation and maintenance of fair competition between clubs.[415]

1222. Alber also stated that as the rules challenged were necessary in order to create competition in the market in question and in order to achieve their objectives, i.e., to ensure the comparability of games results during a season, and did not restrict the free movement of workers disproportionately, and that they are in the interests of competition between clubs, as they increase the attractiveness of games, and should, to this extent, be deemed to be compatible with both the free movement rules and EUCL.[416]

---

the transfer periods that the rules as a whole are disproportionate. In the context of Article 86 of the EC Treaty, a dominant position can be held only by the clubs gathered together in the league. The relevant market could then only be the market in which players are engaged. For there to be a dominant position in the market, however, there must also be an economic connection between the clubs capable of giving rise to an oligopolistic structure in the market. The information provided by the referring court is too concise overall, however, for such conclusions to be reached. It must be taken that neither Article 85 nor Article 86 of the EC Treaty precludes the provisions in question on transfer periods. (Emphasis added).

414. *'It is also the case that trade between Member States may be affected. The concept of trade must not be restricted to trade in goods alone but given a wide interpretation. It must therefore be possible to find that trade is affected in a case in which the exercise of fundamental freedoms is obstructed. Transfer periods generally are liable to affect trade between Member States in so far as they may at certain times prevent changes of club by professional players within the Member States and so - as shown above - restrict freedom of movement for workers'.*

415. *'Since the development of economic activities by the clubs, that is, by undertakings, is obstructed by these transfer rules, there is probably also a restriction of competition within the meaning of Article 85(1) of the EC Treaty. A transfer period prevents clubs from increasing the attractiveness of their product by taking on new players during a certain period. (...)The provisions on transfer periods could, however, be necessary for creating and guaranteeing a competition between the clubs at all. As may be seen from the grounds of justification already put forward in connection with the examination of freedom of movement for workers and effects thereon, the transfer rules as a whole are capable of calling into existence and then guaranteeing fair competition between the clubs.'*, no. 105 (Emphasis added).

416. *'The Court rejected a purely formal application of the competition criterion in the DLG judgment. According to that judgment, the rules of competition law are not to be applied in the abstract, but always by reference to the particular provisions and the economic conditions prevailing in the relevant market. Competition-restricting rules such as in the present case which have the effect of promoting the establishment of competition on the market in question may therefore be compatible with Articles 85 and 86 of the EC Treaty if they are necessary and reasonable for achieving that objective.' (...) "That reasoning may be transposed, at least partially, to the present situation. In so far as the present transfer deadlines do not disproportionately affect freedom of movement for workers, they guarantee comparability of results of matches within a season. That objective is decisive for the competition between clubs which consists in increasing the attractiveness of their matches. Transfer periods are therefore compatible with Article 85 of the EC Treaty to the extent that they may be reconciled with freedom of movement for workers.' 'To sum up, it may be said that transfer*

1223. He added that, as there had been no exemption application, the application under no. 3 of the then Article 85 EC should not be considered, and that as the national court had not provided the necessary matters of fact and law, it was definitively impossible to give an opinion regarding the possible application of the then Article 86 EC to the dispute, i.e., the existence of a collective abuse of dominant position by the clubs.[417]

1224. We shall now consider the position adopted by the ECJ.[418]

1225. Recalling the previous case-law[419] and affirming that the said case-law is based on the declaration regarding sport annexed to the Treaty of Amsterdam,[420] the ECJ commenced by classifying the salaried activity of the basketball player Lehtonen as of an 'economic nature',[421] and therefore subject to community law, i.e.; the principle of non-discrimination on the grounds of nationality (the then Article 6 EC) and of the free movement of workers (the then Article 48 EC).[422]

1226. Thereafter, the ECJ concluded that there was an obstacle to the free movement of workers, to the extent that the rules in question prevent Belgian clubs from fielding players from other Member states in championship games, when they are hired after a certain date.[423]

1227. Following the demonstration of the existence of an obstacle to the free movement of workers, the ECJ sought to ascertain if the same can be justified objectively, and recognised that '*(...) the setting of deadlines for transfers of players may*

---

deadlines are not compatible with Article 85 of the EC Treaty if in particular the comparability of results in a season would be affected by transfers of players before the expiry of the transfer deadline and the transfer period is shorter for professional sportsmen who previously played for a club in another Member State than for professional sportsmen who previously played in third countries. (...)', no. 107.

417. The applicability of the then Art. 86 EC to the case in question presupposes above all the existence of a dominant position. It is clear from the judgment of the ECJ in the Centro Servizi Spediporto case that a mere holding in an entity, which co-ordinates competition does not suffice to create a collective dominant position in the market. On the contrary, it is necessary that the undertakings are sufficiently interlinked in order to adopt the same line of action in the market. In this case, the question is not therefore whether the clubs can, in practice, have major links between them, because of the way they are grouped, but whether they are linked in such a way that they can act independently of the players. The matters of fact and law necessary for a consideration of this question were not provided by the court below. For this reason it is definitively not possible to issue an opinion regarding the application of Art. 86 EC to the dispute, which underlies the main proceedings.
418. Judgment of the ECJ of *13/04/2000, Lehtonen, C-176/96, E.C.R. 2000, p. I-2681.*
419. No. 32.
420. *'That case-law is also supported by Declaration No 29 on sport annexed to the Final Act of the conference which adopted the text of the Treaty of Amsterdam, which emphasises the social importance of sport and calls on the institutions of the European Union inter alia to give special consideration to the particular characteristics of amateur sport. In particular, that declaration is consistent with the above case-law, in that it concerns situations where sport constitutes an economic activity'*, no. 33.
421. No. 39.
422. No. 36.
423. No. 49.

meet the objective of ensuring the regularity of sporting competitions'.[424] The court further commented that it was for the national jurisdictional body to confirm the extent to which objective reasons are at issue, which concern only the sport per se,[425] while it also commented that:

> Late transfers might be liable to change substantially the sporting strength of one or other team in the course of the championship, thus calling into question the comparability of results between the teams taking part in that championship, and consequently the proper functioning of the championship as a whole.[426]

1228. In the aftermath of the Bosman judgment, the ECJ stressed that '(…) measures taken by sports federations with a view to ensuring the proper functioning of competitions may not go beyond what is necessary for achieving the aim pursued'.[427]

The court accordingly concluded that:

> Article 48 of the Treaty precludes the application of rules laid down in a Member State by sportingsports associations which prohibit a basketball club from fielding players from other Member States in matches in the national championship, where they have been transferred after a specified date, if that date is earlier than the date which applies to transfers of players from certain non-member countries, unless objective reasons concerning only sport as such or relating to differences between the position of players from a federation in the European zone and that of players from a federation not in that zone justify such different treatment.

8. The UEFA 'Home-Grown Rule'

1229. Under this UEFA rule, a club competing in the Champions League or Europa League must choose from a squad of twenty-five players, four of whom must have been registered with that club, with four others registered with clubs in the same national association, for a minimum of three years between the ages of 15 and 21.

1230. This rule is a potential breach of competition law in that it restricts the freedom of clubs to compete in their market for quality players. It restrains the abilities of clubs to engage in the market competition for both competition and trophies under Article 101 TFEU and restricts the possibilities for the clubs to compete with each other by engaging players. In normal competitive conditions there would be more players available.

---

424. No. 53.
425. No. 59.
426. No. 54.
427. No. 56.

1231. It should be noted that UEFA's home-grown players rules has not yet been considered by the Commission in the light of EU competition law.[428] Similar schemes aimed at establishing quotas of locally trained players for clubs participating in team sports competitions have been brought to the attention of the Commission since the adoption of UEFA's rules. Each scheme needs to be examined taking into account the specific provisions of the scheme itself, the characteristics of the sport concerned and the general context in which the scheme is proposed.

The European Parliament:

> [r]eaffirms its commitments to the home-grown rule, and considers that could be a model for other professional leagues in Europe; supports further efforts of sports governing bodies that stimulate the training of local young players within the limits of EU law thus strengthening the competitive balance within competitions and the healthy development of the European sports model.[429]

1232. Yvo Belet,[430] in his capacity of MEP sustained that:

> [i] t is very encouraging that the Commission, after a long period of non-committal statements, is finally taking a clear and positive stance on the 'home-grown rule" (ie, sport organisations can require teams to have a minimum number of locally trained players). This is an element the Parliament is adamant about as talented players now often lack opportunities because, instead of investing in expensive training, clubs simply buy comparatively cheap players from abroad.

9. The FIFA '6+5 Rule'

1233. On 30 May 2008, after the 58th FIFA Congress in Sydney, FIFA issued a media release entitled '*FIFA Congress supports objectives of 6+5*'.[431]

1234. The text of the Resolution adopted by the FIFA Congress reads as follows:

> The FIFA Congress, at its meeting in Sydney on 29 and 30 May 2008, decided to:
>
> – fully support the objectives of '6+5' as laid down at the above Congress,
> – request the Presidents of FIFA and UEFA to continue to explore for Europe, together with the world of sport - football's protagonists, but also the International Olympic Committee and the international federations - all possible

428. On 28 May 2008 the Commission only stated that it has no objection to the rules under the prisma of free movement of players and the principle of non-discrimination on grounds of nationality.
429. European Parliament Resolution of 2 Feb. 2011 on the European Dimension of Sport (2011%2087 (INI), para. 72.
430. *When sport is more than just a game*, 20 Sep. 2007, http://www.europeanvoice.com/article/imported/when-sport-is-more-than-just-a-game/58283.aspx.
431. See *http://www.fifa.com/aboutfifa/federation/bodies/media/newsid=783657.html.*

means within the limits of the law to ensure that these crucial sporting objectives be achieved,

- give the FIFA President the mandate to, if necessary, take similar steps on the other continents in cooperation with the relevant Confederation.[432]

1235. FIFA has also indicated that the 6+5 Rule should have an incremental implementation starting at the beginning of the 2010–2011 season to give clubs time to adjust their teams over a period of several years, in accordance with the following calendar:

4+7 for 2010-2011,
5+6 for 2011-2012,
and 6+5 for 2012-2013.

The rule has not been put into practice yet.

1236. As the 6+5 Rule would impose restrictions on European clubs in respect of the use of foreign players, it is reasonable to assume that the FIFA regulation would distort competition in the market for the services of professional football players, i.e., the market where football clubs offer and purchase the economic rights related to the sports performances of professional players.

1237. The obligation that clubs have a minimum number of national players clearly impacts on the market in the economic rights of players' performances by artificially increasing the demand for national players. This would increase the transfer prices and salaries of national players in each country. As a consequence, the new Rule would evidently be to the detriment of medium and low level clubs in the top European national leagues, because those clubs would have to compete with the richest clubs within their leagues to hire more expensive domestic players.

1238. The 6+5 Rule would thus have the effect of distorting competition in the European and national markets in the economic rights to the performances of football players. Taking into account the *Meca-Medina* test, even if it is considered that the 6+5 a 'pure sporting rule', it must still be scrutinised under Article 101 TFUE.

1239. According to FIFA, the 6+5 Rule would have the following objectives: to strengthen sporting competition in European professional football by improving the competitive balance at club level; to encourage the promotion of European junior players; to increase the strength of national teams and to protect national identity at the level of European professional football.

1240. Therefore, FIFA must demonstrate – mainly with data – that the 6+5 is indispensable for the achievement of those goals, since there are no other means for that achievement less restrictive than the national quota system. This will be very

432. *Ibid.*

difficult to demonstrate successfully due the fact that the rule is directly discriminatory on grounds of nationality – eligibility to participate in a certain national team means being national of the country of that team (Cf. Articles 15–18 of the FIFA Regulations Governing the Application of the Statutes). And even if one does not support a total convergence between free movement and competition rules, it is not realistic to sustain efficiencies or a pro-competitive character of such a discriminatory rule.

1241. On 28 May 2008, the Commission declared that the proposed 6+5 FIFA rule was direct discrimination on the grounds of nationality and incompatible with EU Law. The Commission did not analyse the rule under EU Competition Law,

1242. Hans-Gert POETTERING, MEP, a former President of the European Parliament,[433] publicly claimed that the rule infringes EUCL.

1243. However another completely different approach given in an expert opinion needs to be considered.[434]

---

433. He has sustained that *'To take an example, the '6+5' rule proposed by FIFA would not be compatible with Community law because of its inherent direct discrimination on the grounds of nationality, since stipulating a particular number of footballers of a given nationality puts players from other countries at a disadvantage'. 'Where professional sport is concerned, as well as general democratic principles, the rules of European competition law and the relevant regulations on the internal market have also to be taken into account. In the view of the European Parliament, however, applying competition rules to sport unconditionally would result in a growing gulf between sports clubs in which the richest and most popular would benefit, making sports competitions less fair, less exciting and less popular. For this reason, the European Parliament has undertaken to include a new article in the Lisbon Treaty which takes account of this and would make it possible to balance competition law with the specific interests of sport. This is another reason why it is highly desirable for the Lisbon Treaty to enter into force as soon as possible.'* (Emphasis added), *A European Policy on Sports*, by Manolis Mavrommatis, MEP, Published by the EPP-ED Group in the European Parliament, p. 13.

434. This approach is not followed by an Expert Opinion on the Compatibility of the '6+5 Rule' with European Community Law. In its (Summary), one can read the following: © Law Business Research Ltd 1998–2009. All rights reserved. | http://www.lbresearch.com.
87 Lancaster Road, London, W11 1QQ, UK | Tel: +44 207 908 1188 / Fax: +44 207 229 6910, http://www.globalcompetitionreview.com | editorial@globalcompetitionreview.com.
'V. Competition and antitrust law assessment. The "6+5 Rule" is also compatible with competition and antitrust law provisions. It is with good reason that the application of these provisions to professional sport is already questionable or, in any case, that an exemption is accepted for the sector. This is because the "6+5 Rule" constitutes a purely sporting rule of the game that is not subject to the domain of economic competition law. In addition, upon substantial assessment there is no restriction of competition within the meaning of Article 81 EC Treaty. First of all, the definition of the relevant market for the "6+5 Rule" already causes significant difficulties, which is an indication that the application of the competition provisions to the "6+5 Rule" can only be substantiated through a very unclear, overly broad application of the concepts. The only possible market that could be used is the so-called "market for players", but that very wide definition would yield results that would be questionable in practice. In addition, the rule is obviously not a restriction of competition, because it even seeks to uphold balanced sporting competition and it is essential and proportionate to this goal, which the telos of Article 81 EC Treaty precisely allows. The concept is not capable of affecting the trade between EU Member States. Finally, an infringement against Article 81 (1) EC Treaty can be eliminated by application of the de minimis criteria. The effect on the market for players is in any case not appreciable and is moreover proportionate. It is

10. Rules regarding the Training Compensation System

1244. The Bernard Case[435] related to the training compensation system. Bernard, a young football player in the 'espoirs' team of the French club Olympique Lyonnais, refused the offer of a professional contract for one year made by this club and concluded a contract of the same type with the English club Newcastle United FC, whereas under the Charter for 'joueurs espoirs' applicable in France he should have signed his first professional contract at the end of his training, with the club which had trained him.

1245. The ECJ upheld the right of a football club to seek compensation if a young player it has trained signs a professional contract with another club. Such a compensation scheme should be justified by the objective of encouraging the recruitment and training of young players.

1246. One paragraph in this decision is very important and has a major impact on the concept of 'specificity of sport' in general, and 'specificity of football in particular'. Despite the fact that this judgment was not related to EUCL, it is important to make an exegetic analysis of the said paragraph, since its *ratio* can be easily used in the competition law cases.

The said paragraph states as follows:

> 40. In considering whether a system which restricts the freedom of movement of such players is suitable to ensure that the said objective is attained and does not go beyond what is necessary to attain it, account must be taken, as the Advocate General states in points 30 and 47 of her Opinion, of the specific characteristics of sport in general, and football in particular, and of their social and educational function. The relevance of those factors is also corroborated by their being mentioned in the second subparagraph of Article 165(1) TFEU. (Emphasis added).

1247. The first aspect to be stressed is that he Nice Declaration was at the heart of the judgment. The court intentionally did not use the expression in Article 165

---

already doubtful whether "6+5 Rule" falls within the scope of application of the prohibition against the abuse of a dominant position in accordance with Article 82 (1) EC Treaty. Previous jurisprudence of the ECJ can, at any rate, not be understood as inferring that decisions within a sport should be measured against Article 82 EC Treaty. This notwithstanding, it should be noted that FIFA does not have a dominant position with respect to the object of the "6+5 Rule". Without any direct participation of its own on the market for players, FIFA is at the most to be classified as an "association of undertakings", which are not caught by Article 82 EC Treaty. In addition, for systematic and teleological reasons the intended Adoption of the "6+5 Rule" does not fulfil all the conditions required for the finding of an abuse within the meaning of Article 82 (1) EC Treaty. Finally, because any effect on trade is not appreciable, an infringement of Article 82 (1) EC Treaty can be eliminated'.

435. Judgment of the ECJ, *Olympic Lyonnais SASP v. Olivier Bernard and Newcastle United FC*, Case C-325/08, 16 Mar. 2010.

TFEU, and previously mentioned in the *Piau* case [436] – i.e., the *specific nature of sport*. The ECJ chose instead to use the expression *specific characteristics of sport*

1248. We believe this to be more than just a question of semantics, but rather the use of the terminology used in the famous *Nice Declaration*, which has the full title *Declaration on the specific characteristics on sport and its social function in Europe of which account should be taken in implementing common policies.*[437]

1249. The reference made by the ECJ to the *Nice Declaration* is rendered even clearer when we consider the specific reference to paragraph 47 of the conclusions laid down by the Advocate General Sharpson,[438] in which the specific or special character of sport was specifically based on the *Nice Declaration*, in the following terms:

> 47. On the one hand, professional football is not merely an economic activity but also a matter of considerable social importance in Europe. Since it is generally perceived as linked to, and as sharing many of the virtues of, amateur sport, there is a broad public consensus that the training and recruitment of young players should be encouraged rather than discouraged. More specifically, the European Council at Nice in 2000 recognised that 'the Community must … take account of the social, educational and cultural functions inherent in sport and making it special, in order that the code of ethics and the solidarity essential to the preservation of its social role may be respected and nurtured'. (*19*) In addition, the Commission's White Paper on sport (*20*) and the Parliament's resolution on it (*21*) both place considerable stress on the importance of training. (Emphasis added)

1250. Further to the importance, which in our opinion, the ECJ wanted to give to the *Nice Declaration*, it is important to emphasize the terms under which the ECJ introduced Article 165 TFEU: considering it not as the true and innovative legal basis for the concept of specificity of sport, but rather as an instrument which corroborates a previously established understanding that sport has *specific characteristics*.

1251. It seems, at a first glance, that there is a paradoxical subordination of a Treaty provision in relation to a political declaration. One could even argue, based on an even hastier and inattentive reading, that the Court was 'lazy' or cautious, exempting itself from defining a line of thought or reasoning on this issue and that it contented itself with working with a pre-existing one, or, ultimately, one could

436. Cf. *Judgment* of the Court of First Instance of 26 Jan. 2005, *Laurent Piau v. Commission of the European Communities*, n Case T-193/02., ECR 2005, p. II-209, § 105.
437. Cf. *Annex* IV of the Presidency Conclusions for the Nice European *Council*, December 2000. A few months earlier the European Council of Santa Maria da Feira, held on 19 and 20 June, had made the following reference to the expression in question in point 50 of the conclusions, dedicated to sport: '*The European Council requests the Commission and the Council to take account of the specific characteristics of sport in Europe and its social function in managing common policies.*'(Emphasis added).
438. Opinion delivered on 16 Jul. 2009.

also argue that the Court wasted a long awaited opportunity: The opportunity of finding a based guidance in the Primary Law of the EU to define the concept of *specificity of sport.*

1252. However, this is not our view on this matter. We are convinced that what the ECJ truly wanted to be define very clearly was, on the one hand, that the notion of *specificity of sport* had already been sufficiently defined even before sport achieved its place in the Primary law of the EU, and on the other hand, that the TFEU was in line with a notion of continuity by way of strengthening that definition.

1253. Accordingly, it seems that the ECJ is also indicating that the interpretation of the text of Article 165 TFEU namely the expression *specific nature of sport* should be done in accordance with the *Nice Declaration.*

1254. Having said this, we think that with the judgment at stake there is an emergence of a specificity of *(professional)* Football

1255. In addition to the reference to paragraph 47, the Court also made another reference to paragraph 30 of the Sharpson Conclusions, thus indicating it shared or accepted the opinion of the Advocate General. In view of this, it is therefore important, take a closer look at that paragraph, hereby quoted as follows:

> 30. The specific characteristics of sport in general, and football in particular, do not seem to me to be of paramount importance when considering whether there is a prohibited restriction on freedom of movement. They must, however, be considered carefully when examining possible justifications for any such restriction – just as the specific characteristics of any other sector would need to be borne in mind when examining the justification of restrictions applicable in that sector. (Emphasis added)

1256. Linking this paragraph in close articulation with paragraph 40 of the *Olivier Bernard* Judgment, reveals not only the formal recognition of the existence of a *specificity of sport*, but also the existence of a *specificity of football*, as a sporting activity with distinctive and specific characteristics.

1257. In fact, this does not constitute a jurisprudential novelty, since the Court had already pointed out, in paragraph 106 of the Bosman Judgment, that:

> In view of the considerable social importance of sporting activities and in particular football in the Community, the aims of maintaining a balance between clubs by preserving a certain degree of equality and uncertainty as to results and of encouraging the recruitment and training of young players must be accepted as legitimate. (Emphasis added)

1258. At any rate, in our opinion, it is very important to point out the fact that the Court has maintained its view on this matter more than fifteen years after the

Bosman Judgment, with all that entails, namely if we consider how, since then, the economic and entertainment aspects of football have grown exponentially (largely due to the *Bosman* Judgment). It should be noted that the view of the Court has not been hindered by those who argue that football is no longer a cultural, social and entertaining event, but just an economic activity. On the contrary, and rightfully so, the ECJ continues to recognize the significance of football in society.

1259. It should be underlined that the view of the ECJ is far from being fragmentary. We should consider the revealing nature of the reference the ECJ made to the *White Paper on Sport,*[439] mentioned in paragraph 47 of the Conclusions of the Advocate General Sharpson. It is quite revealing that through the twenty-one pages of that important document issued by the European Commission, football is singled out and mentioned on eight different occasions, in contrast to other sports, which are in no occasion individualized.

1260. This reasoning of the European Commission follows another very important document, the Arnaut Report,[440] which despite dealing with sport in general, elected football as a *case study*, and in doing so resorted to arguments which were later included in the Olivier Bernard Judgment:

> 1.18 Due to the economic importance of football there is more potential (and there have been more examples) for rules and practices in football to be examined under European Community law. As confirmed in the Terms of Reference for the Review, football is arguably the only truly global game and its influence cuts across economic, political, social and cultural spheres. Perhaps more than any other sport, football is often seen as 'big business', even though this does not accurately reflect the wider role that it plays in the community. It is necessary to reconcile this business side of football with its specific sporting nature in order to achieve the correct overall balance. (Emphasis added)

1261. There is, in fact, no way of avoiding reality: - there is something different about football, a unique social relevance which justifies calling it 'The King of Sports'. Such relevance must be taken into account, when in face of a rule or conduct prohibited by EU law – namely an infringement of the fundamental liberties or an infringement of EUCL – one has to decide whether there are any justifying causes which, ultimately, lead to the conclusion that the rule or conduct at issue complies with EU Law.

1262. Therefore, there are reasons not to dwell on the recurrent discussion over the characteristics which set this sport apart from other sports – this discussion has prompted the basis for arguing that a specificity of sport exists – and go even further

---

439. Brussels, 11.07.2007, COM (2007) 391 final.
440. Cf. José Luís Arnaut, Independent European Sport Review 2006. The full report is available at http://www.independentfootballreview.com/doc/Full_Report_EN.pdf.

and acknowledge the specificities of a certain sporting activity in particular - football - which set it apart or separate it from sport in general. We are, therefore, before a new concept: the specificity of football.[441]

1263. Perhaps this also helps explain why the ECJ emphasized the *Nice Declaration* in detriment of the TFEU: in fact, while the latter mentions the specificity of sport – sport as a whole, as a reality with characteristics and values shared by all sports – the former allows for mentioning the specificity of a particular sport, *in*

---

441. We believe it not to be too farfetched to argue for a specificity of each sport per se. In support of this understanding is the fact that the Commission believes *that each sport has its specificities and deserves to be treated differently according to these.*(Cf. Commission Staff Working Document The EU and Sport: Background and context Accompanying document to the White Paper on Sport, 2007, p. 43) o or the argument of Advocate General Cosmas, in Case *Deliège*: *On that premise, I shall now address an issue which, in my opinion, is crucial to a precise definition of the economic dimension of a sporting activity. I shall no longer be examining the individual conduct and subjective intentions of sportsmen, but the sporting event itself, viewed objectively, that is to say the specific characteristics of sporting competition. Indeed sportsmen can only be assessed by reference to the competitions they enter, their individual performances being largely meaningless unless combined with success in particular competitions in which they pit themselves against their rivals. The question therefore arises whether sporting activities - in the present case, international Category A judo tournaments - exhibit an economic interest. If the significance of the sports event does not relate purely to sport, in the sense that it does not merely represent confrontation and reward for being the best, but also exhibits an intrinsic economic interest, then the economic dimension of the sporting event is clearly such that the event in itself constitutes an economic activity within the meaning of Article 2 of the Treaty.* (Opinion delivered on 18 Mar. 1999, *Christelle Deliège v. Ligue francophone de judo et disciplines associées ASBL, Ligue belge de judo ASBL, Union européenne de judo and François Pacquée*, in joint cases C- 51/96 and C-191/97, ECR [2000], p. I – 2549, § 54, Emphasis added). In the same way and on the issue of illegal bets, a recent study argues that specific rules of each sport should also take into consideration specific challenges that might be of special relevance in their specific sport (Cf. Examination of threats to the integrity of sports, Oxford Research A/S, April 2010, p. 25). In our opinion, the specificity of each sport also lies in the characteristics and values associated to that sport – this issue has been studied by the International Olympic Committee at the time of the requests for the inclusion of new sports in the programme of the Olympic Games – or also in the degree of the economic aspect of each sport, based on which, for example, there will not be an equal distribution of television revenues among the 28 Olympic Sports Federations which will integrate the Programme of the Summer Olympic Games in London 2012 (Cf. 'Sports federations to review §375 m TV revenue share', http://www.guardian.co.uk/football/feedarticle/9049588). Obviously, what we have just argued, as well as our conviction that there is a 'specificity of spot' is not incompatible with another, rather more peaceful understanding that: there is a common denominator to all sports, based on which the concept of specificity of sport has been built. And it is that common denominator which justifies common positions on the TFEU, of which we would like to point out the *Common position of the Olympic and Sports Movement on the implementation of the new Treaty of the Functioning of the European union (TFEU) on sport (Lisbon Treaty), January 2010*, or even the institutionalization of platforms for the defence of common interests, shared by several sports such as the European Team Sports (ETS), which aggregates basketball (FIBA Europe), handball (EHF), ice hockey (IIHF), volleyball (CEV) and football (UEFA). It is worth mentioning ETS's testimony based on the Bosman Judgment, that the judgments of the Court, on football issues may, due to a snowball effect, have implications to other collective sports, and that is why that entity has been calling for a full recognition of the specificity of sport by all the European Institutions (Cf. Création de l'Association des sports d'équipe européens. Les sports d'équipe unissent leurs forces, uefadirect No. 95, 3.10, pp. 10–11, Cf. also 'Safeguarding the heritage and future of team sport in Europe, July 2008', ETS, July 2008, p. 10.

casu football. In fact, football was the only sport specifically mentioned in that declaration, thus indicating the recognition of its higher relevance. Let us look at the paragraph at issue:[442]

> The European Council is keenly supportive of dialogue on the transfer system between the sports movement, in particular the football authorities, organizations representing professional sportsmen and -women, the Community and the Member States, with due regard for the specific requirements of sport, subject to compliance with Community law. (Emphasis added)

1264. Besides, we believe it is possible to perform an even finer tuning of what is specific in the context of football. We believe that perhaps there is also leeway in arguing that professional football has specific characteristics which set it apart from football as a whole, i.e., there are reasons to defend the existence of something even more specific: a specificity of professional football.

1265. That is indeed the view of the European Parliament, which not only passed a specific resolution on professional football,[443] but also, in that same act, even if only once, specifically mentioned the specificity of professional football:

> F. whereas it is thus the responsibility of the national and European political and sports authorities to ensure that, when Community law is applied to professional football, it does not compromise its social and cultural purposes, by developing an appropriate legal framework, which fully respects the fundamental principles of specificity of professional football, autonomy of its bodies and subsidiarity. (Emphasis added)

1266. In light of what has been said, and when applying EU law to (professional) football we call upon the judge to take into account its specificity.

1267. We would also like to make another call, one aimed at the football authorities: there is still a long way to go in defining concepts such as specificity of sport, specificity of football or specificity of professional football. If football authorities fail to continue to tread that path, they will inadvertently contribute to what they criticize in those who do not recognize its specificity: juridical uncertainty and insecurity.

1268. To be more specific, let us invoke the *Webster*[444] and *Matuzalém*[445] Judgments both by CAS. Both judgments failed in contributing to a further deepening of

442. Pont 16 (Transfers).
443. European Parliament resolution of 29 Mar. 2007 on the future of professional football in Europe (2006/2130 (INI)), OJEU C 27 E of 31 Jan. 2008, pp. 232–240.
444. Arbitral award of the Court of Arbitration for Sport of 30 Jan. 2008, CAS 2007/A/1298,1299 & 1230 – *Heart of Midlothian.v Webster & Wigan Athletic FC.*
445. Arbitral award of the Court of Arbitration for Sport of 19 May 2009, CAS 2008/A/1519 – *FC Shakhtar Donetsk (Ukraine) v/ Mr. Matuzalem Francelino da Silva (Brazil) & Real Zaragoza SAD*

the concept of specificity of sport but also, in our view, the contradictory judgments have shown beyond any doubt that there is still a wide margin for discretionarily in the interpretation of that concept,[446] which has been specifically laid down in Article 17 (1) of the FIFA Regulations on the Status and Transfer of players titled *Consequences of terminating a contract without just cause,* thus the discrepancies in the legal analysis.[447]

1269. In the doctrine, I would like to refer to the commentaries of Michele Colucci,[448] Julien Zylberstein[449] and Frank Hendrickx[450] on the Olivier Bernard

---

(Spain) & FIFA & CAS 2008/A/1520 – Mr. Matuzalem Francelino da Silva (Brazil) & Real Zaragoza SAD (Spain) v/ FC Shakhtar Donetsk (Ukraine) & FIFA.

446. Cf. *Webster* award, § 132: *[t]he specificity of sport is a reference to the goal of finding particular solutions for the football world which enable those applying the provision to strike a reasonable balance between the needs of contractual stability, on the one hand, and the needs of free movement of players on the other hand*; Cf. also Matuzalem award, § 155: *(…) the judging body shall therefore assess the amount of compensation payable by a party under art. 17 para. 1 of the FIFA Regulations keeping duly in mind that the dispute is taking place in the somehow special world of sport. In other words, the judging body shall aim at reaching a solution that is legally correct, and that is also appropriate upon an analysis of the specific nature of the sporting interests at stake, the sporting circumstances and the sporting issues inherent to the single case. (…) professional football is a special sector (…).*
447. *In all cases, the party in breach shall pay compensation. Subject to the provisions of Art. 20 and annex 4 in relation to Training Compensation, and unless otherwise provided for in the contract, compensation for breach shall be calculated with due consideration for the law of the country concerned, the specificity of sport, and any other objective criteria.* (Emphasis added)
448. '*Suppose that the collective agreement at stake would have fallen under EU Law or that the FIFA regulations on training compensation themselves were to be judged in the light of competition law, the question is whether in the Bernard case the Court would have applied the so called Meca Medina test. (…) By applying the Meca Medina test to the Bernard case it is very likely that the payment of damages would have been considered as contrary to the relevant EU competition law. In fact such a measure could have been easily challenged as not adequate and disproportionate to the aim it wants to achieve. In the contrary, a training compensation scheme could have been regarded as legitimate in the light of EU competition law but only if the amount of compensation would have been determined on the basis of clearly defined parameters which take into account the real training costs. With regard to the overall context in which such compensation is foreseen, it could be argued that the general objective of training compensation is legitimate in so far as it aims to encourage the training of youth players. In addition, given the fact that clubs need money to train players, the effect on players' freedom of action could be considered to be, in principle, inherent itself in the sports system. Nevertheless the amount of compensation requested, or more precisely, the criteria Adopted to calculate it, are critical. In fact a compensation which is not considerate as adequate nor justified because it does not reflect the real costs occurred, it could then result in an athlete's unwarranted exclusion from sporting events as well as in the impossibility for some clubs to acquire the players' services. It follows that, in order to avoid the prohibition laid down in art. 101, para. 1 TFEU, the restrictions thus imposed by rules on training compensation must be limited to what is necessary to ensure the proper conduct of competitive sport*' – 'The Bernard Case: an opportunity for all sports stakeholders', in *European Sports Law and Policy Bulletin: The Bernard Case, Sports and Training Compensation*, Issue I-2010, Rome.
449. '*(…) the Court mentioned Article 165 TFEU for the first time. However the reference is hardly a reason for enthusiasm: pushed to the end of the paragraph, Article 165 is used in a subsidiary manner in order to underline the need to take account of the specific characteristics of sport and of its social and educational function. In this respect, it is regrettable that the wording of Article 165 does not explicitly refer to the promotion of young athletes: unless the writers of the Treaty agreed that its very structure prevented its inclusion, there was no obvious reason for excluding it*', 'The Olivier

11. Very Long Exclusivity Periods for Television Broadcasting Rights in Respect of Sporting Events

1270. The exclusivity of television broadcasting rights is questionable from the point of view of EUCL to the extent that once they have been sold to a certain company, they cannot be exercised simultaneously by anyone else.

1271. From the point of view of the organisers of sporting competitions, the sale of exclusive rights is a means to ensure a profit, or an income, in the shortest time possible, while the television operator acquires a product/programme with greater value, which gives it prestige and a greater ability to attract and retain audiences.

1272. Exclusivity, per se, restricts competition insofar as it imposes geographic limitations in relation to the locations where certain economic activities may be carried on. Nevertheless the Commission generally accepts the principle of exclusivity in the ambit of television competitions, as an established commercial practice. The same is also true of the ECJ in relation to control of the cinema.[451]

1273. It is undoubtedly true that exclusivity, when combined with a long period of duration of the contract, may give rise to competition law-related problems, involving breaches of Article 101 TFEU. This is because a long exclusivity period may be considered to restrict competition, if there is a risk of a television operator preventing its competitors from having access to the broadcasting of certain sporting events.

1274. Each agreement has its own characteristics so that it is accordingly impossible to determine an ideal duration for exclusivity agreements, as much depends on the form and objectives of the said agreements[452] the frequency of the events, which

---

Bernard judgment: a significant step forward for the training of players', in European Sports Law and Policy Bulletin: The Bernard Case, Sports and Training Compensation, Issue I-2010, Rome, p. 65.

450. '*This* [para 30 of Advocate General's Conclusions] *seems to confirm the view that the notion of specificity of sport cannot be used as a sort "standard clause" or "style formula" to exclude sport from any further requirement of justifying limitations on the free movement of workers. A mere reference to the specificity of sport is, therefore, not sufficient. It would thus also require that specific reasons for the justification of training compensation are being put forward. It is clear that this possibility of specific justification stand open for any sector of activity in the labour market. One might indeed imagine that other "sectoral" labour markets, such as those of pilots, artists, scientists, etc. are capable of producing a set of specific characteristics on the basis of which a limitation on the free movement by a training compensation schema could be justified'* – 'Justification of training compensation in European football: Bosman and Bernard compared', in European Sports Law and Policy Bulletin: The Bernard Case, Sports and Training Compensation, Issue I-2010, Rome, p. 55.

451. ECJ judgment of 06.10.1982, *Coditel*, 262/81, E.C.R. 1982, p. 3381.

452. An exclusivity agreement for a long period of time may be necessary in order to facilitate entry into a new or developing market, with inherent benefits to consumers arising from access to a new service. Example, in the case of a new project which involves economies of scale and which requires a substantial and risky initial investment, the Commission considers that exclusivity for a

are the subject matter of these agreements.[453] In any event, the Commission states, in Chapter 3 of the Communication entitled 'Guidelines with regard to vertical restrictions',[454] that it does not, in principle, accept exclusivity periods, which exceed five years.

1275. The various commitments or remedies, which can be proposed in order to legitimated exclusivity, can include the following: (i) application of Article 3 – *bis* of the 'Television Without Frontiers Directive',[455] which gives Member states the power to ensure open signal broadcasting of events of significant public interest,

certain period of time may be necessary in order to compensate or ensure a return on the high inherent costs, namely of new technology. The Commission further recognized an exclusivity period of three years in the *Audiovisual, UEFA* and *Bundesliga* cases, as proportionate. In another case, the Commission accepted a five-year exclusivity period for exclusive rights to broadcast Premier League games, agreed between the English Football Federation, the BBC and BSkyB, fundamentally because of the fact that at that time BSkyB had been broadcasting by satellite for only three years [it should be noted however that the Commission nevertheless applied for the elimination of the automatic renewal clause (*English clause*), which made it possible to exclude any rival, because it was certain that this type of clause distorts competition, namely when such clauses are used as a veiled extension of the duration of the exclusivity, which the reallocation of the rights on the expiry of the exclusivity agreement, almost impossible]. The Commission took a contrary view in the *Telepíu* and *Stream* merger, which resulted in the creation of *SkyItalia*, when it only accepted a two-year duration for the exclusivity agreements in respect of football, and imposed a limited scope in order to prevent a disproportionate restriction of competition. In the KNVB/Sport 7 case: the exclusive licence agreement made between the Dutch Football Federation and Sport 7, was considered excessive by the Commission even taking into consideration the need for the Channel to establish itself in Holland and to introduce a certain competition in the broadcasting sector in that country, plus the fact that the agreement did not permit the reallocation of the said right at the end of the seven-year period.

453. For example, a long duration for the Olympic Games, which take place every four years, may be acceptable, and is not comparable, for example, with national football championships, which take place every year, See. Karel Van Miert, 'Sport et concurrence: Développements récents et action de la Commmission', a speech given at the Fórum Européen du Sport, Luxembourg. On this topic See. Dominique Brault, who considers that the Commission should consider the grant of the rights for future Olympic Games, which are currently held on an exclusive basis, as they have been for the past seven years, by EBU, which accordingly excludes some channels, 'À quelles conditions des droits sportifs exclusifs peuvent-ils être concédés?', *Revue Lamy de la Concurrence*, November/December 2005, p. 47.

454. OJEC C 291, of 13/10/2000, pp. 1–44.

455. European Parliament and Council Directive 97/36/EC of 30/06/1997, which amends Council Directive 89/552/EEC regarding the coordination of certain legislative, regulatory and administrative provisions of the Member states regarding the carrying on of television broadcasting activities, OJEC L 202 of 30/07/1997, pp. 60 – 70. This legal framework, which is also required by Art. 8 of the UNESCO Charter and by Arts 17 and 59 of the Olympic Charter, document Adopted by the International Olympic Committee, is characterised by mutual and inverse recognition, i.e., it is the country of origin that has to accept the rules of the host country and that has to complied with the obligations arising from the Treaty and the Directive, so that an event which is considered to be of greater interest in one country (e.g. *Tour de France*) must be transmitted in an open signal in any other Member State of the EU in accordance with the rules of that country, i.e., France in this case. Accordingly, the interest of all potential spectators of sport are given priority to the detriment of the rights of the undertakings involved, notwithstanding the fact that they frequently pay significant sums of money in order to obtain an exclusive right.

thus protecting the right of citizens to be informed via access to television broadcasts of major sporting events; (ii) adoption of legislation like the 1999 Italian legislation, which establishes a 60% plafond of exclusive broadcasting rights per channel, so that each channel may only purchase 10% of the competitions of the most important clubs; (iii) sublicensing provisions, which require the television operator, which has an exclusivity licence, to sub-licence the said rights, in return for payment.[456]

12. Collective or Centralized Sale of Television Broadcasting Rights in Respect of Sporting Events

1276. Not infrequently, the sale of television broadcasting rights in respect of sporting events involves the centralised sale of all rights by a single entity, which is generally the entity which organises or promotes the event, or the aggregation of the rights of all participants in a package or pool which is sold *en bloc*.

1277. Centralisation has clear advantages: (i) it reduces the transaction costs, when compared to bilateral agreements; (ii) it develops the production and distribution of games, which benefits the clubs; (iii) it makes solidarity, via distribution, possible; (iv) it promotes corporate governance; (v) it makes possible to sell a coherent package which covers an entire competition at one point of sale; (vi) it facilitates the task of redistribution.

1278. However, it is our opinion that this is a case of a horizontal restriction of competition which: (i) restricts competition between clubs: in the absence of a centralised system, clubs, which belong to the league, may decide the sale of rights in accordance with their interests – clubs are prevented from undertaking individual sales initiatives with regard to the operation of the rights and their individual financial situation will always be more precarious as it is dependent on the success of the chain; (ii) it restricts competition between television operators: in the absence of this system, a large number of rights would be available to operators, which would mean that a larger number of operators would have the opportunity to enter the market, and that purchasers are compelled to acquire from a single source.

1279. Without prejudice to a necessary case-by-case analysis, the centralised sale of television broadcasting rights in respect of sporting events amounts to a price-fixing mechanism, which restricts price competition and enables clubs to keep prices artificially high and to limit the availability of broadcasting rights and thus strengthens the market power of television operators (only the major media groups

456. That this is a way of reducing the exclusive rights in its object by segmenting them and are thus ensuring that they are never unused and which prevents the purchase of exclusive rights for the sole purpose of preventing access by competitors. In any event, sublicensing per se does not suffice as it must be fair, reasonable and non-discriminatory (it must be available to all those who requested and the prices cannot be excessive all, or, when viewed from the other point of view, the owner of the exclusive rights cannot retain all the valuable rights for itself or charge excessively for them).

have the financial capacity to acquire and operate the rights). Supporters also lose out because they are frequently required to subscribe to *pay TV* or *pay per view*, failing which they will be unable to watch their favourite sport on television, which is frequently the only way available and which undoubtedly reduces spectators' capacity to choose.

1280. We shall now make a brief reference to the decision-making practice of the Commission with regard to this question.

1281. Before going into a case by case approach, it must be highlighted that recently[457] the Commission said that:

> [t]he collective selling of media rights is a good example of financial solidarity and redistribution mechanisms within sports. Collective selling of media rights inherently restricts competition within the meaning of Article 101(1) TFEU. However, collective selling may bring about advantages which may outweigh the negative effects. Joint selling can therefore meet the criteria for an exemption under Article 101(3) TFEU if certain conditions are fulfilled. The Commission recommends sport associations to establish mechanisms for the collective selling of media rights to ensure adequate redistribution of revenues, in full compliance with EU competition law while maintaining the right of the public to information.

1282. As to the cases, the *UEFA* decision of the 23 July, regarding the combined sale of the commercial rights of the UEFA Champions League,[458] in which the Commission considered the relevant market to be that of the '*acquisition and resale of television broadcasting rights in respect of football events which take place regularly each year*', was the first formal exemption decision adopted by the Commission with regard to the combined commercialisation of television rights.

1283. The Bundesliga Decision[459] is equally relevant, in which the issue was the joint sales of broadcasting rights in respect of the German Football League, in which the Commission also granted an exemption from the competition rules. In the Commission's opinion, the traditional centralised sale system amounts to a restriction of competition between clubs and between media undertakings, which accentuates the concentration trends in the sector. However, the exemption was granted, given the commitment proposed by the German Football League to the effect that all broadcasting rights would no longer be sold to a single broadcasting undertaking in a single package, and that the rights would be separated and sold fairly in a series of

457. Communication from the Commission to the European Parliament, the Council, the European Economic and Social Committee and the Committee of the Regions, {SEC(2011) 66 final} {SEC(2011) 67 final}{SEC(2011) 68 final}, point 3.12. 'Sustainable financing of sport'.

458. OJ L 291, de 08/11/2003, pp. 25–55.

459. See. Commission Press Conference, IP/03/1106, Brussels, 24/07/2003 and Decision 2005/396/EC of 19/01/2005, OJ L 134, of 27/05/2005. In this case in which the Commission did not grant an exemption pursuant to no. 3 of Art. 81 EC, but which otherwise took the first ever decision pursuant to Regulation 1/2003.

separate packages, thus avoiding the monopolisation of broadcasting rights by a small number of particular powerful operators. Furthermore, the commitments reduced the ambit and duration of future sales contracts and improved access to content by television and radio channels and for new operators in the media sector. The Commission also took into consideration the fact that in the future it will be possible to broadcast games direct on the Internet and on mobile telephones and of the possibility that first and second division clubs in the Bundesliga could sell certain rights thus intensifying competition and opening up the supply of football events to the consumer.

1284. In the *Champions League* case, the Commission stressed some of the advantages of a centralised system: (i) it favours the so-called minor sports, as the broadcast of an entire competition is guaranteed; (ii) it reduces the transaction and efficiency costs, as there is a single seller with sufficient expertise, so that each club no longer has to have recourse to its own staff; (iii) it assists in the competitive equilibrium of teams; (iv) a competition, which is promoted as a whole by television assists in the solidification and dissemination of a country's culture; (v) if the sale was made by the clubs perhaps only the major/most popular clubs would manage to have their games televised; (vi) it means that production and distribution can benefit the clubs, operators and television viewers, to the extent that it leads to the creation of a single point of sale that the acquisition of a product, which has a brand (a single and distinct product, which cannot be produced individually), and which places the emphasis on the competition as a whole and thus attracts greater external recognition (many viewers like to follow the competition as a whole rather than only one club); (vii) it makes a more effective distribution possible with inherent efficiencies as a consequence of lower transaction costs; (viii) sale without bundling, in different individual packages insures that various media operators can compete for the rights.[460]

1285. The Commission's final decision was as follows:

> The exemption (…) is subject to compliance with the condition that the restriction which prohibits football clubs from selling live broadcasting rights of free access television broadcasting organisations shall not apply whenever a reasonable proposal is not submitted for signature by a television broadcasting organisation.

1286. The Commission made the following proposed various types of remedies for centralised sales agreements:[461] (i) the organisation of a public tender for the sale

460. This is what happened in the UEFA case and in the Bundesliga case, i.e., segmentation of the rights into packages. In the Bundesliga case, Commission Decision of 19/01/2005 is not the grant of an exemption, but a decision with commitments, in accordance with the provisions of Art. 9 of Regulation 1/2003 by virtue of the commitments, which the German Football League proposed according to which television broadcasting rights in respect of the first and second divisions are commercialised in four packets offered to pay or open signal television operators.
461. Torben Toft, 'Broadcasting & EC Competition Law', a speech given at the Sports Law and Business, Conference, Brussels, 31/01/2006.

of the rights on non-discriminatory and transparent terms; (ii) limitation of the duration of vertical exclusivity contracts; (iii) limitation of the subject matter of vertical exclusivity contracts; (iv) returned to the individual clubs of the rights which are not sold by the centralised sales entity; (v) imposition of a prohibition against a single purchaser acquiring all of the packages of rights, which may occur in which there is *ex ante* already a truly dominant operator; (vi) UEFA guaranteed the rights which it was unable to sell centrally, to each of the clubs individually; (vii) division of rights into various packages (the so-called gold, silver and bronze packages); (iv) offer of a specific package of rights for distribution via Internet and mobile telephone; (viii) limitation of the rights operation platform; (vi) sublicensing of all the rights in question, when operators, who dominate the downstream market acquire exclusive rights in respect of neighbouring markets.

1287. In another case, in December 2003,[462] the Commission made a provisional agreement, in proceedings which were commenced in December 2002, with the FA Premier League and BSkyB regarding retransmission rights in respect of football games, *inter alia*, with regard to the combined sale of retransmission rights of games in the English first division.

1288. The Premier League agreed that, as from 2006, the tender procedures with regard to television rights would ensure the presence of at least two organisations, which would broadcast first division games live. The Premier League would create packages of balanced games, which represent the first division as a whole and a single television broadcasting organisation would not be permitted to purchase all the packages. The Premier League also agreed to jointly consider with the Commission the way in which to conduct auctions in order to ensure that potential competitors would not be excluded. BSkyB agreed to grant a sub-licence to another television broadcasting organisation for the re-transmission of a package of up to eight first quality first division games in each season.

1289. However, the truth is that in practice sale in packages does not always result in the healthy competition desired. For example, in August 2003, the English Football Federation commercialised the English league rights for the 2004/2005 and 2006/2007 seasons in the packages each with a different value. However, BSKyB submitted a much higher offer for the packages than its main competitors (ITV and BBC), so that in practice the fragmented form of the sale of rights did not, in the end, prevent exclusivity.

1290. The Commission's reaction to this resulted in negotiations, which were marked by many impasses, which only terminated with the adoption of a decision on the 22 March 2006, pursuant to Article 9 of Regulation 1/2003.[463] Notwithstanding the fact that one of the commitments proposed by the English Football Federation was a requirement that the rights for the 2007/2008 and 2008/2009 seasons would be sold in six packages, the truth, in practice, is that following an open, fair

462. See. The Commission press conference of 16/12/2003, Brussels, IP/03/1748.
463. Decision in Case COMP/C-2/38.173, European Commission, IP/06/356, 22/03/2006.

and competitive tender procedure, four of the said packages (ninety-two games) were gained by BSkyB and 2 (forty-six games) were gained by the Irish pay-TV operator Setanta. Consequently, as were stressed in the Financial Times, it was the British consumers, who lost out, and who were obliged to pay more and to subscribe to or more different television services, in order to be able to see all the games played in their country.[464]

1291. The Commission reacted to this via the publication of a Communication which invited third parties two comment on the commitments provisionally accepted by the English Federation. This procedure also terminated with a commitments decision, which was adopted pursuant to the provisions of Article 9 of Regulation 1/2003.[465]

1292. Various national competition authorities in the Netherlands,[466] Germany[467] and the United Kingdom,[468] have already decided with regard to the subject matter.

13. Agreements for the Joint Purchase of Television Broadcast Rights in Respect of Sporting Events

1293. In the case of joint purchase, there is an aggregation of a certain number of parties interested in the purchase of the television broadcasting rights which, instead of competing to acquire the rights, combine in order to make a single purchase offer. If the offer is successful, there is a subsequent division of the rights acquired, between the entities, which combined for the purposes of the purchase, and naturally also of the costs incurred in respect thereof.

---

464. In an article, published on 13/05/2006, p. 24, Eriko Terazono, wrote the following: '*Brussels, meanwhile, appears to have scored an own goal*'.
465. See. Commission Press Conference, IP/03/1748, 16/12/2003.
466. In the said KNVB case, the Netherlands competition authority considered that the centralised sale, by the Dutch football federation, eliminated competition on the supply side and thus artificially increased prices and left the purchaser without an alternative: either the purchaser purchased the rights in respect of all the games, or it purchased none.
467. After a court, the *Deutscher Fussball-Bund c. Bundeskartellamt, Bundesgerichtshof,* had considered that the centralisation was contrary to CCL, the Parliament approved an exception to be included in the German Competition Law, specifically, Art. 31 of the *Gesetz gegen Wettbewerbsbeschränkungen, GWB,* which provided that the law does not apply to centralised rights for the television broadcasting of sporting events envisaged in the federation bylaws, in the light of the social and political responsibility of such federations, which are also required to promote sport among young people and amateur sport and to ensure adequate receipt distribution arrangements. Torben Toft, *supra.*
468. In 1999, the United Kingdom Restrictive Practice Court decided that the purpose of the restrictions on competition inherent in centralised sale was to promote the public interest and was accordingly in accordance with the Restrictive Trade Practices Act 1976, as (i) there is a reduction of the divide between the large and small clubs; (ii) the increase or reduction of receipts is felt by all; (iii) as centralisation produces more money, the league in question is able to become stronger internationally for the immediate benefit of national consumers.

1294. For example, there are circumstances in which television or radio companies combine in order to jointly acquire television broadcasting rights in respect of sporting events, as in the Audiovisual Sport Case,[469] which involved a joint-venture between two major competitors for the acquisition of the entire television broadcasting rights in respect of football in Spain.

1295. The Eurovision system is also a joint system for the purchase and reciprocal transfer of rights.[470]

1296. Such agreements contain both a horizontal aspect (the agreement between the purchasers to acquire jointly) and a vertical aspect (agreements made with third party suppliers), which involve both the market upstream from the relevant market and the downstream resale market.

1297. The competition law affects depend on the position occupied in the market by the parties to the agreement: for the stronger this position is, the more appreciable of the anti-competitive effects. When the agreement is made between

469. IP (00)1352 de 23/11/2000 – The Commission required the parties to grant a sublicense of the pay-TV rights to all interested operators, which led to a significant reduction in the pay-per-view prices to the consumer.
470. The subject of two different decisions: the Commission considered that the system restricted competition between the members of the EBU and, in practice, excluded private operators from the benefits of exclusivity. However, it granted a five-year exemption on the grounds that the system (i) reduced transaction costs; (ii) offered advantages to small members and made co-ordination between the various channels in each country possible; (iii) facilitated the exchange of programmes between countries; (iv) and contributed to the development of the single European market. Accordingly, the Commission stated in Decision, 2000/400/EC, of 10/05/2000, Case IV/32.150 *– Eurovision, OJEC L 151 of 24/06/2000 p. 18 – 41, pursuant to no. 3 of Art. 81 EC that Art. 81 was not applicable to (i) the joint acquisition of television broadcasting rights in respect of sporting events*; (ii) the allocation of the rights acquired jointly; (iii) signal exchange for Sporting events; (iv) the system of access by organisms, which are not members of EBU to the Eurovision rights to broadcast sporting events; (v) rules regarding sub-licences for the operation of Eurovision rights on subscriber channels. However the exemption granted was subject to conditions and obligations, particularly the condition that EBU and its members jointly acquire sporting event broadcast rights only within the ambit of agreements, which permit them to grant access to third parties, via the grant of sub-licences to operate Eurovision rights on subscriber channels However the SEEI overruled this Commission decision on the grounds that: *'(…)contrary to what the Commission concludes in the contested decision, the sub-licensing scheme does not guarantee competitors of EBU members sufficient access to rights to transmit sporting events held by the latter on the basis of their participation in that purchasing association. Apart from a few exceptions, nothing in the rules or mode of implementation of the scheme enables competitors of EBU members to obtain sub-licences for the live broadcast of unused Eurovision rights. In reality, the scheme merely permits the acquisition of sub-licences to transmit roundups of competitions under extremely restrictive conditions. (…)It follows from all the preceding considerations that the Commission made a manifest error of assessment in the application of Article 81(3)(b) EC in determining that, even if a product market limited to certain major international sports events exists, the sub-licensing scheme guarantees access for third parties which are competitors of the EBUs members to Eurovision rights and consequently avoids the elimination of competition in that market.'*, Judgment of 08/10/2002, *Métropole*, Proceedings consolidated T-185/00, T-216/00, T-299/00 and T-300/00, E.C.R. 2002, p. II-3805, paras 83 and 85.

purchasers, which individually, would not have the financial resources necessary to acquire at the rights, the scenario is generally pro-competitive.

1298. In the *Screensport* case[471] the matters at issue were agreements with regard to a joint enterprise (created by EBU and/or some of its members, together with News International plc, who created the Eurosport sports channel) together with all of the associated contractual provisions between the members of the Eurosport Consortium, on the one hand, and Sky Television plc, Satellite Sports Sales Ltd, Satellite Sports Services and News International plc, on the other hand, which granted the Eurosport unlimited access for ten years to all of the programming, in respect of which the rights belonged to EBU. This arrangement distorted competition, as it gave Eurosport a disproportionate competitive advantage (there was a refusal to grant Screensport sub-licences with regard to sporting events in respect of which EBU and/or its members had acquired exclusive rights, which prevented cable and satellite television companies, such as Screensport, from competing with EBU and/or its members in the market in respect of international sporting broadcasts (intra-community trade was affected in accordance with the provisions of the then Article 85 EC, to the extent that the Eurosport joint purchase system tended to restrict or obstruct access by Screensport, or a similar channel, to that market on equal terms).

14. Restriction of the Television Broadcast of Certain International Games

1299. In July 1998, the Commission initiated non-compliance proceedings in respect of a UEFA regulation with regard to broadcasting times, pursuant to which national federations were required to ensure, whenever broadcasting rights in their territory was sold to another territory with the blocking of certain broadcast times, that the block times were complied with, so that the football events in question could not be broadcast.

1300. The effect of this regulation was to authorise national federations to prohibit the open signal broadcasting of games for the most of the week, and particularly during weekends, so that the Commission accordingly considered the regulation to be a restriction on the production and broadcasting football games, contrary to the then Article 81 EC.[472]

1301. Following this, in July 2000, UEFA agreed to alter the regulation and to limit the prohibition of the broadcast of football games to two and a half hours on

471. OJ L 63, 1991, p. 32.

472. The Commission noted that the Broadcasts Regulations did not have the objective of restricting the opportunities of broadcasting organisations to acquire broadcasting rights in respect of football matches, or to compete with each other in terms of advertising or subscriber revenue, but seek to promote the development of football and competitive diversity, and that there is accordingly no breach of Art. 81 (1) CE. However, it nevertheless acknowledged that the Regulations could, in certain circumstances, potentially lead to situations in which the broadcasting organisations would be unable to broadcast football games live whenever they wished.

Saturday or Sunday, during a national championship. In this way, a balance was created between the interests of the broadcasting organisations, who wished to maximise the rights they had paid for, and the interests of the clubs, throughout the entire game. The revised regulation made it possible not to reduce attendance at games and preserved a certain atmosphere in the stadiums, particularly in the interests of amateur sport. Accordingly, in the light of the limited nature of the prohibition,[473] the Commission closed the case in April 2001.[474,475]

15. Restriction of the Commercialization of Sporting Products

1302. Selective distribution agreements restrict the number of sellers and establish sales 'guidelines', and can accordingly have the effect of reducing competition between the products of a single manufacturer (intrabrand competition), exclude certain forms of distribution and encourage collusion between distributors and producers, to the detriment of consumers.

---

473. Blocked broadcast times vary considerably from one country to another, so that the combination of the various times only rarely result in circumstances in which the broadcasting organisations would be prevented from broadcasting games from a certain source and accordingly broadcasting rights from the said source. This being so, although broadcasting organisations cannot always broadcast a game live, they nevertheless have innumerable opportunities to do live broadcasts of other games in the same championship. In fact, only in very rare cases would a broadcasting organisation, which wished to broadcast the games of a certain country, or championship, be prevented from doing so, added to the fact that broadcasting organisations can broadcast football games live from other national or pan-European tournaments, which are played at different times. As a consequence and independently of the existence of the Broadcasts Regulations, broadcasting organisations may always acquire broadcasting rights in respect of relevant football matches.
474. Commission Decision 2001/478/EC, 19/04/ 2001, OJEC *L 171, 26/06/2001, pp. 12–28.*
475. Further to Patrick Massey:

> [t]he EU Commission acceptance of collective selling of broadcasting rights for football matches, albeit with some modifications in the case of the FAPL and the UEFA Champions League raises some important issues. Such arrangements involve a form of price-fixing, which is generally considered among the most egregious breaches of competition law and not to satisfy the requirements for exemption under Article 81(3). The exemption of such arrangements therefore raises some fundamental policy questions. The Commission correctly concluded in the UEFA Champions League case that collective selling of broadcasting rights was not essential for organisation of a sports league competition. The most commonly advanced argument for collective selling of broadcasting rights is that it promotes greater competitive balance within leagues which is desirable as it enhances the attractiveness of the league for consumers. Previous research provides only weak support for such claims at best. The evidence in the case of the FAPL suggests that competitive balance has declined over time and that it displays less competitive balance than other European football leagues where broadcast rights are sold by individual clubs. A third argument in favour of collective selling is that it promotes solidarity, mainly through the redistribution of income to lower levels of the sport. The degree of solidarity in the case of both the FAPL and the UEFA Champions League seems relatively limited. Given such evidence it may be time to question whether sports leagues should be given special treatment under competition law.

'Are Sports Cartels Different? An Analysis of EU Commission Decisions Concerning Collective Selling Agreements for Football Broadcasting Rights "trick Massey"', *World Competition.*

1303. In the case of sporting products, this restriction of competition can be justified, i.e., when distribution agreements operated so as to improve the economic efficiency of the sector, as certain agreements require the producer, or the distributor, to have a certain sales and after sales service, in the interests of consumers, who are accordingly better informed with regard to the technical characteristics of the product, which may, sometimes, result in the development of the market. Furthermore the distribution of products as top of the range of sporting equipment, i.e., sporting footwear, it may sometimes permit producers to establish and maintain very high sales prices, in order to be able to continue to invest in Research and Development.

1304. In both the *Dunlop* case[476] and the *Tretorn* case,[477] the Commission confirmed that an exclusive distribution system cannot justify the prevention of parallel imports.

1305. In the *Dunlop* case, 'Dunlop Slazenger International Ltd' breached no. 1 of the (then) Article 85 EC by providing, in respect of its commercial relations with its clients, for a general prohibition of the export of its products in order to protect its exclusive distribution network and to apply certain measures in order to ensure the efficacy of the prohibition in relation to some of the said products, i.e., tennis balls, squash balls, tennis rackets and golfing articles, such as (i) refusal to deliver; (ii) dissuasive pricing measures; (iii) marking and monitoring of exported products; (iv) purchase of exported products; and (v) discriminatory use of official references.

1306. In the *Tretorn* case, the CFI confirmed the Commission's decision[478] to the effect that the then Article 85, no. 1 EC cannot, in any circumstances, be declared to be inapplicable to an exclusive distribution agreement in respect of tennis balls, which does not, per se, involve any prohibition against the re-export of the contractual products, in circumstances in which the parties to the agreement are involved in a concerted practice with a view to the restriction of parallel imports destined for an unauthorised retailer.

1307. Also noteworthy are Federation rules, which require member athletes to wear certain clothing, i.e., officially authorised clothing, which can give rise to competition law problems in the relevant market for men and women's equipment for a certain sport. Such rules do create barriers to market entry by limiting or controlling production, markets or technical development in accordance with Article 81, no. 1, paragraph b) EC.

1308. Also in the area of the commercialisation of sports products, should be noted that the regulatory power of the federations has also been used, but no

476. Commission Decision, 18/03/1992, 92/261/CEE, OJ L 131, 16/05/1992, pp. 32–45.
477. SEEI Judgment, 11/12/1996, *Van Megen Sports Group BV –v- Commission*, T-49/95, E.C.R. 1996, p. II-1799.
478. Cases COMP/34590 and COMP/32948 – Decision of 21/12/1994, OJ L 378, 31/12/1994, pp. 45–53.

objective reason, to exclude or obstruct access to the market by certain economic operators. Not infrequently, they require the payment of disproportionate amounts in order to obtain safety certificates for the operator's products, which comply with the same requirements as the 'official' products.

1309. The federations argue that the equipment helps to improve the performance of the athlete and the athletes' image in relation to spectators and that the use of similar equipment (standardised) by all competitors ensures greater fairness and competitive justice, together with other arguments related to safety, which are frequently not objective and are arbitrary and discriminatory.

1310. The former Commission member responsible for competition, Mário MONTI, said, in reply to a parliamentary question regarding 'monopolistic practices with regard to the acquisition of yachting equipment in various Olympic classes',[479] that the imposition of '*strict requirements as to the equipment, which may be used*' may be justified, i.e., '*for safety reasons*' or in order '*to prevent equipment differences from having an improper effect on competition results*'. In such a case there will be no breach of the competition rules.

1311. It is known that in 1995, the FIBT, the International Bobsleigh and Tobogganing Federation, reserved publicity at competition locations and on athletes clothing, to itself, without the agreement of either the competition organisers or the athletes. It is also known that the Commission instructed the French and German Canoeing Federations to lodge a complaint against FISA, the International Rowing Federation. When they approached the Commission these federations alleged abuse of dominant position by FISA, because a rule had been approved at its 1997 Congress according to which the first metres of the boats and the arms of the athletes coats, i.e., the most important areas for publicity purposes, should bear the logos of the FISA sponsors. It is not known whether the complaint was ever lodged.[480]

1312. In another case,[481] the Commission also considered that the selection, by the International Karting Federation of a single supplier of tyres for the three karting championships organised by it, did not restrict competition between producers of tyres for karting, as not only was the selection process objective and fair, but the same did not give rise to a significant risk that the other producers would be excluded from the market.

16. Rules regarding Players' Agents

1313. We refer to the *Piau* Judgment,[482] in which the CFI rejected an appeal against the Commission's decision on the 15 April 2002, which rejected a complaint

479. Written question P-2548/99 asked by Theresa Zabel, of the PPE-DE, of the Commission on 16/12/1999, replied to on 11/01/2000, both published in OJ C 219 E, 01/08/2000, p. 180.
480. 'Professional Sport in the European Union: Regulation and Re-regulation', Ed. Andrew CAIGER and Simon Gardiner, TMC Asser Press, The Hague, 2000, p. 103.
481. Case COMP/E-2/38.316 – *Vega SpA v. CIK-FIA*, Decision of 19/03/2004.
482. ECJ Judgment 26/01/2005, *Piau*, T-193/02, E.C.R. 2005, p. II-209.

submitted by the appellant Laurent Piau regarding of the FIFA rule regarding players' agents.[483]

1314. According to the CFI, the activity of player's agent, the object of which is, according to the amended FIFA Regulation ' (…) to put a player and a club in contact with a view to the conclusion of an employment contract, or two clubs in contact with a view to the conclusion of a transfer contract, for remuneration'' is '(…) consequently an economic activity of the supply of services, which does not have sporting specificity as defined in the case-law (…)'[484] (Emphasis added).

1315. The CFI added that:

> [the] imposition by FIFA, of a licence, the possession of which is required in order to carry on the profession of player's agent creates a barrier to access to the carrying on of the economic activity and thus necessarily affects competitive interplay. To the said extent, the said licence may only be admitted if the conditions listed in [the then] no. 3 of article 81 EC are fully complied with[485] (Emphasis added).

1316. In this context, the CFI concluded that competition is not eliminated by the licence system, to the extent that it '(…) appears to lead more to a qualitative selection in compliance with the aim to professionalise the activity of player's agent, than to a quantitative restriction of access to the said activity (…)'.[486] Moreover, 'as the current conditions with regard to the exercise of the activity of players agent, are characterised by an almost total lack of national regulations and by the lack of a player's agents organisation', '(…) the Commission committed a manifest error when it considered that the restrictions arising from the obligatory character of the licence were likely to benefit from an exemption on the basis of [the then] article 81, no. 3 EC, but nevertheless correctly reserved the right to re-examine the regulation in question. The case made by L. Piau in this regard should therefore be rejected'.[487]

1317. The *Wouters* judgment was cited, by 'analogy',[488] but to compare differing factual circumstances:

---

483. The decision challenged had rejected the complaint of L. Piau on the grounds that there was no sufficient community interest to justify the continuation of the case, to the extent that the most important restrictive provisions complained against had been revoked and the subsisting restrictions could be the subject matter of an exemption pursuant to the provisions of no. 3 of Art. 81 EC, so that Art. 82 EC was not applicable to the specific case. An appeal was subsequently made to the ECJ (OJ C 155, 25/06/2005, p. 5) which was dismissed (OJ C 154, 01/07/2006, p. 3).
484. No. 73.
485. No. 101.
486. No. 103.
487. No. 104.
488. No. 74.

on the one hand, the regulation applicable to the activity of players was adopted by FIFA in the exercise of its own authority and not pursuant to any rule-making powers delegated to it by public authorities within the ambit of a mission of general interest in relation to the sporting activity.

1318. While the doctrine underlines the major importance of this ruling,[489] the Commission[490] refers that the ruling raises some doubts and leads to interrogations

489. Further to Martin Schimke:

> [b] eyond the case discussed, the judgment has fundamental significance for the control under cartel law of association regulations. According to previous legal precedents, association rules could be subject to control under cartel law if they also admit such sensible grounds as the protection of players as justification. Furthermore, the judgment finds that FIFA's activity is, in principle, subject to control under the EU cartel law. In all probability, the findings of this judgment also apply to other international associations in the sphere of professional sport.

'Germany', in *Players' agents World Wide: Legal Aspects*, Edited by R.C.R. Siekmann, R. Parrish, R. Branco Martins and J. W. Soek, p. 246. For Erika Szyszcaz, 'Piau raised the issue of complementarity of the Internal Market and competition rules- "Is sport special?", the regulation of sport ain the European Union', Edited by Barbara Bogusz, Adam Cygan and Erica Szyszczak, p. 27. According to Denis Waelbroeck and Pablo I. Colomo: '[i]n reality, the Piau case does not concern a case of "self-regulation" by already qualified professionals, but a situation where service recipients regulate the activities of service providers', p. 1749. Nicolas focus his analysis of the judgment on the *collective dominance concept. For this author, '[t] he Laurent Piau and Tetra Laval cases could arguably illustrate a change in this paradigm whereby the Community Courts support (i) a more cautious approach ex ante and (ii) a greater admissibility of ex post enforcement under Article 82 EC (now that it is clear that the substantive conditions for collective dominance are the same under 82 and the ECMR, an ex post approach seems easier, given the high standard of proof ex ante). (...) So, does this 'shifting paradigm' approach hold? A few reasons lead me to the conclusion that this approach is misleading. First, as a matter of judicial process, it is much doubtful that the SEEI and the ECJ coordinated themselves in order to reverse the current paradigm. Second, the facts at stake in Laurent Piau (where the SEEI reiterates Airtours) have nothing to do with a situation of oligopolistic coordination. On the contrary, the case is somewhat similar to Compagnie Maritime Belge where the behaviour of the firms was caught under 82 because they were participating to a liner conference through a formal agreement (in Laurent Piau, the clubs were held jointly dominant because of their involvement in an association of undertakings, the FIFA). Third, the SEEI recently recalled with strength its reluctance to the ex post control of anticompetitive parallel behaviour under Article 81 EC (in the Dresdner Bank case, the SEEI reiterated a classic principle pursuant to which conscious parallelism could not be brought under Article 81 EC, unless there was a proof of an agreement/concerted practice.). Finally, even if the statement in Laurent Piau was to be interpreted as an encouragement for the Commission to act under Article 82, there is much uncertainty as to how it would overcome its usual reluctance to condemn purely rational behaviour (sector inquiries, remedies?). To my view, thus, the Laurent Piau case does not change anything to the current state of the law regarding collective dominance under Article 82 EC. In contrast, the Tetra Laval case indisputably shows that the ECJ shares the recent SEEI's concerns with respect to the evidentiary quality of the Commission's merger decisions. The Commission has already shown more cautious in merger cases. In Sony/BMG, for instance, the Commission erred in trying to find a collective dominance outcome and dropped its charges in the course of the proceedings. The high standard of proof upheld in Tetra Laval may thus push the Commission towards even greater caution when examining a risk of future tacit oligopolistic coordination. Rather than a shifting paradigm, the EC Courts rulings illustrate the difficulty to enforce the collective dominance doctrine in oligopolistic settings: (i) under an ex post perspective, the concept seems only applicable where overt agreements between companies are identified, i.e. outside pure tacit collusion settings; (ii) under the ex ante perspective, it will only*

related to the legitimacy of the sport federations to regulate the activity of agents with no certification granted by a public authority.[491] [492] [493]

17. Abuse of Dominant Position in the Exercise of a Regulatory Power

1319. For many years, the *Fédération Internationale d'Automobile* (FIA) exercised its power as a sole world regulatory body in order to obtain commercial benefits and to strengthen its dominant position in the market.

1320. In 1999, the Commission raised objections with regard to the regulations via which FIA abused its powers via the imposition of unnecessary restrictions on

---

increase the - already heavy - onus of proof bearing on the Commission.' – Oligopoly Control after Laurent Piau and Tetra Laval – Shifting Paradigm or just the Same Old Song? António J. Robalo Cordeiro defends that (i) the SEEI makes confusion between two separate realities: on the one hand, FIFA's normative activity as the responsible entity in charge of the regulatory legislation on the exercise of a profession and on the other hand the clubs' conduct when, based on the said legislation, secure the players' services through their agents; (ii) In para. 117 of his Judgment, the SEEI took the view that there was no abuse of a dominant position by FIFA because the restrictions on competition which clearly resulted from the legislation at issue – the principle of the license imposed by FIFA and which restrains the exercise of the profession of agent and constitutes a restriction on competition – could be justified; (iii) This disputable from a legal point of view since the requirements that might justify a restriction on competition in the field of agreements between undertakings cannot be implemented to assess an abuse of a dominant position. The conclusion that an undertaking with significant economic powers has used those powers in order to create difficulties for other competitors to access the market must necessarily lead to condemning such conduct.

490. European Commission, Etude sur les agents Sportifs dans l'Union Européenne : Une étude réalisée pour la Commission européenne (Direction Générale Education et Culture) Novembre 2009.

491. António Robalo Cordeiro opposes this position of the SEEI, which he evaluates as follows: '*It is an approach, which appears to confuse two different realities: on the one hand, FIFA's normative role as the entity responsible for the legislation, which governs a profession, and, on the other hand, the conduct of clubs, when they the contract to obtain the services of players' agents, on the basis of the said legislation.*', *Desporto & Direito - Revista Jurídica do Desporto*, Year II-May/August 2005, pp. 412 and 413. On the other hand, although they consider that clubs appear in the market as corporations, Véronique Sélinsky and Fabrice Rizzo consider that there is no abuse, as the FIFA Regulations only imposes qualitative restrictions, which can be justified, 'Activité des agents de joueurs: la réglementation FIFA validée par le TPICE', *Revue Lamy de la Concurrence* no. 6, January/March 2006, pp. 119–122.

492. In the *Piau* Judgment, the CFI rejected the Commission's position. In the decision appealed against, the Commission has considered that the former Art. 82 EC was not applicable to the specific case on the grounds that FIFA does not operated in the market for the supply of advice to players. By considering that the service provider is not the one in the dominant position but the person who acquires the said services, i.e., the clubs, the CFI admitted the possibility that there could be an abuse of FIFA's collective dominant position, a position about which there is no unanimity among legal theorists.

493. According to the recent Study of Agents sponsored by the Commission, the primary lesson of the Piau case: subject to the assessment of its legitimacy (an issue which was not addressed in the Piau judgment), the existence of a private regulation imposing the possession of a licence for exercising the activity of sports agent can be compatible with the EUCL. Indeed, although constituting a distortion of free competition, such a regulation can be exempted from the prohibition provided by the EUCL when it pursues legitimate objectives and the restrictions it contains are proportionate relative to these objectives, (…).

promoters, track owners, a vehicle manufacturers and drivers, and with regard to certain provisions contained in commercial agreements with the broadcasting organisations.

1321. After long negotiations between FIA and the Commission, certain introductions were made to the said regulations, which ensured: (i) the circumscription the activity of FIA to that of a sports regulatory authority, without any commercial conflicts of interest; (ii) that its capacity as a regulatory body would not be used to obstruct or prevent new competitions, unless this was justified for reasons related to the safe, fair and harmonious organisation of motor sport; and (iii) the strengthening of the internal and external appeal procedures against FIA decisions.

1322. With a view to the prevention of any possible conflicts of interest, FIA sold all its rights in the World Formula One Championship and ceased therefore to have any influence with regard to the commercial exploitation of the Formula One Championship, which permits potential inter and intramural competition between Formula One and similar races and sporting series.

18. Ticketing

1323. Against the background of the 1990 World Football Championship,[494] the Commission decided that:

> [the] FIFA, FIGC, COL Italia, CIT SpA, Italia Tour SpA and 90 Tour Italia SpA breached the provisions of no. 1 of Article 85 of the EEC Treaty in the provisions of the contract dated the 26th of June 1987 on the 11th of Burberry 1988 made between COL Italia, CIT SpA and Italia Tour SpA, of the one part, and 90 Tour Italia SpA, of the other part, which provided for the exclusive worldwide supply to 90 Tour Italia SpA of tickets to the stadiums for the inclusion in tourism packages for the 1990 World Championship. These tickets were part of a general system for the distribution of tickets to the stadiums, which were prepared and produced by COL Italia in accordance with the instructions of FIGC FIFA, following approval by the latter, and which prohibited the sale of the tickets to be included in the said packages, which made it impossible other operators and travel agents to find sources other than 90 Tour Italia SpA.

1324. In the context of the 1998 World Football Championship in France, the Commission[495] concluded that the French organising committee had abused its dominant position by discriminating indirectly on the basis of nationality, as it had

494. See. Art. 1 of the Commission Decision of 27/10/1992, 92/521/CEE, (IV/33.384 and 33.378 – Distribution of tourist packages for the 1990 world football championship), *OJEC L 326, 12/11/1992, p. 31–42.*
495. See. Art. 1 of the Commission Decision of 20/07/1999, 2000/12/EC (Case IV/36.888 – 1998 World Football Championship) *OJEC L 5, 08/01/2000 pp. 55 -74:*

made the sale of tickets to consumers not resident in France subject to the indication of a postal address in France, to which the tickets would be posted.

1325. Subsequently, on the first occasion on which it considered the ticketing system in connection with some Olympic Games, the Commission considered that the agreements regarding the sale of tickets for the 2004 Athens Olympic Games, as notified by the Organising Committee (ATHOC), complied with CCL, even though they provided that the tickets could only be paid for via the Internet using a Visa credit card, to the extent that various sales channels were provided for residents in the European Economic Area (EEA), which, for the first time, could purchase tickets directly from ATHOC via the Internet, and also via any National Olympic Committee or from agents appointed by them. Consumer protection was accordingly ensured.[496]

1326. Finally, a reference to a case of abuse of dominant position. The Organising Committee of the 2006 FIFA World Football Championship, in the ambit of the offer of the conditional opportunity to purchase tickets over the Internet, between the 2 and 30 November 2005, required interested parties to make an advance payment, without any guarantee that they would receive tickets (this would only be revealed in February 2006). Those interested were accordingly deprived of their money for several months and would only be reimbursed if they did not receive tickets, in July 2006, after the deduction of a non-refundable charge.[497] This system was corrected, following complaints by individuals and intervention by the Commission.

1327. Given the Commission's policy of 'pursuing competition cases regarding ticket sales and the Commission's policy of lows on the financial calculations of other' same may take place securely allocation', some authors suggest[498] that: 'Local and international organisers, as well as independent ticket vendors and agents, would be well advised to self-assess their proposed sales arrangements and beware of potential challenges from competitors and fans.'

> The Comité français d'organisation de la Coupe du monde de football 1998 (SEEO) has infringed Article 82 of the EC Treaty and Article 54 of the EEA Agreement by applying discriminatory arrangements in 1996 and 1997 relating to the sale to the general public of entry tickets for World Cup finals matches. Those arrangements involved the imposition of unfair trading conditions on consumers outside France which resulted in a limitation of the market to the prejudice of those consumers in relation to the sale of 393200 tickets through Pass France 98 and 181000 tickets relating to the opening match, quarter and semi-finals, third and fourth-place play-off and the final.

496. See. Commission Press Conference, IP/03/738, Brussels, 23/05/2003.
497. See. written question E-4359/05 asked of the Commission on 22/11/2005 by MEPs Toine Manders and Graf Alexandre Lambsdorff, both of the ALDE.
498. Croce, Riccardo and Sampson, Stephen, 'Section 3: Sports', in *The European Antitrust Review 2010.*

19. Betting/Gambling

1328. Certain activities cannot be object of free competition due to its dangerous nature to the consumers. That has been the case of gambling. However the tendency is increasingly to open this sector to competition not because of the competition in itself (which was the case of sectors like transports, energy, and communications) but mainly as a regulation tool: competition can control the offer by avoiding illegal offer to the consumer with the inherent risks.[499,500]

a. Ladbroke Case

1329. The *Ladbroke* Judgment:[501] the English company Ladbroke contested the fact that it had been for many years prevented from broadcasting images of horse races organised in France by PMU, and considered that the refusal of PMU to granted a licence to exploit the images amounted to an abuse of dominant position. The European Commission did not agree with Ladbroke and considered that they were not in the same geographic market as PMU, and accordingly that the refusal did not amount to abuse. The CFI confirmed the Commission's decision and considered that the criterion of proximity consumers to a betting agency is one of the fundamental aspects in the determination of the relevant market.

b. Santa Casa Case

1330. On 8 September 2009, the ECJ rendered its judgment[502] in a case involving the betting operator Bwin and the Portuguese Football League versus the Portuguese monopolist Santa Casa da Misericórdia de Lisboa. Santa Casa claimed that Bwin's sponsorship agreement with the Portuguese Professional Football League and accompanying advertising activities were illegal due to Santa Casa's monopoly in providing on and offline lottery and betting services in Portugal.

1331. The ECJ has examined the restrictive nature of the freedom to provide services and possible justifications for a national monopoly for the operation of games

---

499. Vilotte, Jean-François, 'Jeux d'argent et de hazard et jeu de la concurrence: Faites vos jeux, rien ne va plus!', pp. 599–605.

500. A recent Council of Europe Convention stressed that the compliance with EU Law is still 'on the agenda': '*34. It should be noted that the Parties have a wide margin of discretion when making policies regarding sports betting, in accordance with applicable law. One consequence of this approach is that the convention aims to be compatible with all types of sports betting market organization (prohibition, monopoly, market open to licenses operators or free market). The reference to compliance with the "applicable law" draws attention to the fact that states must nevertheless abide by the rules in force and in particular the relevant applicable international and European Union law*' (Council of Europe Convention on the Manipulation of Sports Competitions Emphasis added), (CETS No. 215).

501. SEEI Judgment of 12.06.1997, *Tiercé Ladbroke SA –v- Commission*, T-561/93, E.C.R. 1993, p. II-923.

502. *Liga Portuguesa de Futebol Profissional and Baw International Ltd v. Departamento de Jogos da Santa Casa da Misericórdia de Lisboa*, Case C-42/07.

of chance via internet.[503] No analysis was made related to EUCL. However, the Advocate General Yves Bot's Conclusions:[504] have dedicated a brief attention to the topic:

> In my view, Community law does not aim to subject games of chance and gambling to the laws of the market. The establishment of a market which would be as open as possible was intended by the Member States as the basis of the European Economic Community because competition, if it is fair, generally ensures technological progress and improves the qualities of a service or product while ensuring a reduction in costs. It therefore benefits consumers because they can also benefit from products and services of better quality at a better price. In that way competition is a source of progress and development. (…) However, these advantages do not arise in the area of games of chance and gambling. Calling for tenders from service providers in that field, which would necessarily lead them to offer ever more attractive games in order to make bigger profits, does not seem to me a source of progress and development. Likewise I fail to see what progress there would be in making it easier for consumers to take part in national lotteries organised in each Member State and to bet on all the horse races or sporting events in the Union.

Additionally,[505] Yves Bot has pointed out that:

> The last justification [for the prohibition imposed on private operators such as Bwin to provide the service in Portugal] goes beyond market regulation issues. It examines the very nature of market participants and comes to the conclusion that further risks could come from the ambivalent role played by actors like Bwin. Being at the same time sponsors of teams involved in the competition and provider of bets on them, they could be tempted to abuse their position by manipulating competition outcomes for profit reasons.

20. The Creation of Closed/Breakaway Leagues

1332. The traditional European sports model is that there is one national and one international governing body – in most cases a federation – for each sport. This system is underpinned by rules that require teams and individuals not to join other

503. Further to Luca Rebeggiani, in some European countries *'(…) the state monopolies still hold despite of the European competition law and despite of the changing technical environment, especially the rising importance of the internet, which makes it more and more difficult to protect the monopoly. Although the court didn't declare state monopolies as incompatible with European competition law, it forced national legislations at least to be coherent and non-discriminatory'*, 'The Liga Portuguesa Decision of the European Court of Justice – an Economist's view', (…), p. 1.
504. Conclusions delivered on 14 Oct. 2008, paras 245 and 246.
505. 'The Liga Portuguesa Decision of the European Court of Justice – an Economist's view', p. 7.

organisations or to play in other competitions outside the scope of the 'official' governing body. Any breakaway league might lead to the expulsion of those involved from the 'official' governing body.

1333. On the formation of a new league (break-away leagues), the European Parliament[506] has stated that:

> [t]he Commission does not call the monopolistic role of the federations into question, as their international structure is recognised to be the most efficient way of organising sport. In the Mouscroun case the Commission pointed out that also the national geographical organisation of football in Europe is not called into question by community law. It is not clear in what way and to what extend the national associations have to be protected from the scope of the competition laws.

1334. Despite of the above, the rules 'official' governing body aimed to protect the exclusivity of its events and avoid the participation of its affiliates in an event organises by third entity, in the same sport, must be assessed in order to know whether the conditions imposed are proportionate or not. If not Article 101 TFUE would be infringed. Additionally, the monopoly regulatory control of the 'official' governing body must also have strong objective justifications in order not to be considered an abuse of a dominant position under Article 102 TFEU.[507]

21. The Establishment of Salary Caps

1335. Salary caps come in a variety of different forms but can be broadly divided into 'hard' caps and 'soft' caps. 'Hard' caps forbid teams from spending more than a fixed sum on their players; 'soft' caps on the other hand are more flexible and allow clubs to spend a proportion of their individual revenues (but no more) on player's salary. Under a 'soft' cap, the richer the club, the more it can spend on players.

1336. The traditional rationale for salary caps is that in their absence, the survival of the competition or its balance will be at risk because the same well-endowed teams always win. 'Hard' caps, by not allowing the wealthy to buy success, favour competitive balance. On the other hand, 'soft' caps reward efficiency (or the wealthy) who are able to spend more than their poorer rivals at the potential cost of competitive balance.

1337. EU competition law has potential applications to both sorts of caps provided that trade in players' services between Member States is affected. And that is

506. *European Parliament Report 'Professional Sport in the Internal Market'* (PE 358 378), point 4.2.6.
507. According to Ken Foster, '[a] *natural monopoly, sporting organizations have considerable power to crush alternative leagues or rival federations. They can expel clubs, license new entrants and ban players'*, (…) p. 272.

indeed the case. salary caps are inherently collusive – they could be seen as a restriction of Article 101 TFEU on the level of competition for players' services – they restrict the amount clubs can spend on wages thus restricting the supply and demand for players, and influencing the normal rules of the market to determine the salaries – since its object is clearly to restrict ability of club to freely recruit players and may lead to club profit maximisation at the expense of player wages being controlled.

1338. However it would make sense to justify salary caps as a tool to ensure economic viability of teams competing in the league, preserving competitive balance and encouraging youth development.[508,509] A situation of an economic crisis must also be taken into account.[510]

---

508. Further to Riccardo Croce and Stephen Sampson, salary caps (…) *have an inherent potential to breach EC competition rules. They may constitute an anti-competitive agreement or concerted practice between national or international sporting associations and either clubs or players' unions under article 81* [101] *(1) EC. Equally, there is a potential for breaches of article 82 EC, given that sporting associations can be dominant in the market for the competitions they control. Both 'hard' and 'soft' caps are horizontal agreements between competitors which restrict the amount of money that they spend on a key input, or raw material. Both amount to joint purchasing agreements which normally fall within Article 81* [101] *(1) and require justification under Article 81(3). Although the 'hard' cap is very restrictive in character, with no clubs being allowed to exceed the ceiling on expenditure, it is now clear that competition law is not so formalistic that the degree of restrictiveness determines that Article 81(1) applies without further analysis. Similarly, the fact that a 'soft' cap is in formal terms less restrictive than a 'hard' cap because it gives each club the ability to 'cut their coat according to their cloth' does not necessarily mean that it escapes Article 81(1). In both cases, what counts is the effect of the formal restriction on clubs' freedom taking into account all the relevant economic circumstances.*

509. In Gary RICE's opinion:

> [t] he rationale for the cap is to promote competitiveness and parity within the leagues and to control costs. However, if the cap is a percentage of a team's total turnover, the richer clubs will still be spending more than their poorer counterparts. Limiting the team's turnover so that it does not include investment by owners or major shareholders will help to some extent, but the bigger/more successful clubs will still have a larger pool of cash from sponsorship, ticket sales and merchandise than smaller clubs. The proposal comes up against EU competition law and must also not affect the free movement of players between EU Member States. Putting their thinking 'cap', www.beauchamps.ie,

510. *For the European Parliament:*

> Careful consideration should be given to the overall context in which the decision to employ a salary cap was taken. An environment of economic crisis in football would make salary caps more likely to survive legal challenge. In this environment, salary caps may be justified on the grounds that they maintain the economic viability of teams competing in the league and they preserve competitive balance between clubs.

That European institution makes another analysis that must be followed attentively:

> Arguably, salary caps are too economic in nature to fall within the scope of the sporting exception. Therefore salary caps may be subject to a rule of reason analysis and defined as inherent in the proper functioning of sport and thus excluded from the scope of Article 81 [101]. Alternatively, the salary caps may be considered suitable for an exemption under Article 81 [101] (3). Much depends on the nature of the cap (hard or soft), the existence of less restrictive means

22. The 'Player Release' Rule

1339.

When the White Paper was published, player release was identified as a major pending issue because the Charleroi case was then before the ECJ. In Charleroi, a Belgian football club, supported by the G14 group of leading European clubs, contested FIFA's Regulations for the Status and Transfer of Players after a member of its squad was injured playing in an international friendly match.[511] The regulations were challenged under the antitrust provisions of Articles 81(1) and 82 EC, as well as the free movement provisions (…). Under the Regulations, FIFA required clubs to release players selected for national team matches, and clubs were generally not entitled to financial compensation for players' injuries in these games. The clubs, rather than the national associations, were responsible for insuring players against injury sustained while on international duty. Moreover, clubs were afforded no say in the scheduling of international matches.

The Charleroi dispute was resolved out of court in 2008 when the parties agreed a memorandum of understanding. Under the terms of this compromise, G14 agreed to disband so that a wider club group could be formed. In return, FIFA and UEFA gave a number of commitments including to make payments every four years to clubs who provide players for the UEFA European Championships, and to limit the number of qualifying games for the tournament.[512]

---

of achieving the stated objectives and the definition of the market and whether caps have an appreciable affect on it. Some commentators have argued that the softer the cap the harder the law should intervene. If the objective of the cap is to safeguard competitive balance then a hard cap should be preferred as this imposes a flat ceiling on the spending of all clubs whilst a soft cap, which links spending to revenue, disproportionately affects the ability of small clubs to improve their position. This places them at a competitive disadvantage and at risk of closure. Competition law, which is designed to promote competition, could not sanction a system which curtails competition to this level. Consequently, a hard cap is more likely to pass a rule of reason analysis and be defined as falling outside the scope of Article 81 [101]. The fact that a hard cap is more restrictive and less appealing to the larger undertakings and high earners is not relevant under this analysis. So long as players have the rights of free movement to seek alternative employment, a hard cap should not amount to a breach of competition law. To achieve maximum legal certainty in this field the international players union (FIFPro) must give their consent to such a move although high earning players are less likely to consent to a hard cap. Consent could be provided through a collective bargaining agreement with the employers (clubs).–

European Parliament Report 'Professional Sport in the Internal Market' (PE 358 378).

511. Under the FIFA Regulations for the Status and Transfer of Players, it is compulsory for football clubs to release their players for matches of their national teams. Until 2008, these Regulations provided that clubs were responsible for insuring a player during such release period without any entitlement to financial compensation or dames in the event of the players injury. This led to a complaint submitted by the G14 to the Commission – in September 2005, the G-14 (through its Belgian member SA Sporting du Pays Charleroi) sued FIFA under the EU competition rules for restrictive player release rules after Charleroi lost the player Oulmers for eight months when he was injured. A reference for a preliminary ruling was made to the ECJ.
512. Croce, Riccardo and Sampson, Stephen, 'Section 3: Sports', *The European Antitrust Review 2010.*

1340. The following reasoning may help to conclude by an objective justification for this rule, under Article 101 (3) TFEU:

- Clubs are not restricted in their capacity to render the service of providing football games;
- The rule contributes to the improvement of goods: even if the market of national matches is different from the market of club matches and therefore the efficiencies are achieved on separate markets, the group of consumers (fans) affected by the restriction and benefiting from the gains is substantially on the same in both markets;
- The rule allows the fans a fair share of resulting benefits: the fans have the possibility to participate in international events like the FIFA World Cup without an appreciable disadvantage to club matches;
- The rule is indispensable: without the rule of compulsory release, particularly poor and small national associations would have to compete in their international matches without their top stars. Those national associations are not capable to pay compensation for releases players, which are normally top stars, making the compensation expensive. However, the performance of fair competitions demands that every team plays with its best players. The fans are interested in nothing else.

23. The Club Licensing Systems

1341.

> Many sports prescribe licensing systems for clubs and athletes. Robust licensing systems for professional clubs promote good governance in sport. However, they could also constitute restrictions of competition (…) and must be compatible with relevant EU provisions.[513]

1342. The Commission, in 2007[514] already stated in principle in favour of such practices:

> [t]he Commission acknowledges the usefulness of robust licensing systems for professional clubs at European and national levels as a tool for promoting good governance in sport. Licensing systems generally aim to ensure that all clubs respect the same basic rules on financial management and transparency, but could also include provisions regarding discrimination, violence, protection of minors and training.

---

513. Andrej Rogulsky and Samuli Miettinen, 'The EU and sport: the implementation of the White Paper on Sport and future prospects', International Journal of Sport Policy, http://www.informaworld.com/smpp/title~content=t790627367, p. 250.
514. The White Paper on Sport, p. 17.

1343. Focused in the integrity of sport, the Commission, in 2011[515] opined that:

> [i]n team sports, club licensing systems offer a valuable tool to ensure the integrity of competitions. They are also an effective way of promoting good governance and financial stability. The Commission welcomes the adoption of measures aimed at enhancing financial fair play in European football while recalling that such measures have to respect Internal Market and competition rules.

1344. The Committee of Regions[516]*'[f]eels that licensing systems are the responsibility of sporting organizations, provided that such systems are compatible with competition law and internal market provisions'* and the European Economic and Social Committee[517] '(...) agrees that there should be stable licensing systems for professional clubs in the EU, ensuring transparency of their operations.'

1345. The President of the European Parliament[518] made an enthusiastic speech on the topic, specifically in the framework of football, addressed to the UEFA President*: '(...) I congratulate you on UEFA's licensing system, and on your new proposals for financial fair play. These are good policies for European football and I fully support all the initiatives of UEFA and President Platini which are crucial for football in Europe'*. This reasoning was not surprising bearing I mind the support given to UEFA club licensing system by the European Parliament some years earlier, stressing that the system aims at ensuring a level playing-field between clubs and contributing to their financial stability, as well as financial transparency and proper management'. [519]

1346. However, in another occasion[520] the European Parliament went deeper in the legal analysis and invoked the following:

> Licensing is in competition law terms a barrier to entry the market, because of its compulsory character. A licensing-system can only be accepted to the extent that the regulations fulfil the criteria laid down in 81 (3). Entry-barriers, however, are typical for the sports industry. The right to take part is depended on membership and membership is in most cases depended on the possession of

515. Communication from the Commission to the European Parliament, the Council, the European Economic and Social Committee and the Committee of the Regions – Developing the European Dimension in Sport, {SEC(2011) 66 final}{SEC(2011) 67 final}{SEC(2011) 68 final}, point 4.5. – 'Integrity of sporting competitions'.
516. Opinion of the Committee of the Regions on the White Paper on Sport, OJEU C 105, 25.04.2008, pp. 40–45.
517. Opinion of the European Economic and Social Committee on the White paper on sport, *COM(2007) 391 final,* (2008/C 151/12), C 151/36, OJEU 17.6.2008, p. 4.27.
518. Media Release, 05.11.2009, No. 108, UEFA President Michel Platini meets new European Parliament President Jerzy Buzek- Positive meeting in Brussels advances case for specificity of sport.
519. European Parliament resolution of 29 Mar. 2007 on the future of professional football in Europe (2006/2130 (INI)), p. 20.
520. *European Parliament Report 'Professional Sport in the Internal Market' (PE 358 378),* point. 4.2.7.

a license. It is self evident that these kind of rules derive from a need inherent in the organization of competitions. Competitions cannot be free to all. The justification for these 'entry barriers' in the sport industry lies in the unique pyramid sports structure and the required competitive balance among competitors. Because of the (quasi) monopolist power of the league a failure to obtain a licence implicates failure to participate in competitions. A football association may never prevent or impede (new) clubs from taking part in competitions, unless justified on grounds related to the safe, fair or orderly conduct of football. The challenge of these licenses can, in our opinion, only be accepted in case the following criteria are met; non-discriminatory; this means the rules must be equally valid; national association must deal with these issues in a similar matter; objectivity; proportionality; The rules must go no further than is reasonably necessary to protect the legitimate interest of the association; subsidiarity; there are no less restrictive means to pursue the legitimate objectives and, transparency.

24. Territorial Licensing of Sports Content

1347. In the joined cases of *Football Association Premier League v QC Lesire and Karen Murphy v. Media Protection Services Limited,*[521] the ECJ ruled that competition rules prohibited contractual provisions (and indeed national legislation) that prevent viewers in one EU Member State from imposing satellite decoder devices from another Member State in order to watch the services of a foreign broadcaster. Whilst the FAPM could still grant rights on a territorial basis, the relevant provisions in the FAPL's broadcasting licence agreements against the supply of decoding services outside the contracted territory (in the case Greece) were artificially making that territorial exclusivity 'absolute' and therefore infringed Article 101 TFEU. In fact, satellite broadcasting licence agreements may not (by force of Article 101 TFEU) impose restrictions requiring broadcasters to prevent customers using their satellite decoder cards in territories other than those for which the licence is granted.

1348. According to the Advocate General Kokott, the fact that rights-holders of programmes broadcasted via satellite prevent third parties not bound by an agreement to such rights, to watch and show them in other Member States constitutes a restriction to the use of services coming from other EU Member States, particularly the free access to television programmes. This impairment of freedom to provide services is '*particularly intensive*' (§175), as the rights in question not only render the exercise of freedom to provide services more difficult, but also have the effect of partitioning the internal market into separate national markets, neither having into account the specific objective of protecting intellectual property nor the fact that there are time windows which are closed to live broadcasting of certain (Premier League) matches.

521. Judgment of 4 Oct. 2011, *FAPL and Others v. QC Leisure and Others* (C-403/08) and *Karen Murphy v. Media Protection Services Ltd* (C-429/08),ECR 2011, p. I.9083.

1349. In what concerns competition rules, Kokott argued that a contractual obligation linked to a broadcasting licence by which the television operator must prevent his decoder cards from being used outside the territory at issue has the same effect as the agreements which prohibit or limit parallel exports requiring the broadcaster to prevent its satellite decoder cards from being used outside the licensed territory has the same effect as agreements to prevent or restrict parallel exports. She argued further that such a contractual obligation seeks to exclude all competition between television operators through the reciprocal closing of the licensed areas. Therefore, a license with absolute territorial protection is incompatible with the internal market.

1350. As to the competition law aspects of the judgment,[522] one can summarise the reasoning of the CJEU as follows:

- Exclusive territorial licensing agreements are not anti-competitive 'in principle'; the question is whether in a given case the manner in which the exclusive right conferred by that contract is exercised is subject to arrangements the object or effect of which is to prevent or restrict the distribution of the works or to distort competition on the relevant market, in the light of the specific characteristics of that market.
- However, an exclusive territorial licensing agreement will have an anti-competitive object if it contributes to the portioning of the internal market and makes interstate market penetration more difficult – in other words, the exclusive licence restrictions controlling the use by the television viewers of decoder cards by territory are intended to eliminate competition between broadcasters on a territorial basis, affecting the viewers who wish to watch the broadcasts outside the Member State for which the license is granted, an anticompetitive object in contravention of article 101 TFEU.
- The agreements in this case did not qualify for exemption under Article 101 (3) TFEU.[523]

1351. Further to this judgment the Commission opened an investigation into Pay TV services in order to '(…) carefully examine if the principles set out by the Court of Justice should also be applied to other typed of audiovisual content such as the popular films licensed by the US studios.[524]'

522. See Ptbworth, Stuart, '*The Murphy Judgment: Not Quie Full Time for Football Broadcasting Rights*', The Competition Law Review, July 2002, p. 1.
523. See, in particular, paras 138–144 of the judgment.
524. See Joaquín Almunia 'Statement on opening of investigation into Pay TV services', Brussles, 13 Jan. 2014.

25. List of Events of Major Importance

1352. In three separate cases,[525] UEFA and FIFA brought actions before the General Court of the EU relating to the way its broadcasting rights can be marketed in Belgium and the UK. UEFA challenged the Commission's decision to approve the list of the European Championship finals tournament by the UK government; while FIFA challenged the listing of the entire sixty-four matches of the FIFA World Cup by both the Belgian and the UK governments.

1353. The General Court upheld the legality of the Commission's decisions. As to competition law, I will highlight the paragraphs quoted below.

1354. Regarding the FIFA case in which the alleged violation of EUCL was at stake,[526] the Court decided as follows:

> 165. FIFA submits that the contested decision does not contain any analysis relating to the distortion of competition caused by the inclusion of all World Cup matches in the list of events of major importance for United Kingdom society. That distortion consists in a reduction in the number of broadcasters competing to obtain rights to broadcast the World Cup in the United Kingdom, which affects FIFA's earnings as organizer of that event (…)
> (…)
> 169. FIFA adds that the grant of special rights in question to the BBC and ITV, together with their agreement to acquire jointly the rights to broadcast the World Cup, is a measure which is contrary to article 81(1) EC, thus infringing Article 86 (1) EC.
> (…)
> 180. (…) with the authorization of the Office of Communications, only certain broadcasters in the first category, such as the BBC and ITV, will ultimately broadcast the World Cup in the United Kingdom, since their competitors are interested only in exclusive broadcasting and will therefore not submit offers to acquire the relevant rights (…) is not tantamount to a grant of special or exclusive rights to them within the meaning of Article 86 (1) EC. Even assuming that the measures at hand would entail such a result, this would be because of the importance of exclusivity as part of the business model implemented by those broadcasters operating pay television channels and would not in any way stem from the United Kingdom legislation, since the terms of that legislation are applicable without distinction to broadcasters in both categories. It follows that the United Kingdom measures as such do not affect the ability of operators of pay television channels to pursue their activities on

525. Cases T-385/07, *FIFA v. Commission*; T – 55/08, *UEFA v. Commission* and T-68/08, *FIFA v. Commission*, judgments of 17 Feb. 2010.
526. Case T-68/08.

largely equivalent terms as those enjoyed by the BBC or ITV with regard to the acquisition of broadcast rights for the World Cup.

1355. As to the UEFA's case,[527] it is interesting to note the Court's rationale of convergence between the EU free movement rules and EUCL:

> 163. The first complaint concerns the consequences resulting from the fact that, in light of the importance of the exclusivity of broadcasting rights for the EURO matches for those broadcasters coming within the second category established by the United Kingdom legislation, the latter will not be interested in acquiring non-exclusive rights. In UEFA's submission, that leads to restrictions on competition on a number of markets, including the market for acquisition of such rights, the advertising market and the market for broadcasting sporting events by pay television channels, due to the reduction in the number of broadcasters active on those markets. UEFA also complaints that the Commission failed to define those markets and failed to explain its assessment of those restrictions-
>
> 164. It should be observed, in that regard, that the consequences in question result indirectly from the restrictions on freedom to provide services introduced by the United Kingdom measures. Yet, as was held in respect of the fifth plea, restrictions on freedom to provide services resulting from the inclusion of the EURO matches in the list of events of major importance for United Kingdom society are justified by overriding reasons in the public interest and are neither inappropriate nor disproportionate. The effects on the number of potential competitors, which are presented as being an unavoidable consequence of those obstacles to the freedom to provide services, cannot, therefore, be considered to be contrary to the Treaty articles on competition. In those circumstances, the Commission dis not have to conduct a more in-depth analysis of those consequences than that which it did.

26. Sport Organizations as Entities Fulfilling 'Services of General Economic Interest' under Article 106 TFEU

a. General Overview

1356. Article 106(2) TFUE may allow derogation from the prohibitions contained in Article 101(1) TFUE when this is necessary for the achievement of a purpose of general economic interest (public service) that has been entrusted by the State to one undertaking.

1357. The 'service of general economic interest' is an EU law concept that more or less corresponds to the notion of 'public services' that exist in some Member

527. Case T-55/08.

States.[528] The Commission defines this term[529] as referring to market services which Member States subject to specific public service obligations by virtue of general interest criteria. This expression applies to activities that affect and are essential to a large amount of the population both of individual member States and the Community as a whole.

1358. There is no doubt that sport organisations perform a service for the public within a given geographic area, and to ensure that, irrespective of the profitability, all persons enjoy equal access to sport at affordable prices. They are an instrument of public policy, mainly those entrusted by national law or other acts of public authority.[530]

1359. Important documents stress this 'general economic interest' of the sport organisations. Amsterdam Declaration on Sport and Nice Declaration are two relevant examples.

1360. The Amsterdam Declaration on Sport recognises the sports associations' role as social partners:

> The Conference emphasises the social significance of sport, in particular its role in forging identity and bringing people together. The Conference therefore calls on the bodies of the European Union to listen to sports associations when important questions affecting sport are at issue. In this connection, special consideration should be given to the particular characteristics of amateur sport. (Emphasis added)

1361. In its turn, the Nice Declaration[531] states as follows:

> 8. It [The European Council] notes that sport federations have a central role in ensuring the essential solidarity between the various levels of sporting practice, from recreational to the top-level sport, which co-exist there; they provide the possibility of access to sports for the public at large, human and financial support for amateur sports, promotion of equal access to every level of supporting activity for men and women alike, youth training, health protection and measures to combat doping, acts of violence and racist or xenophobic occurrences.

---

528. See Faull & Nikpay, *The EC Law of Competition*, Oxford, 1999, pp. 312–320.
529. See *Commission Green Paper on Services of General Interest*, COM (200039 270 final and *Implementing the Community Lisbon Programs: social services of general interest in the European Union*, COM (2006) 177 final. Art. 36 of the European Charter of Fundamental rights provides that *'[t]the Union recognizes and respects access to services of general economic interest as provided for in national laws and practices, in accordance with the Treaty establishing the European Community, in order to promote the social and territorial cohesion of the Union.'*
530. This is, for instance, the case of Portuguese, Spanish and French Sport Federations.
531. Presidency Conclusions, Nice, (2000), *Declaration on the Specific Characteristics of Sport and its Social Function in Europe, of Which Account Should be Taken in Implementing Common Policies*, Nice European Council Meeting, (12/00).

9. These social functions entail special responsibilities for federations and provide the basis for the recognition of their competence in organising competitions.
10. While taking account of developments in the world of sport, federations must continue to be the key feature of a form of organisation providing a guarantee of sporting cohesion and participatory democracy. (Emphasis added)

Vast specialized doctrine emphasizes the 'general interest' of sport organizations, particular sport federations, namely Bernard Geneste;[532] Charles-Etienne Gudin and Arnaud Parcellier;[533] Frédéric Jolit;[534] Gérad Auneau and Patrick Jacq;[535] Pietro Paulo Mennea;[536] Richard Parrish's[537] and Alberto Palomar Olmeda.[538]

---

532. *'(…) The organization of the sport competitions, the Adoption of decisions strictly linked to the functioning and financing of the representative organs of each sport discipline, the disciplinary power, the rules concerning the delivery of champions' trophies, etc, are part of the mission of general interest committed to the sport federation, and constitute the implementation of public power prerogatives'* (Unauthorized translation; emphasis added), 'Les fédérations sportives face au droit de la concurrence', in *Revue des affaires Européennes*, 9éme Année, 1999/2, Mys & Breesch, éditeurs, p. 150.
533. In their words, *'The right of organising sport competitions is historically inseparable of the pursuit by the federations of a mission of general interest'* (Our unauthorized translation; emphasis added), 'Lórganisation et l'exploitation des activités sportives et le droit communautaire', in *Revue des affaires Européennes, 2001-2002/3 (L'Europe et le sport)*, Bruxelles, Mys & Breesch éditeurs-publishers, p. 372–373.
534. He underlines that *'(…) the positive effects of sport, including the professional one, or training and, generely speaking, education, the "social function" (social cohesion, exemplariness …), the cultural aspects are sufficient indicators that call for the recognition of a specificity, of one certain general interest* (Our unauthorised translation; emphasis added), La compatibilité des aides d'Etat aux clubs sportifs professionnels au regard du droit communautaire', in *Sport et Union européenne*, Bruxelles, Éditions de l'Université de Bruxelles, p. 133.
535. They have the same approach: *'(…) it is widely recognized that the sport movement has (…) a mission of general interest. Should the derogation in Article [86] 2 of the Treaty apply to the sport enterprises, this would allow them to better manage their contradictions'*. (Our unauthorised translation; emphasis added), 'L'application du Droit de la Concurrence aux pratiques sportives (1re partie)', in *Revue de Jurisprudence Commerciale*-Janvier 1995, 39. Année, N. 1, p. 376.
536. *This former Italian Member of the European Parliament, stresses both the sporting and the economic general interest pursuit by the sport federations:* 'Sport federations represent one fundamental structure for the pursuit of the sport activity: these entities not only take in charge the regulation and promotion of sport but are also entities that really provide services and organize major sport events*' (Our unauthorized translation),* Diritto Sportivo Europeo: scritti su alcune problematiche di diritto sportivo europeo, Italia, Delta 3 edizioni, p. 36.
537. *In his view, '[w]*ith further political pressure, the "sporting" justification argument may develop into a 'public interest' justification', Sports law and policy in the European Union, *Manchester, Manchester University Press, 2003, p. 217.*
538. He remarks that *'[a] s long as the sport federations have a role of vertebra of the social activity of sport's structure one can say that it does not exist a radical incompatibility between the sport federation's organizational monopoly and competition law'* (Our unauthorized translation; emphasis added), 'La aplicación al âmbito del deporte de las reglas del Derecho de la competência', in *El modelo europeo del deporte*, Ed. Bosch, Madrid, 2002, p. 240.

b. The *MOTOE* Case

1362. The *MOTOE* case concerned a dispute between the Greek automobile and touring club (ELPA) and an independent Greek motorcycling association (MOTOE). ELPA has a dual role: (i) it is responsible in Greece for the organization of motor sports competitions, and for that purpose created a National Motor-Racing Committee (ETHEAM); (ii) it also participates in the authorisation by a public body of motorcycling events which, under the Greek law, can be issued only with ELPA's consent. When MOTOE sought to organise a number of events in 2000, that consent was refused and consequently the authorisation required too. MOTOE challenged the refusal.

1363. In his Opinion, the Advocate General Kokott[539] stated that:

> the maintenance of effective competition and the ensuring of transparency require a clear separation between the entity that participates in the authorisation by a public body of motorcycling events and, where appropriate, monitors them, on the one hand, and the undertakings that organise and market such events, on the other. That principle of separation is breached where, in circumstances such as those in this case, one and the same entity, namely ELPA and the ETHEAM committee set up by it, not only participates in the public body's authorisation of motorcycling events and is entrusted with monitoring their safety, but is also itself active – in competition with other, independent service providers – in organising and marketing such events.

1364. As to the ECJ ruling, we consider the following paragraphs the most important ones:

> 25. As regards the possible effect of the exercise of public powers on the classification of a legal person such as ELPA as an undertaking for the purposes of Community competition law, it must be noted (…)that the fact that, for the exercise of part of its activities, an entity is vested with public powers does not, in itself, prevent it from being classified as an undertaking for the purposes of Community competition law in respect of the remainder of its economic activities (…)The classification as an activity falling within the exercise of public powers or as an economic activity must be carried out separately for each activity exercised by a given entity.
> (…)
> 27. As regards the effect that the fact that ELPA does not seek to make a profit may have on that classification, it should be noted that (…) the Court stated that the fact that the offer of goods or services is made without profit motive does not prevent the entity which carries out those operations on the market from being considered an undertaking, since that offer exists in competition with that of other operators which do seek to make a profit.
> (…)

539. Opinion delivered on 6 Mar. 2008, *MOTOE v. Elliniko Dimosio*, Case C-49/07, ECR 2008, p. I-4863, para. 102.

28. That is the case of activities engaged in by a legal person such as ELPA. The fact that MOTOE, the applicant in the main proceedings, is itself a non-profit-making association has, from that point of view, no effect on the classification as an undertaking of a legal person such as ELPA. First, it is not inconceivable that, in Greece, there exist, in addition to the associations whose activities consist in organising and commercially exploiting motorcycling events without seeking to make a profit, associations which are engaged in that activity and do seek to make a profit and which are thus in competition with ELPA. Second, non-profit-making associations which offer goods or services on a given market may find themselves in competition with one another. The success or economic survival of such associations depends ultimately on their being able to impose, on the relevant market, their services to the detriment of those offered by the other operators.

(…)

49. On the other hand, a Member State will be in breach of the prohibitions laid down by those two provisions if the undertaking in question, merely by exercising the special or exclusive rights conferred upon it, is led to abuse its dominant position or where such rights are liable to create a situation in which that undertaking is led to commit such abuses (…) . In this respect, it is not necessary that any abuse should actually occur (…) The fact that ELPA's position was a virtual monopoly in the market for organising motorcycle events, it was in breach of Articles 82 and 86(1) of the EC Treaty. Its activities were not automatically abusive (could be justified by objective reasons, such as safety concerns), but the very legal position of ELPA (no recourse for those who were refused consent – such as MOTOE in this case) could give rise to abuse. [540]

27. State Aids

1365. Various Member States of the EU, i.e., those which have a high level of public intervention in the area of sport, provide for legal mechanisms for the grant of public aid to sport, which, in some cases, amounts to a constitutional obligation.[541]

540. For *Samuli MIETTINEN*, '[t]*he MOTOE case involved the combination of regulatory powers and organization of competitions with economic activity in the regulated market. In this respect, the facts are not unlike those related to some similar issues considered in the F1/FIA investigation.*', (…) respectively p, 137, footnote 2, and p. 141.

541. In favour of 'subsidised' sport because of the associated public service aspect, See. Alexandre Husting, 'Quelle reconnaissance pour l''exception' ou pour la 'spécificité' sportive dans la nouvelle Constitution Européenne'?, in *Revue du Marche Commun et de l'Union Européenne*, September 2004, no. 481, p. 519.

1366. However, much public sector support of sport in general and professional sport in particular can be subsumed within the concept of state aid,[542] and is thus likely to give rise to the application of Article 87 EC. When such aid in the area of sport, is incompatible with the common market, it is usually referred to as 'administrative doping'

1367. The following various examples of such aid:

- Aid for the acquisition, construction or improvement of sporting infrastructures, premises and facilities,[543] whether or not in the context of major sporting events,[544] company headquarters or commercial leisure areas.[545]
- Grant by the state of subsidies and other benefits to clubs.[546]

---

542. The undertakings receive revenue, which they would otherwise not receive, or avoid expenses, which they would otherwise have to bear, unlike the other undertakings (competitors). The conditions of the undertakings, which are aided, are improved, not as a consequence of market forces but for exogenous reasons.
543. Canor Quigley and Anthony Collins maintain that state aid to certain sporting infrastructures and events must be considered in accordance with the state aid rules, but stress however that the financing of sports infrastructures, such as a stadium, will not necessarily be deemed to be state aid, when no undertaking benefits from the said finance, or when there are no significant effects on intracommunity trade. The authors also argue that when state aided infrastructures are used to host international sporting events of a commercial nature there will be reason to oppose the application of Art. 83, no. 3, para. d), EC, once it is recognised that the state aid is necessary in order to implement the project, See 'EC State Aid Law and Policy', Oxford-Portland Oregon, 2003, p. 94. Leigh Hancher, Tom Ottervanger and Piet Jan Slot consider that aid to theatres and sports infrastructures ('*cultural aid*') does not fall within the definition of state aid. In another example, they state that if the grant of a stadium to enable the Welsh national rugby team to play a game can attract great tourist income for the capital city Cardiff in just one weekend, this economic benefit should be considered to be too indirect to be considered state aid, *EC State Aids*, Chancery Law Publishing, London, 1999, p. 64 and Rose M. D'Sa, 'European Community Law on State Aid', London, Sweet & Maxwell 1998, p. 148.
544. An inevitable consequence of aid for infrastructures for the organisation of major sporting events is that, after the event, the club, which received the aid, will have the benefit of an infrastructure with increased, capacity, comfort and safety, which may increase public attendance, and thus giving rise to increased revenue.
545. The proper authorities frequently authorise clubs to convert parts of the stadium into spaces for commercial and entertainment activities, so that many stadiums become shopping centres, complementary to the sporting event and contain fitness centres, bars, restaurants, shops, and conference centres, spaces for banquets or concerts, which generate income for the clubs.
546. The national legislation of some Member states provides for state funded support for professional clubs (Belgium, Austria, United Kingdom, Holland, Finland, and Sweden). For example, the German state granted financial aid to the German clubs, when the Kirch company (which was responsible for the television broadcasts) became insolvent. However, the Greek government refused to assist football clubs at the time of the insolvency of *Slpha Digital Synthesis*, which owned the broadcasting rights in respect of the matches of nineteen of the sixteen teams in the Greek first division. We shall list some cases of aid granted to clubs in various EU Member states, with a view to the promotion of the economic, financial and social well-being of the city: *Sixfields Stadium*, the stadium of *Northampton Town* (United Kingdom) was leased for a 150-year term; Kirklees Council (United Kingdom) took out a bank loan of from GBP 3–7 million to ensure the long-term financial stability of second division *Huddersfield Town's* stadium; *Coventry City* (United Kingdom) received permission to construct a New stadium costing GBP 113 million, of which 21 million was paid by the local authority; Chesterfield Borough Council (United Kingdom) made a 183 thousand pound donation to a football club in order to pay to the creditors; in 2002 Real Madrid (Spain)

- Tax regimes – grant by the state of selective benefits, normally via legislation,[547] or of Social Security privileges[548] which are more favourable to certain categories of sporting operators.
- Public sector support for competitive aspects of sport and matches to the detriment of training and recreation.
- Donation/loan or sale of land from the construction of infrastructures.
- Access to the use of public infrastructures.[549]
- Finance in order to bear clubs' travel costs.
- Holdings in the share capital of public limited sports companies.
- State support for infrastructures located around or within the perimeter of stadiums, in order to improve the safety and commercial and sporting access aspects (property and commercial operations).

---

signed an agreement with the President of the Madrid Autonomous Region pursuant to which the planning classification of 120 hectares of land on which the club's sports complex was constructed, was altered, thus increasing the value thereof; Atlético de Bilbao (Spain) received 6 million euros from local authorities in order to solve its financial problems; *Unión Deportiva Melilla* (Spain) received EUR 1.1 million from local authorities in order to reduce its deficit; in 2003,*Vitesse Arnhem* (Holland), received approximately EUR 24 million from the local authority a few hours prior to the close of registrations for the championship, without which the club would not have had the financial resources necessary in order to obtain the necessary licensing in order to be able to compete; in 2002, AZ Alkmaar (Holland) received credit facilities from the local authority.

547. Various tax legislations establish a specific tax regime for one or more sports operators, pursuant to which a supplemental advantage is granted to the sports sector (this is the selective aspect of the aid). Even when the tax regime is only more favourable to players, it is nevertheless state aid granted to undertakings – Commission Decision 94/374 of 02/02/1994 states specifically that measures, which benefit not only workers as such, but also benefit the undertakings on which they depend, amount to state aid. The following are some examples: in the Czech Republic (1992 legislation) and in Luxembourg (1986 legislation), donations made to sports organisations are tax exempt; in Denmark, there has been a VAT exemption for sports organisations since 1996, there has also been a limited exemption in the United Kingdom since 1994; in Finland, non-profit sports organisations have a tax exemption in respect of the income obtained from their main activity and may, exceptionally, also obtain and exemption with regard to commercial activities; in Germany, non-profit sports organisations have certain tax exemptions, i.e., in terms of taxes on trade, property and inheritance (donations are also deductible), André-Noël Chaker, *Study on national sports legislation in Europe*, Council of Europe Publishing, 1999, pp. 121–123. The following are two further examples: Borussia Dortmund, a German club, which is listed on the stock exchange, was authorised to have recourse to legislation, which grants tax incentives to entities, which employ particularly poor workers, or workers, who work during holidays or at night, on the grounds that many games are played at night and during holidays. This enabled the German club to save approximately EUR 1.5 million per annum; in the United Kingdom, legislation has been passed, which reduced the rate payable by clubs on revenue from a redistribution pool, for the benefit of English clubs, many of whom are involved in international competitions.

548. Social security legislation, which permits clubs to save on their payroll bill and places them in an advantageous position in relation to clubs in other countries, to the extent that it enables them to hire more and better human resources and according to have an improved probability of victories.

549. According to the *SFEI* judgment – an ECJ judgment of 03/07/03, consolidated proceedings C-83/01 P, C-93/01 P and C-94/01 P, E.C.R. 2003, p. I-6993 – the provision of equipment (technical or logistic equipment) amounts to state aid, to the extent that the remuneration received in consideration is less than what would be received in normal market conditions.

- State Support recompensed by institutional advertising on the sporting material used by players or on static advertising within stadiums.[550]
- The use of public funds to cover the financial deficits of private sporting entities.[551]
- Sale or leasing of land to clubs at less than the market price.[552]
- Making of grants for the fight against doping.
- Payment by local authorities of specialist technical staff working for clubs (e.g., sports monitors).[553]
- Financing of professional sport from gaming revenues.
- Grant of loans on particularly favourable terms.

a. State Aid to Sport as Viewed by the European Parliament and the European Commission

1368. The first community institution, which devoted attention to and expressed concern about the phenomenon of state aid, was the European Parliament in 1997. It drew attention in a Resolution,[554] to the fact that the equilibrium between clubs and the very nature of the European competitions *'(…) may be adversely affected by distortions of competition connected with existing disparities as regards subsidies and obligations to which the clubs are subject, with particular regard to their obligation to balance their books and to their social security and tax burdens'.*

1369. The Commission was consequently requested, within the ambit of the work of a task force, to examine:

> whether the various schemes for state aid to professional clubs applied in the Member States and the current disparities relating to social security and tax burdens have an effect on the fairness of European competitions and whether the transparency of the financial situation of the various professional clubs in the Community should be guaranteed.

---

550. The Public Accounts Court of the Basque Country audited the aid granted by the Diputacíon Foral de Vizcaya to Atlético de Bilbau in 2002, which consisted of a four-year loan of EUR 6 million in Exchange for the placing of institutional advertising of Vizcaya on the team's tracksuits and the display of the Vizcaya logo as club press conferences, which permitted the club to reduce its deficit substantially. The said audit, which was considered by the Economy Commission of the Basque Parliament to be a *'priority',* also considered both a loan of EUR 9 million to Real Sociedad to finance the works to extend the Zubieta XXI sports complex and a loan of EUR 450,000 for the club to use the Euskadi emblem on club shirts in UEFA competitions, 'Subvenciones bajo sospecha en el Athletic', www.elpais.es, accessed on 29 Nov. 2005.
551. Legislation was approved in Italy, in 1996, to grant financial aid to football clubs, on the grounds of the effect of the *Bosman* judgment on the financial circumstances of sports companies.
552. '*For the use of a piece of land, which is said to have a market price of over DM 100 million, the city of Munich asked Bayern Munich FC for a mere rent of DM6, 079.50 per annum*', Klaus Vieweg, 'Professional Sport in the European Union: Regulation and Re-regulation', Ed. Andrew Caiger and Simon Gardiner, TMC Asser Press, The Hague, 2000, p. 99.
553. André-Noël Chaker, 'Study on national sports legislation in Europe', Council of Europe Publishing, 1999, p. 9.
554. 'Resolution on the role of the European Union in the area of sport', OJ C *200, 30/06/1997, p. 252, para. R.*

1370. The following can be concluded from the various interventions of the European Commission with regard to this matter:

Aid which is incompatible with community law:

(i) Tax pardons
In a decision dated the 22nd of September 1993, the European Commission considered certain tax pardons granted to PMU in relation to the contributions of the employers, who constructed the hippodrome, to be illegal state aid and incompatible with EUCL - for while it is true that horse racing is organised and operated at national racecourses, it is no less true that the bets on these races are organised internationally so that competition and exchanges in the market will increase (PMU traded abroad). France was accordingly required to cancel the aid and to require PMU to recover the aid granted.
(ii) Legislative measures regarding tax and accounting matters, which permit football clubs to set-off their losses against future revenue in respect of a period which is longer than is normally permitted;[555]
The most relevant case happened in Spain, related to state aid to certain professional sport clubs.[556]
(iii) Public sector support for sports infrastructures, when these are intended to be used for the carrying on of economic activities such as sports competitions and concerts, if these compete at community level, i.e., competitions or concerts, which could be held at other sports infrastructures within the EU.[557]

555. As a consequence of the Commission's intervention, the Italian state was required, in 2005, to repeal the legislation, which had been passed at the end of 2002, with regard to urgent provisions in connection with compliance with community and tax collection requirements and accounting procedures, which enabled sports clubs to set-off their recorded past losses against future profits for a longer period than was permitted by the provisions in force, via the reduction of the amortisation rates permitted over 10 years. However, the possible extension of the period during which it is possible to deduct losses amounted to an economic advantage to Italian football clubs. By permitting sports clubs to choose between two alternative taxation systems, the Italian state permitted these taxpayers to opt for the method, which was best suited to them and accordingly agreed to waive part of its tax revenue. The law was altered in 2004, when the measure in question ceased to amount to aid, See. Commission Decision 2006/895/EC, 22/06/2005, regarding the measures planned by Italy in favour of professional sports clubs (the 'salva calcio' decree), OJ L 353, 13/12/2006, p. 16. Alberto Santa Maria disagrees with the Commission's position, and argues, on the basis of the preceding case-law and what had been stated by the former Competition Commissioner Mário Monti regarding the Real Madrid case, to the effect that the measures in question did not amount to state aid, to the extent that they did not involve a transfer of resources of from the state to the clubs, or involve an additional burden for the state. According to this author, the grant of the recapitalisation of clubs does increase their competitiveness, as it does not provide them with additional resources, or enable them to obtain credit, to such an extend that they would become more competitive in the market, 'Professional Sport and Competition', VI Conference on Antitrust Between EC Law and National Law, 13–14 May 2004, Treviso, Ed. by Enrico Adriano Raffaell, Bruyllant Bruxelles and Giuffré Editore, Milan, 2005, p. 285.
556. State aid S.A. 29769 (2013/C) (ex 2013/NN) – Spain, Brussels, 18.12.2013, C (2013) & 436 final.
557. See. Gauthier Ervyn, 'Le respect du droit européen des aides d'Etat dans le sport', available at http://www.droitdusport.be/ViewArticle.php?ref=TOPA00172, accessed on 2 Apr. 2007.

(iv) Concession of guaranteed in favour of clubs on bank loans

That was the case of the loan guarantee of the regional government of Valencia granted to three Valencia professional football clubs – Valencia CF, Hercules CF and Elche CF.[558]

The rationale of the decision was the following:

- The measures granted by the Instituto Valenciano de Finanzas (IVF) consist of State resources and are imputable to Spain;
- The State measures are selective as they are for the benefit of single marketing of one sector (their football clubs benefited from capital injections);
- The advantage for a club playing in the national first league may furthermore have an effect on competition and trade between Member States. These clubs compete for presence in European competitions and are active on the markets for merchandising and TV rights. Broadcasting rights, merchandising and sponsoring are sources of revenue for which first league clubs compete with other clubs within and outside their home country. The more money clubs have available for top players the more success they may have in sport competitions, which promises more revenue from the activities mentioned. Furthermore, the ownership structure of this clubs is international;
- Therefore, the Commission considers at this stage that financial State support ultimately providing an advantage to three professional Valencian football clubs constitutes State aid in the meaning of Article 107 (1) TFEU.[559]

Aid compatible with community law:

(i) Aid in respect of the construction of sports infrastructures within the context of a public service mission,[560] i.e. infrastructures to which there is free and open access to all interested users (the non-selective nature of the aid);[561]

558. State Aid SA. 36387 (2013/C) (ex 2013/NN) – Spain. Alleged aid in favour of three Valencia football clubs.

559. See paras 35–38.

560. In a written question to the Commission on 20/07/2005, regarding a project for the construction of three new football stadiums to be implemented via the formation of a closed-end investment company (SICAF) for investment in infrastructures, asked by MEP Säid El Khadraoui The MEP asked the Commission about the possible application in this case of the criteria formulated by the ECJ in the *Altmark* judgment, and asked '*the lengths to which Member state may go in the grant of aid in the financing of stadiums without breaching the existing competition rules*'. Commencing by stating that the financing of an infrastructure can comply with the 4 conditions listed in the said judgment, the Commission stated that an case-by-case analysis of an infrastructure such as a football stadium, would always focus on the use of the infrastructure, i.e., the extent to which the infrastructure had a public service function or, whether, on the contrary, it serves the economic interests of professional football clubs. In a case of aid for infrastructures in Holland – N 555/04-Holanda, *Martregelen tem behoeve van Sportclubs, Basketball Omniworld Almere en Volleyball Omniworld Almere* – the European Commission stated that aid, which complies with the following criteria are not state aid: (i) the construction of the infrastructure complies with a public tender procedure; (ii) the infrastructure is public, or, if it is private, the management receives no overpayment; (iii) the infrastructures include facilities and equipment for different users, which are let for a market rent.

561. *Ibid.*

A recent example dates back 2013 and is related to the Flemish government plan to subsidize, by way of an aid scheme, the renovation and the construction of multifunctional football stadiums located in Flanders on the region of Brussels Capital.[562]

'The Commission has (...) decided not to raise objection to the measure on the ground that the aid scheme (...) is compatible with (...) Article 107 (3) of the TFEU.[563]'. That European institution considered that 'the public financing of the construction/ renovation of football stadiums under measure therefore pursues public policy objectives, is necessary and proportionate, and does not affect trade and competition between Member States to an extent contrary to the common interest, according to Article 107 (3) (c) TFEU.[564]'

(ii) Aid, which complies with the public sector contracting rules or, granted in the form of a concession, or, if this is impossible, the involvement of the state represented by an independent expert and ensuring that the concessionary pays the appropriate amount;[565]

(iii) Financing of sports training centres for young players taking into consideration the educational and integration objectives pursued and the slight influence on competition between the major clubs;[566]

---

562. State aid SA. 37109 (2013/N) – Belgium Football Stadiums in Flanders, Brussels, 20.11.2013, C (2013) 7889 final.
563. Paragraph 43.
564. Paragraph 42.
565. *Ibid.*
566. A 1999 French law, which authorised grant aid to professional sports clubs for purposes of *'public interest'* was considered by the Commission in a Commission Decision of 25/04/2001 regarding public grant aid to professional sports clubs (118/00). The provisions in question authorised French local authorities to make grants to professional sports clubs, which had training centres for young people, which had been approved by the local authorities, equal to an annual amount of EUR 2.3 million per beneficiary club (football, basketball, rugby and volleyball). The Commission considered that aid in respect of the training of young people was excluded from the application of the community state aid rules, provided that the net training costs are not exceeded and there is a clear separation between the training budget and the budget for the development of the club's economic activity (in order to avoid crossed grant aid with spill-over into professional club's economic activities). The French authorities justified the grant aid on the grounds of the need to *'improve the ethical standards of the sector'* in relation to the training of young sportsmen and women and the combination of school education with sports training and promotion of citizenship, of *'public interest'* (integration in neighbourhoods, proper insertion in school and employment and the prevention of violence). The Commission stressed that the measures in question are within the area of education and can therefore be likened to education and initial training within the meaning of EC Regulation no. 68/2001, regarding the application of Arts 87 and 88 of the EC Treaty and to aid for training and accordingly out with the scope of CCL. We consider that the Commission's position, in which it accepted the *'public interest'* argument, while at the same time limiting the amount of aid allocated to the said public interest, is debatable. We consider further that the fact that various French clubs have earned a lot of money from the international transfer of players trained in their training centres, which places them in an advantageous position in relation to other clubs within the EU, with which they compete in football competitions, and have to bear the cost of the construction and maintenance of their training centres without any aid, is far from irrelevant.

(iv) Regional aid;[567]

(v) Aid to the local projects.

In the case of a construction of a swimming pool in the German city of Dorsten – Case N 258/2000 - *Leisure pool Dorsten* – state resources were used for part of the reconstruction and for all of the modernisation of the swimming pool. The Commission considered that no exceptional factor was at issue and that the aid would not attract visitors from outside the local area (the estimated radius of the significant area was 50 km and the nearest border, with Holland, was far away), i.e., intra-community trade would not be affected. Nevertheless, the European Commission did not lose the opportunity to stress that its analysis would certainly be different in a case involving leisure parks advertised both nationally and internationally.

In another case, which involved a cable railway and ski lift – N 676/2002, Itália Impianti juniviari Valle d'Austa - the European Commission also considered this to be a case of merely local state aid: in this case the infrastructures in respect of which aid was granted were located in an area in which there were few infrastructures of that type and were not capable of attracting visitors, who could use the infrastructures in other member states, as an alternative, because of the small size of the infrastructures, the

567. Decision no. 325/89, of the 2 Jun. 1998, *United Kingdom/Northern Ireland Events Company*, arose following a notice given to the Commission by the United Kingdom Authorities, regarding scheme involving the grant of aid by the Northern Ireland Environment Department. The aid took the form of public sponsorship of events (including horse races and golf tournaments), direct subsidies and bank guarantees. The criterion used in order to select the aid beneficiaries (the event organisers, which were both EU and non-EU) would be the impact of the proposed event on the international image of Northern Ireland, the nature of the event and the extent of the direct and indirect economic and social benefits. The amount of aid to be granted would be EUR 87.6 million for the 1999/2001 period, which was considered to be the minimum amount necessary and would never exceed 50% of the allowable costs (the costs directly associated with the creation and holding of the event). In the light of the nature of the various types of event organisers, which included companies with commercial activities, which traded on international markets, the Commission considered that this was a case of State aid, which might affect intracommunity trade (even though the geographic area where the measure was to be applied was Northern Ireland), plus the fact that the costs of the organisation of the events would amount to a normal routine expense of the State. Nevertheless, the Commission took the difficult situation in Northern Ireland into consideration (30 years of conflict and violence, which have prejudiced the image of the region and have discouraged potential participants, organisers and sponsors, which explains why very few cultural and sporting events of real international quality have taken place during the said period), and decided that a high level of state aid able to change the stereotyped ideas regarding the high level of the risks associated with the organisation of events in the region, was justified. The Commission did no more than rely on its Communication 'Guidelines regarding state for regional purposes' – OJ C 74, 10/03/1998 – which classed Northern Ireland as a region with a special status until 2001, which was exactly the date when the proposed measures would end, which thus rendered it a region, which was eligible for regional aid pursuant to the provisions of the then Art. 92, no. 3, para. a) EC. It is further noted that the budget was considered to be '*relatively modest*' and therefore not likely to distort competition or be contrary to the public interest.

lack of accommodation and the limitations in respect of the ski services available.

(vi) Aid granted in consideration of services provided to the state always at market rates

In 2004 (Case N 555/04, cit), the Commission considered that the contracts for the supply of services, which the Almere local authority in Holland wished to make with the local basketball and volleyball club Omniwordl Almere, were not contrary to Article 87, no. 1 EC, to the extent that the contracts provided that the clubs were required to support education; to stimulate a sporting environment; to support leisure sporting activities and to be involved in the 'marketing of the city'.

(vii) Aid granted to clubs as SMEs in accordance with Regulation (EEC) 70/2001, of the 12th of January for investment in sports infrastructures and job creation;

(viii) Aid to clubs in difficulties;

In a recent case,[568] '[t]*he Commission has receive a considerable number of letters from Dutch citizens alleging that municipalities in the Netherlands award State aid to professional football clubs facing financial difficulties (…) the Commission nourishes[ed] serious doubts whether the aid measures in question can be considered compatible with the internal market pursuant to Article 107 (3) (c) in the light of Article 165 TFEU and the Community Guidelines on State aid rescuing and restructuring firms in difficulty.*'

We consider the following paragraphs very important:

'72. As regards the derogation in Article 107 (3) (c) in favour of aid to facilitate the development of certain economic activities, where such aid does not adversely affect trading conditions to an extent contrary to the common interest, the Dutch activities have argued that this derogation could be applied if the Commission, contrary to the opinion of the Dutch authorities, should find that one of the measures in question constitutes state aid.

73. In its assessment of the notion of 'development of economic activities' in the sports sector, the Commission takes due account of Article 165 (1) and the last incident of Article 165 (2) TFEU which provide that the Union shall contribute to the promotion of European sporting issues, while taking into account of the specific nature of sport, its structures based on voluntary activities and its social and educational function.'

568. State aid SA. 33584 (2013/C) (ex 2011/UN) – The Netherlands municipal aid to the professional Dutch football clubs Vitesse, NEC, Willem II, MVV, PSV and FC Den Bosch in 2008–2011, Brussels, 06.03.2013, C (2'13) 152 final.

(ix) Specific tax regimes, which do not negatively affect the efficacy of tax collection.[569]

A good example of this sort of aids dates back to 2013, and is related to a tax benefit scheme for the Hungarian sport sector. ' *Within specific Hungarian context, state aid to the sport sector could provide a remedy for a well-defined market failure, i.e. situations where individual market investors do not invest even though this would be efficient from a wider economic perspective, e.g., due to the positive spill-over effects. Many of the sport infrastructure facilities in Hungary are in bad situations, not meeting the minimum safety standards and there is no prospect by the private sector to undertake such investments on commercial terms (…) State aid for the sport sector shall also be viewed as a tool to achieve equity objectives: the general public will be an important beneficiary of the measure as ensured by the commitments required by Hungary from the aid recipients (…) and sport has important social and educational function as acknowledged by Article 165 TFEU. Support for sport infrastructures, which potentially entrenches the quality of sport services, which in term can help to ensure people's access to local sport structures (…) the Commission has accordingly decided that the aid measure 'supporting the Hungarian sport sector via tax benefit scheme is compatible with Article 107 (3) (c) TFEU.'*[570]

b. A Prospective Approach

1371. We shall now make some brief comments regarding other possible cases of state aid to sport and indicate possible legal responses thereto.

1372. We commence by stating that it is important not to overlook the fact that one of the grounds for the application of Article 107 TFEU is that intra-community trade is affected. Consequently, the probability that this requirement will be complied with is much greater whenever the aid in question is granted to clubs, which take part in transnational competitions,[571] while it is likely that intracommunity trade will not be affected in other cases.[572]

---

569. On 01.08.2005, the current competition Commissioner Nelie Kroes, in a reply to written question P-2491/05 – asked by Alfredo Antoniozzi, stated, as she had already stated in her reply to question E-1422/05 – asked by Borghezio – that in the light of the information available to her, it could not be concluded that an agreement between SS Lazio and the Italian tax authorities, amounted to state aid, to the extent that the partial cancellation of a tax debt only amounts to state aid when the exceptions envisaged by CL do not apply, i.e., measures, which are likely to be included in a tax regime or tax benefits granted to companies in difficulties, which facilitate tax collection efficacy or preserve the debtors taxpaying capacity.

570. Not. All: SA. 31722, paras 89 and 101.

571. See. Alexandre Husting: '*Le problème du financement public des clubs professionnels se poserait avec une acuité particulière dans le cas d'une rencontre en Coupe d'Europe. Un club ne bénéficiant d'aucune aide publique pourrait deposer une plainte contre un club européen fortement subsidié*', '*Le financement des clubs sportifs professionnels par les collectivités territoriales: aspects*

1373. We also consider that in cases of aid granted by local authorities, the task of checking for the possible existence of state aid involves the evaluation of the local interest of the aid, so that it is appropriate to forecast any increase in the number of people taking part in sport, or who are spectators at local sports competitions, as a consequence of the local aid granted. We also consider that it is relevant to predict the direct and indirect impacts of state aid on local trade and industry, i.e., the following impacts: (i) the media exposure of the towns and cities in question, particularly those, which are not well known; (ii) social insertion and cohesion; (iii) local cultural activity and the promotion of local social activities via sport; (iv) the contribution of sport to town and country planning. Our basic position is that it is of fundamental importance always to ascertain the advantages or benefits to local authorities, which arise from the grant of aid. If there are any, we consider that it is difficult to consider such aid as a state aid in accordance with Article 107 TFEU.

1374. The following are some other cases of state aid to sport, which we consider to be compatible with community law: (i) aid to sports infrastructures the purpose of which is to protect the safety of sports men and women and spectators - e.g., renovation of stadiums; (ii) aid to the promotion of the cultural aspects of sport pursuant to Article 107(3)e) EC - it is noted in this regard that the economic development of specific sectors, whether in crisis or not, as already been invoked as grounds for state aid, specifically in sectors such as the cinema, computer or aeronautical construction industry; (iii) the application of Article 107(3), paragraph d) EC, taking into consideration the cultural impact of sport and its contribution to European society and its cultural heritage; (iv) application of Article 107(3), paragraph e), a residual provision; (v) aid of less than EUR 100,000 on the basis of the *de minimis* rule; (vi) financial aid granted to clubs in difficulties;[573] (vii) aid to small clubs within the ambit of Commission Regulation (EC) no. 70/2001 of 12 January 2001, with regard to the application of Articles 107 and 108 TFEU of the EC Treaty to state aid to small and medium-size enterprises.[574]

1375. Another possibility is the creation of a block exemption Regulation in this area in accordance with and for the purposes of Article 1, no. 1 of 'Council Regulation (EC) no. 994/98, of 07/05/1998, regarding the application of Articles 92 [87] and 93 [88] of the Treaty which created the EEC, to certain categories of horizontal state aid',[575] a tool, which enables the Commission to decide that a category of state aid is no longer subject to the giving of prior notice thereof to the Commission, to the extent that it is automatically considered to be compatible with the common

---

stratégiques et juridiques Sport de haut niveau: sport professionnel en regions', Bordeaux, 2001, Maison des Sciences de l'Homme d'Aquitaine, p. 199.

572. See. Frédéric Jolit, '*Il semble logique de conclure qu'une aide à un club ne disputant pas de compétition européenne n'affecte pas les échanges intra-communautaires et n'est dès lors pas incompatible avec le traité*', 'La compatibilité des aides d'Etat aux clubs sportifs professionnels au regard du droit communautaire', *Sport et Union européenne*, Ed. Jean-Michel de Waele and Alexandre Husting, Éditions de l'Université Libre de Bruxelles, p. 131.

573. OJ C 2888, 1999, p. 2.

574. OJ L 10, 13/1/2001.

575. OJ L 142, 14/5/1998.

market, provided that it complies with certain criteria. Such a regulation would possibly provide a more solid legal basis and avoid unnecessary legal uncertainty.

1376. This final note draws attention to the fact that the recently adopted General Block Exemption Regulation expressly applies to 'tourist activities', which include NACE 92 (recreational, cultural and sporting) activities.

c. The General Block Exemption Regulation (GBER)

1377. In 2014 the Commission, in the framework of a state aid modernisation process, has adopted a revised GBER for state aid, giving to the EU Member States increased flexibility to grant state aid without prior notification and approval by the Commission as from 1 July 2014, provided that certain conditions are met. The GBER sets out the categories if aid and the conditions under which aid measures can benefit from such an exemption.[576]

1378. The adoption of an amended Enabling Regulation enabled the Commission to exempt more categories of aid from the notification requirement. Among seven new categories, the Commission included in Article 55 the 'aid for sport and multifunctional recreational infrastructures'. The full text of this provision reads:

1. Aid for sport and multifunctional recreational infrastructures shall be compatible with the internal market within the meaning of Article 107 (2) of the Treaty and shall be exempted from the notification requirement of Article 108 (3) of the Treaty provided that the conditions laid down in this article and in Chapter I are fulfilled.
2. Sport infrastructure shall not be used exclusively by a single professional sport user. Use of the sport infrastructure by other professional or non-professional sport users shall annually account for at least 20% of time capacity. If the infrastructures is used by several users simultaneously, corresponding fractions of time capacity usage shall be calculated.
3. Multifunctional recreational infrastructure shall consist of recreational facilities with a multi-functional character offering, in particular, cultural and recreational services with the exception of leisure parks and hotel facilities.
4. Access to the sport or multifunctional recreational infrastructures shall be open to several users and be granted on a transparent and non-discriminatory basis. Undertakings which have financed at least 30% of the investment costs of the infrastructure may be granted preferential access under more favourable conditions, provided those conditions are made publicly available.
5. If sport infrastructure is used by professional sport clubs, Member States shall ensure that the pricing conditions for its use are made publicly available.

576. See MEMO/14/369, Brussels, 21 May 2014.

6. any concession or other entrustment to a third party to construct, upgrade and/or operate the sport or multifunctional recreational infrastructure shall be assigned on a open, transparent and non-discriminatory basis, having due regard to the applicable procurement rules.
7. The aid may take the form of :
   (a) investment aid, including aid for the construction or upgrade of sport and multifunctional recreational infrastructure;
   (b) operating aid for sport infrastructure;
8. For investment aid for sport and multifunctional recreational infrastructure the eligible costs shall be the investment costs in tangible and intangible assets.
9. For operating aid for sport infrastructure the eligible costs shall be the operating costs of the provision of services by the infrastructure. Those operating costs include costs such as personnel costs, materials, contracted services, communications, energy, maintenance, rent, administration, etc., but exclude depreciation charges and the costs financing if these have been covered by investment aid.
10. For investment aid for sport and multifunctional recreational infrastructure, the aid amount shall not exceed the difference between the eligible costs and the operating profit of the investment. The operating profit shall be deducted from the eligible costs ex ante, on the basis of reasonable projections, or through a claw-back mechanism.
11. For operating aid for sport infrastructure, the aid amount shall not exceed the operating losses over the relevant period. This shall be ensured ex ante, on the basis of reasonable projections, or through a claw-back mechanism.
12. For aid not exceeding EUR 1 million, the maximum amount of aid may be set, alternatively to the method referred to in paragraphs 10 and 11, at 80% of eligible costs.

28. Mergers

a. General overview

1379. EU decisions have already been taken with regard to mergers of companies involved in sport, i.e., in the area of television,[577] sporting

577. On 13 Nov. 2001, the European Commission authorised the French subscriber television group Canal+ SA and RTL to acquire joint control of the French sports rights agency, Groupe Jean-Claude Darmon SA (GJCD). In the ambit of this operation, Canal+ and RTL formed their own sports rights agencies Sport+ (France) and UFA Sports GmbH (Germany) within the ambit of their joint company GJCD. The Commission considered that the creation of this joint company only involved insignificant and limited overlaps in the market in the acquisition and resale of television broadcasting rights in respect of sports events, which were not such as to strengthen the position of Canal+ in the downstream subscriber television market, or the presence of RTL in Europe, in addition to the fact that KirchMedia and the European Broadcasting Union (EBU) are still solid competitors – See. European Commission Press Conference, IP/01/1579. In 2002, the merger between Fogecable and Via Digital (the two Spanish pay-TV platforms) was notified to the Commission,

goods[578] and in the market known as health and

which accepted the request of the Spanish competition authorities to refer the consideration of the case to them. The transaction was approved by the Spanish authorities, subject to conditions, many of which were related to the acquisition of premium content. Subsequently, the Commission declared in Decision 2004/311/EC, of 2 Apr. 2003, that the merger was compatible with the common market and with the working of the EEA Agreement (case COMP/M.2876 — *Newscorp/ Telepiù*, OJEC L 110, 16/04/2004 pp. 73–125. At issue was the merger project notified to the Commission, pursuant to Art. 4 of the then Council Regulation (EEC) no. 4064/89 of 21 Dec. 1989, regarding the control of mergers, OJ L 257, de 21/9/1990, pursuant to which News Corporation Limited, Australia ('Newscorp') would acquire exclusive control, as per Art. 3 of the said regulation, of the Italian pay-TV channels 'Telepiù' and 'Stream', via a company formed especially for that purpose and a share transfer. The Commission concluded that, subject to compliance by Newscorp with the commitments made, that the merger proposed would neither create nor increase a dominant position, in the market for the offer of pay-TV services, in the markets for the purchase of exclusive rights to major audience films, of football events, which take place every year, in which national teams take part and other sports events, or in the television channels market, which was likely to significantly effect effective competition in the common market or in a substantial part of the said market. In 2006, the Commission approved the acquisition of SLEC Holdings Ltd., the Formula 1 holding company, by CVC Capital Partners Group, although the approval was subject to the sale of the Spanish subsidiary *Dorna,* the promoter of the Motorcycling Championship MotoGP. The following two merger cases are also noteworthy: Case IV/M 110, 10/9/1991 (sport event broadcasting rights) – the Commission was notified of an agreement between ESPN Inc and Canal+, which created a joint company CV 1; Case IV/M. 779, 7/10/1996 (sale of sport and film channels): notice of a merger in which Bertelsmann Aktiengesellschafl Audiofrna SA intended to create a new joint company CLT-UFA; Case IV/M. 1327, 3/12/1998: notification of a merger via which Canal+ and Bank America International Investment Corporation would acquire joint control of NC Nemericable; Case IV/36.237, 3/3/1999: notification of the creation of a new entity (SPS) by TF1, France Télévision; Case IV/36.539, 15/9/1999 (supply of cinema and sports channels): notification of the creation of a joint company, British Interactive Broadcasting Ltd by BSkyB Ltd, BT Holding Limited, Midland Banc plc and Mat Sushita Electric Europe, Ltd; Case COMP/JV.37, 21/3/2001 (sport event broadcasting rights): notification of a merger via which British Sky Broadcasting acquires 34% of Kirch Pay TV Gmbtt & Co; Case COMP/JV.57, 30/4/2002 (acquisition of sports broadcasting rights): notification of a merger project via which TF1 would acquire joint control of TPS together with M6 and the Suez Group; Case COMP/M.3169, 1/7/2003. (sports centres sector): notification of a merger between Bridgeport Capital Limited Group and Schroeder Venture Limited to acquire joint control of Holmes Place.

578. The Competition DG approved an agreement signed on 13 Oct. 2005, involving EUR 485 million, notified pursuant to the national merger legislations of six countries: Austria, Germany, Italy, Poland, Spain and the United Kingdom. The acquisition by Amer's (a Finnish winter sports group) of Salomon (a French sports equipment group, a division of the Adidas-Salomon ski company), without prejudice to essential undertakings being required in order to avoid the restriction of competition in the cross-border ski markets, particularly in Austria, Germany and France – See. www .globalcompetitionreview.com, 28 Oct. 2005 and European Commission Press Conference – IP/0 5/1267. In another case, the Commission authorised the purchase of the US company Reebok International Ltd by its German competitor Adidas-Salomon AG. Notwithstanding the fact that it acknowledged that the operation created horizontal overlaps in the sports footwear market in Europe, the Commission took the position that the different positioning of the companies in terms of price and clientele is not such as to significantly obstruct competition, in the sports footwear segments and in the price range in which the two companies are strongest (mid-price tennis and basketball shoes and trainers), there being no indicators that the merger is the consequence of a price agreement. Adidas is a 'professional and technical brand' while Reebok is oriented to a young and female clientele, in the leisure area and is less well known than Adidas and Nike, the world leader (See. *Bulletin Quotidien Europe* no. 9118, 27/01/2006, p. 15 and European Press Conference – IP/ 06/70, 24/01/2006).

fitness,[579] although it is not an area in which there is a frequent community intervention with regard to the application of EUCL to sport.

1380. As this topic is not comprised in the subject matter of this thesis, we shall not consider the matter further.

b. Case *Lagardère/Sportfive*[580]

1381. On 5 December 2006, the Commission received a notification of a proposed concentration pursuant to Article 4 of Council Regulation (EC) No 139/2004 (Merger Regulation.) by which Lagardère SCA (Lagardère., France) will acquire within the meaning of Article 3(1)(b) of the Merger Regulation control of Sportfive Group SAS (Sportfive., France) by way of acquisition of shares.

1382. On 18 January 2007, the Commission authorized Lagardère's acquisition of Sportfive, a French trader of sports broadcasting rights. Sportfive act as an intermediary between broadcasting rights holders and content users. It is particularly active in trading sports broadcasting rights, notably football, but also provides marketing services for events, especially sports events. Lagardère's main activities are media, broadcasting, and high technologies, and holds a non-controlling stake in Canl + France. The Commission found that the transaction raised no competitive concerns in the respective markets for sports broadcasting rights, TB broadcasting, and sports marketing, finding that there were no horizontal overlaps in the activities of the Parties in any of these markets.

1383. Thus, The Commission has decided not to oppose the notified operation and to declare it compatible with the common market and with the EEA Agreement. This decision is adopted in application of Article 6(1)(b) of Council Regulation (EC) No 139/2004.

c. Case *CVC/SLEC*

1384. In 31 January 2006, the Commission received a notification of a proposed merger pursuant to Article 4 of the Council Regulation No 139/2004 by which the investment fund CVC Capital Partners Group Sarl (CVC, Luxembourg) acquire within the meaning of Article 3(1)(b) of the Council Regulation (EC) No 139/2004 sole control of the whole of the undertaking Speed Investments Limited by means of purchase of shares. Through its control of Speed, CVC will gain control over

579. The European Commission approved the acquisition of Holmes Place, which operates forty-nine health and fitness clubs in the United Kingdom, by the Bridgepoint Capital Group investment fund (the group, which controls Virgin Active, which are in the same business as Holmes Place – twelve health clubs in the United Kingdom and seventy-six in South Africa) and Schroeder Ventures Limited. Although the Commission detected a significant overlap in London between Virgin Active and Holmes Place, the Commission noted that the combined market share did not exceed 20% of the number of privately owned health and fitness facilities with comparable infrastructures in the same area. (See European Commission Press Conference – IP/03/928).

580. COMP/M.4519.

SLEC Holdings Limited (SLEC), which is the holding company of the Formula One group of companies.

1385. The Commission has decided not to oppose the notified operation and to declare it compatible with the common market and with the EEA Agreement subject to some commitments, which include full divestment of the CVC subsidiary Dorna, which holds all rights to the promotion of Moto GP, British Superbikes, the FIM Supercross Championship and the Spanish national motorcycle championship. In addition, CVC has committed not to sell the Spanish TV rights for Moto GP and Formula One before the sale of Dorna.

VIII. Current and Future Cases

A. Financial Fair Play – Striani Case

1386. The text of the complaint lodged by the FIFA agent *Daniel Striani* is not known. We are only aware of the reasoning of his lawyer, Jean-Louis Dupont.[581] Consequently, we only present some arguments in opposition to the majority view which sustains the illegality of the system in question.[582]

1387. These arguments could defend the Financial Fair Play Regulations (FFP) in general and the Break Even Rule (BER) in particular,[583] continuing with '*overriding reasons of general interest*,' thus justifying restrictions to competition law, since they are arguments that could also support the fulfilment of the conditions of Article 101(3) TFEU or an objective justification under Article 102 TFUE. They are also arguments that might help to establish the '*overall context*' of the making, effect and objectives of the FFP rules and in order to know if the restrictions caused are inherent in the pursuit of these objectives, i.e., contribute to evaluate whether the controversial rules fall outside Articles 101(2) and 102 TFEU further to the *Wouters*[584] judgment.

1388. They are also arguments to consider in the assessment of the proportionality of the measures in question, namely in the ambit of competition rules.

---

581. See http://online.wsj.com/article/SB10001424127887324077704578357992271428024.html and http://www.soccernomics-agency.com/?p=454, accessed 28 Jun. 2013.
582. See, *inter alia*, different legal and economic articles and presentations published in the internet written by Andrew Nixon; Ben Van Rompuy; Brian Kennely & Ravi S. Mehta, Christopher A. Flangen; Daniel Geey; Henning Vöpel; Holger Preuss & Mathias Schubert & Kjetil K. Hargen; Thomas Peeters & Stefan Szymanski; and Stephen Weatherhill.
583. The concept of the BER is simple: clubs must not spend more than they earn over a stipulated time frame. The provisions for this are found in Art. 58 of the UEFA FFP as summarised in Annex X: "*The break-even result for a reporting period is calculated as relevant income less relevant expenses*".
584. ECJ Judgment of 19 Feb. 2002, Case C-309/99, ECR 2002, page I-1577.

Article 165 TFEU

1389. There are two passages in Article 165 TFEU which should be invoked here. Firstly, where it alludes to the '*specific nature of sport*' – as demonstrated elsewhere, linking paragraphs 30 and 47 of Advocate General Sharpston's Conclusions,[585] in close articulation with paragraph 40 of *Oliver Bernard*'s judgment,[586] from Article 165 TFEU the specificity of football and even the specificity of professional football can be seen, with their distinctive characteristics, which require a mitigated application of EU Law to football.

1390. The other passage of Article 165 TFUE which must be also highlighted here is that which commits the EU to '*promoting fairness and openness in sporting competitions.*' UEFA competitions can only be fair if there are economic criteria that ensure that the competitions operate normally, have the same number of participants all the time, and that clubs do not pull out as a result of their inability to bear costs, or insufficient funds. The logic of the FFP and its BER is to prevent a financial imbalance between clubs that compete in the same UEFA competitions from becoming a competitive imbalance that jeopardizes the fair nature of the competition. '*Competitors must have equal opportunities, not only at a purely sporting level but at an economic level as well.*'[587] Faced with this, it will be difficult for the Commission or the EU courts, to contradict a mission entrusted to the EU and which could be followed up by an instrument like the FFP.[588]

Soft Law Instruments Enacted by EU Institutions

1391. Further to the objectives listed in Article 2 (2) of the FFP[589] – which eloquently demonstrate the *ratio* of the legislator – i.e. proper adherence to the express decisions of the various EU institutions with regard to the FFP and the previous licensing system, which had identical aims.

---

585. Opinion delivered on 16 Jul. 2009, *Olympique Lyonnais SASP v. Olivier Bernard and Newcastle UFC*, Case C- 25/08, ECR 2010.

586. ECJ Judgment of 16 Mar. 2010, *Olympique Lyonnais SASP v. Olivier Bernard and Newcastle UFC*, Case C-325/08, ECR 2010, p. I-2177.

587. François Mandin, 'La soumission de la norme sportive au droit communautaire,' Dalloz Collection, 1998, 3rd book, p. 32.

588. According to a report of the French Senate, equity and fairness in sport competitions can be achieved by any initiative that leads to the reinforcement of the demands related to good management of professional clubs – see *Sénat, Session Ordinaire 2012-2013, n. 379, Rapport d'information fait au nom de la commission des affaires européennes sur l'Union européenne et le sport professionel*, par Jean-François Humbert, p. 41.

589. To improve the economic and financial capability of the clubs, increasing their transparency and credibility; to place the necessary importance on the protection of creditors by ensuring that clubs settle their liabilities with players, social/tax authorities and other clubs punctually; to introduce more discipline and rationality in club football finances.

1392. The Vice-President of the EU Commission, Joaquim Almunia, in a Joint Statement with UEFA President Michel Platini,[590] stressed that the BER *'reflects a sound economic principle that will encourage greater rationality and discipline in club finances and, in so doing, will help to protect the wider interests of football.'* In turn, the Commissioner M. Barnier[591] drew attention to the *'self-regulatory measures taken by the football sector to reduce the overall debt of clubs.'* The recent Commission communication[592] states that *'club licensing systems offer a valuable tool to ensure the integrity of competitions'* and that the Commission *'welcomes the adoption of measures aimed at enhancing financial fair play in European football.'*

1393. Of equal relevance is the fact that the Commission, in the White Paper on Sport[593] states that the 'legitimate objectives' of sporting rules are normally related to the 'organisation and proper conduct of competitive sport' and may include, for instance 'the ensuring of financial stability of sports' clubs/teams'.

1394. In turn, the European Parliament, in a recent resolution, in the wake of the Disas Report,[594] 'clearly states its support for licensing systems and financial fair play, as they encourage clubs to compete within their actual financial means'. The European Parliament had previously stated regarding the licensing system, that:

> [i]t is self-evident that these kinds of rules derive from a need inherent in the organization of competitions. Competitions cannot be free to all. The justification for these 'entry barriers' in the sports industries lies in the unique pyramid sports' structure and the required competitive balance among competitors.[595]

1395. Furthermore, it also alluded to the objectives of 'financial transparency and proper management'.[596]

EU Case-Law and the Decision Making Practice of the European Commission

590. 'State aid: Vice President Almunia and UEFA President Platini confirm Financial Fair-Play rules in professional football are in line with EU state aid policy', 21 Mar. 2012, IP/12/264.
591. Answer to witten question, 9 Aug. 2010, http://www.europarl.europa.eu/sides/getAllAnswers.do?reference=E-2010-4628&language=SV, accessed 27 Jun. 2013.
592. Communication from the Commission to the European Parliament, the Council, the European Economic and Social Committee and the Committee of the Regions, 'Developing the European Dimension in Sport', Brussels, '18.1.2011 COM(2011) 12 final', '*4.5. Integrity of sporting competitions*'.
593. See 2.1.5.
594. *Report on the European dimension in sport (2011/2087 (INI)), Committee on Culture and Education, Rapporteur: Santiago Disas Ayxela, 18 Nov. 2011, A7-0385/2011.*
595. European Parliament resolution of 29 Mar. 2007 on *the future of professional football in Europe* (2006/2130/INI), para. 20.
596. *The Committee of the Regions also welcomes FFP – see Opinion of the Committee of the Regions on 'Developing the European dimension of sport' (2012/C 9/14), OJEU C 9/74 11.01.2012.*

1396. In the *Deliège* ruling[597] of the European Court regarding a sports competition eligibility rule and its compatibility with the free provision of services, it held that:

> the adoption, for the purposes of an international sports tournament, of one system for selecting participants rather than another must be based on a large number of considerations unconnected with the personal situation of any athlete, such as the nature, the organisation and the financing of the sport concerned. (Emphasis added)

1397. Now, *mutatis mutandis*, where the judgment reads '*international sports tournament*', *UEFA competitions* can clearly be read, in which the framework of the organization and of the financing for football through the FFP can justify a restriction to a fundamental freedom, namely the free provision of services.

1398. Also the *Piau*[598] and *Meca-Medina*[599] decisions should support the analysis of the compatibility of the FFP with EU Law, owing to the similarities between their rulings – the first because it also supported to the international federation eligibility rules based on financial criteria; the second because it focused on federation access rules and continued presence in a sports competition on the grounds of the safeguarding of the integrity of the competition. In either case the existing restrictions of EU Law were justified.

1399. Finally, the *ENIC*[600] case, in which rules that seek to maintain the integrity of the UEFA competitions in order to ensure the uncertainty of the results and consequently to give the public a correct perception of the integrity of UEFA competitions were also at issue, in which the Commission decided not even to apply the Treaty competition rules.

Miscellaneous

1400.

- *Study: The Economic and Legal Aspects of the Transfer of Players, January 2013:*[601] which recommends '*[m]aintain the uncertainty of sports results through better financial accountability and redistribution mechanisms, rewarding excellence as a matter of priority independent of financial strength*'[602] and proposes to

597. ECJ judgment of 11 April 2000, Joined cases C-51/96 and C-191/97, *European Court reports 2000, p. I-02549.*
598. ECJ judgment of 12 Apr. 2005, Case C-265/03, ECR, 2005, p. I-2579.
599. ECJ judgment of 18 Jul. 2006, Case C-519/04 P, OJ C 224 of 16 Sep. 2006, p. 8.
600. COMP 37.806 *ENIC/UEFA*, IP/02/942, 27 Jun. 2002.
601. http://ec.europa.eu/sport/library/documents/f-studies/study-transfers-final-rpt.pdf, accessed 27 Jun. 2013.
602. Page 253.

'[s]*upport the implementation of Financial Fair Play (FFP) rules as an instrument to prevent clubs from financing their position in the transfer market and their sporting results through unacceptable debt levels.*'[603]

- *The current context of the crisis in European football:* the following has already been said in the European Parliament[604] regarding salary caps: '*[a]n environment of economic crisis in football would make salary caps more likely to survive legal challenge. In this environment, salary caps may be justified on the grounds that they maintain the economic viability of teams competing in the league*'. Now, *mutatis mutandis*, the rationale applied to salary caps must also apply to FFP and to the BER, and also to those who claim that FPF mainly cuts wage costs particularly as the crisis in European football is even more serious than it was a few years ago. Moreover, it can even be sustained that mechanisms like the FFP fill a '*vacuum regarding the financial regulation*'[605] in light of the current crisis;
- *Recent case law of the Court of Arbitration for Sport:* in two recent rulings[606] the validity of the FFP was not questioned and the Panel even noted '*how seriously UEFA considers significant breaches*' of such regulations;
- *The protection and benefits of the consumers:* we may consider the words of the UEFA President, Michel Platini: '*I have been deeply convinced, since the start, that a club should not spend more money than it generates (…). You, we, the fans and football lovers, have no interest in seeing clubs, the real heritage of European football, disappear due to risky management*'.[607] As UEFA's competitions are a collective and indivisible product, which is consumed by football fans in general and the fans of the participating clubs in particular, the existence of the FFP is of fundamental importance in order to ensure that these consumers believe in the product, can be spectators with passion and emotion, who are never sure of the result and are completely confident that whoever competes is able to remain in the competition from the beginning to the end, unaffected by mishaps of a financial nature as a consequence of excessive costs, in a context of equality of forces. Competition can only take place within a '*precise*' framework with '*rigid membership rules*'[608] and, '*(…) bearing in mind the specificities of the sports production process, so that the sports competition between the clubs may be as open as possible, the economic competition must be within as narrow a framework as possible.*'[609]

---

603. Page 256.
604. Working Paper, *supra*.
605. Alen Odriozola, 'El deporte profesional y las reglas de mercado. Competencia, ayudas de Estado y libertades comunitárias', in *El deporte profesional*, Edited by Alberto Palomer Olmeda and Ramón Terol Gòmez, Madrid, Bosch, 2009, p. 549.
606. CAS 2012/A/2824 *Besiktas JK v. UEFA*, 16 Oct. 2002; Malaga Case – http://www.tas-cas.org/d2wfiles/document/6818/5048/0/2013.06.1120Media20Release20(English).pdf, accessed 27 Jun. 2013.
607. *Financial Fair Play ensures football's stability (UEFA)*, http://www.uefa.com/uefa/video/videoid=1585436.html? autoplay–true, accessed 27 May 2013.
608. Jacques Fontanel and Liliane Bensahel, Réflexions sur l'économie du sport, Presses Universitaires de Grenoble, 2001, p. 57.
609. Jean-François Bourg, 'L'économie du sport', in *Le Sport en France. Une approche politique, économique et sociale*, Directed by Pierre Arnaud, Les Études de La Documentation Française, 2000, p. 125.

FFP Is the Least Restrictive Means of Achieving UEFA's Aims

1401. FFP is a sort of deepening and extension of the licensing system, that was introduced following the recognition of certain lacunae. The FEP was also agreed between the representatives of the clubs and the players.[610] Therefore, either no stakeholder wanted to find, or was capable of finding a less restrictive means than the FFP, or it can be concluded that the FFP was considered by all to be the most necessary and adequate means to pursue the said objectives.

1402. Certain expenditure is excluded for the purpose of the break-even calculations, namely youth team programmes,[611] since such expenditure is considered to be beneficial in terms of the long-term sustainability and revenue-generation abilities of clubs. It is of fundamental importance to ensure that the BER always prioritized the safeguarding of the superior interests of football. In some cases, this is only possible via restrictive measures and in other cases it is only possible via the non-application of restrictive measures. There is therefore a need for discretionary decisions that ponder and, balance interests and take proportionality into consideration.

In Favour of the TPO

1403. On 2 February 2015, the Spanish and the Portuguese Leagues filed a challenge to have denounced FIFA's 'Third Party Ownership' (TPO) ban withto the European Commission (Directorate General for Competition of the) European Commission.[612]

1404. Apart from an alleged violation of the fundamental freedoms, the complaint states that the outlines that this ban violates EUCL:

> This ban harms clubs, especially those with fewer sources of income, preventing them from sharing the economic rights of their professional players with third parties, and forces them to manage their financial obligations more prudently. This ban also harms dozens of players whose professional careers have been helped along by people, coaches and third party funds. Lastly, this ban completely prohibits third parties from managing footballers' rights, a practice that has been carried out legitimately in the vast majority of the world's professional leagues until now. This restriction on free competition infringes Article 101 of the Treaty of the Functioning of the European Union about the

610. It obtained unanimity at UEFA's Executive Counsel, it received public support from the ECA and FIFPro also strove to defend the rules in question.
611. The investment in the training of young footballers brings us back to para. 106 of the *Bosman* ruling: *'(...) the recruitment and training of young players must be accepted as legitimate."*
612. The FIFA Executive Committee at its meeting on 25 and 26 Sep. 2014 passed a decision of general principle outlining its plan to ban the ownership of player's economic rights by third parties. On 18 and 19 December, the same body approved new provisions to be included in the Regulation on the Status and Transfer of Players.

prohibition of anti-competitive agreements, and Article 102 of the TFUE with regards to FIFA abusing its their dominant position.[613]

Against the TPO

1405. On 31 March 1015, UEFA and FIFPRO have lodged a complaint with the European Commission against TPO:

> on the basis that it is harmful to the interests of players, clubs and fans, and also undermines the standing and integrity of the game (…) Inherent in the practice of TPO is the desire and ability of the so-called 'investors' to control and/or influence the transfer activity of players who are the subject of a TPO arrangement (including players who are not even aware that their 'economic rights' have been sold to a third party). Third parties are driven by a simple motivation, which is to maximise the 'return' on their 'stake' in individual players. UEFA and FIFPro consider that this is not the best interests of players, clubs or the game of football more generally. Players (including young and vulnerable players) can be exposed to the whims of third parties. In the meantime, clubs can be driven into a vicious circle of debt and dependence. The practice of TPO undermines the employment relationship between clubs and players and interferes with important European Union (EU) legal norms.[614]

1406. FIFPro Secretary-General Theo van Seggelen states:

> Despite the ban announced by FIFA, which is welcome, FIFPro is not prepared to rest on its laurels. We see a need to reinforce FIFA's position and create an even stronger argument that improves on the new FIFA regulations. What we and UEFA have put to the European Commission is that by applying basic principles enshrined in EU law all existing TPO arrangements will be declared illegal and therefore not enforceable. This would expand on the rationale behind the implementation of a worldwide TPO ban.

Potential Result of the Complaints

1407. It is extremely difficult to anticipate what the position of the Commission will be in each of these two cases.

1408. According to an agreement signed in 2014 between the Commission and with UEFA,[615] which is – one of the complainants – the Commission seems to opposebe contrary to the TPO:

613. See ww.lfp.es, accessed on 5 Apr. 2015.
614. See www.uefa.org, accessed on 5 Apr. 2015.
615. Arrangement for Cooperation between the UEFA and the European Commission signed in Brussels, 14 Oct. 2014, point 2.8.

> [t]he health and human dignity of athletes must be protected from abusive and unethical practices, commercial or otherwise. It is important that arrangements concerning players, such as the so-called third-party ownership of the 'economic rights' of players, do not threaten the integrity of sporting competition or undermine the relationship of trust and mutual respect that should exist in any relationship of employment.

1409. It is therefore this context it is plausible that the Commission will decide that the ban is legal and proportionate to its aims: i.e., to safeguard the interests of transparency, integrity of the competition, and contractual stability.

1410. Probably the most solid argument is probably that the one related to the need to safeguard a fair competition, to ensure the uncertainty of the results: in theory the outcome of results can be materially affected by the potential conflict of interests between club owners of clubs and owners of the players' economic rights of players. The ability of third parties with an interest in players to influence the clubs that employ those players creates a serious risks that undermining the credibility and integrity of football matches will be undermined games is strong, and could enable having the potential to allow clubs with ties to investors in players to exert some an element control over the transfer market by influencing which clubs players move to. A distortion of competition could may therefore arise.

1411. It can further be argued against TPO that it can unfairly provide clubs with financial power that economic firepower they would otherwise not have if operating in the transfer market alone and without an investment partner.

1412. An opposite approach might consider that (i) the new Article 18*ter* of the FIFA Regulations on the Status and Transfer of Players is a decision of an (association of) undertaking(s) – which means that it falls under EUCL; (ii) the FIFA decision to ban TPO players from playing for their affiliated clubs restricts the market in the supply of the offer of the players, since fewer clubs will have opportunity to contract the major players for their squads – with the result that TPO inevitably the TPO reduces the opportunity of smaller clubs to benefit from the financial support of a third party.

1413. The key aspect for the decision in both cases – and obviously the first decision will affect have a negative effect on the second one – will be the result of the test of proportionality, in order to establish whether Article 101(3) will apply or not. In this context, the evaluation of whether there are less restrictive measures that could be taken in order to prosecute the legitimate objectives at issue, will be decisive. For instance, and so far as potential alternatives to the ban are concerned, the relevant legal theory maintains that:

> [r]ather than prohibition, a better course of action may have been to enforce and enhance the already existing FIFA regulation, Article 18 bis, to ensure

transparency and continue to give clubs access to the often vital source of finance provided by TPO[616]

§2. The Legal Framework of Competition Law in Portugal

I. Introduction

1414. The law governing competition in Portugal is Law no. 18/2003, of 11 June, the *Competition Law* (LdC) the objective of which is to ensure *the efficient functioning of the markets, an effective allocation of resources and the defence of consumer interests.* The LdC prohibits the following Restrictive Anti-Competitive Practices:

(a) agreements between undertakings, decisions of associations of undertakings, concerted practices between undertakings with anti-competitive objectives or effects, e.g., pricing, production limitation or market division cartels;
(b) abuse of a dominant position, such as predatory pricing, discrimination or the closing off of markets;
(c) abuse of economic dependence.

1415. The competition rules are applied either by the AdC or by the community authorities, depending on the case, and there is a right of appeal against their decisions. Natural persons are also entitled to plead failure to comply with competition rules in legal proceedings, not only with regard to the validity of contractual clauses but also in order to claim damages against those, who have committed the violation.

1416. There is another form of control in accordance with Regulation EC no. 139/2004 and Article 8 of the Competition Law. This involves preventive control via the *a priori* analysis of possible negative market effects. It is above all merger operations that are subjected to this type of control. So far as sport is concerned, the sale of broadcasting rights, the formation of undertakings, ticket sales systems and competitions regulations, *inter alia,* may be subject to control.

II. The Application of Portuguese Competition Law to the Sports Sector

1417. The decisions of the AdC with regard to sport have focused mainly on the control of mergers.[617] As a general rule the mergers in the area of sport considered by the AdC have been authorized but conditions and duties have been imposed in some cases.

616. Berry, Richard, 'R.I.P. TPO: Guide to FIFA's ban on third party ownership', www.lawinsport.com, accessed on 24 Jan. 2015.
617. The decisions are available at: www. concorrencia.pt/proc_dec/decididas.asp.

1418. In the first *Sport Tv*[618] case, the (then) Portuguese Competition Council considered, in its opinion regarding the merger involving Sport Tv, that the operation would enable the said company to achieve a dominant position that was likely to prevent, distort or restrict competition in the retail market for broadcasting rights in respect of football games (and game highlights) involving Portuguese teams. It was however possible to reconcile the merger with the maintenance of effective competition, by imposing certain conditions, i.e.:

(a) the duration of the exclusive rights granted to Sport Tv were reduced to three years, thus halving the period initially foreseen;
(b) the renewals of the contracts were not exceed two years;
(c) the contents or sub-licence window granted on an exclusive basis to the State's Radio and Television of Portugal (RTP) was opened to any operator interested, on non-discriminatory terms.

1419. The acquisition of joint control of Sport TV[619] by *PPTV – Publicidade de Portugal e Televisão,* and PT Conteúdos, together with the acquisition of the exclusive rights to broadcast the football games in the 'Super Liga Galp Energia' (the principal Portuguese football tournament), in the 2004/2005 and 2007/2008 seasons, involved rights to broadcast football matches, both complete games and highlights, distributed on pay-per-view television and the use thereof to create multimedia contents, to be distributed via mobile communications and the Internet.

1420. The AdC decided not to oppose the merger and imposed conditions and obligations related to consumer free choice in terms of the distribution of broadcasting rights, and imposed compromise solutions on the grounds that the operation had a negative effect on:

(a) the pay-to-view television market in which the distribution of the Sport Tv channel to the various cable TV operators was required to comply with non-discriminatory terms with regard to marketing, promotions and the provision of the signal. Likewise, the commercial terms were required not to result in the elimination of smaller scale operators from the market, as a consequence of restrictive practices;
(b) the multimedia sports contents for broadcast via *internet* and mobile communications market, in which Sportinveste Multimédia, S.A., is required, in its commercial relations with the various mobile communications and internet operators, to refrain from the ADoPtion of discriminatory practices, i.e., those concerning access to, provision of and the commercial terms on which the said contents are made available.

1421. In addition to these referred mergers there have also been questions regarding restrictive practices in the Gymnasiums and Health Clubs market. On 24

618. Competition Council – Activity Report, 1999, pp. 141 et seq.
619. Case Ccent 47/2003, decision of 8 Apr. 2004.

April 2008, following various complaints and after various preliminary investigative measures, the Portuguese Competition Authority commenced enforcement proceedings against thirty-three undertakings and an association of undertakings, all of which were active in the Gymnasiums and Health Clubs market.

1422. The investigation had its source in the fact that it was noted, during the first quarter of 2008, following the approval of the 2008 State Budget Law (Law no. 67-A/2007, of 31 December), which clarified the inclusion of physical activities and sport in the reduced 5% VAT rate, that most undertakings that operated in the market for the supply of services associated with sport, i.e., physical activity centres, gymnasiums and health clubs, did not pass this reduced tax rate on to consumers, which should have resulted in a reduction of the final price charged for the use of the premises or for the supply of the services in question.

1423. The aim of the investigation was to ascertain whether the said conduct was a consequence of a concerted practice of the economic operators contrary to Article 4 of the Competition Law (prohibition of agreements between undertakings or decisions of associations of undertakings), or whether it was a rational reaction of the businesses to the changes in market in which they operate, which is not prohibited by the competition rules.

1424. The Competition Authority concluded that prior to the legislative change introduced by the 2008 State Budget, gymnasiums and health clubs did not always apply the reduced IVA rate in a homogeneous way to the services they provided, even after the official clarification made by the VAT Department regarding the gymnasium and health club business, in 2006.

1425. The investigation carried out by the Competition Authority did not produce any evidence of exchange of information between the various economic operators, or of any procedural guidelines established by the operators with the largest market share, or by the association of undertakings most representative of the sector.

1426. On the contrary, the economic analysis carried out by the Competition Authority concluded that because of the time lapse discovered and the discrepancy in the application/repercussion of the alteration of the VAT rate during the period in question, that there was no pattern of concerted conduct between the various economic operators investigated. There was accordingly no evidence of the existence of a concerted understanding between the undertakings in question.

1427. The Competition Authority accordingly decided to take no further action on the basis of the enquiry, because it had concluded that there was no evidence of anti-competitive restrictive practices by the undertaking investigated.

III. Application of the Competition Rules to the *Media* Sector

1428. One of the most important cases was the *Controlinveste/Lusomundo Serviços*[620] case, in which the AdC did not oppose the acquisition but imposed conditions (Phase II).

1429. *Controlinveste*, is a holding company active in the media sector, particularly in the sports sector, which controls newspapers, television stations and television broadcast rights of sports events and advertising companies, which had acquired *Lusomundo Serviços*, a sub-holding company of the *Portugal Telecom* Group, also active in the same sector and particularly in the press and radio markets and which controls various Portuguese daily newspapers and a top ranking radio station.

1430. The AdC decided not to oppose the acquisition on the basis of undertakings, which were given because of its concern with regard to the impact of the operation on various relevant markets and particularly the general national daily newspaper market.

1431. In 2004, Reuters submitted a complaint regarding access to the broadcasts of games of the European Football Championship organized in Portugal for news purposes. No action was taken on the complaint because broadcast via various television channels was guaranteed.

1432. In 2008, the press reported that one Portuguese television company had made a complaint to the European Commission alleging abuse by UEFA and Sportfive of a dominant position in relation to the licensing of television broadcast rights with regard to the games in Euro 2008.

1433. Finally, another case is particularly noteworthy, because it is relatively recent and above all, because of its content. We cite the most relevant parts of the Judgment of the Lisbon Court of Appeal of 10 November 2009, which concerns the application of competition law to sport, with the interesting particularity that the issue concerned the relationship between national, EU and federation legislation and regulations.

1434. The case involved proceedings commenced by football club *Vitória Sport Clube* and the Portuguese Football Federation against RTP, in which the former made a claim in damages against the latter for financial and other loss and damage, plus interest. We shall commence by citing the *Summary* of the judgment:

(1) UEFA is a private organisation subject to Swiss law, the regulatory power of which is binding only on those natural or juristic persons that belong to it.
(2) Art. 14 of the version of the UEFA bylaws in force in September 1997, regarding the television broadcasting of football games, and the Television Broadcast

620. Case CCent. 17/2005.

Regulations drawn up to implement the said bylaw provision, are not binding on third parties, i.e. television broadcasting undertakings.
(3) For this reason, the broadcast by a television company of a football match, which does not comply with the conditions imposed by the said regulations is not unlawful and cannot be grounds for a claim in damages by another club prejudiced by the said broadcast.
(4) UEFA is an 'undertaking' for the purposes of the competition rules arising from the EC Treaty.
(5) The UEFA regulations regarding the television broadcasting of football matches that were in force in September 1997 and were notified to the National Federations and football clubs belonging to the said organisation violated the competition rules then defined by Article 85, no. 1 (currently Article 81, no. 1) of the EC Treaty and are therefore null and void.
(6) The nullity of the said regulations would, in any event, prevent the club prejudiced by the television broadcast from making a claim in damages against the television company.

1435. The facts found to have been proved were as follows:

(1) In the 1996/97 season, Vitória Sport Clube (V.S.C.), competed in the National Championship of the 1st Division and achieved a ranking, which entitled it to compete in the UEFA Cup, which gave rise to interest on the part of its members and supporters.
(2) The Bastia/Benfica game took place on 16-9-97, and the V.S.C./Lazio game took place on the same day at 21h00.
(3) RTP obtained the television broadcast rights for the Bastia/Benfica game from Olivedesportos.
(4) On 1-9-97, the FPF asked UEFA how it could oppose the television broadcast of the Bastia/Benfica game.
(5) Only on 15-9-97 did Olivedesportos confirm to RTP the possibility of the television broadcast of the Bastia/Benfica game and inform it that it had acquired the corresponding rights.
(6) UEFA sent a fax to the FPF.
(7) On 12-9-09, V.S.C. sent a fax to the FPF stating, inter alia, that 'this club has become aware that there will be a television broadcast of the abovementioned game to Portugal. As the timing of this game coincides with the Vitória/Lazio match, we inform the federation that we do not authorise this broadcast'.

On 15-9-07, V.C.S. sent a further fax in which it states, inter alia, ' … we reiterate our decision not to authorise the said broadcast, as the Bastia/Benfica game ends after the start of the V.S.C – Lazio game … ';
(8) Given the position adopted by V.S.C., the FPF approached RTP in order to prevent the broadcast of the Bastia/Benfica game.
(9) At RTP's request, FPF faxed it the regulations regarding Article 14 of the UEFA Bylaws – Article 25 of the statement of claim.
(10) The FPF sent a fax to RTP on 16-9-07, in which it stated, inter alia, that ' … in these circumstances we regret to inform you that we do not authorise the

said broadcast pursuant to the provisions of the Regulations applying Article 14 of the UEFA Bylaws'.

(11) The first game (Bastia/Benfica), which commenced at 19h30, was broadcast by RTP and ended at 21h15, so that there was an interval between the end of the first game and the beginning of the Claimant's game of 15 minutes.
(12) RTP did not comply with the requirement of a 45 minute interval between the broad cast of two matches.
(13) There were great expectations on the part of the management of V.S.C. when the VSC/Lazio game was announced, which led it to order 16.200 tickets from the FPF.
(14) The 1st Claimant managed to sell only 9,571 tickets.
(15) The management of the Claimant expected a larger number of people to be present than did in fact attend, so that V.S.C. did not receive an amount, which has yet to be established, corresponding to the difference between the tickets sold and those, which would have been sold had the Bastia/Benfica game not been broadcast.
(16) Were it not for the broadcast of the Bastia/Benfica game a greater, but indeterminate, number of people would have gone to the Afonso Henriques Stadium than were present at the VSC/Lazio game.
(17) The 1st Claimant only received PTE 19.631.500$00.
(18) When it broadcast the said game it was perfectly aware that the broadcast of the said match would be a direct cause of the absence of a larger number of spectators at the 1st Claimant's stadium.
(19) The members of VSC are generally not members of SLB.
(20) It is necessary, in order to compare spectator numbers at football matches, to take various factors into consideration, i.e. the team being played against, and the level of public popularity of that team, the existence of Portuguese players in the adversary team (in the case of foreign teams), the weather and the time of the game.
(21) Vitória Sport Clube has public utility status.
(22) The FPF is a not-for-profit private law juristic person with sports public utility status, the object of which is the promotion, regulation, organization and control, teaching and playing of football in all specialities and competitions.
(23) The Defendant is a public limited company, which is fundamentally in the television business and is the concessionary of the public television service.

1436. We shall now consider the matter of greatest import in the judgment, starting with the two questions that the *Court essentially sought to consider:*

a) *Should the Defendant RTP be held to be civilly liable for the loss and damage sustained by the Claimant V.S.C. because it did not comply with the provisions of the UEFA Television Broadcast Regulations regarding football games, which make the broadcast of games subject to prior authorisation?*
b) *Do the regulations, on which V.S.C. bases its claim, violate the competition rules in art. 83, no. 1 of the EEC Treaty?*

The Regulations regarding television broadcasts issued by UEFA, an organisation subject to the rules of private law can, in no way, bind those, who are not members of the said organisation, or who are not subject to its authority. Furthermore, all regulations with regard to economic activities must comply with the European Union competition rules as defined by the EC Treaty. The said rules have been violated in this case.
So far as the first question is concerned:
(…)
It is not impossible that UEFA (or the FPF), acting by its decision-making bodies, may lay down rules regarding television broadcasting of football games, which, in advance, regulate the times when television broadcasts may take place in order not to conflict with broadcasts of other games. The said regulations may, without prejudice to the question of respect for other rules, i.e. competition law rules, protect interests linked to the said sport and those involved therein, as the revenue from the sale of broadcast rights and tickets or advertising space are important funding sources.
It is accordingly in the interests of clubs and other organisations, or others involved in sport and also in the general interest of sport that a certain level of spectator attendance at football stadiums be encouraged, which can be prejudiced by an absence of rules regarding the times when other football matches are broadcast.

2.3. However such regulations are only binding on the association members.

Indeed it was on the basis that only those involved in a certain sports activity are bound (football player's agents in the case in point) that this Lisbon Court of Appeal stated on 14-10-08 (www.dgsi.pt) that 'the Portuguese Football Federation is entitled to issue regulations regarding the profession of players agent as provided in Law no. 28/98, of 26-6'.

It is natural that an organisation with a pyramid structure, such as UEFA, imposes rules approved by its decision-making bodies on those who freely join such organisations and so bind themselves to comply with the said rules. However, the said rules cannot bind those who are not members of the said organisation. There is no national or international legal basis for UEFA (or any other similar national or transnational organisation) having the power to create obligations and limitations that are binding on those who are not members thereof. Namely, there is no legal basis for the said private regulations being binding on entities, such as RTP, which are television companies and which, as economic agents, are free to make contracts for the broadcast of sports events with any other entities or football clubs.

Certain sport-related organisations, mainly those related to professional football (such as UEFA, FIFA or even FIA), sometimes seek to appear to be sovereign bodies with a supranational scope, but they lack the legitimacy that only the constitutions of the states in which the said organisations operate, or Treaties in International Law, which are signed by states, have to issue universal binding legal provisions.

2.4. In this specific case, the Claimant V.S.C. claims damages based on extra-contractual civil liability from RTP arising from a failure to comply with the provisions of art. 14 of the UEFA Bylaws, which were in force until September 1997 (translated on pages 252 et seq.), and the Television Broadcasts Regulations regarding football matches, approved by UEFA on 18-9-93.

The Claimant V.S.C. considered that RTP by broadcasting the Benfica/Bastia game, failed to comply with the interval period provided in the said regulations in relation to the time when the VSC/Lazio started and failed to obtain the prior consent of the FPF for the said broadcast.

The said Regulation state as follows, inter alia:

- *'If the broadcasting, transmission or reproduction is to another country, and whether the transmission is live or recorded, total or partial, or any new transmissions, the owner of the rights ... may only give its authorisation after having obtained the agreement of the association in the receptor country.*

  The association in the receptor country can refuse to give its agreement if there is a football game to be played on the same day in its territory, in the national football competitions (1st division games or amateur league games), by national representative teams or if one or more club teams are playing in an international competition' (page 252);
- *The chapter regarding the procedure states that 'all producers of television signals shall inform the organising football association, one of the organisations, which belong to the association, or the club, which owns the rights ... of the names and addresses of the television and broadcast organisations interested in broadcasting the said images' (page 253).*

There can be no doubt that the essential aim of the said regulations was to protect interests linked to professional football that could be affected if each football club could make game broadcast contracts with third parties without any limitations or conditions and superimpose them on other games being played at exactly the same time, which would have a negative effect on ticket and advertising revenue and also on the interest in the presence of a certain number of spectators in the stadiums where the games are played.

As we have already stated, it is also easy to understand that the said art. 14 of the UEFA Bylaws and the corresponding Regulations are binding on the National Federations and on their member clubs, which are subject to the penalties provided in the Bylaws and Regulations.

However it is improper to seek to impose the said internal regulations on entities with only an indirect connection with the said sport because they are holders of television broadcast rights. As UEFA is no more than a sports confederation subject to Swiss law it is not possible to base a claim for damages against television companies, or companies that acquire television broadcast rights from clubs in order to resell them to third parties, on a breach of private provisions.

As has already been stated in a Judgment of the Court of 1st Instance of the European Communities, of 26-1-05, regarding another Regulation that was adopted by FIFA,[621] *we can also state that the Television Broadcast Regulations were adopted by UEFA in the exercise of its own powers and not in the exercise of powers delegated to it by the public authorities. The said Regulations cannot therefore become general law that binds other persons or entities that are not members of UEFA.*[622]

2.5. In this case, RTP, SA, acquired the television broadcast rights of this game for Portugal, from Olivedesportos, SA, which it had, in turn acquired them from Bastia football club. There was no agreement between RTP and the FPF or between RTP and V.S.C. regarding the conditions to which the television broadcast of the Lazio/Benfica game would be subject. There is accordingly no breach of any contractual clause, which could give rise to civil liability.

(…)

In a free and competitive market, the Claimant V.S.C. cannot have the caprice to be the sole beneficiary of the exclusivity as to the time when the V.S.C./Lazio game was played or with regard to the need to obtain the prior authorisation of the FPF for the said broadcast. The Claimant V.S.C. was not entitled to require third parties to refrain from broadcasting another football game during the same time period, or at exactly the same time.

(…)

3. So far as the question of violation of the competition rules is concerned:

3.1. RTP pleads that even if it was bound to comply with the said UEFA Bylaws and Television Broadcast Regulations, the judgment should be set aside on the grounds that the said Bylaws and Regulation are null and void as contrary to that part of the EC Treaty that regulates competition.

3.2. In the previous point, we transcribed a substantial part of the regulations regarding the television broadcasting of football games, which require television companies to obtain the prior authorisation of the national association, i.e. the FPF in this case.

621. In the journal *Desporto e Direito*, no. 6, page 395.

622. In an article entitled *Desporto, Estado e Sociedade Civil, Sub Judice*, No. 8, page 23 et seq., José Augusto Garcia Marques, citing another author, states that 'sports federations are indubitably part of the private law organisations that are involved in the management of a public administrative service and exercise public law powers' (page 28), cf. José Augusto Garcia Marques, *Desporto, Estado e Sociedade Civil, Sub Judice*, No. 8, Coimbra, Almedina, 2007, pp. 23 et seq, 28. On the legal nature of *Sports Federations* cf. also the Judgment of the Supreme Administrative Court, of 18 Feb. 1992, *Sub Judice*, No. 8, page 84, and other case law cited by José Manuel Meirim in the same journal, pages 101 and 102, cf. José Manuel Meirim, *Desporto e Constituição, Sub Judice*, No. 8, Coimbra, Almedina, 2007, p. 84, 101, 102. Cf. also Alexandra Pessanha, *As Federações Desportivas. Contributo para o Estudo do Ordenamento Jurídico Desportivo*. Coimbra, Coimbra Editora, 2001, pages 120 and 121, which stresses the public law aspect of sports regulations and public self-regulation.

The said Regulations, on which the Claimant V.S.C. based its claim, have been the subject matter of various considerations, principally by the European Commission.[623]

Given the date on which the facts occurred, the Commission Decision of 16-7-98, which is translated on pages 173 et seq., which states as follows, inter alia, is applicable:

a) *National football associations and their member leagues and the clubs 'by selling football TV rights from which they obtain a considerable and constantly increasing revenue ... have commercialised their product and have become involved in economic competition.*

   Consequently they must accept that the competition rules apply to the sale of TV rights just like any other commercial activity' (§ 99. page 204);

b) *The territorial division of markets 'is a restriction of competition in accordance with art 85, no. 1 of the EC Treaty and art. 53, no. 1 of the EEA Agreement' (§ 105, page. 205);*

c) *'The restrictions of competition created by art. 14 (now art. 44) and the Broadcast Regulations that implement them affect the operation of TV rights for all football played in the common market and in the territory covered by the EEA Agreement.*

   Given the substantial number of rights affected by the UEFA rules, these restrictions appear to affect competition between Member States and the Contracting Parties of the EEA Agreement, to an considerable extent' (§ 111, page 207);

d) *'The said restrictions of competition can affect trade between Member States to a considerable extent given the substantial number of television, advertising and sponsorship rights affected by the UEFA rules.*

   Art. 14 (now art. 44) and the Broadcast Regulations that implement them are accordingly restrictions of competition prohibited by art. 85, no. 1 of the EC Treaty and art. 53, no. 1 of the EEA Agreement' (§ 114, page 208);

e) *'The time window system, obliges all broadcasters to group televised football in the same periods and can therefore have the effect of reducing the viewers programme choices during these periods.*

   It must therefore be concluded that UEFA has not demonstrated that art. 14 (now art. 44) has benefitted consumers' (§ 124, page 210);

f) *'In conclusion, it is concluded that the restrictions on the broadcasting of football in art. 14 (now art. 44) and the Broadcast Regulations that implement them are not, in their current form, indispensable in order to achieve the objective of safeguarding the quality of football games and the attendance thereat' (§ 132, page 212).*

The 'Introduction' to the said Decision states that 'the Commission considers that the system created by art. 44 (formerly art. 14) is part of a market division, which is covered by the prohibition in art. 85 of the EC Treaty and art. 53 of the EEA Agreement'. It also considers that the 'UEFA did not

623. In the case of Portugal, see also the judgment of the Lisbon Appeal Court of 2-11-00, CJ, tome V, page 71, regarding an *assignment of television broadcast rights* with regard to football matches, which was found to be in breach of the competition rules.

produce a convincing case for the grant of an exemption under art. 85, no. 3, of the EC Treaty and art. 53, no. 3, of the EEA Agreement. The Commission accordingly considers that UEFA should abolish art. 44 and will therefore send this statement of objections to UEFA'.[624]

In another and subsequent Decision of 19-4-01 (accessible at http//eur-lex.europa.eu), reference is made to the earlier Decision and it is concluded that the UEFA Regulations regarding television broadcasts, which were in force in September 1997 'infringed Article 81(1) of the EC Treaty and Article 53(1) of the EEA Agreement and that they were not eligible for exemption under Article 81(3) of the EC Treaty and Article 53(3) of the EEA Agreement.'.

The second Decision states that:

- *'Sport is subject to community legislation only to the extent that it is an economic activity in accordance with article 2 of the Treaty'.*
- *'Professional football clubs carry on economic activities and are undertakings for the purposes of no. 1 of art. 81 of the EC Treaty and no. 1 of art. 53 of the EEA Agreement.'*
- *'Each national football association is consequently an association of undertakings'. 'Associations of undertakings' are also undertakings as they carry on economic activities.'*
- *UEFA is 'an association of associations of undertakings and is itself an undertaking to the extent that it carries on economic activities such as the sale of commercial rights with regard to its competitions.'*
- *Therefore, 'UEFA, the national associations and football clubs are consequently undertakings ... despite the fact that some of them are not-for-profit organisations and independently of any cultural or social activities that they may have'.*

3.3. In the light of the lengthy and detailed position argued by the Commission, which affect steps taken by UEFA to correct the situation of non-compliance by the regulations with the competition rules in the European Union, it is easy to examine and analyse the case.

Art. 81, no. 1 of the Treaty (formerly art. 85) provides, subject to the inapplicability of no. 3, 'The following shall be prohibited as incompatible with the common market: all agreements between undertakings, decisions by associations of undertakings and concerted practices which may affect trade between Member States and which have as their object or effect the prevention, restriction or distortion of competition within the common market ... '. The treaty then lists the acts prohibited and states the penalty therefor: i.e. they are void.

The said provision is the most evident sign of one of the major objectives of the European Union as reflected in supremacy of its competition law over any provisions in domestic law or private regulations.

624. In the *BBC/BskyB case*, the European Commission had assumed that an obstruction to intra-community trade had been created as a consequence of the limitation of the broadcast of games to two channels (cited by Alexandre Mestre, in *Desporto e União Europeia*, page 157).

There can be no doubt that despite its specific connection with sport, UEFA (and the National Federations, or the clubs that belong to them) must be considered economic agents or 'undertakings' for the purposes of the subjection of their regulations to the competition rules (and must also be considered to be an 'agreement between undertakings').[625]

It is also clear that the area of television broadcasts of sport and particularly of football matches has sufficient 'community prominence' and not just national prominence, particularly when the Regulations were intended to regulate the broadcast of international games, such as in this case.

A 'relevant market', as required for the application of the competition rules, can also be identified in the area of television broadcasts of sports events, as the segments involved are as follows, the segment linked to the acquisition of the television broadcasting rights of games, upstream, and the segment related to audience rates, advertising revenue, and the number of subscribers of Pay per View television downstream,[626]

The said circumstances (agreement between undertakings, community interest and relevant market) means that it can be stated, in line with the statement of the European Commission in the said Decision dated 16-7-98, that the UEFA Broadcast Regulations in force in September 1997, infringed the provisions of art. 85, no. 1 of the EC Treaty to the extent that it made the television broadcasting of football matches subject to the consent of another party.

Consequently and given the provisions of art. 85, no. 2 the Regulations were void.

Regulations that are void because they infringe the Treaty can never be the basis of a claim for damages based on the breach thereof.

Accordingly, the claim made by the Claimant V.S.C. would also fail on these grounds.

3.4. It might be asserted that the European Commission subsequently altered its position with regard to the said regulations.

The said assertion is true, although it is necessary to put the alteration of the Commission's position in the correct context.

In its Decision dated 19-4-01, the Commission concluded, after having considered the new version of the Broadcast Regulations that were submitted to it by UEFA, that the same did not restrict competition significantly, i.e. 'it has no appreciable restrictive effects on the broadcasting market', and accepted that it 'had no grounds to act pursuant to the provisions of no. 1 of art. 81 of the EC Treaty and no. 1 of art. 53 of the EEA Agreement, with regard to art. 47 of the UEFA Bylaws, as applied by the Broadcast Regulations'.

---

625. This concept, which is duly illustrated by various cases he lists, is assumed by Alexandre Mestre, *supra.*, pages 129 and 133, and he considers therefore that they are subject to the intra-community competition rules, above all, to safeguard the public interest in relation to private interests and because of the necessary importance that must be given to the interest of the community.

626. Alexandre Mestre, *supra.*, pages 137 and 162, summarising the conclusions of the Commission in its said Decision dated 19 Apr. 2001.

The said conclusions were reached with regard to a version of the Regulations, which differed substantially from the version in force in September 1997. The alterations made by UEFA had been 'imposed' by the Commission after having considered successive complaints by third parties alleging infringement of the EC Treaty.

UEFA was 'motivated' to makes the regulations regarding the broadcasting of football matches compatible with the said competition rules, which resulted in the remedying of the infringement of the Treaty.[627]

As the new regulations establish pre-established time periods during which television broadcasts are prohibited, in accordance with the suggestions made by the European Commission, the Commission concluded that the UEFA Regulations no longer violated the Treaty.

Alexandre Mestre, commenting on the Decision dated 19-4-01, stated that 'in the Commission's opinion, the blocking of time periods ensures healthy competition upstream in the television rights acquisition market and downstream in the audience rates markets and the advertising revenue markets dependant thereon and the number of television subscribers per subscription'.[628]

The said subsequent developments only confirmed the infringement of the Treaty arising from the version in force in September 1997, which is the version relevant to this case.

4. *Accordingly, the claim made by the Claimant V.S.C. fails not only because the said regulations do not bind RTP SA, but also because they are void for infringement of the community competition rules.*

   IV – Accordingly the judgment appealed against is set aside and the appeal is granted.'

1437. Another important case was the one that condemned Sport TV of Abuse of Dominant Position.[629]

1438. On 20 June 2013, the Portuguese Competition Authority (PCA) issued a decision fining Sport TV for abusing its dominant position in the premium sports pay-tv market, in breach of *Article 102 Treaty for the Functioning of European Union* (TFEU) and the national equivalent, *Article 11 of the Law no. 19/2012*. The PCA concluded that Sport TV engaged in *price discrimination* in the downstream audio-visual market, especially the pay-tv market, from *January 2005 to April 2011*.

---

627. In another decision dated 23 Jul. 2003, which is available at *http//eur-lex.europa.eu*, the European Commission concluded that 'there are no grounds for acting in accordance with the provisions of no. 1 of art. 81 of the Treaty and no. 1 of art. 53 the EEA Agreement with regard to the joint sale by UEFA applicable to the sponsorships, supplies and licensing of intellectual property rights related to the UEFA Champions League'.
628. *Supra.*, page 162.
629. Dias, Matilde Costa– *Portugal's Sport Tv Case: Abuse of Dominant Position* – World Sports Law Report.

1439. It is relevant to note that during the investigation, there was only one pay-tv premium sports channel in Portugal (Sport TV) which was jointly-owned by Sportinveste, SGPS, S.A. (50%), that has acquired Portuguese Football League and Portuguese Cup broadcasting rights over the last seasons, and by the ZON Multimédia Group (50%), the incumbent pay-tv operator and an important player in '4play' (TV, internet, telephone, mobile phone) and other media and telecommunication markets in Portugal.

1440. The PCA found that Sport TV had entered into contracts with undertakings operating in the pay-tv sector for the distribution of the Sport TV channels with discriminatory conditions for equivalent services, thus violating Article 11 Law no. 19/2012, which states that '*applying dissimilar conditions to equivalent transactions with other trading parties, thereby placing them at a competitive disadvantage, is consider an abuse of dominance'*. Sport TV was found to have imposed '*unfair conditions and limited production, distribution, technical development and investment related to services*', thus harming competition and consumers. The pricing policy of Sport TV allegedly favoured one of the undertakings in the pay-tv retail market – ZON – with which Sport TV had corporate links.

1441. In 2013, the PCA fined Sport TV *EUR 3,700,000* for allegedly applying a discriminatory pricing model in its contracts with pay-tv operators (like Cabovisão, PT, Vodafone) for the distribution of its sports channels. The discriminatory conditions resulted from the *remuneration system* applied by Sport TV, through the *contracts of distribution of TV channels concluded between Sport TV and pay-tv operators*. The first instance Court upheld the Competition Authority's decision, although the fine was reduced to *EUR 2,700,000*. This judgment may still be appealed to the Lisbon Court of Appeal and is therefore not final.

1442. In accordance with the European Court of Justice (ECJ) jurisprudence, the first step in applying Article 102 TFEU involves assessing whether an undertaking is in a *dominant position* and the *degree of market power* it holds. Holding a dominant position confers a special responsibility on the undertaking concerned, the scope of which must be considered in the light of the specific circumstances of each case.

1443. Hence, *dominance* means that an undertaking has the power to harm the competitive process, either by harming consumers (e.g., through higher prices) or by harming competitors (e.g., by offering discounts to customers who would otherwise buy the competitor's goods). It can be said that there are different degrees of dominance; some undertakings are so powerful that they face no competitive constraint, while some dominant undertakings may face competition from others, but are strong enough to keep the smaller competitors isolated. Regardless of the degree, the ECJ measures dominance, first, by considering the undertakings market share, and second, by other factors used to determine the undertaking's position *vis-à-vis* its competitors, customers and consumers.

1444. The Commission has indicated that the list of abuses in Article 102 TFEU is not exhaustive. The types of *abuse* may be classified in two categories: (1) *exploitative* – which includes abuses that aim to harm the customer of the dominant undertaking (e.g., excessive prices); *and (2) exclusionary*, consisting of abuses that are designed to impact negatively on rivals.

1445. These abusive practices are designed to safeguard the undertaking's dominant position and to facilitate subsequent exploitation of dominance, which appears to be the case at stake. According to the PCA's decision, by imposing discriminatory prices and unfair conditions with vertical effects on the downstream media market on the various pay-tv operators, *Sport TV continually restricted other operators from accessing TV sports content.* In fact, from 1 January 2005 until 1 April 2011, *Sport TV* selectively lowered its price in favour of one customer, with whom it had corporate links, and fixed exploitative prices on other pay-tv operators.

1446. The nature of the practices in question affects the competitive structure of the pay-tv market in Portugal and the national coverage of the specified anti-trust practices could also lead to the *isolation of the national market* and, consequently, the *partition of the single market*, thus breaching Article 102 of the TFEU.

1447. The majority of pay-tv operators agreed upon the fact that Sport TV has a very high bargaining power.[630] In fact, this could be explained by *three factors*: (i) the relevance of the channel, (ii) the product substitutability, and (iii) the market positioning.

1448. Regarding the relevance of the channel, it is important to highlight that approximately 51% of pay-tv clients prefer the sports content channels and, consequently, these sports premium channels (along with movies channels) represent 32% of the total revenue of pay-tv market, being generally recognized that the majority of the total revenue comes from the sports content channel. Second, concerning the product substitutability, not only was Sport TV the lone sports channel in the Portuguese market, but it also had the exclusive broadcasting rights over the main football competitions (Portuguese Professional Football League, Portuguese Cup, Champions League and UEFA Cup), and other important sports content, which made it almost impossible to replace. Finally, Sport TV was the single representative of premium sports content channel. Besides, it was jointly-owned by Sportinveste SGPS and ZON Multimédia Group, the biggest market shareholder.

1449. For the reasons described above, it seems clear that Sport TV had easy access to the market of sports broadcasting rights in its relationship with the *player* of media exploitation rights, ZON.

1450. As mentioned before, in Portugal Sports in general and football in particular is a very valuable content in both national television channels and closed signal or pay-tv channels, and has a high price, because it is in short supply. The parties

630. Maksen Consulting Report – *Estudo do acesso a conteúdos no mercado de pay-tv.*

involved in the negotiations seek to maximize their profits and the owners of the broadcasting rights (i.e., the clubs and associations) use strategies designed to increase the sale price, while, on the other hand, the purchasers of these rights are interested in acquiring them on an exclusive basis, to the greatest extent and for the longest period of time possible.

1451. The conflict with the competition rules arises when a single operator sells television rights on an exclusive basis, to the extent that the rights included in the exclusive package are extensive, or because the agreement is made for a long period. This restricts competition and subsequently 'closes' the market, meaning that the prices charged on subscribers can easily be increased.

1452. The Portuguese Professional Football League considered the PCA decision '*a decisive and irreversible step*' for the '*end of the monopoly of television rights*' and towards what is considered to be the '*regular functioning of the market'*. In fact, SPORT TV's monopoly regarding the market of broadcasting rights, in particular national competitions, not only constitutes a breach of antitrust rules, but also an attack on the market economy and free competition.

1453. The PCA's decision is a clear example of the application of the European Courts' reasoning in previous cases regarding abuse of dominant position.[631] Under such jurisprudence, the application by a dominant company of unequal commercial conditions on economic agents without an objective justification, constitutes a breach of antitrust rules.

1454. In accordance with the national law and ECJ jurisprudence regarding the rules applicable to the companies' abuse of dominant position, we can conclude that the fee system applied by Sport TV is in itself a clear sign of the existence of a discriminatory treatment. However, we still have to wait for the Lisbon Court of Appeal's decision, which in my opinion, is likely to uphold that of the PCA.

§3. Gambling and Competition Law

I. Introduction

1455. Gaming activities are subject to a very restrictive legal regime in Portugal. The general rule established by Decree-Law No. 422/89,[632] of 2 December – which was last amended by Decree Law no. 64/2015 of 29 April (Portugal's primary gaming law) is that gaming outside of the legally authorized locations[633] is

631. Notably in *Michelin II* and *Portugal v. Commission* (Cases T-203/01 and C-163/99, respectively).
632. Decree-Law no. 422/89, of 2 December, Art. 9.
633. Decree-Law No. 422/89, of 2 December, Art. 3, no. 2 creates 'gaming zones' in Azores, Algarve, Espinho, Estoril, Figueira da Foz, Funchal, Porto Santo, Póvoa de Varzim, Tróia and Vidago-Pedras Salgadas.

forbidden.[634] However, the State Government reserves the right to operate such activities directly or exceptionally, to licence them to third parties. Currently, only land-based casinos and bingo have been licensed to private operators.

1456. The only entity authorized to offer social games of the State over the internet is the Santa Casa da Misericórdia de Lisboa (Santa Casa), a five century Portuguese religious charitable institution, which holds the monopoly of the State 'Social Games' (Jogos Sociais), according to Decree Law No. 84/85,[635] of 28 March, which includes all lotteries, betting and gambling games in Portugal. Article 2 of Decree-Law No. 282/2003, of 8 November, the legislation that establishes the rules governing the operation of the State's social games on the Internet, grants Santa Casa an exclusive right to operate lotteries and pool betting activities, as well as any other game, via a multi-channel platform that includes the Santa Casa information system, ATMs, the internet, mobile and fixed phones, television,[636] among other means. As at 2015, betting and online games are governed by Decree Law 66/2015 of 29 April, with the exception of social game of the State, which are governed by Decree Law no. 202/2003.

1457. This decree-law also expressly prohibits other parties from offering online gaming in Portugal and gives Santa Casa[637] powers to impose fines on:

(a) illegal operators;
(b) entities that advertise unauthorized operators;
(c) those, who bet in illegal online games.

1458. Additional administrative measures that can be imposed on illegal operators are[638] the seizure of equipment, goods and vehicles used to carry on the said activity, including the seizure and forfeiture of funds intended to fund prizes. The authorities can also close business establishments and ban offending undertakings from operating social games for a maximum period of two years.

1459. Portuguese regulation allows the government and the Santa Casa to take IP blocking measures or impose payment bans against illegal gaming sites. Despite the existence of such a restrictive regime, the Portuguese authorities have not been able to prevent Portuguese players from betting on foreign online gaming sites.

---

634. Except in the circumstances in Arts 6–8 of Decree-Law 422/89, of 3 December. These circumstances are: (i) gaming on Portuguese ships and planes, which can only occur outside the national borders; (ii) gaming when it occurs an important event of touristic interest and; (iii) bingo.
635. The Decree-Law was republished in annexe to Decree-Law No. 317/2002, of 27 December, and was amended by Decree-Law No. 37/2003, of 6 March and recently by Decree Law 114/2011 of 30 November.
636. Including cable, interactive and satellite television.
637. In line with the provisions of Arts 27 et seq. of Decree-Law No. 235/2008, of 3 December.
638. According to Art. 13 of Decree-Law No. 282/2003, of 8 November.

II. The Dispute between *Bwin* and the *Santa Casa da Misericórdia*

1460. The Bwin controversy commenced in August 2005, when Bwin signed a EUR 10.5 million four-year sponsorship agreement with the LPFP. It was agreed, in consideration of this sum, that the top two divisions of the Portuguese Football League would be renamed the 'Bwin Liga' for the 2005/2006 to 2008/2009 seasons.

1461. The Gaming Department Direction of Santa Casa decided to impose a EUR 74,500 fine on Bwin and a EUR 75,000 fine on the Portuguese Football League, as it considered that the sponsorship deal was in breach of the advertisement restrictions established by Decree-Law no. 282/2003, of 8 November. These fines were appealed against and a criminal court in the Portuguese city of Oporto (*Tribunal de Pequena Instância Criminal do Porto*) referred the dispute to the European Court of Justice (ECJ) for a clarification of existing Portuguese gambling law.

1462. The ECJ's judgment on this case (Case 42/07)[639] was eagerly awaited by the online gambling industry throughout Europe as the questions referred to it by the Oporto court were pertinent in many European jurisdictions. The ECJ was expected to issue opinions on the following questions submitted by the Oporto court:

(a) does the monopoly granted to Santa Casa, when relied on against [Bwin], that is to say, against a provider of services established in another Member State in which it lawfully provides similar services, which has no physical establishment in Portugal, constitute an impediment to the free provision of services, in breach of the principles of freedom to provide services, freedom of establishment and the free movement of payments enshrined in Articles 49, 43 and 56 respectively of the EC Treaty?;
(b) is it contrary to Community law, in particular to the abovementioned principles, for rules of domestic law, such as those at issue in the main proceedings, to establish a monopoly in favour of a single body for the operation of lotteries and mutual betting and then to extend that monopoly to 'the entire national territory, including (…) the internet'?

1463. Basically, the Portuguese government supported its position with arguments that have already been raised in other similar ECJ cases regarding state gaming monopolies, such as the Placanica[640] and the Gambelli[641] cases. The basic

639. The Court of Justice of the European Communities, 'Case 42/07)' (Accessed 29 Apr. 2009) http://curia.europa.eu/jurisp/cgi-bin/form.pl?lang=en&newform=newform&alljur=alljur&jurcdj=jurcdj&jurtpi=jurtpi&jurtfp=jurtfp&alldocrec=alldocrec&docj=docj&docor=docor&docop=docop&docav=docav&docsom=docsom&docinf=docinf&alldocnorec=alldocnorec&docnoj=docnoj&docnoor=docnoor&typeord=ALLTYP&allcommjo=allcommjo&affint=affint&affclose=affclose&numaff=&ddatefs=&mdatefs=&ydatefs=&ddatefe=&mdatefe=&ydatefe=&nomusuel=Baw+International&domaine=&mots=&resmax=100&Submit=Submit.
640. ECJ, Judgment of 6 Mar. 2007, joined cases C-338/04, C-359/04 and C-360/04.
641. ECJ, Judgment of 6 Nov. 2003, Case C-243/01.

arguments were the need to limit the gaming on offer, as a way of protecting public interest objectives, such as crime prevention, consumer protection, and to ensure that gaming revenues were destined to projects of social utility.

1464. On the other hand, Bwin and the League argued that the Portuguese government policy is discriminatory[642] and cannot be justified by generic public interest objectives and that the Portuguese government has the burden to prove that it has really been taking measures to reach such objectives. According to their position, Portugal is not pursuing a consistent and systematic policy of restricting gaming activities, as required by the case-law and they are only aiming to increase Santa Casa's revenue from games of chance and gambling, in what is a clear protection of the agent installed in the market. They also claimed that Portugal's restrictive measures are not proportional to the goals they seek to achieve.

1465. Santa Casa and the Portuguese Casino Association also commenced legal proceedings to annul the Bwin sponsorship agreement. That court also referred that case to the ECJ in order to clarify further issues regarding the compatibility of Portugal's gambling monopoly with EU law.

1466. In October 2008, the Advocate General in the case (Advocate General Bot) issued his opinion in the case, stating that while the applicable Portuguese legislation may comply with EU law, it was not enforceable as it had never been notified to the European Commission, in accordance with EU Directive 98/34. In that sense, Advocate General Bot commented that Portugal's 2003 Decree could not be applied in order to fine Bwin and the League, as the law had never been notified in accordance with EU Directive 98/34, requiring draft technical regulations[643] to be submitted to the Commission prior to their enactment.

1467. On the second question referred, Advocate General Bot opined that it was perfectly valid under EU law for a monopoly gambling operator to extend its operation to the internet, provided that the internet offering did not jeopardize underlying social policy concerns justifying that gambling monopoly in the first place.

1468. According to Advocate General Bot:[644]

> Community law does not aim to subject games of chance and gambling to the laws of the market. The establishment of a market which would be as open as

642. For example, one of the mandatory conditions imposed by the Portuguese regulations is the obligation that the potential concessionaries must have a physical commercial establishment in Portugal. This is discrimination because it was not possible to carry on an activity in this segment, because it is illegal to do so in a commercial establishment without a concession.
643. In accordance with the EC directive, Decree-Law 282/2003, of 8 November, forbids the delivery or the use of a service and it is considered to be a 'technical rule'.
644. Opinion of Advocate General Y. Bot, delivered on 14 Oct. 2008, para. 245. http://curia.europa.eu/jurisp/cgi-bin/form.pl?lang=EN&Submit=rechercher&numaff=C-42/07.

> possible was intended by the Member States as the basis of the European Economic Community because competition, if it is fair, generally ensures technological progress and improves the qualities of a service or product while ensuring a reduction in costs. However, these advantages do not arise in the area of games of chance and gambling.

He added:[645]

> Games of chance and gambling, for their part, can only function and continue if the great majority of players lose more than they win. Opening the market in that field, which would increase the share of household budgets spent on gaming, would only have the inevitable consequence, for most of them, of reducing their resources. Therefore limiting the powers of the Member States in the field of games of chance and gambling does not have the aim of establishing a common market and the liberalisation of that area of activity.

In that sense, according to Advocate General Bot, a Member State should be constrained to open to the market of games of chance and gambling only '*if that State treats it, in fact and in law, as a true economic activity from which the maximum profits should be derived.*'

1469. Advocate General Bot also stated that consumer protection and the maintaining of public order may justify measures restricting the freedom to provide betting services in the internet as the risk to consumers and to public order imposed by online gambling are potentially greater than in relation to land-based games.

1470. Additionally, Advocate General Bot's opinion established two conditions that have to be complied with by national courts in order to determine whether an internet gambling monopoly is appropriate for obtaining the objectives of consumer protection and maintaining public order, and left it to the national court to decide whether Portugal has fulfilled the said conditions. The conditions were the following:

(a) the Member State must have the right to effectively direct and control the activities of the entity that has the exclusive right;
(b) the monopoly must not distort the purpose of the measures by seeking to obtain the maximum profit.

1471. Finally, Advocate General Bot concluded that the grant of an internet gambling monopoly to a single not-for-profit entity controlled by a Member State may be a proportionate measure to the attainment of the objectives of consumer protection and maintaining public order, and that such a measure is not, as such, discriminatory.

645. Opinion of Advocate General Y. Bot, delivered on 14 Oct. 2008, paras 248–249.

1472. On 8 September 2009 the Court of Justice handed down its judgment, which commenced by stating that Article 49 of the Treaty requires the elimination of any restriction of the freedom to supply services even if the said restrictions apply equally to services suppliers, who are nationals of the Member State and of other Member States, when the said restriction is likely to prevent or obstruct the activities of service providers established in another Member State, where they legally provide similar services, or to render the said activities less attractive.

1473. Accordingly, national legislation that prohibits a supplier of services such as Bwin, which has its registered office in another Member State, from offering services in the territory of the State, via the Internet, amounts to a restriction of the freedom to supply services enshrined in Article 49 of the Treaty and is contrary to the principles enshrined in the Treaty.

1474. However, the Court acknowledged that, in the absence of harmonization with regard to this issue, the Member States are entitled to establish the objectives of their policy regarding games of chance or fortune and to define the level of protection intended precisely. They are entitled to have recourse to restrictive legal frameworks provided that the same comply with the conditions with regard to proportionality that are well established in the case-law of the Court of Justice.

1475. It is therefore important to consider whether the restrictions on the supply of games of chance or fortune over the Internet, imposed by the Portuguese legislation is appropriate in order to ensure the achievement of the objectives invoked by Portugal and whether the principle of proportionality has been complied with. The restrictions must be applied in a non-discriminatory manner and legislation can only ensure the achievement of the objective invoked, if it really does comply with the intention to attain the objective in a coherent and systematic manner.

1476. According to the Portuguese Government and the Santa Casa, the main objective of Portuguese legislation is to fight crime and more specifically, to protect consumers of games of chance and fortune from fraud by operators, which, according to the case-law of the Court of Justice, can be a matter of supreme public interest, which can justify restrictions regarding the operators authorized to offer services in this particular service. The organization and workings of the Santa Casa are governed by considerations and requirements related to the attainment of objectives that are in the public interest. The Gaming Department of the Santa Casa has even been granted public administrative powers for the commencement, prosecution and enforcement of administrative proceedings with regard to the illegal operation of games of chance and fortune which the Santa Casa has the exclusive right to operate, and which are listed in Decree-Law no. 282/2003, of 8 November.

1477. As the Court acknowledged, a limited authorization of gaming on the basis of exclusivity has the advantage that the operation of the games in channelled to a controlled circuit and that the risks of the operation of the said games for fraudulent or criminal reasons are eliminated.

1478. So far as the examination of the necessary nature of the legal framework in question is concerned, the Court stressed that games of chance and fortune in the Internet sector have not been subjected to community harmonization. A Member State may therefore consider that the fact that an operator offers services legally on the Internet in another Member State, where it has its registered office and is already, in principle, subject to the legal requirements and control of the proper authorities of that Member State, is not sufficient guarantee of the protection of consumers in its country from the risks of fraud and crime, on the grounds of the probable difficulties encountered in this area by the authorities of the host Member State in evaluating the professional qualities and integrity of the operators. Furthermore given the lack of direct contact between the consumer and the operator, games of chance and fortune available on the Internet involve greater and different risks in comparison to the traditional markets for these games, in relation to any frauds against consumers committed by the operators.

1479. The Court of Justice accordingly concluded that Article 49 of the EC Treaty does not prohibit national legislation, like the Portuguese legislation, which prohibits operators such as Bwin, which have their registered office in another Member State, when they legally provide similar services, from offering games of chance and fortune over the Internet, in the territory of the said Member State.

1480. It is noted that the judgment of the Court of Justice makes specific reference to the legal framework introduced by Decree-Law no. 282/2003, which extends the exclusive right granted to the Santa Casa to games offered on an electronic support, i.e., over the Internet, and accordingly prohibits the use of these means by any other operator and as a reflex of the grant of an exclusive concession to the Santa Casa to operate social games. The Court did not take a direct position with regard to the legal framework generally applicable to games of chance and fortune, which was introduced by Decree-Law no. 422/98, of 2 December. However and without prejudice to the fact that some of the grounds of this judgment appear to be specifically influenced by the particular institutional character of the Santa Casa da Misericórdia, the references made to the Portuguese legislation regarding games of chance and fortune as a whole appear to admit the possibility that its *ratio* may be extended to the prohibition of the promotion, organization, operation and advertising of all gaming on the Internet, and not only those which are the subject matter of the exclusive grant to the Santa Casa.

1481. It is necessary, however, to clarify first whether the exclusivity provisions affecting the grant of concessions pursuant to the current Gaming Law, and particularly those for casino games, must be applied to similar games offered via an electronic support, i.e., the Internet.

1482. The case-law of the Court of Justice appears to admit that national legislation, which prohibits the promotion, organization, operation and advertising of any games of chance or fortune, whatever the platform used, which is not authorized or the subject of a concession granted by the Member State, even if the said activity is carried on by an entity established in another Member State, is compatible with community law. The said national legislation must, however always be proportionate, necessary and appropriate for the intended purpose, i.e., the protection of national consumers from the risks of fraud and crime. This judgment of the Court of Justice accordingly confirms the existence of an area that is partially the province of the Member States, i.e., legislation regarding games of chance and fortune.

1483. The fact that the legislation regarding games of chance or fortune is one of the areas in which there are still considerable moral, religious and cultural differences between the Member States was certainly decisive in the cautious posture adopted by the Court of Justice, when it did not consider that the Member State, in which the Internet betting services are provided, is required to recognize the control of these services effected by the Member State where the operator has its registered office. It appears to be a consequence of the Judgment that until such time as standard community legislation is adopted, suppliers of Internet betting services will be subject to the Portuguese prohibition and must refrain from providing their services in Portugal.

Chapter 2. Sponsorship

§1. Sponsorship Contracts

I. Introduction

1484. Sports sponsorship is one of the most significant sports-linked financial activities. With the professionalization of sport, the increasing commercial appetite for the market created by sport began to attract the attention of major businesses, with the consequence that nowadays, the economic impact of sponsorship on sport is, on a par with television broadcasting rights and ticket sales, one of the main sources of funding of professional sport.

1485. Sponsorship is so important for sports institutions that it was one of the main reasons why the scheduling of the events to be televised at the Sydney Olympic Games in 2000 was changed constantly, so that the most popular events could be broadcast on prime time television. It was also the reason why sports, which are more suited to being broadcast on television, such as beach volleyball and the triathlon, were included in the Olympic Games.[646] Klaus Vieweg[647] recalls the polemic that arose when the Olympics were awarded to the city of Atlanta in 1996, when the obvious choice was Athens because the games coincided with the 100th Anniversary of the Olympic Games in the Modern Era, which had commenced in Athens. Apparently, the fact that the headquarters of a well-known brand and one of the main sponsors of the Olympic movement is located in Atlanta was considered by some to be more than a happy coincidence.

1486. Sponsors also manage to secure massive public recognition and exposure for their products and/or services by being associated with the most significant sports events, such as the Olympic Games and the Football World Cup, which generally receive worldwide attention. The economic relevance of sports sponsorship and the connection between businesses and sports organizations have grown and the contracts between them are increasingly complex.

II. Sponsorship Agreements

1487. A sponsorship agreement is a *special type of advertising,*[648] which involves the indirect dissemination of a promotional message,[649] in which the sponsor associates its brand with the fame, celebrity or personality of an individual, team

646. Compare Klaus Vieweg, Patrocínio e Jogos Olímpicos, *Desporto & Direito, No. 5,* Coimbra, Coimbra Editora, 2004, p. 181.
647. For more developments see Klaus Vieweg, Patrocínio e Jogos Olímpicos, *Desporto & Direito, No. 5,* Coimbra, Coimbra Editora, 2004, pp. 179 et seq.
648. Compare Alexandre Libório Dias Pereira, *Contratos de Patrocínio Publicitário ('Sponsoring'),* Revista da Ordem dos Advogados, vol. I, 1998, p. 322.
649. Alexandre Libório Dias Pereira, *Contratos de Patrocínio Publicitário ('Sponsoring'),* Revista da Ordem dos Advogados, vol. I, 1998, p. 320.

or organization and/or with the prestige or fame of a sports event, via the use of a distinctive symbol.[650] In other words, a sponsorship agreement can be defined as a bilateral contract for valuable consideration by which one of the parties, the sponsoree, agrees to collaborate with and to publicize the other party, the sponsor, or its products and brands, in return for the provision of assistance and benefits, in either cash or kind (i.e., via product placement), in relation to the conduct of a sporting activity.[651]

1488. Portuguese law permits this type of contract and makes them subject to the legal framework governing advertising contracts. Article 24 of the Advertising Code defines advertising as *the participation of natural or juristic persons in the financing of any audiovisual, works, programmes [...] whatever the medium used to disseminate it, in order to promote its name or image, its activities, goods or services.* This legal definition includes the references that enable us to identify a sponsorship agreement in a specific case and to submit it to the legal framework governing advertising.

1489. Sponsorship is one of the forms of promotional communication and is one of the operations comprised in the concepts of *advertising* and *advertising activity* defined in the Advertising Code, introduced by Article 3, no. 1 and Article 4 of Decree-Law no. 330/90, of 23 October.[652] According to this legislation governing Advertising, sponsorship is inserted in the section called *special types of advertising.*[653]

1490. Case-law[654] defines a sponsorship agreement as a contract that amounts to the *participation of any persons in the financing of a sports activity, with a view to the promotion of its name or image, or its activities, goods or services, whatever the medium used.*[655] The same Court also defined sponsorship in the following way:

> In the absence of specific legislatory provision in Portugal, advertising sponsorship must be approached as a so-called advertising dissemination contract, i.e. a contract in which one party agrees to work in order to produce an

---

650. The distinctive signs of an undertaking can include its logotype and slogan, *inter alia.*
651. For more details on the subject, see Alexandre Libório Dias Pereira, *Contratos de Patrocínio Publicitário ('Sponsoring'),* Revista da Ordem dos Advogados, vol. I, 1998, pp. 324 et seq.
652. Article 3, no. 1: *Advertising is any type of communication within the ambit of a commercial, industrial, handicraft or liberal activity, with the direct or indirect aim to promote the supply of goods or services, including rights and obligations, or to promote ideas, principles, initiatives or institutions.* Article 4: *Advertising business comprises the series of operations related to the dissemination of an advertising message to its targets and the legal and technical relations arising therefrom between advertisers, advertising agencies and entities that operate advertising supports, or which are in the advertising business.*
653. The Title of Section IV of Chapter II of the Advertising Code.
654. Judgment of the Lisbon Appeal Court dated 30 Apr. 1998, Civil Section, *Pedro Lamy Produções, Lda. v. Chaves, Feist e Cª Lda.*, in Colectânea de Jurisprudência, Year XXIII – 1998, Tome II, pp. 135 et seq.
655. Article 24 of the Advertising Code, introduced by Decree-Law no. 330/90, of 23 October.

advertising result in return for payment by the other party, which is a type of contract for the supply of services.

1491. The *Code on Sponsorship,* of the International Chamber of Commerce defines sponsorship as *all communication by means of which a sponsor provides finance or support of another sort in order to associate its image, organisation, brand, products or services with an event, activity, organisation or person sponsored.*

1492. It follows from Article 1154 of the Civil Code that, in the absence of specific legislative provision, a sports sponsorship agreement is a type of *contract for the supply of advertising services,* within the ambit of a sports activity.

1493. According to the provisions of Article 1156 of the Civil Code, and as there is no specific legislative provision with regard to sponsorship agreements, the provisions of the legal framework governing *agency agreements* is applicable with the necessary adaptations.

1494. So far as breach of contract is concerned, the law distinguishes between, *breach, delayed performance and defective performance.* No. 2 of Article 1170 of the Civil Code provides that, in the absence of just cause, an *agency agreement* may only be revoked by agreement between the parties. When there is just cause *notice to terminate* must be given. This is also termed *unilateral revocation.*

1495. The Law does not define *just cause* but the case-law, in line with the prevailing opinion in legal theory, has considered *that just cause amounts to all subjective or object acts or omissions, which render the continued existence of the contractual relationship impossible, i.e. which creates a situation in which one of the parties cannot be required to continue in the contractual relationship.*[656]

1496. In such contracts, the parties can stipulate the content of their obligations so that the sponsorship will include features of other types of contract, e.g., *a contract for works* or a *rental agreement.*

III. Sponsorship and Patronage

1497. The first model of sponsorship was based on ideas of generosity and donations by the sponsor, similar to patronage, and not on the obligation of the sponsor to provide the agreed performance. The sponsor donated a sum of money to the sponsoree, whose only obligation was to continue with the normal course of its activity as previously carried on.

1498. Such a contract is legally defined as a *patronage agreement.* The *patron* receives important tax benefits, by donating to activities in the areas of culture, the

656. Judgment of Supreme Court of Justice, CJ, Year IV, Tome 2, p. 151.

environment, science or sport, for which it receives nothing in return from the *donee.*

1499. These days, *patronage* is *a special form of advertising* by the patron and the concept of the philanthropic and altruistic nature of *patronage* no longer applies. The obligations of the donee under a patronage arrangement are therefore very clearly defined. A merely passive attitude does not suffice and donees are required to promote the patron's image in exchange for money, products or services.

1500. The main objective of the sponsor, when entering into a sponsorship agreement, is to achieve a favourable recognition of its image via advertising.

1501. Sponsorship agreements are strictly commercial, which distinguishes them from patronage arrangements. It is a bilateral contract, i.e., it involves rights and obligation of both parties.

IV. Sports Sponsorship Agreements

1502. For the purposes of classification and the identification of the legal framework applicable, a sponsorship agreement is a contract that is characterized by the specificity of its *economic and social function,* which limits the application of provisions related to other types of contracts. The vast range of concepts proposed by authors and the case-law is virtually unanimous that the *social and economic function,* or typical core activity, of sponsorship is: the pursuance of an advertising objective via the funding of persons and/or events that have media interest.

1503. A possible definition proposed by legal theory[657] is that, which considers sponsorship to be *the contract whereby a person, termed the sponsoree, agrees, via the sponsoree's participation in an event, to ensure the presence at that event of the brand name or other distinctive signs of another person, termed the sponsor, in order to disseminate the same to the direct and indirect public of the event, in exchange for financial and/or material assistance provided by the sponsor.*

1504. Another definition proposed by legal theory is that which considers a sponsorship agreement to be that which gives rise to *legal relations with an extremely heterogeneous content via which an undertaking (the sponsor) proposes to increase its public profile or to renew, improve or ritualise its institutional image, in the eyes of the general public, in a wide variety of ways, via the creation of a particular connection between its name, brand or symbol and the name, personage, fame, image, activity or undertaking of the sponsoree, in return for payment.*[658]

1505. Sports sponsorship agreements can be classified as follows:

657. Alexandre Libório Dias Pereira, *supra*, p. 324.

658. António Payan Martins, *O Contrato de Patrocínio – Subsídios para o Estudo de um Novo Tipo Contratual,* Direito e Justiça, vol. XII, tome 2, 1998, p. 187 and 188.

(a) *sponsorship of a sports event*, in which the sponsor assumes the obligation to bear the costs of the event, *for example a football match, or a major sports competition*;
(b) *club sponsorship agreement*, in which the typical obligation is the display of the brand name on the team's equipment and promotional activities on the field and at the entrances to sports facilities, or, in which the club also changes its name so as to include the sponsor's name;
(c) *sponsorship of a sportsperson* via the supply of equipment and sporting clothing, which the player is obliged to use. The player also permits the use of his/her name and image for advertising purposes;
(d) *pool sponsorship agreements,* in which a sports federation or body such as the International Olympic Committee grants the exclusive sponsorship of an event to a group of undertakings and gives them the title of Official Sponsor and the exclusive use of advertising locations, in exchange for the supply of sports equipment and other products during the event.

1506. The contracts listed above are related because in all of them the aim is to directly or indirectly advertise or disseminate the name or image of the sponsor and are categorized as *atypical transactions that are an expression of contractual freedom and that are used to satisfy the requirements of modern corporate communications, and play an important role in the economy of the interests of certain groups,*[659] instead of trying to reduce the various types of sponsorship agreement to a single type.

1507. Another form of sponsorship agreement is provided in Article 9 of Decree-Law no. 273/2009, of 1 October, which governs sports development programme contracts and states that sports actors, whose activity as such projects the name of Portugal internationally, and natural or juristic persons, which promote or organize sports events can receive financial sponsorship, to which the rules of sports development programme contracts apply.

1508. Although the sponsorship agreement is an atypical contract, and therefore not mandatorily celebrated in writing, these contracts normally involve large sums of money are therefore usually in writing, so that the applicable law which will govern the contract will normally be stipulated.

V. The Parties

1509. The parties to a sponsorship agreement are the sponsor, or advertiser, whose is interested in promoting itself, and the sponsoree, whose primary interest is to obtain funding.[660] Nowadays, the sportsperson also benefits from the association

659. Alexandre Libório Dias Pereira, *supra*, p. 326. This author makes the proviso that to a certain extent sponsorship agreements fall within the legal type of advertising contracts (see above).
660. Not infrequently, sponsorship also involves a desire for promotion and the advantage of being linked with a certain sponsor.

with a well-known brand, so there is a different approach on how sportspersons choose their sponsors. It is not only about the funding, but it is also about the values of the sponsor. Sponsors normally choose their sponsorees wisely so that the risk of bad advertising can be minimized. Top athletes, those who can bring more value to sponsors, are actually considering carefully which brands they choose to partner with. A weak image or value of the sponsor can also hurt the sponsoree, especially if it happens to be a famous sportsperson. The sponsoree can be a single person or a company.

1510. The other party in the sponsorship contract is the sponsor, which can be one or more persons or companies. If there is more than one sponsor, the sponsorship is termed *pool* sponsorship, which is quite likely to occur in major sporting events, such as the Olympic Games or the World Cup.

1511. The obligations of each party differ on a case-by-case basis, according to the type of sponsorship involved. So far as the sponsor is concerned, the key aspect of its performance is the funding of the sponsoree, which can be in cash, services or kind. In the latter case it can take the form of property transfer or the mere grant of a licence to use property (e.g., equipment). The funding amount is not always fixed and depends on the agreement between the parties and may depend on titles or be subject to the sports performance of the sponsoree.

1512. The contractual performance required of the sponsoree involves a considerable amount of uncertainty and unforeseeability as it is impossible to predict the performance of sportspersons. Accordingly, while the performance required of the sponsor is clear, the sponsoree's performance involves an element of *uncertainty, which is linked to the success of the agreement:* i.e., the number of spectators present at the event, the international success of the club sponsored and any disqualification of the player for doping.

1513. Clauses are included in sponsorship agreement in order to reduce this random element. Such clauses provide that the sponsor's contributions are directly proportional to the result achieved by the sponsoree. This is because the advertising and profile sought by the sponsor, which has complied with its obligations, and therefore has a legitimate interest in the success of the sponsoree, is also directly dependent on the said sporting result.

1514. The sponsoree's primary obligation is the provision of spaces and/or genuine promotion opportunities in order to maximize the sponsor's advertising potential. This also reduces the element of randomness in this type of contract, because the sponsoree is *a priori* unable to guarantee the expected advertising return and accordingly cannot be contractually bound so to do.

1515. The sponsoree's positive and negative obligations are commonly specifically stipulated. For example:

(a) to advertise the sponsor's brand at the various locations at its disposal, i.e., on the players' shirts, sports facility entry tickets or on the sponsoree's promotional material;
(b) to participate in various promotional events organized by the sponsor;
(c) not to make any depreciative statements or to behave in a way that could denigrate the sponsor's image;
(d) to use the equipment provided by the sponsor;
(e) the sponsoree consents to the use by the sponsor of its image, name and emblem;
(f) authorization for the sponsor to call itself an Official Sponsor and to use certain spaces at the event location in order to advertise its products.

1516. It is debated in legal theory[661] whether, in the absence of a contractual clause to that effect, the sponsor can rescind the agreement with just cause when the sponsoree prejudices the sponsor's image, as a consequence of circumstances for which the sponsoree is not liable.

1517. For, so far as the advertising effect sought by the sponsor is concerned, *the sponsoree can only assume an obligation to seek to obtain a result but cannot be obliged to achieve it.*[662] Furthermore the randomness involved in sponsorship agreements involves an allocation of risk, which is more onerous for the sponsor.

1518. According to legal theory, a contract may be rescinded when circumstances *render the achievement of the purpose of the contract impossible, or seriously prejudice the same, in such a way that the continued existence of the contract until the end of the contractual term agreed, or in the case of termination on notice, the term imposed, is not enforceable.*[663]

VI. Personality Rights

1519. Personality rights, such as image rights, have become increasingly important because of the evolution of communications and the importance that questions of image have come to assume in the context of sports advertising.[664]

1520. The taking and dissemination of images in contemporary society has caused a great exposure of those who have achieved prominence in their areas of activity. This has resulted in the fact that the image of such people has a considerable and unexpected value. Sport is no stranger to this phenomenon.

---

661. For further developments see Alexandre Libório Dias Pereira. *Do Patrocínio Desportivo («Sponsoring»).* Revista Desporto e Direito. Year II. Coimbra. Coimbra Editora, 2005, pp. 363 et seq.
662. Alexandre Libório Dias Pereira, *supra,* p. 332, note 50.
663. Article 30, para. b) of the Legal Framework governing Commercial Agency Contracts, Decree-law no. 178/86, of 3 June, as amended by Decree-Law no. 118/93, of 13 April.
664. For more developments on image rights of professional sportspersons, see Sofia de Barros e Carvalhosa. *O Direito de Imagem do Praticante Desportivo Profissional.* Lisbon: Universidade Lusíada Editora, 2008.

1521. Image rights are a fundamental personality right. The person entitled to the right cannot deprive himself of his own image, but can freely deal it. This means that all persons are entitled to the said right, whatever their social, economic and cultural level.

1522. No. 1 of Article 26 of the CRP states expressly that *all persons are entitled to their image* and to *privacy, good name and reputation.*

1523. The legal protection of the right to private life has two aspects: protection against intromission in private life and the prohibition of revelation with regard thereto. Article 70 of the Civil Code establishes general legal protection of personality rights, and prohibits offences against honour, reputation and self-esteem. Article 80 of the said legislation states that *all persons shall respect the intimacy of the private life of others.*

1524. The major characteristic of the right of a person to their image is that it is disposable, despite the fact that it is inalienable and cannot be renounced, i.e., it is possible for a person to deal with their image in such a way that third parties can use it for various purposes, provided that the same are not contrary to the law or public morality, so that a person also has a right to transact their own image.

1525. As is stated above, image rights are specifically regulated by Articles 70, 71 and 79 of the Civil Code, which impose the requirement that a person must consent to the use of his image for commercial purposes. Article 79 of the Civil Code strengthens this right by expressly providing that portraits and images may not be reproduced if this prejudices the honour, reputation or decorum of the person portrayed.

1526. However image rights are subject to limitations. The law dispenses with the said requirement for the consent of the person entitled to the right, when this is justified by reason of the fame of the person in question or matters of public interest. This is understandable because the sole objective of this dispensation is to ensure another right, i.e., the right to information, as enshrined in Article 37 of the CRP.

1527. Nevertheless, it is important to bear in mind that despite the fact that the sportsperson is a public figure or a famous person, the publication or dissemination of images in respect of his or her private life without the person's consent, amounts to unjustified unlawful conduct, which cannot be justified merely on the basis of the duty to inform. There must always be a link between the images, or facts divulged regarding the private life of sportspersons and their professional activity. Furthermore if the public interest in being informed is to prevail there must be communication of information. This is the legal situation that arises from Article 10 of the RJCTPD. In the specific case of football, the applicable CCT provides that the right to use and take commercial advantage of a player's image belongs to the player on a purely individual level and that the player can transfer the right to his employer club, even if the club or sports company reserves the right to use the collective image of all of the players in a team.[665] This is a way of strengthening and safeguarding the scope and protection of the use of a professional player's image rights.

1528. The *right to information* must be exercised in accordance with reasonable criteria in order to prevent the abusive exercise of the right, particularly because it is difficult to delimit the circumstances in which the consent of the holder of image rights is required and the nature and extent thereof. It has been considered that the taking and publication of public images of a sportsperson does not require that person's consent provided they are taken of him in the exercise of his profession, or in some way linked thereto, or as a public figure, provided that this does not interfere with his right to privacy. In other words, the safeguarding of the privacy of the sportsperson as a citizen is one of the absolute limits to the freedom of the press.

1529. The unlawfulness of conduct contrary to the fundamental rights of the sportsperson cannot be negated by the fact that he is a public person, who is famous because of the fact that he is a sportsperson. This was what happened in the case *Luís Figo v. Revista Lux*[666] in which photographs of a visit by the player to Madrid in order to visit his house there, while it was being built, which were taken without the player's consent, were published. This amounted to a violation of his image rights and of his right to privacy. In fact the images published were unconnected with the player's occupation or with his public life and could not be justified because of the fact that the player is a sportsperson, who is well-known to most people. This meant that the lack of the player's consent was decisive.

1530. Clubs and SADs have the same rights as it is considered that the capacity of juristic persons to enjoy their rights includes personality rights with regard to freedom, reputation, credit and social consideration. When the rights to freedom of expression and freedom of the press fail to take those values into consideration, such conduct can give rise to liability in damages, i.e., in cases of defamation of the standing of a juristic person, via the journalistic dissemination of facts likely to reduce confidence as to its compliance with its commitments. Clubs are accordingly entitled to their image, i.e., logotypes, in order to identify their products and services and promote their images as clubs.

1531. The extent of the *right to privacy*[667] can be defined by the person, who is entitled thereto, to the extent that *property rights* are based on the power involved in personal autonomy, which rights become effective when legal assets protected by the constitution become assets with economic value in economic and social life, which can be traded on a market.

---

665. According to the previous legislation – Decree-Law no. 305/95, of 18 November – the right to use a collective image was subject to the consent of the employer. With the amendment of no. 2 of Art. 10 in 1998, the said right became the subject matter of a collective bargaining agreement. In football, the CCT provided that the SJPF is responsible for the commercial exploitation of players' images.

666. Judgment of the Supreme Court of Justice dated 14 Jun. 2005, available at www.dgsi.pt.

667. Article 79 of the Civil Code.

1532. The following are the rights protected by the constitution:

(a) protection of the intimacy of private life;
(b) honour;
(c) the teleological aspect of the right to one's own image. The collateral aspects of these rights can be governed by ordinary legislation.

1533. In sports legislation, Article 10 of the RJCTPD,[668] recognizes that professional sportspersons are entitled to use their public image linked to sports activity and to take steps to prevent third parties from using their public image unlawfully, whether or not the said use is for economic gain.

1534. The sportsperson is entitled to transfer his right to his sports public image to the club for which he plays. This entitlement is provided for in the CCT between the LPFP and the SJPF. This means that images rights, as personality rights per se are inalienable, although the commercial exploitation operation of a player's image is not, so that the said commercial exploitation can be undertaken by the player, or someone else.

1535. When the sponsoree is a juristic person, e.g., a football team, the problem arises as to whether the sponsor can use the individual images of the players and whether they can oppose the publication of images of the team as a whole by the sponsor for advertising purposes. This right to the collective image of all of the players in a team is granted to the club, which is a restriction of the individual right of each player to his image. This is the interpretation provided by clause 38 of the CCT between the LPFP and the SJPF, in accordance with Article 10 of the RJCTPD and the Sportspersons Training Contract, although the player may share in the economic benefits arising therefrom. However, not infrequently, particularly in the case of players with a very high media profile, the consent for the commercial exploitation of the player's image may be given to a third party, which is specialized in such matters.

1536. It should be noted that the assignment of the commercial exploitation of a professional sportsperson's image enables the player to concentrate on, or dedicate himself to, his profession. This is the explanation why the Portuguese legislation does not contain restrictions identical to those in Article 79 of the Civil Code, to the extent that:

> people do not generally have a permanent fame with a commercial value that exceeds the value of an isolated portrait of that person. This is not true of professional sports persons, who become well-known. This explains the frequent display of their portraits for commercial ends. This would be complicated

668. Article 10 of the CCT.

extremely if it was necessary to make an assignment agreement for each specific portrait with a view to the commercial exploitation of the image for the benefit of the player.[669]

The fact that, i.e., the CCT contains no restriction similar to that found in Article 79 of the Civil Code, is understandable, as people in general very rarely have a commercial image of significant value, while this is common in the case of sportspersons.

1537. Accordingly, a contract assigning image rights entirely would be null and void on the grounds that it is contrary to public policy, in accordance with the provisions of Article 81, no. 1 and Article 280, no. 2, of the Civil Code, while the assignment of the commercial exploitation of an image would be permitted by special law.

1538. According to the case-law,[670] the balance between the fundamental rights of freedom of expression and information, on the one hand, and the right to a good name and reputation, on the other, is established via the application of the principle of proportionality. However none of these rights are absolute and they accordingly do not prevail *erga omnes*.

1539. The *right to express thought in words* is a Fundamental Right provided in Article 37 of the CRP, which also guarantees *a right of reply and to rectification and damages for loss and damage sustained*. The connection between these two rights is not always easy to manage because they frequently conflict. This question must be resolved by not prioritizing one to the unjust detriment of the other.

1540. In the absence of better criteria, it is the sense of civic responsibility with which rights are exercised that prevents conflict between them. The case-law[671] considers that freedom of expression cannot be used to attack the right to good name and reputation, except when a matter of public interests is at stake, which prevails over the said right and the facts are revealed in such a way as to as not to exceed what is strictly necessary for the said purpose. If reasonable limits are exceeded, the person in question will be liable in damages.

1541. It is considered that the entitlement to damages in the final part of Article 37 of the CRP does not require the existence of negligence. This criterion is only relevant to the quantum of damages, if intentional conduct cannot be proved.

1542. The use of improper expressions to describe a situation is also unlawful not only when privacy issues are involved but also when improper expressions are used to describe conduct arising from sports activity in which the criterion of

669. Judgment of the Supreme Court of Justice dated 25 Oct. 2005.
670. That is the SCJ judgment of 27 May 1997 available at www.dgsi.pt.
671. The judgment of the Oporto Court of Appeal, of 3 Mar. 2005, available at www.dgsi.pt.

proportionality is not complied with, whatever the nature of the liability of those using them.

1543. Legal theory tends to consider that image rights and the right to privacy are fundamental rights and are innate and inalienable, cannot be renounced and are absolute and opposable *erga omnes*.

1544. If image rights are *a priori* inalienable, the assignment effected by a contract for the commercial exploitation of an image is lawful, as provided in Article 10 of the CCT, which permits the commercial exploitation of public images linked to sports activities. The sportsperson can oppose the use, by another, of his public image arising from his sports activities, for commercial or other economic purposes.

1545. The judgment of the Supreme Court of Justice of 25 October 2005,[672] established a distinction between image rights per se, as a personality right, which is inalienable, and the commercial exploitation of an image, which is not. A person entitled to image rights accordingly has two options: either he handles the commercial exploitation of his image himself, or assigns the mere right to exploit his image for commercial purposes, to another.

1546. Even so, the assignment of the right to exploit an image commercially must be limited in time so that the sportsperson does not effectively renounce his image rights via the assignment and continues to be the person entitled to the right.

§2. Sports and Advertising

I. Advertising Tobacco and Alcohol Brands in Sport

1547. The current legal framework governing the advertising of tobacco is to be found in Law no. 37/2007, of 14 August, which came into force on 1 January 2008 and which, *inter alia,* introduces anti-smoking rules, particularly with regard to protection from passive smoking, the regulations governing the information to be provided regarding tobacco products, health awareness and education, the prohibition of tobacco advertising, promotion and sponsorship, in order to contribute to the reduction of the risks or negative effects associated with the use of tobacco.

1548. Article 2 defines advertising of tobacco as *any form of communication by public or private bodies, within the ambit of a commercial, industrial, handicraft or liberal activity, with the direct or indirect aim to promote a tobacco product or the consumption thereof,* which is similar to the definition in the Advertising Code.

---

672. Available at www.dgsi.pt.

1549. According to Article 16 of the said Law, *all form of advertising and promotion of tobacco and tobacco products, including hidden, dissimulated and subliminal advertising, on Portuguese advertising supports, or supports, which have their registered office in Portugal, including information society services is prohibited [...].* Advertising of tobacco in automatic vending machines is also prohibited, subject to the exceptions in Article 16.

1550. In the case of motor racing, the sport in which tobacco advertising is of greatest significance, as it is traditionally its primary sponsor and one of its most important revenue sources, even after tobacco advertising restrictions began to arise, Decree-Law no. 52/87, of 30 January provided that tobacco brand sponsorship of *motor sports racing events that are part of the World or European Championships of these sports* be permitted exceptionally for five years. This time limit was successively extended by Decree-Laws no. 242/91, of 5 July, 203/95, of 3 August and 178/2001, of 9 June. Nevertheless, the legal framework of Decree-Law no. 52/87, of 30 January, was extended to cover motorbike racing events that are part of the World or European Championships, by Decree-Law no. 346/88, of 29 September.

1551. However tobacco advertising has not been permitted since the coming into force of Decree-Law no. 37/2007, of 14 August, i.e., since 1 January 2008. As João Lima Cluny correctly observes,[673] high profile motor racing events, recognized in Order no. 26326/2006, of the Secretary of State of Youth and Sport, of 29 December, and other such orders, depend on the sponsorship of tobacco brands in order to be able to continue to take place in Portugal. However, given the innumerable exceptions to the prohibition there are serious doubts whether the prohibition enshrined in the law will be complied with.

1552. In the case of the advertising of alcoholic beverages, the corresponding legal framework is to be found in Article 17 of the Advertising Code, introduced by Decree-Law no. 330/90, of 23 October, which was based on Article 15 of European Directive no. 89/552/EEC, of 3 October.

1553. This is a matter that has received special care and attention both nationally and internationally and which is not free of controversy. Advertising of alcoholic beverages is only permitted when:

(a) it is not specifically targeted at minors and specifically does not show them drinking alcoholic beverages;
(b) does not encourage excessive consumption;
(c) does not disparage consumers;
(d) does not suggest that the consumption of alcoholic beverages will lead to social success or result in special aptitudes;

673. João Lima Cluny e Jorge Morais de Carvalho. *Publicidade ao Tabaco e às Bebidas Alcoólicas no Desporto.* João Lima Cluny and Jorge Morais Carvalho. Desporto & Direito, *Revista Jurídica do Desporto. Ano v. Coimbra, Coimbra Editora,* 2008. pp. 411 et seq.

(e) does not suggest that alcoholic beverages have therapeutic properties or stimulant or sedative effects;
(f) does not associate the consumption of alcoholic beverages with physical exercise or the driving of vehicles;
(g) does not emphasise the alcohol content of alcoholic beverages as a positive quality.

1554. There are additional prohibitions, such as the association of alcoholic drinks with Portuguese national symbols, or the broadcasting of advertising for alcoholic beverages on television or radio, between 7 a.m. and 10:30 p.m.

1555. The aim of these provisions is clear, i.e., to ensure that advertising of alcoholic beverages is conducted with great reserve and is subject to clear limits, in order to protect consumers, who are easily influenced.

1556. Finally, it should be noted that according to the legal framework in no. 4 of Article 17 of the Advertising Code, the association of Portuguese national symbols with alcoholic beverages is prohibited, which may cause us to query the cases of sponsorship of the Portuguese national football and rugby teams by brewers.

II. Advertising of Games of Chance or Fortune

1557. Article 21 of the Advertising Code almost completely prohibits advertising of games of chance or fortune and provides that games of chance or fortune cannot be advertised as the essential subject matter of the message, with the exception of the games promoted by the Santa Casa da Misericórdia de Lisboa.

1558. This prohibition includes all types of publicity. The law does not however appear to prohibit advertising of these types of games, when they are not the essential subject matter of the communication. It is therefore possible to consider that the advertisements around sports facilities, or sponsorship of the equipment and kit of sportspersons, which is related to games of chance or fortune but which are linked to sports activity, are not be the essential message and may be permitted.

III. The Combat against Ambush Marketing

1559. At the time of the organization of Euro 2004, Decree-Law no. 86/2004, of 17 April was introduced in order to increase the protection of the distinctive signs of Portuguese commerce by ensuring that the names and symbols created exclusively for the Euro 2004 were not used for advertising or commercial purposes by unauthorized bodies seeking to profit unduly from the values associated with the event. The said legislation also created mechanisms by way of reaction against any uses of symbols, with the intention to damage the profile of the event or masquerading as an Official Sponsor in order to take advantage of the personal benefits inherent therein.

1560. This legislation added little to trademark protection in the strict sense of the phrase, but did concentrate on the penalties to be imposed. The decree-law introduced a system of administrative fines that differed depending on whether the offender was a natural or juristic person and punished the use of the symbols associated with Euro 2004, or any direct or indirect use, of a sign associated with the event, for commercial or advertising purposes and without the authorization of the organizers, in a clear attempt to combat *ambush marketing*.

1561. Decree-Law no. 193/2008, of 6 October, introduced the legal framework to protect the designations of the 2nd Lusophone Games,[674] and the mechanisms to strengthen the direct and indirect fight against unlawful taking advantage of the benefits arising from this sports event. This decree-law established mechanisms to strengthen the direct and indirect fight in any manner against the unlawful obtaining of advantages from the 2nd Lusophone Games, in order to ensure an effective reaction by the proper public authorities against the unlawful use of signs, which damage or devalue their image.

674. The 2nd Lusophone Games took place from the 11–19 Jul. 2009, in Lisbon by decision of the General Assembly of the Association of Olympic Committees in Official Lusophone Countries, which is an excellent opportunity to promote Portugal among those countries.

Chapter 3. Merchandising

§1. Merchandising Contracts

I. Introduction

1562. Merchandising is an activity, which involves all techniques related to the promotion of a product. These techniques include:

(a) the analysis of the relevant market in terms of both business and consumer aspects;
(b) new product research and development;
(c) co-ordination between production, marketing and distribution;
(d) advertising and sale of products.

1563. It is a commercial practice that involves a series of techniques, the aim of which is to improve the sales results of a specific product, or to promote a brand, via a detailed knowledge of the characteristics of the relevant market, combined with the best marketing techniques.

1564. In legal terms, a merchandising agreement is an atypical contract, which is subject to the general contract rules in the Civil Code, as there is no specific legal provision regarding merchandising agreements.

1565. In recent years there has been a massification of sport that gives rise to huge revenue for clubs and their players. One of the main revenue sources is the commercial exploitation of image and brand rights and the sale of sports equipment. This revenue is made possible by the commercial exploitation of these rights, which are assigned by clubs, players and federations to undertakings that are specialized in this business area.

II. Merchandising Agreements

1566. The commercial assignment of rights is normally governed by a sports merchandising agreement, which can, *inter alia*, include the commercial exploitation of sports programmes and events, broadcast rights, brands, symbols and logotypes and other items belonging to the club.

1567. These activities do not fall within the ambit of sponsorship agreements, as the main objective of merchandising agreements is not advertising. In merchandising contracts, the sportsperson, club, or other sports entity is not obliged to advertise an undertaking in exchange for payment, but merely authorizes the commercial exploitation of an image or brand by an undertaking.

1568. Merchandising agreements can therefore be defined as agreements whereby the owner of a brand grants the right to use the same to another undertaking, so that the latter may use the same on its products, which are considerably different in terms of form and purpose from the products for which they were originally registered. In other words, *in a merchandising agreement, one party grants its rights in respect of its distinctive signs to another, for payment, so that the same may be placed on materials or products of third parties, so that the said materials or products gain a high awareness profile, which facilitates the sale thereof.*[675]

1569. The transaction therefore involves two objectives in terms of the use of the brand: the use of the brand creates added value, which attracts the consumer to buy the products and permits the final consumer to use this added value to his benefit.

III. Personality and Corporate Merchandising

1570. Personality merchandising exists when merchandising is associated with the image right of a sportsperson, i.e., the right to use the image of a sportsperson as a brand, in order to add value to products or services, thus taking advantage of its commercial and advertising value.

1571. Corporate merchandising is the use of the brand of a club, via its name or logo, in order to add value to products or services, which are different from those that were originally related to the use of the brand. Accordingly, the sports brands of clubs are protected in the same way as the brands of other undertakings and this includes protection against the improper or unauthorized use thereof by third parties.

IV. Protection of Trademarks

1572. Legal certainty is of decisive importance, not only in the formation of sponsorship agreements, but also in the making of merchandising agreements and similar contracts, because it is not reasonable to grant exclusive rights with regard to names, logotypes and trademarks, if the parties do not have the appropriate legal mechanisms available to them to combat the unauthorized use thereof. The legal protection of trademarks is according one of the prerequisites of their economic value.

1573. The protection of trademarks is guaranteed by industrial property rights, i.e., the Industrial Property Code (CPI), which was published as an annexe to Decree-Law no. 36/2003, of 5 March, i.e., Articles 222 et seq. and was later amended by Decree Law no. 461/2011 of 24 June.

---

675. Ricardo Candeias, *Personalização de Equipa e Transformação de Clube em Sociedade Anónima Desportiva (Contributo para um Estudo das Sociedades Desportivas)*, Coimbra Editora, 2000, p. 135, note 356.

1574. Despite the fact that the clubs have logotypes, by which they can be recognized immediately and which are protected by law, the characteristic colours of a club is perhaps the most important way clubs are identified. Although there is no express provision in the CPI, these colours should also be protected by the law, within the ambit of collective trademarks, enshrined in Article 228 as association or certification trademarks.[676]

1575. In the event of any lacunae in the Portuguese legislation, recourse to EU legislation should be considered, i.e., to the competition law rules, so that sports trademarks can obtain a broader and more extensive legal protection. However, any conflicts between trademarks and above all between the rights of player trademarks and club trademarks can be avoided via the addition of contractual clauses that ensure greater equality between the parties involved. It is the role of the Law to achieve this in order to ensure the legal protection of participants and their financial success.

676. They can be corporate trademarks, signs or indications used in trade to designate the geographic origin of products or services.

Selected Bibliography

Albuquerque, Nuno. 'A Reserva de Jurisdição para as Instâncias Desportivas Prevista na Lei de Bases do Desporto, e a Limitação de Acesso aos Tribunais para a Composição de Eventuais Diferendos Desportivos Quando Estejam em Causa *Questões Estritamente Desportivas'*. Parecer In *Desporto & Direito. Revista Jurídica do Desporto*, Year V, No. 13, Coimbra, Almedina (2007): 49–89.

Almeida, Carlos Ferreira de. *'Introdução ao Direito Comparado'*. 2nd Edition. Coimbra: Almedina, 1998.

Almeida, João Paulo. 'O Desporto Municipal nas Leis de Bases – Contrastes e Continuidades'. *Desporto & Direito. Revista Jurídica do Desporto*, Year V, No. 15, Coimbra, Almedina (2008): 439–465.

Almeida, Teresa. 'Violência Associada ao Desporto – As Normas Tipificadoras de Ilícitos Penais'. *Desporto & Direito. Revista Jurídica do Desporto*, Year II, No. 4, Coimbra, Almedina (2004): 37–45.

Alves, Paulo Farinha, 'Comentários ao Decreto-Lei n.º 10/2009, de 12 de Janeiro (Regime Jurídico do Seguro Desportivo Obrigatório'). *A Nova Legislação do Desporto Comentada*, Wolters Kluwer/Coimbra Editora, Colecção PLMJ, Lisbon (2010): 153–186.

Amado, João Leal. 'Rescisão do Contrato de Jogadores de Futebol'. *Questões Laborais*, Year II, No. 4 (1995): 50–56.

Amado, João Leal. 'Sobre as Sociedades Desportivas e as *Indemnizações de Transferência'*. *Questões Laborais*, no. 11, Year V (1998): 65–72.

Amado, João Leal. 'O Caso Bosman e as Cláusulas de Nacionalidade (Breves Considerações em Torno de um Protocolo)'. *Revista Jurídica da Universidade Moderna*, Year I, No. 1 (1998): 361–383.

Amado, João Leal. 'O Novo Regime do Contrato de Trabalho Desportivo e as *Indemnizações de Transferência'*. *Questões Laborais*, Year V, No. 12 (1998): 226–240.

Amado, João Leal. 'Arbitrabilidade dos Litígios Emergentes do Contrato de Trabalho Desportivo'. *Questões Laborais*, Year VI, No. 13, (1999): 109–112.

Amado, João Leal. 'Desportistas Profissionais e Associativismo Sindical. Algumas Notas, Trabalho e Relações Laborais'. *Cadernos Sociedade e Trabalho*, No. 1 (2001): 109–119.

Amado, João Leal. 'Vinculação *Versus* Liberdade. O Processo de Constituição e Extinção da Relação Laboral do Praticante Desportivo'. Coimbra: Coimbra Editora, 2002.

Amado, João Leal. 'O Caso Jardel e as Especificidades do Contrato de Trabalho Desportivo'. Boletim da Ordem dos Advogados, No. 22 (2002): 12–13.

Selected Bibliography

Amado, João Leal. 'As Cláusulas de Rescisão e a Comissão Arbitral Paritária'. *Desporto & Direito. Revista Jurídica do Desporto*, Year I, No. 1, Coimbra, Almedina (2003): 83–93.

Amado, João Leal. 'Nota ao Acórdão do Supremo Tribunal de Justiça, de 25 de Junho de 2002'. *Desporto & Direito. Revista Jurídica do Desporto*, Year I, No. 2, Coimbra, Almedina (2004): 349–362.

Amado, João Leal. 'Os Fundos de Jogadores: Um Breve Olhar Jus Laboral'. *Desporto & Direito. Revista Jurídica do Desporto*, Year II, No. 4, Coimbra, Almedina (2004): 27–35.

Amado, João Leal. 'Futebol Profissional e Futebolistas Profissionais (A Peculiar Lógica Empresarial Daquele e o Estatuto Jurídico Destes)'. *Temas Laborais*, Coimbra, Coimbra Editora (2005): 155–173.

Amado, João Leal. 'As Condutas Extra-Laborais do Praticante Desportivo Profissional (Alguns Tópicos Sobre as Chamadas *Saídas Nocturnas* dos Praticantes)'. *Temas Laborais*, Coimbra, Coimbra Editora, (2005): 175–179.

Amado, João Leal. 'Algumas Reflexões Sobre o Chamado Caso Nuno Valente'. *Desporto & Direito. Revista Jurídica do Desporto*, Year III, No. 7, Coimbra, Almedina (2005): 29–39.

Amado, João Leal. 'A Opção de Marcelo'. Desporto *& Direito. Revista Jurídica do Desporto*, Year III, No. 8, Coimbra, Almedina (2006): 289–300.

Amado, João Leal. 'Cavalheirismo e Profissionalismo: Notas Soltas a Propósito do *Caso Maciel'*. *Desporto & Direito. Revista Jurídica do Desporto*, Year III, No. 9, Coimbra, Almedina (2006): 437–449.

Amado, João Leal. 'Das Cláusulas de Nacionalidade às Cláusulas de Formação Local: Uma Diferença Insuficiente?'. *Desporto & Direito. Revista Jurídica do Desporto*, Year IV, No. 10, Coimbra, Almedina (2006): 11–28.

Amado, João Leal. 'Treinador de Voleibol: Entre o Regime Laboral Comum e o Regime Especial do Praticante Desportivo? Nótula ao Acórdão do Supremo Tribunal de Justiça de 24 de Janeiro de 2007'. *Questões Laborais*, Year XIII, No. 28 (2006): 259–263.

Amado, João Leal. 'Comentário de Urgência ao Acórdão do Supremo Tribunal de Justiça, de 7 de Março de 2007 (Caso Zé Tó)'. *Desporto & Direito. Revista Jurídica do Desporto*, Year IV, No. 12, Coimbra, Almedina (2007): 501–517.

Amado, João Leal. *Temas Laborais 2*. Coimbra: Coimbra Editora, 2007.

Amado, João Leal. 'Andrew Webster: Uma Pessoa, Não Uma Mercadoria!'. *Desporto & Direito. Revista Jurídica do Desporto*, Year V, No. 14, Coimbra, Almedina (2008): 267–273.

Andrade, Manuel da Costa. 'As Lesões Corporais (e a Morte) no Desporto'. In *Liber Discipulorum Para Jorge de Figueiredo Dias*, Coimbra, Coimbra Editora (2003): 675–720.

Ascensão, José de Oliveira. *O Direito – Introdução e Teoria Geral*, 13th Edition, Lisbon, Almedina, 2008.

Baptista, Albino Mendes. 'É o Regime Laboral Comum Aplicável aos Contratos Entre Clubes e Treinadores Profissionais?'. *Revista do Ministério Público*, Year XX, No. 80, (1999): 129–139.

Baptista, Albino Mendes. 'A Compensação de Antiguidade a que se Refere o Artigo 46º, nº 3, da LCCT, é Aplicável ao Contrato de Trabalho Desportivo?'. *Revista do Ministério Público*, Year XXII, No. 85 (2001): 143–148.

Baptista, Albino Mendes. 'Arbitragem Desportiva. Tribunal Competente Para o Conhecimento da Acção de Anulação de Decisão Arbitral'. *Revista do Ministério Público*, Year XXII, No. 87 (2001): 125–137.

Baptista, Albino Mendes. 'Breve Apontamento Sobre as Cláusulas de Rescisão'. *Revista do Ministério Público*, Year XXIII, No. 91 (2002): 141–147.

Baptista, Albino Mendes. *Grupo Normal de Trabalho, Equipas B e Dever de Ocupação Efectiva do Praticante Desportivo*. Estudos em Homenagem ao Prof. Doutor Raul Ventura, Direito Comercial – Direito do Trabalho, vol. II. Faculdade de Direito da Universidade de Lisboa, 2003: 819–832.

Baptista, Albino Mendes. *Direito Laboral Desportivo – Estudos*, vol. I, Lisbon: Quid Juris, 2003.

Baptista, Albino Mendes. '*Nota ao Acórdão do Supremo Tribunal de Justiça, de 5 de Dezembro de 2002 (Anulação de Decisão da Comissão Arbitral Paritária – Tribunal Competente)'. Desporto & Direito. Revista Jurídica do Desporto*, Year I, No. 1, Coimbra, Almedina (2003): 137–158.

Baptista, Albino Mendes. *Cedência Temporária de Praticantes Desportivos*. Estudos de Direito de Trabalho em Homenagem ao Professor Manuel Alonso Olea. Coimbra, Coimbra Editora, 2004.

Baptista, Albino Mendes. 'O TAS e as Garantias de Imparcialidade e de Independência dos Árbitros'. *Desporto & Direito, Revista Jurídica do Desporto*, Year I, No. 5, Coimbra, Almedina (2005): 193–199.

Baptista, Albino Mendes. *Estudos Sobre o Contrato de Trabalho Desportivo*. Coimbra: Coimbra Editora, 2006.

Baptista, Albino Mendes. 'O Pacto de Preferência na Relação Laboral Desportiva'. *Minerva. Revista de Estudos Laborais*, Year V, No. 9 (2006): 21–50.

Bento, Jorge Olímpio. 'A Propósito da Lei da *Actividade Física'. Desporto & Direito. Revista Jurídica do Desporto*. Year IV, No. 11, Coimbra, Almedina (2007): 167–183.

Brilha, Ana. 'O Novo Regime do Seguro Desportivo – Verdadeira Inovação?'. *Desporto & Direito. Revista Jurídica do Desporto*, Year VI, No. 17, Coimbra, Almedina (2009): 293–299.

Bork, Robert Heron. *The Antitrust Paradox. A policy at War with Itself.* 2nd edition, New York, 1993.

Caiger, Andrew, et al. *Professional Sport in the European Union: Regulation and Re-regulation*, Ed. Andrew Caiger and Simon Gardiner, TMC Asser Press, The Hague, 2000.

Campos, Manuel Fontaine de, 'A venda com exclusividade dos direitos de radiodifusão televisiva das competições e as regras da concorrência'. *IV Congresso do Direito do Desporto*, Memórias, Lisbon (2015): 11–124.

Candeias, Ricardo Marques. 'Nota ao Acórdão do Supremo Tribunal de Justiça, de 3 de Julho de 2003 (Federação Portuguesa de Futebol – Inscrição de Jogador – Certificado Internacional de Jogador – Qualificação do Acto de Inscrição)'. *Desporto & Direito. Revista Jurídica do Desporto*, Year I, No. 3, Coimbra, Almedina (2004): 491–507.

Selected Bibliography

Candeias, Ricardo Marques. 'Notas ao Acórdão do Supremo Tribunal Administrativo, de 25 de Maio de 2005 (Gestão Profissional dos Clubes Desportivos – Responsabilidade Tributária – Presidente do Conselho Fiscal)'. *Desporto & Direito. Revista Jurídica do Desporto*, Year III, No. 7, Coimbra, Almedina (2005): 87–112.

Canivet, Guy. *Le Droit de la Concurrence Appliqué au Sport. Cour de Monsieur Canivet, Sciences Po 2006-2007.*

Canotilho, José Gomes. '*Direito Constitucional e Teoria da Constituição*'. 3rd Edition. Coimbra. Almedina, 1999.

Carvalho, Ana Celeste, 'O Tribunal Arbitral do Desporto, os tribunais administrativos e os poderes do juiz'. *O Direito do Desporto em Perspectiva*, Edited by Ana Celeste Carvalho, Almedina/CEJ/IPDJ (2015): 21–52.

Carvalho, André Dinis de. *Da Liberdade de Circulação dos Desportistas na União Europeia*. Coimbra: Coimbra Editora, 2003.

Carvalho, Maria João Brazão de. 'Que "Justiça Desportiva nos Tribunais?"'. *O Desporto e o Direito: Prevenir, Disciplinar, Punir,* Livros Horizonte, 2001.

Carvalhosa, Sofia de Barros e. *O Direito de Imagem do Praticante Desportivo Profissional*. Lisbon: Universidade Lusíada Editora, 2008.

Castro, José Ribeiro e. *Lei de Bases do Sistema Desportivo, Anotada e Comentada*. Lisbon, Ministério da Educação, 1990.

Chabert, José Manuel. 'Conceito e Regime das Federações Multidesportivas na Lei de Bases do Sistema Desportivo'. *Sub Judice*, No. 8 (1994): 103–112.

Cluny, João Lima. 'A Lei de Bases da Actividade Física e do Desporto e os Direitos dos Consumidores'. *Desporto & Direito. Revista Jurídica do Desporto*, Year IV, No. 11, Coimbra, Almedina (2007): 299–306.

Cluny, João Lima e Jorge Morais Carvalho. 'Publicidade ao Tabaco e às Bebidas Alcoólicas no Desporto'. *Desporto & Direito. Revista Jurídica do Desporto*, Year V, No. 15, Coimbra, Almedina (2008): 391–423.

Constantino, José Manuel. 'A Centralidade das Federações Desportivas no Modelo Europeu do Desporto e os Efeitos nas Políticas Públicas e no Movimento Olímpico'. *Desporto & Direito. Revista Jurídica do Desporto*, Year IV, No. 12, Coimbra, Almedina (2007): 441–449.

Correia, João. 'Princípios para um Novo Contencioso Desportivo'. *I Congresso de Direito do Desporto, Estoril – Outubro de 2004. Memórias*, Coordenação de Ricardo Costa e Nuno Barbosa, Coimbra: Almedina (2005): 77–83.

Correia, João & José Luís Pereira Seixas. 'A Nova Lei de Bases da Actividade Física e do Desporto. Justiça Desportiva: Que Sentido e Que Limites?', *Desporto & Direito. Revista Jurídica do Desporto*, Year IV, No. 11, Coimbra, Almedina (2007): 221–238.

Correia, João Pedro (2015), 'Regime fiscal das SAD (IRC). Direitos de imagem e comissões de agentes de jogadores'. *O Direito do Desporto em Perspectiva*, Edited by Ana Celeste Carvalho,: 53–67.

Correia, Lúcio. 'Contributo para o Estudo da Cláusula Penal/Cláusula de Rescisão no Contrato de Trabalho Desportivo'. *Minerva, Revista de Estudos Laborais*, Year V, No. 8 (2006): 45–142.

Correia, Lúcio. 'O Praticante Desportivo Profissional e o Empresário Desportivo na Nova Lei de Bases da Actividade Física e do Desporto'. *Desporto & Direito.*

Revista Jurídica do Desporto, Year IV, No. 11, Coimbra, Almedina (2007): 273–283.

Correia, Lúcio. 'Algumas Reflexões Sobre o Caso Bueno/Rodriguez. Um Caso de *Rebeldia* à Liberdade de Trabalho do Praticante Desportivo'. *Desporto & Direito. Revista Jurídica do Desporto*, Year IV, No. 12, Coimbra, Almedina (2007): 419–440.

Correia, Lúcio. *Limitações à Liberdade Contratual do Praticante Desportivo*. Lisbon: Livraria Petrony Editores, 2008.

Correia, Lúcio Miguel. 'Comissão Arbitral Paritária – Processo No. 48-CAP/2007 (Contrato de Trabalho Desportivo – Cláusula de Opção – Liberdade de Exercício de Profissão)'. Anotação In *Desporto & Direito. Revista Jurídica do Desporto*, Year V, No. 15, Coimbra, Almedina (2008): 491–518.

Costa, José Manuel Cardoso da. 'Um Tribunal Arbitral do Desporto em Portugal'. Entrevista In *Desporto & Direito. Revista Jurídica do Desporto*, Year V, No. 13, Coimbra, Almedina (2007): 13–19.

Domingues, Paulo de Tarso, 'As sociedades desportivas'. *IV Congresso do Direito do Desporto*. Memórias, Lisboa (2015): 95–110.

Eklund, Elisabeth. *Following the Rules of the Game. A Competition Law Study of the Collective Sale of Sports Broadcasting Rights*. EUI Working Paper Law No. 99/1, European University Institute, Florence-Department of Law, Italy, 1999.

Faria, Pedro e Alves, Ana Grosso, 'Comentários à Lei n.º 50/2007, de 31 de Agosto, que Estabelece um Novo Regime de Responsabilidade Penal por Comportamentos Susceptíveis de Afectar a Verdade, a Lealdade e a Correcção das Competições e do seu Resultado na Actividade Desportiva', *A Nova Legislação do Desporto Comentada*, Wolters Kluwer/Coimbra Editora, Colecção PLMJ, Lisbon (2010): 9–27.

Fátima Ribeiro, Maria de: *Sociedades Desportivas*. Universidade Católica Editora, Porto, 2015.

Faustino, Manuel. 'A Tributação dos Rendimentos Derivados da Prática de Uma Modalidade Desportiva'. *Fisco*, Year IX, No. 82/83 (1997): 43–54.

Figueira, Rita. 'Reflexões Sobre a Liberalização do Mercado no Futebol'. *Desporto & Direito. Revista Jurídica do Desporto*. Year V, No. 13, Coimbra, Almedina (2007): 37–46.

Flynn, Michael A. & Richard J. Gilbert. *The Analysis of Professional Sports Leagues as Joint Ventures. The Economic Journal*, 111, February 2001.

Gaspar, António Henriques. 'A Corrupção no Fenómeno Desportivo'. *Revista Portuguesa de Ciência Criminal*, Year I, No. 1 (1991): 133–135.

Gomes, João Veiga. 'Restrições à Publicidade na Área do Desporto'. *Desporto & Direito, Revista Jurídica do Desporto*, Year VII, No. 19, Coimbra, Almedina (2009): 71–95.

Gonçalves, Jorge Baptista. 'Os Crimes na Lei Sobre a Prevenção e Punição da Violência Associada ao Desporto (Algumas Considerações)'. *I Congresso de Direito do Desporto. Estoril – Outubro de 2004, Memórias*. Coordenação de Ricardo Costa e Nuno Barbosa, Coimbra: Almedina, 2005, 98–121.

Gonçalves, Paulo Leite. 'O Direito de Opção na Prestação do Desportista Profissional'. *Memórias, II Congresso de Direito do Desporto, Almedina, 2006.*

Selected Bibliography

Gonçalves, Pedro. 'A *Soberania Limitada* das Federações Desportivas – Anotação'. *Cadernos de Justiça Administrativa,* No. 59 (2006): 41–61.

Gonçalves, Pedro. 'Imputação ao Gil Vicente FC de Infracção Disciplinar Muito Grave Consistente na Violação do Disposto no Artigo 63º do Regulamento Disciplinar da Liga Portuguesa de Futebol Profissional'. *Desporto & Direito. Revista Jurídica do Desporto*, Year V, No. 13, Coimbra, Almedina (2007): 91–115.

Goulão, Pedro Pardal. 'Contratação de Treinadores de Futebol – A Natureza Efémera Como Legitimação da Ditadura do Termo'. *Desporto & Direito. Revista Jurídica do Desporto*, Year IV, No. 12, Coimbra, Almedina (2007): 377–392.

Guimarães, João Paulo. *Regime Fiscal dos Clubes de Utilidade Pública.* Direito e Desporto. Estudos Fiscais e de Gestão, Coordenação de Glória Teixeira, Coimbra: Almedina, 2007, 15–37.

Jóia, Rogério, 'O sistema de luta contra a dopagem em Portugal'. O Direito do Desporto em Perspectiva, Edited by na Celeste Carvalho, Almedina/CEJ/IPDJ (2015): 149–175.

Latty, Frank. *Le Degré d'Autonomie de la 'Lex Sportiva' à l'Égard de l'Ordre Juridique Communitaire. La Lex Sportiva: Recherche sur le Droit Transnacional*, Martinus Nijhoff Publishers, Leiden-Boston, 2007, 695–764.

Liquito, Neusa Alexandra. *As Taxas de IVA e a Prática de Actividades Desportivas.* Direito e Desporto. Estudos Fiscais e de Gestão, Coordenação de Glória Teixeira, Coimbra, Almedina, 2007, 85–89.

Lopes, J.J. Almeida. 'A Justiça Desportiva: Que Justiça?'. *Revista de Direito Público*, No. 13, 135–140.

Lourenço, Paulo. 'A Lei de Bases da Actividade Física e do Desporto e a Fiscalidade'. *Desporto & Direito. Revista Jurídica do Desporto*, Year IV, No. 11, Coimbra, Almedina (2007): 295–298.

Machado, Ângela Burnay e Lemos, Raquel Sofia. 'Comentários à Lei n.º 27/2009, de 19 de Julho, que Estabelece o Regime Jurídico de Luta Contra a Dopagem no Desporto', *A Nova Legislação do Desporto Comentada*, Wolters Kluwer/ Coimbra Editora, Colecção PLMJ, Lisbon (2010): 187–277.

Madureira, António Bernardino Peixoto & Teixeira, Luís César Rodrigues. '*Futebol – Guia Jurídico'*. Coimbra: Almedina, 1999.

Marques, José Augusto Garcia. *Desporto, Estado e Sociedade Civil*, *Sub Judice*, No. 8, Coimbra, Almedina, 2007.

Marques, Paulo de Moura. 'Comentários ao Decreto-Lei n.º 248-b/2008, de 31 de Dezembro, que Estabelece o Regime Jurídico das Federações Desportivas e as Condições de Atribuição do Estatuto de Utilidade Pública Desportiva', *A Nova Legislação do Desporto Comentada*, Wolters Kluwer/Coimbra Editora, Colecção PLMJ, Lisbon (2010): 53–153.

Martinez, Pedro Romano, *Direito do Trabalho*. 3rd Edition, Lisbon: Almedina, 2006.

Martinez, Pedro Romano. *A Nulidade de Cláusulas de Convenções Colectivas de Trabalho e o Período Experimental no Contrato de Trabalho Desportivo*. Estudos Jurídicos e Económicos em Homenagem ao Professor Doutor António de Sousa Franco, vol. 3, Lisbon: Faculdade de Direito da Universidade de Lisboa, 2006, 735–751.

Martins, António Payan. *O Contrato de Patrocínio – Subsídios para o Estudo de um Novo Tipo Contratual.* Direito e Justiça, vol. XII, tome 2, 1998, p. 187–243.

Martins, João Zenha. 'O Novo Código do Trabalho e os *Contratos de Trabalho em Regime Especial*: Pistas para o Enquadramento do Contrato de Trabalho Desportivo'. *Revista do Ministério Público,* Year XXIV, No. 95 (2003): 31–71.

Martins, João Zenha. *A Mobilidade dos Futebolistas Profissionais: Contributo para o Estudo do Contrato de Trabalho Desportivo*, Tese de Mestrado, 2 vol., Lisbon: Biblioteca da Faculdade de Direito de Lisboa 2003.

Medeiros, Emanuel Macedo. 'Federações Desportivas e Ligas Profissionais: Que Coabitação'. *Desporto & Direito. Revista Jurídica do Desporto,* Year IV, No. 11, Coimbra, Almedina (2007): 239–255.

Meirim, José Manuel. 'A Violência Associada ao Desporto (Aproximação à Legislação Portuguesa)'. *Boletim do Ministério da Justiça,* No. 389 (1989): 5–40.

Meirim, José Manuel. 'Federações Desportivas – Uma Realidade Jurídica (no Confronto Com o Poder Público)'. *Ludens, Ciências do Desporto,* Volume 13, No. 3/4 (1993): 41–51.

Meirim, José Manuel. 'Federações Desportivas – A Sua Natureza Jurídica na Jurisprudência'. *Sub Judice,* No. 8 (1994): 101-102, Publicação em Dezembro de 1995.

Meirim, José Manuel. 'A Violência Associada ao Desporto'. Colectânea de Textos, Lisbon, Ministério da Educação, 1994.

Meirim, José Manuel. 'A Fiscalização da Constitucionalidade dos Regulamentos das Federações Desportivas'. *Revista do Ministério Público,* Year XVII, No. 66 (1996): 117–130.

Meirim, José Manuel. 'A Disciplina das Federações Desportivas no Contencioso Administrativo – Anotação'. *Cadernos de Justiça Administrativa,* No. 4, (1997): 18–23.

Meirim, José Manuel. *Regime Jurídico das Sociedades Desportivas Anotado.* Coimbra. Coimbra Editora, 1999.

Meirim, José Manuel. *Elementos Para uma Leitura Crítica da Legislação Sobre o Desporto.* Lisbon: Confederação do Desporto de Portugal, 2001.

Meirim, José Manuel. *A Federação Desportiva como Sujeito Público do Sistema Desportivo.* Coimbra: Coimbra Editora, 2002.

Meirim, José Manuel. *O Desporto nos Tribunais*, Lisbon: Centro de Estudos e Formação Desportiva, 2002.

Meirim, José Manuel. 'Justice, What Justice?'. *International Sports Law Review*, Sweet & Maxswell's, May 2007, 2/2007, 24–28.

Meirim, José Manuel. 'Os Magistrados Fazem Mal ao Desporto?'. *Julgar*, No. 2 (2007): 55–77.

Meirim, José Manuel. 'A Utilidade Pública Desportiva do *Caso Nuno Assis'*. *Desporto & Direito. Revista Jurídica do Desporto,* Year IV, No. 12, Coimbra, Almedina (2007): 451–470.

Meirim, José Manuel. *Segurança e Seguranças Desportivas.* Lisboa, Livros Horizonte, 2007.

Meirim, José Manuel. *Desporto e Constituição. Sub Judice*, No. 8, Coimbra, Almedina, 2007.

Meirim, José Manuel. *Lei de Bases da Actividade Física e do Desporto – Estudo, Notas e Comentários*. Coimbra, Coimbra Editora, 2007.

Meirim, José Manuel, 'Ainda há questões estritamente desportivas?' *O Direito do Desporto em Perspectiva*, Edited by Ana Celeste Carvalho, Coimbra, Almedina/CEJ/IPDJ (2015): 11–19.

Mestre, Alexandre Miguel. 'Causas de Exclusão da Ilicitude Penal nas Actividades Desportivas'. *Revista Jurídica*, No. 22 (1998): 495–515.

Mestre, Alexandre. *As Transmissões Televisivas de Eventos Desportivos Face ao Direito Comunitário da Concorrência,* Working Paper 8/2001, Faculdade de Direito da Universidade Nova de Lisboa, 2001.

Mestre, Alexandre Miguel. *Desporto e União Europeia. Uma Parceria Conflituante?*. Coimbra: Coimbra Editora, 2002.

Mestre, Alexandre Miguel. *The Law of the Olympic Games,* The Hague, Cambridge University Press/TMC Asser Institute, 2009.

Mestre, Alexandre Miguel, 'Comentários à Lei n.º 39/2009, de 30 de Julho, que Estabelece o Regime Jurídico do Combate à Violência, ao Racismo, à Xenofobia e à Intolerância nos Espectáculos Desportivos, de Forma a Possibilitar a Realização dos Mesmos em Segurança', *A Nova Legislação do Desporto Comentada*, Wolters Kluwer/Coimbra Editora, Colecção PLMJ, Lisbon (2010): 279–353.

Mestre, Alexandre Miguel , *O Desporto na Lei: um percurso pelo ordenamento jurídico estatal português- Guia Prático*, Lisbon, Vida Económica, 2015.

Mestre, Alexandre Miguel, 'O regime jurídico de combate à violência nos espectáculos desportivos'. *O Direito do Desporto em Perspectiva*, Edited by Ana Celeste Carvalho, Coimbra, Almedina/CEJ/IPDJ (2015): 203–233.

Monteiro, António Pinto. 'Sobre as *Cláusulas de Rescisão* dos Jogadores de Futebol'. *Revista de Legislação e de Jurisprudência,* Year CXXXV, No. 3934 (2005): 5–26.

Morgado, Maria José. 'Corrupção e Desporto'. *I Congresso de Direito do Desporto. Estoril – Outubro de 2004, Memórias*, Coordenação de Ricardo Costa e Nuno Barbosa, Coimbra: Almedina, 2005, 87–96.

Morgado, Nuno, 'Comentários ao Decreto-Lei n.º 248-A/2008, de 31 de Dezembro, que Estabelece o Regime de Acesso e de Exercício da Actividade de Treinador Desportivo', *A Nova Legislação do Desporto Comentada*, Wolters Kluwer/Coimbra Editora, Colecção PLMJ, Lisbon (2010): 29–52.

Moura, Paulo Cardoso de. 'Uma Lei de Bases Sem Bases'. *Desporto & Direito. Revista Jurídica do Desporto*, Year IV, No. 11 (2007): 185–197.

Nabais, José Casalta. 'O Regime Fiscal do Desporto Profissional'. *Desporto & Direito. Revista Jurídica do Desporto*, Year I, No. 3 (2004): 411–432.

Neves, Luís Cassiano. 'A Lei de Bases da Actividade Física e do Desporto e a Regulação Desportiva'. *Desporto & Direito. Revista Jurídica do Desporto*, Year IV, No. 11, Coimbra, Almedina (2007): 211–219.

Nogueira Nunes, Henrique, 'Regime fiscal das SAD (IRC). Direitos de imagem e comissões de agentes de jogadores'. *O Direito do Desporto em Perspectiva*, Edited by Ana Celeste Carvalho, Almedina/CEJ/IPDJ (2015): 69–91.

Noll, Roger G. *The Organisation of Sports Leagues*. Oxford Review of Economic Policy, Vol. 19, No. 4, Oxford University Press, 2003.

Nora, José Joaquim Sampaio e. 'Os Fundamentos do Direito Desportivo'. *Boletim do Conselho Distrital de Coimbra da Ordem dos Advogados,* Year III, No. 5, (1998): 13–15.

Oliveira, Nuno Manuel Pinto. 'Clubes de Futebol, Jogadores e Transferências: O Problema da Validade das *Cláusulas de Rescisão*, Anotação ao Acórdão do Supremo Tribunal de Justiça, de 7 de Março de 2007', *Cadernos de Direito Privado*, No. 17 (2007): 65–68.

Palma, Clotilde Celorico. 'O Imposto Sobre o Valor Acrescentado e as Actividades Desportivas'. *Cadernos de Ciência e Técnica Fiscal*, No. 202 (2007) 87–112.

Palma, Maria Fernanda. 'O Caso do Very-Light. Um Problema de Dolo Eventual?'. *Themis*, Year I, No. 1 (2000): 173–180.

Pereira, Alexandre Libório Dias. *Contratos de Patrocínio Publicitário ('Sponsoring').* Revista da Ordem dos Advogados, vol. I, 1998, pp. 317–335.

Pereira, André Gonçalo Dias. 'Assunção do Risco em Actividades Desportivas no Direito Português'. *Desporto & Direito. Revista Jurídica do Desporto*, Year III, No. 9, Coimbra, Almedina (2006): 421–435.

Pereira, André Gonçalo Dias. 'Responsabilidade Civil em Eventos Desportivos'. *Desporto & Direito. Revista Jurídica do Desporto*, Year V, No. 14, Coimbra, Almedina (2008): 227–265.

Pereira, Pedro Barros. 'Federações Desportivas: Uma Realidade em Movimento'. *Desporto & Direito. Revista Jurídica do Desporto*, Year III, No. 9, Coimbra, Almedina (2006): 451–465.

Pessanha, Alexandra. *As Federações Desportivas. Contributo para o Estudo do Ordenamento Jurídico Desportivo*. Coimbra: Coimbra Editora, 2001.

Pessanha, Alexandra. *Reflexões Sobre a Natureza e o Regime Jurídico das Federações Desportivas*. Estudos em Homenagem a Cunha Rodrigues, vol. 2, Coimbra: Coimbra Editora, 2001, 473–514.

Pessanha, Alexandra. 'Nota ao Acórdão do Supremo Tribunal de Justiça, de 17 de Dezembro de 2002 (Federação Desportiva – Tiro aos Pombos – Protecção dos Animais)'. *Desporto & Direito. Revista Jurídica do Desporto,* Year I, No. 1, Coimbra, Almedina, Coimbra, Almedina (2003): 119–135.

Pontes, Sérgio. 'IRC: Implicações na Actividade Desportiva. O Caso Particular do Futebol'. TOC, *Revista da Câmara dos Técnicos Oficiais de Contas*, Year VII, No. 73, (2006): 42–49.

Proença, José Carlos Brandão. *A Conduta do Lesado como Pressuposto e Critério de Imputação do Dano Extracontratual.* Coimbra, Almedina, 1997.

Raposo, Mário Mota. *As Federações Desportivas. O Estatuto de Utilidade Pública Desportiva: Atribuição, Suspensão e Cancelamento*, Lisbon: Instituto do Desporto de Portugal, 2003.

Relógio, Luís Paulo. 'O Papel das Associações de Desportistas Profissionais no Novo Século'. *Desporto & Direito. Revista Jurídica do Desporto*, Year IV, No. 10, Coimbra, Almedina (2006): 29–42.

Relógio, Luís Paulo. 'A Lei de Bases (da Actividade Física e) do Desporto: "Take 3"'. *Desporto & Direito. Revista Jurídica do Desporto*, Year IV, No. 11, Coimbra, Almedina (2007): 199–209.

Ribeiro, Maria João Soares. 'O Treinador nos Tribunais'. *Desporto & Direito. Revista Jurídica do Desporto*, Year IV, No. 12, Coimbra, Almedina (2007): 393–417.
Roberts, Gary R. *The Case for Baseball's Special Antitrust Immunity*. Journal of Sports Economics, Vol. 4, No. 4, November 2003.
Rosário, Alberto Trovão do. *O Desporto em Portugal*. Lisbon: Instituto Piaget, 1996.
Sacadura, Maria Luísa. *Fiscalidade no Desporto*. Lisbon: Editora Erasmos, 1996.
Sacadura, Maria Luísa. *A Tributação do Rendimento dos Praticantes Desportivos*. Direito e Desporto. Estudos Fiscais e de Gestão, Coordenação de Glória Teixeira, Coimbra: Almedina, 2007, 50–62.
Santos, José Carlos Gomes. 'Profissões de Desgaste Rápido'. *Ciência e Técnica Fiscal*, No. 357 (1990): 75–81.
Santos, Renato Dias dos. 'A Arbitragem: Regras Com ou Sem Lei (de Bases)?'. *Desporto & Direito. Revista Jurídica do Desporto*, Year V, No. 15, Coimbra, Almedina (2008): 425–437.
Seixas, José Luís Pereira. 'A Justiça e o Futebol ou a Justiça do Futebol'. *Boletim da Ordem dos Advogados*, No. 22 (2002): 8–11.
Seixas, José Luís Pereira. 'Ocupação Efectiva e Trabalhador Desportivo'. *Revista de Direito e de Estudos Sociais*, Volume XLV, Tomo 1, 2 e 3 (2004): 157–185.
Seixas, José Luís Pereira. 'Justiça Desportiva e a Nova Lei de Bases do Desporto – Algumas Observações'. *Desporto & Direito. Revista Jurídica do Desporto*, Year I, No. 5, Coimbra, Almedina (2005): 155–162.
Silva, Rui Alexandre. 'Da Infracção à Sanção Disciplinar na Regulamentação Desportiva'. *O Desporto e o Direito: Prevenir, Disciplinar, Punir*, Livros Horizonte, 2001.
Silveiro, Fernando Xarepe. 'O Empréstimo Internacional de Futebolistas Profissionais'. *Estudos de Direito Desportivo*. Coimbra, Almedina, 2002.
Silvero, Emílio A. Garcia. 'A Libertação de Desportistas Para as Selecções Nacionais: Aspectos Jurídicos e Económicos', Desporto & Direito Revista Jurídica do Desporto, Year III, No. 9, Coimbra, Almedina (2006).
Teixeira, Glória. *Fiscalidade do Desporto*. Direito e Desporto. Estudos Fiscais e de Gestão, Coordenação de Glória Teixeira, Coimbra: Almedina, 2007, 7–14.
Vieira, José Eduardo Fanha. *O Contrato de Trabalho Desportivo – Colectânea de Legislação e Regulamentação*. Lisbon: CEFD, 2002.
Vieweg, Klaus. Patrocínio e Jogos Olímpicos, *Desporto & Direito, No. 5,* Coimbra, Coimbra Editora, 2004, pp. 179–190.
Weatherhill, Stephen. *Resisting the Pressures of 'Americanization': The influence of European Community Law on the 'European Sports Model. Law and Sport in Contemporary Society'*, Ed. By Steve Grennfield and Guy Osborn, Frank Class, London, 2000.
Xavier, Bernardo. *Curso de Direito do Trabalho*. 2nd Edition, Lisbon: Verbo, 1993.

Index

The numbers here refer to paragraph numbers.

www.ingramcontent.com/pod-product-compliance
Lightning Source LLC
Chambersburg PA
CBHW071410230926
51846CB00001B/46